CookingLight®

ANNUAL
RECIPES 2018

Oxmoor House®

A Year at *Cooking Light*

2017 has been an incredible, and incredibly busy year for *Cooking Light*. We celebrated our big 30th anniversary and took the opportunity to reflect on how far we've come and what's next—not just for the magazine, but for a new generation of conscious consumers and avid food lovers. "Healthy" has changed so much in the past three decades, and we couldn't be more excited to share all the delicious possibilities with you. This year we dove deep into important topics like The Healthy Cook's Guide to Grass-Fed Beef (page 137) and had fun with smart, creative recipes like Muffin-Tin Mains (page 250). Our nutrition experts explored the latest news and trends, including healthy ways to boost metabolism, reduce inflammation, and prevent illness. In September, we debuted an entirely new design of our magazine to bring more joy and focus to the page. We hope you love it as much as we do. And of course, we continued to deliver what you love most about *Cooking Light*: weeknight dinner solutions that are easy, fast, and test kitchen-approved.

This 30th milestone has shown us that the future for a healthy, balanced, and delicious lifestyle is a bright one. We can't wait to share what we have in store for 2018.

Bloody Good Bloody Mary *(page 65)*
Our zingy, tart Bloody Mary has an unexpected star ingredient: pickle juice. This streamlined, homemade mix also slashes the sodium content that you'll find in most bottled mixes.

Here are some highlights from 2017:

- We began the year in January with easy, achievable ways to eat better right now—no more lofty or long-term resolutions. This included recipes with real benefits like Immunity Soup (page 19) and strategies for managing caffeine and sugar cravings. The *Cooking Light* 3-Day Detox (page 26) reset your habits with delicious, streamlined recipes (no gimmicks!) and tips for sticking to the plan. In March we explored all things breakfast and cheered for super tall, super fluffy whole-grain pancakes (page 54).

- April marked the official launch of *Cooking Light* 30 years ago. In What Healthy Means Now (page 76), we examined the past, rich present, and promising future of our relationship with food and nutrition. In short, we're in a golden era, with a passion for whole foods, bold flavors, and plenty of variety. A new guard of inspiring chefs, cookbook authors, and influencers contributed to the issue. We also celebrated spring with essential Easter dishes and one-pot whole-grain meals.

- The vegetable theme of our May issue fit in with *Cooking Light*'s plant-forward mission (and let us express our love for peak spring and early summer produce). This issue included quick, fresh, veggie-laden pizzas (the Garden Greens Pizza, page 112, was a staff favorite), and a preview of our new cookbook, *Everyday Vegetarian*. We showcased thoughtfully composed salads, explored traditional Mexican vegetable dishes, and gave versatile tahini (sesame seed paste) a bigger spotlight.

- Summer arrived in June with bursts of bold color, which we translated into our first-ever Eat by Color summer cookbook. Monochrome recipes in green (Minestrone Verde, page 128), red, yellow (Peach-Thyme Galette, page 133), and purple showed off the natural beauty of the season. July brought us to the backyard with updated cookout classics, like Slow Cooker Bourbon-Peach Baked Beans (page 177), and plenty of grilled favorites.

- September was in many ways a monumental month for us. The look and feel of the magazine received an update from top to bottom. We added more service to our Dinner Tonight section with versatile sides and sauces, timesaving techniques, and efficient shopping lists. We featured a roster of expert columnists like Gina Homolka of Skinnytaste and cookbook author Andrea Nguyen. We also leapt back into the school year with casual dinner ideas like Ann Taylor Pittman's revolutionary Snack Dinner (page 254) and make-ahead lunches.

- Our double issue in November contained a wealth of robust features and company-worthy dishes. We continued to celebrate our 30th birthday with a round up of all-time favorite recipes, as well as the 30 Ways to be a Healthier Cook that we've mastered over the years. The Thanksgiving Cookbook focused on fall produce, with special attention paid to the sides we love, like Pear, Sage, and Golden Raisin Stuffing (page 315) and Sweet Potato Casserole with Pumpkin Seed-Oat Crumble (page 310). A *Cooking Light* Supper Club (going 15 years strong!) shared their wisdom, and we learned how to eat the Mediterranean way.

Every month we hear from you, our faithful readers, who continually empower us through your letters, e-mails, and social media comments to keep doing what we do. We also love to hear stories from our Cooking Light Diet members who inspire us with their weight-loss success and newfound love of cooking. So, to all of you who cook from *Cooking Light* and share your thoughts with us, thank you.

The Editors of *Cooking Light*

Curried Cauliflower Salad with Yogurt *(page 105)*
This Indian-inspired side is a perfect harmony of nutty, sweet, tangy, and spicy. Blooming the curry powder before drizzling it on top of roasted cauliflower deepens its warmth and complex flavor.

Our Favorite Recipes

Not all recipes are created equal.
At *Cooking Light*, only those that have received a passing grade from our Test Kitchen staff and food editors—a group with very high standards—make it onto the pages of the magazine. Each recipe is tested vigorously, often two or three times, to make sure it's healthy, reliable, and tastes the best it possibly can. So, here we've gathered together this past year's most unforgettable recipes. They're the ones we hear about most from readers and the ones we make regularly for our friends and families.

▶ **Red Beans and Rice** *(page 283)*
The ultimate comfort food, this meal-in-a-bowl is filling and flavorful. Pairing one complex carbohydrate with another (the beans and the brown rice) makes this recipe one to reach for when you're looking for an especially satiating dinner.

▼ **Soft-Yolk Muffins with Sausage and Cheese** *(page 250)*
A perfectly soft-cooked egg in a baked muffin may seem like a brilliant feat of engineering, but it couldn't be easier. You get a satisfying meal on the go with the surprise of a creamy, golden yolk in the middle.

Chicken and Butternut Gnocchi *(page 33)*
A complete and wholesome dish in one skillet, gnocchi gets delectably crisp and seared in just a few minutes. This protein-packed meal comes together in only half an hour and requires minimal assembly.

Miso-Ginger Braised Chicken with Bok Choy and Barley *(page 33)* The deep umami flavor of white miso brightened by ginger, green onions, and cilantro makes this a standout chicken dinner and a one-pot wonder that puts your Dutch oven to good use.

All the Green Things Salad *(page 80)*
Our monochromatic salad celebrates everything we love
about spring: delicate herbs, sweet peas, tender asparagus,
and creamy avocado. A zippy lemon dressing binds this
stunning, verdant salad together.

Red Wine-Marinated Steak with Balsamic Onions and Slaw *(page 135)*
Red onions roasted with balsamic vinegar turn a beautiful deep purple, and
become sweet and tangy. Red wine-marinated steak and fresh purple cabbage
slaw stick to the color scheme and round out the plate.

Chocolate-Tahini Banana Bread *(page 103)* Upgrade the familiar banana bread with nutty, rich tahini—a great counter to this sweet quick bread. Sesame is also a good alternative if you're baking for anyone with nut allergies.

Sweet Potato-and-Red Lentil Curry *(page 265)*
The slow cooker works wonders with this fragrant vegetarian stew. Serve over brown rice to catch the coconut-based sauce and top with quick-pickled red onions for a hearty meatless Monday meal.

Creole Shrimp and Creamed Corn *(page 193)*
If you're looking for a new take on shrimp and grits, this crowd-pleasing recipe is all you need. Fresh sweet corn stands in for the grits and balances the smoky, spicy Creole seasoning on the shrimp.

Tomato Gratin Lasagna *(page 194)*
This lighter, brighter take on lasagna is
made for a bounty of juicy summer
tomatoes. Serve it with hearty, crusty
bread so none of the garlicky tomato
juices in the dish go to waste.

Sausage Ragù Over Polenta *(page 47)*
With all the deep flavor of a traditional, slow-simmered ragù, this meal comes together in just 25 minutes. At $1.99 per serving and only 8 ingredients, the creamy polenta and hearty ragú is anything but stingy when it comes to flavor.

Green Gazpacho with Shrimp *(page 205)*
Tomatillos, poblano chiles, and cucumber give this gazpacho its vibrant green color and bold flavor. Use fresh bakery bread to tame the heat and add body to the soup.

Dutch Baby with Strawberries and Pistachios *(page 64)*
This dramatic breakfast centerpiece is perfect for brunch—a great alternative to pancakes. Macerated strawberries and crushed pistachios fill the center for texture and color.

Fluffiest Multigrain Pancakes with Almond Butter Drizzle *(page 54)*
This whole-grain short stack is our tallest yet, with a texture that's both light and creamy. We cut about 36 grams of added sugar by replacing a waterfall of syrup with a maple–almond butter drizzle and fresh fruit.

Summer Salmon Niçoise Salad *(page 172)*
Colorful, simple, and filling—what more could you ask for in a main-dish salad? Use a fork to gently break the salmon fillets into large flakes before topping the salads.

Brownie Energy Bites *(page 23)*
There's absolutely zero added sugar in this indulgent, chocolaty, deceptively sweet snack. Instead, the sweetness comes from energy-packed Medjool dates, while toasted hazelnuts provide a satisfying crunch.

Quick Chicken Pho *(page 52)*
Andrea Nguyen's light, fragrant Vietnamese chicken noodle soup is a soothing and filling way to start your day. Bump up the fresh ginger, basil, and sliced chile to truly wake up the senses.

Turmeric-Pickled Deviled Eggs *(page 81)*
Delicately pickled and beautifully dyed eggs make for a head-turning update on a classic appetizer. Sunny yellow from an all-natural turmeric brine, it's a tangy, vibrant showstopper.

Dijon-Herb Crusted Salmon with Creamy Dill Sauce *(page 86)*
This simple, elegant salmon dish is a perfect date night dinner for two. Panko breadcrumbs create a crisp, golden topper. A tangy, creamy dill sauce is a stellar sidekick.

Rosé-Glazed Strawberry Tart *(page 130)*
Serve this striking tart with any peak season berries—all pair well with the yogurt and cream cheese filling and the bright rosé syrup. Make all the components ahead and assemble just before serving.

Spanish Chorizo Corn Cakes *(page 178)*
Make a big batch of these savory corn cakes ahead and freeze; reheat and top with a fried egg for brunch, sautéed vegetables for dinner, or enjoy on their own as a whole-grain snack.

Quick BBQ Chicken Thighs with Mashed Potatoes *(page 204)*
If you're craving bold BBQ flavor but don't want to heat up your grill, this is a great indoor alternative that doesn't compromise on taste and is ready in 25 minutes. What makes it possible? An easy homemade barbecue sauce that comes together quickly.

Pork Medallions with Fennel-Apple Slaw *(page 247)*
Thinly sliced foods cook faster, making this shortcut version of a fall favorite ready in no time. Pork medallions cook in just five minutes. Sweet potato slices bake in just 10 minutes.

Jalapeño Popper Bean Dip *(page 280)*
We combined two gameday favorites—cheesy pinto bean dip and jalapeño poppers into one crowd-pleasing yet light dish. Serve with mini sweet peppers and sliced cucumbers to offset the heat.

▶ The Big Omega Sandwich *(page 93)*
Wild-caught salmon is rich in omega-3's, which improve your mood and reduce your heart disease risk. It's an added benefit to this impressive makeover, which saves 500mg sodium and 12g fat over a traditional fast food fish sandwich.

Fennel and Blood Orange Salad *(page 303)*
Greens, creamy whites, and jewel tones pop in this company-worthy salad—a fresh hit in a month filled with heartier offerings. Any orange would work well here.

Potato and Parsnip Gratin *(page 310)*
Cheesy, creamy, and bubbly, this indulgent side is a must-have on your holiday table. The secret to this super creamy casserole is to parboil the vegetables first so they absorb less sauce.

Salted Caramel Apple Pie *(page 315)*
A homemade salted caramel sauce elevates this fall standard to something extraordinary. It intensifies the apple flavor rather than make the dessert too sweet.

Cabbage Salad with Miso Vinaigrette *(page 337)*
Crunchy, fresh cabbage is so satisfying, and good for so much more than coleslaws. Miso takes the salad in a savory direction. Pair with simple baked fish for a stunning plate.

Baked Coconut Plantains *(page 359)*
Sarah Copeland skips the fryer and bakes starchy-sweet plantains in fragrant coconut oil until crisp and golden. We couldn't stop eating these.

Korean-Style Short Ribs with Chile-Scallion Rice *(page 375)*
Meaty beef short ribs become fall-apart tender in the slow cooker while a kimchi-laced sauce cooks down into a sticky glaze. It's a restaurant-worthy dish with hardly any of the work.

Molasses Crinkle Cookies *(page 382)*
The classic fall flavor of molasses is the star in these chewy, soft, beautifully spiced cookies. A coat of snowy powdered sugar sets this holiday cookie apart from those caked in rock-hard royal icing.

CONTENTS

Cooking Light® Annual Recipes 2018
Senior Editor: Rachel Quinlivan West, R.D.
Project Editor: Melissa Brown
Designers: Amy Bickell, Olivia Pierce, Matt Ryan
Associate Manager for Project Management
    and Production: Anna Muñiz
Assistant Production Manager: Diane Rose Keener
Copy Editor: Jacqueline Giovanelli
Proofreader: Adrienne Davis
Indexer: Mary Ann Laurens
Fellow: Kaitlyn Pacheco

We welcome your comments and suggestions about
    Time Inc. Books.

Time Inc. Books
Attention: Book Editors
P.O. Box 62310
Tampa, Florida 33662-2310
(800) 765-6400

Cooking Light®
Editor: Hunter Lewis
Digital Director Food @ Time Inc.: Stacey Rivera
Creative Director: Rachel Cardina Lasserre
Executive Editor: Ann Taylor Pittman
Managing Editor: Cindy Hatcher
Assistant Managing Editor: Alice Eldridge Summerville
Food & Nutrition Director: Brierley Horton
Senior Food Editor: Timothy Q. Cebula
Food Editor: Hannah Klinger
Assistant Nutrition Editor: Jamie Vespa
Senior Designer: Hagen Stegall Baker
Senior Designer: Nicole Gerrity
Assistant Designer: Jen Skarda
Senior Designer, Digital: Daniel Boone
Production Director: Liz Rhoades
Copy Director: Jessica Campbell
Production Coordinator: Christina Harrison
Contributors: Marian Cooper Cairns; Jennifer Causey;
    Kira Corbin; Sidney Fry, M.S., R.D.; Kate Johnson;
    Andrea Kirkland, M.S., R.D.; Susan McWilliams;
    Cathy Robbins; Cheryl Slocum; Kathleen Varner;
    Sheri Wilson
Fellows: Zee Krstic, Brianna Riddick, Antara Sinha,
    Arielle Weg

COOKINGLIGHT.COM
Digital Content Manager: Ashley Kappel
Multimedia Editor: Rochelle Bilow
Assistant Editor: Haley Sugg
Associate Editor: Jaime Ritter
Community and Editorial Content Manager,
    Cooking Light Diet: Matthew Moore

ISBN-13: 978-0-8487-5453-2

Printed in the United States of America
10 9 8 7 6 5 4 3 2 1
First Printing 2017

Cover: *Grilled Pork Adobo (page 154) and a simple side salad with
quartered radishes*
Back Cover (left to right): *Chicken Breasts with Brown Butter–
Garlic Tomato Sauce (page 174), Lentil-Tahini Burgers with
Pickled Cabbage (page 102), Beer-Brushed Tofu Skewers with
Barley (page 114)*

START YOUR YEAR OFF LIGHT: 11 WAYS TO EAT BETTER *NOW*

Here's all the food for a fit and happy 2017—savory breakfast waffles, homemade probiotics, satisfying steak dinners, super-nutritious brownies, and more. Our expert editors offer easy-to-keep resolutions and smart strategies to reach peak health while savoring every delicious bite.

1. EAT FOR IMMUNITY

A healthy immune system doesn't come from vitamin C alone; you need a calibrated combination of different nutrients. Certain foods in particular bolster your defenses not only during cold and flu season but all year long. This soothing, hearty soup combines six immunity-boosting ingredients, making each bowlful a prevention powerhouse.

Gluten Free • Kid Friendly Make Ahead • Freezable

Immunity Soup

Hands-on: 30 min. Total: 1 hr.
This recipe yields a big pot of brothy soup that you can make ahead and enjoy for a couple of days; the flavor just gets better over time. You may be wary of the large amount of garlic, but keep in mind that it mellows considerably after being cooked.

2 tablespoons olive oil
1 1/2 cups chopped onion
3 celery stalks, thinly sliced
2 large carrots, thinly sliced
1 pound presliced vitamin D-enhanced mushrooms (such as Monterey Mushrooms)
10 medium garlic cloves, minced
8 cups unsalted chicken stock (such as Swanson)
4 thyme sprigs
2 bay leaves
1 (15-ounce) can unsalted chickpeas, drained
2 pounds skinless, bone-in chicken breasts
1 1/2 teaspoons kosher salt
1/2 teaspoon crushed red pepper
12 ounces curly kale, stems removed, leaves torn

1. Heat oil in a large Dutch oven over medium. Add onion, celery, and carrots; cook, stirring occasionally, 5 minutes. Add mushrooms and garlic; cook, stirring often, 3 minutes. Stir in stock, thyme, bay leaves, and chickpeas; bring to a simmer. Add chicken, salt, and red pepper; cover and simmer until chicken is done, about 25 minutes.
2. Remove chicken from Dutch oven; cool slightly. Shred meat with 2 forks; discard bones. Stir chicken and kale into soup; cover and simmer until kale is just tender, about 5 minutes. Discard thyme sprigs and bay leaves. Serves 8 (serving size: 1 1/2 cups)

CALORIES 253; FAT 6.5g (sat 1g, mono 3g, poly 0.9g); PROTEIN 28g; CARB 22g; FIBER 6g; SUGARS 5g (est. added sugars 0g); CHOL 54mg; IRON 2mg; SODIUM 581mg; CALC 116mg

6 IMMUNITY BOOSTERS

CHICKPEAS
A good source of zinc. As with vitamin D, a zinc deficiency is associated with lowered immunity. Red meat and chicken are also zinc-rich.

DARK LEAFY GREENS
Kale and similar greens are rich in the antioxidant vitamin C. The C, paired with zinc from the chicken and chickpeas, delivers a one-two knockout blow to cold symptoms.

GARLIC
These bulbs contain allicin, one of the world's most powerful antioxidants. A 2014 study found that people who eat garlic every day are nearly two-thirds less likely to catch a cold than non–garlic eaters.

HOT BROTH
Steaming stock makes your nose run, which helps flush out congestion. Broth-based soups also keep you hydrated.

CRUSHED RED PEPPER
Capsaicin, which adds heat, can clear sinuses.

MUSHROOMS
Look for fungi labeled vitamin D–rich; they're grown in ultraviolet light to spur D production. A deficiency in the nutrient has been linked to an increased risk of infection.

2. TRY THESE 6 FOODS IN 2017

Up your game by exploring the food trends that will have you eating better, healthier, and more sustainably.

SWEET POTATO LEAVES
A perfect example of no-waste, root-to-fruit cooking, these tender, lightly peppery leaves work in the same ways you would use spinach or kale. Find them at farmers' markets and Asian groceries.

GRADE B (DARK) MAPLE SYRUP
It's brimming with more antioxidants and deeper maple flavor than Grade A. Available at most supermarkets.

EXO CRICKET FLOUR PROTEIN BARS
Eco-friendly cricket flour packs protein and iron into these chewy, delicious snacks. Find them at exoprotein.com.

FERMENTED VEGGIES
Fermented raw produce delivers gut-healthy probiotics. We love the organic offerings from Caldwell's, such as beets and carrots. wisechoicemarket.com

SKYR
This Icelandic low-fat, high-protein dairy product is loaded with live cultures and is creamy-smooth and even thicker than Greek yogurt. Our faves are Icelandic Provisions and Siggi's, available at stores nationwide.

BEYOND MEAT BURGERS
Vegans and vegetarians rejoice: Beyond Meat's plant-based burgers, with a whopping 20g protein per patty, offer a pretty-darn-close approximation of ground beef taste and texture. Available at Whole Foods.

3. MAKE DINNER CLEAN AND EASY

Clean eating means simple cooking: fresh, seasonal ingredients prepared with minimal fuss so the whole foods can shine. The trick? Do more with less. These three dinners show you exactly how, with smart technique tips to make every bite sing.

Quick & Easy • Gluten Free

Seared Tuna with Shaved Vegetable Salad

Hands-on: 15 min. Total: 15 min.
Shaving raw root veggies into a side-dish salad is a fantastic approach. They're ready in just a few minutes, their earthy flavors stay vibrant, and a simple vinaigrette tenderizes them while retaining some crunch. The tangy, zesty flavor of the vinaigrette complements the meaty tuna so that the fish doesn't need a sauce of its own. Sprinkle with toasted sesame seeds for light crunch, nutty taste, and a healthy dose of minerals like manganese.

¼ cup extra-virgin olive oil, divided
1 tablespoon rice vinegar
1 teaspoon kosher salt, divided
¾ teaspoon Dijon mustard
¾ teaspoon honey
4 ounces baby gold beets, thinly shaved
1 (4-ounce) fennel bulb, trimmed and thinly shaved
4 ounces baby turnips, thinly shaved
1 (6-ounce) Granny Smith apple, very thinly sliced
2 teaspoons toasted sesame seeds
4 (6-ounce) tuna steaks
½ teaspoon black pepper
1 tablespoon torn fennel fronds

1. Combine 2 tablespoons oil, vinegar, ½ teaspoon salt, mustard, and honey in a large bowl. Add beets, fennel, turnips, and apple; toss. Sprinkle salad with sesame seeds.
2. Heat remaining 2 tablespoons oil in a cast-iron skillet over high. Sprinkle tuna with pepper and remaining ½ teaspoon salt; place in hot pan. Cook 90 seconds on both sides (for rare) or until desired degree of doneness. Remove tuna from pan. Slice thinly, and serve with salad; top with fennel fronds. Serves 4 (serving size: 1 tuna steak and about 1¼ cups salad)

CALORIES 366; **FAT** 15.6g (sat 2.4g, mono 11.2g, poly 1.9g); **PROTEIN** 43g; **CARB** 12g; **FIBER** 3g; **SUGARS** 8g (est. added sugars 1g); **CHOL** 66mg; **IRON** 2mg; **SODIUM** 636mg; **CALC** 37mg

Quick & Easy • Gluten Free

Pork Tenderloin with Mushrooms and Onions

Hands-on: 23 min. Total: 23 min.
Use a stainless-steel pan instead of a nonstick here, if possible. A stainless surface will better collect fond (also known as browned bits) from the pork, which is then deglazed to lend rich flavor to the mushrooms and onions as they cook. Cook pork tenderloin on the stovetop instead of oven-roasting it; this gives it a delicious brown crust. Medium heat is key: It browns the pork without burning or toughening the surface before the middle reaches the right temperature.

2 tablespoons canola oil
1 (1-pound) pork tenderloin, trimmed
1 teaspoon kosher salt, divided
¾ teaspoon black pepper, divided
12 ounces sliced shiitake mushroom caps
3 cups frozen pearl onions, thawed
2 tablespoons chopped fresh thyme

1. Heat oil in a large high-sided skillet over medium. Sprinkle pork with ½ teaspoon salt and ½ teaspoon pepper. Add pork to pan; cook, turning occasionally, until browned on all sides and a meat thermometer inserted into thickest portion registers 145°F, about 15 minutes. Remove pork from pan; keep warm.
2. Add mushrooms, onions, thyme, remaining ½ teaspoon salt, and remaining ¼ teaspoon pepper to pan; cook, stirring and scraping pan to loosen browned bits from bottom of pan, until vegetables are soft, about 7 minutes. Cut pork crosswise into thin slices; serve with mushrooms and onions. Serves 4 (serving size: 3 ounces pork and about 1 cup mushroom mixture)

CALORIES 243; FAT 9.8g (sat 1.4g, mono 5.3g, poly 2.5g); PROTEIN 27g; CARB 12g; FIBER 2g; SUGARS 6g (est. added sugars 0g); CHOL 74mg; IRON 2mg; SODIUM 560mg; CALC 25mg

3 MORE CLEAN-COOKING TIPS

QUALITY COUNTS
When you're cooking simple dishes with just a few ingredients, there's no place for inferior products to hide. This is where high-caliber components make all the difference: Flavorful extra-virgin olive oil, pristine produce, and spanking-fresh proteins will shine in these meals.

FASTER FEELS FRESHER
Quick sautés, broiled dishes, flash-sears, and raw salads seem cleaner than long-simmered stews and braises, partly because the flavors of slow-cooked ingredients tend to meld together, while quick-cooked items maintain their distinct tastes, textures, and colors.

VEGGIE VARIETY HELPS
A simple meal shouldn't be boring, and one of the easiest ways to make the plate pop is to include two or more produce items. This gives the dish more color, broadens the flavor spectrum, and helps you take in more vitamins and minerals. Keep it seasonal by remembering the principle "If it grows together, it goes together."

Quick & Easy • Gluten Free
Kid Friendly

Broiled Flat Iron Steak with Brussels Sprouts and Sweet Potatoes

Hands-on: 15 min. Total: 25 min.
This one-pan meal is a crowd-pleaser and testament to how 4 ingredients can come together to form a supremely satisfying dish, ready in a flash. We broil the steak over the veggies so the meat juices baste them as they cook. Choose multifaceted flat iron steak. Butchered from the shoulder (chuck), it gives you the best of both beefy worlds: One end of the cut is tender and mild, while the opposite end has sirloin-like chew and deep, mineral flavor. Slice the dense sweet potato thinly so it cooks at the same rate as the leafy Brussels sprouts.

6 ounces Brussels sprouts, trimmed and halved
6 ounces sweet potatoes, peeled, halved lengthwise, and sliced into thin half-moons
2 tablespoons olive oil, divided
1 (1-pound) flat iron steak, trimmed
2 teaspoons chopped fresh thyme, divided
1 teaspoon kosher salt, divided
¾ teaspoon black pepper, divided

1. Preheat broiler, with oven rack 6 inches from heat.
2. Place Brussels sprouts and sweet potatoes on a rimmed baking sheet; toss with 1 tablespoon oil, and spread in an even layer. Place a wire rack in pan over vegetables. Rub steak with 1½ teaspoons oil, and place on rack in pan over vegetables. Sprinkle steak with 1 teaspoon thyme, ½ teaspoon salt, and half of pepper.
3. Broil 10 minutes. Turn steak over; drizzle with remaining 1½ teaspoons oil, and sprinkle with remaining thyme, salt, and pepper. Broil about 5 minutes or until desired degree of doneness.
4. Remove steak from pan, and let stand 5 minutes. Cut across the grain into thin slices. Place vegetables in a bowl; pour in pan juices, and toss to coat. Serves 4 (serving size: 3 ounces steak and about 1 cup vegetables)

CALORIES 289; FAT 15g (sat 4g, mono 7.9g, poly 0.8g); PROTEIN 26g; CARB 13g; FIBER 3g; SUGARS 3g (est. added sugars 0g); CHOL 39mg; IRON 1mg; SODIUM 574mg; CALC 32mg

4. HYDRATE FOR HEALTH

If you're not a water person, tossing back 64 or more ounces a day can seem punishing. One little trick makes it less daunting, and even kind of fun: the rubber band challenge. At the start of the day, put rubber bands around your water bottle—the number of bands is determined by the size of your bottle and your personal intake goal (on a 20-ounce bottle, you might use three bands). When you finish the bottle, remove a rubber band. Refill and repeat. *Cooking Light* staffers swear by this approach. "It's more about a game than actually drinking water—and hydration is the prize for playing the game," says Senior Designer Nicole Gerrity.

5. CUT DOWN ON SUGAR

When it comes to sugar, how it's delivered makes all the difference. Naturally occurring sugars in fruit, veggies, and even milk typically don't need to be on your worry list, as they come bundled with nutrients, fiber, vitamins, and antioxidant benefits. But added sugars—sweeteners in processed food, from cane sugar to honey and high-fructose corn syrup—deserve scrutiny.

6 WAYS TO USE NATURAL SWEETENERS IN YOUR COOKING

CUT added sugar in half by stirring overripe banana or chopped dates into batters and doughs for quick breads, cookies, muffins, and pancakes.

BALANCE the flavor of acidic tomato sauces by grating in carrots, butternut squash, beets, or sweet potatoes. Beets, apples, and carrots sweeten smoothies and baked goods, too.

USE unsweetened flaked or shredded coconut or coconut milk in cookies, oatmeal, and granola. Keep amounts in check—coconut is a source of saturated fat.

TAKE advantage of fruits that grow sweeter as they ripen: apples, apricots, avocados, bananas, cantaloupes, mangoes, nectarines, papayas, peaches, pears, and plums.

CHOOSE full-fat yogurts as a treat. They're less tangy and so need less added sugar than reduced-fat options.

DRAW out the natural sugars in onions. Cook low and slow to caramelize, and add to burgers in lieu of ketchup or relish.

6. DIY WITH PURPOSE

The do-it-yourself craze for making condiments and other typically store-bought foods is admirable and impressive, but not always practical. Case in point: Seventeen-ingredient homemade Worcestershire sauce? Mmmm, nope. But some foods are absolutely worth making yourself, especially if they're cheap, easy, and more delicious than anything you can buy. Take labneh, the strained Middle Eastern yogurt—it's hard to find at stores and pricey when you do. In our version,

two staple ingredients and one day of giddy anticipation yield the richest, creamiest healthy spread imaginable. And DIY can be incredibly instructive: Scratch-made sauerkraut is like a hands-on class in fermentation science, where you watch cabbage and salt turn day-by-day into tasty relish, with customizable tang and crunch. Try your hand at these two simple projects, and you'll be hooked.

Gluten Free • Make Ahead
Vegetarian

Caraway Kraut

Hands-on: 15 min. Total: 2 weeks
Sauerkraut is an easy entry point to the glories of fermentation. It's easy to make and nearly foolproof, and you can let it ferment to suit your taste (the longer it goes, the softer and more sour it gets).

2 pounds red cabbage, cored and very thinly sliced
2 teaspoons kosher salt
1 teaspoon caraway seeds

1. Place cabbage in a large bowl. Sprinkle with salt. Firmly and vigorously massage cabbage until it wilts, some liquid has pooled in bottom of bowl, and liquid squeezes out when you squeeze a handful, about 10 to 12 minutes. Stir in caraway seeds. Firmly pack cabbage in a 1-quart jar. Start by filling jar about half full; tamp cabbage down with a muddler or wooden spoon to pack it down firmly. Add more cabbage, and repeat the process until it's all in the jar (don't worry—it will fit). Pour liquid from bowl on top of cabbage.
2. Screw on lid, and set jar on a plate or in a bowl. (The kraut will likely bubble over and leak a bit as it ferments.) Let stand at room temperature, out of direct sunlight, until kraut reaches desired flavor and texture, about 1 to 2 weeks. Check every day, starting after 4 days.

When you open the jar, the liquid will likely be bubbling—that means it's working as it should. Refrigerate to stop fermentation once the kraut is to your liking. Store chilled in refrigerator for up to 1 month. Serves 16 (serving size: ¼ cup)

CALORIES 15; **FAT** 0.1g; **PROTEIN** 1g; **CARB** 3g; **FIBER** 2g; **SUGARS** 2g (est. added sugars 0g); **CHOL** 0mg; **IRON** 0mg; **SODIUM** 250mg; **CALC** 24mg

Gluten Free • Kid Friendly
Make Ahead • Vegetarian

Homemade Labneh

Hands-on: 5 min. Total: 24 hr. 5 min.
Labneh (LEB-neigh) has a rich texture similar to whipped cream cheese. Use as a bagel spread, or drizzle with olive oil and sprinkle with Aleppo pepper for a dip.

2 cups plain whole-milk yogurt (not Greek style)
½ teaspoon kosher salt

1. Arrange a double layer of cheesecloth in a strainer (or, alternatively, line a strainer with coffee filters); spoon yogurt into strainer, and place strainer over a bowl so that it rests a few inches above the bottom of the bowl. Lightly cover strainer with plastic wrap. Refrigerate 24 hours.
2. Remove strainer from bowl; discard whey. Spoon labneh into a bowl; stir in salt. Store in refrigerator for up to 1 week. Serves 10 (serving size: 2 tablespoons)

CALORIES 26; **FAT** 1.6g (sat 1g, mono 0.4g, poly 0.1g); **PROTEIN** 2g; **CARB** 1g; **FIBER** 0g; **SUGARS** 3g (est. added sugars 0g); **CHOL** 6mg; **IRON** 0mg; **SODIUM** 110mg; **CALC** 40mg

7. MAKE DESSERT WITH BENEFITS

It's easy to blow your added-sugar budget on a few small bites of dessert—sweets are often loaded with empty calories and void of benefits. Instead, try a treat you can actually feel good about. These rich chocolate-hazelnut bites don't have a grain of added sugar, and they're packed with protein, fiber, and nutrients. Best of all, they taste divine. Naturally sweet dates blended with creamy almond butter, cocoa, and a hint of salt form a perfectly balanced bite (two, in fact) that leaves you satisfied.

**Staff Favorite • Gluten Free
Kid Friendly • Make Ahead
Freezable • Vegetarian**

Brownie Energy Bites

*Hands-on: 20 min. Total: 1 hr. 10 min.
These two-bite treats taste rich and indulgent, with no added sugar. Each also contains 3g fiber and 3g protein. We find one to be satisfying, but don't feel bad about eating two—that's only 222 calories. Store chilled in an airtight container for up to 1 week.*

**¹/₂ cup whole hazelnuts
12 whole Medjool dates, pitted
 and roughly chopped
²/₃ cup almond butter
¹/₃ cup unsweetened cocoa
2 tablespoons water
1 teaspoon vanilla extract
¹/₄ teaspoon kosher salt**

1. Preheat oven to 350°F.
2. Spread nuts on a small rimmed baking sheet. Bake at 350°F until lightly toasted, about 10 minutes, stirring once. Cool 10 minutes. Rub off skins. Reserve 20 hazelnuts. Pulse remaining hazelnuts in a food processor until finely chopped; transfer chopped nuts to a small bowl.
3. Pulse dates in food processor until almost pastelike. Add almond butter, cocoa, 2 tablespoons water, vanilla, and salt; process until well combined. Turn mixture out into a bowl; divide into 20 equal portions. Roll each portion around 1 whole hazelnut to form a ball. (Mixture will be oily.) Roll each brownie ball in chopped hazelnuts to coat. Chill until firm, about 30 minutes. Serves 20 (serving size: 1 brownie bite)

CALORIES 111; **FAT** 7g (sat 0.8g, mono 4.4g, poly 1.4g); **PROTEIN** 3g; **CARB** 12g; **FIBER** 3g; **SUGARS** 9g (est. added sugars 0g); **CHOL** 0mg; **IRON** 1mg; **SODIUM** 47mg; **CALC** 41mg

---

SUGAR: ADDITION BY SUBTRACTION

Last May, the FDA unveiled a new Nutrition Facts label—effective July 2018—that will require major food manufacturers to list grams and a daily value for added sugars on their products (labels now just list total sugar grams without specifying how much was added).

The USDA recommends limiting added sugars to 10% of your daily calories. For a 1,600-calorie diet, that means no more than 160 calories (10 teaspoons/40g) from added sugars. The American Heart Association advises even less: only 100 calories from added sugar daily (6 teaspoons/24g) for women and about 150 calories (9 teaspoons/36g) for men. Most Americans get way more than this, though: We average 19¹/₂ teaspoons of added sugar a day—312 calories' worth—mostly from beverages and packaged snacks.

Of course, you can still have the occasional treat—just get your fix in a smarter way. For instance, a sugar source such as dark maple syrup contains antioxidants. And natural sugars, such as fructose from fruit and lactose from milk, can have the same effect on your cooking and baking as spoonfuls of the white stuff, with less of an impact on your waistline. Satisfy your sugar cravings and cut calories? Now that's sweet.

---

8. START THE DAY SAVORY

Many of us instinctively go for a sweet, starchy breakfast—jam-topped bagels, honey-tinged wheat flakes, syrup-drizzled waffles—but research shows that refined flour and sugar are the worst foods to eat after an overnight fast. "[Sugar] rapidly raises blood sugar at a time the body is least able to process it, with adverse effects throughout the day," says David Ludwig, director of the Optimal Weight for Life Program at Boston Children's Hospital. Concentrated sugars may give you a quick boost, but you'll crash by midmorning, drowsy and unable to concentrate.

The fix: Switch up your morning routine and think savory. A sensible diet has a little wiggle room for added sugars, but don't use them all up by 9 a.m. Breaking the fast with whole grains, berries, and even vegetables gives you a far better chance to hit daily fiber goals, stay full until lunch, and avoid that midmorning slump. Check out our six simple upgrades for standard sweet breakfasts—some save you more than a day's worth of added sugar.

**Quick & Easy • Gluten Free
Vegetarian
Avo-Pico Oatmeal**
The Usual: Instant flavored oatmeal
The Upgrade: 1 cup steel-cut (or overnight) oats topped with ¹/₃ cup thinly sliced avocado + ¼ cup pico de gallo + 1 tablespoon crumbled feta cheese + 1 tablespoon chopped fresh cilantro.
The Savings: 12g added sugar

CALORIES 272; **FAT** 12.3g (sat 3g, mono 6.1g, poly 1.9g); **PROTEIN** 8g; **CARB** 36g; **FIBER** 7g; **SUGARS** 4g (est. added sugars 1g); **CHOL** 8mg; **IRON** 14mg; **SODIUM** 365mg; **CALC** 240mg

Quick & Easy
Egg and Nova Whole-Grain Waffle
The Usual: Refined-flour waffle with butter and syrup
The Upgrade: 1 frozen whole-grain waffle (such as Van's 8 Whole Grains) + ¾ ounce thinly sliced smoked salmon + 1 poached egg + 1½ teaspoons chopped fresh dill + 1½ teaspoons chopped fresh chives.
The Savings: 20g added sugar

CALORIES 173; FAT 8.2g (sat 1.6g, mono 1.8g, poly 1g); PROTEIN 14g; CARB 13g; FIBER 4g; SUGARS 1g (est. added sugars 0g); CHOL 196mg; IRON 2mg; SODIUM 596mg; CALC 58mg

Quick & Easy • Kid Friendly
Pear and Bacon Whole-Grain French Toast
The Usual: 2 pieces of white-bread French toast with berry compote and powdered sugar
The Upgrade: 2 slices whole-grain French toast + 1 slice cooked and crumbled center-cut bacon + ¼ cup thinly sliced pear + 1 tablespoon shaved Parmesan cheese.
The Savings: 45g added sugar

CALORIES 294; FAT 10.7g (sat 3.9g, mono 2.7g, poly 2.1g); PROTEIN 18g; CARB 32g; FIBER 5g; SUGARS 8g (est. added sugars 2g); CHOL 199mg; IRON 2mg; SODIUM 519mg; CALC 151mg

Quick & Easy • Kid Friendly
Vegetarian
Hummus-Zucchini English Muffin
The Usual: White-flour bagel with cream cheese and strawberry jam
The Upgrade: 1 toasted whole-grain English muffin, split + 2 tablespoons hummus + 2 tablespoons shaved carrot + 2 tablespoons shaved zucchini + 2 teaspoons roasted salted sunflower seeds.
The Savings: 30g added sugar

CALORIES 229; FAT 8.7g (sat 1.3g, mono 0.5g, poly 1.8g); PROTEIN 8g; CARB 30g; FIBER 6g; SUGARS 2g (est. added sugars 1g); CHOL 0mg; IRON 3mg; SODIUM 361mg; CALC 90mg

Quick & Easy • Gluten Free
Make Ahead • Vegetarian
Cuke and Tomato Yogurt
The Usual: Yogurt with honey and granola
The Upgrade: ¾ cup plain 2% reduced-fat Greek yogurt (or skyr) + 2 tablespoons thinly sliced cucumber + 6 halved cherry tomatoes + 1 tablespoon toasted walnuts + 1 teaspoon extra-virgin olive oil.
The Savings: 23g added sugar

CALORIES 220; FAT 12.9g (sat 3.4g, mono 4g, poly 4g); PROTEIN 16g; CARB 12g; FIBER 2g; SUGARS 10g (est. added sugars 0g); CHOL 11mg; IRON 1mg; SODIUM 62mg; CALC 132mg

Quick & Easy • Kid Friendly
Vegetarian
Banana-Nut Shredded Wheat
The Usual: Honey-cluster oat cereal
The Upgrade: 2 large shredded wheat biscuits soaked in ½ cup 1% reduced-fat milk + ⅓ cup thinly sliced banana + 1½ teaspoons warm almond butter + 1½ teaspoons toasted sliced almonds + dash of ground cinnamon.
The Savings: 13g added sugar

CALORIES 322; FAT 8.2g (sat 1.5g, mono 3.9g, poly 2g); PROTEIN 12g; CARB 57g; FIBER 9g; SUGARS 13g (est. added sugars 0g); CHOL 6mg; IRON 2mg; SODIUM 72mg; CALC 212mg

9. CAFFEINATE STRATEGICALLY

About that cup of coffee you need first thing in the morning to rev your motor: It's a waste of perfectly good caffeine. Why? Your body's level of cortisol—an energizing hormone triggered by stress and low blood sugar—peaks early in the morning, and the hormone flows freely up until about 10 a.m. Caffeine inhibits cortisol production, leaving you with less energy. So your system comes to rely on caffeine, which is ultimately less effective than a natural "stress hormone" boost. Moreover, you build caffeine tolerance in the long term. The solution is simple: Wean yourself off the early-morning cup, and soon you'll find that hormones get you humming instead. Cortisol levels drop as the day wears on, so your coffee will have the biggest energy impact between 10 a.m. and noon and again in the afternoon starting around 2 p.m.

10. TRADE BOOZE FOR HOMEMADE SODA

There's no shame in a little adult beverage indulgence over the holidays—it's fun, and you earned it. But it can take a toll on mind and body. With party season in the rearview, now's the time for moderation (maybe you even want to try a dry January). But you can still enjoy delicious drinks. These three simple soda bases have just a handful of fresh ingredients and spices that deliver bold flavor and fizzy refreshment with a fraction of the sugar in store-bought soda. And no special equipment is required: Just mix the syrup with seltzer water. To your health!

Gluten Free • Kid Friendly
Make Ahead • Vegetarian
Cinnamon Spice Soda
Hands-on: 7 min. Total: 1 hr. 7 min.
Combine 9 tablespoons brown sugar, ¾ cup water, 6 peppercorns, 4 cinnamon sticks (broken into small pieces), 3 allspice berries, 3 cloves, and 1 crushed cardamom pod in a saucepan over medium-high; bring to a boil, stirring until sugar dissolves. Remove from heat; steep 1 hour. Strain syrup; discard solids. Cool completely. Stir 1½ tablespoons syrup into 1 cup (or more, depending on desired flavor) seltzer water. Store syrup chilled up to 2 weeks. Serves 12

CALORIES 44; **FAT** 0g; **PROTEIN** 0g; **CARB** 12g; **FIBER** 0g; **SUGARS** 10g (est. added sugars 10g); **CHOL** 0mg; **IRON** 4mg; **SODIUM** 3mg; **CALC** 11mg

Gluten Free • Kid Friendly
Make Ahead • Vegetarian
Grapefruit Soda
Hands-on: 15 min. Total: 1 hr. 15 min.
Combine 9 tablespoons sugar; 1 cup water; ⅔ cup fresh pink grapefruit juice; 1 tablespoon fresh lemon juice; and the rinds, peeled in strips, of 2 lemons and 2 large pink grapefruit in a saucepan over medium-high. Bring to a boil, stirring until sugar dissolves. Remove from heat; steep 1 hour. Strain syrup; discard solids. Cool completely. Stir 5 teaspoons syrup into 1 cup (or more, depending on desired flavor) seltzer water. Store syrup chilled up to 2 weeks. Serves 12

CALORIES 43; **FAT** 0g; **PROTEIN** 0g; **CARB** 11g; **FIBER** 0g; **SUGARS** 10g (est. added sugars 9g); **CHOL** 0mg; **IRON** 0mg; **SODIUM** 0mg; **CALC** 4mg

Gluten Free • Make Ahead
Vegetarian
Celery Soda
Hands-on: 14 min. Total: 1 hr. 14 min.
Combine 9 tablespoons sugar; 1½ cups water; ¾ teaspoon celery seed; 4 finely chopped celery stalks; and the rind, peeled in strips, of 1 lemon in a saucepan over medium-high. Bring to a boil, stirring until sugar dissolves. Remove from heat; steep 1 hour. Strain syrup; discard solids. Cool completely. Stir 4 teaspoons syrup into 1 cup (or more, depending on desired flavor) seltzer water. Store syrup chilled up to 2 weeks. Serves 12

CALORIES 38; **FAT** 0g; **PROTEIN** 0g; **CARB** 10g; **FIBER** 0g; **SUGARS** 10g (est. added sugars 10g); **CHOL** 0mg; **IRON** 0mg; **SODIUM** 3mg; **CALC** 6mg

11. RETHINK YOUR DESK PANTRY

Snacks can be a delicious part of a healthy approach to eating, and the number of smarter choices on the market is increasing. We've selected the following options, which keep sodium and calories in check and provide the salty-sweet-crunchy satisfaction to carry you through a busy afternoon, no matter what's on your plate.

7 SNACKS TO BUY NOW

POPCORN INDIANA HIMALAYAN PINK SALT
Just the right balance of salt with only 37 calories per cup.

CHOBANI FLIP PISTACHIO PARADISE GREEK YOGURT
The perfect combo of crunchy pistachio with tart dried cranberries.

QUINN CLASSIC SEA SALT PRETZELS
They're crispy, delicate, and have a true sea salt flavor.

GOLDFISH MADE WITH ORGANIC WHEAT
A lot of flavor in a large serving size: 55 crackers for 140 calories.

I HEART KEENWAH QUINOA CLUSTERS
For sweet snackers: quinoa paired with almonds and a drizzle of dark chocolate.

PETER PAN SIMPLY GROUND
A creamy-crunchy peanut butter that satisfies all texture preferences.

KASHI SAVORY BARS
The sweeter bar trend turns savory. We loved the Basil, White Bean & Olive Oil combo.

THE *COOKING LIGHT* 3-DAY DETOX

Safely detox your diet with simple, delicious recipes. Here's how:

Maybe your diet has been crowded with processed foods, added sugars, and alcohol lately, or you're simply veering far from your normal healthy habits. Any combination of poor choices can leave clothes fitting tighter and you feeling sluggish. This is why diets that claim to cleanse or detox the body have become so popular. The problem is that most plans attempt to do this with extremely low calories and bizarre food restrictions, leaving your body weak and devoid of key nutrients—not the best way to return to good health.

With the *Cooking Light* 3-Day Detox, we don't resort to liquid-only meals or weird food combos to detoxify. In fact, there's not much research to suggest the body needs help ridding itself of toxins; it does this pretty well on its own. Instead, we're helping you tune up your diet with real, unprocessed, nutrient-dense foods. This is meant to be your reset button, and it's streamlined for your busy life. We've delivered delicious recipes and made prep easy, affordable, and quick (most prep clocks in around 20 minutes or less). Our plan helps you jump back into healthy eating with fresh food at a calorie level that keeps pep in your step. Use it post-holidays, following a week of vacation, or any time you need to get back on track. You'll feel energized, nourished, and empowered to continue enjoying a healthier life.

THE 5 PILLARS OF THE *CL* DETOX

There's a lot of misinformation about what to eliminate from your diet—some backed by science and some not. Here are the key principles we used to create this plan.

1 ELIMINATE ADDED SUGARS
The average American consumes an estimated 19½ teaspoons of added sugar daily—that's around 315 calories, empty of nutrients, that may contribute to weight gain and that, research suggests, increases cardiovascular disease risk. Added sugars may give you a quick burst of energy but also cause a drastic spike and dip in blood sugar levels, leaving you feeling weak and unsatisfied.

2 CHOOSE WHOLE OVER PROCESSED
Get more nutrients and avoid added preservatives and dyes by choosing whole or minimally processed foods. For this detox, the term "whole foods" refers to foods unaltered from the state in which they grew (such as an onion or a pear) or foods that have undergone only minimal processing, such as preparation or packaging for convenience or safety (such as trimmed green beans or packaged pork tenderloin).

3 FOCUS ON VEGETABLES
Make vegetables the center of your plate or dish; then supplement with lean protein, starch, or whole grains and heart-healthy fats. You'll end up with a meal that's more filling, thanks to the fiber in the vegetables, and a more balanced plate when it comes to carbs, protein, and fat.

4 DIVERSIFY YOUR CARBS
Carbs aren't bad; in fact, they're key to survival. What has given them a bad name is the fact that most of us overeat them and don't get them from the recommended sources. Focus on carbohydrates sourced primarily from vegetables, fruits, legumes, and beans with a light addition of whole grains.

5 AVOID ALCOHOL
Give your liver a break and cut some calories by skipping the booze for three days. If you're used to a glass of wine with dinner, this may be hard, but consider how much more you'll appreciate that glass of wine after three days of cleansing.

START HERE: TWO SIMPLE GET-AHEAD RECIPES

Prepping these items in advance will make mealtime quick and easy over the next few days.

Gluten Free • Kid Friendly
Make Ahead • Vegetarian

Easy Baked Spaghetti Squash

(used on Day 2 and Day 3)

Hands-on: 6 min. Total: 1 hr. 16 min.
Preheat oven to 350°F. Cut 1 (3-pound) spaghetti squash in half lengthwise. Scrape out and discard seeds and membranes. Place halves, cut sides down, in a large baking dish; add ½ cup water. Bake at 350°F for 45 to 50 minutes or until tender. Remove squash from oven. Turn cut side up; cool for 10 minutes. Scrape inside of squash with a fork to remove spaghetti-like strands. Yield: 4 to 5 cups (serving size: 1 cup)

CALORIES 42; FAT 0.4g (sat 0.1g, mono 0g, poly 0.2g); PROTEIN 1g; CARB 10g; FIBER 2g; SUGARS 4g (est. added sugars 0g); CHOL 0mg; IRON 1mg; SODIUM 28mg; CALC 33mg

WANT TO TRY THE 3-DAY DETOX, BUT CURIOUS HOW TO FEED YOUR FAMILY WHILE FOLLOWING IT? THE PLAN CONSISTS OF NUTRIENT-RICH FOODS THAT ARE HEALTHY FOR ALL AGES, AND MEALS AND RECIPES CAN BE ADAPTED TO FEED MORE. CONSIDER PREPARING ALL MEALS OR AT LEAST THE DINNER MEAL FOR EVERYONE, ADAPTING AS NEEDED FOR TASTE PREFERENCES.

Quick & Easy • Gluten Free Kid Friendly • Make Ahead Vegetarian

All-Purpose Citrus Dressing

(used on Day 1, Day 2, and Day 3)

Hands-on: 5 min. Total: 5 min.
Homemade dressing comes together in minutes and is far healthier, cheaper, and fresher than bottled dressings with added sugars, chemicals, and fillers. Prep ahead and store in a covered jar or container in the refrigerator. If you're cooking for more than one, feel free to double or triple the dressing.

Whisk together 2 tablespoons olive oil, 1 tablespoon fresh lemon juice, 1 tablespoon fresh orange juice, 2 teaspoons Dijon mustard, ½ teaspoon minced fresh garlic, and a dash each of salt and freshly ground black pepper. Refrigerate in an airtight container. Shake well before using. Yield: 5 tablespoons (serving size: 1 tablespoon)

CALORIES 52; **FAT** 5.4g (sat 0.8g, mono 3.9g, poly 0.6g); **PROTEIN** 0g; **CARB** 1g; **FIBER** 0g; **SUGARS** 0g; **CHOL** 0mg; **IRON** 0mg; **SODIUM** 78mg; **CALC** 1mg

A SIMPLE SHOPPING LIST

We kept an eye on price, ease, and reduced food waste. Here's what you'll need to get cooking—all for about $60.

Produce

- ☐ Baby spinach (1 [6-ounce] bag)
- ☐ Bananas (2)
- ☐ Cherry tomatoes (1 pint)
- ☐ Cucumber (1)
- ☐ Garlic (1 head)
- ☐ Lacinato kale (1 bunch)
- ☐ Lemons (2)
- ☐ Oranges (3) or clementines (5)
- ☐ Pears or apples (2)
- ☐ Plain hummus (1 [7-ounce] container)
- ☐ Poultry-blend herbs or fresh rosemary and thyme sprigs (1 package)
- ☐ Red onion (1)
- ☐ Seedless red grapes (1 pound)
- ☐ Spaghetti squash (1 [3-pound])
- ☐ Sweet potato (1 [10- to 12-ounce])
- ☐ Trimmed green beans (1 [12-ounce] bag)

Staples you'll probably have on hand

- ☐ Cooking spray
- ☐ Dijon mustard
- ☐ Garlic powder
- ☐ Olive oil
- ☐ Red wine vinegar
- ☐ Salt and black pepper

Frozen food

- ☐ Frozen mixed berries (12 ounces)

Dairy

- ☐ Crumbled feta cheese (4 ounces)
- ☐ Large eggs
- ☐ Plain 2% reduced-fat Greek yogurt (1 [5.3-ounce] container)

Dry goods

- ☐ Almond butter (1 [1.15-ounce] packet)
- ☐ Cooked quinoa (1 cup)
- ☐ Low-sodium white tuna in water (1 [2.6-ounce] pouch)
- ☐ Unsalted chickpeas (1 [15-ounce] can)

Meat and Seafood

- ☐ Peeled and deveined large shrimp (6 ounces)
- ☐ Pork tenderloin (8 ounces)
- ☐ Wild salmon fillet (6 ounces)

TOTAL COST: $60.34

DAY 1

BREAKFAST
Berry Green Smoothie

LUNCH
Tuna-Quinoa Toss

MIDMORNING SNACK
3 tablespoons hummus with
1/2 cup fresh cucumber slices

AFTERNOON SNACK
1/2 cup grapes

DINNER
Spinach Salad with Roasted
Sweet Potatoes and Easy Herbed
Pork Tenderloin

DAY 1

1,275 Total Calories

Quick & Easy • Gluten Free
Kid Friendly • Vegetarian

Berry Green Smoothie

Hands-on: 10 min. Total: 10 min.
*Smoothies are a quick way to kick-start
your day with extra fruits, vegetables, and
fiber. Avoid juices and powders with added
sugars; instead choose whole ripe fruit to
add a sweet touch naturally. Dairy-free
option: Use a (5.3-ounce) container of
dairy-free soy yogurt alternative.*

1 cup frozen mixed berries
1/2 cup baby spinach
2 tablespoons fresh orange juice
2 tablespoons water
**1 (5.3-ounce) container plain
   2% reduced-fat Greek yogurt**
1 medium-sized ripe banana, sliced

1. Place all ingredients in a blender;
process until smooth. Serves 1
(serving size: 1¾ cup)

CALORIES 297; FAT 3.8g (sat 2g, mono 0.8g,
poly 0.2g); PROTEIN 18g; CARB 54g; FIBER 8g;
SUGARS 33g (est. added sugars 0g); CHOL 15mg;
IRON 2mg; SODIUM 75mg; CALC 229mg

Quick & Easy • Gluten Free
Kid Friendly • Make Ahead

Tuna-Quinoa Toss

Hands-on: 10 min. Total: 10 min.
*A whole-grain protein bowl is the perfect
solution for when lunch needs to be quick—
as well as tasty, filling, and healthy. Cook the
quinoa ahead of time (or buy precooked,
available in pouches near the rice). To
complete the lunch, serve with 1/2 cup
steamed green beans. Dairy-free option:
Use 2 teaspoons toasted chopped walnuts
instead of feta cheese.*

2 teaspoons extra-virgin olive oil
1 teaspoon red wine vinegar
1/2 teaspoon fresh lemon juice
1/2 teaspoon Dijon mustard
Dash of salt
Dash of freshly ground black pepper
1/2 cup cooked quinoa
**1/4 cup unsalted canned chickpeas,
   rinsed and drained**
1/4 cup chopped cucumber
1 tablespoon crumbled feta cheese
5 cherry tomatoes, halved
**1 (2.6-ounce) pouch solid low-sodium
   white tuna in water**

1. Combine first 6 ingredients in
a small bowl, stirring well with a
whisk.
2. Combine quinoa and remaining
ingredients in a bowl. Drizzle with
dressing; toss gently to coat. Serves
1 (serving size: 1¾ cups)

CALORIES 374; FAT 14g (sat 2.9g, mono 7.5g, poly 2.1g);
PROTEIN 27g; CARB 35g; FIBER 6g; SUGARS 4g
(est. added sugars 0g); CHOL 38mg; IRON 3mg;
SODIUM 460mg; CALC 106mg

HYDRATE

Reach for water throughout the day;
don't wait until you feel thirsty. Add a
squeeze of lemon or lime, or toss in
cucumber slices for flavor if you
struggle to get plain water down.

Gluten Free • Kid Friendly
Vegetarian

Spinach Salad with Roasted Sweet Potatoes

Hands-on: 15 min. Total: 45 min.
*This salad is nutrient- and antioxidant-
packed, with healthy doses of fiber, iron,
potassium, vitamin C, and beta-carotene.
You'll save half the potatoes for the next
day's breakfast.*

1 teaspoon olive oil
1/8 teaspoon salt
1/8 teaspoon garlic powder
**1 large sweet potato (10–12 ounces),
   unpeeled and cut into 1/2-inch cubes**
Cooking spray
2 cups baby spinach
**2 tablespoons All-Purpose Citrus
   Dressing (see page 27)**

1. Preheat oven to 400°F.
2. Combine first 4 ingredients in a
bowl; toss to coat. Arrange potato mixture in a single layer on a
foil-lined baking sheet coated with
cooking spray. Coat potato cubes
lightly with cooking spray. Bake at
400°F for 20 to 25 minutes or until
potatoes are crisp on the outside and
tender on the inside, stirring once
after 12 minutes. Combine spinach
and All-Purpose Citrus Dressing,
and toss gently to coat. Arrange
spinach mixture on a plate; top with
half of sweet potatoes. (Refrigerate
the remaining half of sweet potatoes
for Day 2 Breakfast.) Serves 1 (serving size: 2 cups)

CALORIES 251; FAT 14.2g (sat 1.9g, mono 10.2g, poly 1.7g);
PROTEIN 4g; CARB 26g; FIBER 6g; SUGARS 5g
(est. added sugars 0g); CHOL 0mg; IRON 4mg;
SODIUM 447mg; CALC 140mg

Gluten Free • Kid Friendly
Make Ahead

Easy Herbed Pork Tenderloin

Hands-on: 20 min. Total: 50 min.
We suggest buying poultry blend herbs, which will provide a mix of rosemary and thyme in 1 package (instead of buying 2 separate packages). Be sure to reserve half of the pork for the next day's lunch.

1 tablespoon olive oil
1 teaspoon chopped fresh rosemary
1 teaspoon chopped fresh thyme
1 teaspoon minced fresh garlic
8 ounces pork tenderloin, trimmed
1/8 teaspoon salt
**1/8 teaspoon freshly ground
    black pepper**
Cooking spray

1. Preheat grill to medium-high.
2. Meanwhile, combine first 4 ingredients in a ziplock plastic bag. Add pork, turning to coat. Refrigerate 30 minutes. Remove pork from bag; discard marinade. Sprinkle pork with salt and pepper. Place pork on grill grates coated with cooking spray; grill 16 minutes or until desired degree of doneness, turning occasionally. Remove pork from grill; let stand 5 minutes. Thinly slice. (Refrigerate half of pork for Day 2 Lunch.) Serves 2 (serving size: 3 ounces pork)

CALORIES 197; **FAT** 10.3g (sat 1.8g, mono 6.5g, poly 1.4g); **PROTEIN** 24g; **CARB** 1g; **FIBER** 0g; **SUGARS** 0g (est. added sugars 0g); **CHOL** 74mg; **IRON** 1mg; **SODIUM** 209mg; **CALC** 12mg

RETHINK DAIRY

Most cleanse or detox diets eliminate dairy, but unless you have a dairy allergy or intolerance, research doesn't conclusively show that eliminating it improves your health. Our plan includes dairy, but in small amounts—and we suggest substitutes if you opt to go dairy-free.

DAY 2

BREAKFAST
Sweet Potato Home Fries
with Eggs and 1 orange

LUNCH
Winter Salad with Easy Herbed
Pork Tenderloin

SNACK*
1 medium pear or apple
with 1½ tablespoons almond butter

DINNER
Pan-Seared Shrimp
with Rosemary Spaghetti Squash

* On the go? In place of almond butter, go with 12 walnut halves, 22 whole almonds, 10 whole cashews, 45 pistachios, or 10 peanuts.

DAY 2

1,312 Total Calories

Quick & Easy • Gluten Free
Kid Friendly • Vegetarian

Sweet Potato Home Fries with Eggs

Hands-on: 10 min. Total: 10 min.
With the sweet potatoes already roasted the day before, this breakfast is ready in a flash. Serve with 1 orange or 2 clementines to complete the meal.

Cooking spray
**1 cup Roasted Sweet Potatoes
   (see page 28)**
2 large egg whites
1 large egg
Dash of salt
Chopped fresh thyme

---

1. Heat a medium skillet over medium-high. Coat pan with cooking spray. Add Roasted Sweet Potatoes; sauté 4 minutes. Remove from pan; keep warm.
2. Return skillet to medium; coat with cooking spray. Whisk together egg whites, egg, and salt. Add to pan; cook 3 minutes or until soft-scrambled. Serve with potatoes; top with thyme. Serves 1 (serving size: 1 cup potatoes and about ⅔ cup egg mixture)

CALORIES 240; **FAT** 10.3g (sat 2.1g, mono 5.5g, poly 2.1g); **PROTEIN** 15g; **CARB** 22g; **FIBER** 3g; **SUGARS** 4g (est. added sugars 0g); **CHOL** 186mg; **IRON** 2mg; **SODIUM** 543mg; **CALC** 63mg

Quick & Easy • Gluten Free

Winter Salad

with Easy Herbed Pork Tenderloin

Hands-on: 6 min. Total: 6 min.
Kale and spinach provide a hearty salad base for herb-seasoned pork tenderloin, tangy feta, sweet grapes, and a bright, citrusy olive oil dressing. Dairy-free option: Use 2 teaspoons toasted chopped walnuts instead of feta cheese.

2 cups baby spinach
2 cups thinly sliced lacinato kale
¼ cup seedless red grapes, halved
**2 tablespoons All-Purpose Citrus
   Dressing (see page 27)**
1 tablespoon crumbled feta cheese
**3 ounces Easy Herbed Pork
   Tenderloin (recipe at left)**

1. Combine first 5 ingredients in a bowl; toss. Top with pork. Serves 1 (serving size: 3 cups salad and 3 ounces pork)

CALORIES 383; **FAT** 23.7g (sat 4.8g, mono 14.9g, poly 2.9g); **PROTEIN** 29g; **CARB** 15g; **FIBER** 3g; **SUGARS** 8g (est. added sugars 0g); **CHOL** 82mg; **IRON** 4mg; **SODIUM** 511mg; **CALC** 172mg

DETOX YOUR WALLET, TOO

There are several things to consider about grocery costs. First, most foods will provide you with a little extra to eat after the three days end. Second, the grocery list calls for some convenience foods, such as trimmed green beans and cooked quinoa. These save time but also cost a little more, so consider doing the trimming or cooking yourself to cut costs.

TRY CUTTING CAFFEINE

It's ideal to eliminate caffeine along with processed food, added sugar, and alcohol—so if you can do it, go for it! But if the thought holds you back from following the plan, allow yourself one cup of coffee or tea per day. A splash of dairy is fine, but avoid any added sugars or sweeteners, including artificial ones.

SIMPLE SWAPS

There's no magical combination of superfoods in the plan, so it's fine to substitute a food in the same food group for around the same calories, if needed.

PROTEIN
Swap an equal amount of another lean protein (chicken breast, fish, shrimp, or lean steak).

FRUIT
Use an equal amount of another fresh fruit.

VEGETABLES
Sub an equal amount of another low-calorie vegetable (carrots, green beans, zucchini, broccoli, cauliflower, spinach, leafy greens, or cucumber).

QUINOA
Swap an equal amount of other cooked whole grains.

DAIRY
See dairy-free options listed. May add 1 to 2 tablespoons milk, soy milk, or almond milk to coffee, if desired (no sugar, though).

Quick & Easy • Gluten Free
Kid Friendly

Pan-Seared Shrimp with Rosemary Spaghetti Squash

Hands-on: 20 min. Total: 20 min.
For a faster option, you can use an equal amount of raw zucchini noodles or ribbons in place of the spaghetti squash. For a heartier dinner, serve with 1 cup steamed green beans.

2 teaspoons olive oil, divided
6 ounces large peeled and deveined shrimp
¼ cup thinly sliced red onion
½ teaspoon minced fresh garlic
1½ cups Easy Baked Spaghetti Squash (see page 26)
5 cherry tomatoes, halved
1 teaspoon fresh lemon juice
¼ teaspoon chopped fresh rosemary
Dash of salt

1. Heat a medium skillet over medium-high. Add 1 teaspoon olive oil to pan; swirl to coat. Add shrimp; cook 2 minutes on each side or until done. Remove from pan; keep warm. Return skillet to medium-high. Add remaining 1 teaspoon oil to pan; swirl to coat. Add onion and garlic; sauté 4 minutes or until onion is tender. Add squash, tomatoes, juice, rosemary, and salt. Cook 2 minutes or until warmed through. Top with shrimp. Serves 1 (serving size: about 3 cups)

CALORIES 318; FAT 10.7g (sat 1.6g, mono 6.8g, poly 1.6g); PROTEIN 37g; CARB 22g; FIBER 5g; SUGARS 9g (est. added sugars 0g); CHOL 274mg; IRON 2mg; SODIUM 398mg; CALC 178mg

---

DAY 3

BREAKFAST
Berry Green Smoothie

LUNCH
Greek Spaghetti Squash Toss and 1 orange or 2 clementines

SNACK
3 tablespoons hummus with ½ cup cucumber slices and 1 medium apple

DINNER
Roasted Salmon with Kale-Quinoa Salad

DAY 3

1,285 Total Calories

Quick & Easy • Gluten Free
Kid Friendly • Make Ahead
Vegetarian

Greek Spaghetti Squash Toss

Hands-on: 20 min. Total: 20 min.
Eat with 1 orange or 2 clementines. Dairy-free option: Use 4 teaspoons toasted chopped walnuts instead of feta cheese.

1 teaspoon olive oil
¼ cup thinly sliced red onion
½ teaspoon minced fresh garlic
⅓ cup unsalted chickpeas, rinsed and drained
½ teaspoon chopped fresh thyme
6 cherry tomatoes, halved
1½ cups Easy Baked Spaghetti Squash (see page 26)
1 cup baby spinach, torn
Dash of salt
2 tablespoons crumbled feta cheese

1. Heat a medium skillet over medium-high. Add oil to pan; swirl to coat. Add onion and garlic; sauté 4 minutes. Add chickpeas, thyme, and tomatoes; cook 1 minute. Add spaghetti squash, spinach, and salt; toss gently to combine. Cook

2 minutes or until spinach is just wilted. Sprinkle with cheese. Serves 1 (serving size: 3 cups)

CALORIES 272; FAT 10.9g (sat 3.8g, mono 4.6g, poly 1.7g); PROTEIN 11g; CARB 37g; FIBER 10g; SUGARS 13g (est. added sugars 0g); CHOL 17mg; IRON 4mg; SODIUM 516mg; CALC 246mg

Quick & Easy • Gluten Free

Roasted Salmon with Kale-Quinoa Salad

***Hands-on: 15 min. Total: 15 min.** The American Heart Association recommends eating salmon or other fatty fish twice a week to reap the cardio-vascular benefits that the omega-3 fatty acids provide.*

1 (6-ounce) wild salmon fillet
Cooking spray
1 teaspoon olive oil
⅛ teaspoon salt
⅛ teaspoon freshly ground black pepper
1½ cups thinly sliced lacinato kale
½ cup cooked quinoa
1 tablespoon All-Purpose Citrus Dressing (see page 27)
5 seedless red grapes, halved

1. Preheat oven to 425°F.
2. Place salmon on a foil-lined baking sheet coated with cooking spray. Rub evenly with oil, salt, and pepper. Bake at 425°F for 10 minutes or until fish flakes easily when tested with a fork.
3. While fish cooks, combine kale, quinoa, All-Purpose Citrus Dressing, and grapes in a bowl; toss to combine. Let stand 5 minutes. Top with salmon. Serves 1 (serving size: 1½ cups salad and 1 fillet)

CALORIES 453; FAT 19.8g (sat 3g, mono 10.4g, poly 4g); PROTEIN 43g; CARB 27g; FIBER 4g; SUGARS 5g (est. added sugars 0g); CHOL 86mg; IRON 3mg; SODIUM 519mg; CALC 72mg

HEARTY MEATBALL STEW

Add this comforting, 35-minute stew to your winter recipe rotation.

Barbro O'Malley says she's tried "every diet under the sun" in her 81 years, but it wasn't until her daughter-in-law turned her onto the Cooking Light Diet that she finally found a plan that worked for her. "It's just learning to eat properly," she says. "This is the way I should have been eating forever. I think [this diet] really teaches you to eat better, and I'm learning portion control. That's a big thing for me." To celebrate O'Malley's success, we sent her this recipe to try—ideal comfort food for an Indiana winter. "It was easy, delicious, and very hearty. And knowing I can have a 2-cup serving of it—whoopee!"

Quick & Easy • Kid Friendly Make Ahead • Freezable

Spiced Meatball, Butternut, and Tomato Stew

Hands-on: 35 min. Total: 35 min.

1½ whole-wheat bread slices, cubed
⅓ cup 2% reduced-fat milk
1 pound ground sirloin
½ teaspoon ground cumin
½ teaspoon ground coriander
½ teaspoon freshly ground black pepper
½ cup chopped fresh cilantro, divided
⅝ teaspoon kosher salt, divided
2 tablespoons olive oil
1 cup chopped butternut squash
¾ cup chopped yellow onion
1 tablespoon finely chopped fresh garlic
1¼ cups unsalted beef stock
2 cups chopped tomatoes
¾ cup unsalted tomato sauce
1½ cups cauliflower florets

1. Place bread cubes in a bowl; pour milk over bread. Let stand 5 minutes.
2. Gently combine soaked bread cubes, beef, cumin, coriander, pepper, ¼ cup cilantro, and ⅛ teaspoon salt in a medium bowl. Gently shape into 12 (1½-inch) meatballs.
3. Heat a Dutch oven over medium-high. Add oil to pan; swirl to coat. Add meatballs in a single layer; cook, turning to brown on all sides, about 4 minutes. Transfer meatballs to a plate. Add squash, onion, and garlic to pan; cook, stirring occasionally, 3 minutes. Add stock, scraping pan to loosen browned bits. Add remaining ½ teaspoon salt; cook until liquid is reduced by half, about 6 minutes. Add tomatoes and tomato sauce; bring to a simmer. Cook, stirring occasionally, until slightly thickened, 6 to 8 minutes. Stir in cauliflower; cover and cook 3 minutes. Return meatballs to pan; cover and cook just until meatballs are cooked through, 6 to 8 minutes. Sprinkle with remaining ¼ cup cilantro. Serves 4 (serving size: 2 cups)

CALORIES 335; FAT 13.1g (sat 3.3g, mono 7.1g, poly 1.6g); PROTEIN 29g; CARB 29g; FIBER 7g; SUGARS 10g (est. added sugars 1g); CHOL 62mg; IRON 5mg; SODIUM 556mg; CALCIUM 120mg

ONE-DISH CHICKEN DINNERS

We combine America's favorite dinner bird with our favorite way to cook: everything together in one pan for less fuss, easy cleanup, and downright delicious results.

SKILLET

The skillet is chief among one-dish cooking vessels because of its accommodating base and shallow sides: You can sear, sauté, or stir-fry; add liquid for a quick braise; or pop under the broiler for a great crust. This stovetop-to-oven maneuver allows for beautifully browned chicken that's also perfectly cooked (many one-dish meals often sacrifice one for the other).

Kid Friendly
Skillet Chicken and Root Vegetable Potpie

Hands-on: 50 min. Total: 1 hr. 20 min.
You can substitute diced Yukon Gold potatoes and kale or chard for the turnips and turnip greens.

2 tablespoons olive oil, divided
3 (6-ounce) skinless, boneless chicken breasts
1 teaspoon kosher salt, divided
1 teaspoon black pepper, divided
3 cups unsalted chicken stock (such as Swanson), divided
2.8 ounces all-purpose flour (about ½ cup)
1½ cups chopped yellow onion
1 cup diagonally cut carrot
2 teaspoons minced fresh garlic
4 cups coarsely chopped turnip greens or kale (about 3 ounces)
1 pound turnips, peeled and cut into ¾-inch cubes (about 3 cups)
3 tablespoons chopped fresh flat-leaf parsley
½ (14.1-ounce) package refrigerated piecrust
1 large egg white, lightly beaten

1. Heat 1 tablespoon oil in a 10-inch cast-iron or other ovenproof skillet over medium-high. Sprinkle chicken with ½ teaspoon salt and ½ teaspoon pepper. Add chicken to pan; cook 6 minutes on each side. Place chicken on a cutting board; let stand 10 minutes. Shred into large pieces.
2. Preheat oven to 425°F.
3. Combine 2½ cups stock and flour in a bowl, stirring with a whisk. Add remaining 1 tablespoon oil to pan. Add onion, carrot, and garlic; sauté 6 minutes. Add remaining ½ cup stock, scraping pan to loosen browned bits. Stir in turnip greens; cook 1 minute. Stir in remaining ½ teaspoon salt, remaining ½ teaspoon pepper, and flour mixture. Add turnips; bring to a boil. Reduce heat, and simmer 15 minutes or until vegetables are tender. Stir in chicken and parsley. Remove pan from heat.
4. Arrange piecrust over pan, folding edges under as needed. Cut slits in dough to allow steam to escape. Brush with egg white. Bake at 425°F for 20 minutes. Cool 10 minutes. Serves 8 (serving size: about 1¼ cups)

CALORIES 297; FAT 11.9g (sat 3.7g, mono 2.9g, poly 0.7g); PROTEIN 20g; CARB 28g; FIBER 3g; SUGARS 5g (est. added sugars 0g); CHOL 49mg; IRON 1mg; SODIUM 509mg; CALC 58mg

Quick & Easy • Gluten Free
Kid Friendly • Make Ahead
Tuscan Chicken with White Beans and Kale

Hands-on: 22 min. Total: 22 min.
The main, starch, and side are all included in this true one-dish dinner. Feel free to use bumpy lacinato or curly kale; just be sure to remove the tough stems first.

2 tablespoons olive oil
4 (6-ounce) skinless, boneless chicken breast halves
¾ teaspoon kosher salt, divided
½ teaspoon black pepper
1 cup chopped yellow onion
1 cup chopped carrot
2 tablespoons chopped fresh thyme
5 garlic cloves, minced
½ cup dry white wine
8 ounces lacinato kale, stemmed and thinly sliced (about 1 bunch)
1 cup unsalted chicken stock (such as Swanson)
2 teaspoons grated lemon rind
2 (15-ounce) cans unsalted cannellini beans, rinsed and drained
1 (15-ounce) can unsalted diced tomatoes, drained
1 tablespoon unsalted tomato paste

1. Heat oil in a large skillet over medium-high. Sprinkle chicken with ½ teaspoon salt and pepper. Add chicken to pan; cook 4 minutes on each side (chicken will not be cooked through). Remove chicken from pan.

2. Add onion, carrot, thyme, and garlic to pan; sauté 5 minutes. Add wine; cook 2 minutes. Add kale; cook 3 minutes or until wilted. Stir in remaining ¼ teaspoon salt, stock, and remaining ingredients; bring to a simmer. Add chicken; cover, reduce heat, and simmer 4 minutes or until done. Serves 4 (serving size: 4 ounces chicken and 1½ cups bean mixture)

CALORIES 516; **FAT** 13.7g (sat 2g, mono 6.6g, poly 1.6g); **PROTEIN** 52g; **CARB** 43g; **FIBER** 12g; **SUGARS** 8g (est. added sugars 0g); **CHOL** 124mg; **IRON** 5mg; **SODIUM** 609mg; **CALC** 179mg

---

Staff Favorite • Quick & Easy
Kid Friendly

Chicken and Butternut Gnocchi

Hands-on: 15 min. Total: 30 min.
Prepared gnocchi doesn't require boiling; it can go right in the pan.

2 tablespoons olive oil, divided
4 (6-ounce) skinless, boneless chicken thighs, cut into 1-inch pieces
3 cups (½-inch) cubed peeled butternut squash
½ cup chopped yellow onion
1 (12-ounce) package whole-wheat gnocchi
¾ cup unsalted chicken stock (such as Swanson)
2 tablespoons prepared refrigerated pesto
2 teaspoons chopped fresh sage
½ teaspoon chopped fresh garlic
5 ounces baby spinach, chopped
1 ounce Parmesan cheese, grated (about ¼ cup)

1. Heat 1 tablespoon oil in a large skillet over medium-high. Add chicken; cook 5 minutes or until browned. Place chicken in a bowl. **2.** Heat remaining 1 tablespoon oil in pan over medium. Add squash and onion; cook 8 minutes. Add

squash mixture to chicken. Add gnocchi to pan; cook 2 minutes. Add chicken mixture, stock, pesto, sage, garlic, and spinach to pan; cook 1 minute. Top with cheese. Serves 4 (serving size: about 1¼ cups)

CALORIES 526; **FAT** 19.3g (sat 4.5g, mono 9.7g, poly 2.6g); **PROTEIN** 43g; **CARB** 44g; **FIBER** 9g; **SUGARS** 4g (est. added sugars 0g); **CHOL** 165mg; **IRON** 6mg; **SODIUM** 748mg; **CALC** 202mg

---

DUTCH OVEN

The Dutch oven deserves a permanent spot on your stovetop (get one in a cheery color to brighten your kitchen). The base and sides are thicker and stronger than a saucepan, as they're usually made of enamel-coated cast iron. The pan keeps an even heat at any temperature, is oven-safe, and can accommodate a lot of liquid—ideal for seared and braised bone-in chicken pieces or even a whole bird.

Staff Favorite • Make Ahead

Miso-Ginger Braised Chicken with Bok Choy and Barley

Hands-on: 28 min. Total: 1 hr. 28 min.
We call for whole-grain hulled, or hull-less, barley here—pearled barley would overcook as the chicken simmers. You can also use unpearled farro or wheat berries.

1 cup uncooked whole-grain hulled barley
1 tablespoon olive oil
1 (3½- to 4-pound) whole chicken, trimmed of excess fat
¾ teaspoon kosher salt, divided
¾ teaspoon black pepper, divided
8 green onions, cut into 1-inch pieces, light- and dark-green parts divided

3 tablespoons minced peeled fresh ginger
10 medium garlic cloves, smashed
2 cups unsalted chicken stock (such as Swanson)
3 tablespoons white miso
2½ tablespoons rice vinegar
3 heads baby bok choy (about 1 pound), halved lengthwise
¼ cup fresh cilantro leaves

1. Preheat oven to 375°F.
2. Heat a Dutch oven over medium-high. Add barley to dry pan; cook 8 minutes or until deeply browned. Remove from pan.
3. Add oil to pan; swirl. Sprinkle chicken with ½ teaspoon salt and ½ teaspoon pepper. Add chicken to pan, breast side down; cook 6 minutes. Carefully turn chicken over; cook 4 minutes. Remove from pan.
4. Add light-green onion parts, ginger, and garlic to pan; cook 2 minutes, stirring frequently. Add remaining ¼ teaspoon salt, remaining ¼ teaspoon pepper, stock, miso, and vinegar. Bring to a boil, stirring to dissolve miso and loosen browned bits. Add barley and chicken to pan. Cover and bake at 375°F for 45 minutes.
5. Arrange bok choy halves around chicken; cover and bake at 375°F for 15 more minutes. Uncover, and sprinkle dark-green onion parts and cilantro over chicken mixture. Serves 6 (serving size: about 4½ ounces chicken, ½ head bok choy, and about ⅔ cup barley mixture)

CALORIES 506; **FAT** 24.5g (sat 6.4g, mono 10.6g, poly 5.2g); **PROTEIN** 41g; **CARB** 31g; **FIBER** 8g; **SUGARS** 4g (est. added sugars 0g); **CHOL** 135mg; **IRON** 4mg; **SODIUM** 732mg; **CALC** 130mg

---

NESTING BIRD

A whole chicken, nestled in toasted barley and bok choy, lends richness to the miso-spiked broth. The Dutch oven holds all, and maintains steady heat on the stove top and in the oven.

Kid Friendly • Make Ahead

Chicken Stroganoff

Hands-on: 40 min. Total: 40 min.
If stroganoff could restore its Russian creators 200 years ago, this chicken version will restore you on any winter weeknight.

2 tablespoons olive oil, divided
1 pound chicken breast tenders, cut into 1-inch pieces
1 teaspoon kosher salt, divided
³/₄ teaspoon black pepper, divided
2¹/₂ cups unsalted chicken stock, divided (such as Swanson)
1 tablespoon all-purpose flour
1 (8-ounce) package presliced cremini mushrooms
1 tablespoon minced fresh garlic
2 teaspoons chopped fresh thyme
¹/₂ cup dry white wine
6 ounces uncooked wide egg noodles
¹/₂ cup light sour cream
1 tablespoon chopped fresh flat-leaf parsley

1. Heat 1 tablespoon oil in a large Dutch oven over medium-high. Sprinkle chicken with ¼ teaspoon salt and ¼ teaspoon pepper. Add chicken to pan; cook 6 minutes or until done, turning once. Remove from pan.
2. Combine 1 tablespoon stock and flour in a small bowl. Add remaining 1 tablespoon oil to pan over medium-high. Add mushrooms; cook 8 minutes. Stir in garlic and thyme; cook 1 minute. Add wine; cook 2 minutes or until reduced by half, scraping pan to loosen browned bits. Stir in remaining 2 cups and 7 tablespoons stock; bring to a simmer. Add noodles; cook, uncovered, 8 minutes or until done. Stir in flour mixture; cook 1 minute. Remove pan from heat; stir in chicken, remaining ¾ teaspoon salt, remaining ½ teaspoon

pepper, and sour cream. Sprinkle with parsley. Serves 4 (serving size: about 1½ cups)

CALORIES 443; **FAT** 12.8g (sat 3.3g, mono 6.3g, poly 1.8g); **PROTEIN** 39g; **CARB** 39g; **FIBER** 2g; **SUGARS** 5g (est. added sugars 0g); **CHOL** 111mg; **IRON** 3mg; **SODIUM** 681mg; **CALC** 35mg

---

Kid Friendly • Make Ahead

Chicken Adobo

Hands-on: 20 min. Total: 8 hr. 45 min.
Complete the meal with hot cooked brown rice and thinly sliced cucumber and carrots.

2 cups rice vinegar
¹/₄ cup reduced-sodium soy sauce
10 garlic cloves, crushed
8 (6-ounce) bone-in chicken thighs, skinned
3 Thai chiles, halved lengthwise
2 bay leaves
1 (13.5-ounce) can light coconut milk
2 tablespoons canola oil, divided
¹/₂ teaspoon cracked black pepper

1. Place first 7 ingredients in a large ziplock bag. Refrigerate 8 hours or overnight.
2. Remove chicken from bag. Strain marinade over a bowl; discard solids.
3. Heat 1 tablespoon oil in a Dutch oven over medium-high. Add 4 chicken thighs; cook 3 to 4 minutes on each side. Remove from pan. Repeat procedure with remaining oil and chicken.
4. Bring reserved marinade and chicken to a boil in pan. Reduce heat; cover and simmer 12 minutes. Boil cooking liquid 12 minutes. Serve sauce with chicken. Sprinkle with pepper. Serves 8 (serving size: 1 chicken thigh and 2 tablespoons sauce)

CALORIES 264; **FAT** 10.7g (sat 3.4g, mono 3.9g, poly 2.2g); **PROTEIN** 22g; **CARB** 19g; **FIBER** 2g; **SUGARS** 3g (est. added sugars 0g); **CHOL** 96mg; **IRON** 1mg; **SODIUM** 424mg; **CALC** 30mg

---

SLOW COOKER

The slow cooker works a kind of magic over those many hands-free hours. With the right technique, you can avoid dulled flavors and textures; instead, succulent chicken breasts and thighs, plus robust broths and sauces, will emerge. The trick is knowing when and how to add the ingredients so that each improves the next and reaches a tasty crescendo just before you're ready to serve.

Kid Friendly • Make Ahead

Slow Cooker Chicken Cacciatore

Hands-on: 10 min. Total: 8 hr. 10 min.
While the chicken becomes fall-apart tender, briny capers, crushed red pepper, and garlic infuse the tomatoes for a robust marinara sauce.

¹/₂ cup water
1 tablespoon all-purpose flour
2 cups unsalted chicken stock (such as Swanson)
¹/₂ cup white wine
¹/₄ cup chopped fresh oregano
¹/₄ cup drained capers
¹/₂ teaspoon kosher salt
¹/₂ teaspoon crushed red pepper
8 garlic cloves, chopped
1 (28-ounce) container diced tomatoes (such as Pomi)
1 (8-ounce) package cremini mushrooms, quartered
8 (6-ounce) bone-in chicken thighs, skinned (about 3 pounds)
2 tablespoons extra-virgin olive oil
12 ounces uncooked spaghetti, broken in half
5 ounces baby spinach
2 ounces Parmesan cheese, grated (about ¹/₂ cup)

1. Combine ½ cup water and flour in a 6-quart electric slow cooker, stirring with a whisk. Stir in stock and next 8 ingredients (through mushrooms). Add chicken thighs to stock mixture; submerge in liquid. Cover and cook on LOW 7½ hours. Remove chicken. When cool enough to handle, remove bones from chicken; discard bones.

2. Add oil and pasta to slow cooker; cover and cook on HIGH 15 minutes or until pasta is done. Stir in spinach until wilted. Divide pasta mixture among 8 shallow bowls; top evenly with chicken. Sprinkle with Parmesan cheese. Serves 8 (serving size: about 1 cup pasta mixture, 1 chicken thigh, and 1 tablespoon cheese)

CALORIES 490; FAT 13.2g (sat 3.6g, mono 5.8g, poly 2.3g); PROTEIN 44g; CARB 43g; FIBER 4g; SUGARS 2g (est. added sugars 0g); CHOL 166mg; IRON 4mg; SODIUM 569mg; CALC 121mg

Kid Friendly • Make Ahead
Freezable

Slow Cooker Chicken Posole

Hands-on: 10 min. Total: 6 hr. 10 min.
Think of posole as chili's brothier, lighter cousin, a Mexican version of chicken soup. Posole is also a name for the hominy, or rehydrated dried corn, that goes in the dish.

2 cups water
2 cups unsalted chicken stock (such as Swanson)
1 cup chopped yellow onion
½ cup chopped poblano pepper (1 medium)
1 tablespoon ground cumin
2 teaspoons chopped fresh garlic
1 teaspoon dried oregano
1 (28-ounce) can white hominy, drained
2 (10-ounce) bone-in chicken breasts, skinned

⅓ cup finely chopped peeled tomatillos
¼ cup chopped fresh cilantro
1 tablespoon fresh lime juice
¼ teaspoon kosher salt
⅓ cup sliced radishes
1½ ripe avocados, sliced
3 ounces tortilla strips (such as Fresh Gourmet)
¼ teaspoon black pepper

1. Combine first 8 ingredients in a 6-quart electric slow cooker. Add chicken to stock mixture; submerge in liquid. Cover and cook on LOW 6 to 8 hours. Remove chicken from cooker. When cool enough to handle, remove bones, and shred chicken into large pieces.

2. Return chicken to slow cooker; stir in tomatillos, cilantro, juice, and salt. Divide soup among 6 bowls; top evenly with radishes, avocado, tortilla strips, and pepper. Serves 6 (serving size: 1½ cups)

CALORIES 269; FAT 10.4g (sat 1.1g, mono 4.7g, poly 2.8g); PROTEIN 15g; CARB 30g; FIBER 6g; SUGARS 5g (est. added sugars 0g); CHOL 29mg; IRON 2mg; SODIUM 611mg; CALC 35mg

Staff Favorite • Gluten Free
Make Ahead • Freezable

Slow Cooker Chicken Congee

Hands-on: 5 min. Total: 8 hr. 5 min.
The slow cooker does all the work in this comforting rice porridge, breaking down the rice with fragrant ginger and star anise and poaching the chicken until silky. A bit of chili oil is the vibrant kick this dish needs. You can also use Sriracha or a squeeze of fresh lime juice. Cilantro or baby spinach leaves can work in place of the watercress.

8 cups unsalted chicken stock (such as Swanson)
1 cup uncooked jasmine rice

1 tablespoon grated peeled fresh ginger
1½ teaspoons kosher salt
3 pounds bone-in, skin-on chicken breasts
1 Thai chile
1 star anise pod
½ cup roasted, unsalted peanuts, chopped
½ cup chopped green onions
2 tablespoons hot chili oil
2 ounces watercress sprigs
1 ripe avocado, diced

1. Place first 7 ingredients in a 6-quart electric slow cooker. Cover and cook on LOW 7½ hours. Remove chicken. When cool enough to handle, remove skin and bones, and discard. Shred chicken into large pieces.

2. Cover slow cooker, and cook on HIGH 30 minutes or until rice mixture is thickened. Remove chile and star anise; discard. Stir in chicken. Divide rice mixture among 8 bowls. Top servings evenly with peanuts, green onions, chili oil, watercress, and avocado. Serves 8 (serving size: 1¼ cups)

CALORIES 348; FAT 13.6g (sat 2.2g, mono 5.6g, poly 3.9g); PROTEIN 33g; CARB 23g; FIBER 2g; SUGARS 2g (est. added sugars 0g); CHOL 81mg; IRON 2mg; SODIUM 546mg; CALC 26mg

SLOW AND STEADY

The slow cooker ignores the chef's credo of seasoning in stages, but it works. In Slow Cooker Chicken Posole, the cumin, garlic, and oregano stand up to the long, low simmer, infusing the broth and the chicken.

SHEET PAN

The sheet pan quadruples your surface area, letting you roast items in less time and with more delightfully crispy edges. In these recipes, bone-in chicken pieces contribute their juices and keep everything from drying out—call it a self-basting supper. Plus, starchy vegetables caramelize and crisp as they become perfectly tender. Bring the pan straight to the table for a presentation that wows.

Gluten Free • Kid Friendly

Maple-Mustard Roasted Chicken with Squash and Brussels Sprouts

(pictured on page 209)

Hands-on: 20 min. Total: 1 hr.
We give the large bone-in breasts a head start in the oven so they will be perfectly cooked by the time the vegetables are done.

1 tablespoon chopped fresh sage
1 tablespoon Dijon mustard
1 tablespoon pure maple syrup
4 (10-ounce) bone-in, skin-on
    chicken breasts
4 cups cubed peeled butternut
    squash (about 1 pound)
3 large shallots, peeled and quartered
1/2 acorn squash, seeded and cut
    crosswise into slices
8 ounces Brussels sprouts, trimmed
    and halved (about 2 cups)
2 tablespoons unsalted butter, melted
1 tablespoon olive oil
1 1/2 teaspoons kosher salt, divided
1 teaspoon black pepper, divided

1. Place a large rimmed baking sheet in oven; preheat oven to 425°F (leave pan in oven as it preheats).
2. Combine sage, mustard, and syrup in a small bowl; brush evenly over chicken breasts. Carefully remove

pan from oven. Add chicken to pan; bake at 425°F for 20 minutes. Remove pan from oven. Discard any juices from pan.
3. Add butternut squash, shallots, acorn squash, and Brussels sprouts to pan with chicken. Top vegetables with butter, oil, 3/4 teaspoon salt, and 3/4 teaspoon pepper; toss. Spread in an even layer around chicken. Sprinkle chicken with remaining 3/4 teaspoon salt and remaining 1/4 teaspoon pepper. Bake at 425°F for 20 minutes or until chicken is done. Remove bones from chicken before serving; discard. Serves 6 (serving size: 4 ounces chicken and 1 cup vegetables)

CALORIES 376; FAT 14.9g (sat 5.2g, mono 6g, poly 2.3g); PROTEIN 36g; CARB 26g; FIBER 4g; SUGARS 7g (est. added sugars 2g); CHOL 103mg; IRON 3mg; SODIUM 634mg; CALC 97mg

Gluten Free • Kid Friendly

Chimichurri Roasted Chicken with Potatoes and Onions

Hands-on: 10 min. Total: 55 min.
A whole chicken, cut into quarters, lets everyone enjoy their favorite parts of the bird. You can quarter the chicken yourself by removing each breast first, followed by the thigh and leg pieces.

1/2 cup finely chopped shallots
1/3 cup chopped fresh cilantro
1/4 cup olive oil, divided
1/4 cup red wine vinegar, divided
1 1/2 teaspoons kosher salt, divided
3/4 teaspoon crushed red pepper
1 (4 1/2-pound) whole chicken,
    quartered
1 tablespoon paprika
1 pound small red potatoes,
    quartered
2 small red onions, cut into wedges
Cilantro sprigs

1. Preheat oven to 425°F. Line a rimmed baking sheet with foil.
2. Combine shallots, cilantro, 2 tablespoons oil, 2 tablespoons vinegar, 1 teaspoon salt, and red pepper in a small bowl. Carefully remove skin from chicken; reserve. Rub cilantro mixture evenly over chicken. Arrange reserved chicken skin over chicken.
3. Drizzle 1 tablespoon oil over prepared pan. Add paprika and potatoes; toss to coat. Add onions to pan; sprinkle with remaining 1 tablespoon oil and remaining 1/2 teaspoon salt. Arrange chicken quarters, skin side up, on pan. Bake at 425°F for 35 minutes or until chicken is done. Place chicken on a cutting board; let stand 5 minutes. Remove skin from breasts; discard. Cut breasts in half crosswise.
4. Preheat broiler to high.
5. Return pan with vegetables to oven; broil 5 minutes or until vegetables are caramelized. Return chicken to pan; sprinkle with remaining 2 tablespoons vinegar and top with cilantro sprigs. Serves 6 (serving size: about 4 1/2 ounces chicken and 1 cup vegetables)

CALORIES 355; FAT 14.4g (sat 2.5g, mono 8.7g, poly 2.2g); PROTEIN 38g; CARB 17g; FIBER 3g; SUGARS 3g (est. added sugars 0g); CHOL 113mg; IRON 3mg; SODIUM 628mg; CALC 39mg

Quick & Easy • Kid Friendly

Greek Chicken Nachos

Hands-on: 24 min. Total: 33 min.

3 (6-inch) whole-wheat pitas
Cooking spray
2 1/2 tablespoons extra-virgin olive
    oil, divided
2 tablespoons red wine vinegar
1/4 teaspoon freshly ground black
    pepper
4 cups shredded romaine lettuce

1 cup grape tomatoes, halved
1 cup chopped English cucumber
10 pitted kalamata olives, halved
  lengthwise
8 ounces skinless, boneless rotisserie
  chicken breast, shredded (about
  2 cups)
3 ounces part-skim mozzarella
  cheese, shredded (about ¾ cup)
2 ounces feta cheese, crumbled
  (about ½ cup)
2 tablespoons chopped fresh oregano

1. Preheat oven to 400°F.
2. Split each pita in half horizontally
into rounds. Coat cut sides of pitas
with cooking spray. Cut each pita half
into 8 wedges. Arrange half of wedges,
cut sides up, on a baking sheet lined
with foil. Bake at 400°F for 8 minutes
or until browned; remove from pan.
Repeat procedure with remaining
wedges. Cool 10 minutes.
3. Combine oil, vinegar, and pepper
in a medium bowl, stirring with
a whisk. Add lettuce, tomatoes,
cucumber, and olives; toss to coat.
4. Arrange all pita chips on foil-
lined baking sheet so they overlap.
Top with chicken, mozzarella, and
feta. Bake at 400°F for 3 minutes or
until cheese melts. Top with lettuce
mixture and oregano. Serves 6

CALORIES 343; FAT 13.8g (sat 4.5g, mono 6.7g,
poly 1g); PROTEIN 22g; CARB 35g; FIBER 4g;
SUGARS 3g (est. added sugars 0g); CHOL 51mg;
IRON 3mg; SODIUM 553mg; CALC 219mg

Gluten Free • Kid Friendly

Sumac Chicken with Cauliflower and Carrots

Hands-on: 10 min. Total: 55 min.
This sheet pan supper gets a double dose of
bright citrus: thin lemon slices roasted until
tender and fresh lemon juice added to a quick
herb dressing, spooned over the finished dish.

Sumac has a tart, lemony quality as well. It's
fantastic as a rub here but is also delicious in
vinaigrettes or sprinkled over dips.

6 tablespoons olive oil, divided
1 tablespoon sumac
1¼ teaspoons kosher salt, divided
1 teaspoon light brown sugar
1 teaspoon paprika
¼ teaspoon ground red pepper
1 pound cauliflower florets
2 (6-ounce) packages small rainbow
  carrots, halved lengthwise
1 pound bone-in chicken thighs, skinned
1 pound skinless drumsticks
1 small lemon, halved lengthwise and
  thinly sliced
1 small red onion, cut into ¾-inch
  wedges
½ cup finely chopped fresh flat-leaf
  parsley
½ cup chopped fresh cilantro
1 tablespoon fresh lemon juice
1 small garlic clove

1. Preheat oven to 425°F.
2. Combine 3 tablespoons oil, sumac,
1 teaspoon salt, brown sugar, paprika,
and red pepper in a medium bowl.
Place cauliflower and carrots on a
foil-lined baking sheet. Add half of
oil mixture; toss to coat. Add chick-
en thighs, drumsticks, and lemon
slices to pan. Rub remaining oil mixture over chicken. Bake at 425°F for
20 minutes. Stir vegetables. Sprinkle
onion wedges over pan. Bake at
425°F for 20 more minutes or until
chicken is done.
3. Combine remaining 3 tablespoons
oil, remaining ¼ teaspoon salt,
parsley, and remaining ingredients in
a small bowl. Spoon parsley mixture
evenly over chicken and vegetables.
Serves 6 (about 5 ounces chicken
and 1 cup vegetables)

CALORIES 314; FAT 19.7g (sat 3.6g, mono 12.2g,
poly 2.8g); PROTEIN 22g; CARB 13g; FIBER 4g;
SUGARS 6g (est. added sugars 1g); CHOL 108mg;
IRON 2mg; SODIUM 562mg; CALC 61mg

WOW!

Gluten Free • Kid Friendly
Make Ahead

Retro Triple-Layer Parfaits

Hands-on: 30 min. Total: 3 hr.

2 envelopes plus ½ teaspoon
  unflavored gelatin
4¼ cups chilled no-added-sugar
  cranberry-pomegranate juice blend
½ cup cold heavy cream
¼ teaspoon vanilla extract

1. Pour 2 envelopes gelatin over 1 cup
cold juice in a large bowl; let stand
5 minutes. Heat 3 cups juice in a
microwave-safe dish at HIGH 3 to
4 minutes or until scalding hot; pour
over gelatin mixture, stirring until
dissolved. Pour ⅓ cup of mixture into
each of 6 glasses, reserving remaining
mixture. Refrigerate 15 minutes.
2. Place bowl with remaining gelatin
mixture in a larger bowl filled with
ice water. Vigorously whisk mixture
until it becomes a dense, pale-pink
foam and no liquid remains (about
10 minutes). Evenly divide foam
among glasses. Chill 30 minutes.
3. Place remaining ¼ cup juice in a
small microwave-safe dish; sprinkle
with remaining ½ teaspoon gelatin,
and let stand 5 minutes. Microwave
mixture at HIGH 1 to 1½ minutes
or until gelatin is dissolved. Cool.
4. Combine cream and vanilla; whisk
just until the whisk begins to leave
trails in the cream. Add microwaved
gelatin mixture in a steady stream
while whisking; beat just until soft
peaks form. Spoon cream over foamy
gelatin layer in glasses; chill 2 hours
or until all layers are thoroughly set.
Serves 6 (serving size: 1 parfait)

CALORIES 201; FAT 7.4g (sat 4.6g, mono 2.1g,
poly 0.3g); PROTEIN 9g; CARB 25g; FIBER 0g;
SUGARS 23g (est. added sugars 0g); CHOL 27mg;
IRON 0mg; SODIUM 51mg; CALC 18mg

CALDO DE GALLINA FOR THE SOUL

by Shane Mitchell

Steaming Peruvian chicken soup warms this food writer to the core.

North Country winters are harsh. The mercury hovers at -10° Fahrenheit, and the sun negotiates an abridged arc in skies that are more often gray than not. On these days, as the wind roars through pines and rattles the old windowpanes, I seek comfort in the kitchen, one of the warmest rooms in my upstate New York 1820s farmhouse. This is chicken soup weather.

My go-to soup recipe is a treasured souvenir of an extended journey far from home, one I picked up during a research trip to the Peruvian Andes, where Quechua ladies prepare *caldo de gallina*, or hen soup, at stalls in Cusco's San Pedro Market. Here, frugal cooks use tough stewing hens that are long past laying eggs. Older birds are often stringy but create rich stock. They aren't always readily available, though, so I've learned a roaster is a fine alternative, aged enough to produce similarly concentrated flavor with even more meat on its bones. Following breakfast, I set a large stockpot on the stove, and then quarter a chicken, adding the pieces to aromatics in cold, filtered water. I set the soup to simmer, then peel and chop more ingredients to add later.

My dog, Dharma, wants to go out. She doesn't mind subzero temperatures or the onset of a storm, and bounds through the snowdrifts after a squirrel that foolishly attempts to raid the bird feeder. I lower the heat on the stove and pull on an Arctic goose-down parka, then stomp a path to the garage to gather firewood as flurries swirl in the wind.

Dharma returns from her romp. We hustle back inside, snow melting on the heart pine floors. I haul logs into the dining room and start a fire there as the last light fades in the west. The dog flops down next to the blaze. I add potatoes, then noodles, as starchy thickeners. After hours of slow cooking, the chicken breaks down into tender morsels that easily shred with a fork, and the pot liquor turns golden. It smells gamey and herbal, like a cure for homesickness. Peruvians traditionally add a squeeze of lime, fiery chiles, and chopped cilantro before serving. These garnishes brighten the heady broth, adding subtle heat to each mouthful. I spoon some into a bowl as the windows steam up, hiding the blizzard outside for a little while.

Kid Friendly • Make Ahead

Caldo de Gallina (Peruvian Hen Soup)

Hands-on: 20 min. Total: 5 hr. 40 min.
A corner of Cusco's San Pedro Market is devoted to open kitchens where Quechua women make this soup with new-crop potatoes and tough old stewing hens, which can stand up to the long simmering time better than young chickens. We find that widely available roasting hens—older than broilers and fryers—work just fine, growing tender and succulent after hours of stewing. The lime-herb-chile garnish makes the dish sing with flavor.

6 quarts cold water
1 (6-pound) roasting hen, quartered
4 carrots, peeled and chopped
2 celery stalks, trimmed and chopped
2 garlic cloves, chopped
1 large leek, washed and chopped
1 (1-inch) piece ginger, peeled and minced
6 medium Yukon Gold potatoes, peeled and finely chopped
8 ounces dried egg noodles (such as kluski)
2 teaspoons kosher salt
2 tablespoons chopped fresh cilantro
¼ cup chopped fresh chives
1 fresh red Fresno chile, thinly sliced
10 fresh lime quarters

1. Combine first 7 ingredients in a large stockpot or Dutch oven. Bring to a boil over high; reduce heat to medium-low, and simmer 5 hours, skimming froth from surface as necessary. (Add cold water as necessary if soup reduces too much during simmering.)
2. Remove chicken quarters from pan with tongs; place quarters on a plate. Cool 10 minutes. Pull meat from bones, shredding into bite-sized pieces. Discard skin.
3. Add potatoes to the pan. Bring to a boil over medium-high; cook 10 minutes. Stir in egg noodles; cook 10 minutes or until potatoes are tender and noodles are al dente. Stir in shredded chicken and salt. Top each serving with cilantro, chives, and chile; serve with lime. Serves 10 (serving size: about 1½ cups)

CALORIES 322; FAT 7.3g (sat 2.1g, mono 2.2g, poly 1.4g); PROTEIN 29g; CARB 34g; FIBER 4g; SUGARS 3g (est. added sugars 0g); CHOL 101mg; IRON 2mg; SODIUM 583mg; CALC 40mg

ORANGE YOU GLAD

Drew Curren, chef-partner of Elm Restaurant Group in Austin, brightens midwinter meals with a hit of fresh citrus.

What inspired you to char the fruit?
Charring citrus concentrates the flavor while also pulling out the sweetness of the fruit and accentuating the bitterness. In my cooking, bitter is a good flavor that is easily balanced with sweet and savory notes.

Why blend fresh citrus juice with the charred juice and pulp in the relish?
The fresh juice is the acidity, so it's the "vinegar" in the vinaigrette, while the pulp gives it texture. When you add a very little bit of honey and salt, it gives you very deep, rich flavors.

Gluten Free

Shrimp with Grilled Citrus and Leek Relish

Hands-on: 47 min. Total: 47 min.

3 lemons, divided
3 oranges, divided
2 limes, divided
½ grapefruit
2 large leeks, trimmed and
** halved lengthwise**
¼ cup extra-virgin olive oil
2 tablespoons mint leaves, torn
1 teaspoon honey
½ teaspoon kosher salt
1 pound large shrimp (16/20 count),
** peeled and deveined**
4 cups mixed salad greens

1. Slice 1 lemon, 1 orange, and 1 lime crosswise into thin slices. Squeeze juice from 2 lemons, 1 orange, 1 lime, and ½ grapefruit over a strainer into a measuring cup to equal about 1 cup juice. Place juice in a medium bowl. Peel and section remaining orange.
2. Heat a grill pan over high. Add half of fruit slices to pan in a single layer; grill 3 minutes on each side or until lightly charred and caramelized. Add charred fruit slices to juice in bowl. Repeat procedure with remaining fruit slices. Add leek halves to pan; grill 7 minutes, turning to char all sides. Cut leeks crosswise into ½-inch slices; add to fruit in bowl. When fruit slices are cool enough to handle, squeeze juice and charred pulp into bowl; discard remains. Stir in oil, mint, honey, and salt.
3. Add shrimp to grill pan in a single layer in batches; grill 2 minutes on each side or until well marked and done. Place cooked shrimp in a large bowl. Add ½ cup leek mixture; toss to coat. Combine ¾ cup leek mixture and salad greens; toss to coat. Divide greens mixture equally among 4 plates. Top evenly with shrimp and orange sections; drizzle with extra leek mixture, if desired. Serves 4

CALORIES 288; **FAT** 15.4g (sat 2.1g, mono 10.9g, poly 1.5g); **PROTEIN** 17g; **CARB** 22g; **FIBER** 3g; **SUGARS** 10g (est. added sugars 1g); **CHOL** 143mg; **IRON** 1mg; **SODIUM** 423mg; **CALC** 129mg

RED ROOIBOS TEA

If you like tea to be as functional as it is flavorful, red rooibos (ROY-boss) is your new go-to. Smoky, spicy, and naturally sweet, the decaf herbal from South Africa may contain 50% more antioxidants than green tea, plus plenty of essential minerals. Enjoy a steaming mugful, or make ice cubes with it and toss into a cocktail, as we do here, for a flavor infusion as the cubes melt.

Gluten Free • Vegetarian

Red and Pink

Hands-on: 7 min. Total: 5 hr. 7 min.

½ cup brewed red rooibos tea
3 tablespoons bourbon
2 tablespoons fresh red grapefruit
** juice**
1½ teaspoons grenadine
1 tablespoon soda water

1. Pour tea into an ice-cube tray to make 3 to 5 small cubes. Freeze.
2. Combine bourbon, juice, and grenadine in a cocktail glass; stir well. Add soda water; stir. Add tea ice cubes; serve immediately. Serves 1

CALORIES 135; **FAT** 0g; **PROTEIN** 0g; **CARB** 10g; **FIBER** 0g; **SUGARS** 5g (est. added sugars 5g); **CHOL** 0mg; **IRON** 0mg; **SODIUM** 3mg; **CALC** 3mg

TEATIME

If you're serious about loose-leaf tea and want to brew black, green, white, and oolong to perfection, Breville's got you covered. Their new tea maker lets you program water temps and steep times, with a moving tea basket for peak infusion. $250, brevilleusa.com

HORSERADISH

Add a little kick with this potent, pungent sauce.

Staff Favorite • Quick & Easy
Gluten Free • Kid Friendly
Make Ahead • Vegetarian
Broccoli-Apple Slaw

Whisk together ⅓ cup canola mayonnaise, 2 tablespoons apple cider vinegar, 1½ tablespoons prepared horseradish, 1½ teaspoons sugar, 1½ teaspoons grated lemon rind, and ¼ teaspoon salt in a large bowl. Add 2 cups julienne-cut Honeycrisp apple, ¼ cup slivered red onion, and 1 (12-ounce) package broccoli slaw; toss to coat. Serves 6 (serving size: about 1 cup)

CALORIES 78; FAT 3.4g (sat 0g, mono 2.1g, poly 1.3g); PROTEIN 2g; CARB 10g; FIBER 2g; SUGARS 7g (est. added sugars 1g); CHOL 0mg; IRON 1mg; SODIUM 208mg; CALC 33mg

Quick & Easy • Gluten Free
Kid Friendly • Make Ahead
Bacon-Horseradish Deviled Eggs

Cut 12 hard-cooked large eggs in half. Place yolks in a bowl; add ¼ cup plain 2% reduced-fat Greek yogurt, 3 tablespoons canola mayonnaise, 2 tablespoons chopped chives, 2 tablespoons prepared horseradish, ½ teaspoon black pepper, and ¼ teaspoon kosher salt. Mash until smooth; stir in 4 cooked, crumbled bacon slices. Spoon into egg whites. Serves 12 (serving size: 2 egg halves)

CALORIES 100; FAT 6.9g (sat 2g, mono 2.9g, poly 1.4g); PROTEIN 8g; CARB 1g; FIBER 0g; SUGARS 1g (est. added sugars 0g); CHOL 189mg; IRON 1mg; SODIUM 196mg; CALC 34mg

Quick & Easy • Gluten Free
Kid Friendly • Vegetarian
Broccoli with Cheese Sauce

Combine 1 cup evaporated fat-free milk, 1 tablespoon cornstarch, ½ teaspoon grated garlic, ⅜ teaspoon kosher salt, and a dash of ground red pepper in a saucepan; bring to a simmer over medium, stirring until thickened. Reduce heat to low; stir in 1 tablespoon prepared horseradish and 3 ounces shredded sharp cheddar cheese. Serve with 8 cups steamed broccoli. Serves 8 (serving size: 1 cup broccoli and 2½ tablespoons sauce)

CALORIES 96; FAT 3.7g (sat 2.1g, mono 0.9g, poly 0.2g); PROTEIN 7g; CARB 9g; FIBER 1g; SUGARS 5g (est. added sugars 0g); CHOL 12mg; IRON 1mg; SODIUM 220mg; CALC 206mg

Quick & Easy • Gluten Free
Make Ahead • Vegetarian
Horseradish Vinaigrette

Combine ¼ cup extra-virgin olive oil, 3 tablespoons white wine vinegar, 1 tablespoon minced fresh flat-leaf parsley, 1 tablespoon minced shallots, 1 tablespoon prepared horseradish, ½ teaspoon freshly ground black pepper, ½ teaspoon honey, and ⅜ teaspoon kosher salt in a jar. Cover with lid, and shake well to combine. Serves 6 (serving size: about 1½ tablespoons)

CALORIES 84; FAT 9g (sat 1.3g, mono 6.6g, poly 1g); PROTEIN 0g; CARB 1g; FIBER 0g; SUGARS 1g (est. added sugars 1g); CHOL 0mg; IRON 0mg; SODIUM 131mg; CALC 4mg

READY IN 35 MINUTES

GAME PLAN

While pasta cooks:
- Cook sauce.

While sauce simmers:
- Cook chard.

Quick & Easy • Kid Friendly
Vegetarian

Creamy Carrot and Herb Linguine

With Wilted Chard with Red Onion and Pine Nuts
(pictured on page 210)

A quick dunk in the cooking water softens fresh carrot noodles (caroodles!) just enough that you can swirl them through the sauce.

6 ounces uncooked whole-wheat linguine
2 cups carrot noodles or ribbons
2 teaspoons olive oil
½ cup sliced shallots
4 garlic cloves, sliced
2 tablespoons all-purpose flour
2 cups 1% low-fat milk
½ teaspoon kosher salt
½ teaspoon black pepper
2 ounces Parmesan cheese, shaved and divided (about ½ cup)
½ cup fresh whole-wheat breadcrumbs, toasted
¼ cup flat-leaf parsley leaves
2 tablespoons torn tarragon leaves

1. Cook pasta according to package directions, adding carrots during last 3 minutes of cooking. Drain.
2. Heat oil in a medium saucepan over medium-low. Add shallots and

garlic; sauté 5 minutes. Stir in flour; cook 30 seconds. Add milk to pan; bring to a simmer. Cook 5 minutes or until reduced to about 1½ cups. Stir in salt, pepper, and ¼ cup cheese until smooth. Add pasta mixture to milk mixture; toss. Top with breadcrumbs, remaining ¼ cup cheese, parsley, and tarragon. Serve immediately. Serves 4 (serving size: about 1¼ cups)

CALORIES 336; FAT 9.3g (sat 3.3g, mono 3g, poly 1.8g); PROTEIN 16g; CARB 54g; FIBER 7g; SUGARS 11g (est. added sugars 0g); CHOL 18mg; IRON 2mg; SODIUM 613mg; CALC 342mg

Quick & Easy • Gluten Free
Vegetarian

Wilted Chard with Red Onion and Pine Nuts

Don't toss those gorgeous chard stems! Instead, thinly slice and give them a head start in the pan before adding the leaves.

1 (10-ounce) bunch rainbow chard, stems and leaves divided
1 tablespoon olive oil
1 small red onion, cut into ³/₄-inch wedges
¼ teaspoon black pepper
⅛ teaspoon kosher salt
3 tablespoons toasted pine nuts
1½ tablespoons white wine vinegar

1. Thinly slice chard stems. Coarsely chop chard leaves. Heat oil in a skillet over medium-high. Add chard stems and red onion to pan; cook 5 minutes or until just tender, stirring occasionally. Add chard leaves, pepper, and salt; cook 4 minutes, stirring frequently. Remove pan from heat. Sprinkle pine nuts and vinegar over pan; toss to combine. Serves 4 (serving size: ¾ cup)

CALORIES 93; FAT 7.9g (sat 0.8g, mono 3.7g, poly 2.6g); PROTEIN 2g; CARB 5g; FIBER 2g; SUGARS 2g (est. added sugars 0g); CHOL 0mg; IRON 2mg; SODIUM 212mg; CALC 42mg

READY IN
30
MINUTES

GAME PLAN

While stock mixture simmers:
- Cook noodles.
- Make meatballs.

While meatballs cook:
- Make salad.

Quick & Easy • Gluten Free

Miso Noodle Soup with Meatballs

With Baby Bok Choy and Cucumber Salad

Salty, savory miso becomes the backbone of this soup; try adding it to dressings and marinades, too. We add chile-and-honey-spiked pork meatballs to the soup; you could also use shredded rotisserie chicken breast or cubed tofu. Want to get ahead on tomorrow's dinner? Double the meatball mixture, shape half into patties, and sear for Asian-style sliders.

2 teaspoons toasted sesame oil
⅓ cup diagonally sliced green onions, divided
3 garlic cloves, crushed
1 (1-inch) piece ginger, peeled and thinly sliced
3 cups unsalted chicken stock (such as Swanson)
2 ounces uncooked soba noodles
1 teaspoon honey
1 teaspoon sambal oelek (ground fresh chile paste)
6 ounces lean ground pork
2 teaspoons white miso paste
⅓ cup mung bean sprouts
1 red Fresno chile, sliced

1. Heat oil in a medium saucepan over medium. Add ¼ cup green onions, garlic, and ginger; sauté 6 minutes. Add stock; bring to a simmer. Reduce heat to medium-low; cook 8 minutes.
2. Cook noodles separately according to package directions; drain. Rinse with cold water; drain.
3. Combine honey, sambal oelek, and ground pork in a small bowl. Shape pork mixture into 8 meatballs. Remove garlic and ginger from stock mixture; discard. Stir miso into stock mixture. Add meatballs to pan; cook 6 minutes or until done. Add noodles. Divide soup between 2 bowls; sprinkle with remaining green onions, mung bean sprouts, and Fresno chile. Serves 2 (serving size: about 1½ cups)

CALORIES 362; FAT 12.5g (sat 4g, mono 5.4g, poly 2.8g); PROTEIN 30g; CARB 35g; FIBER 2g; SUGARS 8g (est. added sugars 3g); CHOL 64mg; IRON 2mg; SODIUM 550mg; CALC 32mg

Quick & Easy • Vegetarian

Baby Bok Choy and Cucumber Salad

2 teaspoons toasted sesame oil
1 teaspoon rice vinegar
1 teaspoon reduced-sodium soy sauce
½ teaspoon minced fresh garlic
2 cups thinly sliced baby bok choy
½ cup thinly sliced red bell pepper
¾ cup thinly sliced cucumber
2 tablespoons cilantro leaves

1. Combine first 4 ingredients in a bowl. Add bok choy and remaining ingredients; toss to coat. Serves 2 (serving size: about 1½ cups)

CALORIES 67; FAT 5g (sat 0.7g, mono 2g, poly 2.1g); PROTEIN 2g; CARB 5g; FIBER 2g; SUGARS 3g (est. added sugars 0g); CHOL 0mg; IRON 1mg; SODIUM 154mg; CALC 100mg

READY IN 30 MINUTES

....
GAME PLAN
....

While oven preheats:
- Prepare carrot mixture.
- Cook bacon.

While carrot mixture bakes:
- Finish cooking main.

Quick & Easy • Gluten Free

Seared Cod with Bacon, Braised Fennel, and Kale

With Maple-Dijon Roasted Carrots and Mushrooms

Sear the cod fillets first to get a good crust; then add back to the pan, and cover so they steam and impart their juices to the vegetables. Substitute grouper or snapper.

2 center-cut bacon slices, chopped
4 (6-ounce) cod fillets, skinned
1/2 teaspoon kosher salt, divided
1/2 teaspoon black pepper, divided
1 cup thinly sliced fennel
1 cup sliced mini bell peppers
4 cups stemmed, chopped lacinato kale
1/2 cup unsalted chicken stock
1/2 cup chopped fresh flat-leaf parsley
1/4 cup chopped fennel fronds
2 tablespoons apple cider vinegar

1. Cook bacon in a large skillet over medium-high 5 minutes or until crisp. Remove with a slotted spoon. Sprinkle fish with 1/4 teaspoon salt and 1/4 teaspoon pepper. Add fish to drippings in pan; cook 4 minutes on one side or until golden. Remove fish from pan (fish will not be cooked through).

2. Add sliced fennel and bell peppers to pan; sauté 5 minutes. Reduce heat to medium-low. Add kale to pan; arrange fish on top of kale. Add stock to pan; cover and cook 6 to 8 minutes or until kale is wilted and fish flakes easily when tested with a fork. Sprinkle with bacon, remaining 1/4 teaspoon salt, remaining 1/4 teaspoon pepper, parsley, fennel fronds, and vinegar. Serves 4 (serving size: 1 fillet and about 1 cup kale mixture)

CALORIES 205; FAT 6.6g (sat 2.1g, mono 2.6g, poly 1g); PROTEIN 30g; CARB 5g; FIBER 2g; SUGARS 3g (est. added sugars 0g); CHOL 2mg; IRON 1mg; SODIUM 493mg; CALC 63mg

Quick & Easy • Gluten Free
Kid Friendly • Vegetarian

Maple-Dijon Roasted Carrots and Mushrooms

1 tablespoon olive oil
1 teaspoon maple syrup
1/2 teaspoon Dijon mustard
1 (12-ounce) package small carrots with tops, peeled
1 (8-ounce) package cremini mushrooms, halved
2 teaspoons thyme leaves
1/4 teaspoon kosher salt
1/4 teaspoon black pepper

1. Preheat oven to 500°F.
2. Combine oil, maple syrup, and mustard in a medium bowl. Add carrots and mushrooms; toss to coat. Spread carrot mixture in a single layer on a baking sheet. Bake at 500°F for 15 minutes, stirring once after 10 minutes. Sprinkle with thyme, salt, and pepper. Serves 4 (serving size: about 1 cup)

CALORIES 83; FAT 3.7g (sat 0.5g, mono 2.5g, poly 0.5g); PROTEIN 2g; CARB 12g; FIBER 3g; SUGARS 6g (est. added sugars 1g); CHOL 0mg; IRON 1mg; SODIUM 197mg; CALC 42mg

READY IN 35 MINUTES

....
GAME PLAN
....

While broiler preheats:
- Make soup.

While soup simmers:
- Toast bread.
- Make pea mixture.

Quick & Easy • Gluten Free
Kid Friendly

Lemon and Dill Quinoa Chicken Soup

With Ricotta and Sweet Pea Toasts

Quinoa cooks right in the soup without soaking up too much liquid. If you'd like to change to a heartier grain like farro or barley, cook it separately, and stir in during the last 5 minutes of simmering to reheat.

1 tablespoon olive oil
1/2 cup chopped yellow onion
1/2 teaspoon kosher salt
1/2 teaspoon black pepper
4 garlic cloves, sliced
5 cups unsalted chicken stock
1 cup (1/2-inch) diced red potatoes (about 2 medium)
1/4 cup uncooked quinoa
4 ounces skinless, boneless rotisserie chicken breast, shredded (about 2 cups)
1 cup diagonally cut sugar snap peas
1/2 cup chopped tomato
3 tablespoons chopped fresh dill
1 teaspoon grated lemon rind

1. Heat a large saucepan over medium. Add oil to pan; swirl to coat. Add onion, salt, pepper, and garlic to pan; sauté 5 minutes or until onion is tender. Add stock, potatoes, and quinoa; bring to a simmer. Cook 20 minutes or until potatoes are tender and quinoa is done. Stir in chicken and sugar snap peas; cook 5 minutes. Stir in tomato, dill, and lemon rind. Serves 4 (serving size: about 1¼ cups)

CALORIES 238; FAT 5.1g (sat 0.8g, mono 2.9g, poly 1g); PROTEIN 18g; CARB 31g; FIBER 4g; SUGARS 6g (est. added sugars 0g); CHOL 24mg; IRON 2mg; SODIUM 514mg; CALC 49mg

Quick & Easy • Kid Friendly
Vegetarian

Ricotta and Sweet Pea Toasts

We could all use a vibrant dose of green during the cold months. Thankfully, frozen green peas are available year-round. Blend with creamy ricotta and mint for a quick spread on toasted baguette slices. Double the mixture to spread on sandwiches or your morning toast, or use as a dip for whole-grain crackers.

8 (¼-ounce) slices whole-wheat French bread baguette
½ cup frozen green peas, thawed
⅓ cup mint leaves
¼ cup part-skim ricotta cheese
1½ tablespoons extra-virgin olive oil
1 tablespoon fresh lemon juice
¼ teaspoon kosher salt
¼ teaspoon freshly ground black pepper

1. Preheat broiler to high.
2. Arrange bread on a baking sheet; broil 1 minute per side or until toasted.
3. Place peas and remaining ingredients in a mini food processor; pulse until almost smooth. Spread pea mixture evenly over toasts. Serves 4 (serving size: 2 toasts)

CALORIES 111; FAT 6.6g (sat 1.5g, mono 4g, poly 0.6g); PROTEIN 4g; CARB 10g; FIBER 1g; SUGARS 1g (est. added sugars 0g); CHOL 5mg; IRON 0mg; SODIUM 226mg; CALC 52mg

READY IN
35
MINUTES

GAME PLAN

While steak cooks:
▪ Cook pilaf.

While steak rests:
▪ Cook bean mixture.
▪ Assemble bowls.

Quick & Easy • Gluten Free
Kid Friendly

Carne Asada Bowls

With Cilantro and Almond Pilaf

Instead of a fried shell, crunchy tortilla chips mingle in a base of crisp, sturdy romaine. Try leftover mild, crumbly queso fresco in Mexican egg scrambles, burritos, or stuffed poblano peppers.

Cooking spray
1 (12-ounce) flank steak
¾ teaspoon kosher salt, divided
½ teaspoon black pepper, divided
2 teaspoons olive oil
¾ cup chopped white onion
½ cup unsalted chicken stock
1 (15-ounce) can unsalted pinto beans, rinsed and drained
3 cups chopped romaine lettuce
1½ cups chopped tomato
1 ounce tortilla chips
1 ripe avocado, thinly sliced
1½ ounces queso fresco, crumbled (about ⅓ cup)
4 lime wedges

1. Heat a large skillet over medium-high. Coat pan with cooking spray. Sprinkle steak with ¼ teaspoon salt and ¼ teaspoon pepper. Add steak to pan; cook 5 minutes on each side or

until desired degree of doneness. Place steak on a cutting board; let stand 5 minutes. Cut across the grain into slices; cut slices into ¾-inch pieces.
2. Add oil to pan; swirl. Add onion; sauté 2 minutes. Add ¼ teaspoon salt, stock, and beans to pan; bring to a boil. Cook 4 minutes, scraping pan to loosen browned bits.
3. Divide lettuce among 4 shallow bowls. Top evenly with bean mixture, steak, tomato, tortilla chips, and avocado. Sprinkle with remaining ¼ teaspoon salt, remaining ¼ teaspoon pepper, and queso fresco. Serve with lime wedges. Serves 4

CALORIES 369; FAT 15.1g (sat 3.6g, mono 6.9g, poly 1g); PROTEIN 28g; CARB 31g; FIBER 10g; SUGARS 4g (est. added sugars 0g); CHOL 56mg; IRON 4mg; SODIUM 486mg; CALC 133mg

Quick & Easy • Gluten Free
Kid Friendly

Cilantro and Almond Pilaf

1 tablespoon unsalted butter
3 tablespoons sliced almonds
¼ teaspoon ground coriander
¼ teaspoon ground turmeric
1 (8.8-ounce) package precooked brown rice (such as Uncle Ben's)
⅓ cup unsalted chicken stock (such as Swanson)
¼ teaspoon kosher salt
¼ cup chopped fresh cilantro

1. Melt butter in a skillet over medium-high. Add almonds; cook 1 minute. Add coriander, turmeric, and rice; cook 1 minute, stirring constantly. Add stock and salt; bring to a simmer. Cover and cook 2 minutes or until liquid is absorbed. Stir in cilantro. Serves 4 (serving size: about ½ cup)

CALORIES 138; FAT 6.4g (sat 2g, mono 2.1g, poly 0.6g); PROTEIN 4g; CARB 19g; FIBER 2g; SUGARS 0g (est. added sugars 0g); CHOL 8mg; IRON 1mg; SODIUM 138mg; CALC 14mg

SUPERFAST 20-MINUTE COOKING

Quick & Easy • Gluten Free Kid Friendly

Salmon with Potatoes and Horseradish Sauce

You can't go wrong when you start with salmon and a sour cream sauce, especially if the sauce is flavored with dill and horseradish (see page 40 for 4 tasty ways to use up leftover horseradish).

3 tablespoons canola oil, divided
1 pound baby red potatoes, cut into ¼-inch-thick slices
½ cup water
1 teaspoon kosher salt, divided
¾ teaspoon black pepper, divided
4 (6-ounce) skin-on salmon fillets (1 inch thick)
½ cup light sour cream
2 tablespoons chopped fresh dill
1 tablespoon creamy prepared horseradish

1. Heat 1½ tablespoons oil in a large nonstick skillet over medium-high. Add potatoes; cook 8 minutes or until golden, stirring occasionally. Add ½ cup water; bring to a boil. Reduce heat and simmer, partially covered, 8 minutes or until potatoes are tender. Sprinkle with ½ teaspoon salt and ½ teaspoon pepper.
2. Meanwhile, heat remaining 1½ tablespoons oil in a large skillet over high. Sprinkle salmon with remaining ½ teaspoon salt and remaining ¼ teaspoon pepper. Add salmon to pan; cook 4 minutes on each side or until desired degree of doneness.
3. Combine sour cream, dill, and horseradish in a bowl. Serve with salmon and potatoes. Serves 4 (serving size: 1 fillet, about ½ cup potatoes, and about 1½ tablespoons sauce)

CALORIES 457; **FAT** 25.1g (sat 4.7g, mono 11.3g, poly 7.5g); **PROTEIN** 37g; **CARB** 20g; **FIBER** 2g; **SUGARS** 2g (est. added sugars 0g); **CHOL** 105mg; **IRON** 2mg; **SODIUM** 618mg; **CALC** 68mg

Quick & Easy • Gluten Free

Pork Tenderloin with Blue Cheese and Pears

2 tablespoons olive oil
1 (1-pound) pork tenderloin, trimmed and halved crosswise
1 teaspoon kosher salt, divided
½ teaspoon black pepper
2 Bosc pears, cored and cut into ½-inch-thick slices
1 small red onion, cut into 8 wedges
3 tablespoons white balsamic vinegar
1 ounce Gorgonzola cheese, crumbled (about ¼ cup)

1. Preheat oven to 500°F.
2. Heat oil in a large ovenproof skillet over high. Sprinkle pork with ¾ teaspoon salt and pepper. Add pork to pan; cook 5 minutes, turning to brown on all sides. Add the pears and onion to pan, breaking up onion wedges with a spoon. Place pan in the oven.
3. Bake at 500°F for 8 minutes or until onion is tender and a thermometer inserted in thickest part of pork registers 140°F. Remove pork from pan; let stand 3 minutes. Cut into slices.
4. Add remaining ¼ teaspoon salt and vinegar to pan, scraping pan to loosen browned bits. Return pork to pan. Sprinkle with cheese. Serves 4 (serving size: about 3 ounces pork, ½ pear, ¼ onion, and 1 tablespoon cheese)

CALORIES 297; **FAT** 11.3g (sat 3.2g, mono 6.2g, poly 1.1g); **PROTEIN** 26g; **CARB** 21g; **FIBER** 4g; **SUGARS** 13g (est. added sugars 0g); **CHOL** 80mg; **IRON** 1mg; **SODIUM** 640mg; **CALC** 62mg

Quick & Easy • Kid Friendly Make Ahead

Pumpkin Soup with Almonds and Sage

(pictured on page 211)

Canned pumpkin is quite good, saving you lots of time and effort.

2 tablespoons unsalted butter
3 sage leaves
1 (8-ounce) package prechopped onion
¾ cup unsalted, roasted blanched almonds, divided
1 tablespoon all-purpose flour
3 cups unsalted chicken stock, divided
1 (15-ounce) can pumpkin puree
¾ teaspoon kosher salt
⅛ teaspoon ground red pepper
2 tablespoons chopped fresh chives

1. Place butter, sage, and onion in a large saucepan or Dutch oven over medium-high. Cover and cook 7 to 8 minutes or until onion is lightly browned, stirring occasionally.
2. Coarsely chop ¼ cup almonds; set aside. Whisk together flour and ¼ cup stock. Add remaining ½ cup almonds, flour mixture, remaining 2¾ cups stock, pumpkin, salt, and pepper to onion mixture. Bring to a boil. Reduce heat to medium-low, and simmer 5 minutes, stirring occasionally to keep pumpkin mixture from sticking to bottom of pan.
3. Place pumpkin mixture in a blender; remove center piece of blender lid (to allow steam to escape). Secure lid on blender. Place a clean towel over opening in lid. Process until smooth. Ladle soup into bowls; sprinkle with reserved ¼ cup chopped almonds and chives. Serves 4 (serving size: about 1⅔ cups soup, 1 tablespoon almonds, and 1½ teaspoons chives)

CALORIES 288; **FAT** 19.8g (sat 4.9g, mono 10.1g, poly 3.6g); **PROTEIN** 11g; **CARB** 22g; **FIBER** 7g; **SUGARS** 8g (est. added sugars 0g); **CHOL** 15mg; **IRON** 3mg; **SODIUM** 467mg; **CALC** 116mg

Nutty Fried Rice

We incorporate lots of nutty flavor into traditional fried rice using sesame oil, cashews, peanut butter, and sesame seeds.

3 tablespoons toasted sesame oil, divided
3 cups broccoli florets
8 ounces presliced shiitake mushrooms
2 (8.8-ounce) packages precooked brown rice (such as Uncle Ben's)
1/2 cup unsalted, roasted cashews
2 large eggs, lightly beaten
3 tablespoons reduced-sodium soy sauce, divided
1/4 teaspoon freshly ground black pepper
1/4 cup peanut butter
1 tablespoon rice vinegar
1 tablespoon water
1 tablespoon toasted sesame seeds

1. Heat 1 tablespoon oil in a large nonstick skillet over medium-high. Add broccoli and mushrooms; cook 6 minutes. Remove broccoli mixture from pan (do not wipe out pan).
2. Add remaining 2 tablespoons oil to pan. Add rice and cashews; cook 5 minutes. Stir in eggs; cook 1 minute. Stir in broccoli mixture, 1 tablespoon soy sauce, and pepper.
3. Combine remaining 2 tablespoons soy sauce, peanut butter, vinegar, and 1 tablespoon water in a bowl. Top rice mixture with peanut butter mixture, and sprinkle with sesame seeds. Serves 6 (serving size: about 1 cup rice mixture and about 1 tablespoon sauce)

CALORIES 367; FAT 22g (sat 3.6g, mono 9.2g, poly 5.4g); PROTEIN 12g; CARB 36g; FIBER 5g; SUGARS 3g (est. added sugars 0g); CHOL 62mg; IRON 4mg; SODIUM 420mg; CALC 38mg

Shrimp and Black Bean Tacos

A little bit of the black bean liquid brings the chunky mash together. The mash also helps to hold all the filling in place.

2 teaspoons canola oil
3/4 pound medium shrimp, peeled and deveined
1 1/2 teaspoons ground cumin, divided
1/8 teaspoon ground red pepper
1 (15-ounce) can unsalted black beans
1/2 teaspoon chili powder
8 (6-inch) corn tortillas
1 cup hot cooked brown rice
1/2 cup fresh pico de gallo
1/4 cup sliced green onions
1 ripe avocado, thinly sliced
Cilantro leaves

1. Heat oil in a large nonstick skillet over medium-high. Add shrimp, 1 teaspoon cumin, and pepper; cook 5 minutes or until done, stirring occasionally. Remove shrimp from pan. Drain beans in a colander over a bowl, reserving 2 tablespoons liquid. Add beans, reserved liquid, remaining 1/2 teaspoon cumin, and chili powder to pan; cook 3 minutes, mashing beans with a fork.
2. Working with 1 tortilla at a time, heat tortillas over medium-high directly on the eye of a burner 15 seconds on each side. Divide bean mixture, rice, shrimp, pico, onions, and avocado evenly among tortillas. Garnish with cilantro leaves; serve immediately. Serves 4 (serving size: 2 tacos)

CALORIES 408; FAT 11g (sat 1g, mono 4.9g, poly 2.2g); PROTEIN 22g; CARB 61g; FIBER 11g; SUGARS 4g (est. added sugars 0g); CHOL 107mg; IRON 2mg; SODIUM 323mg; CALC 138mg

Upside-Down Shepherd's Pie

To keep things lightning-fast, we serve the veggie-flecked beef mixture on top of a bed of creamy mashed potatoes.

1 tablespoon olive oil
10 ounces 90% lean ground beef
1 cup chopped onion
1/2 cup chopped turnip (about 3 ounces)
1/2 cup chopped carrot (about 1 medium carrot)
2 teaspoons chopped fresh rosemary
4 garlic cloves, minced
2 cups unsalted beef stock
2 tablespoons all-purpose flour
1 cup frozen green peas
1/2 teaspoon black pepper
3/8 teaspoon kosher salt
3 cups frozen mashed potatoes (such as Ore-Ida Steam n' Mash)
1/3 cup 2% reduced-fat milk

1. Heat oil in a large nonstick skillet over medium-high. Add beef; cook 6 to 7 minutes or until browned, stirring to crumble. Add onion, turnip, carrot, rosemary, and garlic to pan; cook 6 minutes or until vegetables are tender, stirring occasionally. Whisk together stock and flour. Add stock mixture to pan; bring to a boil. Reduce heat to medium, and simmer 4 minutes or until thickened. Stir in peas, pepper, and salt.
2. Place potatoes in a microwave-safe dish; cover with plastic wrap. Microwave at HIGH 6 minutes. Add milk to potatoes; mash to desired consistency. Divide potato mixture among 4 shallow bowls. Top with beef mixture. Serves 4 (serving size: about 1/2 cup potatoes and about 1 cup beef mixture)

CALORIES 325; FAT 11.2g (sat 3.6g, mono 5.6g, poly 0.7g); PROTEIN 21g; CARB 34g; FIBER 5g; SUGARS 6g (est. added sugars 0g); CHOL 48mg; IRON 3mg; SODIUM 632mg; CALC 108mg

Turkey and Swiss Sloppy Joes

(pictured on page 211)

This twist on a classic sandwich swaps the sweet, barbecue-style sauce for a white sauce enriched with nutty Swiss cheese.

1 tablespoon canola oil
12 ounces ground turkey breast
2 cups thinly sliced kale
1 cup chopped onion
1 tablespoon chopped fresh thyme
1 teaspoon garlic powder
4 ounces presliced mushrooms
1 1/2 cups 2% reduced-fat milk
1 1/2 tablespoons all-purpose flour
3 ounces Swiss cheese, shredded (about 3/4 cup)
3/4 teaspoon freshly ground black pepper
1/2 teaspoon kosher salt
4 whole-wheat hamburger buns

1. Heat oil in a large nonstick skillet over medium-high. Add turkey; cook 6 minutes or until browned, stirring to crumble. Add kale, onion, thyme, garlic powder, and mushrooms; cook 6 minutes, stirring occasionally.
2. Whisk together milk and flour. Add milk mixture to pan; bring to a boil. Reduce heat to medium-low, and simmer 5 minutes or until thickened. Remove pan from heat; stir in cheese, pepper, and salt. Spoon about 3/4 cup turkey mixture onto each bun. Serves 4 (serving size: 1 sandwich)

CALORIES 404; **FAT** 14.7g (sat 6g, mono 4.8g, poly 2.3g); **PROTEIN** 34g; **CARB** 36g; **FIBER** 5g; **SUGARS** 11g (est. added sugars 4g); **CHOL** 61mg; **IRON** 2mg; **SODIUM** 589mg; **CALC** 351mg

Roasted Cauliflower with Lemon-Caper Vinaigrette

Folks can't get enough of cauliflower's mild, slightly nutty flavor. Here we offer 4 fast and delicious ways to enjoy it.

5 cups small cauliflower florets
3 tablespoons extra-virgin olive oil, divided
1 tablespoon chopped fresh thyme
1 teaspoon grated lemon rind
1 tablespoon fresh lemon juice
1 1/2 teaspoons chopped drained capers
1 teaspoon Dijon mustard
1/2 teaspoon freshly ground black pepper
1/4 teaspoon kosher salt

1. Preheat broiler to high. Combine cauliflower, 1 1/2 tablespoons oil, and thyme in a large bowl. Spread cauliflower mixture in a single layer on a foil-lined baking sheet. Broil 8 to 10 minutes or until browned and tender, stirring once after 4 minutes.
2. Combine remaining 1 1/2 tablespoons oil, rind, juice, capers, mustard, pepper, and salt in a large bowl, stirring with a whisk. Add roasted cauliflower; toss to coat. Serves 4 (serving size: about 1 cup)

CALORIES 132; **FAT** 10.9g (sat 1.7g, mono 8.1g, poly 1g); **PROTEIN** 3g; **CARB** 8g; **FIBER** 3g; **SUGARS** 3g (est. added sugars 0g); **CHOL** 0mg; **IRON** 1mg; **SODIUM** 216mg; **CALC** 34mg

Spiced Roasted Cauliflower and Carrots
Preheat broiler to high. Combine 3 cups small cauliflower florets, 2 cups thinly diagonally sliced carrot, 3 tablespoons olive oil, 3/4 teaspoon ground cumin, 1/2 teaspoon ground cinnamon, 3/8 teaspoon kosher salt, and 1/4 teaspoon freshly ground black pepper in a large bowl. Spread on a foil-lined baking sheet. Broil 8 to 10 minutes, stirring once after 4 minutes. Top with 1/4 cup pomegranate arils and 2 tablespoons chopped fresh cilantro. Serves 4 (serving size: about 3/4 cup)

CALORIES 154; **FAT** 11g (sat 1.6g, mono 8.1g, poly 1.1g); **PROTEIN** 2g; **CARB** 13g; **FIBER** 4g; **SUGARS** 5g (est. added sugars 0g); **CHOL** 0mg; **IRON** 1mg; **SODIUM** 250mg; **CALC** 48mg

Roasted Cauliflower with Red Onions and Oranges
Preheat broiler to high. Combine 3 tablespoons extra-virgin olive oil, 2 tablespoons sherry vinegar, 1 tablespoon chopped fresh oregano, 2 teaspoons grated orange rind, 3/8 teaspoon kosher salt, and 1/4 teaspoon crushed red pepper in a large bowl. Add 4 cups small cauliflower florets and 1 cup vertically sliced red onion; toss. Spread on a foil-lined baking sheet. Broil 8 to 10 minutes, stirring once after 4 minutes. Top with segments of 1 orange. Serves 4 (serving size: about 3/4 cup)

CALORIES 155; **FAT** 10.9g (sat 1.6g, mono 8.1g, poly 1g); **PROTEIN** 3g; **CARB** 13g; **FIBER** 4g; **SUGARS** 6g (est. added sugars 0g); **CHOL** 0mg; **IRON** 1mg; **SODIUM** 214mg; **CALC** 52mg

Roasted Cauliflower with Pumpkin Seeds and Queso Fresco

Preheat broiler to high. Combine 4 cups small cauliflower florets, 2 tablespoons raw pumpkin seeds, 2 tablespoons olive oil, ½ teaspoon black pepper, ⅜ teaspoon kosher salt, and 6 chopped garlic cloves in a large bowl. Spread on a foil-lined baking sheet. Broil 10 minutes or until browned and tender, stirring once after 5 minutes. Top with 3 tablespoons crumbled queso fresco (fresh Mexican cheese). Serves 4 (serving size: about ¾ cup)

CALORIES 146; FAT 11g (sat 2.1g, mono 6.6g, poly 1.8g); PROTEIN 5g; CARB 8g; FIBER 2g; SUGARS 2g (est. added sugars 0g); CHOL 4mg; IRON 1mg; SODIUM 229mg; CALC 66mg

LET'S COOK!

$7.96 FOR FOUR SERVINGS

Sausage Ragù over Polenta

Hands-on: 25 min. Total: 25 min.
Look for bulk sausage, not links, to save the trouble of removing the casings. You can also substitute ground pork, beef, or turkey.

1 tablespoon olive oil
12 ounces bulk pork Italian sausage
½ teaspoon black pepper
2 cups coarsely chopped yellow onion
1½ cups coarsely chopped carrot
3 garlic cloves, chopped
3½ cups water, divided
1 (15-ounce) can unsalted tomato sauce
⅔ cup quick-cooking polenta
1 ounce Parmesan cheese, grated (about ¼ cup)
¼ cup chopped fresh flat-leaf parsley (optional)

1. Heat oil in a large skillet over medium-high. Add sausage; cook 5 minutes or until browned, stirring to crumble. Stir in pepper. Remove sausage mixture to a bowl with a slotted spoon. Remove pan from heat (do not wipe out pan).
2. Combine onion, carrot, and garlic on a cutting board; finely chop. Return pan to medium-high. Add onion mixture to pan; cook 5 to 7 minutes or until tender. Add sausage mixture, ½ cup water, and tomato sauce to pan; cook 1 minute.
3. Bring remaining 3 cups water to a boil in a medium saucepan. whisk in polenta. Reduce heat; cook 3 minutes or until thickened, stirring frequently with a whisk or spoon. Stir in cheese. Serve polenta with pork mixture and parsley, if desired. Serves 4 (serving size: about 1 cup pork mixture and ⅔ cup polenta)

CALORIES 366; FAT 12.7g (sat 4.4g, mono 6.1g, poly 1g); PROTEIN 21g; CARB 37g; FIBER 7g; SUGARS 11g (est. added sugars 1g); CHOL 32mg; IRON 2mg; SODIUM 667mg; CALC 121mg

SLOW COOKER

BBQ Beef-Stuffed Potatoes

(pictured on page 211)

Hands-on: 15 min. Total: 8 hr. 15 min.

Be sure to wrap the potatoes in parchment paper; foil can add a metallic taste to the dish.

¼ cup dark brown sugar
3 tablespoons unsalted tomato paste
2 tablespoons reduced-sodium Worcestershire sauce
1 tablespoon chili powder
1¼ teaspoons kosher salt, divided
1¼ teaspoons black pepper, divided
1½ pounds boneless chuck roast, trimmed
1½ cups vertically sliced red onion
Cooking spray
6 (4-ounce) russet potatoes
2 teaspoons olive oil
3 ounces sharp cheddar cheese, shredded (about ¾ cup)
6 tablespoons light sour cream
¼ cup sliced green onions

1. Combine brown sugar, tomato paste, Worcestershire sauce, chili powder, 1 teaspoon salt, and ¾ teaspoon pepper in a small bowl; rub generously over roast.
2. Place red onion slices in bottom of a 5- to 6-quart slow cooker coated with cooking spray; top with roast.
3. Rub potatoes with oil, remaining ¼ teaspoon salt, and ¼ teaspoon pepper. Wrap each potato in parchment paper; arrange on top of roast. Cover and cook on LOW 8 hours or until tender.
4. Unwrap potatoes; split lengthwise, cutting to but not through the other side. Shred roast with 2 forks, and stir to combine with onion mixture.
5. Top each potato with ½ cup beef mixture, 2 tablespoons cheese, 1 tablespoon sour cream, 2 teaspoons green onions; sprinkle evenly with remaining ¼ teaspoon pepper. Serves 6

CALORIES 385; FAT 12.7g (sat 6.1g, mono 4.9g, poly 0.7g); PROTEIN 32g; CARB 37g; FIBER 3g; SUGARS 12g(est. added sugars 8g); CHOL 92mg; IRON 4mg; SODIUM 687mg; CALC 173mg

IF YOU CAN'T FIND 6 (4-OUNCE) POTATOES, USE 4 (8-OUNCE) RUSSETS, AND CUT EACH IN HALF BEFORE STUFFING.

COOK ONCE, EAT 3X

Enjoy a batch of black-eyed peas tonight, and use them to top fish or stuff squash during the week.

Gluten Free • Kid Friendly Make Ahead

Smoky Black-Eyed Peas

Hands-on: 20 min. Total: 9 hr. 20 min.
Serve these black-eyed peas with collard greens and cornbread for a southern New Year's feast. All three dishes symbolize good fortune; they're also just plain delicious. If you can't find a ham hock, substitute a smoked turkey leg or wing. Add cooked peas to stews or salsa, or sauté with rice, garlic, and bell pepper for hoppin' John. Use leftover ham hock meat as a flavoring agent for greens, beans, and broths.

12 ounces dried black-eyed peas
3 cups unsalted chicken stock (such as Swanson)
2 cups chopped leeks (about 2 medium)
2 cups water
3/4 teaspoon freshly ground black pepper
1/2 teaspoon kosher salt
1 (14- to 16-ounce) smoked ham hock
1/4 cup chopped green onions
Hot sauce (optional)

1. Rinse peas; drain. Place peas in a large bowl; fill with water to cover peas. Let stand at room temperature 8 hours or overnight. Drain.
2. Place peas and next 6 ingredients (through ham hock) in a large Dutch oven; bring to a boil. Reduce heat, and simmer 1 hour or until peas are very tender, stirring occasionally. Remove pan from heat. Remove

hock; cool slightly. Remove meat from bone; discard fat, skin, and bone. Chop meat. Reserve 3 cups pea mixture for Recipes 2 and 3. Add 1/2 cup meat to remaining 3 cups pea mixture (reserve remaining meat for another use). Top with green onions and hot sauce, if desired. Serves 4 (serving size: about 2/3 cup)

CALORIES 200; **FAT** 2.5g (sat 0.7g, mono 0.1g, poly 0.3g); **PROTEIN** 16g; **CARB** 30g; **FIBER** 5g; **SUGARS** 3g (est. added sugars 0g); **CHOL** 15mg; **IRON** 4mg; **SODIUM** 498mg; **CALC** 65mg

Quick & Easy • Gluten Free Kid Friendly

Seared Grouper with Black-Eyed Pea Relish

Hands-on: 10 min. Total: 40 min.
This zingy relish only gets better as it sits; make it a couple of days ahead, if you like. You can also dice the cherry tomatoes and serve the relish with whole-grain tortilla chips for a snack. Use any flaky fish, such as sustainably caught halibut or cod, or try the relish on meaty salmon.

1/4 cup extra-virgin olive oil, divided
2 tablespoons red wine vinegar
1 tablespoon chopped jalapeño
1/2 teaspoon kosher salt, divided
1/2 teaspoon freshly ground black pepper, divided
1 1/2 cups cooked black-eyed peas (from Recipe 1), drained
1 cup quartered cherry tomatoes
1/4 cup finely chopped red onion
1/4 cup chopped fresh flat-leaf parsley
1 ounce chopped pitted Castelvetrano olives (about 1/4 cup)
4 (4-ounce) grouper fillets

1. Combine 3 tablespoons oil, vinegar, jalapeño, 1/4 teaspoon salt, and 1/4 teaspoon black pepper in a bowl. Combine peas, tomatoes, onion, parsley, and olives in a bowl.

Add oil mixture to pea mixture; toss. Let stand at least 10 minutes.
2. Heat remaining 1 tablespoon oil in a large nonstick skillet over medium-high. Sprinkle fillets evenly with remaining 1/4 teaspoon salt and 1/4 teaspoon black pepper. Add fillets to pan; cook 3 minutes on each side or until desired degree of doneness. Place 1 fillet on each of 4 plates; spoon pea mixture evenly over fillets. Serves 4 (serving size: 1 fillet and about 3/4 cup pea mixture)

CALORIES 330; **FAT** 16g (sat 2.4g, mono 10.7g, poly 2g); **PROTEIN** 28g; **CARB** 18g; **FIBER** 4g; **SUGARS** 4g (est. added sugars 0g); **CHOL** 43mg; **IRON** 4mg; **SODIUM** 451mg; **CALC** 81mg

Kid Friendly • Make Ahead

Black-Eyed Pea–Stuffed Acorn Squash

Hands-on: 15 min. Total: 50 min.
Cutting the squashes crosswise instead of from top to bottom is easier, and they take up less space in the baking dish. Trim the ends so the halves sit flat and don't wobble.

2 (1 1/2-pound) acorn squashes, halved crosswise and seeded
2 tablespoons olive oil, divided
1/2 teaspoon kosher salt, divided
1 (1-ounce) slice whole-grain bread
1 1/2 cups cooked black-eyed peas (from Recipe 1), drained
1 cup finely chopped red bell pepper
1 tablespoon chopped fresh thyme
1 teaspoon sherry vinegar
1/2 teaspoon smoked paprika
1/2 teaspoon freshly ground black pepper
1 1/2 ounces goat cheese, crumbled (about 1/3 cup)
1 tablespoon chopped fresh flat-leaf parsley

1. Preheat oven to 400°F. Line an

8-inch square baking dish with foil. Place squash halves, cut sides up, in prepared dish; brush with 1 tablespoon oil, and sprinkle with ¼ teaspoon salt. Bake at 400°F for 25 minutes.

2. Place bread in a food processor; pulse until coarse crumbs form. Heat 1½ teaspoons oil in a small skillet over medium. Add breadcrumbs; cook 3 minutes or until toasted, stirring occasionally. Remove pan from heat.

3. Combine peas and next 6 ingredients (through goat cheese). Divide mixture among squash halves; top with remaining 1½ teaspoons oil, ¼ teaspoon salt, breadcrumbs, and parsley. Serves 4 (serving size: 1 filled squash half)

CALORIES 339; FAT 10.2g (sat 2.7g, mono 5.5g, poly 1.2g); PROTEIN 12g; CARB 56g; FIBER 9g; SUGARS 11g (est. added sugars 0g); CHOL 6mg; IRON 5mg; SODIUM 427mg; CALC 177mg

FREEZE IT

Kid Friendly • Make Ahead
Freezable • Vegetarian

Hearty Tortellini Soup

Hands-on: 40 min. Total: 40 min.
This satisfying main is a great way to reset after a few weeks of meat-centered holiday eating. If freezing, be sure to cool the soup completely before adding the tortellini or they will absorb too much liquid and lose their shape.

2 tablespoons olive oil
2 cups chopped yellow onion (about 1 large)
2 cups chopped fennel bulb (about 1 large)
¼ cup minced fresh garlic
2 (8-ounce) packages sliced cremini mushrooms
2 tablespoons unsalted tomato paste

8 cups unsalted vegetable stock
4 cups water
1 teaspoon freshly ground black pepper
¾ teaspoon kosher salt
2 (15-ounce) cans fire-roasted diced tomatoes, undrained
2 (15-ounce) cans unsalted chickpeas, rinsed and drained
6 cups stemmed, chopped curly kale
1½ (9-ounce) packages whole-wheat 3-cheese tortellini
1½ tablespoons red wine vinegar
⅓ cup chopped fresh flat-leaf parsley

1. Heat oil in a large Dutch oven over medium-high. Add onion, fennel, garlic, and mushrooms; cook 15 minutes or until liquid evaporates, stirring occasionally. Stir in tomato paste; cook 1 minute. Add stock and next 5 ingredients (through chickpeas); bring to a boil. Reduce heat and simmer 5 minutes.
2. Stir in kale. Add tortellini, or follow freezing instructions. Cook 8 minutes or until tortellini are done.
3. Remove pan from heat; stir in vinegar. Divide soup among 12 bowls; sprinkle with parsley. Serves 12 (serving size: about 1½ cups)

CALORIES 269; FAT 7g (sat 1.4g, mono 1.7g, poly 0.5g); PROTEIN 13g; CARB 39g; FIBER 7g; SUGARS 7g (est. added sugars 0g); CHOL 20mg; IRON 2mg; SODIUM 615mg; CALC 114mg

HOW TO

FREEZE
Cool soup completely. Once cool, add tortellini. Freeze flat in a large ziplock freezer bag for up to 2 months.

THAW
Microwave soup in bag at MEDIUM (50% power) for 8 minutes or until pliable.

REHEAT
Pour soup into a large Dutch oven; bring to a simmer over medium heat. Cook 25 minutes or until tortellini are done. Stir in red wine vinegar. Top with parsley.

KITCHEN CONFIDENTIAL

WHITE TURNIPS

Winter white turnips peak from October through February. Like the tender baby turnips of late spring and summer, the smallest bulbs of this root vegetable yield delicate, sweet flavor. (Large turnips can be tough and woody.)

SELECTION: Choose turnips with blemish-free skin. The roots should still be attached, but trim them off when you're ready to cook. Bonus if the greens are also attached—they're delicious, too.

STORAGE: Turnip bulbs will keep in the refrigerator for up to two weeks. Trim the more perishable greens from the bulb right away—use a sharp knife to cut them off at the base where the stems and the bulb intersect. Store the greens separately for up to three days, wrapped in a towel to chill in the crisper drawer.

Quick & Easy • Gluten Free
Vegetarian
Braised Turnips with Greens
Trim and peel **6 small turnips with greens**; reserve and chop the greens. Halve turnips. Heat 1 tablespoon **olive oil** in a large skillet over medium-high. Add turnips, cut sides down; cook 4 minutes or until golden. Turn and add 1 cup **unsalted vegetable stock**, 1 tablespoon **apple cider vinegar**, ⅛ teaspoon **kosher salt**, and ¼ teaspoon **freshly ground black pepper**. Bring to a boil; cover and reduce heat to medium-low. Simmer until turnips are crisp-tender, 5 to 6 minutes. Uncover, increase heat to medium-high, and add greens; cook until liquid reduces by three-fourths and thickens, about 6 minutes. Swirl in 2 teaspoons **cold butter** and 1 teaspoon **honey**. Serves 4 (serving size: about ½ cup)

CALORIES 136; FAT 5.9g (sat 1.7g, mono 3g, poly 0.5g); PROTEIN 3g; CARB 19g; FIBER 4g; SUGARS 7g (est. added sugars 1g); CHOL 5mg; IRON 1mg; SODIUM 244mg; CALC 95mg

WHAT'S THE SECRET TO EXTRA-FLAVORFUL STOCK?

**Staff Favorite • Gluten Free
Kid Friendly • Make Ahead
Freezable**

Rich Brown Chicken Stock

Hands-on: 35 min. Total: 17 hr. 20 min.

**5 pounds chicken wings, separated
  into drumettes and "flats"
4 celery ribs, cut into 1-inch pieces
3 large carrots, peeled and cut into
  1-inch pieces
2 medium yellow onions, unpeeled
  and each cut into 8 wedges
1½ tablespoons olive oil
¾ teaspoon kosher salt
½ teaspoon freshly ground
  black pepper
12 cups water, divided
5 thyme sprigs
2 bay leaves
½ teaspoon black peppercorns
½ bunch fresh parsley**

1. Preheat oven to 425°F.
2. Combine first 4 ingredients in a bowl. Drizzle with oil; season with salt and ground pepper. Arrange in a single layer on 2 rimmed baking sheets or roasting pans. Roast at 425°F for 45 minutes or until browned, stirring after 23 minutes.
3. Reduce oven temperature to 225°F.
4. Transfer wing mixture to a Dutch oven; set aside. Position 1 roasting pan over 2 burners on the stovetop over medium-high heat. Add 1½ cups water; stir, scraping pan to loosen browned bits. Carefully transfer pan contents to Dutch oven. Repeat procedure with 1½ cups water and other pan. Add remaining 9 cups water and remaining ingredients to Dutch oven; transfer to middle rack of oven. Cook, uncovered, 8 hours or overnight.
5. Skim as much fat from top of stock as possible; pour stock through a strainer into a bowl. Discard solids. Cool to room temperature. Cover and refrigerate 8 hours; scrape off and discard fat. Serves 14 (serving size: 1 cup)

CALORIES 19; **FAT** 1.2g (sat 0.3g, mono 0.6g, poly 0.3g); **PROTEIN** 2g; **CARB** 0g; **FIBER** 0g; **SUGARS** 0g; **CHOL** 9mg; **IRON** 0mg; **SODIUM** 86mg; **CALC** 3mg

HOW TO MAKE ROASTED CHICKEN STOCK

Rich, homemade chicken stock will instantly elevate your home cooking. It makes the biggest difference in exceptional gravies and sauces, soups and stews, braises and glazes. With a mostly hands-off method, it couldn't be easier to make—and a batch can last for months. See below for details.

1. CUT UP THE WINGS.
Spread in a single layer with the vegetables for even roasting. Wings have plenty of collagen, which gives the stock body. Browning in the oven intensifies their meaty taste and caramelizes natural sugars in the veggies for deep, sweet flavor. After browning, place the chicken and veggies in a Dutch oven.

2. ADD WATER TO THE ROASTING PAN.
Set over medium-high heat and scrape with a wooden spatula or spoon. This technique, called deglazing, releases the baked-on, deeply browned bits that are packed with concentrated flavor. The bits, also called fond, are as key to the stock's rich flavor as the browned wings and veggies. Add this liquid to the Dutch oven.

3. ADD THE AROMATICS AND WATER.
Simmer, uncovered, in a 225°F oven for eight hours. The fresh herbs, bay leaves, and peppercorns impart another layer of flavor to the stock as it cooks slowly. The low oven temp keeps the liquid from boiling, reducing it just slightly while extracting maximum flavor from the solid ingredients.

4. STRAIN THE SOLIDS.
Drain completely, resisting the urge to press the wings and vegetables to squeeze out any additional liquid—this will release fine particulates that make the stock cloudy and muddy the flavor. Once the strained stock has chilled, a solid layer of fat will form on top, which you can easily skim to make the stock practically fat-free.

WAKE UP YOUR BREAKFAST

We love breakfast because it's so full of potential, setting the tone for the day. From perfect toast and pancakes to foolproof eggs and sausage, these are the new staples to make your mornings brighter.

AMAZING WHOLE-GRAIN MUFFINS

Muffins often waver between two extremes: cupcake-like or dense, dry doorstop. Our version falls squarely in the middle—whole-grain yet still tender, low-sugar yet still sweet.

Kid Friendly • Make Ahead
Freezable • Vegetarian

Browned Butter Whole-Wheat Muffins

Hands-on: 15 min. Total: 40 min.

6 ounces whole-wheat flour
(about 1½ cups)
¼ cup wheat bran
1 teaspoon baking powder
1 teaspoon baking soda
½ teaspoon kosher salt
2 tablespoons unsalted butter
1 cup plain low-fat yogurt
½ cup packed light brown sugar
1 teaspoon vanilla extract
1 medium-sized ripe banana, mashed
(about ½ cup)
1 large egg
Cooking spray

1. Preheat oven to 375°F.

2. Weigh or lightly spoon flour into dry measuring cups; level with a knife. Combine flour, wheat bran, and next 3 ingredients in a bowl.
3. Melt butter in a small skillet over medium; cook 90 seconds or until browned and fragrant, swirling pan frequently. Combine butter, yogurt, sugar, vanilla, banana, and egg in a bowl. Add yogurt mixture to flour mixture, stirring just until combined. Divide batter evenly among 12 muffin cups coated with cooking spray. Bake at 375°F for 22 minutes or until a wooden pick inserted in center comes out clean. Cool in pan 5 minutes. Remove from pan; cool completely on a wire rack. Serves 12 (serving size: 1 muffin)

CALORIES 132; FAT 3g (sat 1.6g, mono 0.8g, poly 0.3g); PROTEIN 4g, CARB 24g, FIBER 2g, SUGARS 12g (est. added sugars 9g); CHOL 22mg; IRON 1mg; SODIUM 242mg; CALC 74mg

MIX IT UP

Add one of these stir-ins to the batter.

Kid Friendly • Make Ahead
Freezable • Vegetarian
Figgy Walnut Muffins
Add ¾ cup sliced dried figs, ½ cup coarsely chopped walnuts, and 1 teaspoon ground cinnamon to muffin batter. Bake as directed. Serves 12 (serving size: 1 muffin)

CALORIES 187; FAT 6.3g (sat 1.9g, mono 1g, poly 2.7g); PROTEIN 5g; CARB 31g; FIBER 4g; SUGARS 17g (est. added sugars 9g); CHOL 22mg, IRON 1mg; SODIUM 243mg; CALC 96mg

Kid Friendly • Make Ahead
Freezable • Vegetarian
Cranberry, Orange, and Pistachio Muffins
Add ½ cup dried cranberries, ½ cup chopped unsalted pistachios, 1½ teaspoons grated orange rind, and ¼ cup fresh orange juice to muffin batter. Bake as directed. Serves 12 (serving size: 1 muffin)

CALORIES 179; FAT 5.4g (sat 1.9g, mono 2g, poly 1.1g); PROTEIN 5g; CARB 30g; FIBER 3g; SUGARS 16g (est. added sugars 11g); CHOL 22mg; IRON 1mg; SODIUM 242mg; CALC 81mg

Kid Friendly • Make Ahead
Freezable • Vegetarian
Cherry-Gingerbread Muffins
Add ½ cup chopped dried cherries, ⅓ cup molasses, 1 teaspoon ground cinnamon, 1 teaspoon ground ginger, and ¼ teaspoon ground allspice to muffin batter. Bake as directed. Serves 12 (serving size: 1 muffin)

CALORIES 180; FAT 3g (sat 1.6g, mono 0.8g, poly 0.3g); PROTEIN 4g; CARB 36g; FIBER 3g; SUGARS 19g (est. added sugars 16g); CHOL 22mg; IRON 1mg; SODIUM 246mg; CALC 95mg

BETTER BREAKFAST

"Healthy" bakery muffins can hide plenty of refined flour and sugar. Ours save about 300 calories and 22g sugar per serving, are 100% whole-grain, and are still tender and moist.

SOOTHING BREAKFAST SOUP

The fragrant noodle soup we love to slurp on cool evenings is actually the breakfast of champions, says cookbook author Andrea Nguyen. "It's a fabulous wake-up call that energizes and satisfies." This is how the soup was always eaten: Pho vendors in Vietnam would start their broths before dawn, open their shops at sunrise, and sell out by midmorning before the day got too hot. Here, Nguyen shares her speedy, streamlined version from *The Pho Cookbook* (Ten Speed Press). Filling and comforting without being heavy, it's the kind of any-weather breakfast that won't leave you in a 10 a.m. food coma.

Staff Favorite • Gluten Free Kid Friendly • Make Ahead

Quick Chicken Pho

Hands-on: 15 min. Total: 45 min.

1 (³/₄-inch) section ginger
2 medium-large green onions
1 small bunch cilantro sprigs
1¹/₂ teaspoons coriander seeds
1 whole clove
3¹/₂ cups unsalted chicken stock
2 cups water
1 (8-ounce) skinless, boneless chicken breast
3 ounces dried flat rice noodles (such as pad Thai)
1 teaspoon fish sauce
¹/₂ teaspoon organic sugar or 1 teaspoon maple syrup (optional)
Freshly ground black pepper (optional)
Basil leaves, mint leaves, mung bean sprouts, sliced red Fresno chile, and lime wedges, for garnish (optional)

1. Peel and slice the ginger crosswise into 4 or 5 coins, then smack with the flat side of a knife. Set aside. Cut the hollow green parts of the green onions into thin rounds to yield 2 to 3 tablespoons; set aside. Cut the leftover white sections into pinkie-finger lengths, bruise, and then add to the ginger.
2. Coarsely chop the leafy tops of the cilantro to yield 2 tablespoons; set aside. Reserve the remaining cilantro sprigs.
3. Add the coriander seeds and clove to a 3- or 4-quart pot over medium; toast 1 to 2 minutes or until fragrant. Add the ginger and green onion mixture; stir 30 seconds or until aromatic. Slide the pot off the heat and cool for about 15 seconds; pour in the stock. Return the pot to the heat; add 2 cups water, cilantro sprigs, and chicken. Bring to a boil over high. Lower the heat, and gently simmer for 30 minutes. While the broth simmers, soak the rice noodles in hot water until pliable and opaque. Drain, rinse, and set aside.
4. After 5 to 10 minutes of simmering, the chicken should be firm and cooked through (it should yield slightly when pressed). Transfer the chicken to a bowl, flush with cold water to stop the cooking; drain. Cool and cut or shred into bite-sized pieces. Cover loosely to prevent drying.
5. When the broth is done, pour it through a fine-mesh strainer positioned over a 2-quart pot (line the strainer with muslin for a super-clear broth). Discard the solids. You should have about 4 cups broth. Add fish sauce and sugar or maple syrup, if needed, to create a strong savory-sweet note.
6. Bring the strained broth to a boil over high. Put the noodles in a noodle strainer or mesh sieve and dunk into the hot broth to heat and soften, 5 to 60 seconds. Lift the noodles from the pot and divide between 2 large bowls. Lower the heat to keep the broth hot while you arrange the chicken on top of the noodles and garnish with the chopped green onions, cilantro, and, if desired, a sprinkling of pepper. Return the broth to a boil before ladling into the bowls. Enjoy with basil, mint, sprouts, chile, and lime, if desired. Serves 2

CALORIES 360; **FAT** 3.1g (sat 0.7g, mono 0.8g, poly 0.5g); **PROTEIN** 35g; **CARB** 47g; **FIBER** 2g; **SUGARS** 6g (est. added sugars 2g); **CHOL** 83mg; **IRON** 2mg; **SODIUM** 577mg; **CALC** 32mg

TOASTS WITH THE MOST

Bread has broken our post-dinner fast for centuries, but overprocessing has given it a bad rap. A return to simple, fresh loaves for morning sustenance is not only tastier, it's better for you, too.

Quick & Easy • Kid Friendly

Banana-Bacon-Nut Toast
(pictured on page 215)

Hands-on: 10 min. Total: 10 min.

1 tablespoon finely chopped pecans
1 bacon slice, cooked and chopped
2 teaspoons almond butter
1 (1-ounce) slice whole-grain bread, toasted
¹/₄ ripe banana, cut diagonally into thin slices

1. Combine pecans and bacon in a bowl. Spread almond butter over bread; top with banana. Sprinkle with about 1 tablespoon bacon mixture (reserve remaining mixture for another use). Serves 1

CALORIES 201; **FAT** 10.5g (sat 1.5g, mono 5.5g, poly 2.8g); **PROTEIN** 7g; **CARB** 22g; **FIBER** 4g; **SUGARS** 6g (est. added sugars 3g); **CHOL** 2mg; **IRON** 1mg; **SODIUM** 167mg; **CALC** 70mg

Kale, Swiss, and Shiitake Toast

Hands-on: 10 min. Total: 10 min.

1 (1-ounce) slice whole-grain bread, toasted
2 ultra-thin Swiss cheese slices (such as Sargento)
1 teaspoon olive oil, divided
2 shiitake mushroom caps, stemmed and thinly sliced
1/4 cup stemmed, thinly sliced lacinato kale
3/4 teaspoon apple cider vinegar
Dash of kosher salt
Dash of freshly ground black pepper

1. Preheat broiler to high.
2. Top bread with cheese. Broil 30 seconds or until cheese melts.
3. Heat 3/4 teaspoon oil in a small skillet over medium-high. Add mushrooms; sauté 4 minutes or until browned.
4. Place kale in a bowl; gently squeeze with your hands until slightly wilted. Add remaining 1/4 teaspoon oil, vinegar, salt, and pepper; toss. Top bread with kale mixture and mushrooms. Serves 1

CALORIES 195; **FAT** 11.1g (sat 4.2g, mono 3.5g, poly 1.1g); **PROTEIN** 10g; **CARB** 14g; **FIBER** 2g; **SUGARS** 2g (est. added sugars 2g); **CHOL** 17mg; **IRON** 1mg; **SODIUM** 271mg; **CALC** 203mg

HOW TO STORE

Keep bread at room temperature in a dry place (sprouted breads should be refrigerated or frozen). If you plan to eat less, slice and freeze the rest in a ziplock plastic freezer bag. Refrigerated bread will go stale faster, but it's not a total loss: Stale and frozen bread makes excellent toast.

Blackberry-Brie Toast

Hands-on: 5 min. Total: 5 min.

1 tablespoon seedless blackberry jam
1 (1-ounce) slice whole-grain bread, toasted
1/2 ounce Brie cheese, cut into pieces
1/4 teaspoon fresh thyme leaves

1. Preheat broiler to high.
2. Spread jam over bread; top evenly with Brie. Broil 30 seconds or until cheese melts. Sprinkle with thyme. Serves 1

CALORIES 173; **FAT** 5.1g (sat 2.7g, mono 1.4g, poly 0.7g); **PROTEIN** 6.7g; **CARB** 25g; **FIBER** 2g; **SUGARS** 14g (est. added sugars 13g); **CHOL** 14mg; **IRON** 1mg; **SODIUM** 197mg; **CALC** 56mg

Apricot-Hazelnut Toast

Hands-on: 5 min. Total: 5 min.

1 tablespoon apricot preserves
1 (1-ounce) slice whole-grain bread, toasted
2 teaspoons chopped hazelnuts
2 teaspoons crumbled goat cheese
1/4 teaspoon fresh thyme leaves

1. Spread preserves over bread. Top with hazelnuts, goat cheese, and thyme. Serves 1

CALORIES 180; **FAT** 6.3g (sat 1.9g, mono 2.9g, poly 1g); **PROTEIN** 6g; **CARB** 26g; **FIBER** 3g; **SUGARS** 11g (est. added sugars 10g); **CHOL** 6mg; **IRON** 1mg; **SODIUM** 145mg; **CALC** 61mg

Apple-Tahini Toast

Hands-on: 5 min. Total: 5 min.

1 tablespoon tahini (sesame paste), stirred well
1 (1-ounce) slice whole-grain bread, toasted
5 thin Granny Smith apple slices
1 teaspoon honey
1/8 teaspoon toasted sesame seeds
1/8 teaspoon ground cinnamon

1. Spread tahini over bread; top with apple slices. Drizzle with honey. Sprinkle with sesame seeds and cinnamon. Serves 1

CALORIES 198; **FAT** 8.6g (sat 1.3g, mono 3g, poly 3.8g); **PROTEIN** 7g; **CARB** 26g; **FIBER** 4g; **SUGARS** 10g (est. added sugars 8g); **CHOL** 0mg; **IRON** 1mg; **SODIUM** 120mg; **CALC** 98mg

Prosciutto-Melon Toast

Hands-on: 5 min. Total: 5 min.

1 tablespoon 1/3-less-fat cream cheese, softened
1 (1-ounce) slice whole-grain bread, toasted
1 1/2 very thin prosciutto slices (about 1/2 ounce)
2 thin cantaloupe slices
Dash of freshly ground black pepper

1. Spread cream cheese over bread, and top with prosciutto and cantaloupe. Sprinkle with pepper. Serves 1

CALORIES 143; **FAT** 5.6g (sat 2.7g, mono 0.9g, poly 0.8g); **PROTEIN** 8g; **CARB** 15g; **FIBER** 2g; **SUGARS** 4g (est. added sugars 2g); **CHOL** 18mg; **IRON** 1mg; **SODIUM** 380mg; **CALC** 43mg

Avocado-Sprout Toast

Hands-on: 5 min. Total: 5 min.

1 (1-ounce) slice whole-grain bread,
   toasted
¼ ripe avocado, sliced
Dash of kosher salt
Dash of freshly ground black pepper
¼ cup alfalfa sprouts
2 teaspoons sunflower seeds
½ teaspoon fresh lemon juice

1. Top bread with avocado; lightly mash. Top with remaining ingredients. Serves 1

CALORIES 169; **FAT** 9.5g (sat 1.2g, mono 4.6g, poly 2.5g); **PROTEIN** 6g; **CARB** 17g; **FIBER** 5g; **SUGARS** 2g (est. added sugars 2g); **CHOL** 0mg; **IRON** 1mg; **SODIUM** 232mg; **CALC** 42mg

Cherry-Ricotta Toast

Hands-on: 8 min. Total: 18 min.

1 cup frozen pitted cherries, thawed
   and halved
½ teaspoon grated lemon rind
½ teaspoon cornstarch
3 tablespoons part-skim ricotta cheese
1 (1-ounce) slice whole-grain bread,
   toasted
2 teaspoons chopped pistachios

1. Place cherries and rind in a microwave-safe bowl; sprinkle with cornstarch. Microwave at HIGH 3 minutes, stirring after 90 seconds. Cool 10 minutes.
2. Spread ricotta over bread; top with ¼ cup compote (reserve remaining compote for another use). Sprinkle with pistachios. Serves 1

CALORIES 187; **FAT** 7.3g (sat 2.9g, mono 2.6g, poly 1.4g); **PROTEIN** 11g; **CARB** 21g; **FIBER** 3g; **SUGARS** 5g (est. added sugars 2g); **CHOL** 14mg; **IRON** 1mg; **SODIUM** 155mg; **CALC** 167mg

DIY BREAKFAST SAUSAGE

In just 25 minutes, you have delicious, freezable patties with 40% less saturated fat and half the sodium of popular commercial brands.

Easy Homemade Breakfast Sausage

Hands-on: 25 min. Total: 25 min.

¼ cup dark maple syrup
1 tablespoon chopped fresh thyme
1 tablespoon chopped fresh sage
1½ teaspoons kosher salt
¾ teaspoon freshly ground
   black pepper
2 garlic cloves, minced
1 pound ground turkey
1 pound ground pork
8 teaspoons canola oil, divided

1. Gently combine all ingredients except oil in a large bowl just until blended. Shape mixture into 16 (3½-inch) patties (about 2 ounces per patty).
2. Heat 2 teaspoons oil in a large skillet over medium-high. Add 4 patties to pan; cook 2½ minutes on each side. Repeat procedure 3 times with remaining oil and remaining patties. Serves 16 (serving size: 1 patty)

CALORIES 151; **FAT** 11g (sat 3g, mono 4.9g, poly 1.8g); **PROTEIN** 10g; **CARB** 4g; **FIBER** 0g; **SUGARS** 3g (est. added sugars 3g); **CHOL** 40mg; **IRON** 1mg; **SODIUM** 213mg; **CALC** 17mg

OUR FLUFFIEST PANCAKES EVER

You'll flip for these irresistible hot cakes. They're quick to make, with a unique texture that's both light and creamy. And when we say fluffy, we mean it: This is our tallest short stack yet.

Fluffiest Multigrain Pancakes with Almond Butter Drizzle

Hands-on: 25 min. Total: 25 min.
These pancakes are wonderfully hearty, thanks to old-fashioned oats and white whole-wheat flour, yet their texture is still fluffy and light, with a beguiling creaminess in the middle. Instead of dousing this short stack with syrup, we opt for a nutty sauce of maple-sweetened almond butter—cutting about 27g added sugars from the typical pancake breakfast. (Sub any nut butter.) Soaking the oats first softens them and helps create that creamy interior. As they soak, you can make the almond butter sauce and measure out the other ingredients.

⅔ cup old-fashioned oats
1⅓ cups nonfat buttermilk
¼ cup warm water
¼ cup natural almond butter
2½ tablespoons maple syrup
3 ounces white whole-wheat flour
   (about ¾ cup)
2 teaspoons baking powder
¼ teaspoon baking soda
¼ teaspoon kosher salt
1 teaspoon vanilla extract
1 large egg, lightly beaten
1⅓ cups fresh raspberries

1. Combine oats and buttermilk in a large bowl; let stand 10 minutes.
2. Meanwhile, combine ¼ cup warm water, almond butter, and 1½ tablespoons syrup, stirring with a whisk until smooth.
3. Weigh or lightly spoon flour into a dry measuring cup; level with a knife. Combine flour, baking powder, baking soda, and salt, stirring well.
4. Heat a large nonstick griddle or nonstick skillet over medium. Stir remaining 1 tablespoon syrup, vanilla, and egg into oat mixture; add flour mixture, stirring just until combined. Spoon a scant ¼ cup batter per pancake onto hot griddle. Cook until tops are covered with bubbles and edges look dry and cooked, about 2 to 3 minutes; turn and cook 1 to 2 minutes on other side. Serve with almond butter sauce and berries. Serves 4 (serving size: 3 pancakes, about 2 tablespoons sauce, and ⅓ cup berries)

CALORIES 324; FAT 11.7g (sat 1.2g, mono 6g, poly 2.9g); PROTEIN 13g; CARB 43g; FIBER 8g; SUGARS 11g (est. added sugars 9g); CHOL 47mg; IRON 3mg; SODIUM 499mg; CALC 320mg

---

CUT THE SUGAR
A typical pancake breakfast contains about 36g added sugars, thanks to syrup. Our nut butter sauce is a smarter choice, offering delicious maple notes while slashing 78% of the added sugar.

GO FOR WHOLE GRAINS
We use white whole-wheat flour and old-fashioned oats, kicking refined flour to the curb. The pancakes still cook up fluffy, with a delightful toasty flavor.

PILE ON THE FIBER
Thanks to whole grains, nut butter, and fresh raspberries, one serving of our pancakes packs in about one-third of your daily fiber needs, helping to keep you fuller longer.

WATCH FOR SNEAKY SODIUM
Because leaveners like baking soda and baking powder harbor lots of sodium, we add just a pinch of salt so you don't blow your daily budget.

HEARTY GRANOLA BOWL

Build a gluten-free breakfast bowl every day with crunchy granola and creamy overnight oats.

Gluten Free • Kid Friendly
Make Ahead • Vegetarian

Blackberry-Citrus Granola Bowl

Hands-on: 10 min. Total: 8 hr. 10 min. (includes soaking)
The best way to cook steel-cut oats during the week? Don't cook them at all. Soak the oats overnight in your milk of choice: The oats will soften and plump in the liquid but remain slightly chewy. Enjoy cold, or heat in the microwave for 30 seconds. Cocoa nibs add a little extra crunch and a wake-up jolt similar to coffee.

2 cups 2% reduced-fat milk or plain, unsweetened almond or soy milk
1 cup uncooked steel-cut oats
1 tablespoon cocoa nibs
1 tablespoon pure maple syrup
1 cup Coconut-Buckwheat Granola (recipe at right)
1 cup blackberries
1 cup red grapefruit and blood orange segments

1. Combine milk and oats in an airtight container; seal. Refrigerate 8 hours or overnight.
2. Add cocoa nibs and maple syrup to oat mixture. Divide oat mixture evenly among 4 bowls; top evenly with granola, blackberries, and citrus segments. Serves 4 (serving size: about ⅔ cup oats mixture, ¼ cup granola, and ½ cup fruit)

CALORIES 403; FAT 14.7g (sat 5g, mono 5.2g, poly 3.3g); PROTEIN 14g; CARB 57g; FIBER 9g; SUGARS 18g (est. added sugars 5g); CHOL 10mg; IRON 3mg; SODIUM 181mg; CALC 190mg

---

Staff Favorite • Quick & Easy
Gluten Free • Kid Friendly
Make Ahead • Vegetarian

Coconut-Buckwheat Granola

Hands-on: 6 min. Total: 36 min.
We change up the classic oat and nut combo with coconut flakes and starchy buckwheat groats. Look for pale-green groats; the toasted, dark-brown buckwheat can have a bitter flavor. You can also skip the buckwheat and add another ½ cup rolled oats.

1½ cups old-fashioned oats
½ cup unsweetened flaked dried coconut
½ cup almonds, coarsely chopped
½ cup unsalted pumpkin seeds
¼ cup uncooked buckwheat groats
2 tablespoons canola oil
2 tablespoons honey
1 teaspoon kosher salt
1 teaspoon ground cinnamon

1. Preheat oven to 375°F.
2. Combine first 5 ingredients in a large bowl. Combine oil, honey, salt, and cinnamon in a bowl, stirring with a whisk. Add honey mixture to oat mixture; stir well to coat. Spread oat mixture in a single layer on a parchment paper–lined baking sheet. Bake at 375°F for 20 minutes or until golden, stirring once after 10 minutes. Cool completely. Serves 12 (serving size: about ⅓ cup)

CALORIES 168; FAT 10.9g (sat 2.9g, mono 4.6g, poly 2.8g); PROTEIN 5g; CARB 15g; FIBER 3g; SUGARS 4g (est. added sugars 3g); CHOL 0mg; IRON 1mg; SODIUM 162mg; CALC 22mg

BEVERAGES WITH BENEFITS

Start and end your day with drinks that give you a boost. Zingy green apple and apple cider vinegar will jump-start your morning; warm coconut milk and turmeric will lull you to sleep.

Quick & Easy • Gluten Free Kid Friendly • Vegetarian

Double-Apple Morning Elixir

Hands-on: 5 min. Total: 5 min.

1 (8-ounce) Granny Smith apple, cored and roughly chopped
½ cup water
2 tablespoons fresh cilantro leaves
2 tablespoons unfiltered apple cider vinegar
1 teaspoon honey

1. Process all ingredients in a blender until well incorporated, about 1½ minutes. Pour through a fine-mesh strainer into an ice-filled glass; discard solids. Serves 1 (serving size: 1 cup)

CALORIES 127; FAT 0.3g (sat 0g, mono 0.1g, poly 0g); PROTEIN 1g; CARB 29g; FIBER 5g; SUGARS 22g (est. added sugars 6g); CHOL 0mg; IRON 0mg; SODIUM 4mg; CALC 12mg

Staff Favorite • Quick & Easy Gluten Free • Vegetarian

Golden Milk Tea

Hands-on: 15 min. Total: 15 min.

2 cups refrigerated unsweetened coconut milk (such as Silk)
1 tablespoon honey
1 tablespoon grated peeled fresh turmeric or 1 teaspoon dried ground turmeric
1 teaspoon grated peeled fresh ginger
⅛ teaspoon ground cardamom
Dash of kosher salt
Dash of freshly ground black pepper

1. Bring all ingredients to a simmer in a small saucepan over medium, stirring often. Remove from heat; cover and let stand 5 minutes. Strain; discard solids. Serves 2 (serving size: 1 cup)

CALORIES 80; FAT 4.6g (sat 4g, mono 0g, poly 0g); PROTEIN 0g; CARB 10g; FIBER 0g; SUGARS 9g (est. added sugars 9g); CHOL 0mg; IRON 1mg; SODIUM 101mg; CALC 453mg

DAY-MAKING DONUTS

Matcha, the trendy green tea powder, infuses baked whole-grain treats and makes a beautiful glaze.

Kid Friendly • Make Ahead Vegetarian

Matcha-Glazed Donuts
(pictured on page 215)

Hands-on: 30 min. Total: 1 hr.
Matcha has a powerfully earthy, bitter flavor, so a little goes a long way. For the most vibrant color, seek out brands like Maeda-en, Aiya, or Eden. You can sub dried cranberries for the goji berries.

6 ounces whole-wheat pastry flour (about 1¾ cups)
½ cup granulated sugar
2¼ teaspoons matcha powder, divided
¾ teaspoon baking powder
¼ teaspoon baking soda
¼ teaspoon salt
½ cup nonfat buttermilk
¼ cup plus 4 teaspoons water
¼ cup butter, melted
½ teaspoon grated lemon rind
1 large egg
Cooking spray
1¼ cups powdered sugar
1 teaspoon fresh lemon juice
2 tablespoons large unsweetened coconut flakes, toasted
2 tablespoons chopped goji berries

1. Preheat oven to 350°F.
2. Weigh or lightly spoon flour into dry measuring cups; level with a knife. Combine flour, granulated sugar, 1½ teaspoons matcha, baking powder, baking soda, and salt. Combine buttermilk, ¼ cup water, butter, rind, and egg, stirring with a whisk. Add buttermilk mixture to flour mixture, stirring until combined.
3. Coat 2 (6-cavity) donut pans with cooking spray. Spoon batter evenly into 12 cavities. Bake at 350°F for 12 minutes or until donuts spring back when lightly pressed. Cool in pan for 2 minutes. Run a thin knife around outside edge of each cavity; invert donuts onto a wire rack. Cool completely.
4. Combine powdered sugar, remaining 4 teaspoons water, remaining ¾ teaspoon matcha powder, and lemon juice, stirring until smooth (add more water, ½ teaspoon at a time, if glaze is too thick). Spread glaze over tops of donuts; sprinkle 6 donuts evenly with coconut and 6 with goji berries. Let stand until glaze is set. Serves 12 (serving size: 1 donut)

CALORIES 195; FAT 5.8g (sat 3.1g, mono 1.6g, poly 0.4g); PROTEIN 3g; CARB 34g; FIBER 2g; SUGARS 21g (est. added sugars 21g); CHOL 26mg; IRON 1mg; SODIUM 158mg; CALC 43mg

CHOOSE YOUR OWN EGGVENTURE

Y ou love eggs. But you need them cooked your way. The following journey leads you to foolproof techniques for egg perfection. Pick a style and then get cracking.

SCRAMBLED

You wake early on Saturday, but your body clock is wound tight, and more sleep ain't happening. It's cold and gloomy outside—perfect for all-day jammies. Your revving metabolism needs fuel, though, and a warm plate of soothing scrambled eggs would be just the thing. Your husband and kids are still asleep. You could wait for them to crawl from bed, then make everyone a big pile of scrambled eggs. But you remember: They like their eggs scrambled differently than how you do them. Very differently. "Hell with them," you think. "I'm making a plate of perfection." You slip stealthily down to the kitchen and heat up your trusty nonstick skillet. Do you:
1. Scramble hot and fast for big, fluffy curds with a tender yet satisfying chew, the kind you get at your favorite breakfast joint downtown? **2.** Cook low and slow, stirring nonstop, for tiny curds and custardy texture, the dreamy-creamy kind chef Jean-Georges Vongerichten serves with a dollop of caviar on top?

Quick & Easy • Gluten Free
Kid Friendly • Vegetarian

1. Diner-Style Scrambled Eggs

Hands-on: 5 min. Total: 5 min.
These are the eggs you probably grew up eating: quick, easy to make, homey, and comforting. A little butter adds richness. We use just a tiny amount of salt here, because it's easy to oversalt eggs. Pull them from the heat the instant they're done so they don't turn tough and rubbery. And as with all egg dishes, dig in right away—they're not getting any better as they cool off.

1 teaspoon unsalted butter
2 large eggs
¼ teaspoon freshly ground black
 pepper
⅛ teaspoon kosher salt

1. Melt butter in an 8-inch nonstick skillet over medium-high until it gets bubbly; diner-style scrambles do not fear heat.
2. While butter melts, break eggs into a small bowl. Use a fork to beat them like they owe you money until completely blended and slightly frothy. Stir in the pepper and salt.
3. Add egg mixture to pan; start pulling the eggs from the sides of the pan into the middle (the edges cook faster than the center). Big, fluffy curds will start to form— exactly what you want. Keep it up, pulling the eggs from around the pan for about 3 minutes. The second all the runny egg is fully set—there's an eggshell-thin line between fluffy, firm eggs and tough, dry ones—pull the pan from the heat and slide the eggs onto your plate. Serves 1

CALORIES 179; **FAT** 13.4g (sat 5.6g, mono 4.7g, poly 2.1g); **PROTEIN** 13g; **CARB** 1g; **FIBER** 0g; **SUGARS** 0g (est. added sugars 0g); **CHOL** 382mg; **IRON** 2mg; **SODIUM** 383mg; **CALC** 59mg

Quick & Easy • Gluten Free
Kid Friendly • Vegetarian

2. Creamy Soft-Scrambled Eggs

Hands-on: 5 min. Total: 5 min.
This style of scramble proves eye-opening for folks used to springy curds—it teaches them how creamy scrambled eggs can be. These taste so rich you'll swear there's cheese in there somewhere. Constant vigilance is the price of perfection here. Stir nonstop for small curds: The bigger the curds, the less creamy the texture. A slight sheen on the finished eggs means they're still wonderfully moist.

1 teaspoon unsalted butter
2 large eggs
¼ teaspoon freshly ground black
 pepper
⅛ teaspoon kosher salt

1. Melt butter in an 8-inch nonstick skillet over medium-low. While butter melts, break eggs into a small bowl. Use a fork to beat them like a red-feathered step-chicken until completely blended and slightly frothy. Stir in pepper and salt.
2. Before the butter starts to froth, add the eggs; cook, stirring quickly and constantly with a heatproof rubber spatula or chopsticks. Be patient; keep stirring. After a few minutes, steam will rise, the eggs will thicken, and small curds will begin to form. If you start to get large curds no matter how quickly you stir, lift the pan from the burner to cool it down, stirring all the while. Cook, stirring constantly, until the eggs hold together in a glistening, custard-soft, and loose mound that can still spread slightly, like risotto. Plate and eat immediately. Serves 1

CALORIES 179; **FAT** 13.4g (sat 5.6g, mono 4.7g, poly 2.1g); **PROTEIN** 13g; **CARB** 1g; **FIBER** 0g; **SUGARS** 0g (est. added sugars 0g); **CHOL** 382mg; **IRON** 2mg; **SODIUM** 383mg; **CALC** 59mg

POACHED

After the kids' Saturday morning basketball game, you bring friends home for an impromptu brunch. One guy suggests poached eggs, because he would—he usually eats out and has no idea how much stress the mere idea of poached eggs puts on the average home cook. Still, pillowy poached eggs would be fantastic. The guy says the top French chefs swear by the swirling vortex method, which delivers perfectly ovoid poached eggs without any raggedy whites. But you don't need Le Cordon Bleu approval; you just want to feed everyone at once, with poached eggs that might look a little shaggy but taste just right, merci beaucoup. Do you:
1. Whisk a deep pot of simmering water into a whirlpool and sculpt each egg to Escoffier-level perfection? **2.** Simmer 2 inches of water in a straight-sided sauté pan and poach everyone's eggs at once?

Quick & Easy • Kid Friendly Vegetarian

1. Swirl-Poached Eggs

Hands-on: 20 min. Total: 20 min.
A little vinegar in the poaching water helps keep the egg whites compact, while the whirlpool and your gentle coaxing do the rest of the work. A gentle blot after the egg is out of the pan keeps water droplets from mixing with the creamy yolk and diluting the flavor and texture.

2 quarts water
1 tablespoon white vinegar
2 large eggs
1/8 teaspoon kosher salt, divided
1/8 teaspoon freshly ground black pepper, divided
1 (2-ounce) slice whole-grain bread, toasted
1 teaspoon extra-virgin olive oil

1. Bring 2 quarts water and vinegar to a gentle simmer in a medium saucepan over medium, about 6 minutes. Adjust heat as necessary to maintain a gentle simmer.
2. Carefully crack eggs into each of 2 small bowls or ramekins, keeping yolks intact. Using a whisk, swirl water in pan in a circular motion until a whirlpool forms. Gently slip 1 egg into center of whirlpool. Using a slotted spoon, swirl water around edge of pan, gently shaping egg as it spins so the egg white forms a tight, neat oval around the yolk. Cook until white is set, about 3 minutes. Using a slotted spoon, remove egg from pan; place on a plate lined with paper towels. Gently blot top of egg with paper towel to dry. Sprinkle with half of salt and half of pepper. Repeat procedure with remaining egg, salt, and pepper.
3. Drizzle toast slice with oil. Top with eggs. Serves 1

CALORIES 336; **FAT** 16.6g (sat 4.3g, mono 7.7g, poly 3.4g); **PROTEIN** 20g; **CARB** 25g; **FIBER** 4g; **SUGARS** 4g (est. added sugars 4g); **CHOL** 372mg; **IRON** 3mg; **SODIUM** 598mg; **CALC** 116mg

Quick & Easy • Kid Friendly Vegetarian

2. Shallow-Poached Eggs

Hands-on: 15 min. Total: 15 min.
The key here is to add the eggs to the water at 30-second intervals and remove in the same order.

1 tablespoon white vinegar
4 large eggs
1/4 teaspoon kosher salt, divided
1/4 teaspoon freshly ground black pepper, divided
2 (2-ounce) slices whole-grain bread, toasted
2 teaspoons extra-virgin olive oil

1. Pour about 2 inches of water into a straight-sided skillet; add vinegar. Bring to a gentle simmer. The liquid temperature will dip as you add eggs; adjust heat as needed to maintain a constant gentle simmer.
2. Break 1 egg into each of 4 small bowls or ramekins. Gently slip 1 egg into simmering water at the 12 o'clock position. Set a timer for 4½ minutes. After 30 seconds, slip the second egg into simmering water at the 3 o'clock position. After another 30 seconds, slip third egg in at 6 o'clock. After another 30 seconds, put fourth egg at 9 o'clock.
3. When the timer reaches 1½ minutes left, the first egg should be done (if the white is just set with no translucent areas, the yolk will still be creamy). Gently remove the first egg with a fish spatula or slotted spoon; place on a plate lined with paper towels, and gently blot top dry with a paper towel. Sprinkle egg with a pinch of salt and pepper. At 30-second intervals, working clockwise, repeat procedure with remaining eggs, salt, and pepper.
4. Drizzle each toast slice with 1 teaspoon oil. Place 2 eggs on each toast slice. Serves 2

CALORIES 336; **FAT** 16.6g (sat 4.3g, mono 7.7g, poly 3.4g); **PROTEIN** 20g; **CARB** 25g; **FIBER** 4g; **SUGARS** 4g (est. added sugars 4g); **CHOL** 372mg; **IRON** 3mg; **SODIUM** 598mg; **CALC** 116mg

BOILED

Your husband pulls the last four eggs from the fridge. He plans to hard-boil them for lunch later in the week. "Then I can make whatever I feel like—egg salad, tuna Niçoise, deviled eggs, the list goes on," he says proudly. You give him points for enthusiasm. And creativity, too. But he hard-boils like a savage, cooking them so long the whites are like industrial-strength latex and the gray-green yolks smell like Satan's breath. So you step in, offering to hard-cook them. Or—or!—you could soft-boil them for supple whites and thick, velvety yolks. That way, both of you can enjoy them hot, right now. Eggless tuna Niçoise is still delicious, right? Do you:
1. Boil water and set the timer for eggs cooked precisely to the second, in what may be the simplest way to coax out their lush textures and rich flavors? **2.** Set the eggs in cold water, bring them to a boil, and then let them rest so the whites are firm but not tough, while the yolks cook through but stay moist?

Quick & Easy • Gluten Free
Kid Friendly • Vegetarian

1. 375-Second Soft-Boiled Eggs

Hands-on: 20 min. Total: 20 min.
It may seem weird to call for a cooking time down to the second, but bear in mind that the temperature difference between a creamy yolk and a solid one is a mere 8°F. If you like your yolks only thickened, without any slightly set parts on the edges, boil them for 6 minutes. Egg yolks cook faster than egg whites, so we call for cold eggs; cold yolks cook slower, insulated in the shells by the whites.

2 quarts water
4 cold large eggs
¼ teaspoon kosher salt
¼ teaspoon freshly ground black pepper

1. Bring 2 quarts water to a boil in a medium saucepan over medium-high. Gently add eggs, straight from the fridge. The boil will halt for a moment as the water temperature drops. When boiling resumes, adjust heat as needed so the eggs don't bounce hard on the bottom of the pan, cracking the shells. Cook 6 minutes and 15 seconds for thick, creamy yolks that have just barely begun to set around the edges. Meanwhile, fill a medium bowl with ice and water. The second the eggs are done, pull them out with a slotted spoon, and plunge them into the ice bath. Let stand 2 minutes. Cut off tops or crack eggs, and remove shells gently; soft-cooked eggs are wobbly and fragile. Sprinkle evenly with salt and pepper after cutting in so the yolks get seasoned, too. Serves 2 (serving size: 2 eggs)

CALORIES 144; **FAT** 9.5g (sat 3.1g, mono 3.7g, poly 1.9g); **PROTEIN** 13g; **CARB** 1g; **FIBER** 0g; **SUGARS** 0g (est. added sugars 0g); **CHOL** 372mg; **IRON** 2mg; **SODIUM** 382mg; **CALC** 57mg

Quick & Easy • Gluten Free
Kid Friendly • Make Ahead
Vegetarian

2. Foolproof Hard-Boiled Eggs

Hands-on: 5 min. Total: 30 min.
Hard-boiling is perfect for eggs that aren't farm-fresh because older eggs peel more easily. This method gives you whites that are firm, not rubbery, and yolks that are cooked through but not dry and flaky. A dip in an ice bath cools any residual heat so green rings don't form around the yolks. We call for a specific amount of water to eliminate variables. Still, water in pots of different materials or thickness may heat and cool at slightly different rates, so if you find the doneness isn't to your liking, simply adjust the time the eggs boil accordingly.

2 quarts water
4 large eggs
¼ teaspoon kosher salt
¼ teaspoon freshly ground black pepper

1. Pour 2 quarts water into a medium saucepan. Gently add eggs, being careful not to crack the shells. Bring water to a boil over high. The minute the water boils, turn off the heat, move the pan to a cold burner, (eliminating the variable of how long it takes your particular burner to cool), and cover the pan. Let stand 12 minutes. Meanwhile, fill a medium bowl with ice and water. After exactly 12 minutes, pull eggs out with a slotted spoon, and plunge them into the ice bath. Let stand 5 minutes, 10 if you're going to store them for later. Gently crack eggs, and remove shells. Sprinkle evenly with salt and pepper after slicing in half so the yolks get seasoned, too. Serves 2 (serving size: 2 eggs)

CALORIES 144; **FAT** 9.5g (sat 3.1g, mono 3.7g, poly 1.9g); **PROTEIN** 13g; **CARB** 1g; **FIBER** 0g; **SUGARS** 0g (est. added sugars 0g); **CHOL** 372mg; **IRON** 2mg; **SODIUM** 382mg; **CALC** 57mg

STUFFED AND TOPPED

The in-laws come to your house unannounced after their weekly worship/Sunday morning news programs/silent, tense car ride (your eggventure, your call). They're verging on hangry—a good breakfast would work wonders for all. Just like you, your mother-in-law loves fluffy, lightly browned omelets stuffed with fresh veggies and a little cheese. Your father-in-law prefers tall slices of quiche with flaky homemade crust. (Not. Happening.) The happy medium? Frittatas! But your father-in-law doesn't know what they are, and he's been wary of Italian food in general ever since you told him what puttanesca means. Do you: **1.** Go Mediterranean and bake simple veggie frittatas, without any pesky omelet-flipping? **2.** Make golden-brown, half-moon omelets, light and fluffy, with a fresh vegetable filling?

CHOOSE YOUR OWN PAN

DO YOU LIKE THE LOW COST OF NONSTICK PANS? ARE YOU OK WITH REPLACING THEM EVERY NOW AND THEN?
You need: Tramontina ProLine 8-inch fry pan. The commercial-grade surface is as durable and stick-proof as you're likely to find, at a price point that's hard to beat. At Costco, a two-pack set (8- and 10-inch) is $25.

DO YOU HATE REPLACING PANS? ARE YOU SERIOUS ENOUGH ABOUT EGGS TO SEASON A PAN YOU CAN USE FOR A LIFETIME?
You need: Mauviel M'Steel 8-inch round frying pan. The carbon steel needs seasoning and light upkeep, but gives you a durable, oven-safe nonstick pan. $40, mauvielusa.com

---

Quick & Easy • Gluten Free
Kid Friendly • Vegetarian

1. Kale and Mushroom Frittata

Hands-on: 10 min. Total: 10 min.
Half the pleasure of a frittata is saying it. Go ahead. Free-tah-tah. For molto fun, stress the first syllable and roll the r. Fr-r-r-r-r-r-r-r-ee-tah-tah. A cast-iron or carbon-steel pan (see "Choose Your Own Pan," at left) is best because broiler heat could damage nonstick skillets.

2 large eggs
1/4 teaspoon freshly ground black pepper, divided
1/8 teaspoon kosher salt, divided
2 teaspoons olive oil
1/2 cup sliced cremini mushrooms
1/2 cup loosely packed baby kale or spinach
1 tablespoon crumbled goat or feta cheese

1. Preheat broiler to high, and set a rack 6 inches from the heat.
2. Break eggs into a small bowl. Use a fork to beat them like a back-talking bass drum until completely blended and slightly frothy. Stir in half the pepper and half the salt.
3. Heat olive oil in an 8-inch cast-iron skillet over medium-high. Add mushrooms to pan; sauté 4 minutes or until nicely browned. Stir in kale and remaining salt and pepper; sauté 30 seconds or until kale is just wilted. Add eggs; stir slowly and tilt the skillet a few times so runny parts hit the pan. After about 2 minutes, when the eggs are lightly browned on the bottom with a few shiny spots still on top, sprinkle with cheese.
4. Place pan under broiler; broil 1 minute or until cheese softens and golden-brown spots appear on egg. Slide frittata onto a plate. Serves 1

CALORIES 269; FAT 21g (sat 5.9g, mono 10.2g, poly 2.9g); PROTEIN 16g; CARB 4g; FIBER 1g; SUGARS 1g (est. added sugars 0g); CHOL 378mg; IRON 2mg; SODIUM 450mg; CALC 147mg

---

Quick & Easy • Gluten Free
Kid Friendly • Vegetarian

2. Half-Moon Browned Omelet

Hands-on: 10 min. Total: 10 min.

2 teaspoons olive oil, divided
1/2 cup sliced cremini mushrooms
1/2 cup loosely packed baby kale or spinach
1/8 teaspoon kosher salt, divided
2 large eggs
1/4 teaspoon freshly ground black pepper
1 tablespoon crumbled goat or feta cheese

1. Heat 1 teaspoon oil in an 8-inch nonstick skillet over medium-high. Add mushrooms; sauté until golden, about 3 minutes. Stir in kale and half of salt; stir about 30 seconds or until kale is just wilted. Place the mushroom mixture on a plate or in a small bowl. Wipe pan clean.
2. Break eggs into a small bowl. Use a fork to beat them until completely blended and slightly frothy. Stir in remaining salt and pepper.
3. Heat remaining 1 teaspoon oil in the same pan, over medium now. Add eggs; stir them around the pan with a heatproof rubber spatula like you're making firm scrambled eggs, pulling from the sides toward the middle. Tilt the pan now and then, lifting the egg disk that forms so runny egg slides off, hits the pan, and firms up. After about 2 minutes, when the eggs are slightly shiny on top in spots, but mostly cooked through, spread the mushroom mixture over half of the eggs; sprinkle with cheese. When the eggs are browned on the bottom, fold them over the filling. Slide omelet onto a plate. Serves 1

CALORIES 269; FAT 21g (sat 5.9g, mono 10.2g, poly 2.9g); PROTEIN 16g; CARB 4g; FIBER 1g; SUGARS 1g (est. added sugars 0g); CHOL 378mg; IRON 2mg; SODIUM 450mg; CALC 147mg

FRIED

Your old college roommate is over for the weekend. The two of you wax nostalgic about late-late-night breakfasts you'd have at the greasy spoon near school. You both always ordered the fried eggs: violently seared on the flattop in raging oil so the edges turned deep brown, lacy, and crunchy, while the yolks ran free and yellow like perps from a crime scene. But in the years since, you've changed in so many ways. Most important, you've developed a taste for gently cooked sunny-side up eggs with inviolably chaste whites. Your roomie still loves old-school eggs, and the chat has made her ravenous. She wants eggs, now. Do you: **1.** Fire up the ol' cast iron and put a hard sizzle on those whites, turning them crispy, crunchy, and every bit as flavorful as the yolks? **2.** Use a little finesse to "fry" and baste those sweet eggs so gently you get wedding-dress whites, tender as a sonnet?

CHOOSE YOUR OWN SPATULA

ARE SCRAMBLED EGGS, OMELETS, AND FRITTATAS YOUR THING? ARE YOU MORE OF A STIRRER THAN A FLIPPER? You need: Mastrad's All-Silicone Spatula. One piece, safe for nonstick pans, and heatproof. $6.95, amazon.com

ARE YOU ALL ABOUT FRIED AND POACHED EGGS? DO YOU SPEND MORE TIME SCOOPING AND LIFTING EGGS THAN STIRRING THEM? You need: Kuhn Rikon's SoftEdge Slotted Fish Turner. The thin, flexible head is coated with silicone, so it won't harm nonstick pans and slips easily under fried or boiled eggs to lift them. $16, surlatable.com

---

Quick & Easy • Gluten Free
Kid Friendly • Vegetarian

1. Frizzled Sunny-Side Up Eggs

Hands-on: 5 min. Total: 5 min.
These are really fun to make, if a little messy. A splatter screen would be a worthwhile investment if this is your egg style of choice. We use plenty of oil here. You don't eat it all, but an abundance of hot oil gives the whites those delicious crisp, brown edges. Also, at higher temps, whole butter could scorch. You'll get slightly better results from a cast-iron pan than a nonstick pan, but as long as the pan and oil are hot enough, either will work.

1 tablespoon canola oil
2 large eggs
1/4 teaspoon freshly ground black pepper
1/8 teaspoon kosher salt

1. Heat oil in an 8-inch nonstick skillet or small cast-iron skillet over medium-high until oil gives off a few wisps of smoke—only a really hot pan will get you good frizzles. Carefully break eggs into pan. (Careful for two reasons: to keep the yolks intact, and to watch for oil splatter. If you have a splatter screen, now's the time to use it.) Sprinkle with pepper and salt. The eggs will hiss, pop, bubble, and flutter wildly. Let them do just that, without moving them an inch, about 4 minutes or until the edges are crisp and beautifully browned and the rest of the whites are set. Remove eggs from pan, leaving excess oil behind. Serves 1

CALORIES 228; FAT 18.9g (sat 3.8g, mono 9.6g, poly 4.5g); PROTEIN 13g; CARB 1g; FIBER 0g; SUGARS 0g (est. added sugars 0g); CHOL 372mg; IRON 2mg; SODIUM 382mg; CALC 58mg

---

Quick & Easy • Gluten Free
Kid Friendly • Vegetarian

2. Pristine Sunny-Side Up Eggs

Hands-on: 5 min. Total: 5 min.
Heat control is crucial here. Too much heat, and the whites will toughen and brown at the edges. Not enough, and the yolks will cook partway through by the time the whites are set. Listen to the pan, and watch the whites for cues that your pan is properly heated. We use a little extra oil in this dish so there's enough for basting. The hot oil baste lets you set the whites without covering the pan and clouding the yolks. Season after the eggs are done so the basting doesn't wash off the salt and pepper.

1 tablespoon canola oil
2 large eggs
1/4 teaspoon freshly ground black pepper
1/8 teaspoon kosher salt

1. Heat oil in an 8-inch nonstick skillet over medium-low. Gently crack eggs into pan. You shouldn't hear a hiss, and the eggs should lie flat and still. If you hear sizzling or the whites flutter or bubble at all, turn down the heat. Cook 3 minutes or until the whites are mostly set, with some still-runny whites near the yolks. Tilt pan toward you so oil pools on the bottom edge; dip a spoon in the oil, and gently baste the uncooked patches of white until they're set. Be careful not to baste the yolks, or they'll cloud over like cataracts. Sprinkle with pepper and salt. Remove eggs from pan, leaving excess oil behind. Serves 1

CALORIES 228; FAT 18.9g (sat 3.8g, mono 9.6g, poly 4.5g); PROTEIN 13g; CARB 1g; FIBER 0g; SUGARS 0g (est. added sugars 0g); CHOL 372mg; IRON 2mg; SODIUM 382mg; CALC 58mg

THE SMOOTHIE MAKEOVER

Order a small chocolate smoothie in a shop, and you could get 430 calories and 77g of sugar—over half of which come from added sugar. In ours, we keep the creamy sweetness while making it dairy-free, packing in nutrients, and cutting added sugar.

Unsweetened chocolate almond milk is the perfect chocolaty base. Vanilla soy yogurt pumps up the protein, while dates offer natural sweetness. The only added sugar in our makeover recipe is the few grams in the yogurt. Finishing with instant coffee heightens the chocolate flavor. The result is a rich chocolate non-dairy smoothie with fewer calories and less added sugar, as well as triple the fiber and double the calcium.

OURS SAVES
128 calories and 44g total sugars over smoothie-shop versions and boosts fiber by 5g

Quick & Easy • Gluten Free
Kid Friendly • Vegetarian

Rich Dark Chocolate Smoothie

(pictured on page 213)

Hands-on: 5 min. Total: 5 min.
This super-chocolaty smoothie is a tasty nondairy option. Dates offer richness and a caramel-like sweetness—naturally—while boosting fiber by about 2g.

3 pitted dates
1 cup unsweetened chocolate almond milk (such as Almond Breeze)
1 cup ice
1 tablespoon unsweetened cocoa powder
1 (5.3-ounce) container vanilla soy yogurt
½ banana, sliced and frozen
Dash of instant coffee (optional)

1. Place dates in a small bowl; cover with hot water. Let stand 3 minutes or until softened; drain.
2. Place milk and dates in a blender; blend 30 seconds or until pureed. Add ice and next 3 ingredients, and, if desired, coffee; blend 30 seconds or until smooth. Serves 1 (serving size: about 2⅓ cups)

CALORIES 302; FAT 7.2g (sat 0.5g, mono 2.7g, poly 2.5g); PROTEIN 9g; CARB 58g; FIBER 7g; SUGARS 37g (est. added sugars 13g); CHOL 0mg; IRON 3mg; SODIUM 200mg; CALC 483mg

Quick & Easy • Gluten Free
Kid Friendly • Vegetarian
Chocolate–Peanut Butter
Decrease chocolate almond milk to ¾ cup and vanilla soy yogurt to ½ cup; add 2 teaspoons natural peanut or almond butter when processing remaining ingredients in Step 2. Serves 1 (serving size: about 2¼ cups)

CALORIES 329; FAT 11g (sat 1.3g, mono 5.7g, poly 4g); PROTEIN 9g; CARB 54g; FIBER 7g; SUGARS 33g (est. added sugars 10g); CHOL 0mg; IRON 3mg; SODIUM 186mg; CALC 368mg

Quick & Easy • Gluten Free
Kid Friendly • Vegetarian
Chocolate-Raspberry
Omit ice. Add ½ cup frozen unsweetened raspberries when processing remaining ingredients in Step 2. Serves 1 (serving size: about 2⅓ cups)

CALORIES 326; FAT 7.2g (sat 0.5g, mono 2.7g, poly 2.5g); PROTEIN 9g; CARB 65g; FIBER 10g; SUGARS 39g (est. added sugars 13g); CHOL 0mg; IRON 3mg; SODIUM 200mg; CALC 491mg

HOW TO PERFECT YOUR SMOOTHIE

Layering ingredients is key to the silkiest, richest blends. Here's how to stack them:

ADD LIQUID FIRST
This lubricates the blender blade and keeps the solids moving. A liquid barrier also keeps the blender from overheating and reduces the noise of the blade as it goes to work.

GREENS GO NEXT
Submerged in the liquid below and weighed down by the solids on top, greens will blend seamlessly into the smoothie rather than tear into small pieces and float around.

FROZEN INGREDIENTS AND OTHER SOLIDS GO LAST
The liquid at the bottom will absorb the pureed solids. Frozen fruit is better than fresh fruit and ice because ice waters down the flavor and texture.

Quick & Easy • Gluten Free
Kid Friendly • Vegetarian

Berry-and-Beet Green Smoothie

Hands-on: 5 min. Total: 5 min.
A lot of people give smoothies a short blend at full power, but that doesn't give the best results. Starting at low speed and gradually increasing power lets the blades work better, breaking the ingredients down evenly and at the same time.

1½ cups unsweetened almond milk
¼ cup fresh orange juice (from 1 orange)
2 cups stemmed coarsely chopped beet greens (from 1 bunch)
1½ cups frozen mixed berries
1 medium-sized raw red beet, peeled and cut into wedges (about 7 ounces)
1 medium-sized frozen banana, broken into large pieces

1. Place almond milk and juice in a blender; top with beet greens, berries, beet, and banana. Start blender at lowest setting and gradually increase to one-third power; process for 30 seconds.
2. Increase to half power; process 30 seconds or until very smooth.
3. Let mixture stand 1 minute before serving. Serves 4 (serving size: about 1½ cups)

CALORIES 84; FAT 1.5g (sat 0.1g, mono 1g, poly 0.1g); PROTEIN 2g; CARB 18g; FIBER 4g; SUGARS 11g (est. added sugars 0g); CHOL 0mg; IRON 1mg; SODIUM 127mg; CALC 111mg

HOW DO I MAKE HOME FRIES THAT AREN'T SOGGY AND BLAND?

1. PICK THE RIGHT SPUD.
For a crisp golden crust on the potatoes, they need to be starchy. The waxy kind, like red potatoes, are less starchy and thus more difficult to make crusty. Yukon Golds are a little starchier, but russets are the best here. They release the most starch, yielding the crunchiest edges; they also absorb flavors wonderfully.

2. PARBOIL FIRST, AND THEN FRY.
Trying to pan-fry raw potato cubes can lead to tough exteriors and undercooked insides. Instead, give the potatoes a head start by parboiling: Cover with cold water, bring to a boil, and simmer 2 minutes. Drain well—wet potatoes won't brown well.

3. COOK VEGGIES SEPARATELY.
Sauté the onion and bell pepper while the potatoes parboil. Try to leave a little crunch on them (texture is half the fun of home fries); it helps to stir them only a couple of times. When they're ready, remove them from the pan and keep warm in a small bowl.

4. FINISH THE POTATOES.
After the veggies are out of the pan, add a layer of oil, and then add the parboiled,

well-drained potatoes. Cook them on their own until they're browned and crisp. Finally, combine them with the sautéed vegetables and seasonings. This way, you get maximum crunch and flavor.

Quick & Easy • Gluten Free
Kid Friendly
Go Big or Go Home Fries

Hands-on: 20 min. Total: 27 min.

1¼ pounds peeled russet potatoes, cut into ½-inch cubes
1 teaspoon sweet paprika
1 teaspoon garlic powder
¾ teaspoon kosher salt
½ teaspoon freshly ground black pepper
2½ tablespoons canola oil, divided
1 cup chopped yellow onion
1 cup chopped red bell pepper
1 teaspoon Worcestershire sauce

1. Place potatoes in a medium saucepan; cover by an inch with cold water. Bring to a boil; lower heat and simmer 2 minutes or until potatoes are not quite tender. Drain well; set aside.
2. Combine paprika, garlic powder, salt, and black pepper in a small bowl. Heat a large cast-iron or nonstick skillet over medium-high; add 1½ teaspoons oil to pan. Add onion and bell pepper; sauté 5 minutes or until lightly browned and crisp-tender. Stir 1 teaspoon paprika mixture into onion mixture; toss well. Place in a small bowl; stir in Worcestershire. Keep warm.
3. Add remaining 2 tablespoons oil to pan over medium-high. Add potatoes; cook 8 minutes or until well browned and crisp, stirring occasionally. Stir in remaining paprika mixture; toss well to coat evenly. Stir in onion mixture. Serve immediately. Serves 4 (serving size: about ¾ cup)

CALORIES 215; FAT 9.1g (sat 0.7g, mono 5.6g, poly 2.6g); PROTEIN 3g; CARB 32g; FIBER 4g; SUGARS 3g (est. added sugars 0g); CHOL 0mg; IRON 1mg; SODIUM 323mg; CALC 22mg

USE IT UP

PURE MAPLE SYRUP

This sweet, rich nectar works wonders with more than just pancakes and waffles.

Quick & Easy • Gluten Free
Kid Friendly
Maple-Bacon-Kale Salad
Cook 2 chopped bacon slices in a small skillet over medium until crisp; remove bacon, reserving 1 Tbsp. drippings in pan. Over low heat, whisk in 2 Tbsp. apple cider vinegar, 1½ Tbsp. maple syrup, 1 Tbsp. olive oil, 1½ tsp. grainy mustard, ¼ tsp. kosher salt, and ¼ tsp. black pepper. Toss warm dressing with 8 oz. sliced lacinato kale (about 6 lightly packed cups); sprinkle evenly with bacon. Serves 4 (serving size: about 1½ cups)

CALORIES 134; FAT 9.1g (sat 2.1g, mono 4.8g, poly 1.1g); PROTEIN 4g; CARB 10g; FIBER 2g; SUGARS 6g (est. added sugars 5g); CHOL 8mg; IRON 1mg; SODIUM 261mg; CALC 98mg

Quick & Easy • Gluten Free
Kid Friendly
Maple-Glazed Salmon
Preheat broiler to high. Combine ¾ tsp. garlic powder, ½ tsp. kosher salt, ½ tsp. smoked paprika, and ⅛ tsp. ground red pepper; sprinkle evenly over 4 (6-oz.) skinless salmon fillets. Arrange fillets on a foil-lined baking sheet coated with cooking spray. Broil 5 minutes. Remove from oven. Brush fillets with 2 Tbsp. maple syrup; broil 1 minute or until desired degree of doneness. Serve with lemon wedges. Serves 4 (serving size: 1 fillet)

CALORIES 268; FAT 9.5g (sat 2.3g, mono 3.4g, poly 2.8g); PROTEIN 36g; CARB 7g; FIBER 0g; SUGARS 6g (est. added sugars 6g); CHOL 89mg; IRON 1mg; SODIUM 335mg; CALC 28mg

Quick & Easy • Gluten Free
Kid Friendly • Vegetarian
Roasted Root Vegetables
Preheat oven to 450°F. Place 4 oz. quartered shallots, 1½ cups diagonally cut carrot, and 1½ cups each turnip and golden beet wedges on a foil-lined baking sheet coated with cooking spray. Drizzle with 2 Tbsp. olive oil; toss to coat. Bake at 450°F for 20 minutes. Add 2 Tbsp. maple syrup, 2 tsp. chopped fresh rosemary, ½ tsp. kosher salt, and ½ tsp. black pepper; stir well to combine. Bake 10 minutes or until tender. Serves 4 (serving size: about ¾ cup)

CALORIES 162; FAT 7.1g (sat 1g, mono 5g, poly 0.8g); PROTEIN 2g; CARB 24g; FIBER 5g; SUGARS 16g (est. added sugars 6g); CHOL 0mg; IRON 1mg; SODIUM 349mg; CALC 61mg

Quick & Easy • Gluten Free
Kid Friendly • Make Ahead
Vegetarian
Maple Mashed Sweet Potatoes
Place 1½ lb. peeled cubed sweet potatoes in a large saucepan; cover with water. Bring to a boil; cook until tender, about 15 minutes. Drain and return to pan; add 1 (5-oz.) can evaporated low-fat milk, 2 Tbsp. maple syrup, ¾ tsp. kosher salt, and ½ tsp. black pepper. Mash with a potato masher to desired consistency. Drizzle with 2 Tbsp. melted butter. Serves 6 (serving size: about ½ cup)

CALORIES 137; FAT 4.3g (sat 2.5g, mono 1g, poly 0.2g); PROTEIN 3g; CARB 22g; FIBER 2g; SUGARS 11g (est. added sugars 4g); CHOL 14mg; IRON 1mg; SODIUM 321mg; CALC 92mg

Quick & Easy • Gluten Free
Vegetarian
Shirred Eggs with Marinara and Feta

Hands-on: 8 min. Total: 23 min.
For a breakfast both simple and special, make shirred eggs. Just crack eggs into small vessels and bake until set, adding flavorful toppers for extra flair. Ramekins will work, but colorful mini cocottes make the dish a dazzler.

4 ounces sourdough bread, cut into
  ¼-inch cubes
2 teaspoons extra-virgin olive oil
4 large eggs
½ teaspoon kosher salt
¼ teaspoon freshly ground
  black pepper
¼ cup lower-sodium marinara sauce
4 teaspoons crumbled feta cheese
2 teaspoons chopped fresh oregano

1. Preheat oven to 375°F.
2. Place bread cubes on a sheet pan; bake at 375°F for 13 minutes or until browned and crisp.
3. Rub ½ teaspoon oil into each of 4 (8-ounce) mini cocottes or ramekins to coat inside. Divide bread cubes among cocottes. Crack one egg into each cocotte. Season each egg with ⅛ teaspoon salt and a dash of pepper. Spoon 1 table-spoon marinara into each. Sprinkle each with 1 teaspoon feta. Place cocottes in oven; bake at 375°F for 12 minutes or until whites are set. Sprinkle with oregano. Drizzle with additional oil, if desired. Serves 4 (serving size: 1 cocotte)

CALORIES 188; FAT 8.9g (sat 2.5g, mono 3.7g, poly 1.5g); PROTEIN 10g; CARB 17g; FIBER 1g; SUGARS 2g (est. added sugars 0g); CHOL 189mg; IRON 2mg; SODIUM 542mg; CALC 64mg

Staff Favorite • Quick & Easy
Kid Friendly • Vegetarian
Dutch Baby with Strawberries and Pistachios

Hands-on: 15 min. Total: 35 min.
The key to the dish's dramatic puff comes from oven spring—the jolt of steam and heat the batter gets when it's poured into the sizzling-hot pan and then goes straight into a cranked-up oven. Make the strawberry mixture first so the fruit has time to macerate and get even juicier.

1 quart fresh strawberries
2 teaspoons powdered sugar
2 teaspoons grated lemon rind,
  divided
2 tablespoons fresh lemon juice
1 tablespoon cornstarch
10 tablespoons fat-free milk
2.25 ounces all-purpose flour (about
  ½ cup)
2 large eggs
1 large egg white
2½ tablespoons butter, melted and
  divided
Cooking spray
2 tablespoons shelled unsalted
  pistachios, crushed

1. Hull and quarter strawberries; place in a medium bowl. Add sugar, 1 tea-spoon lemon rind, and juice; toss.
2. Place a 10-inch cast-iron skillet in oven; preheat oven to 450°F.
3. Place cornstarch, milk, flour, eggs, egg white, remaining 1 teaspoon lemon rind, and 1 tablespoon butter in a blender; blend until smooth.
4. Once oven is preheated, remove pan. Coat pan with cooking spray. Add remaining 1½ tablespoons butter to pan; swirl to coat. Add batter to pan; bake at 450°F for 20 minutes or until batter is very puffed and deeply browned. Remove from oven. Top with strawberry mixture; sprinkle with nuts. Slice into quarters; serve

immediately. Serves 4 (serving size: 1 slice Dutch baby and about ½ cup strawberry mixture)

CALORIES 256; **FAT** 12g (sat 5.6g, mono 3.8g, poly 1.6g); **PROTEIN** 9g; **CARB** 30g; **FIBER** 4g; **SUGARS** 11g (est. added sugars 1g); **CHOL** 113mg; **IRON** 2mg; **SODIUM** 125mg; **CALC** 95mg

LET'S GET SIPPING

Staff Favorite • Quick & Easy
Gluten Free • Make Ahead

Bloody Good Bloody Mary

Hands-on: 7 min. Total: 7 min.
You can't wing it with Bloodies. Random recipes might yield a crazy-thick throat-coater or a thin, insipid glass of blah. And many bottled mixes are sodium bombs. Here's a Bloody blueprint you can trust. Our streamlined version is zingy and sippable, with a fraction of the sodium you'll find in most others. Get mixing; it's noon somewhere. Pickle juice is the secret weapon here, delivering briny tartness. We've tried pickled okra juice and dill pickle juice—both work. Add a little cracked black pepper, if you like.

½ cup low-sodium tomato juice
1 tablespoon dill or okra pickle juice
2 teaspoons fresh lemon juice
1 teaspoon hot sauce (such as Cholula)
¼ teaspoon Worcestershire sauce
1½ ounces vodka

1. Combine all ingredients in a glass; stir well. Add ice. Serve immediately. Serves 1 (serving size: 1 drink)

CALORIES 133; **FAT** 0g; **PROTEIN** 1g; **CARB** 6g; **FIBER** 1g; **SUGARS** 4g (est. added sugars 0g); **CHOL** 0mg; **IRON** 0mg; **SODIUM** 380mg; **CALC** 12mg

"A MAKE-AGAIN RECIPE"

Succulent pork chops with hearty vegetables are guaranteed to become a family favorite.

Cyndie Moran's favorite thing about the Cooking Light Diet is how happy her family has been with the recipes. To celebrate Cyndie hitting the 50-pounds-lost milestone, we sent her and her family this delicious pork chop recipe to try. "This is not a recipe I would normally decide to make, but I'm so glad I did," she says. "It's been years since I've cooked bone-in pork chops. The general consensus was that it was a make-again recipe. My dad is a huge fan of both pork chops and cabbage, so this is on my list of meals to make for his next visit." Cyndie also noted how great this meal would be for a busy weeknight, as it only takes 30 minutes from start to finish. We were thrilled to hear that her kids thought it was delicious, too.

Quick & Easy • Gluten Free
Kid Friendly

Pan-Roasted Pork Chops with Cabbage and Carrots

Hands-on: 18 min. Total: 30 min.
Super-succulent pork chops are browned on the stovetop before being finished in the oven for tenderness. Roasted carrots paired with vastly underrated cabbage create a vibrant vegetable medley that is equal parts flavorful and nutritious. This meal is pretty enough to showcase, yet fast enough for weeknight cooking. Enjoy it with a side of wild rice or roasted potatoes for a well-balanced meal the whole family will love.

4 (6-ounce) bone-in, center-cut pork chops
¾ teaspoon kosher salt, divided
¾ teaspoon black pepper, divided
1 tablespoon unsalted butter
2 cups chopped green and red cabbage
1½ cups diagonally sliced carrot
½ teaspoon caraway seeds
⅓ cup unsalted chicken stock (such as Swanson)
¼ cup apple cider vinegar
3 tablespoons apple jelly
2 tablespoons olive oil

1. Preheat oven to 400°F.
2. Sprinkle pork chops evenly with ½ teaspoon salt and ½ teaspoon pepper. Melt butter in a large oven-proof skillet over medium-high. Add pork chops; cook 4 minutes per side or until desired degree of doneness. Remove from pan; cover to keep warm.
3. Add cabbage, carrot, caraway seeds, remaining ¼ teaspoon salt, and remaining ¼ teaspoon pepper to pan. Stir in stock, scraping bottom of pan to loosen browned bits. Cover and place pan in oven. Bake at 400°F for 12 minutes or until carrots are tender.
4. Remove cabbage mixture from pan; cover to keep warm. Add vinegar, apple jelly, and oil to pan; bring to a boil over medium-high. Cook 3 minutes or until slightly reduced and smooth, stirring with a whisk. Place pork chops and cabbage mixture on each of 4 plates. Drizzle evenly with vinegar mixture. Serves 4 (serving size: 1 pork chop, ¾ cup cabbage mixture, and 1½ tablespoons sauce)

CALORIES 310; **FAT** 16g (sat 4.6g, mono 7.9g, poly 1.6g); **PROTEIN** 24g; **CARB** 17g; **FIBER** 2g; **SUGARS** 12g (est. added sugars 9g); **CHOL** 78mg; **IRON** 1mg; **SODIUM** 459mg; **CALCIUM** 57mg

READY IN
40
MINUTES

····················
GAME PLAN
····················

While broiler preheats:
- Make tomatillo mixture.
- Make sofrito for beans.

While sofrito simmers:
- Assemble chilaquiles.

Quick & Easy • Vegetarian

Zucchini and Spinach Chilaquiles

With Sofrito Pinto Beans

Give this Mexican breakfast classic a verde twist with tomatillos.

1 cup chopped fresh cilantro, divided
2 medium poblano peppers, seeded and chopped
1 (12-ounce) can tomatillos, drained
4 tablespoons water, as needed
2 tablespoons fresh lime juice
1 tablespoon extra-virgin olive oil
2 cups chopped zucchini
1 cup sliced red onion
1 jalapeño, seeded and sliced
2 cups baby spinach, coarsely chopped
4 ounces multigrain tortilla chips (about 4 cups)
2 ounces queso fresco, crumbled (about ½ cup)
¼ cup roasted unsalted pumpkin seeds
1½ tablespoons hot sauce, optional

1. Preheat broiler to high.
2. Place ¾ cup cilantro, peppers, and tomatillos in a food processor; process

20 seconds. Add water, 1 tablespoon at a time, until sauce reaches desired consistency. Stir in juice.
3. Heat oil in a 10-inch cast-iron skillet over medium-high. Add zucchini, onion, and jalapeño; cook 6 minutes. Add spinach, stirring to wilt. Place zucchini mixture in a bowl. Wipe out pan.
4. Arrange tortilla chips in pan; top with tomatillo mixture, zucchini mixture, and cheese. Broil 2 minutes. Top with remaining ¼ cup cilantro, pumpkin seeds, and hot sauce, if desired. Serves 4 (serving size: about 1½ cups)

CALORIES 334; **FAT** 19.7g (sat 4g, mono 9.8g, poly 3g); **PROTEIN** 11g; **CARB** 33g; **FIBER** 8g; **SUGARS** 6g (est. added sugars 0g); **CHOL** 10mg; **IRON** 4mg; **SODIUM** 516mg; **CALC** 209mg

Quick & Easy • Gluten Free
Kid Friendly • Make Ahead
Vegetarian

Sofrito Pinto Beans

We take a shortcut to the rich, deep flavor of slow-simmered beans by starting with a quick sofrito—aromatics sautéed until tender with tomato and vinegar—and adding canned pinto beans. The result is better than any seasoned bean in a can.

1 tablespoon extra-virgin olive oil
1 cup finely chopped yellow onion
1 cup finely chopped red bell pepper
½ cup water
2 tablespoons unsalted tomato paste
1 tablespoon apple cider vinegar
½ teaspoon kosher salt
1 (15-ounce) can unsalted pinto beans, rinsed and drained

1. Heat oil in a large skillet over medium-high. Add onion and pepper; sauté 5 minutes. Stir in ½ cup water, tomato paste, vinegar, and salt; bring to a simmer. Cook 10 minutes or until thickened, stirring occasion-

ally. Stir in beans; cook 3 minutes or until mixture is thoroughly heated. Serves 4 (serving size: about ⅔ cup)

CALORIES 147; **FAT** 3.7g (sat 0.5g, mono 2.7g, poly 0.4g); **PROTEIN** 6g; **CARB** 22g; **FIBER** 7g; **SUGARS** 4g (est. added sugars 0g); **CHOL** 0mg; **IRON** 2mg; **SODIUM** 260mg; **CALC** 64mg

READY IN
30
MINUTES

····················
GAME PLAN
····················

While farro cooks:
- Bring water for eggs to a boil.

While eggs cook:
- Cook tomatoes and kale.

Quick & Easy • Kid Friendly
Vegetarian

Farro Breakfast Bowl

With Blistered Tomatoes with Kale

This meal in a bowl takes its morning cue from soft-boiled eggs and a dollop of yogurt, then goes savory with toasty cumin-scented farro and a creamy avocado.

½ cup uncooked farro
2 large eggs (refrigerator-cold)
2 teaspoons olive oil
½ teaspoon ground cumin
½ teaspoon kosher salt, divided
1 medium-sized ripe avocado, halved and pitted
¼ teaspoon cracked black pepper
3 tablespoons whole-milk plain Greek yogurt
2 lemon wedges

1. Bring a large saucepan filled water to a boil. Add farro; reduce heat to

medium and simmer 20 minutes or until slightly chewy. Drain.
2. Bring a small saucepan of water to a boil. Add cold eggs; reduce heat to medium-low and simmer 6 minutes. Place eggs in a bowl of ice water; let stand 6 minutes or until completely cool. Drain and peel.
3. Heat oil in a small skillet over medium. Add cumin; cook 30 seconds, stirring constantly. Add farro and ¼ teaspoon salt; cook 2 minutes or until lightly toasted. Place ⅔ cup farro mixture in each bowl. Carefully halve one egg over each bowl. Add one avocado half to each bowl. Sprinkle remaining ¼ teaspoon salt and pepper evenly over top. Top each with 1½ table-spoons yogurt. Squeeze 1 lemon wedge over each bowl. Serves 2

CALORIES 396; **FAT** 22g (sat 5.3g, mono 11.8g, poly 3g); **PROTEIN** 15g; **CARB** 37g; **FIBER** 8g; **SUGARS** 1g (est. added sugars 0g); **CHOL** 190mg; **IRON** 2mg; **SODIUM** 588mg; **CALC** 100mg

Quick & Easy • Gluten Free
Kid Friendly • Vegetarian

Blistered Tomatoes with Kale

1 tablespoon olive oil
⅔ cup grape tomatoes
2 cups torn lacinato kale
2 tablespoons thinly sliced shallots
¼ teaspoon kosher salt

1. Heat oil in a cast-iron skillet over medium-high. Add tomatoes; cook 2 minutes, stirring once or twice until blistered in spots. Remove tomatoes from pan. Add kale and shallots to pan; cook 3 minutes, stirring occa-sionally. Stir in salt. Serves 2 (serving size: ⅓ cup tomatoes and ½ cup kale)

CALORIES 84; **FAT** 6.9g (sat 1g, mono 4.9g, poly 0.8g); **PROTEIN** 1g; **CARB** 5g; **FIBER** 2g; **SUGARS** 2g (est. added sugars 0g); **CHOL** 0mg; **IRON** 0mg; **SODIUM** 250mg; **CALC** 36mg

READY IN
30
MINUTES

GAME PLAN

While oven preheats:
- Prepare potato mixture.

While potatoes roast:
- Make sandwiches.

Quick & Easy • Kid Friendly

Sausage, Spinach, and Apple Breakfast Sandwiches

With Parmesan-and-Herb Roasted Potatoes

We swap the classic egg and cheese combo for crisp, tart apple slices and sautéed spinach. Use any bulk turkey breakfast sausage for this sandwich, or try our DIY version on page 54.

3½ tablespoons canola mayonnaise
1½ tablespoons grainy Dijon mustard
1 teaspoon chopped fresh tarragon
2 teaspoons honey
½ teaspoon white vinegar
¼ teaspoon black pepper
6 ounces turkey breakfast sausage
4 cups baby spinach
4 whole-wheat English muffins, split and toasted
½ Granny Smith apple, thinly sliced

1. Combine first 6 ingredients in a small bowl, stirring with a whisk.
2. Heat a medium nonstick skillet over medium-high. Divide and shape sausage into 4 (3-inch) patties. Add patties to pan; cook 3 minutes on each side or until browned and done. Remove patties from pan; keep warm.

Add spinach to pan; cook 1 minute, stirring until wilted.
3. Spread mayonnaise mixture evenly over cut sides of English muffins. Top bottom halves of muffins evenly with patties, spinach, apple slices, and top halves of muffins. Serves 4 (serving size: 1 sandwich)

CALORIES 330; **FAT** 14.3g (sat 2.1g, mono 6.6g, poly 3.7g); **PROTEIN** 15g; **CARB** 36g; **FIBER** 5g; **SUGARS** 6g (est. added sugars 3g); **CHOL** 22mg; **IRON** 4mg; **SODIUM** 800mg; **CALC** 148mg

Quick & Easy • Gluten Free
Kid Friendly • Vegetarian

Parmesan-and-Herb Roasted Potatoes

What would breakfast for dinner be without home fries? Parmesan, garlic, and rosemary make these spuds a little more dressed up than regular hash browns, pairing perfectly with the slightly elevated sausage and apple breakfast sandwiches.

2 tablespoons grated Parmesan cheese
1 tablespoon extra-virgin olive oil
1 teaspoon chopped fresh garlic
1 teaspoon minced fresh rosemary
¼ teaspoon black pepper
⅛ teaspoon kosher salt
1 pound red potatoes, quartered
¼ teaspoon grated lemon rind

1. Preheat oven to 475°F.
2. Combine all ingredients except rind in a medium bowl; toss to coat. Spread potato mixture on a rimmed baking sheet. Bake at 475°F for 20 minutes or until tender, stirring once after 10 minutes. Add rind to potato mixture; toss. Serves 4 (serving size: about ½ cup)

CALORIES 123; **FAT** 4.4g (sat 1g, mono 2.9g, poly 0.4g); **PROTEIN** 3g; **CARB** 19g; **FIBER** 2g; **SUGARS** 2g (est. added sugars 0g); **CHOL** 2mg; **IRON** 1mg; **SODIUM** 123mg; **CALC** 45mg

READY IN
35
MINUTES

········· **GAME PLAN** ·········

While oven preheats:

- Cook tomato mixture.

While tomato and egg mixture bakes:

- Make toasts.

Staff Favorite • Quick & Easy
Gluten Free • Kid Friendly
Vegetarian

Saucy Skillet-Poached Eggs

With Grilled Garlic Toast

If you've ever had Italian eggs in purgatory, this recipe makes a similar Israeli breakfast dish called shakshuka. If you need to stretch the meal, simply add another egg to the pan. Top with any herb, such as cilantro, chives, or oregano.

2 tablespoons extra-virgin olive oil
1 cup chopped yellow onion
1 cup chopped red bell pepper
3 garlic cloves, chopped
1/4 cup water
2 teaspoons red wine vinegar
1 teaspoon chopped fresh oregano
3/4 teaspoon kosher salt
1 (28-ounce) can unsalted crushed tomatoes
1 ounce feta cheese, crumbled (about 1/4 cup)
4 large eggs
1/4 teaspoon freshly ground black pepper
2 tablespoons chopped fresh chives
1 tablespoon fresh oregano leaves

1. Preheat oven to 375°F.
2. Heat oil in a large cast-iron skillet over medium. Add onion and bell pepper; sauté 10 minutes. Add garlic; cook 2 minutes, stirring occasionally. Add 1/4 cup water and next 4 ingredients (through tomatoes). Bring to a simmer; cook 10 minutes or until sauce is slightly thickened. Stir in feta.
3. Form 4 (2-inch) indentations in sauce with the back of a spoon. One at a time, crack eggs into a small custard cup, and gently slip 1 egg into each indentation. Sprinkle black pepper over eggs. Place pan in oven and bake at 375°F for 12 minutes or until whites are set. Sprinkle with chives and oregano. Divide sauce and eggs among 4 shallow bowls. Serves 4 (serving size: 1 egg and about 3/4 cup sauce)

CALORIES 259; FAT 13.5g (sat 3.6g, mono 7.6g, poly 1.7g); PROTEIN 12g; CARB 23g; FIBER 6g; SUGARS 7g (est. added sugars 0g); CHOL 192mg; IRON 1mg; SODIUM 565mg; CALC 87mg

Quick & Easy • Kid Friendly
Vegetarian

Grilled Garlic Toast

8 (1/2-ounce) slices whole-wheat French bread baguette
2 tablespoons extra-virgin olive oil
1 garlic clove, halved

1. Heat a grill pan over medium-high. Brush bread slices with oil. Add bread to pan; cook 1 to 2 minutes on each side or until toasted. Rub 1 side of each bread slice with cut sides of garlic. Serves 4 (serving size: 2 toasts)

CALORIES 122; FAT 7.5g (sat 1.1g, mono 5.4g, poly 0.6g); PROTEIN 2g; CARB 12g; FIBER 0g; SUGARS 1g (est. added sugars 1g); CHOL 1mg; IRON 0mg; SODIUM 145mg; CALC 1mg

READY IN
25
MINUTES

········· **GAME PLAN** ·········

While oven preheats:

- Make syrup mixture.
- Bread chicken.

While chicken bakes:

- Cook waffles.
- Make fruit salad.

Quick & Easy • Kid Friendly

Chicken and Waffles with Kicky Syrup

With Ginger-Lime Fruit Salad

This mash-up actually dates back a couple hundred years, and we can guess why—the sweet, crunchy, and salty trio was surely just as craveworthy then as it is now.

Cooking spray
1/4 cup pure maple syrup
1 tablespoon Sriracha chili sauce
1 teaspoon reduced-sodium soy sauce
1.1 ounces all-purpose flour (about 1/4 cup)
1 large egg, lightly beaten
1 cup naturally sweetened cornflakes, crushed (about 1 ounce)
1/4 cup whole-wheat panko (Japanese breadcrumbs)
4 (4-ounce) chicken breast cutlets
1/4 teaspoon kosher salt
1/4 teaspoon paprika
1 tablespoon butter, melted
4 frozen Belgian or multigrain waffles (such as Van's)
1/4 cup sliced green onions

1. Preheat oven to 425°F. Place a wire rack on a rimmed baking sheet. Coat rack with cooking spray.
2. Combine maple syrup, chili sauce, and soy sauce in a bowl. Place flour in a shallow dish. Place egg in a shallow dish. Combine cornflakes and panko in a shallow dish. Sprinkle chicken with salt and paprika. Dredge chicken in flour, shaking off excess. Dip chicken in egg; dredge in cornflake mixture, pressing to adhere. Place on prepared rack. Drizzle butter over chicken. Bake at 425°F for 10 minutes or until chicken is done and crust is golden.
3. Cook waffles according to package directions. Divide waffles among 4 plates; top evenly with chicken and syrup mixture. Sprinkle with green onions. Serves 4 (serving size: 1 waffle, 1 chicken cutlet, and about 1 tablespoon syrup mixture)

CALORIES 486; FAT 11.9g (sat 2.7g, mono 6g, poly 2.6g); PROTEIN 33g; CARB 64g; FIBER 2g; SUGARS 17g (est. added sugars 16g); CHOL 119mg; IRON 4mg; SODIUM 517mg; CALC 38mg

Quick & Easy • Gluten Free
Kid Friendly • Make Ahead
Vegetarian

Ginger-Lime Fruit Salad

Just a little lime and ginger help to macerate the fresh fruits so they can release their juices.

1 cup chopped ripe mango
1 cup quartered strawberries
1/2 cup blueberries
1 teaspoon grated lime rind
1 tablespoon fresh lime juice
1/2 teaspoon grated ginger

1. Combine all ingredients in a bowl; let stand 5 minutes before serving. Serves 4 (serving size: about 2/3 cup)

CALORIES 49; FAT 0.3g (sat 0.1g, mono 0.1g, poly 0.1g); PROTEIN 1g; CARB 12g; FIBER 2g; SUGARS 9g (est. added sugars 0g); CHOL 0mg; IRON 0mg; SODIUM 1mg; CALC 12mg

SLOW COOKER

RICH AND MEATY PORK RAGÙ

Saucy, fork-tender meat blankets pillowy polenta in this hearty slow cooker main.

**Staff Favorite • Gluten Free
Kid Friendly • Make Ahead
Freezable**

Pork Ragù with Polenta

Hands-on: 20 min. Total: 7 hr. 15 min.
Create a flavorful, golden crust on the pork roast by browning it well before placing it in the slow cooker. Red wine, tomatoes, and plenty of aromatics enrich the ragù with savory depth as it cooks low and slow.

2 tablespoons canola oil
1 (2-pound) boneless pork shoulder roast (Boston butt), trimmed
1 tablespoon kosher salt, divided
1 teaspoon freshly ground black pepper
2 tablespoons minced fresh garlic
1 1/2 tablespoons chopped fresh rosemary
1 1/2 tablespoons chopped fresh oregano
6 medium shallots, halved lengthwise
1/4 cup unsalted tomato paste
1 cup dry red wine
2/3 cup unsalted chicken stock (such as Swanson)
2 tablespoons Dijon mustard
1 (28-ounce) can unsalted whole peeled plum tomatoes, undrained
3 cups stemmed chopped lacinato kale
1 tablespoon red wine vinegar
8 cups water
2 cups stone-ground polenta

1. Heat oil in a large skillet over medium-high. Rub pork evenly with 2 teaspoons salt and pepper. Add pork to pan; cook 5 minutes, turning to brown on all sides. Place pork in a 5- to 6-quart slow cooker; do not wipe out pan.
2. Return pan to medium. Add garlic, rosemary, oregano, and shallots to drippings in pan; cook 3 minutes, stirring occasionally, until shallots are tender and garlic is fragrant. Add tomato paste; cook 1 minute, stirring constantly. Add wine; bring to a boil. Cook 5 minutes or until reduced by half. Combine chicken stock and mustard in a 1-cup glass measure, stirring with a whisk until smooth. Add stock mixture to pan; bring to a boil. Add stock mixture to slow cooker.
3. Add tomatoes to slow cooker, gently mashing with a spoon. Cover and cook on LOW for 7 hours or until pork is very tender. Place pork on a cutting board. Shred into large pieces with 2 forks.
4. Increase slow cooker temperature to HIGH. Stir in remaining 1 teaspoon salt, shredded pork, and kale. Cover and cook on HIGH 5 minutes or until kale is tender. Stir in vinegar.
5. Bring 8 cups water to a boil in a large saucepan over high. Gradually add polenta, stirring with a whisk. Reduce heat and simmer 20 to 30 minutes or until thickened. Serve ragù over polenta. Serves 12 (serving size: about 2/3 cup polenta and 2/3 cup ragù)

CALORIES 267; FAT 8.1g (sat 2.1g, mono 3.9, poly 1.3g); PROTEIN 20g; CARB 28g; FIBER 3g; SUGARS 4g (est. added sugars 0g); CHOL 51mg; IRON 4mg; SODIUM 668mg; CALC 51mg

SUPERFAST 20-MINUTE COOKING

Quick & Easy

Sausage and Broccoli Rabe Flatbreads

(pictured on page 212)

Naan breads are the secret to instant pizza-style flatbreads (no rolling or baking of dough required). Look for whole-grain naan, such as Stonefire, and treat as you would a prepared pizza crust.

4 teaspoons olive oil, divided
12 ounces broccoli rabe, trimmed and coarsely chopped
1 (8.8-ounce) package whole-grain naan (such as Stonefire)
5 ounces spicy turkey Italian sausage, casings removed
1/3 cup pizza sauce (such as Rao's)
1/3 cup part-skim ricotta cheese
1/2 teaspoon freshly ground black pepper

1. Preheat broiler to high.
2. Combine 1 tablespoon oil and broccoli rabe on a rimmed baking sheet. Broil 5 minutes or until broccoli rabe begins to brown. Remove broccoli rabe from pan. Add naan to pan; broil 1 to 2 minutes on each side or until lightly browned.
3. Heat remaining 1 teaspoon oil in a large skillet over medium-high. Add turkey sausage to pan; cook 5 minutes or until browned, stirring to crumble.
4. Spread pizza sauce evenly on 1 side of each naan on baking sheet. Dollop ricotta evenly over top; top evenly with broccoli rabe, sausage, and pepper. Broil 2 to 3 minutes or until cheese melts and broccoli rabe is slightly charred. Cut each flatbread into 4 pieces. Serves 4 (serving size: 2 pieces)

CALORIES 340; **FAT** 12.1g (sat 2.8g, mono 5.4g, poly 1.5g); **PROTEIN** 19g; **CARB** 39g; **FIBER** 6g; **SUGARS** 3g (est. added sugars 2g); **CHOL** 36mg; **IRON** 3mg; **SODIUM** 598mg; **CALC** 126mg

Quick & Easy • Gluten Free
Kid Friendly

Shortcut Shrimp Paella

Fresh shrimp stars in this fast take on paella; you could also use chicken thighs. We swap expensive saffron for turmeric to achieve the yellow color.

2 (8.8-ounce) packages precooked brown rice (such as Uncle Ben's)
1 1/2 tablespoons canola oil
1/2 teaspoon ground turmeric
1 cup sliced red bell pepper
1 cup frozen green peas
1/3 cup water
3/4 teaspoon kosher salt
1/2 teaspoon freshly ground black pepper
1 1/2 pounds medium shrimp, peeled and deveined
Cilantro leaves (optional)

1. Heat rice according to package directions.
2. Heat oil and turmeric in a medium skillet over medium; cook 2 minutes, stirring occasionally. Add rice, bell pepper, and next 4 ingredients (through black pepper); cook 3 minutes. Arrange shrimp over rice mixture; cover and cook 6 minutes or until shrimp are done and rice is slightly crisp. Top with cilantro, if desired. Serves 4 (serving size: 1 1/2 cups)

CALORIES 371; **FAT** 9.9g (sat 0.6g, mono 4.4g, poly 2.7g); **PROTEIN** 30g; **CARB** 43g; **FIBER** 5g; **SUGARS** 3g (est. added sugars 0g); **CHOL** 214mg; **IRON** 2mg; **SODIUM** 662mg; **CALC** 102mg

Quick & Easy • Gluten Free

Beef Tenderloin with Balsamic Asparagus

Beef tenderloin steaks are often considered a special-occasion cut, but when they go on sale (or you're ready for a splurge), this classic preparation is foolproof. Use a timer rather than turning, prodding, or overcooking the steaks, and set the timer again while they rest so you don't slice too soon.

4 teaspoons canola oil, divided
4 (4-ounce) beef tenderloin steaks, trimmed
3/4 teaspoon kosher salt, divided
1/2 teaspoon freshly ground black pepper, divided
1/2 teaspoon paprika
1/4 teaspoon ground cumin
1/4 teaspoon garlic powder
1 pound thin asparagus, cut diagonally into 1-inch pieces
2 teaspoons fresh thyme leaves
1 teaspoon grainy Dijon mustard
2 teaspoons balsamic glaze

1. Heat 1 teaspoon oil in a large skillet over medium-high. Sprinkle steaks evenly with 1/2 teaspoon salt, 1/4 teaspoon pepper, paprika, cumin, and garlic powder. Add steaks to pan; cook 5 minutes on each side for medium-rare or until desired degree of doneness. Remove steaks from pan; let stand 5 minutes.
2. Return pan to medium-high. Add remaining 1 tablespoon oil to pan. Add asparagus; cook 3 minutes. Add remaining 1/4 teaspoon salt, remaining 1/4 teaspoon pepper, thyme, and mustard to pan; toss to coat. Drizzle with balsamic glaze. Serve with steaks. Serves 4 (serving size: 1 steak and about 1/2 cup asparagus)

CALORIES 298; **FAT** 14.4g (sat 4.1g, mono 7.2g, poly 2.1g); **PROTEIN** 38g; **CARB** 6g; **FIBER** 3g; **SUGARS** 2g (est. added sugars 0g); **CHOL** 105mg; **IRON** 7mg; **SODIUM** 457mg; **CALC** 50mg

Herby Pea and Lemon Pasta Salad

This verdant pasta salad signals a fantastic start to spring with a shower of fresh herbs. Mini shell pasta and peas are a perfect pair—the pasta serves as a kind of catcher's mitt for the sweet, bright green peas. You could also use orecchiette, an ear-shaped pasta that serves the same purpose.

6 ounces uncooked small shell pasta
1½ cups frozen green peas, thawed
¼ cup chopped fresh flat-leaf parsley
¼ cup torn fresh mint leaves
¼ cup extra-virgin olive oil
2 tablespoons chopped fresh tarragon
2 tablespoons fresh lemon juice
1 tablespoon chopped fresh thyme
½ teaspoon kosher salt
½ teaspoon freshly ground black pepper
6 ounces shredded skinless, boneless rotisserie chicken breast (about 1½ cups)
¼ cup sliced almonds, toasted

1. Cook pasta according to package directions, omitting salt and fat. Add peas during the last 2 minutes of cooking. Drain.
2. Combine parsley and next 7 ingredients (through pepper) in a large bowl, stirring with a whisk. Add chicken; toss to coat. Add pasta mixture; toss. Sprinkle evenly with almonds. Serves 4 (serving size: about 1¼ cups)

CALORIES 414; FAT 18.5g (sat 2.6g, mono 12.2g, poly 2.7g); PROTEIN 22g; CARB 41g; FIBER 5g; SUGARS 4g (est. added sugars 0g); CHOL 37mg; IRON 3mg; SODIUM 433mg; CALC 59mg

Korean-Style Pork and Rice

Deeply savory gochujang adds a mild heat to the finished dish so kids can still enjoy; look for it on the Asian foods aisle.

2 tablespoons toasted sesame oil
12 ounces lean ground pork
¾ cup finely chopped white onion
¾ cup chopped green onions, divided
4 garlic cloves, finely chopped
⅓ cup water
2 tablespoons gochujang sauce (such as Annie Chun's)
2 tablespoons reduced-sodium soy sauce
1 tablespoon light brown sugar
2 (8.8-ounce) packages precooked brown rice (such as Uncle Ben's)
2 tablespoons chopped fresh cilantro
2 tablespoons rice vinegar
4 lime wedges

1. Heat oil in a large skillet over high. Add pork; cook 5 minutes or until browned, stirring to crumble. Add white onion, ¼ cup green onions, and garlic; cook 4 minutes. Add ⅓ cup water; cook 1 minute, scraping pan to loosen browned bits. Remove from heat; stir in remaining ½ cup green onions, gochujang, soy sauce, and brown sugar.
2. Heat rice according to package directions.
3. Place ½ cup pork mixture and ¾ cup rice in each of 4 bowls; top with cilantro, vinegar, and lime wedges. Serves 4

CALORIES 429; FAT 17.4g (sat 4g, mono 2.7g, poly 2.9g); PROTEIN 23g; CARB 49g; FIBER 5g; SUGARS 7g (est. added sugars 5g); CHOL 64mg; IRON 1mg; SODIUM 532mg; CALC 30mg

Caesar-Crusted Chicken Salad

(pictured on page 211)

1½ tablespoons Dijon mustard
1½ ounces Parmesan cheese, grated and divided (about 6 tablespoons)
1 anchovy fillet, minced
Cooking spray
4 (6-ounce) skinless, boneless chicken breasts
¼ teaspoon kosher salt
¼ teaspoon freshly ground black pepper
¼ cup whole-wheat panko (Japanese breadcrumbs)
2 romaine lettuce hearts, halved
2 tablespoons olive oil, divided
2 teaspoons fresh lemon juice

1. Preheat broiler to high.
2. Combine mustard, 3 tablespoons cheese, and anchovy in a bowl. Heat a grill pan over medium-high; coat with cooking spray. Sprinkle chicken with salt and pepper; add to pan, and cook 4 minutes. Turn, brush with mustard mixture, top with panko, and coat with cooking spray. Place pan in oven; broil 7 minutes or until chicken is done. Let stand 5 minutes. Cut into slices.
3. Return pan to medium-high. Brush cut sides of lettuce with 1 tablespoon oil. Grill lettuce, 2 halves at a time, for 2 minutes.
4. Place 1 chicken breast and ½ lettuce heart on each of 4 plates. Top lettuce evenly with remaining 1 tablespoon oil, juice, and remaining 3 tablespoons cheese. Serves 4

CALORIES 359; FAT 14.8g (sat 3.6g, mono 7.4g, poly 1.5g); PROTEIN 44g; CARB 10g; FIBER 2g; SUGARS 3g (est. added sugars 0g); CHOL 134mg; IRON 2mg; SODIUM 572mg; CALC 156mg

Parmesan Carrots with Lemon-Parsley Dressing

Steaming and sautéing the carrots in the same pan is the time-saving trick to making them tender and beautifully glazed.

½ cup water
¼ cup chopped shallots
14 ounces medium carrots, cut diagonally into 1½-inch pieces (about 2½ cups)
2 tablespoons olive oil
3 tablespoons chopped fresh flat-leaf parsley
1½ tablespoons fresh lemon juice
2 teaspoons pine nuts, toasted
¼ teaspoon black pepper
3 tablespoons shaved Parmesan cheese

1. Combine ½ cup water, shallots, and carrots in a medium skillet over medium-high heat; bring to a boil. Reduce heat to low and simmer, partially covered, 6 minutes or until carrots are tender. Increase heat to medium-high and cook, uncovered, 4 minutes or until liquid evaporates. Add oil; cook 4 minutes or until carrots are lightly browned, stirring occasionally. Stir in parsley and remaining ingredients. Serves 4 (serving size: about ½ cup)

CALORIES 127; **FAT** 9g (sat 1.6g, mono 5.5g, poly 1.3g); **PROTEIN** 2g; **CARB** 11g; **FIBER** 3g; **SUGARS** 5g (est. added sugars 0g); **CHOL** 3mg; **IRON** 1mg; **SODIUM** 126mg; **CALC** 67mg

Quick & Easy • Gluten Free
Vegetarian
Balsamic Onion and Thyme Carrots
Heat 1 Tbsp. olive oil in a skillet over medium-high. Add 2 cups sliced yellow onion and a dash of baking soda; cook 10 minutes. Add ½ cup water and 14 oz. carrots, cut into 1½-in.

pieces, to pan; bring to a boil. Reduce heat and simmer, partially covered, 6 minutes. Increase heat to medium-high; cook, uncovered, 4 minutes or until liquid evaporates. Add 2 Tbsp. balsamic vinegar, 1 Tbsp. olive oil, 1 Tbsp. chopped fresh thyme, ¼ tsp. kosher salt, and ¼ tsp. black pepper. Serves 4 (serving size: about ½ cup)

CALORIES 124; **FAT** 7g (sat 1g, mono 4.9g, poly 0.8g); **PROTEIN** 1g; **CARB** 15g; **FIBER** 3g; **SUGARS** 7g (est. added sugars 0g); **CHOL** 0mg; **IRON** 1mg; **SODIUM** 180mg; **CALC** 45mg

Quick & Easy • Gluten Free
Kid Friendly • Vegetarian
Sweet-and-Sour Carrots
Combine ½ cup water and 14 oz. carrots, cut into 1½-in. pieces, in a skillet over medium-high; bring to a boil. Reduce heat and simmer, partially covered, 6 minutes. Increase heat to medium-high; cook, uncovered, 4 minutes or until liquid evaporates. Add ¼ cup (½-in.-diced) green onions, 1 Tbsp. toasted sesame oil, and 3 sliced garlic cloves; cook 3 minutes. Stir in 2 Tbsp. apple cider vinegar, 2 Tbsp. sweet chili sauce, and ¼ tsp. kosher salt. Top with ½ tsp. sesame seeds. Serves 4 (serving size: ½ cup)

CALORIES 72; **FAT** 3.8g (sat 0.5g, mono 1.4g, poly 1.6g); **PROTEIN** 1g; **CARB** 9g; **FIBER** 2g; **SUGARS** 4g (est. added sugars 1g); **CHOL** 0mg; **IRON** 0mg; **SODIUM** 177mg; **CALC** 39mg

Quick & Easy • Gluten Free
Kid Friendly • Vegetarian
Tarragon Carrots with Green Beans
Combine 1 cup halved haricots verts (French green beans), ½ cup water, and 14 oz. carrots, cut into 1½-in. pieces, in a skillet over medium-high heat; bring to a boil. Reduce heat and simmer, partially covered, 6 minutes or until carrots are just tender. Increase heat to medium-high; cook, uncovered, 4 minutes or until liquid evaporates. Add 2 Tbsp. unsalted butter; cook 2 minutes, stirring to coat. Stir in 1½ Tbsp. chopped fresh tarragon,

¼ tsp. kosher salt, and ¼ tsp. black pepper. Serves 4 (serving size: about ¾ cup)

CALORIES 93; **FAT** 6g (sat 3.7g, mono 1.5g, poly 0.3g); **PROTEIN** 1g; **CARB** 10g; **FIBER** 3g; **SUGARS** 4g (est. added sugars 0g); **CHOL** 15mg; **IRON** 0mg; **SODIUM** 178mg; **CALC** 42mg

Quick & Easy • Gluten Free

Salmon and Spinach Salad

Tarragon and fresh fennel both have the same faint licorice flavor, but they don't overwhelm this simple spring salad.

3 tablespoons extra-virgin olive oil
4 (6-ounce) salmon fillets, skinned
¾ teaspoon kosher salt, divided
½ teaspoon freshly ground black pepper, divided
2 tablespoons chopped fresh tarragon
2 tablespoons white wine vinegar
1 teaspoon finely chopped garlic
¾ cup very thinly sliced fennel bulb
½ cup fresh mint leaves
½ cup fresh flat-leaf parsley leaves
1 (6-ounce) package baby spinach

1. Heat 1½ teaspoons oil in a large skillet over medium-high. Sprinkle fillets evenly with ½ teaspoon salt and ¼ teaspoon pepper. Add fillets to pan; cook 4 to 5 minutes on each side or until desired degree of doneness. Cool 5 minutes. Break fillets into large flakes with a fork.
2. Combine remaining 2½ tablespoons oil, remaining ¼ teaspoon salt, remaining ¼ teaspoon pepper, tarragon, vinegar, and garlic in a large bowl, stirring with a whisk. Add fennel, mint, parsley, and spinach; toss to coat. Arrange spinach mixture on plates; top with salmon. Serves 4 (serving size: about 1½ cups salad and 4.5 ounces salmon)

CALORIES 359; **FAT** 20g (sat 3.5g, mono 11.3g, poly 4.3g); **PROTEIN** 38g; **CARB** 4g; **FIBER** 2g; **SUGARS** 1g (est. added sugars 0g); **CHOL** 90mg; **IRON** 3mg; **SODIUM** 487mg; **CALC** 91mg

$9.15 FOR FOUR SERVINGS

Quick & Easy
Kid Friendly

Chicken Piccata with Crispy Garlic

(pictured on page 214)

Hands-on: 30 min. Total: 30 min.

6 ounces uncooked whole-grain angel hair pasta
¼ cup fresh flat-leaf parsley, divided
¼ cup olive oil, divided
2 tablespoons fresh lemon juice
1 pound chicken breast cutlets
¾ teaspoon salt, divided
½ teaspoon freshly ground black pepper, divided
1.1 ounces all-purpose flour (about ¼ cup), divided
2 tablespoons sliced garlic
1½ cups unsalted chicken stock
2 tablespoons capers, drained

1. Cook pasta according to package directions; drain. Place in a bowl with 2 tablespoons parsley, 2 tablespoons oil, and 1 tablespoon juice; toss. Sprinkle chicken with ½ teaspoon salt and ¼ teaspoon pepper. Place 3 tablespoons flour in a shallow dish. Dredge chicken in flour, shaking off excess.
2. Heat remaining 2 tablespoons oil and garlic in a large skillet over medium; cook 4 minutes or until garlic is crisp and golden. Remove garlic from pan with a slotted spoon; reserve. Increase heat to medium-high. Add chicken; cook 3 minutes on each side or until done. Remove chicken from pan.
3. Add remaining 1 tablespoon flour and ¼ cup of the stock to pan, stirring with a whisk. Add remaining 1¼ cups stock and capers; bring to a boil. Cook 3 minutes. Stir in remaining 2 tablespoons parsley, 1 tablespoon juice, ¼ teaspoon salt, and ¼ teaspoon pepper. Top pasta with chicken, sauce, and garlic. Serves 4 (serving size: ¾ cup pasta, 1 chicken cutlet, and 3 tablespoons sauce)

CALORIES 460; FAT 17.8g (sat 2.5g, mono 10.7g, poly 2g); PROTEIN 34g; CARB 40g; FIBER 4g; SUGARS 2g (est. added sugars 0g); CHOL 83mg; IRON 3mg; SODIUM 654mg; CALC 38mg

FREEZE IT!

CREAMY CHICKEN CASSEROLE

Freeze one or two pans of this rice-and-veggie bake for an easy last-minute main.

Kid Friendly • Make Ahead
Freezable

Creamy Chicken-and-Wild Rice Casserole

Hands-on: 35 min. Total: 1 hr. 10 min.
For 3 cups cooked wild rice, simmer 1½ cups rice in 6 cups water for 45 minutes; drain. Or try a frozen cooked wild rice blend, such as Engine 2 from Whole Foods.

1 tablespoon olive oil
1½ pounds skinless, boneless chicken breasts
2 teaspoons kosher salt, divided
1 teaspoon black pepper, divided
Cooking spray
¼ cup all-purpose flour
5 cups 2% reduced-fat milk, divided
1½ cups sliced leeks
1 cup chopped carrots
½ cup chopped celery
1 tablespoon fresh thyme leaves
2 (8-ounce) packages presliced cremini mushrooms
¼ cup chopped fresh flat-leaf parsley
1 ounce ⅓-less-fat cream cheese, softened
3 cups hot cooked wild rice
3 green onions, sliced
½ cup sliced almonds

1. Preheat oven to 350°F.
2. Heat oil in a large skillet over medium-high. Sprinkle chicken with 1 teaspoon salt and ½ teaspoon pepper. Add chicken to pan; cook 3 minutes on each side. Divide chicken between 2 square (8-inch) baking dishes coated with cooking spray. Bake at 350°F for 10 minutes or until done. Cool and chop.
3. Return skillet to medium-high. Combine flour and ½ cup milk in a bowl. Add leeks and next 4 ingredients (through mushrooms) to pan; cook 13 minutes or until browned and tender. Stir in flour mixture, remaining 4½ cups milk, and parsley; cook 3 minutes. Stir in cream cheese until smooth; cook 2 minutes or until slightly thickened. Combine chicken, remaining 1 teaspoon salt, remaining ½ teaspoon pepper, mushroom mixture, rice, and green onions in a bowl. Coat baking dishes with cooking spray. Divide chicken mixture between dishes; top evenly with almonds. Follow freezing directions, or bake at 350°F for 30 minutes or until browned and bubbly. Serves 8 (serving size: about 1¼ cups)

CALORIES 335; FAT 10.9g (sat 3.5g, mono 4.6g, poly 1.7g); PROTEIN 29g; CARB 32g; FIBER 4g; SUGARS 2g (est. added sugars 0g); CHOL 62mg; IRON 2mg; SODIUM 633mg; CALC 240mg

HOW TO

FREEZE
Cool mixture completely. Cover with heavy-duty aluminum foil or airtight lids. Freeze up to 2 months.

THAW
Uncover and microwave at MEDIUM (50% power) 15 minutes or until thawed.

REHEAT
Cover and bake at 450°F for 25 to 30 minutes or until thoroughly heated.

DINNER MADE EASIER

Quality shortcut ingredients make a satisfying meal with next to no prep.

Quick & Easy • Kid Friendly

Warm Bacon-Dijon Lentil Salad with Goat Cheese Crostini

Hands-on: 15 min. Total: 30 min.
Precooked lentils reheat in a warm sherry vinaigrette for a French-inspired main.

3 bacon slices
1/2 cup minced shallots
2 garlic cloves, minced
3 tablespoons water
3 tablespoons sherry vinegar
1 tablespoon Dijon mustard
1/2 teaspoon sugar
1/2 teaspoon black pepper
1/4 teaspoon kosher salt
1 1/4 cups precooked lentils
1/2 teaspoon grated lemon rind
2 teaspoons fresh lemon juice
1 teaspoon chopped fresh thyme
3 ounces goat cheese, softened (about 1/3 cup)
8 (1/2-ounce) whole-wheat French bread baguette slices, toasted
6 cups baby arugula (about 4 ounces)

1. Cook bacon in a skillet over medium-high 6 minutes or until crisp. Remove bacon from pan; chop. Reduce heat to medium-low. Add shallots and garlic to drippings in pan; sauté 4 minutes. Remove pan from heat; stir in the water, vinegar, mustard, sugar, pepper, and salt. Stir in lentils. Return pan to medium-low; cook 1 minute or until warmed.

2. Combine rind, juice, thyme, and goat cheese in a bowl. Spread mixture evenly over toasted baguette slices. Divide arugula evenly among 4 plates. Top with lentil mixture and baguette slices. Sprinkle bacon evenly over salads. Serves 4 (serving size: about 1 1/2 cups salad and 2 crostini)

CALORIES 343; **FAT** 9g (sat 5.3g, mono 2.5g, poly 0.8g); **PROTEIN** 16g; **CARB** 34g; **FIBER** 7g; **SUGARS** 5g (est. added sugars 1g); **CHOL** 22mg; **IRON** 4mg; **SODIUM** 562mg; **CALC** 148mg

COOK ONCE, EAT 3X

Bake a fleet of spuds for stuffed bakers tonight, and then transform them into crispy cakes and creamy risotto.

Gluten Free • Kid Friendly
Make Ahead

BBQ-Stuffed Baked Sweet Potatoes

Hands-on: 22 min. Total: 1 hr. 42 min.

9 (8-ounce) sweet potatoes
5 teaspoons olive oil, divided
1 (12-ounce) pork tenderloin, trimmed
1 teaspoon black pepper, divided
3/4 teaspoon kosher salt, divided
1/2 cup unsalted ketchup
1/4 cup apple cider vinegar
2 teaspoons yellow mustard
1/2 teaspoon onion powder
1/2 teaspoon garlic powder
1/4 cup sour cream
1/4 cup thinly sliced green onions

1. Preheat oven to 400°F.
2. Pierce sweet potatoes with a fork; rub with 2 teaspoons oil. Wrap each potato in foil. Bake at 400°F for

1 hour or until tender. Reserve 5 roasted potatoes for Recipes 2 and 3.
3. Heat remaining 1 tablespoon oil in a large ovenproof skillet over high. Sprinkle pork with 1/4 teaspoon pepper and 1/4 teaspoon salt. Add pork to pan; cook 6 to 8 minutes, turning to brown on all sides. Place pan in oven; bake at 400°F for 18 minutes or until a thermometer inserted in center registers 145°F. Let stand 10 minutes. Cut pork into bite-sized pieces.
4. Bring remaining 3/4 teaspoon pepper, remaining 1/2 teaspoon salt, ketchup, and next 4 ingredients (through garlic powder) to a simmer in a small saucepan over medium; cook 10 minutes or until thickened, stirring occasionally. Add pork; toss to coat.
5. Unwrap remaining 4 potatoes. Partially split potatoes in half lengthwise. Top potatoes evenly with pork mixture, sour cream, and onions. Serves 4 (serving size: 1 stuffed potato)

CALORIES 362; **FAT** 9g (sat 3g, mono 4g, poly 0.8g); **PROTEIN** 21g; **CARB** 47g; **FIBER** 5g; **SUGARS** 18g (est. added sugars 10g); **CHOL** 65mg; **IRON** 2mg; **SODIUM** 516mg; **CALC** 73mg

Kid Friendly

Sweet Potato Cakes with Chicken and Poblano Relish

Hands-on: 32 min. Total: 47 min.

2 poblano peppers, halved lengthwise and seeded
2 cups cherry tomatoes, halved
3/4 cup thinly vertically sliced red onion
5 tablespoons olive oil, divided
2 tablespoons fresh lime juice
1/2 teaspoon kosher salt
3 roasted sweet potatoes (from Recipe 1), peeled and mashed
1/2 cup quick-cooking oats

1/4 teaspoon ground red pepper

2.1 ounces all-purpose flour (about 1/2 cup)

1 large egg, lightly beaten

6 ounces skinless, boneless rotisserie chicken breast, shredded and warmed

2 tablespoons chopped fresh cilantro

1. Preheat broiler to high.

2. Place poblano peppers on a foil-lined baking sheet; broil 8 minutes. Wrap in foil; let stand 10 minutes. Peel and coarsely chop. Combine peppers, tomatoes, onion, 2 table-spoons oil, juice, and salt in a bowl. Combine potatoes, oats, red pepper, flour, and egg in a bowl.

3. Heat 1½ tablespoons oil in a large skillet over medium-high. Spoon about 1/3 cup potato mixture into pan. Repeat 3 times to form 4 cakes. Cook 3 to 4 minutes on each side. Remove from pan; keep warm. Repeat procedure with remaining 1½ tablespoons oil and potato mixture. Top cakes evenly with poblano mixture, chicken, and cilantro. Serves 4 (serving size: 2 cakes, ½ cup relish, and about 1/3 cup chicken)

CALORIES 466; FAT 21g (sat 3.4g, mono 14.6g, poly 2.5g); PROTEIN 20g; CARB 51g; FIBER 7g; SUGARS 9g (est. added sugars 0g); CHOL 83mg; IRON 3mg; SODIUM 464mg; CALC 66mg

---

Gluten Free • Kid Friendly

Sweet Potato-and-Mushroom Risotto

Hands-on: 52 min. Total: 52 min.
When two starchy, creamy elements combine, the result is pure comfort. Pureed sweet potatoes give this risotto a golden hue and a subtle sweetness. For crunch, try sprinkling each serving with crumbled bacon or toasted nuts (hazelnuts or pecans would be delicious).

2 roasted sweet potatoes (from Recipe 1), peeled

2 tablespoons olive oil

3 cups thinly sliced shiitake mushrooms

1 cup finely chopped yellow onion

2 tablespoons chopped fresh sage, divided

5 garlic cloves, minced

1½ cups uncooked Arborio rice

5 cups unsalted chicken stock (such as Swanson), divided

1 teaspoon kosher salt, divided

2 tablespoons chopped fresh flat-leaf parsley

3/4 teaspoon freshly ground black pepper

1 ounce mascarpone cheese (1/4 cup)

1 ounce Parmesan cheese, grated (about 1/4 cup)

1. Place sweet potatoes in a food processor; process until smooth.

2. Heat oil in a Dutch oven over high. Add mushrooms, onion, 1½ tablespoons sage, and garlic; sauté 5 minutes. Add rice; cook 1 minute, stirring constantly. Stir in 1 cup sweet potato puree, 2 cups stock, and ½ teaspoon salt; bring to a boil (reserve remaining puree). Reduce heat to medium-high; simmer 8 minutes or until liquid is reduced by half, stirring frequently.

3. Add remaining 3 cups stock and ½ teaspoon salt; cook 25 minutes or until rice is tender, stirring occasionally. Remove pan from heat; stir in reserved sweet potato puree, parsley, pepper, and mascarpone. Divide risotto evenly among 6 shallow bowls; sprinkle with remaining 1½ teaspoons chopped sage and Parmesan cheese. Serves 6 (serving size: about 1¼ cups)

CALORIES 343; FAT 8.8g (sat 2.6g, mono 3.6g, poly 0.6g); PROTEIN 11g; CARB 57g; FIBER 5g; SUGARS 5g (est. added sugars 0g); CHOL 10mg; IRON 1mg; SODIUM 552mg; CALC 82mg

---

WOW!

Staff Favorite • Quick & Easy Gluten Free • Kid Friendly Vegetarian

Waffle Iron Hash Browns

Hands-on: 10 min. Total: 24 min.
For hash browns that are crisp on the outside and buttery on the inside, look to your waffle iron—this works with both Belgian and traditional waffle irons. Serve as is, or try with Greek yogurt and chives.

1½ pounds peeled russet potatoes, shredded

1/2 teaspoon kosher salt

1/2 teaspoon freshly ground black pepper

1/4 teaspoon garlic powder

1/4 teaspoon onion powder

1½ tablespoons unsalted butter, melted

1. Preheat a waffle iron to medium-high.

2. Squeeze potatoes between paper towels to remove excess liquid. Toss potatoes with salt, pepper, garlic powder, and onion powder. Brush both sides of waffle iron evenly with butter.

3. Add potatoes to iron, evenly mounded. Close iron, pressing lightly (iron may not close completely right away); cook 2 minutes.

4. Press iron to close completely; cook 12 minutes or until golden brown and crisp. Serves 4 (serving size: 1/4 waffled hash brown)

CALORIES 178; FAT 4.5g (sat 2.8g, mono 1.1g, poly 0.2g); PROTEIN 3g; CARB 33g; FIBER 3g; SUGARS 1g (est. added sugars 0g); CHOL 12mg; IRON 1mg; SODIUM 249mg; CALC 16mg

WHAT HEALTHY MEANS NOW

When *Cooking Light* launched 30 years ago, "healthy" meant eat this (reduced-calorie margarine), not that (actual butter). Enjoying all the food you love was not the guiding principle. Three decades and a few billion boneless, skinless chicken breasts later, the definition has evolved from prescriptive to progressive. Thanks to our growing national food obsession and access to fresher ingredients, home cooks are finding inspiration everywhere—from the produce aisle to the chef's table—in order to cook delicious food that makes them feel good. In so many ways, healthy is becoming mainstream. Celebrate the rise of healthy food and the big 3-0 with us by joining the party—and the conversation—by tagging your best food pics with #TheNewHealthy on Facebook and Instagram. You're the nutritional gatekeeper, after all—you define it every day.

HEALTHY IS...

... whole grains. From toothsome pasta to artisanal loaves of bread, whole grains add intrigue and nutritional heft.

... balance, including a celebratory splurge every now and then—bring on the rib roast!

... plant-based food. There's never been a more exciting time to eat vegetables—so eat more of them.

A NEW TURN AT THE TABLE

The dinner plate, a symbol of nurturing and domestic plenty, is as reliable a time capsule as fashion or pop music. Trends are easy to spot—and easy to mock, as one decade's go-to dish becomes the next decade's punch line. (Hold the microwave-steamed veggies, please—forever.) From fat-phobic to plant-forward, here's how the national plate has evolved—and where it's heading.

1987: THAT WAS THEN...

If you were mindful enough to cook light back in 1987, odds are you were motivated by fearful headlines. Cholesterol and fat, the dietary Joker and Penguin of the decade, lurked in every (delicious) dish, poised to drive us to an early grave. Traditional staples like beef, butter, and eggs were sacrificed on the altar of "lean" cuisine. In their place came starches naturally low in fat, and lean poultry, fish, and reduced-calorie margarines (we could believe it was not butter).

SKINLESS, BONELESS CHICKEN BREAST
This lean protein became the weeknight staple. Usually grilled or baked, it was prepared with little to no fat. Serving size was skimpy: Back then, skinless, boneless breasts averaged about 4 ounces each, roughly half the size they are today.

SKIM MILK
Though milk consumption had already begun the downward trend still going on today, most people thought of skim milk as a fortified beverage essential to good health—not just something to pour over cereal or in coffee. The low- to no-fat dairy treatment extended to yogurt and sour cream as well.

STEAMED VEGETABLES
Steaming offered a fat-free, foolproof way to cook, and countertop steamers were hugely popular. Indulgence came in the form of a pat of margarine. Unless you grew your own, fresh herbs were hard to come by, so dried was the best option. Dash of Mrs. Dash, anyone?

REFINED GRAINS AND STARCHES
Carbs became the star of the show, often making up half the plate. With the focus on fat content rather than nutrient density, refined grains like white rice and pasta were popular "healthy" choices. If you were interested in whole grains, you were generally limited to brown rice and oats.

2017: THIS IS NOW...

Forget deprivation. Healthy eating is no longer about what we shouldn't include on the plate, but a celebration of eating just about everything. Variety is the new mantra. We seek out ingredients that bring balance, color, and texture to our meals. We crave richer, bolder flavors. An abundance of fresh, whole foods helps keep dinnertime fun and delicious.

WHOLE GRAINS
Nutty, chewy farro and other ancient grains bring texture and earthy intrigue. Add a few forkfuls of fermented sauerkraut for gut-healthy, probiotic-rich tang.

GO GREEN
Vegetables dominate half the plate, providing crunchy, creamy, and toothsome textures. Handfuls of herbs bring a burst of freshness to sugar snaps, peas, and asparagus.

OMEGA-3–RICH FATTY FISH
Portion sizes of meat and poultry entrées continue to shrink in favor of sustainable fish high in unsaturated fat. If you can find them, seek out wild salmon varieties like sockeye, coho, and king—or try mackerel or sardines.

FULL-FAT DAIRY
Keep portions (and sat fat) in check by deploying a smart dollop of sour cream or yogurt for satiating creaminess.

UNSATURATED FATS
Embrace the health and flavor benefits of good-for-you fats, including olive oil and avocado in the salad and omega-3 fats in the fish.

RED WINE
We opt for red due to resveratrol, a compound in red grapes that may help reduce cardiovascular disease risk, fight cancer, preserve memory, and more.

2047: THIS IS NEXT

A sneak peek of your supper 30 years from now may very well elicit a "Jiminy Cricket!" Which is fitting, given your burger (and bread and pasta) could be made of bugs. Meat consumption will shrink due to dwindling resources, shifting from the center of the plate to the role of condiment. Depleted of many wild fish, the oceans will offer up a different bounty: a host of sustainable aquaculture, including iodine-rich salty greens from sea beans to seaweed. They will also become our primary source for drinking water. The American diet will eschew processed convenience food and embrace from-scratch cooking from a diverse array of plants, including cover crops, seasonal veg, ancient grains, and plenty of good, healthy fats.

CRICKET FLOUR

A standby Mexican bar snack that's already being used in protein bars for its nutritive punch, the cricket will find favor as a milled meat substitute as large-animal farming subsides. ($14 for ¼ pound, amazon.com)

MICRO-LIVESTOCK

Expect to see more goat, rabbit, guinea pig, and grasscutter (a large rodent in the porcupine family). These are delicacies in much of the world and leave less of an environmental "hoofprint" than large-animal production.

SEA BEANS

We'll be savoring more cultivated, Earth-friendly, vitamin- and mineral-rich seaweed and foraged sea vegetables like crunchy, juicy, salty sea beans (aka samphire).

SPECIALTY PLANTS

Rarities like watermelon radishes and Japanese eggplant will become commonplace as people hunger for variety. Some plants will be fortified or bred to produce all essential nutrients, including B12, so that even vegan diets are nutritionally complete.

COVER CROPS

Given the limited supply of soil still packed with nutrients, soil health will be more important than ever. To avoid a global dust bowl, cover crops such as cowpeas and alfalfa will find their way to more tables as they hold our land from drifting off into the sky.

Staff Favorite • Quick & Easy
Kid Friendly

Wild Salmon with Horseradish-Mustard Sauce

Hands-on: 5 min. Total: 20 min.
Wild salmon tends to be leaner than farmed, making it trickier to cook; brushing the fillets with oil helps to keep them moist. Look for fresh salmon starting in mid-May, or find it year-round in your freezer case. If using farmed salmon, look for fish caught in U.S. waters. We love the richness of full-fat sour cream here, but you can use reduced-fat if that's what you have.

2 tablespoons olive oil, divided
4 (6-ounce) wild salmon fillets (about 1-inch thick)
1 tablespoon chopped fresh thyme
¾ teaspoon kosher salt, divided
¾ teaspoon black pepper, divided
½ cup whole-milk sour cream
1½ teaspoons prepared horseradish
1½ teaspoons grainy Dijon mustard

1. Brush 1 tablespoon oil over tops of fillets; sprinkle evenly with 1 teaspoon thyme, ½ teaspoon salt, and ¼ teaspoon pepper. Heat a large nonstick skillet over medium-high. Add remaining 1 tablespoon oil to pan; swirl to coat. Add fillets to pan, skin side down; cook 3 minutes or until skin begins to brown. Turn fillets over; cook 2 to 3 minutes or until desired degree of doneness.
2. Combine sour cream, horseradish, mustard, remaining 2 teaspoons thyme, remaining ¼ teaspoon salt, and remaining ½ teaspoon pepper, stirring well. Serve with salmon. Serves 4 (serving size: 1 fillet and about 2 tablespoons sauce)

CALORIES 314; FAT 18g (sat 5.3g, mono 8.7g, poly 2.8g); PROTEIN 35g; CARB 1g; FIBER 0g; SUGARS 1g (est. added sugars 0g); CHOL 92mg; IRON 1mg; SODIUM 512mg; CALC 101mg

---

Staff Favorite • Quick & Easy
Kid Friendly • Make Ahead
Vegetarian

Farro-Kraut Pilaf

Hands-on: 10 min. Total: 10 min.
Sauerkraut livens up this whole-grain side with crunch, tang, and a little bit of fermentation funk. Use refrigerated, probiotic-rich sauerkraut; shelf-stable versions have been pasteurized, killing any gut-friendly bacteria.

2 tablespoons olive oil
½ cup chopped shallots
2 garlic cloves, minced
1 (8-ounce) package precooked farro (such as Simply Balanced)
¼ teaspoon kosher salt
¼ teaspoon freshly ground black pepper
½ cup thinly sliced radishes
½ cup packed refrigerated red sauerkraut

1. Heat oil in a large skillet over medium. Add shallots and garlic; sauté 3 minutes. Add farro, salt, and pepper; cook until lightly toasted, stirring occasionally, about 2 minutes. Remove from heat; let stand 1 minute. Stir in radishes and sauerkraut. Serves 4 (serving size: about ⅔ cup)

CALORIES 184; FAT 7.8g (sat 0.9g, mono 4.9g, poly 0.7g); PROTEIN 5g; CARB 31g; FIBER 5g; SUGARS 2g (est. added sugars 0g); CHOL 0mg; IRON 0mg; SODIUM 308mg; CALC 14mg

HAVE NO FEAR

Fat was public health enemy number one when *Cooking Light* launched in 1987. Now it's sugar. Our take: Nutrition science continues to evolve, so hedge your nutritional bets by eating a variety of whole foods, including fish loaded with healthy fats.

HEARTY ONE-POT WHOLE GRAINS

Use one dish to turn super-nourishing whole grains into veggie-packed family dinners without the fuss.

**Gluten Free • Kid Friendly
Make Ahead**

Cajun Red Beans and Brown Rice with Andouille

Hands-on: 30 min. Total: 11 hr.

1 pound dried red kidney beans
1 tablespoon olive oil
6 ounces andouille sausage, sliced
1 cup chopped green bell pepper
1 cup chopped yellow onion
1 cup chopped celery
1/4 cup chopped green onions
1 tablespoon minced fresh garlic
1 tablespoon chopped fresh thyme
2 teaspoons chopped fresh sage
1/2 teaspoon ground red pepper
6 cups water
4 cups unsalted chicken stock
1 teaspoon kosher salt
1 bay leaf
1 cup uncooked long-grain brown rice
1/4 cup chopped fresh flat-leaf parsley
Parsley leaves (optional)
Hot sauce (optional)

1. Rinse beans, and place in a bowl with water to cover by 2 inches. Let stand 8 hours or overnight. Drain.
2. Heat oil in a Dutch oven over medium-high. Add andouille; cook, stirring occasionally, until browned, about 3 minutes. Using a slotted spoon, transfer andouille to a bowl, reserving drippings in pan. Add bell pepper, onion, celery, chopped green onions, garlic, thyme, sage, and red pepper to pan; cook, stirring occasionally, until softened and browned, about 7 minutes. Add beans, 6 cups water, stock, salt, and bay leaf; bring to a boil. Reduce heat to medium, and simmer, uncovered, until beans are mostly tender, about 1½ hours.
3. Stir in andouille and rice; cover and cook 1 hour or until rice is tender. Remove from heat; discard bay leaf. Stir in chopped parsley. Top with parsley leaves and serve with hot sauce, if desired. Serves 8 (serving size: about 1 cup)

CALORIES 357; FAT 5.7g (sat 1.5g, mono 1.5g, poly 0.7g); PROTEIN 22g; CARB 57g; FIBER 16g; SUGARS 4g (est. added sugars 0g); CHOL 13mg; IRON 6mg; SODIUM 484mg; CALC 107mg

Kid Friendly • Make Ahead

Umami Broth with Buckwheat and Vegetables

Hands-on: 30 min. Total: 40 min.
The richness of the broth comes from miso, onion, ginger, and garlic cooked in sesame oil.

2 tablespoons toasted sesame oil
2 tablespoons red miso
1 cup diced sweet onion
1 (1-inch) piece fresh ginger, peeled and grated
3 garlic cloves, minced
4 cups water
4 cups unsalted chicken stock (such as Swanson)
1 ounce dried shiitake mushrooms
4 large eggs in shells
1/2 cup uncooked buckwheat groats, rinsed and drained
1 medium carrot, cut into 1/4-inch-thick half-moons
12 ounces baby bok choy, stalks sliced crosswise into 1/2-inch pieces, leaves left whole
2 green onions, cut into 1-inch pieces
2 tablespoons rice vinegar

1. Heat oil in a large saucepan over medium-high. Add miso, onion, and ginger; sauté 10 minutes or until browned and fragrant. Add garlic; sauté 2 minutes. Add 4 cups water, stock, and mushrooms. Bring to a boil.
2. Carefully drop eggs into broth; reduce heat to medium. Simmer 7 minutes. Using a slotted spoon, transfer eggs to a bowl filled with ice water. Let stand 1 minute. Peel eggs.
3. Add buckwheat and carrot to broth; increase heat to medium-high, and bring to a boil. Reduce heat to medium-low; simmer 15 minutes or until buckwheat is tender.
4. Add bok choy and green onions; cook until tender, about 5 minutes. Stir in vinegar. Ladle soup evenly into 4 bowls. Cut eggs in half lengthwise; place 2 egg halves on each bowl of soup. Serves 4 (serving size: 2 cups soup and 2 egg halves)

CALORIES 301; FAT 12.7g (sat 2.6g, mono 4.7g, poly 4.2g); PROTEIN 16g; CARB 33g; FIBER 5g; SUGARS 7g (est. added sugars 0g); CHOL 186mg; IRON 3mg; SODIUM 644mg; CALC 136mg

Wheat Berry "Ribollita"

Hands-on: 30 min. Total: 1 hr. 30 min.
Classic ribollita is a Tuscan dish of leftover minestrone warmed up with chunks of bread tossed into it; here, we use wheat berries in place of bread for a lovely chewy texture.

1 (28-ounce) can whole peeled plum tomatoes, drained and divided
3 tablespoons olive oil, divided
1½ cups finely chopped yellow onion
2 tablespoons minced fresh garlic
½ teaspoon crushed red pepper
1 cup chopped carrot
1 cup chopped celery
2 cups chopped cremini mushrooms
6 cups water
¾ cup uncooked wheat berries
1¾ teaspoons kosher salt
¾ teaspoon black pepper
1 (15-ounce) can unsalted cannellini beans, drained and rinsed
1 (2-ounce) Parmesan cheese rind
5 cups loosely packed baby arugula (about 5 ounces)
2 tablespoons sherry vinegar
1 ounce Parmesan cheese, shaved (about ⅓ cup)

1. Remove 3 tomatoes from can, and finely chop to equal ½ cup. Heat 2 tablespoons oil in a Dutch oven over medium-high. Add chopped tomatoes, onion, garlic, and red pepper. Cook, stirring often, until tomatoes are caramelized and deep red, about 7 minutes. Add carrot, celery, and mushrooms; cook, stirring occasionally, until browned, about 8 minutes. Add 6 cups water, wheat berries, salt, black pepper, beans, rind, and remaining tomatoes; bring to a boil. Reduce heat to medium; partially cover, and simmer 40 minutes or until wheat berries are tender, stirring occasionally.

2. Add arugula and vinegar; cook 1 minute or until arugula just wilts, stirring constantly. Discard Parmesan rind. Ladle soup evenly into 8 bowls. Top servings evenly with shaved Parmesan; drizzle evenly with remaining 1 tablespoon oil. Serves 8 (serving size: about 1 cup)

CALORIES 225; **FAT** 7.6g (sat 1.6g, mono 4.1g, poly 0.7g); **PROTEIN** 9g; **CARB** 30g; **FIBER** 7g; **SUGARS** 6g (est. added sugars 0g); **CHOL** 5mg; **IRON** 2mg; **SODIUM** 573mg; **CALC** 124mg

Mediterranean Chicken and Bulgur Skillet

Hands-on: 25 min. Total: 45 min.
You'll be delighted by the incredible results from this one-pot wonder: tender, fluffy bulgur; creamy feta; and moist chicken. You don't even need a sauce since there's so much flavor in the pan. It's a complete meal, though you could serve it with a side salad if you'd like.

4 (6-ounce) skinless, boneless chicken breasts
¾ teaspoon kosher salt, divided
½ teaspoon freshly ground black pepper, divided
1 tablespoon olive oil, divided
1 cup thinly sliced red onion
1 tablespoon thinly sliced garlic
½ cup uncooked bulgur
2 teaspoons chopped fresh or ½ teaspoon dried oregano
4 cups chopped fresh kale (about 2½ ounces)
½ cup thinly sliced bottled roasted red bell peppers
1 cup unsalted chicken stock (such as Swanson)
2 ounces feta cheese, crumbled (about ½ cup)
1 tablespoon coarsely chopped fresh dill

1. Preheat oven to 400°F.
2. Sprinkle chicken with ½ teaspoon salt and ¼ teaspoon black pepper. Heat 1½ teaspoons oil in a 10-inch cast-iron or other ovenproof skillet over medium-high. Add chicken to pan; cook until browned on both sides, about 3 minutes per side. Transfer chicken to a plate.
3. Add remaining oil to pan. Add onion and garlic; cook, stirring occasionally, until lightly browned, about 5 minutes. Add bulgur and oregano; cook, stirring often, until fragrant and toasted, about 2 minutes. Add kale and bell peppers; cook, stirring constantly, until kale begins to wilt, about 2 minutes. Add stock and remaining ¼ teaspoon each salt and black pepper; bring to a boil. Remove from heat.
4. Nestle chicken into bulgur mixture; place skillet in oven. Bake at 400°F until a meat thermometer inserted in thickest portion of chicken registers 165°F, 12 to 15 minutes. Remove from oven. Sprinkle with feta. Let stand 5 minutes. Sprinkle with dill, and serve immediately. Serves 4 (serving size: ¾ cup bulgur mixture and 1 chicken breast)

CALORIES 369; **FAT** 11.3g (sat 3.6g, mono 4.3g, poly 1.3g); **PROTEIN** 45g; **CARB** 21g; **FIBER** 1g; **SUGARS** 3g (est. added sugars 0g); **CHOL** 137mg; **IRON** 2mg; **SODIUM** 663mg; **CALC** 141mg

NEW EASTER ESSENTIALS

These six modern classics will make your spring more delicious than ever.

Celebrate the first big holiday feast of the year with this collection of new essentials. From a make-ahead breakfast casserole and killer asparagus side dish to a fresh twist on carrot cake, these recipes are destined to become family traditions. Go ahead: Celebrate green vegetables, embrace distinct textures, and amp up all the flavors. After all, spring is finally here!

Staff Favorite • Quick & Easy Gluten Free • Kid Friendly Make Ahead • Vegetarian

All The Green Things Salad

Hands-on: 25 min. Total: 25 min. This salad is full of lovely green spring produce, with textures ranging from crunchy to creamy. You can make the zippy lemon dressing and blanch, drain, and chill the peas and asparagus up to 2 days ahead, but combine all the elements shortly before serving to preserve the color of the avocado and the crunch of the greens.

1½ cups frozen green peas
1 pound asparagus, trimmed and cut diagonally into 2½-inch pieces (4 cups)
12 ounces sugar snap peas, trimmed (about 4 cups)
3 tablespoons minced shallots
3 tablespoons extra-virgin olive oil
1½ teaspoons grated lemon rind
2 tablespoons fresh lemon juice
1 tablespoon Dijon mustard
¾ teaspoon kosher salt
½ teaspoon freshly ground black pepper
4 ounces pea tendrils, pea shoots, or watercress (about 5 cups)
1 cup loosely packed fresh flat-leaf parsley leaves
½ cup torn fresh mint leaves
1 firm, ripe avocado, cubed

1. Bring a large Dutch oven filled with water to a boil over high. Add green peas, asparagus, and sugar snap peas; boil until crisp-tender, about 3 minutes. Drain and rinse well with cold water; drain well.
2. Whisk together shallots, oil, rind, juice, mustard, salt, and pepper in a large bowl. Add blanched vegetables; toss well to coat. Add pea tendrils, parsley leaves, mint leaves, and cubed avocado; toss gently to combine. Serves 8 (serving size: 1 cup)

CALORIES 137; FAT 7.9g (sat 1.1g, mono 5.4g, poly 0.9g); PROTEIN 5g; CARB 14g; FIBER 6g; SUGARS 5g (est. added sugars 0g); CHOL 0mg; IRON 3mg; SODIUM 251mg; CALC 63mg

Kid Friendly • Make Ahead Vegetarian

Spinach-Artichoke Strata

Hands-on: 30 min. Total: 9 hr. 20 min. This get-ahead dish plays off the appeal of spinach-artichoke dip. Assemble the night before; in the morning, let the strata stand while the oven preheats, and then pop it in.

1½ tablespoons canola oil, divided
1 (9-ounce) package frozen artichoke hearts, thawed
4 garlic cloves, minced, divided
1 pound fresh spinach
2½ cups 1% low-fat milk
1 teaspoon kosher salt
½ teaspoon freshly ground black pepper
6 large eggs
12 ounces whole-grain or whole-wheat baguette, cut into ¾-inch cubes
3 ounces garlic-and-herb spreadable cheese (such as Boursin), crumbled
Cooking spray
3 ounces Swiss cheese, shredded (about ¾ cup)

1. Heat 1½ teaspoons oil in a Dutch oven over medium-high. Add artichokes and 2 garlic cloves; sauté until fragrant and softened, about 4 minutes. Remove from pan. Add remaining 1 tablespoon oil and 2 garlic cloves; cook, stirring often, 30 seconds. Add spinach gradually, tossing constantly until spinach wilts, about 3 minutes. Transfer spinach to a strainer to cool.
2. Whisk together milk, salt, pepper, and eggs in a large bowl. Squeeze spinach to remove excess moisture. Add spinach, artichokes, bread, and garlic-and-herb cheese to milk mixture; toss well to combine. Spoon bread mixture into a 13- x 9-inch glass or ceramic baking dish coated with cooking spray; sprinkle with

Swiss cheese. Cover, and chill 8 hours or overnight.
3. Preheat oven to 350°F. Let the strata stand at room temperature while the oven preheats.
4. Uncover strata, and bake at 350°F until set and lightly browned around the edges, about 45 minutes. Remove from oven; let stand 5 to 10 minutes. Serves 9 (serving size: 1 piece)

CALORIES 281; FAT 13.8g (sat 6g, mono 3.6g, poly 1.5g); PROTEIN 15g; CARB 25g; FIBER 4g; SUGARS 4g (est. added sugars 0g); CHOL 146mg; IRON 3mg; SODIUM 578mg; CALC 254mg

Gluten Free • Kid Friendly Make Ahead

Honey-Baked Pork Roast

(pictured on page 218)

Hands-on: 30 min. Total: 4 hr. 15 min.
Instead of the traditional cured ham that's full of sodium and nitrates, bake the flavors of honey-baked ham into a pork picnic roast. You can season it up to 2 days in advance for even better flavor. The cooked roast cuts like ham, with firm, juicy slices that go perfectly with a simple honey-mustard sauce. We use a skin-on picnic roast here, which is cheaper than a Boston butt roast.

1 (5-pound) bone-in pork picnic half roast
6½ tablespoons honey, divided
¼ cup packed brown sugar
2 teaspoons kosher salt
1 teaspoon freshly ground black pepper
1 teaspoon ground cinnamon
½ teaspoon ground ginger
¼ teaspoon ground cloves
⅓ cup canola mayonnaise
¼ cup Dijon mustard
¼ cup apple cider vinegar
⅜ teaspoon ground red pepper

1. Preheat oven to 300°F.
2. Trim tough outer skin layer from pork, leaving as much fat as possible intact. Discard skin. Rub 2½ tablespoons honey over pork. Combine sugar, salt, pepper, cinnamon, ginger, and cloves in a bowl; rub mixture evenly over all sides of pork. Place pork, fat side up, in a foil-lined broiler pan.
3. Bake at 300°F until a thermometer inserted in thickest portion registers 170° to 180°F, about 3 to 3½ hours. Remove from oven; let stand 15 minutes before cutting into thin slices.
4. Combine remaining ¼ cup honey, mayonnaise, and remaining ingredients; serve sauce with pork. Serves 16 (serving size: about 3 ounces pork and about 2½ teaspoons sauce)

CALORIES 277; FAT 16.7g (sat 5.7g, mono 7.6g, poly 1.9g); PROTEIN 19g; CARB 12g; FIBER 0g; SUGARS 10g (est. added sugars 7g); CHOL 70mg; IRON 1mg; SODIUM 422mg; CALC 29mg

Staff Favorite • Gluten Free Kid Friendly • Make Ahead Vegetarian

Turmeric-Pickled Deviled Eggs

Hands-on: 40 min. Total: 4 hr. 45 min.
Deviled eggs get way more interesting when the eggs are pickled in a tangy turmeric-spiked brine that also dyes them a lovely color. The longer the eggs stay in the brine, the firmer they become and the more vibrant the color gets. For a tangier flavor, use brine instead of water to loosen the filling.

2 cups water
1 cup apple cider vinegar
2 tablespoons grated fresh turmeric or 1 tablespoon dried ground turmeric
2⅜ teaspoons kosher salt, divided
12 hard-cooked large eggs, peeled
¾ teaspoon Madras curry powder
¼ teaspoon ground cumin
¼ cup canola mayonnaise
¼ cup plain 2% reduced-fat Greek yogurt
2 tablespoons chopped fresh chives
Additional chopped fresh chives (optional)

1. Combine 2 cups water, vinegar, turmeric, and 2 teaspoons salt in a bowl or large jar. Add eggs; chill 4 to 8 hours, turning occasionally to "stir." Drain eggs; pat dry with paper towels.
2. Heat a small skillet over medium. Add curry powder and cumin; cook, stirring constantly, until fragrant, about 1 minute. Cool.
3. Cut eggs in half crosswise; carefully remove yolks, and place in a mini food processor. Cut a sliver off each rounded bottom of egg white (so eggs will sit flat); place egg whites on a platter. Add mayonnaise, yogurt, curry mixture, and remaining ⅜ teaspoon salt to processor; pulse until smooth, adding 1 or 2 tablespoons water if mixture becomes too thick. Add chives; pulse to combine. Divide filling evenly among egg whites; top with additional chives, if desired. Serves 12 (serving size: 2 egg halves)

CALORIES 88; FAT 6.1g (sat 1.6g, mono 2.6g, poly 1.4g); PROTEIN 7g; CARB 1g; FIBER 0g; SUGARS 0g; CHOL 186mg; IRON 1mg; SODIUM 200mg; CALC 33mg

Herbed Ricotta, Asparagus, and Phyllo Tart

(pictured on page 216)

Kid Friendly • Vegetarian

Hands-on: 25 min. Total: 50 min.
If working with phyllo dough fills you with fear, don't worry—this recipe is beginner-friendly. You just lay flat sheets of dough on top of each other for a rustic edge.

3/4 cup part-skim ricotta cheese
1/4 cup chopped fresh flat-leaf parsley
1 1/2 tablespoons 1% low-fat milk
1 tablespoon thyme leaves
1 garlic clove, grated
1/2 teaspoon kosher salt, divided
**12 (14- x 9-in.) frozen phyllo pastry
    sheets, thawed**
3 1/2 tablespoons olive oil, divided
**1 1/2 pounds medium asparagus
    spears, trimmed to 6 1/2 inches long**
**1 ounce Parmigiano-Reggiano
    cheese, shaved (about 1/4 cup)**

1. Preheat oven to 400°F.
2. Stir together ricotta, parsley, milk, thyme, garlic, and 3/8 teaspoon salt.
3. Place 1 phyllo sheet on a baking sheet lined with parchment paper. (Cover remaining dough to keep it from drying.) Lightly brush phyllo sheet with oil, and top with another sheet. Repeat layers with remaining phyllo sheets and oil, reserving 1 teaspoon oil to brush on asparagus.
4. Spread ricotta mixture on phyllo stack, leaving a 1/2-inch border. Arrange asparagus side by side over ricotta mixture; brush with remaining 1 teaspoon oil. Bake at 400°F until phyllo is browned and crisp, 22 to 25 minutes. Sprinkle with remaining 1/8 teaspoon salt; top with shaved cheese. Serves 8 (serving size: 1 piece)

CALORIES 174; FAT 9.9g (sat 2.9g, mono 5.7g, poly 0.9g); PROTEIN 7g; CARB 15g; FIBER 2g; SUGARS 2g (est. added sugars 0g); CHOL 10mg; IRON 3mg; SODIUM 286mg; CALC 136mg

Browned Butter Carrot Cake with Toasted Pecans

(pictured on page 217)

Kid Friendly • Make Ahead
Freezable • Vegetarian

Hands-on: 45 min. Total: 1 hr. 30 min.
The Bundt pan makes for a much easier dessert, freeing you from the fuss of stacking and frosting layers. You can bake the cake ahead and freeze it, unglazed: Wrap the cooled cake in plastic wrap, and freeze in a ziplock plastic freezer bag for up to 3 months (glaze the thawed cake).

1/2 cup unsalted butter
**11 ounces whole-wheat pastry flour
    (about 3 cups)**
1 tablespoon baking powder
1 1/2 teaspoons ground cinnamon
3/4 teaspoon table salt
1/8 teaspoon ground cloves
1 1/4 cups granulated sugar
1/3 cup canola oil
1 1/4 teaspoons vanilla extract, divided
2 large eggs
**3/4 cup plus 3 tablespoons fat-free
    evaporated milk, divided**
2 cups finely shredded peeled carrots
Baking spray with flour
**3 ounces 1/3-less-fat cream cheese,
    softened**
3/4 cup powdered sugar
**3 tablespoons chopped pecans,
    toasted**

1. Preheat oven to 350°F.
2. Melt butter in a small saucepan over medium; continue cooking until butter is browned and fragrant, about 4 minutes. Cool to room temperature.
3. Weigh or lightly spoon flour into dry measuring cups; level with a knife. Whisk together flour, baking powder, cinnamon, salt, and cloves. Place browned butter, granulated sugar, oil, and 1 teaspoon vanilla in a large bowl; beat with an electric mixer on medium speed until well blended, about 2 minutes. Add eggs, 1 at a time, beating well after each addition. With mixer on low speed, gradually add flour mixture to butter mixture, alternating with 3/4 cup evaporated milk, beginning and ending with flour mixture. Stir in carrots. Coat a (10-cup) Bundt pan with baking spray; spoon batter evenly into prepared pan.
4. Bake at 350°F until a wooden pick inserted in center comes out clean, about 45 minutes. Cool in pan on a wire rack 10 minutes. Remove cake to wire rack; cool completely.
5. Place cream cheese in a medium bowl. Add powdered sugar, remaining 3 tablespoons evaporated milk, and remaining 1/4 teaspoon vanilla; beat on medium-high speed until smooth. Spoon glaze over cooled cake. Sprinkle with pecans. Serves 16 (serving size: 1 slice)

CALORIES 298; FAT 13.5g (sat 5.1g, mono 5.2g, poly 1.9g); PROTEIN 5g; CARB 41g; FIBER 3g; SUGARS 24g (est. added sugars 22g); CHOL 43mg; IRON 1mg; SODIUM 257mg; CALC 82mg

3 STEPS FOR CARROT CAKE SUCCESS

BROWN THE BUTTER
Cooking butter until browned intensifies its flavor, making it nutty and caramel-rich.

FINELY SHRED THE CARROTS
Use the smaller holes on the box grater for more delicate strands that incorporate better into the batter.

CHOP THE NUTS JUST RIGHT
Try not to chop the pecans too finely; you want to be sure to get some hearty crunch and not end up with dust.

10-MINUTE VEGGIE WRAPS

Here's a superbly simple, plant-powered lunch you can lean on.

Lynn Nelson discovered the Cooking Light Diet via happenstance at a Hudson News airport kiosk. Now, after losing 30 pounds, Lynn says receiving her weekly menus means "there is never a reason to be bored. There are so many options, and the recipes are great. That has really surprised me." Because we know make-ahead, portable lunches can be a challenge for busy folks like Lynn, we sent her the recipe for this fast and fresh veggie wrap. Between the ease of preparation and how well the wrap held up the next day, Lynn was sold. She has added these to her weekday recipe routine. Lynn says, "This recipe is now in my favorites, and it's such an easy meal you can make ahead if you're in a time crunch."

**Quick & Easy • Kid Friendly
Make Ahead • Vegetarian**

Spinach, Hummus, and Bell Pepper Wraps

Hands-on: 10 min. Total: 10 min.
Make this super-simple wrap the night before, wrap in parchment paper or plastic wrap, and store in the fridge.

**2 (1.9-ounce) whole-grain flatbreads
(such as Flatout Light)
1/2 cup roasted garlic hummus
1 small red bell pepper, thinly sliced
1 cup firmly packed baby spinach
1 ounce crumbled tomato-and-basil
feta cheese (about 1/4 cup)**

1. Spread each flatbread with 1/4 cup hummus, leaving a 1/2-inch border around the edge.
2. Divide the bell pepper evenly between the flatbreads; top each with 1/2 cup spinach and 2 tablespoons cheese. Starting from one short side, roll up the wraps. Cut each wrap in half, and secure with wooden picks. Serves 2 (serving size: 1 wrap)

CALORIES 258; **FAT** 12.1g (sat 2.9g, mono 5.6g, poly 3g); **PROTEIN** 15g; **CARB** 34g; **FIBER** 13g; **SUGARS** 7g (est. added sugars 0g); **CHOL** 10mg; **IRON** 3mg; **SODIUM** 793mg; **CALCIUM** 78mg

LET'S COOK

$11.14
FOR FOUR
SERVINGS

**Quick & Easy
Gluten Free
Kid Friendly • Make Ahead**

Spiced and Seared Flank Steak with Carrot Mash and Snap Peas

Hands-on: 20 min. Total: 23 min.

**2 cups water
2 cups finely chopped carrot
2 tablespoons unsalted butter
1 tablespoon light sour cream
3/4 teaspoon salt, divided
1 teaspoon garlic powder
1 teaspoon paprika
3/4 teaspoon freshly ground black
pepper, divided
1 pound flank steak
1 tablespoon olive oil, divided
1 (12-ounce) package frozen steam-
in-bag sugar snap peas
1 tablespoon unseasoned rice vinegar**

1. Bring 2 cups water and carrots to a boil in a medium saucepan over medium-high. Cover and cook 15 minutes or until tender; drain. Place carrots in a bowl with butter, sour cream, and 1/4 teaspoon salt; mash with a fork until almost smooth.
2. Combine remaining 1/2 teaspoon salt, garlic powder, paprika, and 1/2 teaspoon pepper in a small bowl; rub over steak. Heat 1 1/2 teaspoons oil in a large nonstick skillet over medium-high. Add steak to pan; cook 5 minutes on each side. Let stand 5 minutes. Cut across the grain into slices.
3. Cook snap peas according to package directions. Add remaining 1 1/2 teaspoons oil and snap peas to pan; cook 3 minutes or until lightly browned, stirring frequently. Stir in remaining 1/4 teaspoon pepper and vinegar. Serve snap peas with carrot mash and steak. Serves 4 (serving size: 3 ounces steak, about 1/3 cup carrot mixture, and 3/4 cup peas)

CALORIES 333; **FAT** 16.1g (sat 6.8g, mono 6.3g, poly 1g); **PROTEIN** 28g; **CARB** 18g; **FIBER** 6g; **SUGARS** 9g (est. added sugars 0g); **CHOL** 87mg; **IRON** 4mg; **SODIUM** 588mg; **CALC** 116mg

HERE, WE UPDATED THE USUAL PEAS-AND-CARROTS SIDE DISH WITH A FRESHER TAKE.

SALLY AND SUZY'S DISH

by Colu Henry

A dear friend's cherished pasta recipe comes to mean far more than just dinner.

I graduated from Emerson College in 1999 and was eager to start a career as a cabaret singer (yes, it's the truth). There was never any question that I would move to New York following graduation. I arrived late that summer and rented an apartment in the only neighborhood I could afford: Astoria, Queens.

Although I spent much of my youth visiting the city and living close by, I didn't have many friends upon arrival. An old boyfriend who had also moved around that time suggested I meet Suzy, a new girl he had started dating from his hometown of Seattle. I enthusiastically agreed, and a bread-baking date at my apartment sealed the deal. (It was a classic white sandwich loaf from the *Joy of Cooking*, if you're wondering.) We have been dearest friends ever since.

I went on to live with Suzy for four years in Fort Greene, Brooklyn. It was in that apartment that we discovered the joys of hosting Sunday suppers together. We had the pleasure of cooking for others and corralling large groups of friends around tables pushed together to toast the week past and usher in the next. Mind you, those Monday mornings always started with a headache after one too many bottles of wine from the previous night. It was at one of those dinners that Suzy introduced me to a recipe from her mother, Sally: Pasta with Shrimp in Tomato Cream, which Sally would make for Suzy every time she visited.

It was their tradition of making this dish that in turn chartered ours.

At a time when buying shrimp felt like a luxury (yes, even the frozen kind), guests or no guests, this soulful pasta was one Suzy and I turned to after a terrible day, for a night in to catch up, or when we needed to make our way back from some silly spat. This recipe became so dear that Suzy put it in a cookbook my friends collaborated on and gave to me as an engagement gift.

Years later, I learned that Sally had adapted the recipe from a Junior League of Seattle cookbook, *Simply Classic*, which made it all the more endearing. The cookbook still opens automatically to that recipe and shows signs of wear and tear on just that one page.

Sally passed away a few years ago after a valiant fight with idiopathic pulmonary fibrosis. It was devastating. I learned recently that Suzy and her brother Dan now gather on Sally's birthday and the anniversary of her death and make this cherished dish to honor her. My version of this recipe is my tribute to Suzy and to Sally. Make it for someone you love.

Kid Friendly

Pasta with Shrimp in Tomato Cream

Hands-on: 25 min. Total: 36 min.
Use this recipe to start your own loving tradition. You can add your own touches, such as swapping in whole-grain pasta for a nutrition boost or trying goat cheese in place of feta. If you don't have dry vermouth on hand, you can substitute dry sherry or a dry white wine like Sauvignon Blanc.

8 ounces fusilli pasta
2 tablespoons canola oil or extra-virgin olive oil
1 pound peeled and deveined medium shrimp
1 teaspoon kosher salt, divided
1/2 teaspoon freshly ground black pepper, divided
3 garlic cloves, thinly sliced
3 green onions, thinly sliced (dark green slices kept separate)
1/2 cup dry vermouth
1/2 cup unsalted chicken stock (such as Swanson)
1/2 cup heavy cream
1/2 cup dry-packed sun-dried tomatoes, thinly sliced
1 tablespoon tomato paste
2 ounces feta cheese, crumbled (about 1/2 cup)
1/4 cup chopped fresh flat-leaf parsley
1/4 cup chopped fresh basil, divided

1. Cook pasta according to package directions; drain well. Set aside.
2. Heat a large skillet over medium-high. Add oil. Sprinkle shrimp with 1/2 teaspoon salt and 1/4 teaspoon pepper. Add to pan; sauté 2 minutes or until just done. Place shrimp in a large bowl.
3. Add garlic and white and light green onion slices to pan; sauté 2 minutes. Add to shrimp in bowl.
4. Reduce heat to medium. Stir in vermouth, stock, cream, tomatoes, and tomato paste. Bring to a boil; cook 5 minutes or until reduced by half, stirring well. Increase heat to medium-high. Add pasta, shrimp mixture, cheese, parsley, 2 tablespoons basil, and remaining 1/2 teaspoon salt and 1/4 teaspoon pepper; toss to combine. Place about 1 1/2 cups pasta mixture in each of 6 bowls; top evenly with dark green onion slices and remaining 2 tablespoons basil. Serves 6

CALORIES 367; FAT 16.2g (sat 7.1g, mono 5.8g, poly 1.8g); PROTEIN 19g; CARB 34g; FIBER 2g; SUGARS 5g (est. added sugars 0g); CHOL 134mg; IRON 2mg; SODIUM 590mg; CALC 140mg

READY IN
40
MINUTES

···
GAME PLAN
···

While pilaf simmers:
- Grill chicken and vegetables.

While pilaf stands:
- Assemble salads.

Quick & Easy • Gluten Free
Kid Friendly

Grilled Lemon Chicken Salad

With Orzo and Herb Pilaf

2 medium lemons
1¹⁄₂ tablespoons chopped fresh oregano
1¹⁄₂ tablespoons canola oil
2 teaspoons minced fresh garlic
4 (6-ounce) skinless, boneless chicken breasts
Cooking spray
³⁄₄ teaspoon kosher salt, divided
¹⁄₂ teaspoon freshly ground black pepper, divided
8 ounces thin asparagus
8 green onions, trimmed
2 tablespoons extra-virgin olive oil
1¹⁄₂ tablespoons white wine vinegar
1 (5-ounce) package arugula

1. Grate lemon rinds to equal 2 teaspoons; halve lemons crosswise and reserve. Combine rind, oregano, canola oil, and garlic in a large bowl. Add chicken; toss to coat.

2. Heat a grill pan over medium-high. Coat pan with cooking spray. Sprinkle chicken with ¼ teaspoon salt and ¼ teaspoon pepper. Add chicken to pan; cook 5 minutes on each side or until done. Add lemon halves to pan, cut sides down; cook 4 minutes. Remove chicken and lemons from pan. Cut chicken into slices.

3. Coat asparagus and green onions with cooking spray; add to pan. Cook 3 to 4 minutes or until charred and tender, turning occasionally. Cut asparagus and green onions into 2-inch pieces.

4. Combine remaining ½ teaspoon salt, remaining ¼ teaspoon pepper, olive oil, and vinegar in a large bowl. Add asparagus, green onions, and arugula; toss. Serve with chicken and lemon halves. Serves 4 (serving size: 1 chicken breast and about 1½ cups salad)

CALORIES 342; **FAT** 17g (sat 2.3g, mono 9.5g, poly 3.1g); **PROTEIN** 40g; **CARB** 7g; **FIBER** 2g; **SUGARS** 2g (est. added sugars 0g); **CHOL** 124mg; **IRON** 2mg; **SODIUM** 452mg; **CALC** 108mg

IF YOU'VE NEVER THROWN FRESH LEMONS ON THE GRILL, TRY IT: THE SLIGHT CHAR MAKES THEM JUICIER AND INTENSIFIES THEIR TARTNESS.

Quick & Easy • Kid Friendly
Make Ahead

Orzo and Herb Pilaf

If you'd like to sub whole-grain, unpearled farro for the orzo, reverse the cooking method: Simmer the farro until done, drain, and then sauté for a couple minutes in the onion mixture before serving.

1¹⁄₂ tablespoons unsalted butter
¹⁄₂ cup chopped yellow onion
³⁄₄ cup uncooked orzo
1¹⁄₂ cups unsalted chicken stock (such as Swanson)
¹⁄₄ teaspoon kosher salt
¹⁄₄ teaspoon freshly ground black pepper
1 cup halved heirloom cherry tomatoes
3 tablespoons chopped fresh flat-leaf parsley
1 tablespoon chopped fresh dill

1. Melt butter in a medium saucepan over medium-high. Add onion; sauté 3 minutes. Add orzo; cook 2 minutes, stirring frequently. Stir in stock, salt, and pepper; bring to a boil. Cover, reduce heat, and simmer 10 to 12 minutes or until liquid is almost absorbed.

2. Remove pan from heat; let stand, covered, 5 minutes. Fluff with a fork. Stir in tomatoes, parsley, and dill. Serves 4 (serving size: about ½ cup)

CALORIES 181; **FAT** 5g (sat 2.8g, mono 1.1g, poly 0.2g); **PROTEIN** 6g; **CARB** 28g; **FIBER** 2g; **SUGARS** 4g (est. added sugars 0g); **CHOL** 11mg; **IRON** 0mg; **SODIUM** 174mg; **CALC** 14mg

READY IN 30 MINUTES

GAME PLAN

While oven preheats:
- Prepare panko mixture.
- Prepare yogurt sauce.

While fish bakes:
- Cook radish mixture.

Staff Favorite • Quick & Easy
Kid Friendly

Dijon-Herb Crusted Salmon with Creamy Dill Sauce

With Warm Buttered Radish and Edamame Salad

We add the crumbly panko topping to the fish after it bakes so the crust doesn't burn before the fish is cooked through.

2 (6-ounce) salmon fillets, skinned (about 1½ inches thick)
¼ teaspoon kosher salt
¼ teaspoon freshly ground black pepper
¼ cup whole-wheat panko (Japanese breadcrumbs)
1 tablespoon finely chopped fresh flat-leaf parsley
1 tablespoon canola oil
2 teaspoons chopped fresh thyme
1 teaspoon Dijon mustard
2 tablespoons plain 2% reduced-fat Greek yogurt
2 teaspoons chopped fresh dill
1½ teaspoons 2% reduced-fat milk
1 teaspoon red wine vinegar

1. Preheat oven to 450°F.

2. Arrange fish on a parchment paper–lined baking sheet. Sprinkle with salt and pepper. Bake at 450°F for 10 minutes or until desired degree of doneness. Remove pan from oven. Turn on broiler.
3. Combine panko, parsley, oil, thyme, and Dijon in a small bowl. Spoon panko mixture over fish, pressing to adhere. Place pan in oven; broil 1 to 2 minutes or until topping is browned.
4. Combine yogurt, dill, milk, and vinegar in a small bowl. Serve with fish. Serves 2 (serving size: 1 fillet and about 1½ tablespoons sauce)

CALORIES 359; FAT 18.6g (sat 2.5g, mono 8.1g, poly 6g); PROTEIN 37g; CARB 9g; FIBER 1g; SUGARS 1g (est. added sugars 0g); CHOL 95mg; IRON 2mg; SODIUM 398mg; CALC 51mg

Quick & Easy • Gluten Free
Vegetarian

Warm Buttered Radish and Edamame Salad

Radishes lose their pepperiness once sautéed and turn a faint rosy pink. For a boost of protein, we use edamame.

1½ tablespoons unsalted butter
1 cup radishes, quartered
½ cup frozen shelled edamame, thawed
2 tablespoons chopped fresh chives
⅛ teaspoon kosher salt
⅛ teaspoon freshly ground black pepper

1. Melt butter in a medium skillet over medium-high. Add radishes; sauté 4 minutes or until tender. Add edamame; cook 1 minute. Stir in chopped chives, salt, and black pepper. Serves 2 (serving size: about ½ cup)

CALORIES 139; FAT 10.2g (sat 5.5g, mono 2.2g, poly 0.4g); PROTEIN 5g; CARB 7g; FIBER 3g; SUGARS 2g (est. added sugars 0g); CHOL 23mg; IRON 1mg; SODIUM 164mg; CALC 49mg

READY IN 35 MINUTES

GAME PLAN

While barley mixture simmers:
- Cook chicken and mushroom mixture.

While chicken mixture cooks:
- Prepare soy sauce mixture.

Quick & Easy • Kid Friendly

Chicken, Mushroom, and Bok Choy Bowls

With Scallion-and-Cilantro Barley

A little ground chicken goes a long way here. Brown leftover chicken and stir into chili or pasta sauce, tuck into tacos, or add to casseroles.

2 tablespoons canola oil, divided
8 ounces ground chicken
1 (8-ounce) package cremini mushrooms, finely chopped
½ cup shiitake mushroom caps, sliced
6 heads baby bok choy, quartered
½ cup sliced green onions
1 tablespoon chopped peeled fresh ginger
3 tablespoons reduced-sodium soy sauce
1 tablespoon unseasoned rice vinegar
1 tablespoon honey
¼ cup unsalted roasted peanuts, chopped

1. Heat 1 tablespoon canola oil in a cast-iron skillet over medium-high. Add chicken; cook 5 minutes or until browned, stirring to crumble. Add mushrooms; cook 6 minutes, stirring occasionally. Remove chicken mixture from pan; keep warm.

2. Return pan to medium-high. Add remaining 1 tablespoon oil; swirl. Add bok choy; cook 3 to 4 minutes or until lightly browned, turning occasionally. Add green onions and ginger; sauté 2 minutes. Stir in chicken mixture.

3. Combine soy sauce, vinegar, and honey in a small bowl. Divide chicken mixture among 4 shallow bowls; top evenly with soy sauce mixture and peanuts. Serves 4 (serving size: about 1¼ cups)

CALORIES 271; FAT 16.9g (sat 2.6g, mono 8.9g, poly 4.1g); PROTEIN 19g; CARB 16g; FIBER 4g; SUGARS 9g (est. added sugars 4g); CHOL 49mg; IRON 3mg; SODIUM 588mg; CALC 206mg

Quick & Easy • Kid Friendly
Make Ahead

Scallion-and-Cilantro Barley

6 green onions
1 tablespoon canola oil
1³⁄₄ cups unsalted chicken stock (such as Swanson)
1 cup uncooked quick-cooking barley
¹⁄₄ teaspoon kosher salt
¹⁄₄ teaspoon freshly ground black pepper
¹⁄₂ cup chopped fresh cilantro
4 lime wedges

1. Slice white parts of green onions to measure ¹⁄₃ cup. Cut green parts of green onions to measure ¹⁄₂ cup. Heat oil in a medium saucepan over medium. Add white parts of green onions; sauté 5 minutes. Add stock, barley, salt, and pepper; bring to a boil. Cover, reduce heat, and simmer 10 minutes or until barley is tender. Stir in green parts of green onions and cilantro. Serve with lime wedges. Serves 4 (serving size: about ²⁄₃ cup)

CALORIES 173; FAT 3.9g (sat 0.3g, mono 2.2g, poly 1g); PROTEIN 6g; CARB 32g; FIBER 5g; SUGARS 1g (est. added sugars 0g); CHOL 0mg; IRON 1mg; SODIUM 181mg; CALC 18mg

READY IN
40
MINUTES

GAME PLAN

While oven preheats:
- Cook broccoli mixture.
- Prepare carrot mixture.

While carrots bake:
- Prepare cakes.

Staff Favorite • Quick & Easy
Kid Friendly • Make Ahead
Freezable • Vegetarian

Broccoli, Cheddar, and Brown Rice Cakes

With Sweet-and-Spicy Carrots and Peas
(pictured on page 215)

These crispy cakes are inspired by cheesy broccoli-and-rice casserole, right down to the layer of melted cheddar cheese on top.

Cooking spray
1 tablespoon unsalted butter
³⁄₄ cup chopped yellow onion
4 garlic cloves, chopped
³⁄₄ cup unsalted vegetable stock (such as Swanson)
12 ounces fresh broccoli florets, cut into ¹⁄₂-inch pieces
1 (8.8-ounce) package precooked brown rice (such as Uncle Ben's)
¹⁄₄ cup whole-wheat panko (Japanese breadcrumbs)
1 tablespoon grainy mustard
¹⁄₂ teaspoon black pepper
³⁄₈ teaspoon kosher salt
3 ounces preshredded reduced-fat sharp cheddar cheese, divided (about ³⁄₄ cup)
2 large eggs, lightly beaten
Sliced green onions (optional)

1. Preheat oven to 450°F. Coat a baking sheet with cooking spray.
2. Melt butter in a large skillet over medium-high. Add onion and garlic; sauté 4 minutes. Add stock and broccoli. Bring to a boil; cook 3 minutes.
3. Heat rice according to package directions. Combine broccoli mixture, rice, panko, mustard, pepper, salt, and ¹⁄₂ cup cheese in a large bowl. Stir in eggs. Divide and shape broccoli mixture into 8 (2¹⁄₂-inch) patties. Arrange patties on prepared pan; coat patties with cooking spray. Bake at 450°F for 15 minutes. Top with remaining ¹⁄₄ cup cheese, and bake at 450°F for 4 more minutes or until cheese melts. Garnish with green onions, if desired. Serves 4 (serving size: 2 cakes)

CALORIES 280; FAT 10.6g (sat 5.2g, mono 3g, poly 1.1g); PROTEIN 15g; CARB 33g; FIBER 5g; SUGARS 2g (est. added sugars 0g); CHOL 113mg; IRON 2mg; SODIUM 554mg; CALC 268mg

Quick & Easy • Gluten Free
Kid Friendly • Vegetarian

Sweet-and-Spicy Carrots and Peas

1 tablespoon canola oil
¹⁄₂ teaspoon light brown sugar
¹⁄₄ teaspoon ground cumin
¹⁄₈ teaspoon ground red pepper
1 (12-ounce) package small carrots
1³⁄₄ cups snow peas
¹⁄₄ teaspoon kosher salt

1. Preheat oven to 450°F.
2. Combine oil, brown sugar, cumin, red pepper, and carrots on a rimmed baking sheet. Bake at 450°F for 12 minutes. Add snow peas to pan; bake 5 more minutes or until vegetables are tender and lightly browned. Sprinkle with salt. Serves 4 (serving size: ¹⁄₂ cup)

CALORIES 84; FAT 3.8g (sat 0.3g, mono 2.2g, poly 1.1g); PROTEIN 2g; CARB 11g; FIBER 3g; SUGARS 6g (est. added sugars 1g); CHOL 0mg; IRON 1mg; SODIUM 180mg; CALC 45mg

READY IN 35 MINUTES

······················

GAME PLAN

······················

While bread cubes toast:

■ Cook bacon mixture.

While bread puddings bake:

■ Prepare salad.

Quick & Easy • Kid Friendly
Make Ahead

Spinach, Cheese, and Bacon Bread Puddings

With Bibb, Radicchio, and Asparagus Salad
(pictured on page 215)

You just can't go wrong with a savory bread pudding—think of it as a cross between holiday stuffing and a cheesy breakfast casserole. For a vegetarian spin, skip the bacon, sub vegetable stock for chicken stock, and add shiitake or cremini mushrooms.

**8 ounces multigrain bread, cut into
 ³⁄₄-inch cubes (about 6 cups)**
1 tablespoon olive oil
¹⁄₂ cup chopped white onion
1 teaspoon minced fresh garlic
4 center-cut bacon slices, chopped
8 ounces fresh baby spinach
³⁄₄ cup 1% low-fat milk
**¹⁄₄ cup unsalted chicken stock
 (such as Swanson)**
3 large eggs, lightly beaten
**2¹⁄₂ ounces fontina cheese, grated
 and divided (about ²⁄₃ cup)**
Cooking spray

1. Preheat oven to 400°F.
2. Arrange bread cubes in a single layer on a baking sheet. Bake at 400°F for 7 minutes or until toasted.
3. Heat oil in a large skillet over medium-high. Add onion, garlic, and bacon; cook 8 minutes or until bacon is crisp, stirring occasionally. Add spinach; cook 1 to 2 minutes, stirring until wilted. Place spinach mixture in a bowl.
4. Add milk, stock, eggs, and ¹⁄₃ cup cheese to spinach mixture, stirring to combine. Add bread; toss to coat. Divide bread mixture evenly among 4 (7-ounce) ramekins coated with cooking spray. Place ramekins on a baking sheet; top evenly with remaining ¹⁄₃ cup cheese. Bake at 400°F for 20 minutes or until browned. Serve immediately. Serves 4 (serving size: 1 bread pudding)

CALORIES 355; **FAT** 16.1g (sat 5.8g, mono 5.5g, poly 2.5g); **PROTEIN** 20g; **CARB** 34g; **FIBER** 5g; **SUGARS** 8g (est. added sugars 0g); **CHOL** 167mg; **IRON** 4mg; **SODIUM** 563mg; **CALC** 408mg

CHOOSE BREAD FROM THE BAKERY SECTION RATHER THAN THE AISLE; IT WILL ABSORB MORE LIQUID AND HAVE A BETTER TEXTURE AFTER SOAKING AND BAKING.

Quick & Easy • Vegetarian

Bibb, Radicchio, and Asparagus Salad

Just a little radicchio provides a colorful contrast to the tender, delicate Bibb lettuce, though its slight bitterness may be too much for some kids. Swap in thinly sliced red cabbage if you like.

2 tablespoons extra-virgin olive oil
1 tablespoon apple cider vinegar
2 teaspoons Dijon mustard
2 teaspoons honey
¹⁄₄ teaspoon kosher salt
**¹⁄₄ teaspoon freshly ground black
 pepper**
2 cups thinly sliced radicchio
1 cup diagonally sliced asparagus
**1 head Bibb lettuce, leaves separated
 and torn (about 6 ounces)**

1. Combine first 6 ingredients in a medium bowl, stirring with a whisk. Add radicchio, asparagus, and Bibb lettuce; toss to coat. Serves 4 (serving size: ¹⁄₂ cup)

CALORIES 90; **FAT** 6.9g (sat 1g, mono 4.9g, poly 0.8g); **PROTEIN** 2g; **CARB** 7g; **FIBER** 1g; **SUGARS** 4g (est. added sugars 3g); **CHOL** 0mg; **IRON** 1mg; **SODIUM** 187mg; **CALC** 25mg

SUPERFAST 20-MINUTE COOKING

Staff Favorite • Quick & Easy
Gluten Free • Kid Friendly
Vegetarian

Arugula, Egg, and Charred Asparagus Salad

4 large eggs in shells
$3/4$ teaspoon kosher salt, divided
$1/2$ teaspoon black pepper, divided
1 tablespoon extra-virgin olive oil
12 ounces medium asparagus, trimmed
$1/4$ cup plain whole-milk Greek yogurt
1 tablespoon fresh lemon juice
1 tablespoon water
1 (5-ounce) package baby arugula

1. Preheat broiler to high.
2. Bring a small saucepan filled with water to a boil. Carefully add eggs; cook 8 minutes. Place eggs in a bowl filled with ice water; let stand 2 minutes. Peel eggs, cut into quarters, and sprinkle with $1/4$ teaspoon salt and $1/8$ teaspoon pepper.
3. Combine olive oil, $1/4$ teaspoon salt, $1/4$ teaspoon pepper, and asparagus on a baking sheet; spread in a single layer in pan. Broil 3 minutes or until lightly charred. Remove asparagus mixture from pan; cut into 2-inch pieces.
4. Combine remaining $1/4$ teaspoon salt, remaining $1/8$ teaspoon pepper, yogurt, juice, and 1 tablespoon water. Add arugula; toss. Arrange arugula mixture on a platter; top with asparagus mixture and eggs. Serves 4 (serving size: about 2 cups salad and 1 egg)

CALORIES 148; FAT 10.1g (sat 3.3g, mono 4.4g, poly 1.6g); PROTEIN 10g; CARB 6g; FIBER 2g; SUGARS 3g (est. added sugars 0g); CHOL 189mg; IRON 3mg; SODIUM 446mg; CALC 119mg

---

Quick & Easy • Kid Friendly

Chicken Potpie Tartines

A creamy chicken and vegetable mixture tops toast for a quick twist on potpie. Matchstick-cut carrots, frozen peas, and rotisserie chicken save time, as does a wide skillet for sautéing the vegetables and building the sauce. Need ideas for the leftover peas in the package? See page 96 for 4 great recipes.

3 tablespoons olive oil
1 (8-ounce) package cremini mushrooms, quartered
1.1 ounces unbleached all-purpose flour (about $1/4$ cup)
$2 1/4$ cups unsalted chicken stock (such as Swanson)
$3/4$ cup frozen green peas, thawed
$1/2$ cup matchstick-cut carrots
$3/8$ teaspoon kosher salt
$1/4$ teaspoon black pepper
6 ounces skinless, boneless rotisserie chicken breast, shredded (about $1 1/2$ cups)
4 ($1 1/2$-ounce) whole-wheat bread slices, toasted
2 tablespoons chopped fresh flat-leaf parsley

1. Heat oil in a large nonstick skillet over medium-high. Add mushrooms; cook 6 minutes or until browned, stirring occasionally. Sprinkle flour over mushrooms; cook 1 minute, stirring constantly. Add stock; cook 4 minutes or until slightly thickened. Stir in peas, carrots, salt, pepper, and chicken; cook 2 minutes or until thoroughly heated.
2. Spoon chicken mixture over toasted bread slices. Sprinkle evenly with parsley. Serves 4 (serving size: 1 bread slice and about $1 1/4$ cups chicken mixture)

CALORIES 332; FAT 13.4g (sat 2.2g, mono 8.2g, poly 2.5g); PROTEIN 23g; CARB 32g; FIBER 5g; SUGARS 5g (est. added sugars 2g); CHOL 37mg; IRON 2mg; SODIUM 610mg; CALC 95mg

---

Quick & Easy • Kid Friendly

Pork Stir-Fry with Snow Peas

A great stir-fry uses only 2 or 3 vegetables in the base, ensuring all elements shine through as well as leaving enough room in the pan for a good sear.

2 tablespoons canola oil
8 ounces pork tenderloin, trimmed and cut into $1/2$-inch-thick pieces
$1/2$ teaspoon kosher salt
$1/4$ teaspoon black pepper
$2 1/2$ tablespoons reduced-sodium soy sauce
2 teaspoons light brown sugar
1 tablespoon toasted sesame oil
1 cup chopped red bell pepper
2 cups snow peas, diagonally sliced
2 (8.8-ounce) packages precooked brown rice (such as Uncle Ben's)
1 tablespoon toasted sesame seeds
Lime wedges

1. Heat canola oil in a wok or large nonstick skillet over medium-high. Sprinkle pork with salt and black pepper. Add pork to pan; cook for 5 minutes or until browned, stirring frequently. Remove pork from pan.
2. Combine soy sauce and sugar in a small bowl, stirring with a whisk. Add sesame oil to pan; swirl. Add bell pepper; cook 3 minutes or until crisp-tender, stirring occasionally. Add pork, soy sauce mixture, and snow peas to pan; cook 1 minute, stirring frequently.
3. Heat rice according to package directions. Divide rice among 4 bowls; top with the pork mixture, and sprinkle with sesame seeds. Serve with lime wedges. Serves 4 (serving size: $3/4$ cup rice and $3/4$ cup pork mixture)

CALORIES 380; FAT 15.7g (sat 1.6g, mono 6.8g, poly 4.2g); PROTEIN 19g; CARB 44g; FIBER 5g; SUGARS 5g (est. added sugars 2g); CHOL 37mg; IRON 3mg; SODIUM 646mg; CALC 42mg

Chimichurri Chicken Thighs with Potatoes

An herb-packed chimichurri sauce makes this meat-and-potatoes main vibrant and exciting. Double the mixture and spoon it over grilled steak or fish on another night. For less heat in both the chimichurri and the potatoes, remove the seeds from the Fresno chile.

2 tablespoons water
12 ounces fingerling potatoes, halved
5 tablespoons extra-virgin olive oil
8 skinless, boneless chicken thighs (about 1½ pounds)
1 teaspoon kosher salt, divided
¾ teaspoon black pepper, divided
1 red Fresno chile, halved crosswise
1 cup fresh flat-leaf parsley leaves
1 cup fresh cilantro leaves
1 tablespoon chopped shallots
2 garlic cloves
2 tablespoons fresh lemon juice

1. Place 2 tablespoons water and potatoes in a microwave-safe bowl; cover and microwave at HIGH 4 minutes or until almost tender.
2. Heat 2 tablespoons oil in a large nonstick skillet over medium-high. Sprinkle chicken with ½ teaspoon salt and ½ teaspoon black pepper. Add chicken to pan; cook 5 minutes on each side. Remove from pan; keep warm.
3. Cut half of chile into thin slices; finely chop remaining half. Add potatoes and chile slices to drippings in pan; cook 4 minutes. Stir in ¼ teaspoon salt and ⅛ teaspoon black pepper.
4. Place chopped chile, parsley, cilantro, shallots, and garlic in a mini food processor; pulse to combine. Add remaining 3 tablespoons oil, ¼ teaspoon salt, ⅛ teaspoon black pepper, and juice; process until smooth. Serve with chicken and potatoes. Serves 4 (serving size: 2 thighs, ½ cup potato mixture, and 2 tablespoons cilantro mixture)

CALORIES 433; **FAT** 24.9g (sat 4.4g, mono 15.1g, poly 4.2g); **PROTEIN** 36g; **CARB** 17g; **FIBER** 2g; **SUGARS** 2g (est. added sugars 0g); **CHOL** 160mg; **IRON** 3mg; **SODIUM** 669mg; **CALC** 52mg

Roasted Red Pepper and Pine Nut Salad

Spring mix, a blend of small, tender lettuces, is an ideal base for side salads with a more delicate profile (think herbs, berries, and nuts rather than croutons, pungent cheeses, or big, crunchy vegetables). This Mediterranean version would be a perfect side for citrus-and-herb baked chicken and Greek-style roasted potatoes.

2 tablespoons extra-virgin olive oil
1 tablespoon red wine vinegar
⅛ teaspoon kosher salt
⅛ teaspoon ground red pepper
1½ teaspoons chopped fresh oregano
2 cups loosely packed spring mix
2 cups loosely packed baby spinach
½ cup bottled roasted red bell peppers, drained and chopped
2½ tablespoons toasted pine nuts
2 tablespoons crumbled feta cheese

1. Combine oil, vinegar, salt, red pepper, and oregano in a large bowl, stirring with a whisk. Add spring mix, spinach, and roasted bell peppers; toss gently to coat. Sprinkle salad with pine nuts and crumbled feta. Serves 4 (serving size: about 1 cup)

CALORIES 118; **FAT** 11.6g (sat 2g, mono 6.2g, poly 2.8g); **PROTEIN** 2g; **CARB** 2g; **FIBER** 1g; **SUGARS** 1g (est. added sugars 0g); **CHOL** 4mg; **IRON** 1mg; **SODIUM** 170mg; **CALC** 47mg

Radish and Parmesan Salad
Combine 2 Tbsp. extra-virgin olive oil, 1 Tbsp. fresh lemon juice, ⅛ tsp. kosher salt, and ⅛ tsp. black pepper in a large bowl, stirring with a whisk. Add 4 cups spring mix, ¾ cup sliced watermelon radishes or other radishes, and ¼ cup shaved Parmesan cheese; toss to coat. Serves 4 (serving size: about 1 cup)

CALORIES 100; **FAT** 8.5g (sat 1.8g, mono 5g, poly 1.1g); **PROTEIN** 3g; **CARB** 4g; **FIBER** 1g; **SUGARS** 2g (est. added sugars 0g); **CHOL** 5mg; **IRON** 1mg; **SODIUM** 228mg; **CALC** 78mg

Avocado and Almond Salad
Combine 2 Tbsp. extra-virgin olive oil, 1 Tbsp. chopped shallots, 1 Tbsp. Champagne vinegar, 1 tsp. chopped fresh thyme, 1 tsp. Dijon mustard, ⅛ tsp. kosher salt, and ⅛ tsp. black pepper in a large bowl. Add 4 cups spring mix, ½ cup diced ripe avocado, and 3 Tbsp. toasted sliced almonds; toss. Serves 4 (serving size: about 1 cup)

CALORIES 133; **FAT** 11.9g (sat 1.6g, mono 8g, poly 1.9g); **PROTEIN** 3g; **CARB** 6g; **FIBER** 3g; **SUGARS** 2g (est. added sugars 0g); **CHOL** 0mg; **IRON** 1mg; **SODIUM** 155mg; **CALC** 43mg

Berry and Walnut Salad
Combine 3 Tbsp. whole buttermilk, 1 oz. softened goat cheese, 1 tsp. honey, ¼ tsp. kosher salt, and ⅛ tsp. black pepper in a large bowl. Add 4 cups spring mix, 1 cup quartered strawberries, ½ cup fresh blueberries, and 2 Tbsp. toasted chopped walnuts; toss. Serves 4 (serving size: about 1¼ cups)

CALORIES 91; **FAT** 4.4g (sat 1.5g, mono 0.8g, poly 1.9g); **PROTEIN** 4g; **CARB** 10g; **FIBER** 2g; **SUGARS** 7g (est. added sugars 1g); **CHOL** 5mg; **IRON** 1mg; **SODIUM** 229mg; **CALC** 61mg

TIME-SAVING PASTA SALAD

Quality meets convenience in this speedy springtime main.

Quick & Easy • Kid Friendly

Tortellini, Chicken, and Arugula Salad

Hands-on: 10 min. Total: 20 min.

1 (9-ounce) package refrigerated cheese tortellini (such as Buitoni), cooked according to package directions
8 ounces skinless, boneless rotisserie chicken breast, shredded (about 2 cups)
1 garlic clove, finely chopped
1/8 teaspoon kosher salt
3 tablespoons extra-virgin olive oil
1/2 teaspoon grated lemon rind
2 tablespoons fresh lemon juice
1/2 teaspoon granulated sugar
1/2 teaspoon black pepper
3 cups baby arugula
1/3 cup thinly sliced shallots
3/4 ounce Parmesan cheese, shaved (about 1/4 cup)

1. Place tortellini and chicken in a large bowl.
2. Combine garlic and salt on a cutting board. Mash with the side of a knife to form a paste. Place in a small bowl. Add oil, rind, juice, sugar, and pepper; stir with a whisk.
3. Add 2 tablespoons dressing to tortellini and chicken; toss to coat. Gently fold in arugula, shallots, and remaining dressing. Sprinkle with shaved Parmesan cheese. Serves 4 (serving size: 1½ cups)

CALORIES 400; FAT 18g (sat 4.9g, mono 9.6, poly 2.1g); PROTEIN 27g; CARB 35g; FIBER 3g; SUGARS 4g (est. added sugars 1g); CHOL 77mg; IRON 2mg; SODIUM 629mg; CALC 184mg

---

PREWASHED BABY ARUGULA
Prewashed greens let you grab a handful and go. Build a salad, wilt into sautés, or blend into a pesto.

TORTELLINI
Look to Buitoni pasta packs for quick meals on their own or to help you elevate salads and soups.

ROTISSERIE CHICKEN
One of your best supermarket allies for fast and fresh weeknight meals.

KID-FRIENDLY SWEET-AND-SOUR CHICKEN

The slow cooker makes this family favorite so easy. Make it ahead for busy weeknights.

Kid Friendly • Make Ahead Freezable

Sweet-and-Sour Chicken Bowl

Hands-on: 20 min. Total: 3 hr. 20 min.
If ketchup goes with every chicken dinner in your family, try these saucy, sweet, and tangy chicken thighs instead. The meat becomes incredibly tender in the slow cooker so you can easily slip out the bones and cut the chicken into bite-sized pieces for kids.

2½ pounds bone-in chicken thighs, skinned
1/4 cup cornstarch
1 tablespoon canola oil
2 green onions
1/4 cup unsalted ketchup
1/4 cup honey
2 tablespoons reduced-sodium soy sauce
2 teaspoons grated fresh ginger
2 teaspoons minced garlic (about 2 cloves)
3/4 teaspoon kosher salt
1/2 cup plus 1 tablespoon rice vinegar
2 (8.8-ounce) pouches precooked whole-grain brown rice (such as Uncle Ben's Ready Rice)
3 cups packaged cabbage-and-carrot coleslaw
3/4 cup thinly sliced radishes
1 tablespoon toasted sesame oil

1. Place chicken thighs in a large ziplock plastic freezer bag; sprinkle with cornstarch, and seal. Shake bag until chicken is evenly coated. Remove chicken; shake off excess cornstarch.
2. Heat canola oil in a large nonstick skillet over medium-high. Add chicken, and cook 3 minutes on each side or until browned. Place in a 5- to 6-quart slow cooker.
3. Thinly slice green parts of green onions; set aside. Finely chop white parts of green onions; stir together white parts, ketchup, honey, soy sauce, ginger, garlic, salt, and ½ cup vinegar in a medium bowl. Pour sauce over chicken in slow cooker. Cover and cook on HIGH for 3 hours, or on LOW for 7 hours and 30 minutes, until chicken is tender and cooked through. Remove chicken from slow cooker; cool slightly. Carefully remove bones from each thigh; discard bones.
4. Heat rice according to package directions. Stir together coleslaw, radishes, sesame oil, and remaining 1 tablespoon vinegar.
5. Divide cooked rice among 6 bowls. Top with coleslaw mixture and chicken. Drizzle with sauce from slow cooker; sprinkle evenly with green onion slices. Serves 6 (serving size: about ½ cup rice, 1½ chicken thighs, ½ cup coleslaw mixture, and 3 tablespoons sauce)

CALORIES 479; FAT 14.3g (sat 2.6g, mono 6.5g, poly 4.1g); PROTEIN 41g; CARB 47g; FIBER 3g; SUGARS 16g (est. added sugars 14g); CHOL 178mg; IRON 3mg; SODIUM 636mg; CALC 38mg

COOK ONCE, EAT 3X

This big batch of spinach-basil pesto stays vibrant for days. Stir it into pasta, spread it onto chicken, or dollop it over soup.

Kid Friendly • Make Ahead

Spinach Pesto Pasta with Shrimp

Hands-on: 45 min. Total: 50 min.
Pesto tends to go army-green if made ahead. We blanch the spinach and basil to preserve color without diluting flavor. Fresh tomato adds moisture and a mild acidity to the sauce.

Pesto:
2 cups packed fresh baby spinach
1 cup packed fresh basil leaves
1/2 cup loosely packed fresh flat-leaf parsley
1/2 cup seeded chopped plum tomato
6 tablespoons chopped toasted walnuts
2 teaspoons fresh lemon juice
1/2 teaspoon kosher salt
1/2 teaspoon freshly ground black pepper
1 1/2 ounces Parmesan cheese, grated (about 1/3 cup)
1 garlic clove, chopped
2 tablespoons extra-virgin olive oil

Pasta:
8 ounces uncooked whole-wheat penne pasta
1 pound fresh asparagus, cut into 2-inch pieces

1 tablespoon olive oil
1 tablespoon unsalted butter
1 pound large fresh shrimp, peeled and deveined
1/4 teaspoon ground red pepper
1/4 teaspoon freshly ground black pepper
1/2 cup halved multicolored grape tomatoes
1/4 teaspoon kosher salt

1. To prepare pesto, bring a large saucepan filled with water to a boil. Add spinach and basil; cook 20 seconds. Remove spinach mixture to a bowl filled with ice water (reserve water in pan); let stand 30 seconds. Drain and pat dry with paper towels.
2. Place parsley and next 7 ingredients (through garlic) in a food processor; process until finely chopped. Add spinach mixture and 2 tablespoons oil; process to combine. Place ¾ cup pesto in a small bowl; place plastic wrap directly on pesto. Reserve for Recipes 2 and 3.
3. To prepare pasta, return water in pan to a boil. Add pasta; cook according to package directions, adding asparagus during last 5 minutes of cooking. Drain in a colander over a bowl, reserving ¾ cup cooking liquid.
4. Heat 1 tablespoon oil and butter in a large skillet over medium-high until butter melts. Sprinkle shrimp with red pepper and ¼ teaspoon black pepper. Add shrimp to pan; cook 1 to 2 minutes on each side or until done. Remove shrimp from pan.
5. Add pasta mixture and reserved ¾ cup cooking liquid to pan; cook 1 minute. Stir in remaining 6 tablespoons pesto, shrimp, grape tomatoes, and ¼ teaspoon salt. Divide pasta mixture among 4 bowls. Serves 4 (serving size: 1¾ cups)

CALORIES 409; FAT 15.5g (sat 3.6g, mono 5.6g, poly 4.4g); PROTEIN 27g; CARB 50g; FIBER 9g; SUGARS 3g (est. added sugars 0g); CHOL 154mg; IRON 5mg; SODIUM 443mg; CALC 163mg

Quick & Easy • Kid Friendly

Pesto Chicken with Blistered Tomatoes

Hands-on: 30 min. Total: 30 min.
Here, pesto acts as a binder, helping the crispy panko topping stick to the chicken.

2 1/2 tablespoons olive oil, divided
4 (6-ounce) skinless, boneless chicken breasts, pounded to 1-inch thickness
1/2 teaspoon kosher salt, divided
1/2 teaspoon black pepper, divided
1/4 cup whole-wheat panko (Japanese breadcrumbs)
2 tablespoons grated Parmesan cheese
1 tablespoon unsalted butter, melted
6 tablespoons spinach pesto (from Recipe 1)
3 cups multicolored cherry tomatoes
1 garlic clove, thinly sliced
1 teaspoon red wine vinegar

1. Preheat broiler to high.
2. Heat 1 tablespoon oil in a large ovenproof skillet over medium-high. Sprinkle chicken with ¼ teaspoon salt and ¼ teaspoon pepper. Add chicken to pan; cook 5 minutes on each side. Remove pan from heat.
3. Combine panko, cheese, and butter in a bowl. Spread pesto over chicken in pan; top with panko mixture, pressing to adhere. Place pan in oven; broil 2 minutes or until browned.
4. Heat remaining 1½ tablespoons oil in a skillet over medium-high. Add tomatoes; cook 6 minutes or until softened. Add garlic; cook 30 seconds, stirring constantly. Stir in remaining ¼ teaspoon salt, remaining ¼ teaspoon pepper, and vinegar. Serve with chicken. Serves 4 (serving size: 1 chicken breast and about ½ cup tomato mixture)

CALORIES 419; FAT 22.7g (sat 5.5g, mono 10.6g, poly 4g); PROTEIN 43g; CARB 11g; FIBER 3g; SUGARS 4g (est. added sugars 0g); CHOL 137mg; IRON 2mg; SODIUM 525mg; CALC 95mg

Vegetable Soup Au Pistou

Hands-on: 30 min. Total: 45 min.
A traditional French pistou is a nut-free pesto, but the spinach pesto is delicious here. Don't rinse the beans after draining; any remaining starches will help bring the soup together.

2 bacon slices, chopped
1½ cups chopped yellow onion
1 cup chopped celery
1 cup chopped carrots
1½ teaspoons minced fresh garlic
5 cups unsalted chicken stock
1 tablespoon chopped fresh thyme
2 teaspoons chopped fresh sage
2 cups chopped zucchini
1 cup chopped haricots verts
    (French green beans)
1 (15.5-ounce) can unsalted cannellini
    beans, drained
1 tablespoon fresh lemon juice
½ teaspoon freshly ground
    black pepper
¼ teaspoon kosher salt
6 tablespoons spinach pesto
    (from Recipe 1)

1. Cook bacon in a large saucepan over medium-high 4 minutes or until crisp. Add onion, celery, carrots, and garlic; cook 7 minutes, stirring occasionally. Add stock, thyme, and sage; bring to a boil. Cook 10 minutes or until reduced to about 5 cups.
2. Reduce heat to medium-low. Add zucchini, haricots verts, and cannellini beans; cook 5 minutes. Stir in juice, pepper, and salt. Divide soup among 4 bowls; top each serving with spinach pesto. Serves 4 (serving size: about 2 cups soup and about 1½ tablespoons spinach pesto)

CALORIES 296; **FAT** 12.7g (sat 3.1g, mono 4.8g, poly 3.2g); **PROTEIN** 16g; **CARB** 32g; **FIBER** 9g; **SUGARS** 9g (est. added sugars 0g); **CHOL** 12mg; **IRON** 3mg; **SODIUM** 612mg; **CALC** 146mg

RECIPE MAKEOVER

THE ULTIMATE FISH SANDWICH MAKEOVER

There are concrete benefits of regular consumption of omega-3-rich fish. Here, we swap out the standard white fish in a fast-food fish-wich in favor of omega-3-charged salmon. A yogurt-blended aioli offers a jolt of spice to kick your metabolism into high gear.

OURS SAVES
500mg sodium and 12g fat, and it packs nearly double the protein of fast-food fish-wiches.

The Big Omega Sandwich

Hands-on: 20 min. Total: 50 min.

1 pound (1-inch-thick) boneless,
    skin-on wild-caught salmon fillets
⅓ cup whole-wheat panko
    (Japanese breadcrumbs)
1 large egg, lightly beaten
1½ tablespoons chopped shallots
1 tablespoon chopped drained capers
1 tablespoon chopped fresh flat-leaf
    parsley
1 garlic clove, minced
2 teaspoons chopped fresh dill
2 teaspoons fresh lemon juice
1 teaspoon smoked paprika
½ teaspoon ground red pepper
¼ cup canola mayonnaise, divided
⅜ teaspoon kosher salt, divided

3 tablespoons plain 2% reduced-fat
    Greek yogurt
1 teaspoon Sriracha chili sauce
½ teaspoon white vinegar
2 teaspoons olive oil
4 whole-wheat hamburger buns,
    toasted
8 thin red onion slices
1 cup firmly packed arugula

1. Preheat broiler with oven rack 6 inches from heat. Place salmon, skin side down, on a foil-lined baking sheet. Broil 5 minutes. Set aside until cool enough to handle.
2. Place panko, egg, shallots, capers, parsley, garlic, dill, lemon juice, smoked paprika, red pepper, 2 tablespoons mayonnaise, and ¼ teaspoon salt in a large bowl. Mix to combine.
3. Remove and discard salmon skin; place salmon in a bowl, and mash with a fork. Add to panko mixture. Using your hands, mix until well combined. Shape mixture into 4 (¾-inch-thick) patties (5 ounces each). Place patties on a parchment paper–lined baking sheet. Cover and chill 30 minutes.
4. Combine yogurt, Sriracha, vinegar, remaining 2 tablespoons mayonnaise, and remaining ⅛ teaspoon salt in a small bowl. Set aside.
5. Heat oil in a large nonstick skillet over medium-high. Place salmon patties in skillet; reduce heat to medium, and cook 4 to 5 minutes per side or until browned.
6. Spread aioli on cut sides of buns. Top each bottom bun with 1 patty. Top patties with onion slices and arugula; cover with top halves of buns. Serves 4 (serving size: 1 bun, about 1 tablespoon aioli, 1 salmon patty, 2 onion slices, and ¼ cup arugula)

CALORIES 394; **FAT** 16.8g (sat 2.3g, mono 7.3g, poly 5.7g); **PROTEIN** 30g; **CARB** 30g; **FIBER** 4g; **SUGARS** 5g (est. added sugars 4g); **CHOL** 110mg; **IRON** 3mg; **SODIUM** 681mg; **CALC** 94mg

**Kid Friendly • Make Ahead
Freezable**

Chicken-and-Vegetable Hand Pies

(pictured on page 219)

Hands-on: 35 min. Total: 1 hr. 20 min.

**14 ounces white whole-wheat flour
    (about 3½ cups) plus 2 tablespoons
1 tablespoon kosher salt, divided
1 teaspoon baking powder
10 tablespoons ice-cold water
⅔ cup plus 2 tablespoons extra-
    virgin olive oil, divided
1½ pounds ground chicken
4 ounces haricots verts (French green
    beans), cut into ¼-inch pieces
¾ cup finely chopped carrot
1 tablespoon chopped fresh thyme
1 tablespoon minced fresh garlic
½ cup fresh or frozen green peas,
    thawed
1½ cups unsalted chicken stock
1 tablespoon chopped fresh flat-leaf
    parsley, plus more for garnish
¾ teaspoon black pepper
1 large egg, beaten
1 teaspoon water
Cooking spray**

1. Place 3½ cups flour, 1½ teaspoons salt, and baking powder in a food processor; pulse until combined. Stir together 10 tablespoons ice-cold water and ⅔ cup oil. With processor running, slowly pour water-and-oil mixture through food chute, processing until dough is crumbly. Turn dough out onto a lightly floured surface. Knead 1 minute. Press into a 5-inch disk; wrap in plastic wrap, and chill 30 minutes.
2. Preheat oven to 400°F. Heat 1 tablespoon oil in a large nonstick skillet over medium-high. Add chicken; cook, stirring often, until no

longer pink, about 5 minutes. Place chicken and pan drippings in a bowl.
3. Without wiping pan, heat remaining 1 tablespoon oil over medium-high; add haricots verts, carrot, thyme, and garlic; cover, and cook, stirring occasionally, 5 minutes or until tender. Add chicken and drippings back to pan; stir in peas. Sprinkle with remaining 2 tablespoons flour; stir to coat. Add stock and bring to a boil; cook 3 to 4 minutes or until thickened. Fold in parsley, pepper, and remaining 1½ teaspoons salt.
4. Whisk together egg and 1 teaspoon water in a bowl. Remove dough from refrigerator; let stand 5 minutes. Divide dough into 12 equal portions (about 2 ounces each), shaping each into a ball. Roll each ball into a 6-inch circle on a lightly floured surface. Spoon ⅓ cup chicken mixture onto center of each circle. Brush edges of dough circles with egg wash; fold dough over filling to form half-moons. Press edges together to seal. Brush remaining egg mixture over tops of pies and score tops to vent, or follow freezing instructions. Line a baking sheet with parchment paper; lightly coat paper with cooking spray. Place pies on prepared pan.
5. Bake at 400°F for 22 to 25 minutes or until crust is lightly browned. Top with additional parsley, if desired. Serves 12 (serving size: 1 pie)

CALORIES 347; FAT 20.2g (sat 3.5g, mono 12.7g, poly 3.0g); PROTEIN 17g; CARB 24g; FIBER 4g; SUGARS 1g (est. added sugars 0g); CHOL 57mg; IRON 2mg; SODIUM 628mg; CALC 42mg

HOW TO

FREEZE
Freeze on a baking sheet for 12 hours or until solid. Transfer to a ziplock plastic freezer bag; freeze up to 6 months.

THAW
Not necessary! Bake straight from frozen.

REHEAT
Place frozen pies on a parchment paper-lined baking sheet. Brush with egg wash; score. Bake at 450°F for 32 minutes.

GET YOUR GOAT

Bright-flavored, smooth, tangy, and spreadable, goat cheese is a treat on its own. But it also shines in a simple olive oil, garlic, and herb marinade. Serve over toasted baguette slices.

**Gluten Free • Kid Friendly
Make Ahead • Vegetarian**

Marinated Goat Cheese

Hands-on: 15 min. Total: 8 hr. 55 min.

**1½ tablespoons chopped fresh thyme
1½ tablespoons chopped fresh chives
1 tablespoon chopped fresh rosemary
½ teaspoon crushed red pepper
2 garlic cloves, smashed
1 (3- x 1-inch) strip lemon rind
2 cups extra-virgin olive oil
1 (12-ounce) log fresh plain goat
    cheese**

1. Combine first 7 ingredients in a small saucepan over low; cook 20 minutes. Let oil mixture cool to room temperature in pan.
2. Slice cheese log into 24 (¼-inch-thick) rounds. Pour some of the cooled oil mixture into a 13- x 9-inch glass or ceramic baking dish to cover bottom. Place cheese rounds in dish in a single layer. Pour remaining oil mixture over cheese to cover, distributing herbs and pepper on top of cheese rounds. Cover pan with plastic wrap; refrigerate 8 hours or overnight. Serve cheese with a slotted spoon, reserving oil for another use. Serves 12 (serving size: 2 marinated cheese rounds)

CALORIES 92; FAT 7.8g (sat 4.4g, mono 2.7g, poly 0.3g); PROTEIN 5g; CARB 0g; FIBER 0g; SUGARS 0g; CHOL 13mg; IRON 1mg; SODIUM 130mg; CALC 42mg

FOR THE LOVE OF COD

Maine chef Justin Walker shares his son's most-requested home-cooked dish, a bright, fresh mélange of spring veggies and mild, flaky fish.

So this is a Walker family fave?
This dish was one of the few things my son would eat when he was 1½. And it had to be seasoned just right, and have lots of olive oil.

This particular version feels like spring on a plate. How do you achieve that?
These are classic spring components—spring onions, fennel, fresh herbs—that we love to use coming out of the winter. This dish is healthy. And it's not complicated; it doesn't take hours of prep.

Any tips for cooking cod to perfection?
Cod in particular is a very lean fish, so you need to cook it slowly and gently. The moist heat in this recipe keeps it from drying out. Cook it to just before it's completely done, and then let the residual heat finish it—it'll be absolutely perfect that way.

**Staff Favorite • Gluten Free
Kid Friendly**

Cod with Fennel and Fingerling Potatoes

Hands-on: 15 min. Total: 48 min.

3 cups purple Peruvian and banana fingerling potatoes, halved lengthwise
¼ cup extra-virgin olive oil
½ cup thinly sliced fennel bulb
½ cup thinly sliced spring onions, green and white parts
2 tablespoons minced fresh garlic
1 tablespoon chopped fresh tarragon
1¼ teaspoons kosher salt, divided
½ teaspoon black pepper, divided
½ cup dry white wine
½ cup unsalted chicken stock (such as Swanson)
2 Meyer lemon slices
6 (6-ounce) cod loin fillets
Meyer lemon wedges (optional)

1. Place potatoes in a small saucepan; cover with cold water by 1 inch. Place pan over medium-high; bring to a simmer and cook 1 minute or until potatoes are not quite fully tender. Drain well; sprinkle with ¼ teaspoon salt and set aside.
2. Heat oil in a large skillet over medium-high. Add fennel, onions, garlic, tarragon, ½ teaspoon salt, and ¼ teaspoon pepper; sauté 4 minutes or until vegetables are tender. Add wine, stock, and lemon slices; bring to a simmer. Sprinkle cod with remaining ½ teaspoon salt and remaining ¼ teaspoon pepper. Add potatoes and cod to pan, nestling cod into sauce. Cover, reduce heat, and simmer 5 minutes or until fish is done. Divide potato mixture evenly among 6 bowls; top each serving with 1 fish fillet. Serve with lemon wedges, if desired. Serves 6 (serving size: about ½ cup potato mixture and 1 cod fillet)

CALORIES 293; FAT 10.5g (sat 1.5g, mono 7.4g, poly 1.3g); PROTEIN 32g; CARB 14g; FIBER 3g; SUGARS 2g (est. added sugars 0); CHOL 73mg; IRON 1mg; SODIUM 508mg; CALC 44mg

LET'S GET SIPPING

A SIPPER FOR SPRING

We give the Gin Rickey a seasonal twist with ripe strawberries. Full fruit flavor balanced by bracing gin and spritzy soda water is a tasty way to ring in spring.

**Quick & Easy • Gluten Free
Make Ahead • Vegetarian**

Strawberry-Lime Rickey

Hands-on: 5 min. Total: 7 min.
At its core, gin is essentially juniper-flavored vodka. London Dry gins like Beefeater feature strong piney flavor and a hint of citrus—they work nicely in a rickey and other classic gin cocktails. A more botanically brewed brand like Hendrick's suits the fruit here just fine.

⅔ cup hulled strawberries, quartered
2 teaspoons sugar
1 lime
3 ounces gin
½ cup chilled soda water

1. Combine strawberries and sugar in a pint glass. Cut lime in half. Slice one half into quarters; add quarters to strawberry mixture. Squeeze juice of other lime half into strawberry mixture; discard squeezed lime. With a muddler or wooden spoon, muddle strawberry mixture until well blended and sugar has dissolved. Add gin to glass; cover and shake well for 30 seconds. Pour strawberry mixture through a strainer evenly into 2 glasses. Add ice to each glass; top each glass with ¼ cup soda water. Serves 2 (serving size: about ⅔ cup)

CALORIES 126; FAT 0.2g (sat 0g, mono 0g, poly 0.1g); PROTEIN 0g; CARB 6g; FIBER 1g; SUGARS 6g (est. added sugars 4g); CHOL 0mg; IRON 0mg; SODIUM 14mg; CALC 14mg

FROZEN GREEN PEAS

Pop into dishes for fresh color and sweet flavor.

**Quick & Easy • Gluten Free
Kid Friendly • Make Ahead
Vegetarian**
Green Pea and Parsley Hummus
Place 1⅓ cups thawed frozen green peas, ½ cup chopped fresh flat-leaf parsley, ½ cup tahini, ¼ cup warm water, 2 Tbsp. extra-virgin olive oil, 2 Tbsp. fresh lemon juice, ¾ tsp. kosher salt, and 2 chopped garlic cloves in a mini food processor; process until smooth. (Blend in more water, 1 Tbsp. at a time, if hummus is too thick.) Serve with raw vegetables. Serves 8 (serving size: ¼ cup)

CALORIES 139; **FAT** 11.5g (sat 1.6g, mono 5.5g, poly 3.9g); **PROTEIN** 4g; **CARB** 7g; **FIBER** 2g; **SUGARS** 1g \(est. added sugars 0g); **CHOL** 0mg; **IRON** 1mg; **SODIUM** 212mg; **CALC** 33mg

**Staff Favorite • Quick & Easy
Kid Friendly • Vegetarian**
Indian-Spiced Pea Fritters
Combine 1½ cups coarsely mashed thawed frozen green peas, ¾ cup whole-wheat panko, ½ cup chopped green onions, 1 tsp. garam masala, ¾ tsp. kosher salt, ¼ tsp. ground red pepper, and 2 large eggs. Heat 2 Tbsp. canola oil in a nonstick skillet over medium-high. Scoop mixture by ¼-cupfuls into pan to form 4 fritters; cook 3 minutes per side. Repeat. Serve with ¼ cup plain 2% reduced-fat Greek yogurt. Serves 4 (serving size: 2 fritters and 1 Tbsp. yogurt)

CALORIES 268; **FAT** 17.4g (sat 2g, mono 9.8g, poly 4.5g); **PROTEIN** 9g; **CARB** 19g; **FIBER** 4g; **SUGARS** 4g (est. added sugars 0g); **CHOL** 94mg; **IRON** 2mg; **SODIUM** 477mg; **CALC** 50mg

Quick & Easy • Gluten Free
Cod with Herbed Pea Relish
Combine 1 cup thawed frozen green peas, 1½ Tbsp. chopped fresh oregano, 2 Tbsp. chopped shallots, 2 Tbsp. capers, 2 Tbsp. fresh lime juice, 2 Tbsp. olive oil, ¼ tsp. kosher salt, and ¼ tsp. crushed red pepper. Sprinkle ¼ tsp. kosher salt over 4 (6-oz.) cod fillets. Heat a nonstick skillet over medium-high. Add 1 Tbsp. olive oil and cod; cook 4 minutes per side. Serves 4 (serving size: 1 fillet and ¼ cup relish)

CALORIES 224; **FAT** 11g (sat 1.6g, mono 7.5g, poly 1.4g); **PROTEIN** 24g; **CARB** 7g; **FIBER** 2g; **SUGARS** 2g (est. added sugars 0g); **CHOL** 67mg; **IRON** 1mg; **SODIUM** 485mg; **CALC** 32mg

**Quick & Easy • Kid Friendly
Vegetarian**
Pasta with Pea Puree
Cook 8 oz. whole-grain linguine per directions. Drain, reserving ½ cup pasta water. Cook 2½ Tbsp. butter in a skillet over medium until browned. Place browned butter, 1 cup thawed frozen green peas, ½ cup pasta water, ½ cup fresh mint leaves, 1 tsp. lemon rind, ¾ tsp. kosher salt, and 1 garlic clove in a food processor, and process until smooth; toss with pasta. Top with ¼ cup shaved Parmesan. Serves 4 (serving size: 1 cup)

CALORIES 303; **FAT** 10.7g (sat 5.8g, mono 2.4g, poly 0.4g); **PROTEIN** 13g; **CARB** 45g; **FIBER** 8g; **SUGARS** 4g (est. added sugars 0g); **CHOL** 24mg; **IRON** 4mg; **SODIUM** 552mg; **CALC** 103mg

WOW!

**Quick & Easy • Gluten Free
Kid Friendly • Make Ahead
Vegetarian**

Grilled Pineapple Lemonade

Hands-on: 20 min. Total: 30 min.
This twist on classic lemonade is the divine union of fruity and smoky flavors. Naturally sweet pineapple goes into the drink, allowing us to use less added sugar. We use an indoor grill pan, but if your outdoor grill is already fired up, use it to lend extra smoky depth. Add a boozy spin with a dash of rum or tequila.

6 ounces fresh pineapple, sliced
4 cups hot water
3 tablespoons granulated sugar
³/₄ cup fresh lemon juice (4 large lemons)

1. Heat a grill pan over medium-high. Add pineapple slices in a single layer, and cook 5 to 6 minutes on each side, until dark char marks appear. Set grilled pineapple slices aside to cool.
2. Combine 4 cups hot water and sugar in a large pitcher, and stir with a whisk until sugar is dissolved.
3. Place pineapple and lemon juice in a blender; process until relatively smooth.
4. Pour pineapple mixture through a fine-mesh strainer into pitcher with sugar mixture; discard solids. Stir well until fully blended. Serve over ice. Serves 6 (serving size: about 1 cup)

CALORIES 45; **FAT** 0.1g; **PROTEIN** 0g; **CARB** 12g; **FIBER** 0g; **SUGARS** 10g (est. added sugars 6g); **CHOL** 0mg; **IRON** 0mg; **SODIUM** 7mg; **CALC** 10mg

MEXICAN VEGETABLE COOKING

At its roots, Mexican cooking is one of the world's most plant-forward cuisines. Culinary ambassador Margarita Carrillo Arronte shares the key ingredients and time-honored techniques to make smoky salsas, satisfying veggie tacos, and saucy enchiladas sing with bold flavor.

There are many misconceptions in the U.S. about Mexican food. This idea that it's greasy, unhealthy, cheap—that's absolutely wrong," says Margarita Carrillo Arronte. For more than 30 years, Carrillo has extolled the virtues of true Mexican cuisine as a restaurateur, author, TV host, and indefatigable ambassador. "We have a real treasure in our food, and it's completely mingled with the culture."

In fact, many plant-based cornerstones of the global kitchen are native to Mexico: corn, beans, chiles, tomatoes, avocados, even chocolate and vanilla. "We didn't have any chicken, pork, sheep, cows—all of that was brought by the Spaniards," says Carrillo. "We had turkey and wild rabbits, but no dairy animals, which is why many inhabitants of this part of the world are intolerant to lactose."

Today, produce remains at the heart of Mexican cuisine. The complex sauces that often take center stage aren't enriched with butter and cheese, but with fresh and dried chiles, nuts, and seeds. Mexican cooks use chiles more for flavor than fire. Unlike cuisines that have adapted to accommodate vegetarian diets, the reverse is true in Mexico, says Carrillo. "Mexico had a very developed cuisine when the Spanish came, and lots of our cuisine was vegetarian. The more indigenous you go, the more vegetarian the dishes."

Besides ingredients, there are certain techniques that are key to Mexican flavors. Nixtamalization, the process by which corn is soaked in an alkaline solution to make it more digestible and nutritious (and easily ground into masa for tortillas), originated in Mesoamerica millennia ago; this process is a daily part of the Mexican diet. Early cooks pounded sauces in lava-stone mortars called *molcajetes*, but blenders are a huge time-saver, even if some say the flavors aren't quite the same.

The process of dry roasting is so common, especially in preparing chiles, tomatoes, tomatillos, onions, and garlic, that it has its own word in Mexico: *tatemado*. It creates concentrated, lightly charred flavors that enhance almost every recipe here.

Mastering these techniques will broaden your perceptions of Mexican food and give you flexibility in the kitchen—most vegetables go with most sauces, and you can tuck almost anything into a tortilla, after all.

MEXICAN PANTRY

1 / CILANTRO
Strong, sweet-sour, and citrusy flavor. Lends bright, clean freshness.

2 / CORN TORTILLAS
Ubiquitously used as a wrap for fillings. The most authentic house-made tortillas have undergone nixtamalization (see info at left). For store-bought, we like La Tortilla Factory.

3 / WHITE ONION
A fundamental staple in Mexican cooking. Because they're milder than yellow onions, they're also ideal for raw garnishes.

4 / JICAMA
This root veggie, with a crunchy raw texture and lightly sweet, mild flavor, brings textural interest to many Mexican dishes.

5 / TOMATILLOS
Small, green, husk-wrapped relatives of the tomato. Mostly used cooked, they deliver bright, zippy tang to salsas—especially salsa verde—and stews.

6 / DRIED MEXICAN OREGANO
A relative of lemon verbena, it's very different from Mediterranean oregano—more pungent and grassy and less sweet.

7 / QUESO FRESCO
Translated as "fresh cheese," it's crumbly, salty, and mildly tangy.

8 / CANNED CHIPOTLES IN ADOBO
Dried smoked jalapeño peppers in a tangy tomato puree. Their deep flavor lends an umami note to veggie dishes.

This salsa's smoky flavor comes as much from the *tatemado* technique of charring the vegetables as from the smoked chipotle chiles.

Gluten Free • Make Ahead
Freezable • Vegetarian

Salsa Chipotle

Hands-on: 10 min. Total: 20 min.
Charring the veggies brings complexity to this simple sauce. You can also blacken them in a dry cast-iron skillet set over high heat, turning occasionally. The tomato skins will be easy to remove once they've charred.

8 ounces plum tomatoes
$1/2$ medium-sized white onion, cut into $1/2$-inch-thick slices
2 garlic cloves
1 tablespoon chopped canned chipotle chile in adobo sauce
$1/2$ teaspoon kosher salt
$1/4$ teaspoon granulated sugar
1 tablespoon olive oil

1. Preheat broiler to high with oven rack 6 inches from heat. Place tomatoes, onion, and garlic on a broiler pan; broil for 8 minutes or until mostly blackened, turning occasionally. Peel tomatoes; discard peels. Place tomatoes in a blender. Add onion mixture, including juices, to blender. Add chipotle, salt, and sugar; cover with blender lid, and let mixture stand 5 minutes. Process until very smooth, stopping occasionally to scrape down sides.
2. Heat oil in a medium skillet or saucepan over medium; carefully add the tomato sauce (sauce will splatter). Cook 5 minutes or until salsa thickens, stirring occasionally. Cool and serve. Serves 8 (serving size: about 2 tablespoons)

CALORIES 26; FAT 1.9g (sat 0.2g, mono 1.2g, poly 0.2g); PROTEIN 0g; CARB 2g; FIBER 0g; SUGARS 1g (est. added sugars 1g); CHOL 0mg; IRON 0mg; SODIUM 132mg; CALC 6mg

Quick & Easy • Vegetarian

Purslane in Green Salsa

Hands-on: 30 min. Total: 30 min.
While purslane's gently tart flavor and soft, slightly succulent texture make it distinct, a mix of torn watercress, spinach, and chard in equal portions will give you a similar taste.

5 cups water
1 pound tomatillos, husked and rinsed
2 serrano chiles, stemmed and seeded
$1/2$ large white onion, coarsely chopped
3 garlic cloves
1 cup chopped fresh cilantro, divided
3 tablespoons canola oil
2 pounds purslane, stemmed
$1/2$ teaspoon kosher salt

1. Bring 5 cups water to a boil in a large saucepan. Add tomatillos, chiles, onion, and garlic; cook 5 minutes or until tender. Drain well; place tomatillo mixture in a blender. Add $1/2$ cup cilantro; process until smooth, stopping to scrape down sides.
2. Heat oil in a deep skillet or saucepan over medium-high. Carefully add tomatillo sauce (it will splatter); bring to a simmer. Reduce heat to medium. Add purslane; cook 2 minutes or until just wilted, stirring constantly. Stir in salt and remaining $1/2$ cup cilantro. Serves 6 (serving size: about $3/4$ cup)

CALORIES 122; FAT 8.4g (sat 0.6g, mono 4.6g, poly 2g); PROTEIN 4g; CARB 11g; FIBER 2g; SUGARS 4g (est. added sugars 0g); CHOL 0mg; IRON 4mg; SODIUM 231mg; CALC 111mg

The salsa verde that flavors the purslane would make a terrific table salsa; just leave out the leaves.

In Mexico City's Narvarte neighborhood, most of the taquerias offer a version of this spicy, nutty sauce.

Quick & Easy • Gluten Free
Make Ahead • Freezable
Vegetarian

Peanut Salsa

Hands-on: 10 min. Total: 40 min.
Pair this rich salsa with grilled shrimp, pork, or poultry.

3 dried pasilla or guajillo chiles (about $1^{1}/2$ ounces), stemmed and seeded
2 dried ancho chiles (about $1^{1}/2$ ounces), stemmed and seeded
$3/4$ cup chopped white onion
3 cups boiling water
1 cup unsalted dry-roasted peanuts
1 tablespoon light brown sugar
$1^{1}/2$ teaspoons kosher salt
$1^{1}/2$ cups water

1. Heat a large skillet over medium-high. Add chiles; cook 90 seconds or until fragrant. Place chiles in a heatproof bowl; add onion. Cover with 3 cups boiling water; let stand 30 minutes. Drain well; place in blender. Add peanuts, sugar, salt, and $1^{1}/2$ cups water; process until smooth, stopping to scrape down sides. Serves 24 (serving size: about 2 tablespoons)

CALORIES 52; FAT 3g (sat 0.5g, mono 1.6g, poly 0.6g); PROTEIN 2g; CARB 4g; FIBER 1g; SUGARS 1g (est. added sugars 1g); CHOL 0mg; IRON 0mg; SODIUM 122mg; CALC 10mg

Hibiscus-Stuffed Chiles with Walnut Sauce

Hands-on: 35 min. Total: 1 hr. 25 min.
Traditional chiles en nogada use a pork filling, but hibiscus flowers—typically used in a tart drink—make a surprisingly hearty filling. You can find them at Mexican grocers and specialty stores like Trader Joe's. Mexican cooks often use fresh green walnuts, briefly available in autumn, which have a creamier texture and less bitterness; standard walnuts work well, too. We add a touch of sugar to the sauce here to balance the slight bitterness of the nuts.

Sauce:
1¼ cups roasted unsalted walnut halves
3 ounces goat cheese or fresh ricotta cheese (about ¾ cup)
1 tablespoon white wine vinegar
1½ teaspoons dry sherry
1½ teaspoons granulated sugar
½ teaspoon kosher salt
⅓ cup plus 2 tablespoons fat-free milk, divided
Chiles:
8 large poblano chiles
Cooking spray
1 cup dried hibiscus flowers (also known as Jamaica), rinsed and drained
1½ teaspoons olive oil
2 cups chopped white onion
1 tablespoon dried Mexican oregano leaves, crumbled
6 garlic cloves, minced
2 cups chopped tomato
2 cups grated peeled jicama
½ cup grated peeled carrot
1 tablespoon chopped canned chipotle chile in adobo sauce
½ teaspoon kosher salt
Dash of ground cinnamon
3½ cups cooked long-grain white rice, at room temperature
½ cup loosely packed fresh cilantro leaves
2 tablespoons pomegranate arils

1. To make sauce, place walnuts in a bowl; cover with boiling water. Let walnuts soak 15 minutes. Drain, and rub walnuts with a clean dish towel to remove as much walnut skin as possible. Discard skins.
2. Place walnuts, cheese, vinegar, sherry, sugar, salt, and ⅓ cup milk in a blender; process until smooth. (Sauce will be very thick, more scoopable than pourable.) Stir in remaining milk, 1 tablespoon at a time, to thin sauce, if desired.
3. To make chiles, preheat broiler to high with oven rack 6 inches from heat. Place chiles on a baking sheet; coat chiles with cooking spray. Broil 10 minutes or until blistered on all sides, but not completely charred, turning after 5 minutes; place in a bowl; cover tightly with plastic wrap. Reduce oven to 400°F.
4. Bring a small saucepan of water to a boil over high. Add hibiscus flowers; remove from heat. Let stand 30 minutes. Drain flowers well; coarsely chop.
5. Heat oil in a large skillet over high. Add onion; sauté 2 minutes or until lightly browned. Reduce heat to medium-high. Add oregano and garlic; sauté 5 minutes. Increase heat to high; stir in tomato, jicama, carrot, chipotle, salt, and cinnamon. Bring to a simmer, and cook, stirring occasionally, until liquid is absorbed, about 2 minutes. Place tomato mixture in a large bowl; cool 10 minutes. Stir in chopped hibiscus and rice. Cool to room temperature.
6. Remove chiles from bowl. Peel; discard skins. Using scissors, cut a slit lengthwise in each chile. (Do not cut through the opposite side of the chile.) Remove and discard seeds.
7. Stuff each chile with about 1 cup rice mixture. Place stuffed chiles, cut sides up, on an aluminum foil–lined baking sheet coated with cooking spray. Bake at 400°F for 15 minutes or until filling is heated through. Place 1 stuffed poblano on each of 8 plates. Top each with about 2 tablespoons walnut sauce. Sprinkle evenly with cilantro and pomegranate arils. Serves 8

CALORIES 363; **FAT** 16.1g (sat 3g, mono 3.1g, poly 9g); **PROTEIN** 10g; **CARB** 47g; **FIBER** 6g; **SUGARS** 13g (est. added sugars 5g); **CHOL** 5mg; **IRON** 2mg; **SODIUM** 333mg; **CALC** 110mg

Esquites (Corn Salad)
(pictured on page 220)

Hands-on: 20 min. Total: 30 min.
Roasting the corn under the broiler adds a little smoky flavor and also a "meatier" texture, more like the corn used in Mexico, which is less sugar-sweet than ours. You can also grill the corn over high heat.

6 ears fresh corn
¼ cup chopped fresh cilantro
2 tablespoons fresh lime juice
2 tablespoons canola mayonnaise
2 serrano chiles, stemmed, seeded, and minced
1 ounce Cotija or feta cheese, finely crumbled (about ¼ cup)

1. Preheat broiler to high with oven rack 6 inches from heat. Place corn on a broiler pan or rimmed baking sheet; broil 8 minutes or until blackened in spots, turning once or twice. Cool. Cut kernels from cobs to equal about 3 cups; place kernels in a large bowl. Add cilantro, juice, mayonnaise, chiles, and cheese; toss well to coat. Serve salad chilled or at room temperature. Serves 6 (serving size: about ½ cup)

CALORIES 93; **FAT** 3.6g (sat 1.2g, mono 1.4g, poly 0.9g); **PROTEIN** 3g; **CARB** 14g; **FIBER** 2g; **SUGARS** 5g (est. added sugars 0g); **CHOL** 6mg; **IRON** 0mg; **SODIUM** 104mg; **CALC** 34mg

Quick & Easy • Vegetarian

Creamy Poblano Tacos

(pictured on page 220)

Hands-on: 30 min. Total: 30 min.
Look for chayote in Mexican markets, or substitute zucchini.

6 large poblano chiles (about 1¹/₂ pounds)
2 tablespoons canola oil
1 medium-sized white onion, cut into ¹/₄-inch slices
1 tablespoon minced fresh garlic
¹/₃ cup Mexican crema or sour cream
³/₄ teaspoon kosher salt
12 (5-inch) corn tortillas, warmed
¹/₂ cup sliced radishes
1 ear corn, grilled and kernels removed
1 chayote, peeled, grilled, and diced (optional)

1. Preheat broiler to high with oven rack 6 inches from heat. Broil chiles 8 minutes or until blackened, turning frequently. Place in a bowl; cover with plastic wrap. Let stand 15 minutes. Peel, seed, and slice chiles into ¹/₄-inch-wide strips.
2. Heat oil in a skillet over medium-high. Add onion; sauté 5 minutes. Add sliced chiles and garlic; sauté 2 minutes. Stir in crema and salt; cook 1 minute. Divide chile mixture among tortillas; top with radishes, corn, and chayote, if using. Serves 6 (serving size: 2 tortillas and about 1 cup filling)

CALORIES 255; **FAT** 9g (sat 0.4g, mono 3g, poly 2.3g); **PROTEIN** 6g; **CARB** 44g; **FIBER** 6g; **SUGARS** 5g (est. added sugars 0g); **CHOL** 8mg; **IRON** 0mg; **SODIUM** 325mg; **CALC** 50mg

CREAMY POBLANO TACOS

Roasted poblano chiles are one of the most distinctive scents and tastes of the Mexican kitchen—irresistible when combined with cream or cheese.

MORELIA-STYLE ENCHILADAS

Enchiladas in Mexico are simply folded or rolled tortillas napped in a chile sauce, not the baked casserole as in the U.S.

Vegetarian

Morelia-Style Enchiladas

Hands-on: 40 min. Total: 40 min.

2 dried ancho chiles (about ³/₄ ounce), stemmed and seeded
2 dried guajillo chiles (about ¹/₂ ounce), stemmed and seeded
1 cup boiling water
2¹/₂ tablespoons canola oil, divided
¹/₂ medium-sized white onion, thinly sliced
2 garlic cloves, minced
¹/₂ tablespoon apple cider vinegar
1 teaspoon light brown sugar
¹/₂ teaspoon Mexican ground oregano
4¹/₂ cups water, divided
1¹/₄ teaspoons kosher salt, divided
1 large russet potato (about 8 ounces), cut into ¹/₄-inch-thick half-moons
1 large carrot (about 8 ounces), cut into ¹/₄-inch-thick half-moons
12 (5¹/₂-inch) corn tortillas
4 ounces queso fresco, crumbled (about 1 cup)
2 tablespoons Mexican crema or sour cream
³/₄ cup shredded cabbage
6 tablespoons diced white onion
6 tablespoons chopped fresh cilantro

1. Heat a large skillet over high; add chiles; cook 90 seconds or until fragrant, turning often. Place in a large heatproof bowl. Cover with 1 cup boiling water; let stand 30 minutes. Drain well; place chiles in a blender.
2. Heat 1¹/₂ teaspoons oil in a medium skillet over medium. Add onion and garlic; cook 20 minutes, stirring occasionally. Place onion mixture in blender; add vinegar, brown sugar, oregano, ¹/₂ cup water, and ³/₄ teaspoon salt; process until very smooth, stopping to scrape down sides. Pour mixture through a fine-mesh strainer into a bowl; discard solids. Return mixture to pan; bring to a simmer. Cook 5 minutes or until warm, stirring frequently.
3. Combine potato and remaining 4 cups water in a medium saucepan over high; bring to a boil. Add carrot; reduce heat to medium. Cook 10 minutes or until tender. Drain well; set aside.
4. Heat a large nonstick skillet over medium-high. Using tongs, place 2 tortillas in pan; cook 3 minutes or until dry, turning often. Dip tortillas lightly in chile mixture; place on a plate. Repeat process with remaining tortillas.
5. Heat a large nonstick skillet over medium-high. Add remaining 2 tablespoons oil. Add potato mixture, remaining chile mixture, and remaining ¹/₂ teaspoon salt; sauté 5 minutes or until vegetables are browned. Spoon 3 tablespoons potato mixture into each tortilla; fold in half. Place 2 enchiladas on each of 6 plates; sprinkle each enchilada with about 1 tablespoon cheese; top each serving with 1 teaspoon crema, 2 tablespoons cabbage, 1 tablespoon diced white onion, and 1 tablespoon cilantro. Serves 6 (serving size: 2 enchiladas)

CALORIES 356; **FAT** 14.7g (sat 2.8g, mono 6.5g, poly 3.4g); **PROTEIN** 11g; **CARB** 49g; **FIBER** 5g; **SUGARS** 5g (est. added sugars 1g); **CHOL** 16mg; **IRON** 1mg; **SODIUM** 581mg; **CALC** 187mg

SMOOTH OPERATOR

Look out, peanut butter: Tahini is the new pantry spread of our dreams. This creamy, rich sesame seed butter gives a nutty appeal to desserts and savory depth to soups, sauces, and marinades. Call it liquid gold in a jar.

Quick & Easy • Gluten Free
Make Ahead • Vegetarian

Tahini Sauce

Hands-on: 10 min. Total: 20 min.
We use chef Michael Solomonov's method of steeping fresh garlic in lemon juice to remove its bite and let the tahini shine through. Use this sauce to make a killer hummus. Blend it with a can of chickpeas, some water, olive oil, salt, and cumin until very smooth. We love it with toasted pita.

3 tablespoons fresh lemon juice
2 teaspoons minced fresh garlic
½ teaspoon kosher salt
½ cup tahini (sesame seed paste), well stirred
6 tablespoons ice water

1. Combine first 3 ingredients in a bowl; let stand 10 minutes. Add tahini to garlic mixture, stirring with a whisk to combine (mixture will be very thick). Add 6 tablespoons ice water, 2 tablespoons at a time, stirring after each addition until incorporated and sauce reaches desired consistency. Serves 16 (serving size: 1 tablespoon)

CALORIES 46; **FAT** 4g (sat 1.5g, mono 1.7g, poly 1g); **PROTEIN** 2g; **CARB** 0g; **FIBER** 0g; **SUGARS** 0g; **CHOL** 0mg; **IRON** 0mg; **SODIUM** 63mg; **CALC** 12mg

Vegetarian

Sesame-Ginger-Chickpea-Stuffed Sweet Potatoes

Hands-on: 40 min. Total: 1 hr. 40 min.
Sesame, especially toasted sesame oil, is a key flavor in many Asian cuisines. It makes sense that tahini would fit here too, especially as a finishing touch for roasted sweet potatoes with Sriracha.

4 medium-sized sweet potatoes (about 8 ounces)
1 teaspoon canola oil
1 (15-ounce) can unsalted chickpeas, rinsed and drained
2 teaspoons toasted sesame oil
1 teaspoon garlic powder
½ teaspoon kosher salt, divided
½ teaspoon ground ginger
3 tablespoons tahini (sesame seed paste), well stirred
1 teaspoon grated peeled fresh ginger
1 teaspoon grated fresh garlic
1 teaspoon rice vinegar
3 tablespoons hot water
4 teaspoons Sriracha chili sauce
2 teaspoons water
¼ cup thinly sliced green onions
½ teaspoon white and black sesame seeds

1. Preheat oven to 400°F.
2. Rub potatoes with canola oil; pierce liberally with a fork. Bake at 400°F for 1 hour or until tender. Cool. Split potatoes in half lengthwise. Gently score flesh with the tip of a knife.
3. Place chickpeas on a baking sheet; pat dry with paper towels. Add sesame oil; toss. Sprinkle with garlic powder, ¼ teaspoon salt, and ground ginger; toss. Bake at 400°F for 30 minutes, stirring every 10 minutes.
4. Combine tahini, fresh ginger, fresh garlic, and vinegar in a bowl. Add 3 tablespoons hot water; stir until loose and smooth.
5. Combine Sriracha and 2 teaspoons water in a bowl. Drizzle about 2 teaspoons tahini mixture over each sweet potato half; sprinkle with remaining ¼ teaspoon salt. Top with chickpea mixture, remaining tahini mixture, Sriracha mixture, green onions, and sesame seeds. Serves 4 (serving size: 2 stuffed sweet potato halves)

CALORIES 413; **FAT** 10.6g (sat 1.3g, mono 4.1g, poly 4.1g); **PROTEIN** 12g; **CARB** 69g; **FIBER** 12g; **SUGARS** 10g (est. added sugars 1g); **CHOL** 0mg; **IRON** 3mg; **SODIUM** 495mg; **CALC** 136mg

TIP

Make sure to stir tahini well in the jar before you measure (it should be pourable). If the paste is still too thick, add a splash of water to the jar and keep stirring until the mixture is loose and smooth.

Tahini-Marinated Chicken Thighs with Cucumber-and-Tomato Salad

Hands-on: 20 min. Total: 8 hr. 20 min.
Adding tahini to the marinade makes the chicken buttery tender without an overwhelming amount of sesame flavor in the finished dish. It also helps the chicken to char nicely on the grill.

Chicken:
1/4 cup tahini (sesame seed paste), well stirred
3 tablespoons finely chopped fresh flat-leaf parsley
3 tablespoons olive oil
3 tablespoons water
1 tablespoon finely chopped fresh rosemary
2 teaspoons grated lemon rind
2 tablespoons fresh lemon juice
1/2 teaspoon crushed red pepper
1 garlic clove, finely grated
1 small shallot, finely grated
8 skinless, boneless chicken thighs (about 1 1/2 pounds)
Cooking spray
1/2 teaspoon kosher salt
Salad:
1 1/2 cups chopped cucumber
1 1/2 cups chopped tomato
1 cup coarsely chopped fresh flat-leaf parsley
1/4 cup chopped fresh mint
1 tablespoon fresh lemon juice
1 teaspoon olive oil
1/4 teaspoon kosher salt
2 cups hot cooked brown rice

1. To prepare chicken, combine first 10 ingredients in a bowl. Place 1/4 cup tahini mixture in a small bowl; reserve. Place remaining tahini mixture and chicken in a large ziplock plastic bag; seal, turning to coat chicken.

Refrigerate 8 hours or overnight.
2. Preheat grill to medium (350°F to 450°F). Coat grill grate with cooking spray. Remove chicken from marinade; discard marinade. Sprinkle chicken with salt. Arrange chicken on grill grate; cover and cook 4 minutes on each side or until done. Arrange chicken on a platter; drizzle with reserved 1/4 cup tahini mixture.
3. To prepare the salad, combine cucumber and next 6 ingredients (through 1/4 teaspoon salt) in a bowl, and toss gently to combine. Serve cucumber salad with chicken and rice. Serves 4 (serving size: 2 chicken thighs, 1/2 cup salad, and 1/2 cup rice)

CALORIES 448; **FAT** 18.6g (sat 3.5g, mono 9g, poly 31g); **PROTEIN** 39g; **CARB** 31g; **FIBER** 4g; **SUGARS** 3g (est. added sugars 0g); **CHOL** 160mg; **IRON** 4mg; **SODIUM** 544mg; **CALC** 76mg

Lentil-Tahini Burgers with Pickled Cabbage

(pictured on page 219)

Hands-on: 30 min. Total: 50 min.
Look for steamed, vacuum-packed lentils in the grain aisle for the best texture in the burgers, or cook, drain, and refrigerate your own the night before.

2 cups finely shredded red cabbage (about 5 1/2 ounces)
3 tablespoons red wine vinegar
3/4 teaspoon kosher salt, divided
1 teaspoon sesame seeds
4 teaspoons olive oil, divided
1/2 cup finely chopped yellow onion
1/4 cup tahini (sesame seed paste), well stirred and divided
1/2 teaspoon ground cumin
1/2 teaspoon freshly ground black pepper

8 ounces precooked lentils (about 1 1/3 cups)
1/2 cup grated peeled carrot
1/4 cup chopped fresh cilantro
3 tablespoons plain 2% reduced-fat Greek yogurt
2 teaspoons fresh lemon juice
1/2 small garlic clove, grated
2 teaspoons water
4 (1 1/2-ounce) whole-wheat hamburger buns, toasted

1. Combine cabbage, vinegar, and 1/2 teaspoon salt in a bowl; let stand 20 minutes. Drain; stir in sesame seeds.
2. Heat 1 teaspoon oil in a skillet over medium-high. Add onion; sauté 3 minutes.
3. Place remaining 1/4 teaspoon salt, 2 tablespoons tahini, cumin, pepper, and lentils in a mini food processor; pulse 4 to 5 times or until coarsely chopped. Combine cooked onion, lentil mixture, carrot, and cilantro in a bowl. Divide and shape lentil mixture into 4 patties (3 ounces each).
4. Heat remaining 1 tablespoon oil in pan over medium-high. Add patties; cook 4 minutes on each side.
5. Combine remaining 2 tablespoons tahini, yogurt, juice, and garlic in a bowl. Stir in water, 1 teaspoon at a time, until sauce reaches desired consistency. Spread yogurt mixture over cut sides of buns; top bottom halves with patties, cabbage, and top halves of buns. Serves 4 (serving size: 1 burger)

CALORIES 349; **FAT** 15.5g (sat 2.3g, mono 6.9g, poly 5.1g); **PROTEIN** 13g; **CARB** 44g; **FIBER** 10g; **SUGARS** 8g (est. added sugars 2g); **CHOL** 1mg; **IRON** 4mg; **SODIUM** 748mg; **CALC** 116mg

TIP

Why does tahini turn to a gluey paste when liquid is added? Tahini is made of carbs, and carbs stick to water molecules like, well, glue. Keep slowly adding liquid and stirring; the sauce will start to absorb the liquid and smooth out.

Chocolate-Tahini Banana Bread

Hands-on: 10 min. Total: 1 hr. 20 min.
Bananas and peanut butter are a likely duo, but bananas and tahini? Mind-blowing. For those with nut allergies, tahini is a great, slightly more complex, substitute.

Cooking spray
**1½ cups mashed ripe banana
(about 3 bananas)**
**⅓ cup plain nonfat yogurt
(not Greek-style)**
**⅓ cup tahini (sesame seed paste),
well stirred**
**3 tablespoons unsalted butter,
melted**
1 teaspoon vanilla extract
2 large eggs
½ cup granulated sugar
½ cup packed light brown sugar
**6 ounces white whole-wheat flour
(about 1½ cups)**
¾ teaspoon baking soda
½ teaspoon kosher salt
**2 ounces bittersweet baking
chocolate, finely chopped**
1 teaspoon white sesame seeds
1 teaspoon black sesame seeds

1. Preheat oven to 350°F. Coat a 9- x 5-inch loaf pan with cooking spray.
2. Combine banana and next 5 ingredients in a bowl; beat with an electric mixer at medium speed. Add sugars; beat until combined.
3. Weigh or lightly spoon flour into dry measuring cups; level with a knife. Combine flour, baking soda, and salt in a bowl, stirring with a whisk. Add flour mixture to banana mixture; beat just until combined. Fold in chocolate. Pour batter into prepared pan; sprinkle with sesame seeds.
4. Bake at 350°F for 55 minutes or until a wooden pick inserted in the center comes out clean. Cool in pan 10 minutes on a wire rack. Remove bread from pan; cool completely. Serves 16 (serving size: 1 slice)

CALORIES 187; **FAT** 7.2g (sat 2.8g, mono 1.9g, poly 1.5g); **PROTEIN** 4g; **CARB** 28g; **FIBER** 2g; **SUGARS** 17g (est. added sugars 14g); **CHOL** 29mg; **IRON** 1mg; **SODIUM** 149mg; **CALC** 37mg

Tahini-Carrot Soup with Pistachios

Hands-on: 15 min. Total: 35 min.
Luscious, velvety carrot soup gets its body from tahini, not yogurt or cream. Tahini's ability to stand in for dairy makes it a go-to for vegans and those who keep kosher.

1 tablespoon olive oil
**1 large yellow onion, chopped
(about 2 cups)**
½ teaspoon kosher salt
½ teaspoon smoked paprika
¼ teaspoon ground turmeric
2 garlic cloves, chopped
1 pound carrots, peeled and chopped
**3 cups unsalted chicken or vegetable
stock (such as Swanson)**
**3 tablespoons tahini (sesame seed
paste), well stirred**
8 teaspoons Tahini Sauce (page 101)
**6 tablespoons unsalted pistachios,
coarsely chopped**
2 teaspoons fresh oregano leaves

1. Heat oil in a large Dutch oven over medium-high. Add onion; sauté 5 minutes. Stir in salt, paprika, turmeric, and garlic; cook 1 minute. Add carrots; cook 1 minute. Stir in stock; bring to a boil. Reduce heat to medium-low; cover and simmer 20 minutes or until carrots are tender.
2. Place carrot mixture and 3 tablespoons tahini in a blender. Remove center piece from blender lid (to allow steam to escape); secure lid on blender. Place a clean kitchen towel over opening in lid (to avoid splatters). Process until smooth. Place soup into each of 4 bowls. Drizzle 2 teaspoons Tahini Sauce over each serving. Top each serving with 1½ tablespoons pistachios and ½ teaspoon oregano leaves. Serves 4 (serving size: about 1¼ cups)

CALORIES 273; **FAT** 17.6g (sat 2.4g, mono 8.5g, poly 5.9g); **PROTEIN** 10g; **CARB** 23g; **FIBER** 6g; **SUGARS** 9g (est. added sugars 0g); **CHOL** 0mg; **IRON** 2mg; **SODIUM** 464mg; **CALC** 90mg

Tahini-Date Shake

Hands-on: 10 min. Total: 4 hr. 20 min.
Dates are naturally so sweet that using frozen yogurt in the shakes proved too cloying; we opt instead for plain whole-milk yogurt frozen in ice-cube trays.

**2 cups vanilla whole-milk yogurt
(not Greek-style)**
1 cup boiling water
**8 Medjool dates, pitted and chopped
(about ½ cup)**
1 cup crushed ice (about 6 ice cubes)
**¼ cup tahini (sesame seed paste),
well stirred**
¼ teaspoon ground cinnamon
⅛ teaspoon kosher salt

1. Spoon yogurt into an empty ice-cube tray; freeze 4 hours or overnight.
2. Place 1 cup boiling water and dates in a bowl; let stand 10 minutes.
3. Place date mixture in a blender; blend 30 seconds or until smooth. Add frozen yogurt cubes, crushed ice, tahini, cinnamon, and salt to blender; blend until smooth. Divide mixture among 4 glasses; chill 5 minutes before serving. Serves 4 (serving size: about ¾ cup)

CALORIES 273; **FAT** 12g (sat 3.6g, mono 3g, poly 3.5g); **PROTEIN** 7g; **CARB** 37g; **FIBER** 4g; **SUGARS** 14g (est. added sugars 0g); **CHOL** 15mg; **IRON** 1mg; **SODIUM** 125mg; **CALC** 211mg

THE ART OF THE SALAD

A beautiful salad is a master class in contrasts—think tart citrus with earthy-sweet beets, crunchy cucumber with creamy feta. Channeling six veggie-loving chefs, food editor Hannah Klinger creates five salads that are balanced, colorful, and brilliantly simple.

1. STICK TO THE SEASON

Keep salad combos seasonal by using what naturally grows together so peak produce can shine. "Salads are the perfect way to show off the bounty of the season or celebrate a beloved ingredient." —Suzanne Goin

Quick & Easy • Gluten Free Kid Friendly • Vegetarian

Spring Vegetable and Herb Salad

Hands-on: 15 min. Total: 20 min.
Asparagus, radishes, peas, and delicate herbs create a salad that celebrates the bounty of late spring.

1 cup radishes, halved lengthwise
1 cup (1-inch) pieces asparagus
1 (8-ounce) package sugar snap peas, trimmed
1½ tablespoons unsalted butter
1 teaspoon grated lemon rind
½ teaspoon kosher salt, divided
½ teaspoon black pepper, divided
2 cups loosely packed baby arugula
2 cups loosely packed fresh flat-leaf parsley leaves
1 cup torn fresh mint
1 tablespoon extra-virgin olive oil
5 teaspoons fresh lemon juice

1. Bring a large saucepan filled with water to a boil over medium-high. Add radishes, asparagus, and snap peas; cook 3 minutes or until crisp-tender. Drain. Plunge radish mixture into a bowl filled with ice water; let stand 2 minutes. Drain.
2. Heat a small saucepan over medium. Add butter to pan; cook 2 minutes or until lightly browned and fragrant. Remove pan from heat; stir in rind, ¼ teaspoon salt, and ¼ teaspoon pepper.
3. Combine arugula, parsley, and mint in a large bowl. Add remaining ¼ teaspoon salt, remaining ¼ teaspoon pepper, oil, and 1 tablespoon juice; toss. Arrange arugula mixture on a platter; top with radish mixture. Drizzle with butter mixture and remaining 2 teaspoons juice. Serve immediately. Serves 6 (serving size: about 1¼ cups)

CALORIES 89; **FAT** 5.6g (sat 2.2g, mono 2.5g, poly 0.5g); **PROTEIN** 3g; **CARB** 8g; **FIBER** 4g; **SUGARS** 3g (est. added sugars 0g); **CHOL** 8mg; **IRON** 3mg; **SODIUM** 192mg; **CALC** 86mg

2. KEEP IT SIMPLE

Resist the "kitchen sink" approach unless every item has a purpose. "I never like things to be mushed together. Every ingredient must have its own identity yet still work together as a whole." —Yotam Ottolenghi

Quick & Easy • Vegetarian

Beet, Lemon, and Walnut Salad

Hands-on: 10 min. Total: 1 hr. 10 min.

1 tablespoon sugar
2 large lemons, peeled and sectioned (about ¾ cup)
4 large beets, roasted and peeled (about 5 ounces each)
½ cup loosely packed fresh flat-leaf parsley leaves
¼ cup coarsely chopped walnuts, toasted
1½ ounces goat cheese, crumbled (about ⅓ cup)
2 tablespoons walnut or olive oil
⅜ teaspoon flaky sea salt (such as Maldon)
¼ teaspoon freshly ground black pepper

1. Combine sugar and lemon segments; let stand at room temperature 1 hour. Remove segments from bowl with a slotted spoon (reserve lemon juice mixture for another use).
2. Thinly slice beets crosswise into ⅛-inch-thick rounds. Arrange beet slices, lemon segments, and parsley on a large platter. Sprinkle with walnuts and goat cheese. Drizzle with oil. Sprinkle with salt and pepper. Serves 6 (serving size: about ½ cup)

CALORIES 147; **FAT** 9.4g (sat 1.8g, mono 1.9g, poly 5.3g); **PROTEIN** 4g; **CARB** 14g; **FIBER** 4g; **SUGARS** 9g (est. added sugars 2g); **CHOL** 3mg; **IRON** 1mg; **SODIUM** 254mg; **CALC** 44mg

3. CHOOSE A THEME

Carefully selected elements make a salad feel like a real dish, not an obligatory vegetable serving. "I have to choose an ethnicity. When flavors complement each other, it's more satisfying." —Jenn Louis

Staff Favorite • Gluten Free Vegetarian

Curried Cauliflower Salad with Yogurt

Hands-on: 40 min. Total: 50 min.
Composed salads are more thoughtful than fussy; this one couldn't be easier to assemble. They're also more about what's left out (no ubiquitous cherry tomatoes or carrots) than what's included. Every ingredient here fits the Indian-inspired theme.

¼ cup olive oil, divided
½ teaspoon kosher salt, divided
1 head cauliflower, cut into florets (about 6 cups)
1 teaspoon Madras curry powder
2 teaspoons unseasoned rice vinegar
1 cup plain low-fat yogurt (not Greek-style)
¼ cup unsalted pistachios, coarsely chopped
¼ cup golden raisins
¼ cup loosely packed fresh cilantro leaves

1. Preheat oven to 425°F.
2. Combine 2 tablespoons oil, ¼ teaspoon salt, and cauliflower in a large bowl; toss to coat. Spread cauliflower mixture in a single layer on a rimmed baking sheet. Bake at 425°F for 30 minutes or until browned and tender, stirring occasionally.
3. Heat remaining 2 tablespoons oil in a skillet over medium. Add curry powder; cook 1 minute, stirring frequently. Remove pan from heat; let stand 10 minutes. Stir in vinegar.
4. Spoon about 3 tablespoons yogurt onto each of 6 small plates; spread into an even layer with the back of a spoon. Top yogurt evenly with cauliflower; sprinkle with pistachios, raisins, and cilantro. Drizzle curry mixture evenly over salads; sprinkle with remaining ¼ teaspoon salt. Serves 6 (serving size: about ¾ cup)

CALORIES 181; FAT 12.3g (sat 2.1g, mono 8g, poly 1.7g); PROTEIN 6g; CARB 15g; FIBER 3g; SUGARS 9g (est. added sugars 0g); CHOL 2mg; IRON 1mg; SODIUM 222mg; CALC 109mg

4. STRIVE FOR BALANCE

Round out crunchy with soft, acidic with fatty, spicy with creamy. "I'll soften a hearty or bitter green with avocado, a creamy dressing, or a soft cheese." —Sara Jenkins

Quick & Easy • Kid Friendly

Kale-Buttermilk-Caesar with Frizzled Eggs

Hands-on: 20 min. Total: 20 min.
Classic salads like Caesar don't go out of style, but they can certainly be updated. We swap romaine for lacinato kale and use tangy buttermilk in place of mayo. A second hit of anchovy in the hot oil gives the croutons extra savory depth as they toast in the pan.

3½ tablespoons extra-virgin olive oil, divided
2 oil-packed anchovy fillets, drained and divided
3 ounces whole-grain bread, cut into ½-inch cubes (about 1½ cups)
1 garlic clove, finely chopped
½ teaspoon kosher salt, divided
¼ cup whole buttermilk
1 tablespoon fresh lemon juice
½ teaspoon Dijon mustard
½ teaspoon freshly ground black pepper, divided
6 large eggs
1 bunch lacinato kale, stemmed
½ ounce Parmesan cheese, shaved

1. Heat 1½ tablespoons oil in a large skillet over medium. Add 1 anchovy fillet to pan; cook 30 seconds or until anchovy has melted into the oil, stirring frequently. Add bread to pan; cook 3 minutes or until browned and toasted on all sides, stirring occasionally. Place croutons in a bowl. Remove pan from heat (do not wipe out pan).
2. Finely chop remaining anchovy fillet. Add garlic to anchovy on cutting board; sprinkle with ¼ teaspoon salt. Mash with the side of a knife to form a paste. Combine garlic mixture, 1½ tablespoons oil, buttermilk, juice, mustard, and ¼ teaspoon pepper in a small bowl, stirring with a whisk.
3. Heat remaining 1½ teaspoons oil in pan over medium. Crack eggs over pan; cook 3 minutes or until whites are set. Remove pan from heat.
4. Cut the larger kale leaves in half crosswise (leave any smaller leaves whole). Place kale in a large bowl; massage gently with your hands 1 minute or until slightly wilted. Drizzle half of buttermilk mixture over kale; toss. Divide kale mixture among 6 plates; top evenly with croutons, Parmesan, remaining buttermilk mixture, and eggs. Sprinkle eggs evenly with remaining ¼ teaspoon salt and remaining ¼ teaspoon pepper. Serves 6 (serving size: about 1¼ cups)

CALORIES 208; FAT 14.5g (sat 3.4g, mono 8g, poly 2.2g); PROTEIN 10g; CARB 9g; FIBER 2g; SUGARS 2g (est. added sugars 0g); CHOL 190mg; IRON 2mg; SODIUM 404mg; CALC 103mg

5. SEEK OUT CRUNCH

Just as a salad would be naked without dressing, it would be incomplete without crunch. "Texture plays a big role in creating a memorable salad, especially crunchy textures." —Scott Crawford

Quick & Easy • Gluten Free
Kid Friendly • Vegetarian

Crunchy Cucumber, Feta, and Almond Salad

Hands-on: 10 min. Total: 10 min.
Crunchy and crisp vegetables signify freshness—they taste as vibrant as they look. Fewer ingredients let you enjoy every kind of crunch without overwhelming the palate.

4 cups coarsely chopped romaine lettuce heart (about 1)
2½ cups (½-inch) diced English cucumber (about 1 medium)
½ cup unsalted roasted almonds, coarsely chopped
2 ounces feta cheese, crumbled (about ½ cup)
2 tablespoons chopped fresh dill
2 tablespoons extra-virgin olive oil
2 tablespoons white wine vinegar
1 teaspoon Dijon mustard
½ teaspoon kosher salt
½ teaspoon freshly ground black pepper

1. Combine lettuce, cucumber, almonds, and feta in a large bowl; toss. Combine dill and remaining ingredients in a small bowl, stirring with a whisk. Add dill mixture to lettuce mixture; toss to coat. Serves 8 (serving size: about 1½ cups)

CALORIES 110; FAT 9.5g (sat 1.9g, mono 5.6g, poly 1.5g); PROTEIN 3g; CARB 4g; FIBER 2g; SUGARS 2g (est. added sugars 0g); CHOL 6mg; IRON 1mg; SODIUM 203mg; CALC 73mg

LET'S GET COOKING

DRESS FOR SUCCESS

Few food upgrades are as easy as going from bottled salad dressing to homemade vinaigrette. Combine a few pantry staples together, and you've got an additive-free, lower-sodium dressing that keeps for a week or longer. There's more flavor (and fewer calories) in these than their store-bought counterparts; conventional vinaigrettes use up to four times as much oil as vinegar, while we use them in equal portions for extra zest.

Quick & Easy • Make Ahead
Vegetarian
Lemon Vinaigrette
Combine 6 Tbsp. extra-virgin olive oil, 6 Tbsp. fresh lemon juice, ½ tsp. kosher salt, and ½ tsp. freshly ground black pepper in a jar. Seal lid; shake well for 30 seconds or until blended. Add fresh chopped herbs, if desired. Serves 6 (serving size: 2 Tbsp.)

CALORIES 130; FAT 14g (sat 2g); SODIUM 160mg

Quick & Easy • Make Ahead
Vegetarian
Mustard-Chive Vinaigrette
Combine 6 Tbsp. extra-virgin olive oil, 6 Tbsp. fresh lemon juice, 2 Tbsp. chopped fresh chives, 1 Tbsp. Dijon mustard, ¼ tsp. kosher salt, and ¼ tsp. black pepper in a jar. Seal lid; shake well for 30 seconds or until blended. Serves 6 (serving size: 2 Tbsp.)

CALORIES 132; FAT 14.1g (sat 2g); SODIUM 140mg

Quick & Easy • Make Ahead
Vegetarian
Spicy Soy Vinaigrette
Combine 6 Tbsp. fresh lemon juice, 4 Tbsp. canola oil, 2 Tbsp. toasted sesame oil, 1 Tbsp. reduced-sodium soy sauce, 2 tsp. toasted sesame seeds, and 1 tsp. Sriracha chili sauce

in a jar. Seal lid; shake well for 30 seconds or until blended. Serves 6 (serving size: 2 Tbsp.)

CALORIES 133; FAT 14.3g (sat 1.4g); SODIUM 113mg

SPRING IN A BOWL

Atlanta chef and vegetable savant Steven Satterfield shows how to let the season's tender new produce shine.

What makes this dish so fresh, clean, and distinct from stewed, braised, or roasted winter dishes?
When you've been working with turnips and rutabagas for months, it's nice to have spring produce again—it's so tender. These spring veggies are great when shaved raw. Even some of the dense roots, like beets, that you'd always think to cook can be fantastic shaved.

It's one of those vegetarian recipes where you don't miss meat at all. How do you pull that off?
It's hearty, it's delicious, and it's satisfying. We've served it as a family meal [to staff] at Miller Union. The farro has a great nutty toothsome-ness. We try to serve vegetarian dishes that go beyond something like the grilled portobello mushroom as a burger dish you find on menus so often. A grilled portobello mushroom can be very good, but as a burger dish, it's often not very interesting.

We like using both beet root and greens in the same dish, an approach you take in your cookbook [*Root to Leaf*, Harper Collins, $45]. What's the thinking?
Arugula can work well in this dish also, but if you're going to use beets, use the tops if they're fresh. The flavor is great, and it's a good way to use the whole plant.

Spring Vegetable Grain Bowl

Hands-on: 30 min. Total: 50 min.
This dish is all about clean flavors and distinct textures. Farro provides satisfying chew, while the raw shaved veggies soften slightly in the vinaigrette to become perfectly crisp-tender. To blanch the peas, cook in boiling water for 1 minute or until crisp-tender, and then dunk in an ice bath for 1 minute to stop the cooking. A mandoline or vegetable peeler makes quick work of thinly slicing vegetables.

1½ cups uncooked farro
3 cups water
1¼ teaspoons kosher salt, divided
2 tablespoon extra-virgin olive oil
1 tablespoon sherry vinegar or white wine vinegar
½ cup roughly chopped beet greens or arugula
¼ cup blanched English peas
2 baby carrots, thinly sliced
1 green onion, thinly sliced
1 celery stalk, thinly sliced
1 small red beet, peeled and thinly sliced
2 ounces goat cheese, crumbled (about ½ cup)
¼ cup chopped fresh flat-leaf parsley

1. Combine farro, 3 cups water, and ¾ teaspoon salt in a small saucepan over medium-low; cook, covered, 25 minutes or until farro becomes tender. Place farro in a strainer; drain well.
2. Place hot farro in a large bowl. Add remaining ½ teaspoon salt, oil, vinegar, greens, peas, carrots, onion, celery, and beet; stir gently to combine. Top evenly with cheese and parsley. Serves 5 (serving size: about 1 cup)

CALORIES 344; FAT 9.9g (sat 2.5g, mono 4.9g, poly 0.6g); PROTEIN 11g; CARB 49g; FIBER 10g; SUGARS 2g (est. added sugars 0g); CHOL 5mg; IRON 3mg; SODIUM 572mg; CALC 64mg

WASTE LESS PRODUCE

10 smart ways to get the most from fresh fruits and veggies.

1. SAVE STALKS
Stalks from broccoli and cauliflower aren't just edible—they're eye-openingly delicious. Peel the tough outer layer from the stems (save peels for stock; see below), and then shave into salads, or sauté, roast, or steam them just as you would the florets.

2. PICKLE AND PRESERVE
Turn surplus veggies into a quick pickle to use throughout the week—or a sealed batch to last months. A simple brine of vinegar, salt, and sugar punched up with common pantry spices and fresh aromatics makes magic happen.

3. MAKE STOCK
Save tough outer peels and snipped parts of turnips, rutabagas, squash, and beans; mushroom stems; bell pepper scraps; and other odds and ends to make vegetable stock. Mix in some fresh-cut veggies to round out flavor and cut bitterness. Cover with water, and simmer 45 minutes.

4. GET TO KNOW YOUR CRISPER
Crispers on newer fridges are often humidity controlled, or designed for one bin to be high humidity (sometimes marked "vegetables") and the other low (marked "fruits"). Store vegetables that wilt or shrivel in the high-humidity drawer: celery, carrots, broccoli, cauliflower, green beans, beets, radishes, asparagus, and leafy greens. Berries are also good here, as they're very sensitive to ethylene. If your fridge doesn't have humidity controls, both drawers are high humidity. Use the top shelf for items that prefer low humidity, and keep them in ziplock bags with a few holes slit in them.

5. GIVE UGLY PRODUCE SOME LOVE
Buy misshapen "ugly" fruits and vegetables whenever you can. While not exactly ready for their close-up, they're just as tasty as their comelier counterparts. Think big picture: The more they sell, the less they'll be wasted nationwide. That's no small potatoes.

continued

6. USE SMART APPS

Clever apps like Ample Harvest (ampleharvest.org) connect you to food pantries where you can donate produce (great for people with backyard gardens). Others like Handpick (handpick.com) provide recipes that utilize exactly what you have on hand.

7. TRY SHOCK TREATMENT

Sometimes you can revive wilted greens, herbs, celery, and other items with a one-minute dip in an ice bath. If that doesn't work, turn unspoiled but wilting produce into a tasty mash or pureed soup.

8. FIRE IT UP

Toss citrus peels into your fireplace to infuse your home with a delicious aroma. Dried grapefruit, lemon, lime, and orange peels work great as kindling—their oils help ignite the wood.

9. START SAVING TOWARD A SMOOTHIE

Put any fruit leftovers—overripe peeled bananas, halves of apples and pears, uneaten grapes or berries—in a ziplock plastic bag in the freezer. When you have enough stored up, blend them into a smoothie.

10. SNACK AS YOU COOK

Toss potato, carrot, and parsnip peels with a little oil, salt, and pepper, and bake at 400°F for 10 minutes or until browned and crisp. They're delicious, and they also make great crunchy garnishes for soups and salads.

Quick & Easy • Vegetarian

Roasted Veggie Stalk Salad

Hands-on: 5 min. Total: 22 min.
Preheat oven to 425°F; place a sheet pan in oven. Toss 1 cup thinly sliced, peeled broccoli stems and 1 cup thinly sliced peeled cauliflower stems with 2 tsp. extra-virgin olive oil, ¼ tsp. kosher salt, and ¼ tsp. freshly ground black pepper. Place mixture on sheet pan; roast 18 minutes or until browned and tender. Toss with 2 tsp. red wine vinegar and 2 tsp. chopped fresh chives. Serve over mixed greens, if desired. Serves 4 (serving size: ⅓ cup)

CALORIES 40; **FAT** 3.6g (sat 0.5g); **SODIUM** 129mg

Make Ahead • Vegetarian

Quick Pickled Red Onion

Hands-on: 4 min. Total: 1 hr. 34 min.
Combine ½ cup water, ¼ cup apple cider vinegar, 2 tsp. brown sugar, 1 tsp. whole black peppercorns, ¾ tsp. kosher salt, ½ tsp. mustard seed, 1 star anise, and 1 garlic clove in a small saucepan; bring to a simmer. Pour vinegar mixture over 1 cup thinly sliced red onion and 1 fresh dill frond in a clean, heatproof jar. Cool. Cover and chill at least 1 hour or up to 2 weeks. Serves 12 (serving size: about 2 tsp.)

CALORIES 5; **FAT** 0g; **SODIUM** 37mg

NOTE FROM THE EDITOR

PASS THE PLANTS, PLEASE

In this business, I hear a lot of absurd judgments, like "kale is so last year." That's ridiculous, when you think about it: How can a delicious plant species like *Brassica oleracea* go out of style when less than one in five Americans are eating enough vegetables?

It's no secret that we should all be eating a more diverse plant-based diet filled with more fresh produce, nuts, seeds, and whole grains—and less meat—to hedge our nutritional bets against diet-related diseases.

For many screwed up reasons, convenient, affordable food in this country means highly processed food, which is exactly the opposite of how it should be. Make real, simple food, and take inspiration from cultures in Mexico, Greece, Italy, and Korea, where plant-based cuisines have nourished the masses on the cheap and served as preventive medicine for centuries. Stew a pot of fragrant beans; sauté fistfuls of greens with garlic and olive oil; make a hot pot with tofu, kimchi, and rich stock.

And hold the judgment, please. Shred some kale and anoint it with one of my go-to recipes: a garlicky, lemony dressing reinforced with anchovies, capers, and cumin. Even after I've spent hours smoking a pork shoulder or roasting a prime rib for a dinner party, it's this dressing that friends ask me to send them the next day. I've included it here for you.

Quick & Easy • Make Ahead

That Kale Salad Dressing

Hands-on: 15 min. Total: 15 min.
If you can find Meyer lemons, juice one and seed the other, chopping up the entire fruit to make a thicker, more vibrant sauce. This recipe makes enough to dress 2 bunches of shredded lacinato kale mixed with 1 cup of finely grated Parmesan.

4 anchovy fillets
2 garlic cloves
2 tablespoons drained capers
1 tablespoon Dijon mustard
½ teaspoon crushed red pepper
½ teaspoon ground cumin
¼ teaspoon kosher salt
¼ teaspoon black pepper
Grated rind and juice of 2 lemons
½ cup extra-virgin olive oil

1. Place first 3 ingredients in a mini food processor (or blender). Add remaining ingredients and process for 1 minute. Refrigerate in a sealed jar for up to 1 week. Serves 8 (serving size: about 2 tablespoons)

CALORIES 132; **FAT** 13.8g (sat 1.9g, mono 9.9g, poly 1.5g); **PROTEIN** 1g; **CARB** 2g; **FIBER** 0g; **SUGARS** 0g; **CHOL** 2mg; **IRON** 0mg; **SODIUM** 230mg; **CALC** 11mg

GROW. HARVEST. COOK.

GET SCHOOLED ON PEAS

Fresh peas are in season and at the market in early spring. Read on for gardening tips and shopping advice.

Quick & Easy • Kid Friendly
Make Ahead • Vegetarian

Pea Pappardelle Pasta

Hands-on: 10 min. Total: 15 min.
Sugar snaps, green peas, and pea shoots enrich this dish with sweet flavor and a bounty of pleasing textures. Look for pea shoots at your local farmers' market or Asian market, or substitute watercress.

6 ounces fresh sugar snap peas
8 ounces uncooked dried egg pappardelle pasta or fettuccine
1 cup shelled fresh or frozen green peas, thawed
3 tablespoons extra-virgin olive oil
1 teaspoon grated lemon rind
1 tablespoon fresh lemon juice
1/2 teaspoon kosher salt
1/4 teaspoon black pepper
1/8 teaspoon crushed red pepper
3/4 cup pea shoots
2 1/2 ounces ricotta salata or pecorino romano cheese, shaved (about 1 cup)
2 tablespoons torn fresh basil

1. Bring a large pot of water to a boil over high. Add snap peas, and cook until bright green, about 1 minute. Using a slotted spoon, place snap peas in a bowl of ice water. Add pasta to boiling water; cook for 4 minutes or until al dente, adding green peas during the last 30 seconds. Drain and cool for 5 minutes.

2. Drain snap peas, and cut in half diagonally.
3. In a large bowl, combine oil, rind, juice, salt, black pepper, and crushed red pepper. Stir with a whisk. Add pasta mixture, snap peas, and pea shoots; toss to coat. Top with cheese and basil. Serves 4 (serving size: 1 2/3 cups)

CALORIES 418; FAT 17.3g (sat 4.4g, mono 9.2g, poly 2.2g); PROTEIN 14g; CARB 51g; FIBER 5g; SUGARS 5g (est. added sugars 0g); CHOL 49mg; IRON 4mg; SODIUM 578mg; CALC 94mg

Quick & Easy • Gluten Free
Kid Friendly • Make Ahead
Vegetarian

Pea and Wasabi Dip

Hands-on: 5 min. Total: 5 min.
This blend is a zippy alternative to hummus; serve with crudités or crackers. Sweet green peas offset the kicky heat of wasabi (which you'll find on the Asian foods aisle).

2 cups fresh or frozen green peas, thawed
1/2 cup firmly packed fresh flat-leaf parsley leaves
1/3 cup extra-virgin olive oil
1 teaspoon grated lime rind
2 tablespoons fresh lime juice (about 1 lime)
3/4 teaspoon kosher salt
1/2 teaspoon wasabi paste
1/2 teaspoon sesame seeds

1. Place peas, parsley, oil, rind, juice, salt, and wasabi in a food processor; process for 1 minute, stopping to scrape down the sides as needed, until almost smooth. Place in a serving bowl; sprinkle with sesame seeds. Serves 8 (serving size: 3 tablespoons)

CALORIES 110; FAT 9.6g (sat 1.4g, mono 6.7g, poly 1.4g); PROTEIN 2g; CARB 5g; FIBER 2g; SUGARS 2g (est. added sugars 0g); CHOL 0mg; IRON 1mg; SODIUM 225mg; CALC 15mg

HOW TO SHOP

1. ACT FAST
The prime time for purchasing fresh peas is early spring. To relish the freshness and peak nutrition, snap them up quickly and prepare them ASAP, as their sweetness begins to decline as soon as pods are picked. At your own farmers' market, you can ask if peas were grown organically.

2. KNOW WHAT TO LOOK FOR
With sugar snap peas and garden (green) peas, look for bright, glossy pods with a "plump factor." For snow peas, seek out glossy pods that are flat, not plump, with crisp crunch.

3. KEEP COOL
Keep fresh shelled peas refrigerated if you can't enjoy them immediately. For garden peas, keep them in their pods and wait to shell until right before using in order to get the brightest flavor and texture.

HOW TO GROW

1. PICK A SUNNY SPOT
Use a tall trellis, or poke multibranched twigs deep into soil for a natural lattice. Clingy tendrils grasp vertical supports as pea plants climb up. Check the seed packet for plant height (bush or climbing), though all types benefit from support.

2. SOW WHEN IT'S COOL
Plant early, usually one month before the last frost date is forecast in your region. Soak seeds in lukewarm water overnight for a jump start. Sow seeds two to three weeks apart for a continuous crop.

3. GET READY TO PICK
Look for pods to harvest within two months, choosing firm, glossy green ones. Sugar snaps and garden peas should be plump, with large peas inside; pick snow peas when flat and crisp. Try the young tendrils and leaves—they're delicious in salads or lightly sautéed.

TAKE THE PIE ROAD

Our expert guide to creating healthy homemade pizza

As a country, we love our pizza. In fact, in 2014 the USDA reported about one in eight Americans eats pizza on any given day. But our love of pie typically comes loaded with too much saturated fat and sodium. Studies show that pizza ranks as one of the top three contributors of sodium to the American diet. Clocking in at an average of 750 calories per pizza-eating session, our favorite Netflix accompaniment has a reputation for being a hefty calorie-bomb, too. Until now, that is.

We like to think of pizza as a blank canvas that's full of healthy potential. Trying to eat more veggies? Pile them onto a pizza. A disk of dough is the perfect platform to showcase a bounty of fresh produce, lean proteins, and healthy oils. And perhaps the best news is that you have the power to maximize the nutritional value of your pizza by making a few healthy choices. From the whole-grain crust to the plant-based toppings, velvety cheese, and flurry of fresh herbs, these crave-worthy, handcrafted pizzas make skipping delivery easy as pie.

THE ROLE OF GLUTEN

Flour contains wheat proteins, which, when agitated in the presence of water, combine to form gluten, a protein that adds strength and pliability to dough. Dough without gluten is lower in protein and can fall apart more easily when not handled carefully.

Quick & Easy • Kid Friendly Vegetarian

Mushroom and Arugula Pizza

Hands-on: 15 min. Total: 30 min.
Mushrooms stand in for cured meat toppers, adding meaty, umami-rich flavor while shaving off sodium and saturated fat.

1 tablespoon olive oil
1 shallot, thinly sliced
2 cups sliced fresh cremini mushrooms
1½ cups sliced fresh portobello mushrooms
2 teaspoons minced fresh garlic
¼ teaspoon kosher salt, divided
12 ounces fresh deli whole-wheat pizza dough
1⅓ ounces goat cheese, crumbled (about ⅓ cup)
3 ounces part-skim mozzarella cheese, shredded (¾ cup)
1 cup packed arugula
1 teaspoon fresh lemon juice
1 teaspoon truffle oil (optional)

1. Place a pizza stone or baking sheet in oven. Preheat oven to 500°F. (Do not remove pizza stone while oven preheats.)
2. Heat oil in a large nonstick skillet over medium. Add shallots, and cook, stirring occasionally, until soft, 1 to 2 minutes. Add mushrooms and garlic; cook, stirring often, until liquid has almost evaporated, 5 to 6 minutes. Remove from heat. Sprinkle with ⅛ teaspoon salt, and set aside.
3. Roll dough into a 13-inch circle on a piece of parchment paper; pierce with a fork. Sprinkle goat cheese on top; spread mushroom mixture over cheese. Top with mozzarella.
4. Place dough (on paper) on preheated stone; bake at 500°F for 13 to 14 minutes.
5. Toss arugula with lemon juice. Top pizza with arugula mixture; drizzle with truffle oil, if desired, and sprinkle with remaining ⅛ teaspoon salt. Cut into 8 slices. Serves 4 (serving size: 2 slices)

CALORIES 339; **FAT** 15.4g (sat 4.5g, mono 8.5g, poly 1.4g); **PROTEIN** 15g; **CARB** 40g; **FIBER** 4g; **SUGARS** 2g (est. added sugars 0g); **CHOL** 18mg; **IRON** 1mg; **SODIUM** 661mg; **CALC** 197mg

Quick & Easy • Kid Friendly Vegetarian

Tomato-Ricotta Pizza

Hands-on: 15 min. Total: 35 min.

2 cups halved cherry tomatoes
1 tablespoon canola oil
12 ounces fresh deli whole-wheat pizza dough
¾ cup part-skim ricotta cheese
2 tablespoons refrigerated pesto
2 tablespoons 1% low-fat milk
1 garlic clove, grated
2 ounces feta cheese, crumbled (½ cup)
¼ cup torn fresh basil

1. Place a pizza stone or baking sheet in oven. Preheat oven to 500°F. (Do not remove while oven preheats.)
2. Combine tomatoes and oil on a foil-lined baking sheet. Bake at 500°F for 7 minutes.
3. Roll dough into a 13-inch circle on parchment paper; pierce with a fork. Place dough (on paper) on preheated stone. Bake at 500°F for 4 minutes.
4. Combine ricotta, pesto, milk, and garlic; spread over dough, leaving a ½-inch border. Sprinkle with feta. Bake at 500°F for 10 minutes.
5. Top with tomatoes. Bake at 500°F for 4 minutes. Top with basil. Cut into 8 slices. Serves 4 (serving size: 2 slices)

CALORIES 342; **FAT** 14.3g (sat 4.9g, mono 5.9g, poly 1.8g); **PROTEIN** 15g; **CARB** 43g; **FIBER** 4g; **SUGARS** 3g (est. added sugars 0g); **CHOL** 22mg; **IRON** 1mg; **SODIUM** 594mg; **CALC** 198mg

Quick & Easy • Kid Friendly
Vegetarian

Banh Mi Pizza

Hands-on: 20 min. Total: 35 min.

1 cup apple cider vinegar
1 cup water
1/2 cup granulated sugar
1/2 teaspoon kosher salt
1 cup matchstick-cut carrots
1/2 English cucumber, thinly sliced
1/3 cup thinly sliced radishes
1/2 fresh jalapeño, thinly sliced
12 ounces fresh deli whole-wheat
    pizza dough
1/2 teaspoon reduced-sodium soy
    sauce or tamari
1 1/2 tablespoons sesame oil, divided
5 ounces part-skim mozzarella
    cheese, shredded (about 1 1/4 cups)
1 1/2 tablespoons canola mayonnaise
1/2 teaspoon Sriracha chili sauce
1/2 cup loosely packed cilantro leaves

1. Place a pizza stone or baking sheet in oven. Preheat oven to 500°F. (Do not remove while oven preheats.)
2. Combine vinegar, 1 cup water, sugar, and salt in a saucepan. Bring to a simmer over medium-high; cook, stirring occasionally, until sugar and salt dissolve. Stir in carrots, cucumber, radishes, and jalapeño. Remove from heat; let stand 10 minutes. Drain and set aside.
3. Roll dough into a 13-inch circle on a piece of parchment paper; pierce with a fork. Brush soy sauce and 1 tablespoon sesame oil over dough. Place dough and paper on preheated stone. Bake at 500°F for 6 minutes.
4. Sprinkle mozzarella evenly over dough. Bake at 500°F for 5 minutes.
5. Combine mayonnaise, Sriracha, and remaining 1 1/2 teaspoons sesame oil.
6. Spread pickled vegetables over pizza; drizzle with mayo mixture. Sprinkle with cilantro. Cut into 8 slices. Serves 4 (serving size: 2 slices)

CALORIES 354; **FAT** 15.2g (sat 4.3g, mono 6.4g, poly 3.4g); **PROTEIN** 15g; **CARB** 43g; **FIBER** 4g; **SUGARS** 5g (est. added sugars 3g); **CHOL** 23mg; **IRON** 0mg; **SODIUM** 690mg; **CALC** 293mg

BUILD A BETTER PIZZA

Good pizza starts with good dough. Whether homemade (Supremely Veggie Pizza, page 112) or store-bought, the dough must contain the right ratio of flour, water, yeast, and salt that creates the coveted crisp-chewy texture. Look to store-bought dough for pizzeria quality and convenience—we certainly do. Out of the package, the dough should be smooth and springy. We prefer whole-grain crusts, which add nutty flavor and toasty complexity while slipping in a few servings of whole grains.

SUPERMARKET DOUGH TASTE TEST

WHOLE FOODS WHOLE WHEAT
Taste: Earthy profile, bran-forward flavor

Texture: Soft crust, hearty chew, sturdy base for ample toppings

Pliability: Silky smooth and easy to roll out and mold

Nutrition (per 2 oz.)
Calories 130
Protein 4g Fiber 1g
Sodium 260mg

TRADER JOE'S WHOLE WHEAT
Taste: Pleasantly nutty, toasty flavor

Texture: Crisps up well; texture comparable to a pita

Pliability: Dough is a little tacky and sticky but easy to work with.

Nutrition (per 2 oz.)
Calories 120
Protein 4g Fiber 4g
Sodium 170mg

TRADER JOE'S GARLIC & HERB
Taste: Powerful rosemary and garlic flavor; best with few toppings

Texture: Crisps up well; texture comparable to a pita

Pliability: Dough is tacky and more difficult to work with.

Nutrition (per 2 oz.)
Calories 140
Protein 4g Fiber 1g
Sodium 280mg

WHOLLY WHOLESOME GLUTEN FREE
Taste: Neutral flavor lets toppings shine.

Texture: Delightfully chewy; pale in color with minimal browning

Pliability: Weak structure; difficult to roll out without breaking apart.

Nutrition (per 2 oz.)
Calories 110
Protein 2g Fiber 4g
Sodium 200mg

TACKLE THE TOPPINGS

THE INSPIRATION for pizza-topping nirvana can come from one trip to your local farmers' market. Take advantage of seasonal vegetables to add freshness and nutritional heft to your homemade pie. Not only do our pizzas (recipes begin on page 110) run the gamut when it comes to tasty, plant-heavy toppings, they're also weeknight-fast and won't break the sodium or calorie bank. We can't promise there will be leftovers, but we can guarantee each slice will be love at first bite.

THE SAUCE should be light and simple. Using fresh roasted tomatoes or unsalted canned whole tomatoes in place of traditional pizza sauce can save up to 150mg sodium per serving.

THE CHEESE acts as the glue, helping to bind your toppings to the dough. Part-skim mozzarella is mild and melty, making it our top pick. Part-skim ricotta can serve as both the sauce and cheese when thinned out and made creamier with a splash of milk.

THE VEGGIE TOPPINGS need not be elaborate, but they should fill nutritional gaps for the day. Parbaking the dough can prevent the crust from getting weighed down and soggy when adding vegetables such as cherry tomatoes or zucchini.

THE FINISHER should add bright flavor and fresh dimension. Add a handful of arugula to slip in some extra leafy greens, a drizzle of Sriracha-spiked mayonnaise for a spicy punch, or fresh herbs for a wispy, flavor-packed garnish.

Garden Greens Pizza

Hands-on: 15 min. Total: 25 min.
This springtime pie taps into some of the season's superior produce for a vibrant, fresh take on pizza.

12 ounces fresh deli whole-wheat pizza dough
8 cups water
1 cup medium-thick asparagus spears, trimmed and cut diagonally in half
1 cup sugar snap peas
$2/3$ cup part-skim ricotta cheese
2 tablespoons 1% low-fat milk
1 garlic clove, grated
3 ounces part-skim mozzarella cheese, shredded ($3/4$ cup)
1 small zucchini, shaved lengthwise into thin slices using a mandoline or vegetable peeler (about 1 cup)
1 teaspoon fresh lemon juice
$1/4$ teaspoon kosher salt
$1/2$ teaspoon grated lemon rind
$1/4$ cup torn fresh basil
$1/8$ teaspoon freshly ground black pepper

1. Place a pizza stone or baking sheet in oven. Preheat oven to 500°F. (Do not remove pizza stone while oven preheats.)
2. Roll dough into a 13-inch circle on a large piece of parchment paper; pierce well with a fork. Place dough (on paper) on preheated stone. Bake at 500°F for 4 minutes.
3. Bring 8 cups water to a boil in a large saucepan. Add asparagus and peas; cook 2 minutes. Drain, and plunge into ice water; drain. Pat dry.
4. Combine ricotta, milk, and garlic in a small bowl. Spread mixture over dough, leaving a ½-inch border.
5. Top pizza with mozzarella, asparagus, and peas. Bake at 500°F for 10 minutes.
6. Toss zucchini with lemon juice and salt. Top pizza with zucchini mixture, lemon rind, basil, and black pepper. Cut into 8 slices. Serves 4 (serving size: 2 slices)

CALORIES 317; **FAT** 10.4g (sat 4.5g, mono 3.9g, poly 1.0g); **PROTEIN** 17g; **CARB** 44g; **FIBER** 4g; **SUGARS** 5g (est. added sugars 0g); **CHOL** 31mg; **IRON** 1mg; **SODIUM** 689mg; **CALC** 256mg

PREP POINTERS

1. REST refrigerated dough at room temperature for at least 30 minutes to relax the gluten and make the dough easier to roll out.

2. CRANK the oven temperature to 500°F, or as high as you can go without broiling, to achieve the best results.

3. PIERCE the rolled-out dough with a fork to prevent it from bubbling up as it bakes.

4. SPRINKLE cornmeal underneath the dough to keep it from sticking to the pizza stone and to get the bottom of the crust extra crispy.

5. BUILD your pizza on a sheet of parchment paper, and then carefully place the pizza and paper on top of your hot stone or baking sheet to avoid the need for a pizza peel. This also promotes crisping.

RECIPE MAKEOVER

The supreme pizza takes a virtuous U-turn as a hearty, veggie-loaded pizza. By skipping sodium-laden meats, we pack one full serving of vegetables into each square, doubling the fiber of most pizza chain offerings. Every bit as satisfying as its meaty counterparts, our pie will delight the most devout of carnivores.

OURS SAVES
5g saturated fat and 300mg sodium over popular pizza chain supreme pizzas

Supremely Veggie Pizza

Hands-on: 45 min.
Total: 25 hr. 45 min.
The dough develops a focaccia-like texture from a 24-hour rest in the refrigerator.

1 cup warm water (100° to 110°F)
5.4 ounces bread flour (1$1/4$ cups)
5 ounces white whole-wheat flour (about 1$1/4$ cups)
1 ($1/4$-ounce) envelope active dry yeast
$1/4$ cup olive oil, divided
$3/4$ teaspoon kosher salt, divided
Cooking spray
1 Japanese eggplant, cut into $1/4$-inch-thick slices
1 cup thinly sliced zucchini
1 cup thinly sliced yellow squash
1 cup thinly sliced red onion
1 red bell pepper, thinly sliced
$3/4$ cup jarred pizza sauce
2 cups chopped fresh spinach
5 ounces part-skim mozzarella cheese, shredded (about 1$1/4$ cups)

1. Place ¾ cup warm water in the bowl of an stand mixer fitted with the dough hook attachment. Add flours; mix on medium speed until combined, about 20 seconds. Cover, and let stand 20 minutes.

2. In a small bowl, mix yeast and remaining ¼ cup water; let stand until bubbly, about 5 minutes. Add yeast mixture, 1 tablespoon oil, and ½ teaspoon salt to flour mixture; mix until a soft dough forms. Place dough in a large bowl coated with cooking spray; place plastic wrap coated with cooking spray directly on surface of dough. Chill 24 hours.

3. Let dough stand 1 hour, covered, until dough reaches room temperature. Place dough on a lightly floured surface; roll into a 14- x 11-inch rectangle. Press dough into bottom and partially up sides of a 13- x 9-inch metal baking pan coated with cooking spray.

4. Place a baking sheet in oven on bottom rack. Preheat oven to 450°F. (Do not remove baking sheet while oven preheats.)

5. Toss together eggplant, zucchini, squash, 1½ teaspoons oil, and remaining ¼ teaspoon salt on a separate rimmed baking sheet; spread in a single layer. Bake at 450°F for 15 minutes or until tender, turning once halfway through.

6. Heat 1½ teaspoons oil in a large nonstick skillet over medium-high. Add onion and bell pepper. Cook, stirring often, until tender, about 4 to 5 minutes.

7. Spread pizza sauce over dough, leaving a ½-inch border; top evenly with spinach. Sprinkle mozzarella over spinach. Arrange eggplant, zucchini, and squash slices alternately over cheese. Top evenly with onion and bell pepper mixture. Brush remaining 2 tablespoons oil over dough border. Place baking pan on preheated baking sheet; move to middle oven rack. Bake at 450°F for 22 to 23 minutes. Cut into 6 squares. Serves 6 (serving size: 1 square)

CALORIES 382, FAT 13.9g (sat 3.8g, mono 7.7g, poly 1.3g); PROTEIN 15g; CARB 48g; FIBER 7g; SUGARS 9g (est. added sugars 2g); CHOL 15mg; IRON 3mg; SODIUM 579mg; CALC 226mg

MUST-MAKE SPRING SUCCOTASH

Fresh, flavorful, and ready in 20 minutes, this vegetarian main is a family favorite.

Minnesota mom Sue Given credits the Cooking Light Diet with making a remarkable difference in her life. "I'm so much healthier now, and I'm able to be a much better mom for my kids," she says. "Seriously, that's the best part."

Sue also tells us that the "cherry on top" of the CL Diet is that her kids love the recipes, too. We sent her this quick succotash recipe to test drive; the whole family loved it. According to Sue's husband, the leftovers he enjoyed for lunch the next day "tasted even better!" Sue labels this recipe as a "must-make" and recommends bringing it to a picnic or potluck this season, as it holds up well and is easy to transport. Great idea, Sue!

EDAMAME ADDS HEARTY TEXTURE AND A HIT OF PLANT-BASED PROTEIN.

Quick & Easy • Gluten Free
Kid Friendly • Make Ahead
Vegetarian

Feta-Herb Edamame Succotash

Hands-on: 15 min. Total: 20 min.
We're ready for the glories of summer produce, but since it's not quite the season, frozen vegetables and year-round grape tomatoes do the job. This veggie-packed entrée is light yet satisfying, and it holds up great when prepared a day in advance.

1 tablespoon olive oil
1 medium-sized yellow onion, chopped (about 1 cup)
2 cups frozen shelled edamame, thawed
1½ cups frozen corn kernels, thawed
1 cup grape tomatoes, halved lengthwise
1 ounce feta cheese, crumbled (about ¼ cup)
2 tablespoons chopped fresh dill
2 tablespoons chopped fresh flat-leaf parsley
2 tablespoons sherry vinegar
½ teaspoon kosher salt
¼ teaspoon freshly ground black pepper

1. Heat a large nonstick skillet over medium-high. Add oil to pan; swirl to coat. Add onion, and cook, stirring occasionally, until tender, about 4 minutes.

2. Add edamame; cook, stirring constantly, 2 minutes. Add corn; cook, stirring constantly, 2 minutes. Remove from heat. Transfer to a bowl; cool 10 minutes. Stir in tomatoes, feta, dill, parsley, vinegar, salt, and pepper. Serves 4 (serving size: about 1 cup)

CALORIES 218; FAT 8.6g (sat 1.3g, mono 3.5g, poly 3.3g); PROTEIN 14g; CARB 23g; FIBER 7g; SUGARS 7g (est. added sugars 0g); CHOL 8mg; IRON 3mg; SODIUM 318mg; CALC 85mg

EASY MEATLESS MAINS

This month, we share our new cookbook, *Everyday Vegetarian: A Delicious Guide for Creating More Than 150 Meatless Dishes.* You'll find both globally inspired recipes and dishes close to home—all streamlined for busy cooks.

Vegetarian

Beer-Brushed Tofu Skewers with Barley

(pictured on page 219)

Hands-on: 45 min. Total: 45 min.
If you don't have barley, serve with brown rice, quinoa, or farro. You can also cook the tofu on a stovetop grill pan—just be sure to turn your oven vent on high, as the honey-based glaze will create some smoke.

1 (12-ounce) bottle brown ale
1/4 cup honey
1/2 teaspoon crushed red pepper
12 ounces extra-firm tofu, drained, cut into 1 1/2-inch cubes, and patted dry
Cooking spray
1 teaspoon black pepper, divided
3/4 teaspoon kosher salt, divided
1 zucchini (about 10 ounces), cut lengthwise into 1/2-inch-thick planks
1 pint cherry tomatoes, halved
3 cups loosely packed arugula (about 2 1/2 ounces)
2 cups cooked barley
3 tablespoons extra-virgin olive oil
1 tablespoon sherry vinegar

1. Preheat grill to high (450°F to 550°F).
2. Bring beer, honey, and red pepper to a boil in a saucepan over medium-high. Cook, stirring occasionally, 20 to 25 minutes or until reduced to 1/2 cup.
3. Thread tofu cubes onto 4 (6-inch) skewers. Coat with cooking spray. Sprinkle with 1/2 teaspoon pepper and 1/4 teaspoon salt. Brush tofu and zucchini with beer mixture. Arrange tofu skewers and zucchini in a single layer on grill grate coated with cooking spray. Grill tofu, brushing often with beer mixture, 2 to 3 minutes per side or until grill marks appear. Cook zucchini 3 to 4 minutes per side or until tender and grill marks appear. Remove from grill; coarsely chop zucchini.
4. Toss together zucchini, tomatoes, arugula, barley, oil, vinegar, and remaining 1/2 teaspoon each pepper and salt in a large bowl. Top barley mixture with tofu. Serves 4 (serving size: 1 2/3 cups barley mixture and 1 tofu skewer)

CALORIES 382; FAT 16.7g (sat 2.2g, mono 11.5g, poly 2.4g); PROTEIN 12g; CARB 49g; FIBER 5g; SUGARS 22g (est. added sugars 17g); CHOL 0mg; IRON 3mg; SODIUM 384mg; CALC 204mg

Kid Friendly • Vegetarian

Broccolini, Red Pepper, and Roasted Garlic Frittata

Hands-on: 35 min. Total: 45 min.

2 tablespoons canola oil
11 to 12 garlic cloves
6 large eggs, lightly beaten
1/2 cup low-fat cottage cheese
1 (8-ounce) bunch Broccolini
1 medium red bell pepper, sliced into thin strips
1/2 cup vertically sliced sweet onion
2 tablespoons chopped fresh flat-leaf parsley
1 tablespoon chopped fresh oregano
1/2 teaspoon kosher salt
1/4 teaspoon freshly ground black pepper

1. Heat a small saucepan over medium-low. Add oil and garlic; cook, stirring occasionally and adjusting the heat as needed to keep garlic from browning too quickly, 25 to 30 minutes or until garlic is very soft. Drain oil into a small bowl; reserve oil. Place garlic cloves, eggs, and cottage cheese in a food processor; process until smooth. Transfer mixture to a medium bowl.
2. Preheat broiler with oven rack 6 inches from heat. Trim Broccolini stems from tops; cut tops and stems into bite-size pieces. Heat a 10-inch nonstick ovenproof skillet over medium-high. Add 1 1/2 teaspoons reserved garlic oil to pan; swirl to coat. Add Broccolini stems, bell pepper, and onion; cook, stirring often, 5 minutes or until vegetables are slightly tender. Add Broccolini tops; cook 5 to 6 minutes or until Broccolini is bright green and bell peppers are tender. Fold vegetable mixture, parsley, oregano, salt, and black pepper into egg mixture.
3. Heat 1 1/2 teaspoons garlic oil in skillet over medium-high; swirl to coat. Pour egg mixture into skillet; cook 30 seconds. Reduce heat to medium-low; cook, without stirring, until eggs are partially cooked, about 4 minutes.
4. Transfer skillet to oven; broil until eggs are set and top of frittata is lightly browned, about 5 minutes. Remove from oven; run a spatula around edges of frittata to loosen. Cut into 8 wedges. Serve immediately. Serves 4 (serving size: 2 wedges)

CALORIES 222; FAT 15.1g (sat 3.2g, mono 7.3g, poly 3.5g); PROTEIN 15g; CARB 12g; FIBER 2g; SUGARS 5g (est. added sugars 0g); CHOL 282mg; IRON 2mg; SODIUM 457mg; CALC 128mg

Double Barley Posole

Hands-on: 45 min. Total: 1 hr. 10 min.
This hearty soup gets its name from the pearl barley used in the soup as well as the barley used in the beer that's stirred in.

2 tablespoons olive oil
8 ounces cremini mushrooms, quartered
1 cup chopped red bell pepper
1/2 cup chopped yellow onion
1 tablespoon minced fresh garlic
1 tablespoon chopped fresh thyme
1 tablespoon all-purpose flour
1 (12-ounce) bottle pilsner beer
3 1/2 cups unsalted vegetable stock
3/4 cup chopped peeled butternut squash (about 4 1/2 ounces)
1/2 cup uncooked pearl barley
1 teaspoon black pepper
1/8 teaspoon kosher salt
1 (15-ounce) can white hominy, rinsed and drained
1/2 cup chopped zucchini
1 ripe avocado, diced
1/4 cup packed fresh cilantro leaves
1/4 cup light sour cream
4 lime wedges

1. Heat oil in a Dutch oven over medium-high. Add mushrooms; cook, stirring occasionally, until mushrooms begin to release their liquid, about 5 minutes. Add bell pepper and onion; cook, stirring occasionally, until onion is translucent, about 4 minutes. Add garlic, thyme, and flour; cook, stirring often, 1 minute. Stir in beer; cook until liquid is reduced and glossy, about 7 minutes. Stir in vegetable stock, squash, barley, black pepper, and salt; bring to a boil. Reduce heat to medium-low; cover and cook until barley is tender, about 40 minutes. Stir in hominy and zucchini; simmer until zucchini is tender but still bright green, about 5 minutes.

2. Divide soup evenly among 4 bowls; top servings evenly with diced avocado, cilantro, sour cream, and lime wedges. Serves 4 (serving size: 1 1/2 cups)

CALORIES 417; **FAT** 17.5g (sat 3.4g, mono 10.2g, poly 2.3g); **PROTEIN** 11g; **CARB** 58g; **FIBER** 13g; **SUGARS** 8g (est. added sugars 0g); **CHOL** 8mg; **IRON** 3mg; **SODIUM** 662mg; **CALC** 92mg

TARTINE ALL DAY

Elisabeth Prueitt's new cookbook delivers simple, hearty food for busy but conscientious family cooks, along with signature sweet treats.

Elisabeth Prueitt wants to inspire people to get in their kitchens and cook. Prueitt, co-founder of Tartine Bakery & Cafe and Tartine Manufactory in San Francisco and co-author of *Tartine*, aims to do just that in her new solo book, *Tartine All Day: Modern Recipes for the Home Cook*. With 200 practical, delicious recipes, it's a book meant to live in the kitchen, one she hopes will make people "want to jump up and make something."

Prueitt herself is a busy working mom, and so her cooking has become more simplified over the years. Recipes like Spring Risotto and Pan-Roasted Eggplant are easy yet elegant, while dishes like Ceci Cacio e Pepe (roasted chickpeas flavored like the pasta dish cacio e pepe) showcase Prueitt's creativity. Nowhere does her innovation shine more, though, than with her desserts. A classically trained pastry chef with gluten intolerance, Prueitt has gone through "years of trial and error and finding new grains to work with" to perfect her gluten-free desserts. A robust chapter showcases some of her favorites. Featured here is one of the simplest and most beautiful desserts from the book.

Champagne Gelée with Strawberries

Hands-on: 10 min. Total: 1 hr. 10 min.
Unlike some classic gelatin desserts, this one—relying on a high-quality sparkler—is quite elegant.

3 cups Champagne, prosecco, or cava, divided
4 1/2 teaspoons powdered unflavored gelatin
6 tablespoons plus 2 teaspoons sugar
1 pint strawberries

1. Pour 1/4 cup Champagne into a small saucepan; sprinkle gelatin evenly over top. (It will become soft and absorb the liquid.) Heat mixture over low, stirring constantly, until gelatin dissolves completely.
2. In a large bowl, combine 6 tablespoons sugar and remaining 2 3/4 cups Champagne. It will foam, but the bubbles will subside after a minute. Stir in gelatin mixture, making sure it is evenly incorporated. Pour into a square or rectangular container so that the liquid is about 1 to 2 inches deep. Cover and chill in refrigerator until set, about 1 hour. The longer it chills, the more set it will become.
3. Shortly before serving, hull and quarter strawberries; toss with remaining 2 teaspoons sugar. Let stand 5 minutes, tossing occasionally to coat strawberries in juices.
4. Once gelée is set, use a knife to cut it into a crosshatch pattern in order to create small cubes. Top gelée cubes with macerated strawberries and serve. Serves 6 (serving size: about 1/2 cup gelatin and 1/3 cup strawberries)

CALORIES 160; **FAT** 0.2g (sat 0g, mono 0g, poly 0.1g); **PROTEIN** 2g; **CARB** 20g; **FIBER** 1g; **SUGARS** 16g (est. added sugars 14g); **CHOL** 0mg; **IRON** 0mg; **SODIUM** 4mg; **CALC** 9mg

SAVORING SPRING

by David Bonom

Cookbook author David Bonom recalls how an annual road trip through Amish country led to family bonding and a beloved dessert.

My mother baked twice a year: her apple pie at Thanksgiving, and then when the crocuses peeped out of the ground in the spring, she'd make her rhubarb-apple crisp.

One day every year, seemingly out of the blue, Mom would announce that we were heading to Amish country for the farmers' market on the weekend. On the drive there, we'd play games: The first of us to spot an Amish person got a quarter, and 50 cents went to the first horse and buggy sighting.

The minute we arrived at the market, my mother would make a beeline for the rhubarb. She would pick only the stalks that were thick and deep red, with crisp, green, chard-like leaves. It didn't seem to matter to her that by the time we got home, the leaves would be faded and limp.

The morning after our outing, our "work" would begin. We'd sit around the table and nod our heads as my mother—every year—explained the leaves were poisonous as she trimmed them off. With her hand guiding mine, we would cut the stalks into thick slices that we'd toss into a big white bowl along with peeled, sliced McIntosh apples, lots of sugar, and a little flour. (In the ensuing years I learned that McIntosh are not the best baking apples, but they were my mother's favorite and the only type she ever used to make her crisp.)

My favorite part was making the topping. It was simple: flour, sugar, and margarine. (My mother was a Depression-era baby, so butter was, even in the 1970s, a luxury not to be "wasted" in a baked good.) As the baby of the family, I got the best job: mushing the topping into clumps to scatter over the crisp before it went in the oven.

Then we would wait, and the intoxicating, sweet smell of rhubarb, apples, and sugar filled the house. It always felt like a torturous eternity until the crisp not only baked but was also cool enough for me to take that first spoonful.

My mother has been gone many years now, but I carry on her rite of spring with my own children. And while I think of her every year as we sit around our table trimming the stalks (and yes, I always remind the kids the leaves are poisonous), I have to admit to tweaking her recipe. I use Golden Delicious or Honeycrisp apples, which hold their shape and offer better apple flavor when cooked; I put oats in the topping for texture; and I use brown sugar for deeper flavor. Oh—and I got rid of the margarine (sorry, Mom!) and replaced it with just enough butter to hold the topping together.

But one thing will never change: I still use the first rhubarb of spring from the farmers' market, and, like my mother, I choose only stalks with bright, lively leaves—even if they might wilt by the time I bring them home. Because sometimes cooking is about tradition more than logic—and our family thinks tradition tastes better.

Kid Friendly • Vegetarian

Mom's Rhubarb-Apple Crisp

Hands-on: 13 min. Total: 1 hr. 8 min.
Honeycrisp and Golden Delicious apples hold their shape well and won't get too mushy after baking. Brown sugar lends deep molasses flavor to the topping.

Cooking spray
12 ounces fresh or frozen rhubarb, thawed, cut into 1/2-inch-thick slices
1 1/4 pounds Golden Delicious or Honeycrisp apples, peeled, cored, and diced
2/3 cup granulated sugar
2.1 ounces all-purpose flour (about 1/2 cup), divided
1 teaspoon vanilla extract
1/4 teaspoon ground cinnamon
2/3 cup old-fashioned rolled oats
1/2 cup light brown sugar (not packed)
3 tablespoons unsalted butter, softened and cut into small pieces

1. Preheat oven to 375°F. Coat a 6-cup, preferably oval, baking pan or dish with cooking spray.
2. Combine rhubarb, apples, granulated sugar, 2 tablespoons flour, vanilla extract, and cinnamon; toss well. Place in prepared baking dish.
3. Combine remaining 6 tablespoons flour, oats, and brown sugar; mix well. Add butter to mixture; rub in with your hands until the mixture begins to hold in clumps when compressed. Sprinkle oat mixture evenly over rhubarb mixture in baking dish.
4. Bake at 375°F until topping is golden brown, filling is thick and bubbly, and fruit is tender, about 50 to 55 minutes. (Cover loosely with foil if the top begins to brown too quickly.) Cool 15 minutes before serving. Serves 12

CALORIES 161; **FAT** 3.4g (sat 1.9g, mono 0.9g, poly 0.3g); **PROTEIN** 2g; **CARB** 32g; **FIBER** 2g; **SUGARS** 22g (est. added sugars 12g); **CHOL** 8mg; **IRON** 1mg; **SODIUM** 4mg; **CALC** 35mg

MEDITERR-ANEAN BREAD SALAD

Fresh and fast, this meatless main redefines the art of convenience cooking.

Quick & Easy • Kid Friendly
Vegetarian

Chickpea Panzanella

Hands-on: 10 min. Total: 20 min.
We toast the bread in the oven, but if you already have the grill cranked up, this salad easily transitions to an outdoor dish. If your bakery carries whole-grain ciabatta, use it for a nutrition boost.

1 (8-ounce) ciabatta loaf
2 cups cherry tomatoes, halved
1 (15-ounce) can unsalted chickpeas, drained and rinsed
1 (8.5-ounce) can quartered artichoke hearts, drained
3 ounces feta cheese, crumbled (about ³⁄₄ cup)
¹⁄₂ cup thinly sliced red onion
¹⁄₄ cup chopped fresh basil, plus more for garnish
¹⁄₄ cup extra-virgin olive oil
1¹⁄₂ tablespoons red wine vinegar
¹⁄₂ teaspoon dried oregano
¹⁄₄ teaspoon black pepper
¹⁄₈ teaspoon kosher salt

1. Preheat oven to 350°F. Remove and discard crust from ciabatta; cut bread into ¹⁄₂-inch cubes. Spread bread cubes in an even layer on a baking sheet. Bake at 350°F for 12 minutes or until toasted and golden.
2. Combine toasted bread, tomatoes, chickpeas, artichoke hearts, feta, onion, and basil in a large bowl.
3. In a separate smaller bowl, combine oil, vinegar, oregano, pepper, and salt. Stir with a whisk. Pour over salad; toss to combine. Garnish with chopped fresh basil. Serves 5 (serving size: 2 cups)

CALORIES 347; **FAT** 16g (sat 4.2g, mono 8.8g, poly 1.8g); **PROTEIN** 11g; **CARB** 40g; **FIBER** 6g; **SUGARS** 3g (est. added sugars 0g); **CHOL** 15mg; **IRON** 2mg; **SODIUM** 599mg; **CALC** 132mg

PARSLEY, THE UNSUNG PASTA HERO

This garnishing green gets its moment in the spotlight in a simple weeknight main.

Quick & Easy • Kid Friendly
Vegetarian

Pretty "Parslied" Spaghetti

Hands-on: 15 min. Total: 25 min.
Try embellishing this dish with lemon zest, toasted nuts, sun-dried tomatoes in oil, or even sardines.

1 tablespoon plus ¹⁄₄ teaspoon kosher salt, divided
8 ounces uncooked spaghetti
5 teaspoons olive oil, divided
4 garlic cloves, thinly sliced
1¹⁄₂ cups chopped fresh flat-leaf parsley
2¹⁄₂ ounces grated Parmesan cheese (about ²⁄₃ cup)
¹⁄₄ teaspoon black pepper

1. Bring a large saucepan of water and 1 tablespoon salt to a boil. Add pasta; cook 7 minutes or until al dente. Drain in a colander over a bowl, reserving 1¹⁄₂ cups cooking liquid.
2. Heat 1 tablespoon oil in a skillet over medium. Add garlic; cook 2 minutes or until pale golden-brown.
3. Scoop pasta directly into the skillet, tossing to coat. Add parsley and Parmesan, and toss until all the pasta strands are covered. Add 1 to 1¹⁄₂ cups reserved pasta cooking liquid to pan as needed to loosen sauce. Sprinkle with remaining ¹⁄₄ teaspoon salt and pepper. Drizzle with remaining 2 teaspoons olive oil. Serves 4 (serving size: about 1 cup)

CALORIES 348; **FAT** 11.6g (sat 3.7g, mono 5.5g, poly 1.2g); **PROTEIN** 13g; **CARB** 47g; **FIBER** 3g; **SUGARS** 2g (est. added sugars 0g); **CHOL** 15mg; **IRON** 3mg; **SODIUM** 600mg; **CALC** 201mg

LEFTOVER FLAT-LEAF PARSLEY IS LIKELY LURKING IN YOUR CRISPER. THIS UNASSUMING HERB HAS A BRIGHT, GRASSY PERSONALITY THAT, COMBINED WITH CHEESE, GARLIC, AND GOOD OLIVE OIL, MAKES THIS DISH SING.

READY IN 25 MINUTES

....
GAME PLAN
....

While tofu cooks:

■ Prepare stock mixture.

While cauliflower mixture cooks:

■ Prepare rice.

Quick & Easy • Vegetarian

Szechuan Tofu with Cauliflower

With Orange-Scallion Brown Rice

We combine everything you love about Chinese takeout—the sweet and spicy sauce; the super-crispy tofu; and the crisp-tender, caramelized vegetables—into a single quick main. Instead of pressing the tofu, we toss the cubes in a little cornstarch to absorb extra moisture and create a crispy crust.

12 ounces extra-firm tofu, drained and cut into 3/4-inch cubes
3 tablespoons cornstarch, divided
2 tablespoons canola oil
1 cup unsalted vegetable stock
3 tablespoons reduced-sodium soy sauce
1 tablespoon sherry vinegar
1 1/2 teaspoons hoisin sauce
3 cups cauliflower florets
2 cups thinly diagonally sliced celery
6 garlic cloves, thinly sliced
1 1/2 tablespoons unsalted ketchup
1/2 teaspoon crushed red pepper
1/2 cup thinly sliced green onions

1. Pat tofu dry with paper towels. Place 7 teaspoons cornstarch in a large bowl. Add tofu; toss to coat. Remove tofu from bowl. Heat oil in a large nonstick skillet over medium-high. Add tofu; cook 6 minutes or until golden and crisp, stirring occasionally. Remove tofu to a plate with a slotted spoon.
2. Combine remaining 2 teaspoons cornstarch and 1/4 cup stock in a bowl, stirring with a whisk until smooth. Stir in remaining 3/4 cup stock, soy sauce, vinegar, and hoisin.
3. Add cauliflower to remaining oil in pan; cook 3 minutes or until lightly browned, stirring occasionally. Add celery and garlic; sauté 2 minutes. Add ketchup and pepper; cook 1 minute, stirring to coat. Add stock mixture to pan; bring to a boil. Cook 2 minutes or until liquid is slightly thickened. Add cooked tofu; toss. Top with green onions. Serves 4 (serving size: about 1 cup)

CALORIES 271; FAT 12.9g (sat 1.7g, mono 5.5g, poly 5.1g); PROTEIN 13g; CARB 27g; FIBER 4g; SUGARS 5g (est. added sugars 1g); CHOL 0mg; IRON 2mg; SODIUM 612mg; CALC 120mg

Quick & Easy • Vegetarian

Orange-Scallion Brown Rice

Perk up precooked brown rice with fresh orange rind, a faintly floral note that's welcome in stir-fries and other classic Asian dishes. If you like, add chopped toasted almonds or peanuts for extra crunch.

2 (8.8-ounce) packages precooked brown rice (such as Uncle Ben's)
1 tablespoon toasted sesame oil
1/2 cup chopped green onions
1 teaspoon grated orange rind
1/4 teaspoon kosher salt
1/4 teaspoon black pepper

1. Heat rice in microwave according to package directions.
2. Heat oil in a large skillet over medium-high. Add green onions; sauté 2 minutes. Stir in rind, salt, and pepper; cook 1 minute. Stir in rice; cook 3 minutes or until thoroughly heated. Serves 4 (serving size: about 3/4 cup)

CALORIES 204; FAT 6.2g (sat 0.5g, mono 1.5g, poly 1.5g); PROTEIN 5g; CARB 36g; FIBER 3g; SUGARS 0g (est. added sugars 0g); CHOL 0mg; IRON 1mg; SODIUM 135mg; CALC 10mg

READY IN 25 MINUTES

....
GAME PLAN
....

While oven preheats:

■ Prepare potato mixture.
■ Cook veggie mixture.

While potatoes bake:

■ Poach eggs.

Quick & Easy • Gluten Free

Shiitake and Asparagus Sauté with Poached Eggs

With Herbed Roasted New Potatoes

Date-night dinner need not center around meat. Here, earthy, meaty shiitake mushrooms balance lemony asparagus and a rich, perfectly poached egg.

2 tablespoons olive oil
1/3 cup thinly sliced shallots
1 tablespoon chopped fresh thyme
2 cups sliced shiitake mushroom caps (about 6 ounces)
5 ounces trimmed fresh asparagus
3 garlic cloves, thinly sliced
1/2 cup unsalted chicken stock (such as Swanson)
2 teaspoons unsalted butter

2 teaspoons fresh lemon juice
³/₈ teaspoon kosher salt
½ teaspoon black pepper, divided
1 teaspoon white vinegar
2 large eggs (in shells)

1. Heat oil in a large skillet over medium-high. Add shallots, thyme, and mushrooms; cook 4 minutes or until lightly browned. Add asparagus and garlic; cook 2 minutes. Add stock; cook 2 to 3 minutes or until liquid has reduced to about 2 tablespoons. Remove pan from heat; stir in butter, lemon juice, salt, and ¼ teaspoon pepper.
2. Fill a skillet two-thirds full with water. Add vinegar; bring to a simmer. Break each whole egg into a custard cup, and pour each gently into pan; cook 3 minutes or until desired degree of doneness. Carefully remove eggs using a slotted spoon.
3. Divide mushroom and asparagus mixture evenly between 2 plates. Top each serving with 1 egg. Sprinkle remaining ¼ teaspoon pepper over eggs. Serves 2

CALORIES 303; FAT 22.7g (sat 5.9g, mono 12.7g, poly 2.6g); PROTEIN 12g; CARB 16g; FIBER 5g; SUGARS 6g (est. added sugars 0g); CHOL 196mg; IRON 3mg; SODIUM 478mg; CALC 74mg

Quick & Easy • Gluten Free
Kid Friendly • Make Ahead
Vegetarian

Herbed Roasted New Potatoes

Double this recipe to serve with scrambled eggs for tomorrow's breakfast.

1 tablespoon chopped fresh thyme
2 teaspoons olive oil
¼ teaspoon kosher salt
¼ teaspoon black pepper
8 ounces baby red potatoes, cut into wedges
1 tablespoon chopped fresh flat-leaf parsley

1. Preheat oven to 425°F.
2. Combine first 5 ingredients in a bowl; toss to coat. Spread potato mixture in a single layer on a parchment paper–lined baking sheet. Bake at 425°F for 20 minutes or until tender, stirring once after 10 minutes. Top with parsley. Serves 2 (serving size: about ½ cup)

CALORIES 122; FAT 4.7g (sat 0.7g, mono 3.3g, poly 0.6g); PROTEIN 2g; CARB 19g; FIBER 2g; SUGARS 1g (est. added sugars 0g); CHOL 0mg; IRON 1mg; SODIUM 262mg; CALC 20mg

READY IN
40
MINUTES

GAME PLAN

While peppers broil:
- Prepare salad.

While peppers stand:
- Cook tomato mixture.
- Cook polenta.

Quick & Easy • Gluten Free
Make Ahead

Chicken and Poblano Stew with Polenta

With Avocado Salad with Honey-Lime Vinaigrette

Think of this saucy chicken stew as a Mexican twist on Italian comfort food, especially when served over creamy polenta. Poblano chiles become smoky and lose some of their intensity when broiled. Wrap the peppers in the same foil used to line the pan, and let stand so that the steam can loosen the skins before you peel them.

3 poblano peppers
2 tablespoons olive oil, divided
2 cups thinly sliced yellow onion
2 tablespoons chopped fresh oregano
8 medium garlic cloves, minced
2 cups chopped tomato
2 tablespoons adobo sauce from canned chipotle chiles in adobo
¾ teaspoon kosher salt, divided
1 tablespoon fresh lime juice
4 ounces skinless, boneless rotisserie chicken breast, shredded (about 1 cup)
3 cups whole milk
¾ cup uncooked quick-cooking polenta

1. Preheat broiler to high.
2. Place peppers on a foil-lined baking sheet; rub with 1½ teaspoons oil. Broil 10 minutes or until blackened on all sides, turning occasionally. Wrap peppers in foil; let stand 10 minutes. Unwrap; remove skins and seeds. Coarsely chop peppers.
3. Heat remaining 1½ tablespoons oil in a large skillet over high. Add onion, oregano, and garlic; sauté 3 minutes. Add tomato, adobo sauce, and ½ teaspoon salt; cook 4 minutes, stirring occasionally. Stir in peppers, juice, and chicken; cook 2 to 3 minutes or until slightly thickened.
4. Bring milk to a boil in a saucepan over medium-high. Reduce heat to medium-low; add remaining ¼ teaspoon salt and polenta, whisking constantly. Cook 2 minutes or until thickened, stirring constantly. Place ¾ cup polenta in each of 4 shallow bowls; top each serving with ¾ cup chicken mixture. Serves 4

CALORIES 389; FAT 14.4g (sat 4.6g, mono 6.7g, poly 1.3g); PROTEIN 19g; CARB 47g; FIBER 5g; SUGARS 15g (est. added sugars 0g); CHOL 43mg; IRON 2mg; SODIUM 619mg; CALC 259mg

continued

Avocado Salad with Honey-Lime Vinaigrette

2 tablespoons extra-virgin olive oil
1¹⁄₂ tablespoons fresh lime juice
2 teaspoons honey
¹⁄₄ teaspoon kosher salt
¹⁄₈ teaspoon ground red pepper
1 romaine lettuce heart, chopped (about 3 cups)
1 cup thinly sliced radishes (about 5 medium)
1 ripe peeled avocado, diced

1. Combine first 5 ingredients in a large bowl. Add remaining ingredients; toss. Serves 4 (serving size: about ¾ cup)

CALORIES 143; **FAT** 12.4g (sat 1.7g, mono 8.7g, poly 1.3g); **PROTEIN** 1g; **CARB** 8g; **FIBER** 4g; **SUGARS** 4g (est. added sugars 3g); **CHOL** 0mg; **IRON** 1mg; **SODIUM** 137mg; **CALC** 24mg

READY IN
25
MINUTES

GAME PLAN

While snap pea mixture stands:
- Prepare cakes.

While cakes cook:
- Prepare salad.

Zucchini and Shrimp Cakes with Snap Pea Relish

With Black-Eyed Pea Salad

Just a little shrimp goes a long way in these spring-inspired cakes. If using frozen shrimp, make sure to thaw completely before peeling and chopping; otherwise the shrimp will fall apart. You can use fresh basil instead of tarragon.

1 cup chopped sugar snap peas (about 3 ounces)
¹⁄₄ cup diced Vidalia or other sweet onion
3 tablespoons olive oil, divided
1¹⁄₂ teaspoons red wine vinegar
³⁄₄ teaspoon kosher salt, divided
¹⁄₂ teaspoon black pepper, divided
2 medium zucchini, trimmed (about 1 pound)
1 cup whole-wheat panko (Japanese breadcrumbs)
1¹⁄₂ teaspoons chopped fresh tarragon
6 ounces large fresh or frozen thawed shrimp, peeled, deveined, and finely chopped
1 large egg, lightly beaten

1. Combine snap peas, onion, 1 tablespoon oil, vinegar, ½ teaspoon salt, and ¼ teaspoon pepper in a bowl. Let stand 10 minutes.
2. Shred zucchini on the large holes of a box grater. Place shredded zucchini on a clean kitchen towel; squeeze well to remove excess liquid. Combine zucchini, remaining ¼ teaspoon salt, remaining ¼ teaspoon pepper, panko, tarragon, shrimp, and egg in a bowl.
3. Heat remaining 2 tablespoons oil in a large nonstick skillet over medium-high. Spoon ¼ cup zucchini mixture loosely into a dry measuring cup. Add mixture to pan; flatten slightly. Repeat procedure 7 times to form 8 cakes. Cook 3 minutes on each side or until golden brown. Serve cakes with snap pea mixture. Serves 4 (serving size: 2 cakes and about ⅓ cup snap pea mixture)

CALORIES 234; **FAT** 13.1g (sat 2g, mono 8.6g, poly 1.4g); **PROTEIN** 12g; **CARB** 17g; **FIBER** 2g; **SUGARS** 5g (est. added sugars 0g); **CHOL** 100mg; **IRON** 1mg; **SODIUM** 495mg; **CALC** 64mg

Black-Eyed Pea Salad

Unsalted canned black-eyed peas give the salad heft and texture, a great pairing for the light, crispy cakes. Bulk up any leftovers with more arugula, sliced cucumbers, and red bell pepper for a satisfying lunch salad.

1 cup halved grape tomatoes
2¹⁄₂ tablespoons canola mayonnaise
2 tablespoons red wine vinegar
¹⁄₂ teaspoon kosher salt
¹⁄₄ teaspoon freshly ground black pepper
1 (15-ounce) can unsalted black-eyed peas, rinsed and drained
2 cups baby arugula (about 2 ounces)

1. Combine first 6 ingredients in a large bowl, stirring to coat. Add arugula; toss gently to combine. Serves 4 (serving size: about ¾ cup)

CALORIES 109; **FAT** 3.3g (sat 0g, mono 1.5g, poly 1g); **PROTEIN** 6g; **CARB** 15g; **FIBER** 4g; **SUGARS** 2g (est. added sugars 0g); **CHOL** 0mg; **IRON** 2mg; **SODIUM** 334mg; **CALC** 52mg

READY IN
40
MINUTES

GAME PLAN

While pasta cooks:
- Cook sauce.

While sauce simmers:
- Prepare salad.

Quick & Easy • Kid Friendly
Make Ahead

Mostly Veggie Pasta with Sausage

With Black Pepper-Parmesan Wedge Salad

Spaghetti sauce is typically mostly meat, about a pound of ground beef bound by a scant amount of marinara. Here, we reverse the ratio, using sausage as the flavor agent instead of the base and adding plenty of vegetables.

8 ounces uncooked whole-wheat spaghetti
1 tablespoon olive oil
6 ounces hot turkey Italian sausage, casings removed
2 cups chopped yellow onion
6 garlic cloves, minced
1½ cups chopped cremini mushrooms (about 4 ounces)
2 small yellow squash, halved lengthwise and cut into ¼-inch slices (about 7 ounces each)
1 tablespoon unsalted tomato paste
1 tablespoon chopped fresh oregano
2 cups small broccoli florets
½ teaspoon kosher salt
¼ teaspoon crushed red pepper
1 (14-ounce) can unsalted whole peeled tomatoes, undrained
¼ cup torn fresh basil leaves

1. Cook pasta according to package directions, omitting salt and fat. Drain.
2. Heat oil in a large nonstick skillet over medium-high. Add sausage; cook 4 minutes, stirring to crumble. Add onion and garlic; cook 3 minutes. Add mushrooms and squash; cook 4 minutes. Stir in tomato paste and oregano; cook 1 minute.
3. Add broccoli, salt, pepper, and tomatoes to pan; bring to a boil. Reduce heat, and simmer 10 minutes, breaking up tomatoes with a spoon. Spoon sauce over pasta; top with basil. Serves 4 (serving size: ½ cup pasta and ¾ cup sauce)

CALORIES 391; FAT 9.7g (sat 0.8g, mono 2.9g, poly 1g); PROTEIN 21g; CARB 62g; FIBER 12g; SUGARS 11g (est. added sugars 0g); CHOL 25mg; IRON 5mg; SODIUM 547mg; CALC 121mg

Quick & Easy • Gluten Free
Kid Friendly • Vegetarian

Black Pepper-Parmesan Wedge Salad

¼ cup canola mayonnaise
3 tablespoons nonfat buttermilk
1 tablespoon fresh lemon juice
¾ teaspoon black pepper
1 ounce Parmesan cheese, finely grated and divided (about ⅔ cup)
1 small head iceberg lettuce, cut into 4 wedges
1 tablespoon finely chopped chives

1. Combine first 4 ingredients and ⅓ cup Parmesan cheese in a bowl. Top lettuce wedges evenly with dressing, remaining ⅓ cup Parmesan cheese, and chives. Serves 4 (serving size: 1 lettuce wedge and about 2 tablespoons dressing)

CALORIES 92; FAT 5.9g (sat 1.1g, mono 2.8g, poly 1.6g); PROTEIN 4g; CARB 6g; FIBER 2g; SUGARS 3g (est. added sugars 0g); CHOL 6mg; IRON 1mg; SODIUM 260mg; CALC 102mg

LET'S COOK

$11.14
FOR FOUR
SERVINGS

Quick & Easy
Gluten Free
Kid Friendly

Shrimp Paella

Hands-on: 15 min. Total: 20 min.
Precooked rice and ground turmeric speed up this Spanish shrimp dish and keep cost in check. Let the rice sizzle in the pan to get the prized crispy layer.

2 tablespoons canola oil
½ teaspoon ground turmeric
1 cup chopped red bell pepper
1 cup frozen green peas
1 tablespoon minced fresh garlic
2 (8.8-ounce) packages precooked brown rice (such as Uncle Ben's)
3 tablespoons unsalted chicken stock (such as Swanson)
¾ teaspoon kosher salt
½ teaspoon freshly ground black pepper
12 ounces frozen medium shrimp, thawed, peeled, and deveined
2 tablespoons fresh lemon juice

1. Heat oil in a large skillet over medium-high. Add turmeric; cook 1 minute, stirring constantly. Add bell pepper, peas, and garlic to pan; cook 2 minutes, stirring occasionally.
2. Stir in rice; spread in an even layer. Cook, without stirring, 3 minutes. Reduce heat to medium. Stir in stock, salt, and pepper. Spread rice mixture in an even layer in pan. Cook, without stirring, 7 minutes.
3. Arrange shrimp on top of rice mixture; cover and cook 3 to 4 minutes or until shrimp are done. Drizzle lemon juice over shrimp and rice. Serve immediately. Serves 4 (serving size: about 5 shrimp and 1 cup rice mixture)

CALORIES 336; FAT 10.8g (sat 0.7g, mono 4.5g, poly 2.2g); PROTEIN 19g; CARB 44g; FIBER 5g; SUGARS 3g (est. added sugars 0g); CHOL 107mg; IRON 2mg; SODIUM 544mg; CALC 62mg

SUPERFAST 20-MINUTE COOKING

Quick & Easy • Gluten Free
Kid Friendly • Make Ahead

Honey-Dijon Chicken Paillards with Zucchini Slaw

(pictured on page 219)

"Paillard" is a French term for any cut of meat that's been sliced or pounded thin, a brilliant shortcutting technique for plump chicken breasts.

3 tablespoons extra-virgin olive oil
1 tablespoon honey
1 teaspoon Dijon mustard
1 teaspoon kosher salt, divided
³⁄₄ teaspoon black pepper, divided
4 (6-ounce) skinless, boneless chicken breasts, split horizontally into 8 cutlets
1¹⁄₂ tablespoons red wine vinegar
1¹⁄₂ cups grape tomatoes, halved
1 (8-ounce) zucchini, grated on the large holes of a box grater (about 1¹⁄₂ cups)
¹⁄₂ cup chopped fresh flat-leaf parsley
2 tablespoons finely chopped shallots
2 tablespoons chopped fresh oregano

1. Combine 1 tablespoon oil, honey, mustard, ¹⁄₂ teaspoon salt, and ¹⁄₂ teaspoon pepper in a small bowl. Pat chicken dry with paper towels. Add chicken to honey mixture; toss to coat. Heat a large skillet over medium-high. Add 4 chicken cutlets to pan; cook 3 minutes on each side or until done. Repeat procedure with remaining 4 cutlets.
2. Combine remaining 2 tablespoons oil, remaining ¹⁄₂ teaspoon salt, remaining ¹⁄₄ teaspoon pepper, and vinegar in a medium bowl. Add tomatoes and remaining ingredients; toss. Serve with chicken. Serves 4 (serving size: 2 chicken breast cutlets and about ³⁄₄ cup slaw)

CALORIES 345; **FAT** 15.3g (sat 2.5g, mono 9.3g, poly 1.7g); **PROTEIN** 40g; **CARB** 10g; **FIBER** 2g; **SUGARS** 8g (est. added sugars 4g); **CHOL** 124mg; **IRON** 1mg; **SODIUM** 586mg; **CALC** 51mg

---

Quick & Easy • Kid Friendly
Vegetarian

Mini Mozzarella-and-Kale Pita Pizzas

(pictured on page 223)

We split the pitas in half before toasting so the crusts can get extra crisp.

6 (1-ounce) miniature whole-wheat pita rounds (such as Toufayan)
3 tablespoons extra-virgin olive oil
¹⁄₂ cup thinly sliced shallots
1 tablespoon sliced garlic
6 ounces baby kale
¹⁄₂ cup pizza sauce (such as Rao's)
2¹⁄₂ ounces preshredded 2% reduced-fat Italian cheese blend (about ²⁄₃ cup)
1¹⁄₂ ounces fresh mozzarella cheese, shredded (about ¹⁄₃ cup)
¹⁄₄ cup heirloom cherry tomatoes, sliced
¹⁄₂ teaspoon black pepper
¹⁄₈ teaspoon kosher salt

1. Preheat broiler to high with oven rack in middle position.
2. Split each pita in half horizontally to get 12 rounds. Arrange rounds, cut sides up, on a baking sheet; drizzle with 2 tablespoons oil. Broil 2 to 3 minutes or until lightly toasted.
3. Heat remaining 1 tablespoon oil in a large skillet over medium-high. Add shallots and garlic; sauté 2 minutes or until browned. Stir in kale; cook 2 minutes or until wilted. Remove pan from heat.
4. Spread about 2 teaspoons pizza sauce over each pita round; top evenly with kale mixture, cheeses, and tomatoes. Sprinkle evenly with pepper and salt. Broil 4 to 5 minutes or until cheeses are melted. Serves 4 (serving size: 3 mini pizzas)

CALORIES 349; **FAT** 18.7g (sat 5.1g, mono 8.3g, poly 1.6g); **PROTEIN** 14g; **CARB** 35g; **FIBER** 6g; **SUGARS** 4g (est. added sugars 0g); **CHOL** 18mg; **IRON** 3mg; **SODIUM** 571mg; **CALC** 210mg

---

Quick & Easy • Gluten Free
Kid Friendly

Pan-Roasted Pork with Baby Vegetable Salad

A mandoline is the best tool for shaving the vegetables into thin, even slices, but the salad would be just as delicious with thinner shaved ribbons (using a vegetable peeler) or slightly thicker slices (using a sharp knife). If you don't have pecorino romano, you can substitute Parmesan cheese.

3 tablespoons extra-virgin olive oil
1 (1-pound) pork tenderloin, trimmed
1 teaspoon kosher salt, divided
1 teaspoon paprika
³⁄₄ teaspoon black pepper, divided
1 tablespoon chopped fresh tarragon
1 tablespoon chopped fresh dill
1 tablespoon fresh lemon juice
1 teaspoon honey
¹⁄₃ cup frozen green peas, thawed
1 cup (¹⁄₈-inch-thick) strips zucchini (about 5 ounces)
1 cup (¹⁄₈-inch-thick) strips yellow squash (about 3 ounces)
1 cup (¹⁄₈-inch-thick) strips small carrots (about 2 ounces)
1 cup thinly sliced radishes (about 2 ounces)
2 tablespoons shaved pecorino romano cheese

1. Preheat oven to 500°F.

2. Heat 1 teaspoon oil in an oven-proof skillet over medium-high. Sprinkle pork with ½ teaspoon salt, paprika, and ⅜ teaspoon pepper. Add pork to pan; cook 5 minutes, turning to brown on all sides. Place pan in oven; bake at 500°F for 8 minutes or until a thermometer inserted in the thickest portion registers 145°F. Place pork on a cutting board; let stand 5 minutes. Cut into medallions; drizzle with 2 teaspoons oil and ⅛ teaspoon pepper.

3. Combine remaining 2 tablespoons oil, remaining ½ teaspoon salt, remaining ¼ teaspoon pepper, tarragon, dill, lemon juice, and honey in a medium bowl. Add peas, zucchini, squash, carrots, and radishes; toss. Sprinkle with cheese. Serve with pork. Serves 4 (serving size: 3 ounces pork and about ¾ cup salad)

CALORIES 295; **FAT** 16.1g (sat 3.3g, mono 9g, poly 1.5g); **PROTEIN** 26g; **CARB** 11g; **FIBER** 2g; **SUGARS** 6g (est. added sugars 1g); **CHOL** 76mg; **IRON** 2mg; **SODIUM** 608mg; **CALC** 44mg

Quick & Easy • Gluten Free
Kid Friendly • Vegetarian

Feta-and-Walnut Blistered Green Beans

Charring is a great technique for coaxing extra flavor from vegetables without adding calories. Here, slender green beans stay crisp and fresh while taking on a hint of bitter and smoke for balance.

2 tablespoons extra-virgin olive oil, divided
1 pound haricots verts (French green beans), trimmed
3 tablespoons fresh flat-leaf parsley leaves
1 teaspoon grated orange rind
2 tablespoons fresh orange juice

¼ cup chopped walnuts, toasted
2 tablespoons crumbed feta cheese
½ teaspoon freshly ground black pepper
⅜ teaspoon kosher salt

1. Preheat broiler to high with oven rack in top position.

2. Combine 1½ teaspoons oil and beans on a rimmed baking sheet. Broil 5 minutes or until beans are lightly charred and tender, stirring occasionally.

3. Combine remaining 1½ tablespoons oil, parsley, rind, and juice in a bowl. Stir in beans and nuts. Place bean mixture on a platter; top with feta, pepper, and salt. Serves 4 (serving size: about ¾ cup)

CALORIES 161; **FAT** 12.8g (sat 2.2g, mono 5.8g, poly 4.3g); **PROTEIN** 4g; **CARB** 10g; **FIBER** 4g; **SUGARS** 5g (est. added sugars 0g); **CHOL** 4mg; **IRON** 2mg; **SODIUM** 232mg; **CALC** 79mg

Quick & Easy • Gluten Free
Kid Friendly • Vegetarian
Garlic-and-Sesame Green Beans
Preheat broiler to high with oven rack in top position. Combine 2 Tbsp. toasted sesame oil and 1½ Tbsp. reduced-sodium soy sauce in a medium bowl. Add 1 lb. trimmed haricots verts (French green beans) to soy sauce mixture; toss to coat. Spread bean mixture in a single layer on a rimmed baking sheet. Add 6 sliced garlic cloves; toss. Broil 5 minutes or until beans are lightly charred and tender, stirring occasionally. Place bean mixture on a platter; sprinkle with 1 Tbsp. toasted sesame seeds. Serves 4 (serving size: about ½ cup)

CALORIES 117; **FAT** 8.3g (sat 1.2g, mono 3.4g, poly 3.6g); **PROTEIN** 3g; **CARB** 10g; **FIBER** 4g; **SUGARS** 4g (est. added sugars 0g); **CHOL** 0mg; **IRON** 1mg; **SODIUM** 224mg; **CALC** 55mg

Quick & Easy • Gluten Free
Kid Friendly • Vegetarian
Chickpea-and-Mint Green Beans
Preheat broiler to high. Place 1 (15-oz.) can unsalted chickpeas, rinsed and drained, on a rimmed baking sheet; rub with a clean kitchen towel to loosen skins. Add 2 Tbsp. extra-virgin olive oil and 1 lb. trimmed haricots verts to pan; toss. Broil 5 minutes, stirring occasionally. Combine bean mixture, ½ tsp. black pepper, ⅜ tsp. kosher salt, and ¼ tsp. ground cumin in a medium bowl; toss. Place bean mixture on a platter; sprinkle with 3 tablespoons chopped fresh mint. Serves 4 (serving size: ½ cup)

CALORIES 203; **FAT** 7.9g (sat 1g, mono 4.9g, poly 0.9g); **PROTEIN** 8g; **CARB** 27g; **FIBER** 7g; **SUGARS** 5g (est. added sugars 0g); **CHOL** 0mg; **IRON** 2mg; **SODIUM** 212mg; **CALC** 88mg

Quick & Easy • Gluten Free
Kid Friendly
Prosciutto-and-Almond Green Beans
Preheat broiler to high. Place 4 (¼-oz.) thin prosciutto slices between paper towels; microwave at HIGH 1½ minutes or until crisp. Break into pieces. Place 1½ Tbsp. extra-virgin olive oil, 2 tsp. chopped fresh thyme, and 1 lb. trimmed haricots verts on a baking sheet; toss. Broil 5 minutes, stirring occasionally. Place bean mixture on a platter; top with prosciutto, 2 Tbsp. sliced toasted almonds, 1 tsp. fresh thyme leaves, ¼ tsp. black pepper, and ⅛ tsp. kosher salt. Serves 4 (serving size: about ¾ cup)

CALORIES 113; **FAT** 7.7g (sat 1.2g, mono 4.7g, poly 1.2g); **PROTEIN** 5g; **CARB** 9g; **FIBER** 4g; **SUGARS** 4g (est. added sugars 0g); **CHOL** 6mg; **IRON** 1mg; **SODIUM** 257mg; **CALC** 53mg

Crispy Potato Cakes with Smoked Salmon

Frozen shredded potatoes are a fast cook's friend: They need no draining or thawing. Serve for brunch with a side of fruit.

¼ cup plus 1 tablespoon very thinly sliced green onions, divided
¼ teaspoon kosher salt
1 pound shredded refrigerated or frozen potatoes (such as Simply Potatoes)
2 large eggs, lightly beaten
1½ tablespoons all-purpose flour
2 tablespoons canola oil, divided
4 ounces cold-smoked salmon
3 tablespoons light sour cream (optional)

1. Combine 3 tablespoons green onions, salt, potatoes, and eggs in a large bowl. Stir in flour.
2. Heat 1 tablespoon oil in a large nonstick skillet over medium-high. Spoon ⅓ cup potato mixture loosely into a dry measuring cup. Add to pan; flatten slightly. Repeat procedure 3 times to form 4 cakes. Cook 4 minutes on each side or until browned and crisp. Place cakes on a platter. Repeat procedure with remaining 1 tablespoon oil and remaining potato mixture until you have 8 cakes.
3. Top cakes evenly with salmon, sour cream, if desired, and remaining 2 tablespoons green onions. Serves 4 (serving size: 2 cakes)

CALORIES 283; **FAT** 13.7g (sat 2.8g, mono 6.2g, poly 3.3g); **PROTEIN** 13g; **CARB** 27g; **FIBER** 2g; **SUGARS** 1g (est. added sugars 0g); **CHOL** 112mg; **IRON** 1mg; **SODIUM** 574mg; **CALC** 42mg

SLOW COOKER

SUCCULENT STUFFED PORK

High-flavor ingredients embellish a lean cut in this elegant slow cooker main.

Gluten Free • Kid Friendly
Make Ahead

Pork Loin Stuffed with Spinach and Goat Cheese

(pictured on page 221)

Hands-on: 40 min. Total: 8 hr. 10 min.

2 tablespoons olive oil, divided
½ cup thinly sliced shallots
1 tablespoon sliced garlic
1 tablespoon chopped fresh thyme
1 (5-ounce) package fresh baby spinach
3 ounces goat cheese (about ⅔ cup), at room temperature
2 tablespoons chopped fresh chives
2 tablespoons chopped fresh flat-leaf parsley
1 teaspoon grated lemon rind
1 (3-pound) boneless pork loin
1½ teaspoons kosher salt, divided
1 teaspoon black pepper, divided
¼ cup apricot preserves
2 tablespoons unsalted butter
1 tablespoon Dijon mustard
2 teaspoons apple cider vinegar

1. Heat 1 tablespoon oil in a large nonstick skillet over medium-high. Add shallots, garlic, and thyme; cook 5 minutes, stirring often, until shallots are caramelized. Add spinach; cook 1 minute, stirring constantly, until wilted. Remove from heat.
2. Combine goat cheese, chives, parsley, and lemon rind in a small bowl.

3. Holding a knife flat and parallel to a cutting board, cut horizontally through center of pork loin, cutting to, but not through, other side. Open flat, as you would a book. Starting at the center seam, cut horizontally through each half, cutting to, but not through, other side. Open flat on either side. Place pork between 2 sheets of plastic wrap; pound to an even ½-inch thickness using a meat mallet or small, heavy skillet. Remove plastic wrap.
4. Season with ½ teaspoon salt and ½ teaspoon pepper. Spread goat cheese mixture evenly over pork; top with shallot mixture. Roll up pork jelly-roll fashion. Tie with kitchen twine at 1-inch intervals. Sprinkle with remaining 1 teaspoon salt and remaining ½ teaspoon pepper.
5. Wipe pan clean. Heat remaining 1 tablespoon oil over medium-high. Add pork; cook 3 minutes per side or until browned. Place stuffed pork in a 5-quart slow cooker.
6. Add apricot preserves, butter, and mustard to pan; reduce heat to medium. Cook 1 minute, stirring constantly, until butter melts. Pour over pork loin in slow cooker. Cover and cook on LOW 7 to 8 hours, or until a meat thermometer inserted in thickest portion of pork registers 145°F.
7. Place pork on a cutting board; let stand 15 minutes. Skim and discard fat from sauce in slow cooker. Pour sauce into a saucepan; bring to a boil over medium-high. Cook 5 minutes, until reduced to about 1 cup. Stir in vinegar.
8. Remove and discard twine. Slice pork into 12 slices; serve with sauce. Serves 12 (serving size: 1 slice of pork and about 4 teaspoons sauce)

CALORIES 206; **FAT** 10.7g (sat 4g, mono 4.3g, poly 0.9g); **PROTEIN** 20g; **CARB** 7g; **FIBER** 1g; **SUGARS** 5g (est. added sugars 3g); **CHOL** 66mg; **IRON** 1mg; **SODIUM** 354mg; **CALC** 45mg

COOK ONCE, EAT 3X

Skip the fryer: Bake a batch of chickpea cakes for stuffed pitas tonight, then crumble onto pizza and a salad during the week.

Kid Friendly • Make Ahead Vegetarian

Falafel Pita Sliders

Hands-on: 25 min. Total: 8 hr. 40 min.
We make falafel patties instead of balls because the wide, flat surface area gets extra crisp when seared and baked, a lighter approach to shallow frying. Use any stuffers you like for the sandwiches, or load up as the Israelis do with a chopped cucumber and tomato salad, pickled cabbage, and tahini sauce like the one on page 101.

Falafel:
6 cups water
2 cups dried chickpeas (garbanzo beans)
2 cups finely chopped white onion
1 cup chopped fresh cilantro
1 cup chopped fresh flat-leaf parsley
1/4 cup fresh lemon juice
8 garlic cloves
1 tablespoon ground cumin
1 teaspoon kosher salt
1 teaspoon freshly ground black pepper
1/2 teaspoon baking soda
1/4 teaspoon ground red pepper
Cooking spray

Pita Sliders:
1/4 cup plain 2% reduced-fat Greek yogurt
1/4 cup canola mayonnaise
2 tablespoons chopped fresh dill
1/4 teaspoon freshly ground black pepper
8 (1-ounce) miniature whole-wheat pita rounds (such as Toufayan)
1 medium tomato, thinly sliced
2 cups loosely packed baby arugula (about 2 ounces)
1 small red onion, very thinly sliced

1. To prepare falafel, combine 6 cups water and chickpeas in a large bowl; let stand at room temperature 8 hours or overnight. Drain.
2. Preheat oven to 450°F.
3. Place chickpeas, onion, and next 9 ingredients (through ground red pepper) in a food processor; pulse until coarsely chopped. Divide and shape mixture into 16 (1/2-inch-thick) patties (about 1/3 cup per patty).
4. Heat a large cast-iron skillet over medium-high. Coat pan with cooking spray. Place 8 patties in pan; coat patties with cooking spray. Cook 2 to 3 minutes on each side or until browned. Place on a wire rack set on a baking sheet. Repeat procedure with cooking spray and remaining patties. Place baking sheet in oven; bake at 450°F for 10 minutes. Reserve 8 falafel patties for Recipes 2 and 3.
5. To prepare pita sliders, combine yogurt, mayonnaise, dill, and 1/4 teaspoon black pepper in a bowl. Cut off top fourth of each pita (reserve for another use). Spoon about 1 tablespoon yogurt mixture into each pita pocket; top with 1 falafel patty, 1 tomato slice, 1/4 cup arugula leaves, and about 1/4 cup red onion slices. Serves 4 (serving size: 2 filled pita pockets)

CALORIES 379; **FAT** 8.5g (sat 0.7g, mono 3.1g, poly 3.2g); **PROTEIN** 17g; **CARB** 63g; **FIBER** 14g; **SUGARS** 10g (est. added sugars 0g); **CHOL** 1mg; **IRON** 6mg; **SODIUM** 642mg; **CALC** 132mg

Quick & Easy • Kid Friendly Make Ahead • Vegetarian

Falafel Pizza

Hands-on: 15 min. Total: 25 min.
When a Middle Eastern main takes a trip to Italy via the Mediterranean, you get this fantastic vegetarian pizza. The chopped falafel toasts until crisp while the pizza bakes. Sun-dried tomatoes and kalamata olives give this quick pizza its bold, intense flavor.

1 (12-inch) whole-grain prebaked pizza crust (such as Mama Mary's)
1/2 cup lower-sodium marinara sauce
2 ounces part-skim mozzarella cheese, shredded (about 1/2 cup)
1 cup thinly sliced yellow bell pepper
1/4 cup chopped sun-dried tomatoes
1/2 teaspoon crushed red pepper
1/2 ounce pitted kalamata olives, finely chopped (about 2 tablespoons)
4 cooked falafel patties (from Recipe 1), chopped
1/4 cup chopped fresh oregano
1 teaspoon fresh lemon juice

1. Preheat oven to 425°F.
2. Place pizza crust on a baking sheet. Spread sauce evenly over crust, leaving a 1/2-inch border. Top evenly with cheese, bell pepper, sun-dried tomatoes, crushed red pepper, olives, and falafel; bake at 425°F for 7 to 8 minutes or until crust is browned and crisp. Sprinkle with oregano and lemon juice. Cut into 8 slices. Serves 4 (serving size: 2 slices)

CALORIES 358; **FAT** 11.7g (sat 2.4g, mono 2.9g, poly 3.8g); **PROTEIN** 14g; **CARB** 57g; **FIBER** 10g; **SUGARS** 10g (est. added sugars 1g); **CHOL** 9mg; **IRON** 5mg; **SODIUM** 754mg; **CALC** 218mg

WHY DRIED CHICKPEAS?

The secret to the best falafel is to use dried chickpeas that have been soaked but not simmered. They retain more starch than cooked or canned, ideal for getting the crispiest cakes. Conversely, for the best hummus, start with dried soaked chickpeas and simmer for 30 minutes with a pinch of baking soda until fall-apart tender. Drain and blend while slightly warm.

Falafel, Feta, and Tomato Salad

Hands-on: 15 min. Total: 15 min.
Think of chopped falafel as a tasty, protein-packed crouton—it adds texture to the salad and instantly turns a simple side into a substantial main dish. We chose a Mediterranean theme here, but you could use any nuts, cheeses, or vegetables you like.

1/4 cup extra-virgin olive oil
2 tablespoons red wine vinegar
1/2 teaspoon kosher salt
1/2 teaspoon freshly ground black pepper
2 pounds tomatoes, sliced crosswise into 1/2-inch-thick slices
4 cups loosely packed arugula
1 cup sliced cucumber
3/4 cup thinly sliced red onion
1/2 cup torn fresh mint
4 cooked falafel patties (from Recipe 1), cut into 1/2-inch pieces
2 ounces feta cheese, crumbled (about 1/2 cup)
1/4 cup pine nuts, toasted

1. Combine first 4 ingredients in a large bowl, stirring with a whisk. Add tomatoes; toss gently to coat. Let stand 2 minutes. Arrange tomatoes on a platter so that slices overlap slightly. Reserve remaining vinaigrette in bowl.
2. Add arugula, cucumber, onion, mint, and falafel to reserved vinaigrette to bowl; toss gently to coat. Arrange falafel mixture over tomatoes; sprinkle evenly with feta and pine nuts. Drizzle any remaining vinaigrette over salad. Serves 4 (serving size: about 3 cups)

CALORIES 386; FAT 25.1g (sat 4.8g, mono 13.4g, poly 5.1g); PROTEIN 12g; CARB 32g; FIBER 9g; SUGARS 12g (est. added sugars 0g); CHOL 13mg; IRON 5mg; SODIUM 560mg; CALC 202mg

---

FREEZE IT!

FLAKY FISH WITH A TOASTY TWIST

Our freezer-friendly nuggets give store-bought ones a run for their money.

Quinoa-Crusted Fish Nuggets with Tartar Sauce

Hands-on: 15 min. Total: 30 min.
Any firm white fish will work, such as grouper, halibut, flounder, or cod. Use rice flour to make gluten-free nuggets.

Cooking spray
1 cup uncooked white quinoa
1/4 cup all-purpose flour
1 teaspoon paprika
1/2 teaspoon dried thyme
3/4 teaspoon freshly ground black pepper, divided
1/4 cup nonfat buttermilk
1 large egg
1 pound skinless flounder or cod fillets, cut into 1-inch pieces
1/4 cup canola mayonnaise
1/4 cup plain 2% reduced-fat Greek yogurt
2 tablespoons chopped dill pickles
1 tablespoon white wine vinegar
1 teaspoon grainy mustard
1 teaspoon chopped fresh dill

1. Preheat oven to 425°F. Line a baking sheet with parchment paper; lightly coat with cooking spray.
2. Cook quinoa in a large skillet over medium-high, stirring occasionally, for 3 to 4 minutes, until toasted and fragrant. Remove from heat; cool 10 minutes. Transfer to a food processor; process for 20 seconds or until finely ground.
3. Stir together flour, paprika, thyme, and 1/2 teaspoon black pepper in a shallow dish. Stir together buttermilk and egg in a second shallow dish. Place ground quinoa in a third shallow dish.
4. Dredge fish pieces in flour mixture; shake off excess. Dip fish in egg mixture; dredge in quinoa, pressing to adhere. Place fish in a single layer on prepared baking sheet. Lightly coat breaded fish pieces with cooking spray.
5. Bake at 425°F for 13 minutes, turning once after 7 minutes, until golden and cooked through.
6. Meanwhile, stir together mayonnaise, yogurt, pickles, vinegar, mustard, dill, and remaining 1/4 teaspoon black pepper in a small bowl. Serve with fish nuggets. Serves 4 (serving size: 5 nuggets and 2 tablespoons sauce)

CALORIES 343; FAT 10.6g (sat 1.4g, mono 3.9g, poly 3.7g); PROTEIN 24g; CARB 36g; FIBER 4g; SUGARS 4g (est. added sugars 0g); CHOL 99mg; IRON 3mg; SODIUM 565mg; CALC 91mg

---

HOW TO

FREEZE
Prepare recipe as directed through Step 4, omitting cooking spray. Freeze until solid. Place nuggets in a ziplock plastic bag; return to freezer.

THAW
Bake from frozen!

REHEAT
Place frozen nuggets in a single layer on a baking sheet lined with greased parchment paper; lightly coat nuggets with cooking spray. Bake at 425°F for 15 minutes, turning once halfway through.

WOW!

Staff Favorite • Quick & Easy
Gluten Free • Kid Friendly
Make Ahead • Vegetarian

Jackfruit Tostadas

Hands-on: 20 min. Total: 35 min.
Jackfruit is a nutrient-rich, tree-borne fruit that easily shreds to mimic the texture of pulled pork. It's gluten-free and a favorite ingredient for vegetarians. Look for young green jackfruit found canned at Asian supermarkets.

1 cup white vinegar
1 cup water
1 teaspoon granulated sugar
¾ teaspoon kosher salt, divided
½ cup thinly sliced carrot
½ cup very small cauliflower florets
⅓ cup thinly sliced radishes
6 (6-inch) corn tortillas
1 (14-ounce) can jackfruit in brine, drained and rinsed
1 tablespoon grated lime rind
¼ cup fresh lime juice (from 2 limes)
2 teaspoons chipotle chile powder
2 teaspoons ground cumin
1 garlic clove, minced
¼ teaspoon black pepper
⅓ cup chopped fresh cilantro

1. Preheat oven to 400°F. Combine vinegar, 1 cup water, sugar, and ½ teaspoon salt in a saucepan. Bring to a simmer; cook until sugar and salt dissolve. Stir in carrot, cauliflower, and radishes. Remove from heat.
2. Cut 4 circles from each tortilla with a 2-inch round cutter. Place on a baking sheet. Bake at 400°F for 9 minutes.
3. Place jackfruit in a bowl, and shred. Stir in lime rind, juice, chile powder, cumin, garlic, pepper, and remaining ¼ teaspoon salt. Place in a nonstick skillet; cook over medium-high, stirring often, 3 to 5 minutes.
4. Top each baked tortilla circle with 1 teaspoon jackfruit mixture and a

few pickled vegetables. Sprinkle with cilantro. Serves 8 (serving size: 3 tostadas)

CALORIES 58; **FAT** 1.5g (sat .03g, mono .8g, poly .6g); **PROTEIN** 1g; **CARB** 10g; **FIBER** 2g; **SUGARS** 1g (est. added sugars 0g); **CHOL** 0mg; **IRON** 1mg; **SODIUM** 184mg; **CALC** 23mg

USE IT UP

HOISIN SAUCE

Easy weeknight ideas that use the rest of the jar.

Staff Favorite • Quick & Easy
Kid Friendly
Easy Sesame-Hoisin Salmon
Preheat oven to 400°F. Combine 2 Tbsp. hoisin sauce, 1 Tbsp. brown sugar, 1 Tbsp. reduced-sodium soy sauce, 1 Tbsp. rice vinegar, 2 tsp. toasted sesame oil, 1 tsp. grated fresh ginger, and ¼ tsp. crushed red pepper. Place 4 (6-oz.) salmon fillets in a baking dish coated with cooking spray; sprinkle with ¼ tsp. kosher salt. Pour sauce over salmon. Bake at 400°F for 15 minutes, basting occasionally. Sprinkle with 2 Tbsp. sliced green onions. Serves 4 (serving size: 1 fillet)

CALORIES 294; **FAT** 12g (sat 2.4g, mono 4.1g, poly 4.4g); **PROTEIN** 37g; **CARB** 8g; **FIBER** 0g; **SUGARS** 6g (est. added sugars 5g); **CHOL** 89mg; **IRON** 1mg; **SODIUM** 489mg; **CALC** 26mg

Kid Friendly • Make Ahead
Sweet BBQ Drumsticks
Preheat oven to 400°F. Boil ¼ cup hoisin sauce, ¼ cup orange juice, 2 Tbsp. honey, 1 Tbsp. fresh lime juice, ¼ tsp. kosher salt, and 2 minced fresh garlic cloves 2 minutes; reserve ¼ cup. Place 8 (4-oz.) skinned chicken drumsticks on a foil-lined baking sheet coated with cooking spray; brush with half of remaining sauce. Bake at 400°F for 40 minutes or until done, turning and brushing with other half of sauce after

20 minutes. Serve with reserved ¼ cup sauce. Serves 4 (serving size: 2 drumsticks)

CALORIES 230; **FAT** 5.5g (sat 1.3g, mono 1.9g, poly 1.4g); **PROTEIN** 26g; **CARB** 18g; **FIBER** 1g; **SUGARS** 14g (est. added sugars 12g); **CHOL** 118mg; **IRON** 1mg; **SODIUM** 529mg; **CALC** 23mg

Quick & Easy • Kid Friendly
Make Ahead • Vegetarian
Pan-Roasted Carrots
Cut 1 lb. medium carrots in half lengthwise. Heat a large cast-iron skillet over medium-high. Add 2 Tbsp. olive oil and 1½ tsp. unsalted butter to pan; swirl to coat. Add carrots in a single layer; cook without stirring for 5 minutes. Stir, and arrange in a single layer; cook without stirring for 5 more minutes. Combine 2 Tbsp. water, 1 Tbsp. hoisin sauce, 1½ tsp. maple syrup, and ¼ tsp. kosher salt; add to pan, and cook 1 minute or until carrots are glazed. Serves 4 (serving size: about ⅔ cup)

CALORIES 139; **FAT** 9.2g (sat 2g, mono 5.3g, poly 0.9g); **PROTEIN** 1g; **CARB** 14g; **FIBER** 3g; **SUGARS** 8g (est. added sugars 3g); **CHOL** 4mg; **IRON** 0mg; **SODIUM** 255mg; **CALC** 40mg

Quick & Easy • Kid Friendly
Make Ahead
Hoisin Sloppy Joes
Heat a large nonstick skillet over medium-high. Add 1 lb. 90% lean ground beef, ½ cup chopped red onion, and 4 minced garlic cloves; cook 5 minutes, stirring to crumble. Stir in ¼ cup water, ¼ cup hoisin sauce, 2 Tbsp. ketchup, 1½ tsp. Sriracha chili sauce, and ¼ tsp. kosher salt; cook 3 minutes. Divide mixture evenly among 4 whole-wheat hamburger buns; serve with red onion slices, if desired. Serves 4 (serving size: 1 sandwich)

CALORIES 379; **FAT** 14g (sat 4.9g, mono 5.4g, poly 1.6g); **PROTEIN** 28g; **CARB** 36g; **FIBER** 4g; **SUGARS** 11g (est. added sugars 6g); **CHOL** 74mg; **IRON** 4mg; **SODIUM** 794mg; **CALC** 79mg

SUMMER COOKBOOK
EAT BY COLOR

GREEN

Lush and verdant, the peas, herbs, and peppers of summer offer glorious bursts of freshness and boost the nutrition of salads, soups, and drinks.

Minestrone Verde

(pictured on page 223)

Hands-on: 29 min. Total: 29 min.
Brothy and light, this is a perfect summer soup. A quick and easy pesto adorns each bowl for a burst of herbal freshness. In a pinch, you can use purchased pesto.

1 cup coarsely chopped fresh basil (from about 3 bunches)
2 tablespoons shredded Parmigiano-Reggiano cheese
1 tablespoon pine nuts
1 garlic clove, chopped
2 tablespoons extra-virgin olive oil, divided
2 cups thinly sliced leeks
2 small zucchini, sliced into half-moons
4 cups unsalted chicken stock
8 ounces refrigerated tortellini
3 cups coarsely chopped fresh baby spinach (about 3 ounces)
1 cup frozen green peas, thawed
1 teaspoon fresh lemon juice
1/4 teaspoon kosher salt
1/4 teaspoon freshly ground black pepper

1. Process basil, cheese, pine nuts, and garlic in a food processor until finely chopped. Add 1½ tablespoons oil; process until very finely chopped and fully combined, stopping to scrape sides of bowl as necessary. Set aside.
2. Heat remaining 1½ teaspoons oil in a medium Dutch oven over medium. Add leeks; cook, stirring often, until softened, about 6 minutes. Stir in zucchini; cook, stirring occasionally, until zucchini is just tender but not browned, about 4 minutes. Add chicken stock, and increase heat to medium-high. Bring to a boil; reduce heat to medium-low, and simmer 8 minutes.
3. Meanwhile, cook tortellini in a stockpot of boiling water 3 minutes less than package directions, omitting salt and fat. Drain.
4. Add tortellini, spinach, and peas to soup. Cook until spinach is wilted, about 1 minute. Stir in lemon juice and salt. Ladle soup into 4 bowls. Top each serving with pesto, and sprinkle evenly with pepper. Serves 4 (serving size: about 1½ cups soup and about 1 teaspoon pesto)

CALORIES 354; FAT 13.8g (sat 3.8g, mono 6.8g, poly 1.9g); PROTEIN 18g; CARB 42g; FIBER 5g; SUGARS 8g (est. added sugars 0g); CHOL 32mg; IRON 4mg; SODIUM 614mg; CALC 237mg

Shaved Cucumber Greek Salad

Hands-on: 15 min. Total: 15 min.
Besides being crisp and cool, cukes offer up lots of vitamin C.

2 English cucumbers
1 pound Green Zebra tomatoes, cut into 3/4-inch wedges
2/3 cup pitted Castelvetrano olives
1/2 cup sliced green onions
1 1/2 ounces feta cheese, crumbled (about 1/3 cup)
2 teaspoons fresh oregano leaves
3 tablespoons extra-virgin olive oil
2 tablespoons Champagne vinegar or white wine vinegar
1/2 teaspoon cracked green peppercorns
1/8 teaspoon kosher salt

1. Shave cucumbers into long strips using a vegetable peeler to equal about 6 cups. Arrange cucumber strips, tomatoes, and olives on a large platter. Sprinkle with green onions, feta, and oregano. Drizzle with oil and vinegar. Sprinkle with green pepper and salt. Serves 8 (serving size: about 3/4 cup)

CALORIES 100; FAT 8g (sat 1.7g, mono 5.4g, poly 0.8g); PROTEIN 2g; CARB 5g; FIBER 2g; SUGARS 3g (est. added sugars 0g); CHOL 5mg; IRON 1mg; SODIUM 272mg; CALC 55mg

Snap Pea Salad with Whipped Ricotta

Hands-on: 15 min. Total: 15 min.
Look for pea tendrils or shoots at your farmers' market or Asian markets; you can substitute watercress or arugula.

8 ounces sugar snap peas
$^2/_3$ cup part-skim ricotta cheese
1 teaspoon grated lemon rind, divided
$^1/_2$ cup pea tendrils or shoots
$^1/_4$ cup sliced fresh chives
2 tablespoons torn fresh mint
2 tablespoons coarsely chopped fresh dill
2 teaspoons fresh lemon juice
1 tablespoon extra-virgin olive oil
$^1/_4$ teaspoon fine sea salt
$^1/_4$ teaspoon freshly ground black pepper

1. Bring a medium saucepan of water to a boil over high. Add peas, and cook just until bright green and barely tender, about 1 minute. Immediately transfer peas to a bowl of ice water; let stand 5 minutes. Drain well. Thinly slice lengthwise.
2. Process ricotta and ½ teaspoon lemon rind in a food processor until smooth and creamy, about 15 seconds. Spread mixture on a serving platter.
3. Toss together sliced snap peas, pea tendrils, chives, mint, dill, and lemon juice in a large bowl. Arrange on top of ricotta mixture. Drizzle with oil, and sprinkle with salt, pepper, and remaining ½ teaspoon lemon rind. Serves 4 (serving size: ½ cup)

CALORIES 108; **FAT** 6.5g (sat 2.5g, mono 2.7g, poly 0.3g); **PROTEIN** 6g; **CARB** 7g; **FIBER** 2g; **SUGARS** 5g (est. added sugars 0g); **CHOL** 17mg; **IRON** 1mg, **SODIUM** 197mg, **CALC** 103mg

Shishito and Shrimp Skewers with Chimichurri

Hands-on: 25 min. Total: 25 min.
Ridged shishito peppers are usually pleasantly bitter with mild to medium heat, but watch out: Every so often, you'll get one that packs a fiery punch.

1 cup firmly packed fresh flat-leaf parsley leaves
1 cup firmly packed fresh cilantro leaves
$^1/_4$ cup firmly packed fresh basil leaves
2 garlic cloves
$^1/_2$ teaspoon grated lemon rind
2 tablespoons fresh lemon juice
$^1/_4$ teaspoon crushed red pepper
4 tablespoons extra-virgin olive oil, divided
$^3/_4$ teaspoon kosher salt, divided
1$^1/_2$ pounds large shrimp (about 24), peeled and deveined (tails on)
16 (2-inch) shishito peppers (about 3 ounces)
$^1/_4$ teaspoon black pepper
Cooking spray

1. Preheat grill to medium-high (about 450°F).
2. Process parsley, cilantro, basil, and garlic in a food processor until finely chopped. Add lemon rind, juice, crushed red pepper, 3 tablespoons oil, and ¼ teaspoon salt; process until finely chopped and well combined.
3. Toss together shrimp and ¼ cup herb mixture. Thread 4 shrimp onto each of 6 (8-inch) skewers; thread 8 peppers onto each of 2 (8-inch) skewers. Drizzle skewers with remaining oil; sprinkle with black pepper and remaining ½ teaspoon salt.
4. Place skewers on grill grates coated with cooking spray; grill just until shrimp are done and peppers are charred, 2 to 3 minutes per side.

Brush skewers with remaining herb mixture before serving. Serves 4 (serving size: 6 shrimp and 4 peppers)

CALORIES 265; **FAT** 16g (sat 2.2g, mono 11g, poly 1.6g); **PROTEIN** 24g; **CARB** 5g; **FIBER** 1g; **SUGARS** 1g (est. added sugars 0g); **CHOL** 214mg; **IRON** 2mg; **SODIUM** 623mg; **CALC** 127mg

Honeydew-Jalapeño Margaritas

(pictured on page 225)

Hands-on: 10 min. Total: 2 hr. 10 min.
This slushy sipper offers sweet honeydew flavor with a nice slow burn from jalapeño-infused tequila.

$^1/_2$ cup silver tequila
1 jalapeño pepper, sliced
5 tablespoons fresh lime juice, divided
1 tablespoon turbinado sugar
1 teaspoon grated lime rind
$^1/_2$ teaspoon coarse sea salt
$^1/_2$ pound (about 1$^1/_2$ cups) frozen honeydew melon cubes
1$^1/_2$ cups ice cubes
$^1/_2$ cup water
1 tablespoon light agave syrup

1. Combine tequila and jalapeño in a bowl; let stand 2 to 4 hours. Pour through a small wire-mesh strainer into a bowl. Discard solids.
2. Place 2 tablespoons lime juice in a shallow dish. Stir together sugar, rind, and salt in a second shallow dish. Dip rims of 4 chilled 8-ounce glasses in lime juice then dip in sugar mixture.
3. Process infused tequila, honeydew, ice cubes, water, agave syrup, and remaining 3 tablespoons lime juice in a blender until smooth, about 1 minute. Pour evenly into prepared glasses. Serves 4 (serving size: 1 cup)

CALORIES 127; **FAT** 0.1g (sat 0g, mono 0g, poly 0.1g); **PROTEIN** 0g; **CARB** 14g; **FIBER** 1g; **SUGARS** 12g (est. added sugars 7g); **CHOL** 0mg; **IRON** 0mg; **SODIUM** 296mg; **CALC** 7mg

RED

Bring on the tomatoes, the strawberries, the beets. These crimson beauties make for stunning dishes rich in lycopene, vitamin C, and folate.

Staff Favorite • Make Ahead

Rosé-Glazed Strawberry Tart

Hands-on: 35 min. Total: 3 hr. 35 min.
The rectangular tart pan makes for a striking presentation, but if you don't have one, you can use a 9-inch tart pan or pie plate.

Crust:
⅓ cup almond meal
8 graham cracker sheets (about 4¼ ounces)
2 tablespoons sugar
⅛ teaspoon table salt
1 large egg white
1 tablespoon unsalted butter, melted
Baking spray with flour
Filling:
1 (8-ounce) package ⅓-less-fat cream cheese, softened
⅓ cup sugar
⅓ cup plain 2% reduced-fat Greek yogurt
1 teaspoon grated lemon rind
½ teaspoon vanilla extract
Glaze:
1 cup rosé wine
2 tablespoons sugar
Additional ingredients:
3 cups sliced strawberries (about 16 ounces)
Fresh mint leaves (optional)

1. Preheat oven to 350°F.
2. To prepare crust, spread almond meal in an even layer on a rimmed baking sheet. Bake at 350°F until lightly browned and fragrant, about 6 minutes. Cool 10 minutes.
3. Process almond meal, graham crackers, 2 tablespoons sugar, and salt in a food processor until finely ground, about 20 seconds. Place egg white in a small bowl; whisk until foamy. Add egg white and melted butter to food processor; pulse just until crumbs are moist, 3 to 4 times. (Do not overprocess.) Coat a 13½- x 4-inch tart pan with removable bottom with baking spray. Press crumb mixture into bottom and up sides of prepared pan. Place tart pan on a baking sheet.
4. Bake crust at 350°F until lightly browned, about 10 to 12 minutes. Cool completely on a wire rack, about 30 minutes.
5. To prepare filling, beat cream cheese and ⅓ cup sugar with a mixer on medium speed until light and fluffy and sugar is dissolved, 1 to 2 minutes. Add yogurt, lemon rind, and vanilla, and beat until blended and smooth. Spread filling evenly in cooled crust. Cover and chill until firm, about 2 hours.
6. To prepare glaze, bring wine and 2 tablespoons sugar to a boil in a small saucepan over medium-high, stirring occasionally until sugar dissolves. Cook until syrupy and reduced to about 2½ tablespoons, about 12 minutes. Cool 10 minutes.
7. Arrange strawberry slices in rows over filling; drizzle with rosé glaze. Garnish with mint leaves, if desired. Serve immediately. Serves 8 (serving size: 1 slice)

CALORIES 264; **FAT** 12.1g (sat 5.1g, mono 3.9g, poly 1.7g); **PROTEIN** 6g; **CARB** 33g; **FIBER** 2g; **SUGARS** 23g (est. added sugars 16g); **CHOL** 25mg; **IRON** 1mg; **SODIUM** 209mg; **CALC** 72mg

Quick & Easy • Gluten Free

Red Snapper with Chunky Tomato-Watermelon Salsa

Hands-on: 25 min. Total: 25 min.
To get the skin crisp, forgo a nonstick skillet in favor of a stainless-steel or cast-iron one; reach for a 12-inch skillet (or larger) so the fish doesn't get overcrowded—or cook in 2 batches if using a smaller pan.

1½ cups halved cherry tomatoes (about 8½ ounces)
1½ cups diced seedless watermelon (about 8½ ounces)
¼ cup finely chopped red onion
1 red Fresno chile, finely chopped
2 tablespoons finely chopped cilantro
1 tablespoon finely chopped mint
2 tablespoons fresh lime juice
3 tablespoons canola oil, divided
¾ teaspoon kosher salt, divided
4 (6-ounce) skin-on red snapper fillets
½ teaspoon black pepper

1. Stir together tomatoes, watermelon, red onion, chile, cilantro, mint, lime juice, 1 tablespoon canola oil, and ¼ teaspoon salt in a medium bowl. Set aside.
2. Pat fish dry with paper towels. Cut 3 shallow slits into the skin side of each fillet. Sprinkle fillets with pepper and remaining ½ teaspoon salt. Heat remaining 2 tablespoons oil in a large stainless-steel or cast-iron skillet over high. Add fillets, skin side down, and cook until skin is browned and crisp, about 5 minutes. Turn fillets; cook until lightly browned and done, 1 to 2 minutes. Serve fish immediately, skin side up, topped with salsa. Serves 4 (serving size: 1 snapper fillet and about ¾ cup salsa)

CALORIES 374; **FAT** 13.6g (sat 1.4g, mono 7.2g, poly 4.1g); **PROTEIN** 38g; **CARB** 27g; **FIBER** 4g; **SUGARS** 20g (est. added sugars 0g); **CHOL** 63mg; **IRON** 2mg; **SODIUM** 483mg; **CALC** 99mg

Grilled Red Curry Chicken and Bell Peppers

Hands-on: 25 min. Total: 2 hr. 25 min.
We use a combination of peppers for different flavor notes—mini bell peppers for sweetness and Fresnos for moderate spice. Fresnos look like red jalapeños but are less spicy; use the latter if you want more heat.

¼ cup red curry paste
¼ cup canola oil
2 tablespoons fresh lime juice
1 tablespoon sambal oelek
  (ground fresh chile paste)
2 teaspoons finely chopped garlic
8 boneless, skinless chicken thighs
  (1½ pounds)
12 miniature red bell peppers
  (about 9 ounces)
8 red Fresno chiles
2 large shallots (about 3 ounces),
  peeled and halved
Cooking spray

1. Whisk together first 5 ingredients. Place chicken and half (about ⅓ cup) of the curry paste mixture in a large ziplock plastic bag. Reserve remaining mixture. Seal bag, removing any excess air, and massage mixture into chicken. Chill 2 to 24 hours, turning occasionally.
2. Preheat grill to medium-high (about 450°F).
3. Coat bell peppers, Fresno chiles, and shallots with cooking spray, and place in a single layer on grill grate. Grill bell peppers and Fresno chiles, uncovered, until charred, turning occasionally, 6 to 8 minutes. At the same time, grill shallots until charred, 2 to 3 minutes. Place bell peppers, Fresno chiles, shallots, and 2 tablespoons reserved curry paste mixture in a large bowl, and toss to coat.

4. Remove chicken from marinade; discard marinade in bag. Place chicken on grill grate, and grill, uncovered, until done, 5 to 6 minutes per side. Arrange vegetables and chicken on a platter; top with remaining curry paste mixture. Serves 4 (serving size: 2 chicken thighs, ½ shallot, 3 bell peppers, and 2 Fresno chiles)

CALORIES 423; FAT 22.2g (sat 3g, mono 11.8g, poly 6g); PROTEIN 36g; CARB 19g; FIBER 4g; SUGARS 9g (est. added sugars 0g); CHOL 160mg; IRON 3mg; SODIUM 648mg; CALC 40mg

Lobster Roll Bruschetta

Hands-on: 25 min. Total: 25 min.
Though we love the sweet flavor of lobster in this appetizer, you can easily substitute ½ pound of shrimp with delicious results.

½ cup red wine vinegar
1 tablespoon granulated sugar
⅛ teaspoon crushed red pepper
2 small shallots, peeled and cut into
  thin rings
2 (8-ounce) lobster tails
Cooking spray
1 (10-ounce) French bread baguette,
  split lengthwise
¼ cup extra-virgin olive oil
2 cups chopped tomato
  (about 2 large tomatoes)
1½ tablespoons fresh lemon juice
1 tablespoon chopped fresh flat-leaf
  parsley
1 tablespoon chopped fresh basil
½ teaspoon kosher salt
½ teaspoon freshly ground black
  pepper
6 tablespoons canola mayonnaise

1. Stir together vinegar, sugar, and crushed red pepper in a medium microwave-safe bowl. Microwave at HIGH until hot and sugar has melted, 1 to 2 minutes. Add shallots. Let stand 5 minutes; drain.

2. Preheat grill to medium-high (about 450°F).
3. Using a sharp knife, cut lobster tails in half lengthwise; coat flesh with cooking spray. Place lobster tails, flesh side down, on grill grates; grill, uncovered, until grill marks appear, about 4 minutes. Turn lobster tails over, and grill, uncovered, until flesh is opaque, about 2 minutes. Remove from grill, and cool 10 minutes.
4. Meanwhile, lightly coat bread with cooking spray. Cut each bread piece in half. Place bread, cut side down, on grill grate; grill, uncovered, until toasted, about 1 to 2 minutes.
5. Remove meat from lobster tails, and chop. Discard shells. Stir together lobster meat, oil, tomato, lemon juice, parsley, basil, salt, and black pepper in a medium bowl.
6. Spread 1½ tablespoons mayonnaise on cut side of each bread piece; top evenly with lobster mixture and pickled shallot. Cut each bread piece into 5 slices. Serves 20 (serving size: 1 slice)

CALORIES 110; FAT 6.5g (sat 0.6g, mono 4.2g, poly 1.5g); PROTEIN 4g; CARB 9g; FIBER 1g; SUGARS 2g (est. added sugars 1g); CHOL 9mg; IRON 1mg; SODIUM 200mg; CALC 19mg

Rosy Beet-and-Quinoa Salad

Hands-on: 15 min. Total: 50 min.
This earthy whole-grain salad holds up well,
so it's a good make-ahead option; just bring
it to room temperature before serving for
the best flavor.

1¼ cups water
¼ cup dry white wine
1¼ cups uncooked quinoa
3 small red beets (about 8 ounces),
   peeled and cut into ½-inch wedges
   (about 1½ cups)
2 cups thinly sliced radicchio
   (½ medium head)
¼ cup chopped fresh dill
3 tablespoons pine nuts, toasted
3 tablespoons extra-virgin olive oil
1½ tablespoons red wine vinegar
1 teaspoon kosher salt
½ teaspoon freshly ground black
   pepper
2 ounces goat cheese, crumbled
   (about ½ cup)

1. Bring 1¼ cups water and wine to
a boil in a medium saucepan over
high. Stir in quinoa and beet wedges;
reduce heat to medium-low, cover,
and simmer until quinoa and beets
are tender, about 15 minutes. Fluff
with a fork, and transfer to a medium bowl. Cool for 30 minutes.
2. Stir radicchio, dill, pine nuts, oil,
vinegar, salt, and pepper into quinoa
mixture. Sprinkle with goat cheese.
Serves 4 (serving size: 1¼ cups salad
and 2 tablespoons cheese)

CALORIES 413; **FAT** 21.2g (sat 4.3g, mono 10.8g,
poly 5g); **PROTEIN** 12g; **CARB** 42g; **FIBER** 6g;
SUGARS 7g (est. added sugars 0g); **CHOL** 7mg;
IRON 4mg; **SODIUM** 598mg; **CALC** 63mg

YELLOW

Mild summer squash, juicy peaches, crunchy
bell peppers, and sweet corn bring benefits
galore to the table. It's time to dig in to
the golden treats of the summer garden.

Yellow Squash Pasta with Caramelized Lemon

Hands-on: 20 min. Total: 3 hr. 20 min.
Look for lemons with thinner skins (smoother,
shinier skins are often thinner); you'll get a
nice citrus hit with each bite, but charring
the slices softens the flavor so it's not over-
powering. Serve right after tossing everything
together, as the squash will start to wilt.

1½ pounds yellow squash
   (about 3 large squash)
3 medium lemons, divided
1½ tablespoons olive oil, divided
¼ teaspoon kosher salt, divided
⅛ teaspoon sugar
½ cup roughly chopped celery leaves
¾ ounce Parmigiano-Reggiano
   cheese, finely grated (about ¼ cup)
½ teaspoon freshly ground black
   pepper

1. Trim squash ends, and halve
squash crosswise. Using a spoon,
carefully scoop out inner seeds from
each squash, removing as little flesh
as possible. Cut squash into large
noodles using a spiralizer. Place
squash noodles between 2 layers of
paper towels. Let stand at room temperature until dry, about 3 hours.
2. Transfer noodles to a medium
bowl. Grate rind from 1 lemon to
equal ½ teaspoon. Cut same lemon
in half; squeeze juice to equal 1
tablespoon. Set aside rind and juice.
Trim tops and bottoms of remaining
2 lemons, and slice into half-moons.
3. Heat 1½ teaspoons oil in a large
nonstick skillet over medium-high.
Add lemon slices; sprinkle evenly
with ⅛ teaspoon salt. Sprinkle sugar
over lemons. Cook, stirring occasionally, until lemons are browned
on the edges and caramelized, 4 to
5 minutes.
4. Add caramelized lemon slices to
squash noodles. Add celery leaves,
cheese, lemon rind, lemon juice, pepper, and remaining ⅛ teaspoon salt;
toss gently to combine. Drizzle with
remaining 1 tablespoon oil. Serve
immediately. Serves 4 (serving size:
¾ cup)

CALORIES 97; **FAT** 7.9g (sat 2.1g, mono 4.1g, poly 0.6g);
PROTEIN 2g; **CARB** 6g; **FIBER** 2g; **SUGARS** 1g
(est. added sugars 0g); **CHOL** 5mg; **IRON** 0mg;
SODIUM 230mg; **CALC** 67mg

Peach-Thyme Galette

(pictured on page 222)

Hands-on: 45 min. Total: 1 hr. 45 min.
Rustic, free-form edges give this dessert a beautiful look. The crust is made with whole-wheat pastry flour, which is finely milled and thus perfect for pastries.

4 to 5 tablespoons ice water
½ teaspoon rice vinegar
¼ teaspoon vanilla extract
5⅞ ounces whole-wheat pastry flour (about 1⅔ cups), divided
¼ cup hazelnut meal
¼ teaspoon kosher salt
4½ tablespoons Demerara or turbinado sugar, divided
¼ cup cold unsalted butter, cut into pieces
1½ tablespoons cornstarch
1¾ pounds firm ripe peaches, peeled, pitted, and sliced into thin wedges (4 to 5 medium peaches)
2 tablespoons peach preserves
1 tablespoon honey
1½ teaspoons fresh thyme leaves

1. Preheat oven to 400°F.
2. Combine ice water, vinegar, vanilla, and ⅓ cup flour in a small bowl; stir with a fork until well blended to form a slurry.
3. Whisk together hazelnut meal, salt, 2 tablespoons sugar, and remaining 1⅓ cups flour in a medium bowl. Cut in butter with a pastry blender or 2 knives until mixture resembles coarse meal. Add slurry; stir just until moist. Turn dough out onto a lightly floured surface; knead lightly 5 times. Gently press dough into a 4-inch circle on heavy-duty plastic wrap. Cover with more plastic wrap. Carefully roll dough into a 12-inch round; freeze 10 minutes.
4. Remove dough from freezer; remove and discard top piece of plastic wrap. Let stand until pliable, about 1 minute. Invert dough round onto a baking sheet lined with parchment paper; remove and discard remaining plastic wrap.
5. Stir together cornstarch and 2 tablespoons sugar; sprinkle over dough, leaving a 2-inch border around edge. Arrange peaches in a spokelike pattern on cornstarch mixture, leaving a 2-inch border around edge. Fold edges of dough over peaches, pinching gently to close any cracks.
6. Stir together preserves and honey in a small microwave-safe bowl; microwave at HIGH until soft, about 20 seconds. Brush preserves mixture over peaches and dough edges. Sprinkle dough edges with remaining 1½ teaspoons sugar.
7. Bake at 400°F until crust browns, about 35 minutes. Remove from oven; sprinkle with thyme. Cool 10 minutes, and slice into 8 wedges. Serves 8 (serving size: 1 wedge)

CALORIES 243; FAT 8.5g (sat 3.8g, mono 3.2g, poly 0.6g); PROTEIN 4g; CARB 40g; FIBER 5g; SUGARS 21g (est. added sugars 12g); CHOL 15mg; IRON 2mg; SODIUM 67mg; CALC 29mg

Corn Cakes with Bacon and Turmeric Yogurt

Hands-on: 30 min. Total: 30 min.
Serve these sweet-savory cakes as a hearty side dish (they would be great with grilled shrimp) or as a lighter entrée with a side salad. Or turn them into an appetizer by making smaller cakes.

2 center-cut bacon slices, chopped
2¾ cups fresh corn kernels (about 4 ears)
1¼ cups finely chopped yellow squash
⅓ cup chopped green onions (white parts only)
2 large eggs, lightly beaten
¼ cup plain yellow cornmeal
¾ teaspoon freshly ground black pepper
⅜ teaspoon kosher salt, divided
¼ cup plain low-fat yogurt (not Greek-style)
1 tablespoon pure maple syrup
½ teaspoon ground turmeric

1. Heat a large cast-iron skillet over medium. Add bacon; cook, stirring often, until crisp, about 8 minutes. Drain on paper towels; reserve drippings in pan.
2. Increase heat to medium-high. Add corn and squash to drippings; cook until lightly charred and al dente, about 2 minutes. Transfer to a large bowl; cool 10 minutes. Add onions, eggs, cornmeal, pepper, ¼ teaspoon salt, and cooked bacon to corn mixture; stir to combine. Let mixture stand 5 minutes, stirring occasionally.
3. Stir together yogurt, maple syrup, turmeric, and remaining ⅛ teaspoon salt in a small bowl. Set aside.
4. Heat pan over medium. Drop batter by ¼-cupfuls into pan, flatten slightly with a spatula, and cook until firm and browned on each side, about 2 minutes per side. Serve with turmeric-yogurt mixture. Serves 4 (serving size: 3 corn cakes and 1 tablespoon yogurt mixture)

CALORIES 219; FAT 7.3g (sat 2.7g, mono 1.5g, poly 1.1g); PROTEIN 10g; CARB 33g; FIBER 4g; SUGARS 11g (est. added sugars 3g); CHOL 98mg; IRON 2mg; SODIUM 334mg; CALC 69mg

Yellow Bell Pepper Gazpacho

Hands-on: 15 min. Total: 1 hr. 15 min.
This soup just screams "summer" with its bright, refreshing flavor and cool temperature. You can make the soup a day ahead and keep it chilled; just give it a good whisk or another turn in the blender before serving.

1³/₄ **pounds yellow bell peppers (about 4 medium)**
1¹/₂ **pounds yellow tomatoes (about 2 large tomatoes)**
1¹/₂ **cups peeled seeded chopped cucumber**
2 garlic cloves
2 tablespoons sherry vinegar
³/₄ **teaspoon kosher salt**
5 tablespoons olive oil, divided
1¹/₂ **tablespoons fresh lemon juice**
2 tablespoons thinly sliced green onions (white parts only)

1. Dice bell peppers to equal ¼ cup; reserve. Dice tomatoes to equal ¼ cup; reserve. Roughly chop remaining bell peppers and tomatoes, and place in a blender. Add cucumber, garlic, vinegar, salt, 3 tablespoons oil, and 1 tablespoon lemon juice to blender; process on high until very smooth, 1 to 2 minutes. Chill 1 hour.
2. Stir together reserved ¼ cup bell peppers and ¼ cup tomatoes in a small bowl. Add onion slices and remaining 1½ teaspoons lemon juice, and toss. Ladle chilled soup into each of 6 bowls. Top each serving with pepper-tomato mixture, and drizzle with remaining 2 tablespoons oil. Serves 6 (serving size: 1 cup soup, about 1½ tablespoons relish, and ½ teaspoon oil)

CALORIES 161; FAT 11.9g (sat 1.6g, mono 8.3g, poly 1.3g); PROTEIN 3g; CARB 13g; FIBER 2g; SUGARS 4g (est. added sugars 0g); CHOL 0mg; IRON 1mg; SODIUM 270mg; CALC 35mg

Cantaloupe-White Balsamic Sorbet

(pictured on page 223)

Hands-on: 15 min. Total: 5 hr. 10 min.
This sorbet is refreshing, with an almost creamy texture. The white balsamic vinegar is subtle, but it adds a depth of flavor that enhances the melon.

1 pound chopped peeled ripe cantaloupe (about 2¹/₂ cups)
3 tablespoons white balsamic vinegar
¹/₈ **teaspoon kosher salt**
³/₄ **cup water, divided**
3 tablespoons sugar
3 tablespoons honey

1. Process cantaloupe, vinegar, salt, and ½ cup water in a blender until smooth.
2. Combine sugar, honey, and remaining ¼ cup water in a saucepan over medium; cook, stirring constantly, until sugar is dissolved, 2 to 4 minutes. Remove from heat, and cool 10 minutes.
3. Stir together cantaloupe mixture and honey mixture in a medium bowl until combined. Cover and chill until cold, about 30 minutes.
4. Pour mixture into freezer bowl of a 1-quart electric ice-cream maker, and proceed according to manufacturer's instructions. (Instructions and times will vary.) Transfer to a freezer-safe container, and freeze until easily scooped, at least 4 hours. Serves 6 (serving size: ½ cup)

CALORIES 87; FAT 0.1g (sat 0g, mono 0g, poly 0.1g); PROTEIN 1g; CARB 23g; FIBER 1g; SUGARS 21g (est. added sugars 15g); CHOL 0mg; IRON 0mg; SODIUM 56mg; CALC 7mg

PURPLE

It's time you got to know anthocyanin, a powerful antioxidant that's found in the gorgeous indigo pigmentation of certain fresh produce.

Smoked Potato Salad

Hands-on: 20 min. Total: 1 hr. 20 min.

3 cups cherry wood chips, soaked and drained
2 pounds baby purple potatoes
1¹/₂ **cups thinly sliced purple radishes (about 6 ounces)**
5 tablespoons extra-virgin olive oil
¹/₄ **cup apple cider vinegar**
2 tablespoons grainy mustard
4 teaspoons light brown sugar
1 teaspoon kosher salt
1 teaspoon ground cumin
³/₄ **teaspoon chipotle chile powder**

1. Preheat a gas grill to medium (about 400°F) on one side, or push hot coals to one side of a charcoal grill. Place a disposable aluminum pan directly on the burner on lit side of the gas grill, and add soaked wood chips to pan, or scatter wood chips on hot coals of charcoal grill; heat until wood chips are smoking.
2. Place potatoes in a disposable aluminum pan; place on grates over unlit side of grill. Grill, covered,

20 minutes. Rotate pan halfway; grill, covered, until potatoes are tender, 20 to 30 more minutes. Cut potatoes into ¾-inch pieces. Place in a large bowl; add radishes.

3. Whisk together oil and remaining ingredients in a small bowl. Pour dressing over potatoes and radishes; toss to coat. Serves 8 (serving size: about ¾ cup)

CALORIES 179; FAT 8.9g (sat 1.2g, mono 6.2g, poly 0.9g); PROTEIN 3g; CARB 23g; FIBER 3g; SUGARS 3g (est. added sugars 2g); CHOL 0mg; IRON 1mg; SODIUM 337mg; CALC 22mg

Staff Favorite • Gluten Free

Red Wine– Marinated Steak with Balsamic Onions and Slaw

Hands-on: 40 min. Total: 5 hr. 45 min.
Cook this with either hanger or flank steak, whichever you prefer. The onions add a hit of umami, but feel free to omit them.

2 cups dry red wine (such as Merlot)
1 tablespoon fennel seeds
1 teaspoon crushed red pepper
3 thyme sprigs
1 (2-pound) flank steak, trimmed
5 small red onions (about 2¼ pounds), peeled and each cut into 8 wedges, root end intact
½ cup balsamic vinegar
¼ cup water
2 teaspoons kosher salt, divided
1½ teaspoons freshly ground black pepper, divided
6 cups thinly sliced red cabbage
¼ cup thinly sliced green onions
3 tablespoons extra-virgin olive oil
3 tablespoons red wine vinegar

1. Place red wine, fennel seeds, crushed red pepper, and thyme sprigs in a small saucepan; bring to a simmer over high. Reduce heat to medium, and simmer, stirring occasionally, until reduced to ¾ cup, about 10 minutes. Cool completely, about 10 minutes. Pour wine mixture through a fine wire-mesh strainer; discard solids. Place steak in a large ziplock plastic bag. Add wine mixture, seal bag, and turn to coat steak. Marinate in refrigerator, turning occasionally, 4 hours or overnight.

2. Preheat oven to 400°F.
3. Place red onion wedges in a 13- x 9-inch glass baking dish. Add vinegar, ¼ cup water, ¼ teaspoon salt, and ½ teaspoon black pepper; cover with foil. Bake at 400°F for 45 minutes; turn onions over. Uncover and bake until liquid is syrupy and onions are tender, about 20 minutes. Remove and discard root ends from onion wedges; separate the onion wedges into "petals."

4. Preheat grill to high (450° to 550°F).
5. Remove steak from marinade; discard marinade. Sprinkle steak with 1½ teaspoons salt and remaining 1 teaspoon black pepper. Place steak on oiled grill grates, and grill, uncovered, until desired degree of doneness, 5 to 6 minutes per side. Let stand 5 minutes. Slice crosswise against the grain.

6. Combine cabbage, green onions, oil, red wine vinegar, and remaining ¼ teaspoon salt in a bowl. Toss to coat. Place cabbage mixture on a platter with steak, onions, and any accumulated juices from the steak. Serves 8 (serving size: 3 ounces steak, about 1 cup onions, and about ¾ cup cabbage mixture)

CALORIES 297; FAT 13.1g (sat 4g, mono 6.9g, poly 0.9g); PROTEIN 25g; CARB 17g; FIBER 4g; SUGARS 9g (est. added sugars 0g); CHOL 68mg; IRON 2mg; SODIUM 544mg; CALC 72mg

Gluten Free • Make Ahead
Vegetarian

Grilled Eggplant and Purple Cauliflower Caponata

Hands-on: 15 min. Total: 45 min.
Purple cauliflower is becoming more widely available at farmers' markets; white cauliflower would also be delicious here.

8 ounces purple cauliflower florets
½ cup thinly sliced shallots
1 tablespoon sugar
3/8 teaspoon kosher salt
1 pound Japanese eggplant, cut into 1-inch-thick rounds (about 2 medium)
Cooking spray
1 cup chopped seeded Cherokee purple tomatoes
½ cup loosely packed fresh purple basil leaves
¼ cup red wine vinegar
¼ cup extra-virgin olive oil
3 tablespoons capers, drained
1 ounce pitted kalamata olives, chopped (about 9 olives)

1. Place cauliflower, shallots, sugar, and salt in a large bowl; toss to coat. Let stand 30 minutes.
2. Preheat grill to medium-high (about 450°F).
3. Generously coat eggplant with cooking spray. Place in a single layer on oiled grill grates; grill, covered, until tender, 5 to 6 minutes, turning occasionally. Cut into 1-inch cubes. Add eggplant, tomatoes, basil, vinegar, oil, capers, and olives to cauliflower mixture; toss well. Let stand 10 to 15 minutes. Serve with a slotted spoon. Serves 8 (serving size: about ½ cup)

CALORIES 115; FAT 8.1g (sat 1.2g, mono 6.1g, poly 0.8g); PROTEIN 2g; CARB 9g; FIBER 3g; SUGARS 5g (est. added sugars 1g); CHOL 0mg; IRON 1mg; SODIUM 235mg; CALC 20mg

Blueberry-Lavender Yogurt Pops

Hands-on: 30 min. Total: 4 hr. 30 min.
These just might be the most sophisticated ice pops we've ever had. Reach for regular whole-milk yogurt here instead of Greek yogurt; the texture is looser, and the flavor is richer and less tart.

2 cups fresh blueberries
2 tablespoons sugar
6 tablespoons honey
⅓ cup water
2 teaspoons dried culinary lavender
 or 3 fresh lavender sprigs
2 (2-inch) lemon rind strips
2¼ cups whole-milk plain yogurt
 (not Greek-style)

1. Place berries and sugar in a small saucepan over medium. Cook, stirring occasionally and pressing to break up berries, until juices release completely, 10 to 12 minutes. Cool completely.
2. Meanwhile, place honey, ⅓ cup water, lavender, and rind in a small saucepan. Cover and bring to a boil over medium-high. Remove from heat; let stand 15 minutes. Pour through a fine sieve; discard solids. Cool completely.
3. Stir together lavender syrup and yogurt in a bowl. Spoon yogurt mixture and blueberry mixture alternately into 10 (3-ounce) ice-pop molds, beginning and ending with yogurt mixture. Swirl gently. Freeze until solid, 4 hours or overnight. Serves 10 (serving size: 1 frozen pop)

CALORIES 99; **FAT** 1.9g (sat 1.2g, mono 0.5g, poly 0.1g); **PROTEIN** 2g; **CARB** 20g; **FIBER** 1g; **SUGARS** 18g (est. added sugars 13g); **CHOL** 7mg; **IRON** 0mg; **SODIUM** 26mg; **CALC** 69mg

Blackberry Gin Fizz

Hands-on: 10 min. Total: 35 min.
For the perfect layer of creamy froth on top of each cocktail, be prepared to shake the cocktail shaker (with no ice) vigorously; the half-and-half helps set the egg white for a more stable foam.

4 cups fresh blackberries (about
 1 pound)
2 tablespoons sugar
2 tablespoons fresh lemon juice
10 tablespoons gin, divided
2 large pasteurized egg whites,
 divided
2 tablespoons half-and-half, divided
1 cup chilled club soda, divided
Mint sprigs (optional)

1. Place berries and sugar in a saucepan over medium. Cook, stirring occasionally to break up berries, until juices release completely, about 15 minutes. Pour through a fine sieve, pressing to release liquid; discard solids. (You will have about 1 cup liquid.) Cool mixture completely; stir in lemon juice.
2. Place half of the blackberry syrup, 5 tablespoons gin, 1 egg white, and 1 tablespoon half-and-half in a cocktail shaker. Shake vigorously until frothy, about 15 seconds. Divide evenly between 2 glasses. Top each serving with ¼ cup club soda. Repeat with remaining ingredients. Garnish with mint, if desired. Serves 4 (serving size: about ¾ cup)

CALORIES 161; **FAT** 0.9g (sat 0.5g, mono 0.3g, poly 0g); **PROTEIN** 3g; **CARB** 15g; **FIBER** 1g; **SUGARS** 12g (est. added sugars 6g); **CHOL** 3mg; **IRON** 0mg; **SODIUM** 44mg; **CALC** 22mg

LET'S COOK

Kicky Black Bean Burgers

Hands-on: 30 min. Total: 30 min.
If you don't have a food processor, you can sub about ⅔ cup plain breadcrumbs for the torn bun.

1 (15-ounce) can unsalted black
 beans, drained and rinsed
5 (1¼-ounce) whole-wheat
 hamburger buns, toasted and
 divided
¾ teaspoon ground cumin
½ teaspoon garlic powder
¼ teaspoon salt
¼ teaspoon black pepper
1 large egg, lightly beaten
1 large egg white, lightly beaten
2 tablespoons canola oil
2 ounces sliced pepper-Jack or
 Monterey Jack cheese
½ cup fresh refrigerated pico de gallo
4 lettuce leaves

1. Place beans in a large bowl; mash with a fork. Place 1 toasted bun, torn, in a food processor; pulse until fine crumbs form. Stir breadcrumbs, cumin, and next 5 ingredients (through egg white) into beans.
2. Divide and shape bean mixture into 4 (1-inch-thick) patties. Heat oil in a large skillet over medium-high. Add patties to pan; cook 4 minutes on each side or until browned.
3. Divide cheese evenly among patties; cook 1 minute or until cheese melts. Top bottom halves of remaining 4 buns evenly with patties, pico de gallo, lettuce, and top halves of buns. Serves 4 (serving size: 1 burger)

CALORIES 360; **FAT** 15.1g (sat 3.5g, mono 5.4g, poly 3.2g); **PROTEIN** 16g; **CARB** 43g; **FIBER** 10g; **SUGARS** 7g (est. added sugars 2g); **CHOL** 59mg; **IRON** 3mg; **SODIUM** 654mg; **CALC** 222mg

THE HEALTHY COOK'S GUIDE TO GRASS-FED BEEF

With a nutrition profile closer to salmon than grain-fed beef and flavor bold enough to seem like a different animal altogether, grass-fed beef should be a staple in your repertoire. But you may be cooking it wrong. Here's what you need to know about this robust red meat.

COST

Grass-fed beef typically costs between $2 and $3 more per pound than grain-fed—because it costs more to raise livestock this way: Grass-fed beef ranchers can take up to 12 months longer to get their beef to market without the aid of antibiotics, hormones, and feedlot diets that slash production costs. Moreover, most grass-fed beef comes from relatively small, family-owned herds that lack the economy of scale of feedlot cattle businesses.

FLAVOR

To generalize, grass-fed beef tastes different from grain-fed in that it's often pleasantly gamy and a little mineral- and lamb-like in flavor. But to generalize is to miss much of what makes grass-fed meat so unique. Its flavor depends on the particular breed of cattle, how and where it was raised, and exactly what it ate. Cattle that ate clover and alfalfa in Colorado will taste different from Black Angus in Georgia fed a rotational mix of bluegrass, sorghum, and legumes.

LABELING

Here's a quick guide to beef label terms. For grass-fed beef that meets the highest standards, look for products certified by independent accrediting bodies such as Certified Humane and A Greener World's Animal Welfare Approved.

CERTIFIED GRASS-FED BY AGW
The strictest standard. Animal Welfare Approved ensures the cattle are 100% grass-fed, kept to high welfare standards, have not routinely been given antibiotics or hormones, and have been slaughtered humanely.

CERTIFIED GRASS-FED BY THE AMERICAN GRASS-FED ASSOCIATION Same standards as the AWA certification but no welfare and slaughter requirements.

HUMANE/HUMANELY RAISED/HIGH WELFARE Label phrases without legal, regulated definitions. Beware of these claims without independent third-party certification from groups like Animal Welfare Approved and Certified Humane.

GRASS-FINISHED Vague term that doesn't preclude cattle eating grain for much of their lives or being given antibiotics or hormones.

Quick & Easy • Gluten Free
Kid Friendly
Olive Oil–Basted Grass-Fed Strip Steak

Hands-on: 25 min. Total: 25 min.
We developed this technique specifically for lean grass-fed steaks. Turn them frequently to cook evenly and prevent the exterior from toughening. Baste after every turn so the sizzling surface stays moist.

3 tablespoons olive oil, divided
2 (8-ounce) 1$\frac{1}{2}$-inch-thick grass-fed New York strip steaks, trimmed
1 teaspoon kosher salt, divided
1 teaspoon freshly ground black pepper, divided
1 (3-inch) rosemary sprig
1 garlic clove, crushed
Fresh rosemary leaves (optional)

1. Heat a grill pan over medium-high. Brush 1 tablespoon oil on steaks; sprinkle with ½ teaspoon each salt and pepper.
2. Add rosemary sprig, garlic, and 1 tablespoon oil to pan. Add steaks; cook 9 minutes or until desired degree of doneness, turning steaks and basting with oil once every minute.
3. Place steaks on a cutting board; let stand 5 minutes. Slice steaks across grain; place on a platter. Drizzle with juices from cutting board and remaining 1 tablespoon oil. Sprinkle with remaining ½ teaspoon each salt and pepper. Garnish with rosemary leaves, if desired. Serves 4 (serving size: about 3 ounces)

CALORIES 224; FAT 13.2g (sat 2.6g, mono 8.5g, poly 1.2g); PROTEIN 26g; CARB 0g; FIBER 0g; SUGARS 0g; CHOL 62mg; IRON 2mg; SODIUM 543mg; CALC 13mg

Grass-Fed Beef Sirloin Kebabs

Hands-on: 25 min. Total: 25 min.
Feel free to prep the sauce and skewer the beef ahead of time.

½ cup plain 2% reduced-fat Greek yogurt
2 tablespoons chopped fresh dill
1 tablespoon grated lemon rind
1 tablespoon fresh lemon juice
1 teaspoon kosher salt, divided
1 pound grass-fed top sirloin steak, trimmed
2 tablespoons olive oil
1 teaspoon ground coriander
1 teaspoon freshly ground black pepper
8 (8-inch) skewers
Cooking spray
Chopped green onions (optional)

1. Preheat grill to high (450° to 550°F). Combine yogurt, dill, rind, juice, and ¼ teaspoon salt in a small bowl; stir well.
2. Cut steak into 16 (4- x 1-inch) strips. Toss with oil; sprinkle with coriander, pepper, and remaining ¾ teaspoon salt. Thread 2 strips onto each skewer.
3. Place skewers on grill grate coated with cooking spray. Grill, uncovered, 90 seconds on each side or until slightly charred. Serve with yogurt sauce. Garnish with onions, if desired. Serves 4 (serving size: 2 kebabs and 2 tablespoons sauce)

CALORIES 216; **FAT** 10.5g (sat 2.5g, mono 6.1g, poly 0.8g); **PROTEIN** 29g; **CARB** 2g; **FIBER** 1g; **SUGARS** 1g (est. added sugars 0g); **CHOL** 64mg; **IRON** 2mg; **SODIUM** 552mg; **CALC** 37mg

Juicy Grass-Fed Beef Burgers

Hands-on: 30 min. Total: 30 min.
In addition to the mayo mixed into the patties, we also stir in caramelized onions to help with juiciness and offer a flavor boost.

1 teaspoon canola oil
¾ cup finely chopped yellow onion
¼ cup canola mayonnaise, divided
1 teaspoon garlic powder
1 teaspoon freshly ground black pepper
1 pound 93% lean grass-fed ground sirloin
Cooking spray
4 (½-ounce) cheddar cheese slices
3 tablespoons ketchup
4 whole-wheat hamburger buns, toasted
4 (¼-inch-thick) tomato slices
4 Bibb lettuce leaves
1 ounce dill pickle slices

1. Heat oil in a small skillet over medium-high. Add onion; sauté 2 minutes. Reduce heat to medium; cook onion 5 minutes or until soft and caramelized, stirring frequently. Remove from heat; cool 5 minutes.
2. Combine caramelized onions, 2 tablespoons mayonnaise, garlic powder, pepper, and ground beef in a bowl, stirring just until combined. Gently shape mixture into 4 (⅓-inch-thick) patties.
3. Heat a grill pan or cast-iron skillet over high. Coat pan with cooking spray. Add patties; cook 3 minutes. Turn patties. Top each with 1 cheese slice; cook 2 minutes or to desired degree of doneness.
4. Spread ketchup evenly on bottom halves of buns. Spread remaining 2 tablespoons mayonnaise evenly on top halves of buns. Top bottom buns evenly with patties, tomato slices, lettuce leaves, and pickles. Cover with top halves of buns. Serves 4 (serving size: 1 burger)

CALORIES 423; **FAT** 19.5g (sat 6.3g, mono 4.7g, poly 2.7g); **PROTEIN** 32g; **CARB** 28g; **FIBER** 2g; **SUGARS** 8g (est. added sugars 3g); **CHOL** 80mg; **IRON** 4mg; **SODIUM** 682mg; **CALC** 183mg

NUTRITION

You may find yourself surprised at the numbers for grass-fed beef. The fat profile is closer to that of salmon than grain-fed beef. Grass-fed beef also has less than half the saturated fat of dark-meat chicken and a far better ratio of omega-6 to omega-3 polyunsaturated fats (the ideal ratio is less than 4).

G/100G OF MEAT	TOTAL FAT, G	SATURATED FAT, G	RATIO OF OMEGA-6 TO OMEGA-3 POLY-UNSATURATED FATS
GRASS-FED BEEF	1.87	0.80	1.54
GRAIN-FED BEEF	3.65	1.58	5.01
CHICKEN BREAST, SKINLESS	1.10	0.39	16.25
CHICKEN THIGH	7.20	2.09	17.64
PORK CHOP	3.38	1.22	27.45
SALMON, FARM RAISED	7.52	1.41	0.80

Source: Susan K. Duckett, PhD, professor at Clemson University

Grass-Fed Flat Iron Steak with Grilled Ratatouille

Hands-on: 35 min. Total: 35 min.
Grain-fed flat iron steaks are a relatively tender cut. But with grass-fed steak's lower fat content, we find pounding the meat before cooking ensures tenderness.

2 (8-ounce) grass-fed flat iron steaks
1 teaspoon kosher salt, divided
1 teaspoon freshly ground black pepper, divided
2 cups grape tomatoes, halved
2 tablespoons balsamic vinegar
1 (10-ounce) yellow squash, cut into ½-inch-thick rounds
1 (10-ounce) zucchini, cut into ½-inch-thick rounds
4 green onions, trimmed
1 (10-ounce) eggplant, cut crosswise into ½-inch-thick rounds
Cooking spray
2 tablespoons thinly sliced fresh mint
2 tablespoons extra-virgin olive oil
½ cup loosely packed fresh basil leaves

1. Place steaks in a single layer on a sheet of plastic wrap on a cutting board. Top with another sheet of plastic wrap. Using a meat mallet or small heavy skillet, pound steaks to ¼-inch thickness. Discard plastic wrap. Sprinkle steaks evenly with ½ teaspoon each salt and pepper.
2. Preheat grill to high (450° to 550°F). Combine tomatoes, vinegar, and remaining ½ teaspoon each salt and pepper in a large bowl.
3. Coat squash, zucchini, green onions, and eggplant with cooking spray. Place vegetables in a single layer on grill grate coated with cooking spray. Grill squash and zucchini, uncovered, 2 minutes or until tender and grill marks appear. Grill green onions 2 minutes or until charred and slightly tender, turning occasionally. Grill eggplant 3 minutes on each side or until tender and grill marks appear. Coarsely chop green onions. Place eggplant, squash, zucchini, and chopped green onions in bowl with tomato mixture; toss to combine.
4. Place steaks in a single layer on grill grate coated with cooking spray; grill, uncovered, 2 minutes. Turn steaks; grill 1 minute or until desired degree of doneness. Place steaks on a cutting board; let stand 5 minutes. Thinly slice steaks against the grain.
5. Add mint and oil to vegetable mixture; toss to coat. Add basil; toss to coat. Divide vegetable mixture and steak slices among 4 plates. Serves 4 (serving size: about 3 ounces steak and about 1½ cups vegetables)

CALORIES 271; FAT 11.3g (sat 2.6g, mono 6.6g, poly 0.9g); PROTEIN 29g; CARB 14g; FIBER 5g; SUGARS 8g (est. added sugars 0g); CHOL 62mg; IRON 4mg; SODIUM 569mg; CALC 83mg

SOURCING

If grass-fed beef isn't available at your local markets, we recommend ordering from these quality online retailers that ship nationwide.

PRE-BRANDS.COM
Available both in stores and online through Amazon Fresh, Pre Brands sources Hereford and Angus beef from New Zealand and Australia.

BUTCHERBOX.COM
Sign up for a subscription service that delivers a customized assortment of beef cuts to your doorstep each month.

GREENSBURY.COM
Certified organic beef sourced from a collective of family farms in the Dakotas.

GRASSLANDBEEF.COM
The site for U.S. Wellness Meats, which sources meat throughout the country. One of the broadest offerings we've found, including some cuts not available from other purveyors, like organ meat, brisket, oxtail, and beef cheeks.

KICKS LIKE A MULE

A classic Moscow mule—spicy ginger beer, tart lime, and vodka served in a chilled copper mug—is as frosty and refreshing as a snow cone. This fresh twist uses barrel-aged bourbon and a hint of mint for a mule with Kentucky-style giddyap.

Bourbon Mule

Hands-on: 4 min. Total: 4 min.
Copper mugs are in: Find them at Crate and Barrel ($19.95, crateandbarrel.com).

1½ ounces bourbon
1 tablespoon fresh lime juice
½ cup light ginger beer (such as Fever-Tree Naturally Light)
1 mint sprig
1 lime slice

1. In a copper mug or highball glass, combine bourbon and lime juice. Fill cup with ice. Add ginger beer; stir gently to combine. Garnish with mint sprig and lime slice. Serves 1

CALORIES 148; FAT 0g; PROTEIN 0g; CARB 14g; FIBER 0g; SUGARS 6g (est. added sugars 6g); CHOL 0mg; IRON 0mg; SODIUM 2mg; CALC 2mg

THE GINGER BEER YOU NEED

Mules call for ginger beer, a non-alcoholic brew that's spicier and more complex than ginger ale. Fever-Tree's Naturally Light Ginger Beer has just 10g of sugar per 200-milliliter bottle, the ideal balance for its intense ginger heat. Available at most supermarkets.

THE SALAD DAYS

by Hugh Acheson

The advent of summer triggers a garden-fresh craving for chef Hugh Acheson.

I grew up in Canada, a land of vivid seasons. Though not from a very culinary-minded family, I remember clearly the cadence of summer produce: when the first blueberries came, the arrival of tiny *fraises des bois* (wild strawberries that punctuate the forests of Ontario and Quebec), the plump blackberries that would come soon after, and the final push of raspberries, sweet from the heat in August. We knew that the good tomatoes arrived late in July and waited for the "peaches and cream" corn from the roadside stand—literally a truck with a bounty that would sell us some of the harvest from the Simpsons' family farm north of Toronto. At age 6, I knew the pattern of our agrarian community.

Savory summer is that time of tomatoes and corn and basil, all of which pile up in wonderful abundance a bit earlier now that I live in the American South. When you have bounty, you need a dish that is easy to prepare, that the whole brood enjoys multiple times in a week, yet will still pique palates and encapsulate the beauty and purity of the season. I make a simple salad about four times a week that is an ode to that trio of tomatoes, corn, and basil—a dish that my family eats up with gusto. It is a salad for hot nights with a cold simple beer. The tomatoes should be ripe and plump, the corn should be tender and cut from the cob right before eating, and the basil should be crimped from the tops of the plants, a cutting that allows them to keep on trucking through the remaining hot months of summer.

So in balancing the heady plumpness of tomatoes, the natural sweetness of corn, and the beautifully angular, peppery notes of fresh basil, we need a unifying vinaigrette—a marinating vehicle of great olive oil and puckery vinegar. I don't want citrus juice in this vinaigrette, as that seems contrary to what tomatoes meld with, and citrus has nothing to do with this seasonal bliss. But I do want the bold and bracing flavor of great red wine vinegar—bonus points if you make your own. I want big shavings of real Parmigiano-Reggiano cheese, not finely grated powder that would lump up with the vinaigrette. I want a hint of mustard and a secret little dollop of miso and soy sauce for an umami jolt that shows earthiness and makes you smile.

This should be a staple dish, an essential part of a summer spread. Welcome to 'mater country.

Staff Favorite • Kid Friendly
Vegetarian

Corn, Tomato, and Basil Salad

Hands-on: 14 min. Total: 44 min.
While corn and tomatoes are at their peak later in the summer, you can enjoy this simple salad all season long. White miso—the kind that's lowest in sodium—adds a powerful umami punch to the mix, enhancing the meaty flavor that tomatoes and Parmigiano-Reggiano cheese provide. Salting the tomatoes and letting them stand draws out their juices so they'll meld with the dressing when you combine all the components.

2 large ripe heirloom tomatoes, cored and cut into 1-inch dice, or 1 diced heirloom tomato and 1 cup halved cherry tomatoes
1/2 teaspoon kosher salt
1/3 cup extra-virgin olive oil
1 tablespoon minced flat-leaf parsley
3 tablespoons red wine vinegar
1 tablespoon grainy mustard
1 tablespoon reduced-sodium soy sauce
1 tablespoon white miso
1 medium shallot, peeled and minced
2 cups fresh yellow and white corn kernels
1/4 cup shaved Parmigiano-Reggiano (about 1 ounce)
2 tablespoons coarsely chopped fresh flat-leaf parsley
12 fresh basil leaves, torn into small pieces

1. Place tomatoes in a large bowl. Sprinkle with salt; let stand 30 minutes at room temperature.
2. Combine oil and next 6 ingredients (through shallot) in a pint jar. Seal jar; shake 30 seconds or until blended.
3. Add vinaigrette, corn, cheese, chopped parsley, and basil to tomatoes. Toss gently to combine; serve immediately. Serves 8 (serving size: about 3/4 cup)

CALORIES 150; FAT 10.9g (sat 2g, mono 7.6g, poly 1.1g); PROTEIN 3g; CARB 11g; FIBER 2g; SUGARS 4g (est. added sugars 0g); CHOL 3mg; IRON 1mg; SODIUM 306mg; CALC 39mg

NOTE FROM THE EDITOR

COLOR THEORY

The greens arrive at the market first, harbingers of spring and the strawberry-reds and rhubarb-pinks to come. Soon enough, green peas, favas, and butter lettuces usher in purple berries and eggplants. Blushing, fragrant yellow peaches and musky melons beckon; in come fire-engine-red peppers and riots of juicy tomatoes. And so forth.

Eat by color. It's a mantra that becomes easier to follow every week as the market tables and supermarket stalls groan heavier with seasonal variety. This weekend, I'll head to my local market in search of fat stalks of late-season asparagus and spring onions. I'll wilt them over a charcoal fire and serve them with a smoky, nutty romesco sauce reddened with charred peppers, bound with toasted bread, and emboldened with garlic. It's a simple, colorful segue into summer.

Quick & Easy • Make Ahead
Vegetarian

Romesco Sauce

Hands-on: 20 min. Total: 25 min.
This all-purpose condiment, a riff on the classic Catalonian recipe, goes well with just about anything charred on the grill, from sweet spring onions and fat spears of asparagus to fish, shrimp, steak, and pork chops. Use this recipe as a baseline and change it up however you see fit. You can make it spicy or tangy, smooth or chunky.

4 garlic cloves, unpeeled
2 red bell peppers
1 red jalapeño or Fresno chile
1 (1½-inch-thick) slice crusty bread
5 tablespoons olive oil, divided
⅓ cup Marcona almonds
2 tablespoons sherry or red wine vinegar
1 tablespoon smoked paprika
¾ teaspoon kosher salt
1 ripe medium tomato, cored

1. Preheat broiler to high. Arrange garlic, bell peppers, chile, and bread on a foil-lined baking sheet. Drizzle vegetables with 1 tablespoon oil. Broil, turning occasionally, until vegetables are nicely charred and softened and bread is toasted, about 8 minutes for peppers and garlic and 4 minutes for bread. Transfer peppers and chile to a medium bowl; cover with the used foil and let steam.
2. Tear bread into small pieces. Peel garlic. Finely chop bread, garlic, and almonds in a food processor. Peel, stem, and seed peppers and chile. Add remaining ¼ cup oil, peppers and chile, vinegar, paprika, salt, and

tomato to processor; process until almost smooth. Serve at room temperature or cover and refrigerate for up to 2 days. Serves 12 (serving size: about 2 tablespoons)

CALORIES 96; FAT 7.9g (sat 1g, mono 5.5g, poly 1.2g); PROTEIN 2g; CARB 5g; FIBER 1g; SUGARS 1g (est. added sugars 0g); CHOL 0mg; IRON 1mg; SODIUM 148mg; CALC 15mg

THE COOKING LIGHT DIET

MAKE-AHEAD SUMMER SALAD

Our 20-minute, portable pasta toss stands up beautifully to summer heat.

Christy Price sought out the Cooking Light Diet in the hopes of feeling comfortable in her own skin again. Having now lost 50 pounds, she attributes her success to a dedicated exercise regimen and the delicious recipes offered through the Cooking Light Diet.

We were interested in having Christy, an important member of the Cooking Light Diet community, preview our recipe for Tortellini Salad with Zucchini and Peas. "It was really good!" she says. "The lemon in the dressing brought out the other flavors, and made it taste like a fantastic summer salad." She was surprised that the salad tasted even better the next day: "The flavors had melded a bit more, and the lemon was more powerful, having soaked into the zucchini. I'm definitely making this when I crave something cooler for lunch this summer." Sounds like a great way to offset summer's sweltering heat.

Quick & Easy • Kid Friendly
Make Ahead • Vegetarian

Tortellini Salad with Zucchini and Peas

Hands-on: 20 min. Total: 20 min.
'Tis the season for zucchini. Make the most of it in this light and summery salad where it's just barely wilted.

1 (9-ounce) package refrigerated whole-wheat 3-cheese tortellini (such as Buitoni)
⅔ cup frozen peas
2 medium zucchini
2 tablespoons olive oil, divided
2 garlic cloves, minced
1 teaspoon grated lemon rind plus 1 tablespoon fresh lemon juice
½ teaspoon kosher salt
½ teaspoon freshly ground black pepper
Small fresh basil leaves (optional)

1. Cook pasta according to package directions, omitting salt and fat; add peas for the last 6 minutes. Drain, and cool 10 minutes; place pasta and peas in a medium bowl.
2. Using a vegetable peeler, shave zucchini into ribbons.
3. Heat 1½ teaspoons oil in a medium skillet over medium. Add garlic; cook, stirring constantly, 30 seconds. Remove from heat. Add zucchini; stir constantly until zucchini is slightly softened, about 1 minute. Add zucchini mixture to tortellini mixture in bowl.
4. Combine rind, juice, salt, pepper, and remaining 1½ tablespoons oil. Drizzle over tortellini mixture; toss gently to coat. Sprinkle with basil, if desired. Serves 4 (serving size: 1 cup)

CALORIES 302; FAT 14g (sat 3.2g, mono 6.8g, poly 1.6g); PROTEIN 12g; CARB 34g; FIBER 7g; SUGARS 5g (est. added sugars 0g); CHOL 39mg; IRON 2mg; SODIUM 561mg; CALC 115mg

GATEWAY FISH

Cooking in trout-rich Greenville, South Carolina, chef Teryi Youngblood turns picky eaters into seafood lovers.

CL: What's behind your choice of trout in this dish instead of, say, snapper, striped bass, or mackerel?
TY: I call trout the gateway fish. It's perfectly mild and delicate, the way fish should taste. If you want to convince people to enjoy fish, trout is the one to cook. It's simple enough to appeal to finicky eaters, but sophisticated enough to serve at a dinner party. And that skin is so crunchy and delicious, I'd almost eat the skin off every trout we served if I could.

CL: How did you design this dish so that even busy cooks can pull it off on a weeknight?
TY: As a working mom, I love a fast, healthy meal that doesn't require a lot of work. This dish doesn't take a lot of prep. You can chop the mise en place ahead of time and even make the tomato vinaigrette in advance, so it makes for a quick weeknight dinner.

Gluten Free

Chard-Stuffed Trout with Charred Tomato Vinaigrette

Hands-on: 37 min. Total: 53 min.

2 large tomatoes, cut into ¹/₂-inch-thick slices
¹/₄ cup fresh flat-leaf parsley leaves
2 tablespoons capers, drained
6 tablespoons olive oil, divided
1 tablespoon chopped fresh rosemary
2 tablespoons fresh lemon juice
2 tablespoons red wine vinegar
2 garlic cloves
¹/₂ teaspoon kosher salt, divided
³/₄ teaspoon freshly ground black pepper, divided
1 red bell pepper, stemmed, seeded, and sliced into thin strips
1 yellow bell pepper, stemmed, seeded, and sliced into thin strips
1 shallot, thinly sliced
3 garlic cloves, thinly sliced
1 bunch chard, leaves and top portions of stems thinly sliced
¹/₄ cup chopped fresh basil
4 (6-ounce) butterflied boneless trout, heads and tails removed
¹/₄ cup pitted Niçoise olives
5 thyme sprigs

1. Heat a large cast-iron pan or grill pan over high. Add tomato slices to pan; cook 6 minutes on each side or until well charred. Place tomatoes in a blender. Add parsley, capers, ¹/₄ cup olive oil, rosemary, juice, vinegar, 2 garlic cloves, ¹/₄ teaspoon salt, and ¹/₄ teaspoon pepper; blend until smooth.
2. Heat a large nonstick skillet over medium-high. Add 1 tablespoon oil to pan. Add bell peppers, shallots, and sliced garlic cloves; sauté 4 minutes or until tender. Add chard; sauté 2 minutes or until just wilted. Remove from heat; stir in chopped basil.
3. Sprinkle trout inside and out evenly with remaining ¹/₄ teaspoon salt and remaining ¹/₂ teaspoon pepper. Place about ¹/₂ cup chard mixture in each butterflied trout, and fold halves back together.
4. Preheat oven to 400°F. Spread charred tomato mixture in bottom of a 9- x 13-inch glass or ceramic baking dish. Sprinkle olives over tomato mixture; spread thyme sprigs over mixture. Heat remaining 1 tablespoon oil in large nonstick skillet over medium-high. Add 2 stuffed trout to pan; cook 2 minutes or until skin is golden brown. Turn trout over; cook 2 minutes. Place browned trout in prepared baking dish. Repeat procedure with remaining 2 trout. Place baking dish in oven; bake at 400°F for 12 minutes or until trout is just cooked through. Serves 4 (serving size: 1 stuffed trout)

CALORIES 460; **FAT** 30g (sat 5.2g, mono 19.1g, poly 4.5g); **PROTEIN** 33g; **CARB** 15g; **FIBER** 5g; **SUGARS** 6g (est. added sugars 0g); **CHOL** 88mg; **IRON** 3mg; **SODIUM** 665mg; **CALC** 193mg

CHAMPAGNE TASTE

Two things to know about Champagne (aka Ataulfo) mangoes: They're at peak season now, and they make other mangoes seem a little blah. Smaller than green-red Tommy Atkins, these yellow-skinned mangoes have creamy texture, floral fragrance, and ethereal sweetness with honey and vanilla notes, making them the ideal summer sweet treat.

Quick & Easy • Gluten Free Kid Friendly • Make Ahead Vegetarian

Champagne Mangoes with Lime and Sea Salt

Hands-on: 4 min. Total: 4 min.
Combine 2 cups diced Champagne (or Ataulfo) mango and 1 tablespoon fresh lime juice; toss well to coat. Divide mango mixture among 4 small bowls. Sprinkle each serving with a dash of Aleppo pepper or crushed red pepper flakes and a dash of Maldon sea salt. Serves 4 (serving size ¹/₂ cup)

CALORIES 51; **FAT** 0.3g (sat 0.1g, mono 0.1g, poly 0.1g); **PROTEIN** 1g; **CARB** 13g; **FIBER** 1g; **SUGARS** 11g (est. added sugars 0g); **CHOL** 0mg; **IRON** 0mg; **SODIUM** 61mg; **CALC** 10mg

GROW. HARVEST. COOK.

GET SCHOOLED: RADISHES

Seventh-grader Steven Constanza shares with us what a kick radishes are to grow—and eat. See sidebar at right for tips on gardening, shopping for, and preparing these peppery treats.

Quick & Easy • Gluten Free
Kid Friendly • Make Ahead
Vegetarian

Miso-Glazed Radishes

Hands-on: 15 min. Total: 15 min.

1½ tablespoons rice vinegar
1½ tablespoons white miso
3 cups quartered radishes
   (12 ounces), with root and 1-inch stem attached
Cooking spray
1 tablespoon unsalted butter
1 tablespoon granulated sugar
2 tablespoons chopped cilantro
½ teaspoon black or white sesame seeds

1. Whisk together vinegar and miso in a bowl. Heat a large cast-iron skillet over medium. Generously coat radishes and skillet with cooking spray. Add radishes to skillet; cook, stirring occasionally, 10 minutes or until just tender. Add butter, and sprinkle with sugar; cook 30 seconds, stirring to coat. Remove from heat; add miso mixture, and stir until radishes are completely coated. Add cilantro; toss to combine. Sprinkle with sesame seeds. Serves 4 (serving size: ½ cup)

CALORIES 68; **FAT** 3.5g (sat 1.9g, mono 0.9g, poly 0.4g); **PROTEIN** 1g; **CARB** 8g; **FIBER** 1g; **SUGARS** 6g (est. added sugars 3g); **CHOL** 8mg; **IRON** 0mg; **SODIUM** 210mg; **CALC** 26mg

HOW TO SHOP

Drop a bundle in your basket, and aim to use both the roots and the greens.

1. BUY BEFORE IT GETS TOO HOT.
Available year-round at most grocers, radishes are at their peak in spring and fall. Those grown in hot summer climates can get a little spicy. Some of Steven's harvests were "like peppers ... sometimes [they] feel like they are burning your tongue."

2. GAUGE FRESHNESS.
When shopping at local farm stands, it's easy to ask the grower about freshness; he or she can tell you the day the radishes were harvested. At stores, look for firm radishes with leaves still attached. Seek bundles with greens that are vibrant and not at all wilted.

3. TRY A VARIETY.
Color and shape vary, from globes of Easter Egg and Pink Beauty to long, slender types such as French Breakfast. Harvests of red, pink, and white make for candy-like displays at the school's student-run market and jazz up your own salads and crudités platters. For the showiest option, seek out watermelon radishes, which have a magenta interior.

HOW TO GROW

If you can sow, you can grow radishes!

1. SOW IN A SUNNY SPOT.
Choose light, rich soil in a bed or large pot. Gently push the large seeds ½-inch deep into soil at least 1 inch apart. Allow 6 inches between rows, as the tops can grow 6–12 inches tall and wide.

2. CHOOSE GOOD COMPANIONS.
Mix and match varieties like those Steven and his classmates grew, such as Easter Egg and D'Avignon. Plant with rows of quick-growing lettuces and longer-to-mature carrots, creating elbow room for the carrots as you harvest.

3. PICK QUICK.
Beloved by beginners for big seeds, easy sowing, and fast harvest time, radishes give near-instant gratification when seedling leaves appear in just a few days. Harvest when roots are almost the size of golf balls (or pinky fingers, for slender varieties), about 45–50 days.

Quick & Easy • Gluten Free
Kid Friendly • Make Ahead
Vegetarian

Radish Carpaccio

Hands-on: 10 min. Total: 10 min.
We love the interplay of crunchy, peppery radishes with refreshingly tangy yogurt spread. If you can, use a variety of radishes for more color.

⅓ cup plain 2% reduced-fat Greek yogurt
1½ ounces goat cheese, softened
½ teaspoon grated lemon rind
4 teaspoons olive oil, divided
5 ounces very thinly sliced radishes (about 8 small radishes)
¼ teaspoon flaky sea salt
2 tablespoons torn fresh mint leaves
¾ teaspoon za'atar (optional)

1. Whisk together yogurt, goat cheese, lemon rind, and 2 teaspoons oil until smooth. Spread on a platter. Top with radish slices, and drizzle with remaining 2 teaspoons oil. Sprinkle radishes with salt, mint, and za'atar, if desired. Serves 4 (serving size: 1 cup)

CALORIES 89; **FAT** 7.3g (sat 2.5g, mono 4.1g, poly 0.5g); **PROTEIN** 4g; **CARB** 2g; **FIBER** 1g; **SUGARS** 1g (est. added sugars 0g); **CHOL** 6mg; **IRON** 0mg; **SODIUM** 214mg; **CALC** 39mg

ABOUT OUR PARTNERS

School gardens are trending, and we couldn't be happier—they're a great way to expose kids to fresh food and encourage healthier eating. That's why we've partnered with Birmingham, Alabama–based Jones Valley Teaching Farm. Through their work with seven local elementary, middle, and high schools, JVTF staffers engage students in project-based learning centered on fresh vegetables and fruits. Their outposts resonate with kids where computers can't: in the sunshine and in the dirt. Visit jvtf.org to learn more, or go to edibleschoolyard.org for resources in your area.

READY IN 40 MINUTES

....
GAME PLAN

While pasta shells cook:
- Cook eggplant mixture.

While stuffed shells bake:
- Cook green bean mixture.

Quick & Easy • Kid Friendly
Make Ahead • Vegetarian

Ratatouille-Stuffed Shells

With Green Bean and Radish Sauté

Jumbo stuffed shells are your weeknight answer to homemade lasagna: Instead of endless layers, spoon a single vegetable mixture into each shell, and bake 12 minutes or until the cheese melts.

16 uncooked jumbo pasta shells
1 tablespoon olive oil
3/4 cup chopped onion
1 tablespoon minced fresh garlic
1 1/2 cups diced eggplant
1 cup diced red bell pepper
3/4 cup diced zucchini
3/4 cup chopped plum tomato
1/2 cup canned unsalted chickpeas, rinsed and drained
1 3/4 cups low-sodium marinara sauce (such as Dell'Amore), divided
1/2 cup plus 2 tablespoons torn fresh basil, divided
3/4 teaspoon freshly ground black pepper
1/2 teaspoon kosher salt
Cooking spray
4 ounces preshredded Italian 5-cheese blend (about 1 cup)

1. Preheat oven to 450°F.
2. Cook pasta according to package directions, omitting salt and fat. Drain.
3. Heat oil in a large skillet over medium-high. Add onion and garlic; sauté 2 minutes. Add eggplant and bell pepper; cook 4 minutes, stirring occasionally. Add zucchini, tomato, and chickpeas; cover and cook 4 minutes. Remove pan from heat; stir in 1 cup marinara, 1/2 cup basil, black pepper, and salt.
4. Coat a 2-quart glass or ceramic baking dish with cooking spray. Spread remaining 3/4 cup marinara over bottom of dish. Spoon about 2 tablespoons vegetable mixture into each pasta shell. Arrange filled shells in dish; sprinkle with cheese. Bake at 450°F for 12 minutes. Top with remaining 2 tablespoons basil. Serves 4 (serving size: about 4 stuffed shells)

CALORIES 370; FAT 11.8g (sat 4.1g, mono 4.3g, poly 1.4g); PROTEIN 16g; CARB 50g; FIBER 6g; SUGARS 11g (est. added sugars 0g); CHOL 20mg; IRON 4mg; SODIUM 586mg; CALC 275mg

Quick & Easy • Gluten Free
Kid Friendly • Vegetarian

Green Bean and Radish Sauté

Rather than boiling the green beans, we sauté them and let the liquid evaporate so the beans are crisp-tender and lightly seared.

1/4 cup water
2 tablespoons olive oil
12 ounces green beans, trimmed
1/2 cup thinly sliced radishes
1/2 teaspoon kosher salt
1/4 teaspoon freshly ground black pepper
3 tablespoons chopped fresh flat-leaf parsley

1. Heat 1/4 cup water and oil in a large skillet over medium-high. Add beans to pan; cover and cook 5 minutes. Add radishes, salt, and pepper; uncover and cook 3 minutes or until liquid almost evaporates. Remove pan from heat; sprinkle with parsley. Serves 4 (serving size: about 3/4 cup)

CALORIES 90; FAT 7.2g (sat 1.1g, mono 5g, poly 1.1g); PROTEIN 2g; CARB 7g; FIBER 3g; SUGARS 3g (est. added sugars 0g); CHOL 0mg; IRON 1mg; SODIUM 252mg; CALC 40mg

READY IN 25 MINUTES

....
GAME PLAN

While water comes to a boil:
- Cook prosciutto.
- Make vinaigrette.

While bread toasts:
- Make tapenade.

Quick & Easy • Gluten Free
Kid Friendly

Fresh Pea, Prosciutto, and Herb Salad

With Lentil Tapenade Crostini

Build the salad on large slices of red, ripe tomato for a main that looks and feels more substantial.

4 cups water
2/3 cup frozen shelled edamame
1/4 cup fresh or frozen shelled green peas, thawed
4 ounces haricots verts (French green beans), trimmed and halved diagonally
2 thin slices prosciutto (about 1 ounce)
2 tablespoons extra-virgin olive oil
1 1/2 tablespoons white wine vinegar

1 tablespoon chopped fresh tarragon
1 tablespoon chopped fresh mint
1/8 teaspoon kosher salt
1/4 teaspoon freshly ground black
   pepper
1 cup baby arugula
1 medium heirloom tomato, cut into
   1/2-inch slices

1. Bring 4 cups water to a boil in a small saucepan. Add edamame, peas, and haricots verts; cook 3 minutes or until crisp-tender. Drain; rinse under cold water. Drain.
2. Wrap prosciutto in a paper towel. Microwave at HIGH 1 minute or until crisp. Cool slightly. Break into large pieces.
3. Combine oil, vinegar, tarragon, mint, salt, and pepper in a medium bowl, stirring with a whisk. Add edamame mixture; toss to coat. Add arugula; toss. Arrange tomato slices on a platter; top with arugula mixture and prosciutto. Serves 2 (serving size: about 1 1/2 cups)

CALORIES 273; FAT 17.6g (sat 2.5g, mono 10.6g, poly 1.9g); PROTEIN 13g; CARB 18g; FIBER 7g; SUGARS 7g (est. added sugars 0g); CHOL 11mg; IRON 3mg; SODIUM 550mg; CALC 94mg

Quick & Easy • Make Ahead

Lentil Tapenade Crostini

Precooked lentils are a healthy cook's ally, adding instant fiber and protein to any dish while saving nearly 30 minutes of stovetop simmering. Here we pulse the lentils in a food processor as part of a rustic tapenade for crostini.

1/4 cup steamed lentils (such as
   Melissa's)
1 tablespoon extra-virgin olive oil
3 pitted Castelvetrano olives
1 garlic clove, coarsely chopped
4 (1/4-ounce) whole-wheat French
   bread baguette slices, toasted
1/4 teaspoon fresh thyme leaves
1/8 teaspoon crushed red pepper

1. Place lentils, olive oil, olives, and garlic in a mini food processor; pulse 3 times or until coarsely chopped. Spread lentil mixture evenly over bread; sprinkle with thyme and pepper. Serves 2 (serving size: 2 crostini)

CALORIES 190; FAT 8.3g (sat 1.1g, mono 5g, poly 1g); PROTEIN 8g; CARB 22g; FIBER 6g; SUGARS 2g (est. added sugars 0g); CHOL 0mg; IRON 3mg; SODIUM 193mg; CALC 24mg

READY IN
40
MINUTES

GAME PLAN

While steak marinates:
- Grill corn, bell pepper, and shallots.

While steak grills:
- Finish corn salad.

Quick & Easy • Gluten Free
Kid Friendly • Make Ahead

Grilled Chile-Lime Flank Steak

With Grilled Corn and Bell Pepper Salad

1/2 cup chopped fresh cilantro stems
3 tablespoons fresh lime juice
3 tablespoons olive oil, divided
3/4 teaspoon crushed red pepper,
   divided
1 pound flank or skirt steak, trimmed
Cooking spray
1/2 teaspoon kosher salt
1/4 cup vertically sliced red onion
1/4 cup loosely packed fresh cilantro
   leaves
1 tablespoon sliced garlic
4 lime wedges

1. Preheat grill to high (450° to 550°F).
2. Place cilantro stems, juice, 1 1/2 tablespoons oil, and 1/2 teaspoon crushed red pepper in a mini food processor; process until smooth. Place cilantro mixture in a shallow dish; add steak, turning to coat. Let stand 10 minutes.
3. Coat grill grate with cooking spray. Remove steak from marinade; discard marinade. Sprinkle steak with salt. Add steak to grill; cook 4 minutes on each side for medium-rare or until desired degree of doneness. Place steak on a cutting board. Let stand 5 minutes. Cut across the grain into thin slices.
4. Place steak on a platter; sprinkle with remaining 1/4 teaspoon crushed red pepper, onion, cilantro leaves, and garlic. Drizzle with remaining 1 1/2 tablespoons oil. Serve steak with lime wedges. Serves 4 (serving size: about 3 ounces steak)

CALORIES 294; FAT 20.1g (sat 5.1g, mono 12.9g, poly 1.4g); PROTEIN 24g; CARB 3g; FIBER 0g; SUGARS 1g (est. added sugars 0g); CHOL 74mg; IRON 3mg; SODIUM 318mg; CALC 19mg

continued

Quick & Easy • Gluten Free
Kid Friendly • Make Ahead
Vegetarian

Grilled Corn and Bell Pepper Salad

Get the most out of your grill space by adding a little char to every element of this quick, fresh corn salad. Add all the vegetables at once; remove each as it finishes cooking.

Cooking spray
2 large ears fresh yellow corn, husks removed
1 medium-sized red bell pepper
1 medium-sized yellow bell pepper
1 medium shallot, peeled and halved lengthwise
3 tablespoons chopped fresh flat-leaf parsley
2 tablespoons extra-virgin olive oil
1 tablespoon apple cider vinegar
1/4 teaspoon kosher salt
1/4 teaspoon freshly ground black pepper
3/4 ounce Cotija cheese, crumbled (about 3 tablespoons)

1. Preheat grill to high (450° to 550°F).
2. Coat grill grate and corn, bell peppers, and shallots with cooking spray. Add vegetables to grill. Grill corn 14 minutes, turning after 7 minutes. Grill bell peppers 10 minutes, turning occasionally. Grill shallots 8 minutes, turning after 4 minutes. Remove vegetables from grill; cool 5 minutes.
3. Cut corn kernels from ears and place in a bowl. Cut bell peppers into 3/4-inch pieces; add to corn. Chop shallots; add to corn mixture. Add parsley, oil, vinegar, salt, and pepper to corn mixture; toss. Sprinkle with cheese. Serves 4 (serving size: about 1 cup)

CALORIES 144; **FAT** 9.2g (sat 2.1g, mono 5.5g, poly 1.1g); **PROTEIN** 4g; **CARB** 14g; **FIBER** 2g; **SUGARS** 6g (est. added sugars 0g); **CHOL** 6mg; **IRON** 1mg; **SODIUM** 213mg; **CALC** 86mg

READY IN 35 MINUTES

GAME PLAN

While rice simmers:
- Broil okra and bell pepper.
- Prepare shrimp.

While bell pepper stands:
- Cook shrimp.

Staff Favorite • Quick & Easy
Gluten Free

Charred Shrimp and Okra Bowl

With Toasted Jasmine Rice

2 1/2 tablespoons extra-virgin olive oil, divided
2 tablespoons coarse yellow cornmeal
10 ounces fresh whole okra, halved lengthwise
1 large red bell pepper, halved
2 teaspoons honey
1 teaspoon salt-free Creole seasoning (such as Tony Chachere's)
8 ounces large shrimp, peeled and deveined
1 1/2 cups chopped tomato
1/2 cup sliced red onion
1/2 cup loosely packed fresh flat-leaf parsley leaves
1/4 cup thinly diagonally sliced celery
1 tablespoon red wine vinegar
3/4 teaspoon kosher salt
8 thin slices red Fresno chile

1. Preheat broiler to high with oven rack 6 inches from heat. Line a rimmed baking sheet with foil.
2. Combine 1 tablespoon oil, cornmeal, and okra in bowl. Place okra and bell pepper halves, skin side up, on prepared pan. Broil 10 minutes. Wrap bell pepper in foil; let stand 10 minutes. Peel and chop.
3. Line pan with foil. Combine honey, Creole seasoning, and shrimp in a bowl; add to pan. Broil 2 to 3 minutes on each side or until done.
4. Combine okra, bell pepper, shrimp mixture, tomato, and remaining ingredients in a bowl; toss. Serves 4 (serving size: about 1 1/2 cups)

CALORIES 206; **FAT** 9.5g (sat 1.3g, mono 6.3g, poly 1.1g); **PROTEIN** 11g; **CARB** 21g; **FIBER** 5g; **SUGARS** 8g (est. added sugars 3g); **CHOL** 71mg; **IRON** 2mg; **SODIUM** 465mg; **CALC** 117mg

Quick & Easy • Gluten Free
Kid Friendly • Make Ahead
Vegetarian

Toasted Jasmine Rice

2 tablespoons olive oil
1/3 cup thinly sliced shallots
1 cup uncooked jasmine or basmati rice
1 3/4 cups unsalted chicken stock (such as Swanson)
1/2 teaspoon kosher salt
1/4 teaspoon freshly ground black pepper
1 bay leaf
1/4 cup finely chopped fresh flat-leaf parsley

1. Heat oil in a medium saucepan over medium-high. Add shallots; sauté 3 minutes. Add rice; cook 2 minutes, stirring to coat. Add stock, salt, pepper, and bay leaf to pan with rice; bring to a boil.
2. Reduce the heat; cover, and simmer 18 minutes or until liquid is absorbed. Remove pan from heat; let stand 5 minutes. Discard bay leaf. Stir in parsley. Serves 4 (serving size: about 3/4 cup)

CALORIES 240; **FAT** 6.8g (sat 0.9g, mono 4.9g, poly 0.7g); **PROTEIN** 5g; **CARB** 39g; **FIBER** 2g; **SUGARS** 2g (est. added sugars 0g); **CHOL** 0mg; **IRON** 1mg; **SODIUM** 301mg; **CALC** 31mg

READY IN
35
MINUTES

········· **GAME PLAN** ·········

While chicken grills:

- Microwave potatoes.
- Prepare dressing.

While potatoes grill:

- Prepare salad.

Quick & Easy • Gluten Free
Kid Friendly

Grilled Chipotle Chicken and Sweet Potato Toss

With Dilly Cucumber Salad with Yogurt

Adobo sauce, what surrounds the chipotle chiles in the can, is a fantastic single-ingredient wet rub for grilled chicken, smoky with just a touch of heat that won't be overwhelming for kids.

Cooking spray
4 (6-ounce) skinless, boneless
   chicken breasts
1 tablespoon adobo sauce from
   canned chipotle chiles in adobo
3/4 teaspoon kosher salt, divided
3/4 teaspoon freshly ground black
   pepper, divided
1 tablespoon water
1 (8-ounce) sweet potato, peeled and
   cut lengthwise into 1/2-inch-thick
   slices
1 cup canned unsalted chickpeas,
   rinsed and drained
3 tablespoons chopped green onions
3 tablespoons extra-virgin olive oil
2 tablespoons fresh lime juice
2 tablespoons torn fresh basil
   (optional)

1. Preheat grill to medium-high
(350° to 450°F).
2. Coat grill grate with cooking
spray. Rub chicken with adobo sauce;
sprinkle with 1/2 teaspoon salt and
1/2 teaspoon pepper. Arrange chicken
on grill grate; cook 5 minutes on
each side or until done.
3. Place 1 tablespoon water and
sweet potato slices in a microwave-
safe bowl; cover with plastic wrap.
Microwave at HIGH 5 minutes
or until almost tender. Pat potato
slices dry; coat with cooking spray.
Arrange on grill; cook 3 to 5 minutes
or until tender and grill marks
appear. Remove from grill; cut into
1/2-inch pieces.
4. Combine remaining 1/4 teaspoon
salt, remaining 1/4 teaspoon pepper,
chickpeas, green onions, oil, juice,
and basil, if using, in a large bowl.
Add sweet potato; toss. Serve with
chicken. Serves 4 (serving size: 1
chicken breast and about 3/4 cup salad)

CALORIES 420; FAT 15.6g (sat 2.5g, mono 9.3g,
poly 1.7g); PROTEIN 43g; CARB 25g; FIBER 5g;
SUGARS 3g (est. added sugars 0g); CHOL 124mg;
IRON 2mg; SODIUM 526mg; CALC 71mg

Quick & Easy • Gluten Free
Kid Friendly • Vegetarian

Dilly Cucumber Salad with Yogurt

1 medium English cucumber, halved
   lengthwise and seeded
1 cup grape tomatoes, sliced
1/2 cup vertically sliced red onion
2 tablespoons chopped fresh dill,
   divided
1/2 teaspoon kosher salt
1/4 teaspoon black pepper
4 teaspoons plain 2% reduced-fat
   Greek yogurt
2 tablespoons extra-virgin olive oil
1 tablespoon red wine vinegar

1. Cut cucumber halves diagonally
into thin slices. Combine cucumber,
tomatoes, onion, 1 tablespoon dill,

salt, and pepper in a bowl; toss. Top
with yogurt, remaining 1 tablespoon
dill, oil, and vinegar. Serves 4 (serving size: about 2/3 cup)

CALORIES 88; FAT 7.2g (sat 1.1g, mono 5.4g, poly 0.6g);
PROTEIN 1g; CARB 5g; FIBER 1g; SUGARS 3g
(est. added sugars 0g); CHOL 0mg; IRON 0mg;
SODIUM 246mg; CALC 22mg

SUPERFAST 20-MINUTE COOKING

Quick & Easy • Gluten Free
Kid Friendly

BLT Salad

*Macerate tomatoes with salt before building
this salad, and you'll be amazed at the
difference: The salt concentrates the tomato
flavor and helps loosen the tomato juices.*

2 cups halved multicolored cherry
   tomatoes
1/8 teaspoon kosher salt
1/4 cup canola mayonnaise
1 1/2 tablespoons fresh lemon juice
2 teaspoons chopped fresh dill
1/2 teaspoon freshly ground black
   pepper
2 cups loosely packed arugula
2 bacon slices, cooked and finely
   crumbled

1. Combine tomatoes and salt in a
large bowl. Let stand 5 minutes.
2. Combine mayonnaise, juice, dill,
and pepper in a bowl with a whisk.
3. Add arugula to tomato mixture;
toss. Divide tomato mixture among
4 plates. Drizzle mayonnaise mixture
over salads. Sprinkle evenly with
bacon. Serves 4 (serving size: 1 cup)

CALORIES 77; FAT 5.6g (sat 0.6g, mono 3.1g,
poly 1.7g); PROTEIN 2g; CARB 4g; FIBER 1g;
SUGARS 2g (est. added sugars 0g); CHOL 4mg;
IRON 0mg; SODIUM 242mg; CALC 26mg

continued

Quick & Easy • Gluten Free
Kid Friendly • Vegetarian
Southern Tomato Salad
Combine 2 cups halved multicolored cherry tomatoes and ⅛ tsp. kosher salt in a bowl. Let stand 5 minutes. Add 1 cup sliced fresh peaches, 1½ Tbsp. olive oil, 1 Tbsp. fresh mint leaves, 2 tsp. apple cider vinegar, and ⅛ tsp. kosher salt; toss. Top with ¼ tsp. black pepper and 1 oz. crumbled goat cheese. Serves 4 (serving size: ¾ cup)

CALORIES 96; **FAT** 7g (sat 1.8g, mono 4.4g, poly 0.6g); **PROTEIN** 2g; **CARB** 7g; **FIBER** 2g; **SUGARS** 5g (est. added sugars 0g); **CHOL** 3mg; **IRON** 0mg; **SODIUM** 157mg; **CALC** 21mg

Quick & Easy • Gluten Free
Kid Friendly • Vegetarian
Caprese Tomato Salad
Combine 3 cups halved multicolored cherry tomatoes and ⅛ tsp. kosher salt in a large bowl. Let stand 5 minutes. Add ½ cup fresh basil leaves, 1 Tbsp. extra-virgin olive oil, 1 Tbsp. balsamic vinegar, ½ tsp. black pepper, ¼ tsp. kosher salt, and 1 oz. diced fresh mozzarella cheese (about ⅓ cup); toss. Serves 4 (serving size: ¾ cup)

CALORIES 80; **FAT** 5.8g (sat 1.8g, mono 2.7g, poly 0.4g); **PROTEIN** 2g; **CARB** 5g; **FIBER** 2g; **SUGARS** 4g (est. added sugars 0g); **CHOL** 5mg; **IRON** 1mg; **SODIUM** 207mg; **CALC** 23mg

Quick & Easy • Gluten Free
Kid Friendly • Vegetarian
Greek Tomato Salad
Combine 2 cups halved multicolored cherry tomatoes and ⅛ tsp. kosher salt in a large bowl. Let stand 5 minutes. Add 1 cup chopped English cucumber, ½ cup thinly sliced red onion, ¼ cup chopped kalamata olives, 2 Tbsp. fresh oregano leaves, 2 Tbsp. olive oil, 1½ Tbsp. red wine vinegar, and ⅛ tsp. crushed red pepper; toss. Serves 4 (serving size: ¾ cup)

CALORIES 109; **FAT** 9.2g (sat 1.2g, mono 6.9g, poly 0.9g); **PROTEIN** 1g; **CARB** 6g; **FIBER** 1g; **SUGARS** 3g (est. added sugars 0g); **CHOL** 0mg; **IRON** 0mg; **SODIUM** 181mg; **CALC** 28mg

Quick & Easy • Gluten Free
Kid Friendly

Seared Salmon with Balsamic-Blistered Tomatoes

Both fresh tomatoes and balsamic vinegar benefit from a little high heat in the pan.

1½ tablespoons olive oil, divided
4 (6-ounce) salmon fillets, about 1 inch thick
1 teaspoon kosher salt, divided
1 teaspoon freshly ground black pepper, divided
⅔ cup thinly sliced shallots
3 cups cherry tomatoes
½ cup torn basil leaves, divided
2 tablespoons balsamic vinegar

1. Preheat oven to 500°F. Line a rimmed baking sheet with foil.
2. Heat 1 tablespoon oil in a large cast-iron skillet over high. Sprinkle fillets evenly with ½ teaspoon salt and ½ teaspoon pepper. Add fillets to pan; cook 4 minutes on one side or until golden brown. Place fillets, seared side up, on prepared baking sheet; bake at 500°F for 4 minutes or until desired degree of doneness.
3. Return skillet to medium-high. Add remaining 1½ teaspoons oil to pan. Add shallots, and sauté 2 minutes. Add remaining ½ teaspoon salt, remaining ½ teaspoon pepper, tomatoes, and ¼ cup basil; cook 2 minutes or until tomatoes begin to break down. Stir in vinegar, and cook 1 minute.
4. Place 1 fillet on each of 4 plates; top evenly with tomato mixture and remaining basil. Serves 4 (serving size: 1 fillet and ½ cup tomato mixture)

CALORIES 338; **FAT** 15.1g (sat 2.8g, mono 7.3g, poly 3.9g); **PROTEIN** 38g; **CARB** 11g; **FIBER** 2g; **SUGARS** 6g (est. added sugars 0g); **CHOL** 90mg; **IRON** 2mg; **SODIUM** 571mg; **CALC** 52mg

Quick & Easy • Gluten Free

Seared Pork Chops with Poblano Peperonata

5 teaspoons olive oil, divided
4 (6-ounce) bone-in center-cut pork loin chops
¾ teaspoon kosher salt, divided
½ teaspoon freshly ground black pepper
1 cup sliced red onion
5 garlic cloves, thinly sliced
1 poblano chile, seeded and thinly sliced (about ¾ cup)
1 red bell pepper, seeded and thinly sliced (about 1½ cups)
1 yellow bell pepper, seeded and thinly sliced (about 1½ cups)
3 tablespoons chopped fresh flat-leaf parsley
3 tablespoons red wine vinegar
2 tablespoons capers, rinsed and drained
¼ teaspoon crushed red pepper

1. Heat 1½ teaspoons oil in a large skillet over high. Sprinkle pork with ½ teaspoon salt and black pepper. Cook 3 minutes on each side or until desired degree of doneness. Remove pork from pan; keep warm.
2. Reduce heat to medium-high. Add remaining 3½ teaspoons oil, onion, garlic, poblano, and bell peppers to pan; cook 4 minutes or until tender, stirring occasionally. Increase heat to high. Stir in remaining ¼ teaspoon salt, parsley, and remaining ingredients; cook 1 minute or until liquid is reduced by half. Serve pepper mixture with pork. Serves 4 (serving size: 1 chop and ½ cup pepper mixture)

CALORIES 263; **FAT** 12.7g (sat 2.8g, mono 6.6g, poly 1.7g); **PROTEIN** 26g; **CARB** 11g; **FIBER** 3g; **SUGARS** 4g (est. added sugars 0g); **CHOL** 75mg; **IRON** 1mg; **SODIUM** 519mg; **CALC** 48mg

Roasted Goat Cheese-Stuffed Portobellos

Serve with a mixture of sautéed sliced snap peas, radishes, and hot cooked brown rice. To make this a vegetarian main, simply skip the prosciutto.

4 large portobello mushroom caps, stemmed and dark gills removed
Cooking spray
³/₄ teaspoon freshly ground black pepper, divided
³/₄ cup whole-wheat panko (Japanese breadcrumbs), divided
1 tablespoon olive oil
2 tablespoons chopped fresh chives
1¹/₂ teaspoons grated lemon rind
1 teaspoon fresh lemon juice
¹/₄ teaspoon kosher salt
4 ounces goat cheese, crumbled (about 1 cup)
2 ounces thinly sliced prosciutto, torn into 1-inch pieces

1. Preheat oven to 500°F. Line a rimmed baking sheet with foil.
2. Coat mushrooms with cooking spray; place, top sides down, on prepared pan. Top with ½ teaspoon pepper. Bake at 500°F for 4 minutes.
3. Combine 6 tablespoons panko and oil in a small bowl. Combine remaining 6 tablespoons panko, chives, rind, juice, salt, and goat cheese in a bowl. Spoon ¼ cup goat cheese mixture into each mushroom; top with panko mixture. Bake at 500°F for 3 minutes. Top with prosciutto and remaining ¼ teaspoon pepper. Serves 4

CALORIES 204; **FAT** 11.5g (sat 5.1g, mono 4.5g, poly 0.8g); **PROTEIN** 13g; **CARB** 14g; **FIBER** 3g; **SUGARS** 3g (est. added sugars 0g); **CHOL** 21mg; **IRON** 2mg; **SODIUM** 488mg; **CALC** 48mg

Blackened Grouper Sandwiches with Rémoulade

(pictured on page 223)

Firm white fish like grouper, tilapia, and mahi mahi are perfect for crusty sandwiches because they won't fall apart after cooking.

1 teaspoon paprika
³/₄ teaspoon freshly ground black pepper
¹/₄ teaspoon kosher salt
4 (6-ounce) grouper fillets
2 tablespoons canola oil
¹/₄ cup canola mayonnaise
1¹/₂ tablespoons sweet pickle relish
1 tablespoon grainy mustard
1 tablespoon unsalted ketchup
4 (2-ounce) whole-wheat hoagie rolls, split
4 romaine lettuce leaves
8 plum tomato slices

1. Preheat broiler to high with oven rack 8 inches from the heat.
2. Combine paprika, pepper, and salt in a small bowl. Rub spice mixture evenly over fillets.
3. Heat oil in a large nonstick skillet over medium-high. Add fillets to pan; cook 3 to 4 minutes on each side.
4. Combine mayonnaise, relish, mustard, and ketchup in a bowl. Arrange rolls, cut sides up, on a baking sheet; broil 1 minute or until toasted. Spread mayonnaise mixture over cut sides of rolls. Top bottom halves of rolls with lettuce, tomato, fillets, and top halves of rolls. Serves 4 (serving size: 1 sandwich)

CALORIES 435; **FAT** 15.3g (sat 1.4g, mono 7.8g, poly 5.2g); **PROTEIN** 38g; **CARB** 36g; **FIBER** 5g; **SUGARS** 8g (est. added sugars 2g); **CHOL** 63mg; **IRON** 3mg; **SODIUM** 751mg; **CALC** 115mg

Crab-Stuffed Avocados

We couldn't resist stuffing cup-shaped avocado halves, here gently seared until lightly caramelized. Sweet crabmeat dressed with zingy lemon and tarragon is a nice complement to the buttery avocado; chopped cooked shrimp or shredded chicken breast would also work. You could also fill the halves with a fresh summer squash salad or black bean salsa.

¹/₂ cup canola mayonnaise
¹/₄ cup fresh lemon juice
3 tablespoons chopped fresh tarragon
¹/₂ teaspoon freshly ground black pepper
12 ounces lump crabmeat, shell pieces removed
Cooking spray
2 ripe avocados, halved and pitted

1. Combine first 4 ingredients in a bowl; gently fold in crab.
2. Heat a large cast-iron skillet over medium-high. Coat pan with cooking spray. Place avocado halves, cut sides down, in pan; cook 2 minutes or until lightly browned.
3. Place avocado halves, cut sides down, on a cutting board; cut a very small slice from the bottom of each half so that it stands flat. Turn over; spoon about ½ cup crab mixture into each avocado half. Serves 4 (serving size: 1 filled avocado half)

CALORIES 266; **FAT** 18.8g (sat 1.6g, mono 11.4g, poly 4.2g); **PROTEIN** 17g; **CARB** 7g; **FIBER** 5g; **SUGARS** 1g (est. added sugars 0g); **CHOL** 83mg; **IRON** 1mg; **SODIUM** 556mg; **CALC** 96mg

SANDWICH, MEET PASTA

The classic BLT becomes a simple, summery weeknight main.

Quick & Easy • Kid Friendly

BLT Pasta

Hands-on: 10 min. Total: 30 min.
Slab bacon lets you get a thicker dice than presliced bacon that will hold its own in the pasta; if it's hard for you to find, just use thick-cut sliced bacon. Peppery watercress wilts well yet maintains a little crunch. Arugula would also work.

1 tablespoon plus $^3/_8$ teaspoon kosher salt, divided
10 ounces uncooked mezze rigatoni or penne pasta
2 ounces slab bacon, cut into $^1/_2$-inch dice
1 tablespoon olive oil
1 pound red or yellow cherry tomatoes, halved (about 3 cups)
$^1/_2$ teaspoon freshly ground black pepper, divided
5 ounces watercress, coarsely chopped
1 ounce pecorino Romano cheese, grated

1. Bring a large saucepan filled with water and 1 tablespoon salt to a boil. Add pasta and cook 10 minutes or until al dente. Drain in a colander over a bowl, reserving 1 cup pasta cooking liquid.
2. Place bacon and olive oil in a 12-inch skillet over medium-low; cook 8 minutes or until the bacon is crisp, stirring occasionally. Remove bacon from pan (do not wipe out pan).
3. Heat pan over medium. Add tomatoes, ¼ teaspoon salt, and ¼ teaspoon pepper to drippings in pan; cook 5 minutes or until tomatoes are tender and almost melt, scraping pan to loosen browned bits. Stir in half of the cooked bacon.
4. Increase heat to medium-high. Add pasta to pan; toss to coat. Add ½ cup reserved pasta cooking liquid and watercress, stirring until watercress wilts. Add ¼ to ½ cup reserved pasta cooking liquid to pan as needed to loosen sauce. Divide pasta mixture among 4 shallow bowls; sprinkle evenly with remaining ⅛ teaspoon salt and remaining ¼ teaspoon pepper. Top servings evenly with remaining half of bacon and cheese. Serves 4 (serving size: about 1¾ cups)

CALORIES 400; **FAT** 12.5g (sat 4.5g, mono 5g, poly 1.4g); **PROTEIN** 15g; **CARB** 58g; **FIBER** 4g; **SUGARS** 6g (est. added sugars 0g); **CHOL** 17mg; **IRON** 3mg; **SODIUM** 581mg; **CALC** 132mg

SPEEDY BBQ CHICKEN TACOS

Easy assembly and bold flavors join forces for a dinner the whole family will love.

Quick & Easy • Gluten Free
Kid Friendly • Make Ahead

BBQ Chicken-and-Black Bean Tacos

(pictured on page 224)

Hands-on: 15 min. Total: 25 min.
A kid-friendly mix of quality convenience items and bright produce imparts fresh taste with minimal legwork.

2 teaspoons olive oil
$^2/_3$ cup diced red bell pepper
$^3/_4$ cup frozen whole kernel sweet corn, thawed
$^3/_4$ cup canned unsalted black beans, rinsed and drained
12 ounces skinless, boneless rotisserie chicken breast, shredded (about 2$^1/_2$ cups)
$^1/_3$ cup organic barbecue sauce (such as Annie's)
10 (6-inch) corn tortillas
$^1/_2$ cup plain 2% reduced-fat Greek yogurt
3 tablespoons chopped fresh cilantro leaves, plus more for garnish
1 tablespoon fresh lime juice
$^1/_4$ teaspoon kosher salt

1. Heat oil in a large nonstick skillet over medium. Add bell pepper; cook, stirring occasionally, until tender, 5 to 6 minutes. Stir in corn and black beans; cook until warmed through, 2 to 3 minutes. Set aside.
2. Place shredded chicken and barbecue sauce in a microwave-safe bowl. Mix until thoroughly coated. Loosely cover, and microwave at HIGH 1 minute or until warmed through.
3. Warm tortillas according to package directions. Place 3 tablespoons chicken mixture in center of each tortilla. Top each tortilla with 3 tablespoons bell pepper mixture.
4. Place yogurt, cilantro, lime juice, and salt in a small bowl. Whisk to combine. Dollop each taco with about 1 tablespoon yogurt mixture. Sprinkle tacos with cilantro. Serves 5 (serving size: 2 tacos)

CALORIES 331; **FAT** 6.6g (sat 1.1g, mono 2.4g, poly 1.6g); **PROTEIN** 27g; **CARB** 45g; **FIBER** 6g; **SUGARS** 6g (est. added sugars 1g); **CHOL** 60mg; **IRON** 1mg; **SODIUM** 465mg; **CALC** 78mg

EASIEST FRUIT CRUMBLE

Look to the slow cooker for the comfort of fruit pie without making piecrust.

Kid Friendly • Make Ahead Vegetarian

Blackberry-Peach Slow Cooker Crumble

Hands-on: 20 min. Total: 3 hr. 20 min. Topped with a scoop of vanilla ice cream or Greek yogurt, this simple dessert is a great way to satisfy the sweet tooth while reaping the nutritional benefits of summer fruit. Keep the peach slices no less than ½ inch thick; any smaller, and they may lose their shape when cooked.

1 cup old-fashioned rolled oats
3 ounces white whole-wheat flour (about ¾ cup)
½ cup packed light brown sugar
2 teaspoons ground cinnamon
½ teaspoon ground nutmeg
½ teaspoon kosher salt
½ cup unsalted butter, melted and cooled to room temperature
Cooking spray
3 pounds peaches, peeled and cut into 1-inch slices
3 cups blackberries (about 14 ounces)

1. Combine oats, flour, brown sugar, cinnamon, nutmeg, and salt in a large bowl. Stir with a whisk. Add melted butter; stir until combined. Set aside 1 cup of mixture.
2. Coat a 4- to 5-quart slow cooker with cooking spray. Place peaches, blackberries, and remaining oat mixture in slow cooker; stir to combine. Sprinkle peach mixture evenly with reserved 1 cup oat mixture. Lightly coat top with cooking spray.
3. Cook on LOW for 3 hours, until fruit is bubbly and top is browned. Serves 12 (serving size: ⅔ cup)

CALORIES 217; **FAT** 9.2g (sat 5g, mono 2.5g, poly 0.8g); **PROTEIN** 3g; **CARB** 33g; **FIBER** 5g; **SUGARS** 20g (est. added sugars 9g); **CHOL** 20mg; **IRON** 1mg; **SODIUM** 101mg; **CALC** 37mg

USE IT UP

LIGHT COCONUT MILK

Tasty ways to use up the leftovers, whether you have a little or a lot left in the can

Kid Friendly • Make Ahead Freezable • Vegetarian
Coco-Zucchini Bread
Preheat oven to 350°F. Combine 1½ cups shredded zucchini, ¾ cup brown sugar, ⅔ cup light coconut milk, ¼ cup coconut oil, and 2 large eggs. Combine 8 oz. (2 cups) whole-wheat flour, 1 tsp. baking soda, ¾ tsp. salt, and ¾ tsp. cinnamon. Stir in zucchini mixture; spoon into a greased 8- x 4-inch loaf pan. Bake for 50 to 55 minutes. Serves 16 (serving size: 1 slice)

CALORIES 127; **FAT** 4.8g (sat 3.6g, mono 0.4g, poly 0.2g); **PROTEIN** 3g; **CARB** 18g; **FIBER** 2g; **SUGARS** 9g (est. added sugars 9g); **CHOL** 23mg; **IRON** 1mg; **SODIUM** 197mg; **CALC** 16mg

Quick & Easy • Kid Friendly Make Ahead
Chicken Chowder
Heat 1 Tbsp. olive oil in a saucepan over medium-high. Add 1 cup diced onion, 1 Tbsp. thyme, and 12 oz. chopped skinless, boneless chicken breast; sauté 5 minutes. Add 2 cups unsalted chicken stock, 1½ cups corn, 1 tsp. kosher salt, and ½ tsp. black pepper; cook 10 minutes. Combine ¾ cup canned light coconut milk and 1 Tbsp. all-purpose flour; stir into soup until thickened. Serves 4 (serving size: about 1⅓ cups)

CALORIES 239; **FAT** 8.7g (sat 3.3g, mono 3.3g, poly 1g); **PROTEIN** 24g; **CARB** 18g; **FIBER** 2g; **SUGARS** 6g (est. added sugars 0g); **CHOL** 1mg; **IRON** 1mg; **SODIUM** 605mg; **CALC** 19mg

Staff Favorite • Quick & Easy Gluten Free • Kid Friendly Vegetarian
Soft Serve Nice Cream
Place 4 frozen sliced bananas, 4 soft pitted Medjool dates (soak in hot water if firm), ½ cup canned light coconut milk, and ½ tsp. kosher salt in a food processor. Process until smooth, scraping sides of bowl occasionally. Spoon about ¾ cup soft serve into each of 4 bowls; top each with 1 Tbsp. toasted unsweetened coconut flakes. Serves 4

CALORIES 179; **FAT** 5.3g (sat 4.6g, mono 0g, poly 0.1g); **PROTEIN** 2g; **CARB** 35g; **FIBER** 4g; **SUGARS** 19g (est. added sugars 0g); **CHOL** 0mg; **IRON** 1mg; **SODIUM** 251mg; **CALC** 9mg

Quick & Easy • Gluten Free Kid Friendly • Vegetarian
Fruit and Nut Smoothie
Place 1 cup ice cubes, ⅔ cup fresh orange juice, ½ cup frozen mango cubes, ⅓ cup sliced strawberries, ¼ cup toasted walnut halves, and ¼ cup canned light coconut milk in a blender; process until smooth. Serves 1 (serving size: about 2 cups)

CALORIES 350; **FAT** 19.8g (sat 4.4g, mono 2.3g, poly 12g); **PROTEIN** 7g; **CARB** 43g; **FIBER** 5g; **SUGARS** 31g (est. added sugars 0g); **CHOL** 0mg; **IRON** 2mg; **SODIUM** 18mg; **CALC** 52mg

FREEZER-PLEASER CHICKEN ENCHILADAS

Throw a restaurant-style fiesta on the fly with tangy tomatillos and smoky sauce.

Gluten Free • Kid Friendly
Make Ahead • Freezable

Roasted Chili Verde Chicken Enchiladas

Hands-on: 55 min. Total: 1 hr. 30 min.
Skip red enchilada sauce in favor of homemade chili verde in this Mexican classic. The heat level of poblanos can range from mild to spicy; removing the seeds lessens the kick.

Cooking spray
2 pounds tomatillos, husks removed
4 poblano chiles, halved lengthwise, ribs and seeds removed
1 large yellow onion, quartered
6 garlic cloves
1 cup firmly packed fresh cilantro leaves and stems
2 teaspoons ground cumin
1 teaspoon kosher salt, divided
1 teaspoon freshly ground black pepper, divided
2 tablespoons olive oil
8 bone-in, skinless chicken thighs (about 4 pounds)
16 (6-inch) corn tortillas
6 ounces reduced-fat Mexican blend cheese, shredded (about 1¹⁄₂ cups)
¹⁄₂ cup plain 2% reduced-fat Greek yogurt
¹⁄₂ cup chopped fresh cilantro

1. Preheat broiler with oven rack 6 inches from heat. Coat a rimmed baking sheet with cooking spray. Place tomatillos, poblanos, onion, and garlic on prepared baking sheet. Broil for 12 minutes, turning vegetables after 6 minutes, until well charred. Let stand 5 minutes. Scrape mixture and any accumulated juices into a blender. Add cilantro leaves and stems, cumin, and ½ teaspoon each salt and black pepper; process until smooth.
2. Heat oil in a Dutch oven over medium-high. Sprinkle chicken with remaining ½ teaspoon each salt and black pepper. Place chicken in a single layer in Dutch oven, meaty sides down. Cook until browned, 5 to 6 minutes. Transfer to a plate.
3. Pour tomatillo mixture into Dutch oven. Bring to a boil over medium-high. Cook until sauce thickens slightly, 3 to 5 minutes. Return chicken to Dutch oven; reduce heat to medium-low; simmer until a thermometer inserted in thickest portion registers 165°F, 12 to 15 minutes. Place chicken on a plate; let stand 5 minutes. Set aside 2 cups tomatillo mixture. Shred chicken and return to Dutch oven; discard bones. Toss meat to coat.
4. Preheat oven to 350°F. Coat 2 (11- x 7-inch) baking dishes with cooking spray. Spread ¼ cup reserved tomatillo mixture in the bottom of each dish. Spoon ¼ cup chicken mixture into each tortilla; fold into thirds, and arrange in dishes (8 enchiladas in each). Spread ¾ cup reserved tomatillo mixture over enchiladas in each dish. Sprinkle each with ¾ cup cheese. Coat 2 pieces of aluminum foil with cooking spray, and cover each dish. Follow freezing directions, or continue to step 5.
5. Bake at 350°F for 15 minutes, until heated through. Remove foil. Increase heat to broil. Broil for 1 to 2 minutes, until cheese is golden and bubbly. Top each serving with 1 tablespoon yogurt

and 1 tablespoon chopped cilantro. Serves 8 (serving size: 2 enchiladas)

CALORIES 379; **FAT** 13.7g (sat 3.8g, mono 3.1g, poly 4.3g); **PROTEIN** 25g; **CARB** 44g; **FIBER** 7g; **SUGARS** 8g (est. added sugars 0g); **CHOL** 79mg; **IRON** 2mg; **SODIUM** 497mg; **CALC** 316mg

HOW TO

FREEZE
Cover dish with heavy-duty aluminum foil or an airtight lid. Freeze up to 2 months.

THAW
Remove foil; reserve. Place dish in microwave. Microwave on MEDIUM for 20 minutes, until thawed.

REHEAT
Cover dish with reserved foil. Bake at 350°F for 30 minutes, until cheese is melted and a thermometer inserted in center registers 160°F. Remove foil during last 5 minutes.

WOW!

Staff Favorite • Kid Friendly
Make Ahead • Vegetarian

Smoky Carrot Dogs with Nacho Sauce

Hands-on: 20 min. Total: 9 hr. 20 min., including 8 hours soaking
We've embellished the humble carrot to mimic the smoky taste and snappy texture of a hot dog. To lend a dairy-free cheesy flavor to plant-based nacho sauce, we use nutritional yeast; look for it in health food stores or well-stocked specialty grocers. Our recipe saves 8g sat fat over standard cheese dogs without losing any of the flavor.

³⁄₄ cup raw cashews
8 large carrots, rinsed
2 tablespoons canola oil
1 tablespoon reduced-sodium tamari or soy sauce

2 teaspoons liquid smoke (optional)
1½ teaspoons smoked paprika
1 teaspoon garlic powder
1 teaspoon onion powder
¼ cup jarred salsa
¼ cup unsweetened almond milk
3 tablespoons nutritional yeast
¼ teaspoon cayenne pepper
¼ teaspoon ground cumin
¼ teaspoon ground turmeric
¼ teaspoon kosher salt
1 tablespoon water
8 whole-wheat hot dog buns, lightly toasted
2 small jalapeños, thinly sliced
¼ cup diced red onion

1. Place cashews in a bowl with water to cover by 1 inch. Let stand 8 hours or overnight.
2. Preheat oven to 450°F. Line a 13- x 9-inch baking dish with aluminum foil. Trim ends from carrots to fit hot dog buns. Using a vegetable peeler, peel carrots, and round edges to create a hot dog shape.
3. Place oil, tamari, liquid smoke (if desired), paprika, garlic powder, and onion powder in a small bowl. Stir with a whisk. Place carrots in a single layer in prepared baking dish. Pour oil mixture over carrots; rub to coat on all sides. Bake at 450°F for 35 minutes, tossing every 15 minutes.
4. Drain cashews. Place cashews, jarred salsa, almond milk, yeast, cayenne pepper, cumin, turmeric, and salt in a high-powered blender. Process until creamy, 2 to 3 minutes. Stir in up to 1 tablespoon water, 1 teaspoon at a time, until desired consistency is reached.
5. Place 1 roasted carrot in each bun. Top each with 2 tablespoons nacho sauce; top evenly with jalapeño slices and diced red onion. Serves 8 (serving size: 1 carrot dog)

CALORIES 228; FAT 7.8g (sat 1.3g, mono 4g, poly 1.9g); PROTEIN 8g; CARB 32g; FIBER 4g; SUGARS 7g (est. added sugars 1g); CHOL 0mg; IRON 3mg; SODIUM 412mg; CALC 120mg

GET-AHEAD COOKING

COOK ONCE, EAT 3X

Fresh, intensely aromatic curry paste is easy to make at home. Use it in marinades, broths, and sauces.

Gluten Free • Kid Friendly
Make Ahead

Curried Grilled Chicken Thighs

Hands-on: 20 min. Total: 8 hr. 30 min.
Curry paste is a flavor powerhouse, full of roasted aromatics, earthy spices, fiery chiles, and more. Yellow curry powder is commonly used in green curry paste recipes, serving as the flavor backbone; it's convenient, too, providing lots of spices in a single handy ingredient. You can substitute 1 tablespoon lemongrass paste (found near the fresh herbs) for the fresh stalks; simply add right to the food processor instead of roasting.

Curry Paste:
1 large garlic bulb, top ½ inch removed
1 large shallot (about 4 ounces), peeled and halved
1 (3-inch) piece peeled fresh ginger
1 (3-inch) piece fresh lemongrass, halved lengthwise
½ cup chopped fresh cilantro stems
2½ tablespoons canola oil
4 teaspoons curry powder
2½ teaspoons ground turmeric
¾ teaspoon ground coriander
5 green Thai chiles or 1 medium jalapeño, stems removed
Chicken:
¾ cup canned light coconut milk
1½ tablespoons canola oil
8 skinless, boneless chicken thighs (about 1½ pounds)
Cooking spray
¾ teaspoon kosher salt

½ teaspoon freshly ground black pepper
3 tablespoons chopped fresh cilantro leaves
2 tablespoons chopped unsalted roasted peanuts
4 lime wedges

1. To prepare the curry paste, preheat oven to 375°F.
2. Wrap garlic and shallot in foil. Wrap ginger and lemongrass in foil. Bake at 375°F for 1 hour or until very tender and fragrant. Cool.
3. Squeeze pulp from garlic cloves into a food processor; discard skins. Add shallot, ginger, lemongrass, cilantro, and next 5 ingredients (through chiles) to food processor; process until combined. Reserve 5 tablespoons curry paste for Recipes 2 and 3. Reserve ⅓ cup curry paste for another use.
4. To prepare chicken, combine remaining 6 tablespoons curry paste, milk, and 1½ tablespoons oil in a large ziplock plastic bag. Add chicken; seal. Refrigerate 8 hours or overnight.
5. Preheat grill to medium (350°F to 400°F). Coat grill grate with cooking spray. Remove chicken from marinade; discard marinade. Sprinkle chicken evenly with salt and pepper. Arrange chicken on grill; cook 5 minutes on each side or until done. Place chicken on a platter; top with cilantro leaves and peanuts. Serve with lime wedges. Serves 4 (serving size: 2 thighs)

CALORIES 371; FAT 19.9g (sat 3.4g, mono 9.9g, poly 4.8g); PROTEIN 36g; CARB 12g; FIBER 3g; SUGARS 2g (est. added sugars 0g); CHOL 160mg; IRON 2mg; SODIUM 530mg; CALC 50mg

Staff Favorite • Quick & Easy
Gluten Free • Kid Friendly

Curry-Poached Cod with Snap Pea Slaw

Hands-on: 30 min. Total: 30 min.
While a lot of curry paste makes a fantastic marinade, just a little can make a light, fragrant poaching liquid for delicate cod fillets.

1 cup unsalted chicken stock
$\frac{1}{2}$ cup dry white wine
3 tablespoons fresh curry paste (from Recipe 1)
4 garlic cloves, crushed
1 bay leaf
4 (6-ounce) skinless cod fillets
$\frac{2}{3}$ cup sugar snap peas, thinly diagonally sliced
$\frac{1}{2}$ cup thinly sliced yellow bell pepper
$\frac{1}{4}$ cup thinly sliced shallots
$1\frac{1}{2}$ ounces canned bamboo shoots, drained and thinly sliced
1 small red Fresno chile, seeded and thinly sliced
2 tablespoons fresh lime juice
2 tablespoons extra-virgin olive oil
$\frac{1}{2}$ teaspoon kosher salt, divided

1. Bring first 5 ingredients to a boil in a large skillet. Reduce heat; add fish, cover, and simmer 8 to 10 minutes or until fish flakes easily when tested with a fork. Remove pan from heat.
2. Combine snap peas and next 5 ingredients in a bowl; toss. Stir in 1 tablespoon oil and $\frac{1}{4}$ teaspoon salt. Place 1 fillet in each of 4 shallow bowls; sprinkle evenly with remaining $\frac{1}{4}$ teaspoon salt. Add about 3 tablespoons poaching liquid to each bowl. Top each serving with about $\frac{1}{3}$ cup snap pea mixture. Drizzle with remaining 1 tablespoon oil. Serves 4

CALORIES 277; FAT 10.1g (sat 1.3g, mono 7g, poly 1.6g); PROTEIN 29g; CARB 11g; FIBER 2g; SUGARS 4g (est. added sugars 0g); CHOL 80mg; IRON 2mg; SODIUM 401mg; CALC 51mg

Staff Favorite • Quick & Easy
Gluten Free • Vegetarian

Thai Sweet Potato Noodle Bowls

Hands-on 25 min. Total: 25 min.
Add fresh curry paste to canned coconut milk and nut butter, and you have an instant, wonderfully complex satay sauce. Use as a dip, in stir-fries, or drizzled on this bowl.

$2\frac{1}{2}$ tablespoons toasted sesame oil, divided
2 medium sweet potatoes, spiralized into thick noodles (about 8 cups)
1 cup thinly sliced red bell pepper
$\frac{3}{4}$ teaspoon kosher salt, divided
$\frac{1}{2}$ cup water, divided
3 cups baby spinach
8 ounces extra-firm tofu, cut into $\frac{1}{2}$-inch cubes
$\frac{1}{2}$ cup canned light coconut milk
3 tablespoons almond butter
2 tablespoons fresh curry paste (from Recipe 1)
$\frac{1}{4}$ cup chopped unsalted cashews
4 lime wedges

1. Heat $1\frac{1}{2}$ tablespoons oil in a large nonstick skillet over medium-high. Add sweet potato noodles, bell pepper, and $\frac{1}{2}$ teaspoon salt; sauté 5 minutes. Add $\frac{1}{4}$ cup water; cover and cook 3 minutes. Uncover and cook 2 minutes. Stir in spinach until wilted. Place potato mixture in a bowl.
2. Add remaining 1 tablespoon oil to pan. Add tofu; sauté 4 minutes, stirring occasionally.
3. Combine remaining $\frac{1}{4}$ cup water, remaining $\frac{1}{4}$ teaspoon salt, coconut milk, almond butter, and curry paste in a bowl. Add $\frac{1}{2}$ cup sauce to potato mixture; toss. Divide potato mixture among 4 bowls; top evenly with tofu, remaining $\frac{1}{2}$ cup sauce, and cashews. Serve with lime wedges. Serves 4 (serving size: about $1\frac{1}{2}$ cups)

CALORIES 357; FAT 24.4g (sat 3.7g, mono 11.7g, poly 8.3g); PROTEIN 12g; CARB 27g; FIBER 6g; SUGARS 6g (est. added sugars 0g); CHOL 0mg; IRON 3mg; SODIUM 448mg; CALC 144mg

WHY TRY HOMEMADE?

Our case for making condiments from scratch usually boils down to flavor and sodium: Store-bought curry paste contains about 350mg per serving compared to 4mg in our fresh paste. Omitting salt in the paste lets you use it where it matters—directly on the chicken, instead of in a marinade that'll be discarded later. The shelf life is shorter (about two weeks in the fridge), but the big flavor and salt savings are worth it. Extend use by freezing in ice-cube trays for up to three months.

KITCHEN CONFIDENTIAL

Make Ahead

Grilled Pork Adobo

Hands-on: 17 min. Total: 2 hr. 17 min.
We cook the marinade down so none of the flavors go to waste.

$\frac{1}{3}$ cup white vinegar, divided
$\frac{1}{3}$ cup reduced-sodium soy sauce
2 tablespoons brown sugar
2 tablespoons canola oil
2 bay leaves
$\frac{1}{2}$ cup vertically sliced red onion
1 serrano chile, halved lengthwise
2 (8-ounce) bone-in pork loin chops
Cooking spray
$\frac{1}{4}$ cup thinly sliced green onions

1. Combine 2 tablespoons vinegar and next 5 ingredients (through red onion) in a large ziplock plastic bag. Add 1 serrano chile half to bag; reserve other half for another use. Seal bag; shake well to dissolve sugar. Add pork to bag; refrigerate 2 to 8 hours, turning occasionally.
2. Heat grill to medium-high (about 450°F). Remove pork and red onion from bag; pat pork dry. Strain marinade into a small saucepan over

medium heat; discard solids. Add red onion and remaining vinegar to pan; cook 5 minutes or until liquid is syrupy and reduced by half.
3. Place pork on grill grate coated with cooking spray; grill 3 minutes. Turn pork; baste top of pork with reduced marinade. Grill 3 minutes or until desired degree of doneness. Place on a serving platter; let stand 10 minutes. Slice pork off bone; cut meat into thin slices. Drizzle pork with remaining reduced marinade. Sprinkle with green onions. Serves 4 (serving size: about 3 ounces pork and ¼ cup onion mixture)

CALORIES 263; FAT 13.2g (sat 2.4g, mono 6.7g, poly 2.7g); PROTEIN 25g; CARB 11g; FIBER 1g; SUGARS 9g (est. added sugars 5g); CHOL 71mg; IRON 1mg; SODIUM 573mg; CALC 37mg

HOW TO MARINATE

A little oil, some tangy acid, and plenty of salty liquid and zesty aromatics make the best mix for infusing flavor into meat. Here's how to do it.

1 MARINADE ONLY GOES SO DEEP.
The flavor won't penetrate much more than a small fraction of an inch into the meat no matter how long you marinate, so relatively brief soaks from one to eight hours are best.

2 KEEP ACIDS TO A MINIMUM.
Vinegar and citrus juices lend zesty flavor, but they also break down proteins and can make the meat dry and tough. Stick to about 2 tablespoons per pound. Use oil to distribute flavor. Add a little oil to the marinade to help oil-soluble flavors from aromatics like garlic, onion, and herbs soak into the meat.

3 SALT FOR DEEPER FLAVOR.
Salt will penetrate meat more deeply than the rest of the flavorings in a marinade, brining as it soaks. Salt-rich ingredients like soy sauce and fish sauce work wonders, but a ½ teaspoon of kosher salt (per pound of meat) dissolved into a marinade will help as well.

Quick & Easy • Make Ahead
Vegetarian
Blanched Pesto

Hands-on: 17 min. Total: 17 min.
This approach makes pesto that's less grassy and intense than raw basil versions, with rounded, balanced flavor. It's good to use a mellow, mild olive oil here so it doesn't detract from the fresh herbs. If you don't care for the hot taste of raw garlic, you can take the edge off the cloves by blanching them along with the basil. We use sunflower seed kernels here because they are far less expensive than the pine nuts traditionally used, and their flavor is similarly rich and sweet. If you have pine nuts already on hand, feel free to use them instead.

6 cups fresh basil leaves
2 garlic cloves, peeled
2 tablespoons unsalted sunflower seed kernels, toasted
¼ cup plus 1 tablespoon extra-virgin olive oil
¼ teaspoon kosher salt
2 ounces finely grated Parmigiano-Reggiano cheese (about ½ cup)

1. Bring a large Dutch oven filled with water to a boil over high. Fill a large bowl with ice water. Place basil leaves in a metal strainer. Place strainer in pan, using tongs to quickly submerge all basil leaves; cook 5 seconds or just until leaves turn bright green. Carefully remove strainer with leaves from pan; drain. Immediately plunge strainer with leaves in ice water bath. Let stand 10 seconds. Remove basil; drain well. Spread basil leaves on a clean, dry dish towel; gently blot dry with another towel.
2. Place basil, garlic cloves, sunflower seeds, oil, and salt in a food processor; process until smooth. Add cheese and process until blended. Serves 12 (serving size: about 1 tablespoon)

CALORIES 85; FAT 8g (sat 1.6g, mono 5g, poly 1.1g); PROTEIN 2g; CARB 2g; FIBER 0g; SUGARS 0g; CHOL 4mg; IRON 1mg; SODIUM 126mg; CALC 79mg

WHAT'S THE SECRET TO DELICIOUS PESTO THAT STAYS BRIGHT GREEN?

1 START BY BLANCHING.
Giving fresh basil a quick dip in boiling water followed by an ice bath results in brilliant, emerald-green pesto that keeps its color far longer than basil that goes straight into the blender. Place the basil in a heatproof strainer, and then into boiling water to make the leaves easy to scoop out quickly.

2 SHOCK AND DRY.
Immediately after pulling the leaves from the pot—as soon as they become bright green—dunk them into an ice bath for 10 seconds to stop the cooking. Drain well, spread the leaves onto a clean, dry dish towel, and gently blot dry with another towel. A little water content will remain—and that's actually good for the pesto, as you'll see.

3 BLEND TO A PUREE.
Combine basil, toasted seeds or nuts, garlic, salt, and olive oil in a food processor, and and blend until smooth. The small amount of residual water on the leaves from blanching will emulsify with the oil. Finally, add the cheese—it further emulsifies with the water and oil to make the pesto wonderfully creamy.

4 BASK IN THE GREEN GLOW.
The end result is noticeably brighter than raw pesto, and it's made to stay that way. Blanched pesto won't brown if you add a squeeze of lemon or toss it with hot pasta. What's more, its flavor is rounder and more mellow than conventional basil pesto, which can taste a little "hot," between peppery uncooked basil and the pungent raw garlic.

CLASH OF THE COOKOUT TITANS

We give classic cookout dishes—burgers, grilled chicken, potato salad, coleslaw, and corn on the cob—two different delicious takes and pit them head-to-head. Decide the winners, and assemble your greatest picnic-table spread of all time.

GRILLED BURGERS vs SMASHED SLIDERS

The all-American classic is the no-frills star of cookouts from sea to shining sea: flame-kissed juicy beef with old-school fixings (hello, iceberg!) and a pickle-flecked special sauce. Smashed sliders are the plucky upstarts, with beef pressed on a ripping-hot pan for patties with crunchy, caramelized crust and incredible flavor. Plus, cheese!

Quick & Easy • Kid Friendly

All-American Grilled Burger

Hands-on: 20 min. Total: 20 min.

1/4 cup finely chopped iceberg lettuce
3 tablespoons unsalted ketchup
3 tablespoons finely chopped reduced-sodium dill pickle (about 1 1/2 spears)
1 tablespoon grainy mustard
1 teaspoon hot sauce
1 pound 90% lean ground sirloin
1/2 teaspoon kosher salt
1/2 teaspoon freshly ground black pepper
Cooking spray
4 iceberg lettuce leaves
4 (1.8-ounce) sesame seed hamburger buns, lightly toasted
4 (1/4-inch-thick) heirloom tomato slices
4 thin white onion rings

1. Preheat grill to medium-high (about 450°F). Combine first 5 ingredients in a small bowl.
2. Gently shape ground sirloin into 4 (4-inch-wide) patties. Sprinkle evenly with salt and pepper. Coat grill grate with cooking spray. Place patties on grate; grill 4 minutes on each side or to desired degree of doneness.
3. Place 1 lettuce leaf on bottom half of each bun. Top each with about 2 1/2 tablespoons sauce, 1 patty, 1 tomato slice, and 1 onion ring. Cover with top halves of buns. Serves 4 (serving size: 1 burger)

CALORIES 381; **FAT** 13.8g (sat 4.9g, mono 5.2g, poly 1.3g); **PROTEIN** 29g; **CARB** 34g; **FIBER** 2g; **SUGARS** 7g (est. added sugars 2g); **CHOL** 74mg; **IRON** 4mg; **SODIUM** 685mg; **CALC** 115mg

Quick & Easy • Kid Friendly

Smashed Double Cheeseburger Sliders

Hands-on: 20 min. Total: 20 min.

2 tablespoons unsalted ketchup
1 tablespoon canola mayonnaise
3/4 teaspoon black pepper, divided
3/4 teaspoon sugar
3/4 teaspoon kosher salt
12 ounces 93% lean ground sirloin
2 garlic cloves, minced
Cooking spray
2 ounces shredded cheddar cheese (about 1/2 cup)
8 whole-wheat slider buns, toasted
8 thin plum tomato slices
16 thin, small red onion slices
8 small romaine lettuce slices

1. Combine ketchup, mayonnaise, and 1/4 teaspoon pepper in a bowl.
2. Place sugar, salt, remaining 1/2 teaspoon pepper, beef, and garlic in a bowl; gently combine. Divide into 16 (3/4-ounce) balls; lightly coat with cooking spray.
3. Heat a large cast-iron skillet over high. Coat pan with cooking spray.

Add 4 beef balls to pan; use a large offset spatula to press each portion into a 2-inch-wide patty. Cook until well browned, about 1 minute. Turn patties; top each with 1½ teaspoons cheese. Cover pan; cook 30 seconds or until cheese melts. Remove patties from pan; arrange in stacks of 2. Repeat procedure with remaining beef balls and cheese.

4. Top each bottom bun with 1½ teaspoons ketchup mixture, 2 patties, 1 tomato slice, 2 onion slices, and 1 lettuce leaf. Cover with bun tops. Serves 4 (serving size: 2 sliders)

CALORIES 284; FAT 13g (sat 4.5g, mono 4.2g, poly 2.2g); PROTEIN 24g; CARB 19g; FIBER 1g; SUGARS 4g (est. added sugars 3g); CHOL 61mg; IRON 2mg; SODIUM 631mg; CALC 135mg

SMOKED CORN vs GRILL-STEAMED CORN

Smoke 'em if you got 'em: A low and slow fire releases the fragrance of applewood to burnish the corn with bronze highlights and a mellow-sweet smoky flavor. Or use the husks like a natural steamer to lock in all the sweetness and keep the kernels tender and juicy. Then give the golden ears a dusting of fruity Aleppo pepper and citrusy cilantro.

Kid Friendly • Vegetarian

Applewood-Smoked Corn on the Cob

Hands-on: 15 min. Total: 45 min.
We love the warm, slightly sweet smoky flavor that applewood gives the corn. Hickory chips might overpower here, but cherry chips would also work.

1 cup applewood chips
4 large ears fresh corn with husks
2 tablespoons unsalted butter, softened
½ teaspoon salt
½ teaspoon freshly ground black pepper

1. Prepare a charcoal or gas grill for indirect heat. If using a charcoal grill, carefully push hot coals to one side of grill, and close grill lid. Bring temperature to 275°F to 300°F. If using a gas grill, turn all burners to high, and close grill lid. Bring internal temperature to 275°F to 300°F; turn off one side of gas grill.

2. Wrap applewood chips in an aluminum foil packet, and use a skewer to poke 10 holes through foil.
3. Pull husks back from corn, keeping husks intact; remove and discard silks. Tie husks together with kitchen twine or a long strip of husk to form a handle for each ear of corn.
4. Place foil packet with wood chips over coals or lit burner; close lid, and heat until smoke starts to fill grill. Place corn on grate over unlit side of grill. Cover and grill 30 minutes or until corn is tender and kernels are lightly browned, maintaining temperature between 275°F and 300°F. Remove corn from grill. Stir together butter, salt, and pepper; evenly brush over corn. Serves 4 (serving size: 1 ear)

CALORIES 139; FAT 7.2g (sat 4g, mono 1.9g, poly 0.7g); PROTEIN 3g; CARB 19g; FIBER 2g; SUGARS 6g (est. added sugars 0g); CHOL 15mg; IRON 1mg; SODIUM 311mg; CALC 5mg

Quick & Easy • Gluten Free Vegetarian

Grill-Steamed Corn with Cilantro and Chile Powder

(pictured on page 227)

Hands-on: 30 min. Total: 50 min.
Aleppo is a fruity Middle Eastern pepper with moderate heat. Sub ½ teaspoon crushed red pepper flakes, if desired.

4 large ears fresh corn with husks
2 tablespoons extra-virgin olive oil
2 tablespoons finely chopped fresh cilantro
¾ teaspoon Aleppo chile powder
½ teaspoon salt
4 lime wedges

1. Preheat grill to medium-high (about 450°F). Place corn on grill grate; grill, uncovered, 15 minutes or until husks are charred and corn is tender. Remove corn from grill; let stand 10 minutes. Pull husks back; discard silks. Brush corn with oil. Sprinkle with cilantro, chile powder, and salt. Serve with lime wedges. Serves 4 (serving size: 1 ear)

CALORIES 151; FAT 8.2g (sat 1.3g, mono 5.4g, poly 1.3g); PROTEIN 3g; CARB 20g; FIBER 2g; SUGARS 7g (est. added sugars 0g); CHOL 0mg; IRON 1mg; SODIUM 333mg; CALC 5mg

TANGY POTATO SALAD
vs CREAMY POTATO SALAD

Nothing brings a starchy potato salad to life like tangy vinaigrette—zesty mustard and white wine vinegar deliver a one-two punch to the palate. But everyone loves the cool comfort of a creamy mayo-based potato salad, especially when a little yogurt livens up the dressing and roasted red pepper adds a touch of sweetness and velvety texture.

Quick & Easy • Gluten Free
Make Ahead • Vegetarian

Yukon Gold Potato Salad

Hands-on: 29 min. Total: 53 min.
A middle ground between waxy red potatoes and starchy russets, buttery Yukon Golds are great in potato salad.

2 large red bell peppers
1¼ pounds Yukon Gold potatoes,
   cut into ¾-inch cubes
4 large eggs
⅓ cup chopped green onions
¼ cup canola mayonnaise
¼ cup chopped fresh flat-leaf parsley
3 tablespoons plain 2% reduced-fat
   Greek yogurt
2 tablespoons chopped fresh dill
2 teaspoons Dijon mustard
⅛ teaspoon table salt

1. Preheat broiler with oven rack in top position. Cut peppers in half, and discard seeds and stems. Place bell peppers, cut sides down, on an aluminum foil–lined baking sheet. Broil 10 minutes or until well charred. Cover pan tightly with foil, and let stand 10 minutes. Uncover peppers; remove and discard skins. Chop peppers; place in a medium bowl.
2. Place potatoes in a medium saucepan. Cover with water by 3 inches; bring to a boil. Reduce heat to medium; cook 5 minutes or until al dente. Add whole eggs; cook 10 minutes or until potatoes are tender. Drain potatoes;

plunge eggs into ice water. Let eggs stand 10 minutes.
3. Add green onions and remaining ingredients to bell peppers; stir to combine. Peel cooked eggs; chop. Add potatoes to bell pepper mixture; toss to coat. Add eggs to potato mixture; stir gently to combine. Serves 4 (serving size: about 1 cup)

CALORIES 244; **FAT** 9g (sat 1.7g, mono 4.2g, poly 2.4g); **PROTEIN** 10g; **CARB** 30g; **FIBER** 6g; **SUGARS** 6g (est. added sugars 3g); **CHOL** 187mg; **IRON** 2mg; **SODIUM** 324mg; **CALC** 53mg

Quick & Easy • Gluten Free
Make Ahead • Vegetarian

Fingerling Potato Salad with Mustard Vinaigrette

Hands-on: 10 min. Total: 30 min.
Little fingerling potatoes are fantastic in potato salads, in part because their skin-to-flesh ratio is much smaller than big potatoes, so there's more dynamic textural difference in every bite.

¼ cup extra-virgin olive oil
3 tablespoons white wine vinegar
2 tablespoons grainy mustard
¾ teaspoon freshly ground black
   pepper
¼ teaspoon kosher salt
1¼ pounds multicolored fingerling
   potatoes, halved
½ cup thinly sliced red onion
2 tablespoons finely chopped fresh
   chives

1. Combine first 5 ingredients in a large bowl.
2. Place potatoes in a medium saucepan. Cover with water by 3 inches; bring to a boil. Reduce heat to medium-low; cook 20 minutes or until potatoes are tender. Drain well. Add hot potatoes to dressing; toss gently to coat. Add onion and chives; toss. Serves 4 (serving size: about 1 cup)

CALORIES 231; **FAT** 13.5g (sat 1.9g, mono 9.9g, poly 1.4g); **PROTEIN** 2g; **CARB** 26g; **FIBER** 4g; **SUGARS** 3g (est. added sugars 0g); **CHOL** 0mg; **IRON** 1mg; **SODIUM** 301mg; **CALC** 8mg

CONDIMENT SMACKDOWN

SAUERKRAUT VS SWEET RELISH
Kraut brings the crunch to a picnic table spread. We like Bubbies: It's naturally fermented, with no added sugar. For sweet relish, we love that Cascadian Farm's organic blend has no artificial colors or preservatives—rare in store-bought relish.

YELLOW MUSTARD VS DIJON
Good old yellow mustard doesn't get enough love these days, but ballparks and backyard barbecues are where it shines. For our money, French's is the gold standard. As for Dijon, France's Maille delivers bold but balanced flavor, perfect for salads or sandwiches.

DILL PICKLES VS BREAD & BUTTER
Vlasic Kosher Dill Spears are everything you want from a snack pickle: crispy, crunchy, juicy, and zesty. At the other end of the pickle spectrum, Mt. Olive's Old-Fashioned Sweet Bread & Butter Chips offer the ideal sweet-tart flavor balance and firm, snappy texture.

Tangy Beer-Can Chicken

Hands-on: 1 hr. Total: 2 hr. 45 min.
The can method keeps the bird moist while it grills because liquid in the can forms steam inside the cavity. Any canned beverage will work, since it won't really impart any noticeable flavor to the chicken. We like the bright, tangy flavor of good old-fashioned yellow mustard here.

2 tablespoons olive oil
1 teaspoon freshly ground black pepper
1 teaspoon kosher salt
1 (5-pound) whole chicken
1 (12-ounce) can beer or soft drink
¼ cup yellow mustard
2 tablespoons honey
2 tablespoons apple cider vinegar
1 tablespoon tomato paste
¼ cup fresh flat-leaf parsley leaves

1. Preheat a gas grill to medium (about 400°F) on one side, or push hot coals to one side of a charcoal grill.
2. Combine first 3 ingredients in a small bowl. Starting at the neck cavity, loosen and lift chicken skin from breasts and legs with fingers. Rub oil mixture under loosened skin. Open beer can; pour out ¾ cup beer, reserving for another use. Place chicken upright onto can, fitting can into cavity. Pull legs forward to form a tripod, so chicken stands upright. Place chicken upright on grill grate over unheated side. Cover and grill 1 hour and 30 minutes or until a thermometer inserted in thigh registers 165°F, rotating chicken once.
3. Combine mustard, honey, vinegar, and tomato paste in a small bowl.
4. Place chicken and can on a cutting board; let stand 15 minutes. Remove and discard skin and can. Cut chicken into pieces; place on a platter. Drizzle with sauce, and sprinkle with parsley. Serves 6 (serving size: about 4 ounces chicken and 1 tablespoon sauce)

CALORIES 248; **FAT** 9.5g (sat 1.8g, mono 4.9g, poly 1.4g); **PROTEIN** 32g; **CARB** 7g; **FIBER** 1g; **SUGARS** 6g (est. added sugars 5g); **CHOL** 119mg; **IRON** 1mg; **SODIUM** 519mg; **CALC** 20mg

Gluten Free • Kid Friendly

Herb-Rubbed Chicken Under a Brick

Hands-on: 30 min. Total: 1 hr. 15 min.
Brick-pressed chicken cooks quickly and evenly, a great boon to a barbecue host. The key is to spatchcock—or butterfly—the bird (see our illustrated step on page 185), and then press it down flat on the grill with a foil-wrapped brick or cast-iron skillet.

2 tablespoons finely chopped fresh flat-leaf parsley
2 tablespoons finely chopped fresh tarragon
1 tablespoon finely chopped fresh thyme
3 tablespoons olive oil
1¼ teaspoons kosher salt
1¼ teaspoons black pepper
½ teaspoon ground cumin
1 (5-pound) whole chicken
Cooking spray
4 lemon wedges

1. Preheat a gas grill to medium (about 400°F) on one side, or push hot coals to one side of a charcoal grill. Combine first 7 ingredients in a small bowl.
2. Place chicken, breast side down, on a cutting board. Using poultry shears, cut along both sides of backbone; remove backbone. (Discard backbone, or reserve for stock.) Turn chicken breast side up; open the underside of chicken like a book. Using the heel of your hand, press firmly against breastbone until it cracks. Tuck wing tips under. Loosen and lift skin from chicken with fingers; spread herb mixture under skin.
3. Coat grill grate with cooking spray. Place chicken on grate, skin side down, over hot side of grill. Place an aluminum foil–wrapped brick or a cast-iron skillet on chicken to flatten. Grill chicken 8 minutes or until well browned. Turn chicken over, and move to unheated side of grill. Place brick or skillet on chicken. Cover, and grill 35 minutes or until a thermometer inserted in thickest part of breast registers 165°F. Remove from grill; let stand 10 minutes. Remove and discard skin; cut chicken into pieces. Serve with lemon wedges. Serves 6 (serving size: about 4 ounces chicken)

CALORIES 241; **FAT** 11.5g (sat 2.1g, mono 6.4g, poly 1.6g); **PROTEIN** 32g; **CARB** 1g; **FIBER** 0g; **SUGARS** 0g; **CHOL** 119mg; **IRON** 1mg; **SODIUM** 494mg; **CALC** 18mg

Classic slaw can cool you down, a creamy yet crisp respite from summer temps and grill-charred meats. This one amps up the black pepper and uses rough-chopped cabbage for a fresh look and mouthfeel. Or let your slaw bring the heat with a touch of chipotle chile in adobo, infusing the bright citrus and bitter radicchio with charred jalapeño smokiness.

**Quick & Easy • Gluten Free
Make Ahead • Vegetarian**

Creamy Black Pepper Coleslaw

Hands-on: 15 min. Total: 15 min.
Cutting the cabbage coarsely gives the dish a different look from shredded-cabbage slaws. A full teaspoon of black pepper lends pleasant warm heat without overpowering. Make the dish up to a day ahead if you like—the veggies will stay crisp and the flavors will meld as the slaw chills.

¼ cup canola mayonnaise
2 tablespoons apple cider vinegar
1 tablespoon water
2 teaspoons grainy mustard
1 teaspoon freshly ground black
   pepper
1 teaspoon minced fresh garlic
¼ teaspoon kosher salt
3 cups coarsely chopped
   green cabbage
1 cup matchstick-cut carrot
½ cup fresh flat-leaf parsley leaves

1. Combine first 7 ingredients in a medium bowl. Add cabbage, carrot, and parsley; toss to coat. Serves 4 (serving size: ¾ cup)

CALORIES 77; **FAT** 4.1g (sat 0g, mono 2.4g, poly 1.5g); **PROTEIN** 2g; **CARB** 8g; **FIBER** 3g; **SUGARS** 3g (est. added sugars 1g); **CHOL** 0mg; **IRON** 1mg; **SODIUM** 315mg; **CALC** 40mg

---

**Quick & Easy • Gluten Free
Make Ahead • Vegetarian**

Smoky-Spiced Slaw

Hands-on: 15 min. Total: 15 min.
A little chipotle pepper in the dressing lends smoky heat to the dish. A touch of sugar and tangy lime juice balance the pleasant bitterness of radicchio. You can make this slaw up to a day ahead. The radicchio will soften a little as it chills, but the broccoli and cabbage stay crunchy.

2 tablespoons fresh lime juice
2 tablespoons extra-virgin olive oil
2 teaspoons finely chopped chipotle
   pepper in adobo sauce
2 teaspoons minced fresh garlic
½ teaspoon sugar
¼ teaspoon salt
3 cups sliced red cabbage
1 cup thinly sliced radicchio
1 cup broccoli slaw

1. Combine first 6 ingredients in a medium bowl. Add cabbage, radicchio, and broccoli slaw; toss to coat. Serves 4 (serving size: ¾ cup)

CALORIES 91; **FAT** 6.9g (sat 1g, mono 4.9g, poly 0.7g); **PROTEIN** 2g; **CARB** 7g; **FIBER** 2g; **SUGARS** 3g (est. added sugars 1g); **CHOL** 0mg; **IRON** 1mg; **SODIUM** 193mg; **CALC** 42mg

---

NUTRITION MADE EASY

ALT. MEATS 2.0

Eat less meat to improve your health and the environment.

Just as obesity and diet-related chronic diseases are on the rise, so are concerns about the environmental impact of food production. Our Western, meat-centric diets are a major contributor to greenhouse gas emissions, deforestation, and climate change. Animal food production occupies 70% of all agricultural land and requires the greatest amount of water of any protein source to produce, accounting for roughly 27% of our total water footprint. What's more, the livestock sector is estimated to generate more greenhouse gas emissions than the transport sector, with ruminants, such as beef and lamb, producing the most. Replacing meat with plant-based alternatives even one day per week can reduce your carbon footprint. A 2014 European study showed that if we replaced up to 50% of animal-derived foods with plant-based foods, we would cut up to 40% of our greenhouse gas emissions and use nearly a quarter less land. So embrace more meatless meals. And don't worry, we'll help: Here, we show you fresh, innovative ways to swap out meat for nutrient-dense plant-based alternatives. Viva la plant!

MORE PLANTS, LESS MEAT: SUSTAINABLE HEALTH

Plant-forward eating has become the model for healthful, sustainable living—perhaps thanks to the Mediterranean diet, which had it right all along. This way of eating emphasizes the need to move nuts, legumes, and whole grains to the center of the plate; let produce take precedence; and shrink portions and frequency of animal-based protein. A plant-forward diet has been linked to a lower risk of obesity, heart disease, type 2 diabetes, Alzheimer's, and certain types of cancer, and it has even been shown to contribute to longer life spans in Mediterranean and Asian regions. Eating more plants also helps you get more of vitamins A, C, and E, folate, potassium, calcium, and magnesium, nutrients which are frequently underconsumed.

Because of this growing interest in plant foods, most grocery stores now stock more faux meat products. Crafted with the intent to replicate the meat experience, these products are often highly processed; look for ones without artificial flavors and colors and less than 20% daily value of sodium. Also, try experimenting with more whole-food ingredients or traditionally prepared forms of soy, such as tempeh or tofu (see information at right).

SOY PRIMER

Soy foods aren't just good for you: They're environmentally savvy, requiring 88% less water than cattle production and delivering the highest protein density for fossil fuel usage. In 2016, 94% of all soybeans grown in the United States were genetically engineered (a process used, in this case, to make soy more herbicide-tolerant), according to the USDA. Research shows genetically engineered soybeans and soy products (think tofu, oil, etc.) are safe to eat, but if you're concerned, choose soy foods that are certified organic or labeled non-GMO.

POWER-HOUSE PLANT PROTEINS

Add a variety of these plants to your diet and you won't come up short on protein. Our picks are minimally processed and nutrient-packed, making them sustainable for you and the planet.

1. TOFU

Made from soy milk that has been coagulated and either curdled and pressed into blocks (similar to the process of cheesemaking) or left in its natural coagulated state to retain moisture (silken).

HOW IT'S SOLD

Located in the refrigerated produce section of most grocery stores and supermarkets, you'll find silken and block tofu in soft, firm, medium-firm, or extra-firm textures, depending on water content and density.

BEST USES

Silken: Requires delicate handling, as consistency is similar to poached egg whites. Use raw and blend into soups, smoothies, or creamy desserts.

Soft (block-style): Use to bulk up soups or stews, or blend into desserts.

Medium (block-style): Press/drain excess water before pan-searing or baking. Add to stir-fries, salads, or breakfast scrambles.

Firm/extra-firm (block-style): Press/drain excess water before pan-searing, baking, or grilling. Use in place of chicken, beef, or pork in almost any recipe.

NUTRITION HIGHLIGHTS

Rich in calcium because of the precipitating agent, calcium sulfate, used in the coagulating process. Protein content ranges from about 4g in 3 ounces of silken tofu to 10g in 3 ounces of extra-firm block-style tofu.

2. TEMPEH

Fermented soybeans packed into cakes; this tofu counterpart originated in Indonesia. Because the whole bean is used, tempeh is less processed than tofu and is a richer source of protein.

HOW IT'S SOLD

Located in the refrigerated produce section of most specialty markets, tempeh is sold in vacuum-sealed packs and is available in different flavor varieties, some with whole grains or flax seeds added.

BEST USES

Tempeh has a mild nutty flavor and firm texture. Crumble it up and use it in place of ground meat, or cut it into slices or cubes to replace chicken, turkey, pork, or lamb.

NUTRITION HIGHLIGHTS

The fermentation process gives tempeh a probiotic boost and makes its zinc and iron more available for your body to use (by reducing a compound called phytate). Three ounces offers 16g protein (equal to 3 ounces of turkey breast meat) and 7g or 8g fiber, depending on the variety. Tempeh is higher in magnesium and potassium than tofu and is a richer source of omega-3 fatty acids.

3. PULSES

Pulses (dried peas, beans, and lentils) are affordable, nutrient-packed, and have one of the lowest carbon footprints of any food. They rely less on chemical fertilizers due to their ability to recycle nutrients from the atmosphere back into the soil, making them a highly sustainable choice. Pulses provide up to 9g protein per ½ cup cooked, and although not a complete source of protein (due to inadequate quantities of some essential amino acids), they are also rich in fiber, iron, folate, potassium, and magnesium.

4. WHOLE GRAINS

Amaranth, quinoa, wheat berries, teff, bulgur, spelt, and kamut are rich sources of plant protein, boasting up to 6g per ½ cup cooked. Quinoa is technically a seed and is one of the few plant-based sources of complete protein, containing all nine essential amino acids.

5. NUTS AND SEEDS

While nutrient compositions vary, nuts and seeds are rich sources of heart-healthy unsaturated fats, fiber, protein, essential vitamins and minerals, and a wide variety of key health-promoting compounds like carotenoids, polyphenols, and phytosterols. Hemp seeds triumph their seedy cousins with a whopping 9g protein per ounce (that's more than chicken, beef, or pork).

OUR FAVORITE NEW PLANT PRODUCTS

The total market for plant-based foods now tops $5 billion in annual sales with a trajectory to keep soaring.

1 BURGERS
Hilary's Bean Burgers
Whole grains and legumes lend hearty meatlike texture to tasty patties that are ready in minutes.

MAYO
Sir Kensington's Fabanaise
Made with aquafaba (chickpea liquid, see page 185) to create a smooth sandwich upgrade.

JACKFRUIT
Upton's Bar-B-Que Jackfruit
A tree-borne fruit with a fiesty kick that resembles the texture and flavor of pulled pork.

RICOTTA
Kite Hill Ricotta
Almond milk and cultures add sweet and salty overtones and a buttery, smooth finish.

Gluten Free • Make Ahead
Vegetarian

Churrasco-Style Tofu Steaks with Hemp Chimichurri

Hands-on: 30 min. Total: 45 min.
Be sure to press and drain as much liquid as possible before cooking the tofu (see step 2); it will better absorb the spices from the dry rub and reach its full grilling potential. Hemp seeds lend quality plant protein to zesty chimichurri and are a rich source of heart-healthy fats and fiber.

1 cup packed fresh flat-leaf parsley leaves
1 cup packed fresh cilantro leaves
2 tablespoons hemp seeds
1 tablespoon red wine vinegar
1 tablespoon fresh lime juice
1 garlic clove
¼ teaspoon crushed red pepper
1 teaspoon kosher salt, divided
5 tablespoons extra-virgin olive oil, divided
2 (14-ounce) packages extra-firm block-style tofu, drained
2 teaspoons garlic powder
1 teaspoon onion powder
1 teaspoon smoked paprika
1 teaspoon ground cumin
½ teaspoon black pepper
Cooking spray

1. Preheat oven to 400°F. Place parsley, cilantro, hemp seeds, vinegar, lime juice, garlic, red pepper, ½ teaspoon salt, and ¼ cup oil in a food processor; process until smooth. Set aside.
2. Press tofu with paper towels until very dry. Slice each block in half diagonally. Stand each half on cut side, and split each into thirds, creating 12 equal triangles. Place in a single layer on paper towels.

3. Combine garlic powder, onion powder, smoked paprika, cumin, black pepper, and remaining ½ teaspoon salt in a bowl. Rub spice mixture evenly on each side of tofu steaks. Spray steaks with cooking spray.
4. Heat remaining 1 tablespoon oil in a grill pan over medium-high. Cook tofu steaks in single-layer batches until deep char marks appear, 3 to 5 minutes on each side. Transfer to a baking sheet.
5. Bake tofu steaks at 400°F for 5 minutes. Place tofu steaks on each of 6 plates. Top each serving with herb mixture. Serves 6 (serving size: 2 tofu steaks and about 1 tablespoon sauce)

CALORIES 278; **FAT** 21g (sat 3.3g, mono 10.8g, poly 6.8g); **PROTEIN** 14g; **CARB** 8g; **FIBER** 1g; **SUGARS** 0g (est. added sugars 0g); **CHOL** 0mg; **IRON** 3mg; **SODIUM** 329mg; **CALC** 119mg

Quick & Easy • Kid Friendly
Vegetarian

Tempeh Gyros with Tzatziki

Hands-on: 20 min. Total: 30 min.
Tempeh's toothsome texture and boundless flavor adaptability make it an excellent stand-in for lamb meat. Braising the tempeh removes its bitter edge and infuses it with deep umami flavor. Silken tofu blends into a velvety-smooth consistency, lending body and creaminess to tzatziki sauce. Our veggie-centric version packs in 22g plant protein and saves 300mg sodium over the traditional meaty street-cart meal.

1 (8-ounce) package tempeh
1 tablespoon olive oil
½ cup water
¼ cup minced yellow onion
2 tablespoons reduced-sodium soy sauce or tamari
1 teaspoon chopped fresh rosemary
1 teaspoon chopped fresh oregano
4 garlic cloves, minced and divided

1/4 teaspoon black pepper, divided
3/4 cup silken tofu (about 6 ounces)
1/2 cup peeled and grated English
   cucumber
1 tablespoon fresh lemon juice
1 tablespoon chopped fresh dill
1/2 teaspoon white wine vinegar
1/4 teaspoon kosher salt
4 (1.9-ounce) whole-grain flatbread
   wraps (such as Flatout Flatbread
   Light Original)
1/2 cup vertically sliced red onion
1 medium tomato, thinly sliced

1. Slice tempeh lengthwise into
8 (1/4-inch-thick) slices.
2. Heat oil in a large nonstick skillet
over medium. Place tempeh slices in
pan, and cook until golden-brown, 3
to 4 minutes on each side.
3. Meanwhile, stir together 1/2 cup
water, minced onion, soy sauce,
rosemary, oregano, 2 minced garlic
cloves, and 1/8 teaspoon black pepper
in a small bowl.
4. Add soy sauce mixture to tempeh
in pan. Cover, and reduce heat to
medium-low. Braise tempeh, turning
occasionally, until liquid has mostly
evaporated and tempeh has absorbed
the flavors, about 10 minutes.
5. Process silken tofu and remaining
2 garlic cloves in a high-powered
blender until smooth. Place in a
bowl. Stir in cucumber, lemon juice,
dill, vinegar, salt, and remaining
1/8 teaspoon black pepper.
6. Divide tempeh evenly among
flatbreads, and top each with about
2 tablespoons tzatziki. Divide onion
slices and tomato evenly among
gyros. Serves 4 (serving size: 1 wrap)

CALORIES 333; FAT 12.8g (sat 1.9g, mono 4.8g,
poly 4.8g); PROTEIN 22g; CARB 37g; FIBER 4g;
SUGARS 3g (est. added sugars 0g); CHOL 0mg;
IRON 4mg; SODIUM 722mg; CALC 137mg

Staff Favorite • Quick & Easy
Gluten Free • Kid Friendly
Vegetarian

"Huevos" Soy-Cheros

Hands-on: 25 min. Total: 30 min.
In this vegetarian take on huevos rancheros,
cooking crumbled tofu in a skillet achieves
the fluffy texture of scrambled eggs, while
turmeric adds the quintessential golden
hue. Our version saves 20g sat fat over
the classic and provides 35% of your daily
fiber goal.

10 ounces extra-firm block-style tofu,
   drained
1 teaspoon ground turmeric
1 teaspoon garlic powder
1/2 teaspoon chili powder
1/4 teaspoon kosher salt
2 tablespoons water
2 teaspoons olive oil
1 cup sliced red bell pepper
1 cup sliced green bell pepper
5 ounces soy chorizo, diced or
   crumbled (about 3/4 cup)
1 (14.5-ounce) can fire-roasted diced
   tomatoes, undrained
1 cup rinsed and drained canned
   unsalted pinto beans
10 (6-inch) corn tortillas
2 tablespoons lime juice (from 1 lime)
1 ripe avocado, sliced
1/4 cup packed fresh cilantro leaves

1. Press tofu with paper towels until
very dry. Place on a cutting board;
use a fork to crumble. Set aside.
2. Combine turmeric, garlic powder,
chili powder, and salt in a bowl. Stir
in 2 tablespoons water. Set aside.
3. Heat oil in a large nonstick skillet
over medium. Add bell peppers;
cook 5 minutes or until softened.
Move peppers to one side of pan,
and add tofu to empty side. Cook
2 minutes; add turmeric mixture to
tofu, and stir to evenly distribute.
Cook 5 minutes or until tofu is

lightly browned. Gently toss peppers
with tofu.
4. Heat a separate large skillet
over medium-high. Add soy chorizo; cook 3 to 4 minutes or until
browned. Stir in tomatoes and
beans; cook 2 minutes or until
heated through.
5. Working with 1 tortilla at a time,
heat over medium-high directly on
eye of a burner until warmed and
charred, about 15 seconds per side.
6. Place 2 tortillas on each of 5
plates. Top each with 2/3 cup chorizo
mixture and 1/2 cup tofu mixture.
Drizzle evenly with lime juice.
Top with avocado slices; sprinkle
with cilantro. Serves 5 (serving size:
2 tacos)

CALORIES 353; FAT 15g (sat 1.8g, mono 7.2g,
poly 3.7g); PROTEIN 15g; CARB 43g; FIBER 10g;
SUGARS 5g (est. added sugars 0g); CHOL 0mg;
IRON 4mg; SODIUM 591mg; CALC 169mg

SHEDDING LIGHT ON SOY

Despite misconceptions, current
research suggests two to four servings
of soy foods per day can have positive
health benefits, such as lowering LDL
cholesterol and improving bone health.
Experts attribute much of soy's health
benefits to its rich amount of isofla-
vones. Soy also contains all nine
essential amino acids, making it nutritionally equivalent to animal protein.
Plus, 1/2 cup of cooked soybeans contains 15g protein, approximately twice
that of other legumes. Soy also delivers
soluble and insoluble fiber and
omega-3 fatty acids.

AS AMERICAN AS GAZPACHO

By José Andrés

Through an iconic cold soup, star chef José Andrés discovers deep roots that connect his Spanish heritage with his Washington, D.C., home.

Sunday mornings in the summertime, I absolutely love going to the farmers' market. I go early enough to speak with the farmers—some of them I've known for years—and I also know that the best produce will be sold out if I get there too late. I wake up my three daughters to come along; they're still sleepy as we get in the car to go to Dupont Circle, where the Freshfarm market has been every week since we first lived in the neighborhood many years ago. This time of year, the bounty of the market is amazing: aromatic peaches, juicy watermelons, and all the local produce that makes D.C. a wonderful food city.

We hit my favorite vegetable stand and smell the crisp green cucumbers and the ripe, heavy heirloom tomatoes. My daughter, Carlota, tells me she thinks these must be the ripest, most perfect tomatoes in the world—they smell so much sweeter than the hothouse tomatoes in December. We pick out produce for the week, and of course we get ingredients for gazpacho. My wife, Patricia (aka Tichi), has a recipe that is our family favorite, and even though we know it by heart, just for fun I go to my library to look at a gazpacho recipe written in 1824 by Mary Randolph. I found it when I bought her first-edition cookbook, *The Virginia Housewife*, and it blew my mind—a soup I have

forever known to be Spanish, written in one of the first American cookbooks. Randolph's recipe calls for fresh tomatoes and cucumbers, pepper, salt, onions, and stewed tomatoes. It's different from Tichi's, but it's always incredible to me to think about our shared culinary legacies. All around the world, we share food, culture, and history. On a hot summer day, it's good we don't have to turn on the stove to make the soup. Instead, we put it all in a blender—tomatoes, cucumbers, bell pepper, some good sherry, a healthy splash of Spanish olive oil. A quick blend and it's done, and then into a pitcher in the fridge. Now it's time to enjoy the rest of the day outside, kicking around a football, with glasses of cold gazpacho waiting for us. It's not a sit-down dish for us, but a standing one, a salad in a glass. This is summertime in my home, the same as my wife's growing up, and maybe even the same as Mary Randolph's almost 200 years ago, just down the road in Virginia.

Staff Favorite • Make Ahead Vegetarian

Tichi's Gazpacho

Hands-on: 20 min. Total: 50 min.
High-quality olive oil will make a big difference here. You can find Spanish extra-virgin olive oil at reasonable prices at Trader Joe's, but any flavorful variety you have on hand will work.

1/2 **cup extra-virgin olive oil**
1/2 **cup oloroso sherry**
1/4 **cup sherry vinegar**
1 1/4 **teaspoons kosher salt**
3 **pounds ripe tomatoes, quartered**
1 **English cucumber, peeled and chopped**
1 **green bell pepper, stemmed, seeded, and chopped**

2 **garlic cloves**
1 **cup rustic whole-wheat bread, sliced into 1-inch cubes**
1/4 **cup diced English cucumber**
6 **multicolored cherry tomatoes, quartered**
Edible flowers or microgreens (optional)

1. Place first 8 ingredients in a food processor or blender (work in 2 batches if needed); process until tomato mixture is well blended. Pour the tomato mixture through a medium strainer into a large pot or pitcher, using a ladle to gently press the mixture through the strainer. Chill strained mixture at least 30 minutes in refrigerator.
2. Preheat oven to 450°F. Place bread cubes on a sheet pan; toast cubes at 450°F for 7 minutes or until golden-brown and crisp, turning once. Cool 5 minutes. Ladle about 1/2 cup tomato mixture into each of 12 small bowls or glasses. Divide bread cubes evenly among bowls. Top each serving with 1 teaspoon diced cucumber and 2 cherry tomato quarters. Top each serving with small edible flowers or microgreens, if desired. Serves 12 (serving size: about 1/2 cup)

CALORIES 142; **FAT** 9.8g (sat 1.4g, mono 7.3g, poly 1g); **PROTEIN** 2g; **CARB** 9g; **FIBER** 2g; **SUGARS** 4g (est. added sugars 0g); **CHOL** 0mg; **IRON** 1mg; **SODIUM** 240mg; **CALC** 24mg

CHERRY BLISS

Cherry season has arrived at Bardenhagen Farms in Suttons Bay, Michigan. Friend of the farm and chef, Mario Batali, shares his experience from a recent visit. In the kitchen, we cook up a summer menu to celebrate the cherry in all its glory, from cocktails to barbecue sauce.

Nestled between Lake Leelanau and Grand Traverse Bay on Michigan's northern peninsula is a stunning landscape of cherry orchards, home to the most incredible, ruby-red fruits you will ever taste. The deliciousness dates back to the 1950s, when Vernon Bardenhagen planted the first cherry tree on his family's land, Bardenhagen Farms, which has been a success since the end of the Civil War and a special place I've adored visiting during my summers in Michigan.

Vernon's legacy now lives on through his son, Jim, who is the quintessence of a relentlessly dedicated Midwestern farmer. His effort to protect other local farms has let the treasured terrain thrive, popularizing Traverse City's nickname as the Cherry Capital. Every July during the peak of harvest season, cherry lovers from around the world attend the city's National Cherry Festival, where they can taste just about every Michigan-grown variety. The plump, sour Balaton cherry and the sweet, golden Emperor Francis make my mouth water even now. Perhaps what I love most about visiting an orchard are the crimson stains that line the winding roads, a result of a farmer's swift turn (causing cherries to fly out of the truck) and a true symbol of summer.

When I bite into a perfectly tart cherry—whether it's by the handful on the beach or in my wife Susi's iconic pie—I'm transported into a dreamy state where I can fully relish the agricultural identity of Northern Michigan. It's really something to see how one adventurous farmer turned a small Midwestern town into a beloved gastronomic destination.

Staff Favorite • Gluten Free
Kid Friendly • Make Ahead
Freezable • Vegetarian

Vanilla Frozen Yogurt with Fresh Cherry Swirl

Hands-on: 30 min. Total: 5 hr.
Creamy and luscious with a touch of tart, this simple fro-yo was a clear staff favorite. A combination of half-and-half, plain whole-milk yogurt, and a little corn syrup gives the frozen yogurt its supersmooth texture.

1¼ cups fresh sweet cherries, pitted and coarsely chopped (about 8 ounces)
1 tablespoon light brown sugar
2 teaspoons fresh lemon juice
3 cups plain whole-milk yogurt
½ cup half-and-half
⅓ cup granulated sugar
2 tablespoons light corn syrup
1 teaspoon vanilla bean paste

1. Bring cherries and brown sugar to a boil in a small saucepan over medium; cook 2 minutes or until cherries begin to soften. Reduce heat to medium-low; cook 13 minutes or until syrupy.

Stir in lemon juice. Remove pan from heat; cool. Place cherry mixture in an airtight container; refrigerate 1 hour or until chilled.
2. Meanwhile, place a 9- x 5-inch loaf pan in freezer; freeze at least 30 minutes. Combine yogurt, half-and-half, granulated sugar, corn syrup, and vanilla bean paste in a bowl; stir with a whisk until smooth. Chill yogurt mixture 1 hour.
3. Pour yogurt mixture into the freezer can of an ice cream freezer; freeze according to manufacturer's instructions. Spread half of frozen yogurt in bottom of loaf pan. Dollop half of cherry mixture over top; swirl into frozen yogurt with the tip of a knife. Repeat procedure with remaining half of frozen yogurt and remaining half of cherry mixture. Gently press a piece of parchment paper directly on top of frozen yogurt; wrap tightly with plastic wrap. Freeze 4 hours or until firm. Serves 8 (serving size: about ½ cup)

CALORIES 148; **FAT** 4.8g (sat 3g, mono 0.5g, poly 0.1g); **PROTEIN** 4g; **CARB** 24g; **FIBER** 0g; **SUGARS** 22g (est. added sugars 14g); **CHOL** 13mg; **IRON** 0mg; **SODIUM** 54mg; **CALC** 134mg

Cherry-Basil Lemonade Spritzers

Hands-on: 25 min. Total: 55 min.
Instead of the neon cocktail-cherry garnish, fresh cherries star in this refreshing lemon-and-vodka sipper. Macerating the cherries in sugar helps to soften their thick skins and release their juices, which become gorgeously syrupy in the pan.

2 cups fresh sweet cherries, pitted and halved (about 13 ounces)
1/2 cup sugar
4 cups water, divided
6 basil sprigs
1 (1/2-inch) piece peeled fresh ginger, thinly sliced
2/3 cup fresh lemon juice (from 6 medium lemons)
1 1/2 cups vodka
3 cups chilled seltzer water
8 basil sprigs (for garnish)

1. Combine 1½ cups of the cherries and sugar in a small saucepan; let stand 10 minutes or until juices have released, stirring occasionally. Place pan over medium-high. Add 1 cup water, 6 basil sprigs, and ginger to pan; bring to a boil. Cook 10 minutes or until sugar dissolves and cherries have broken down. Remove pan from heat. Gently mash cherry mixture with a potato masher or a fork. Let stand 30 minutes at room temperature.
2. Strain cherry mixture through a mesh sieve over a large pitcher; discard solids. Add remaining 3 cups water, lemon juice, and vodka to pitcher; stir gently to combine. Stir in remaining ½ cup fresh cherries. Add seltzer water to pitcher just before serving. Pour cherry mixture into each of 8 ice-filled glasses. Garnish each glass with a small basil sprig. Serves 8 (serving size: about 1 cup)

CALORIES 175; FAT 0.2g; PROTEIN 1g; CARB 20g; FIBER 1g; SUGARS 18g (est. added sugars 13g); CHOL 0mg; IRON 0mg; SODIUM 23mg; CALC 19mg

Mixed Grain, Cherry, and Snap Pea Salad

Hands-on: 20 min. Total: 35 min.
Fresh cherries take the place of tomatoes in this triple-grain salad. Bulgur, quinoa, and brown rice make for a nutty, wonderfully textured base, though you can omit the bulgur and double the quinoa for a gluten-free version. Extra crunch comes from fresh snap peas and red onion.

1 3/4 cups water, divided
1/2 cup uncooked bulgur, rinsed and drained
1/2 cup uncooked quinoa, rinsed and drained
3 tablespoons extra-virgin olive oil
2 tablespoons white balsamic vinegar
3/4 teaspoon kosher salt
1/2 teaspoon freshly ground black pepper
1 1/2 cups fresh sweet cherries, pitted and halved (about 10 ounces)
1 1/2 cups sugar snap peas, trimmed and cut into 1/2-inch pieces (about 6 ounces)
1/2 cup thinly sliced red onion
1/4 cup chopped fresh mint
1 (8.8-ounce) package precooked brown rice (such as Uncle Ben's)
2 ounces goat cheese, crumbled (about 1/2 cup)

1. Bring 1 cup water to a boil in a small saucepan over medium-high; add bulgur. Reduce heat; cover, and simmer 10 minutes or until liquid is absorbed. Remove pan from heat; let stand 5 minutes. Spoon bulgur onto a parchment paper–lined baking sheet.
2. Bring quinoa and remaining 3/4 cup water to a boil in a small saucepan over medium-high. Reduce heat; cover, and simmer 12 minutes or until liquid is absorbed. Add quinoa to bulgur on baking sheet; cool to room temperature.
3. Combine oil, vinegar, salt, and pepper in a small bowl, stirring with a whisk. Combine bulgur mixture, cherries, snap peas, onion, mint, and rice in a large bowl. Add oil mixture to bulgur mixture; toss. Sprinkle with goat cheese. Serves 8 (serving size: about 1 cup)

CALORIES 211; FAT 8.3g (sat 1.9g, mono 4.3g, poly 1.2g); PROTEIN 6g; CARB 30g; FIBER 4g; SUGARS 6g (est. added sugars 0g); CHOL 3mg; IRON 2mg; SODIUM 220mg; CALC 42mg

Grilled Sweet Potatoes with Fresh Cherry Salsa

Hands-on: 20 min. Total: 20 min.

2 medium sweet potatoes, cut into 3/4-inch-thick wedges (about 18 ounces)
1 tablespoon canola oil
2 teaspoons ground cumin
5/8 teaspoon kosher salt, divided
Cooking spray
2 cups fresh sweet cherries, pitted and coarsely chopped (about 13 ounces)
3/4 cup fresh corn kernels
1/4 cup thinly sliced green onions
1/4 cup thinly sliced white onion
2 1/2 tablespoons chopped fresh cilantro
1 1/2 tablespoons fresh lime juice
1/2 jalapeño, thinly sliced

1. Preheat grill to medium-high (about 450°F).
2. Fill a large saucepan with water to a depth of 1 inch; bring to a boil. Insert steamer basket. Add sweet potato wedges; cover, and steam 10 minutes. Combine potatoes, oil, cumin, and ¼ teaspoon salt in a bowl; toss.
3. Coat grill grate with cooking spray. Add potatoes to grill; grill 2 minutes on each side or until tender. Place potatoes on a platter.
4. Combine remaining ⅜ teaspoon salt, cherries, and remaining ingredients in a bowl; spoon over potatoes. Serves 6 (serving size: about 4 potato wedges and ⅓ cup salsa)

CALORIES 149; FAT 2.9g (sat 0.3g, mono 1.6g, poly 0.8g); PROTEIN 3g; CARB 30g; FIBER 4g; SUGARS 12g (est. added sugars 0g); CHOL 0mg; IRON 1mg; SODIUM 252mg; CALC 42mg

Quick & Easy • Make Ahead

Grilled Chicken Drumsticks with Bourbon-Cherry BBQ Sauce
(pictured on page 228)

Hands-on: 1 hr. Total: 1 hr. 40 min.

3 cups fresh or frozen sour cherries, pitted and thawed (about 20 ounces)
¼ cup water
2 tablespoons sugar
⅓ cup honey
⅓ cup unsalted ketchup
¼ cup unsalted tomato paste
¼ cup unseasoned rice vinegar
3 tablespoons bourbon
1½ teaspoons kosher salt
1 teaspoon black pepper
1 teaspoon onion powder
½ teaspoon dry mustard
⅛ teaspoon ground red pepper
4 pounds chicken drumsticks, skinned (about 16)
Cooking spray

1. Place cherries in a food processor; pulse until almost smooth. Bring cherry puree, ¼ cup water, and sugar to a boil in a saucepan over medium-high. Reduce heat to low; simmer 20 minutes. Strain mixture through a fine-mesh sieve over a bowl to yield about 1 cup liquid; discard solids.
2. Add cherry liquid to pan; bring to a boil. Stir in honey and next 9 ingredients (through ground red pepper). Reduce heat to medium-low; cook 10 minutes or until slightly thickened, stirring occasionally. Cool. Place 1 cup sauce in a bowl; reserve.
3. Preheat grill to medium-high (about 450°F).
4. Coat grill grate and drumsticks with cooking spray. Arrange drumsticks on grate; cover and grill 8 minutes, turning occasionally. Reduce heat to medium. Brush drumsticks with remaining sauce; cook 12 minutes or until done, turning and brushing every 3 minutes. Serve with reserved 1 cup sauce. Serves 8 (serving size: 2 drumsticks and about 2 tablespoons sauce)

CALORIES 389; FAT 9.9g (sat 2.5g, mono 3.3g, poly 2.3g); PROTEIN 45g; CARB 28g; FIBER 1g; SUGARS 23g (est. added sugars 17g); CHOL 206mg; IRON 2mg; SODIUM 585mg; CALC 39mg

Kid Friendly • Make Ahead
Vegetarian

Sweet-and-Sour Cherry Tartlets
(pictured on page 226)

Hands-on: 30 min. Total: 2 hr. 10 min.

4.25 ounces unbleached all-purpose flour (about 1 cup)
2 ounces white whole-wheat flour (about ½ cup)
½ teaspoon kosher salt, divided
4½ tablespoons chilled unsalted butter, diced
¼ cup ice water
2 tablespoons chilled vodka
5 tablespoons plus 2 teaspoons turbinado sugar
2 tablespoons cornstarch
2½ cups fresh or frozen sour cherries, thawed and drained, pitted and halved (about 16 ounces)
2½ cups fresh sweet cherries, pitted and halved (about 16 ounces)
2 teaspoons fresh lemon juice
1 large egg white, lightly beaten

1. Weigh or lightly spoon flours into dry measuring cups; level with a knife. Place flours and ¼ teaspoon salt in a food processor; pulse to combine. Add butter; pulse 6 times or until mixture resembles coarse meal. Add ¼ cup water and vodka; pulse 6 times or until dough comes together. Turn dough out onto a lightly floured surface; gently knead 1 to 2 times. Divide dough into 12 equal portions; shape each portion into a ball and press flat. Roll each dough portion into a 4½-inch circle. Arrange dough circles on a baking sheet lined with plastic wrap; cover and chill 1 hour or until firm.
2. Preheat oven to 375°F with oven rack in lower middle position.
3. Unwrap dough circles; fit 6 circles into 6 (4-inch) tart pans. Using a 1¼-inch star-shaped cutter, cut a star from the center of each of the remaining 6 dough circles. Refrigerate tart shells and lids until ready to use; refrigerate stars, if using.
4. Combine remaining ¼ teaspoon salt, 5 tablespoons of the sugar, and cornstarch in a large bowl. Add cherries and lemon juice; toss. Spoon about ½ cup cherry mixture into each shell; top with dough lids, pressing edges to seal. Brush with egg white; sprinkle with 2 teaspoons sugar. Arrange tartlets on a foil-lined baking sheet; bake at 375°F for 35 to 40 minutes or until golden and bubbly. Cool 10 minutes. Remove tartlets from pans; cool completely. Serves 6 (serving size: 1 tartlet)

CALORIES 289; FAT 9.3g (sat 5.6g, mono 2.3g, poly 0.5g); PROTEIN 5g; CARB 47g; FIBER 4g; SUGARS 20g (est. added sugars 8g); CHOL 23mg; IRON 2mg; SODIUM 173mg; CALC 28mg

DROP IT LIKE IT'S HOT

Put all those peppers you grew or grabbed at the farmers' market to great use in sauces that are so potent, only a dab'll do.

THAI

Make Ahead

Homemade Sriracha

Hands-on: 20 min. Total: 55 min.
If you're like us, you'll want to eat this on just about everything—burgers, eggs, and more.

1 pound fresh red chiles (such as jalapeño, serrano, or red Fresno), seeded and chopped
1/2 cup garlic cloves
1/2 cup white vinegar
3 tablespoons brown sugar
3/4 teaspoon kosher salt
4 to 7 tablespoons warm water
1 teaspoon fish sauce

1. Combine the first 5 ingredients in a medium saucepan. Cover, and cook over medium-low 25 to 30 minutes or until tender, stirring occasionally.
2. Transfer chile mixture to a blender; add ¼ cup warm water and fish sauce. Remove center piece of blender lid (to allow steam to escape); secure lid on blender, and place a clean towel over opening in lid. Process until smooth; add up to 3 tablespoons more water, 1 tablespoon at a time, if necessary. Serve immediately, or refrigerate in an airtight container up to 7 days. Makes 1¾ cups (serving size: 1 tablespoon)

CALORIES 10; **FAT** 0.1g; **PROTEIN** 0g; **CARB** 2g; **FIBER** 0g; **SUGARS** 2g (est. added sugars 1g); **CHOL** 0mg; **IRON** 0mg; **SODIUM** 69mg; **CALC** 5mg

SOUTHERN U.S.

Staff Favorite • Gluten Free
Make Ahead • Vegetarian

Fermented Jalapeño Hot Sauce

Hands-on: 10 min. Total: 48 hr.
30 min. *Use this sauce on eggs, tacos, sandwiches, or grilled vegetables.*

1½ cups chopped jalapeños (about 6 ounces)
¼ cup chopped white onion
3 garlic cloves, crushed
2 cups water
2 teaspoons kosher salt

1. Place jalapeños, onion, and garlic in a large glass jar with a tight-fitting lid.
2. Combine 2 cups water and salt in a saucepan; bring to a boil over high, stirring until salt dissolves. Cool to room temperature.
3. Pour salted water over jalapeño mixture. Cover with lid; set on counter in a cool place away from direct sunlight for 2 to 3 days, stirring once a day.
4. Process mixture in a blender until smooth. Serve immediately, or refrigerate in an airtight container up to 2 weeks. Makes 2 cups (serving size: 2 teaspoons)

CALORIES 1; **FAT** 0g; **PROTEIN** 0g; **CARB** 0g; **FIBER** 0g; **SUGARS** 0g; **CHOL** 0mg; **IRON** 0mg; **SODIUM** 81mg; **CALC** 1mg

INDONESIAN

Gluten Free • Make Ahead
Vegetarian

Sambal Oelek

Hands-on: 20 min. Total: 45 min.
Traditional versions of this sauce contain sugar, but we left it out for a more straightforward flavor. Serve with noodle bowls or rice dishes.

1 tablespoon canola oil
1 pound fresh red chiles (such as jalapeño or serrano), seeded and chopped
1/3 cup rice wine vinegar
1½ teaspoons kosher salt
3 tablespoons water

1. Heat oil in a medium saucepan over medium. Add chiles; cook 10 minutes, stirring often. Add vinegar and salt; cook 5 minutes, stirring occasionally.
2. Remove from heat; cool 10 minutes. Transfer mixture to a food processor; add 3 tablespoons water. Pulse until nearly smooth, 3 to 4 times. Serve immediately, or refrigerate in an airtight container up to 1 week. Makes 1¼ cups (serving size: 2 teaspoons)

CALORIES 9; **FAT** 0.5g (sat 0g, mono 0.3g, poly 0.2g); **PROTEIN** 0g; **CARB** 1g; **FIBER** 0g; **SUGARS** 1g (est. added sugars 0g); **CHOL** 0mg; **IRON** 0mg; **SODIUM** 96mg; **CALC** 2mg

ISRAELI

Quick & Easy • Gluten Free
Make Ahead • Vegetarian

Zhug

Hands-on: 10 min. Total: 10 min.
Originally from Yemen and now one of the "national sauces" of Israel, zhug (pronounced "schoog") is great with grains, falafel, or grilled fish or meat.

3 cups chopped fresh cilantro leaves and stems
2 tablespoons water
2 tablespoons extra-virgin olive oil
1 tablespoon fresh lemon juice
1¹⁄₂ teaspoons kosher salt
1¹⁄₂ teaspoons honey
¹⁄₂ teaspoon ground cumin
¹⁄₄ teaspoon ground coriander
¹⁄₄ teaspoon ground cardamom
6 jalapeños, seeded and chopped
2 garlic cloves

1. Pulse all ingredients in a food processor until thick. Serve immediately, or refrigerate in an airtight container up to 1 week. Makes 1¼ cups (serving size: 2 teaspoons)

CALORIES 11; **FAT** 1g (sat 0.1g, mono 0.7g, poly 0.1g); **PROTEIN** 0g; **CARB** 1g; **FIBER** 0g; **SUGARS** 0g; **CHOL** 0mg; **IRON** 0mg; **SODIUM** 98mg; **CALC** 3mg

CARIBBEAN

Staff Favorite • Quick & Easy
Gluten Free • Make Ahead
Vegetarian

West Indies–Style Hot Sauce

Hands-on: 10 min. Total: 25 min.

1 tablespoon olive oil
1 cup chopped carrots
¹⁄₂ cup chopped onion
4 garlic cloves, minced
2 ounces habanero chiles
6 tablespoons water
¹⁄₄ cup white vinegar
¹⁄₄ cup fresh lime juice
¹⁄₂ teaspoon kosher salt

1. Heat oil in a medium skillet over medium. Add carrots, onion, and garlic; cook 10 minutes or until tender, stirring often. Remove from heat; cool 10 minutes. Transfer to a blender. Add chiles, 6 tablespoons water, vinegar, juice, and salt; process until smooth. Serve immediately, or refrigerate in an airtight container up to 7 days. Makes 1¼ cups (serving size: 1 teaspoon)

CALORIES 4; **FAT** 0.2g (sat 0g, mono 0.2g, poly 0g); **PROTEIN** 0g; **CARB** 1g; **FIBER** 0g; **SUGARS** 0g; **CHOL** 0mg; **IRON** 0mg; **SODIUM** 18mg; **CALC** 2mg

NOTE FROM THE EDITOR

ON THE SUMMER PLAYLIST

Every summer, my backyard patio becomes the staging ground for impromptu family weeknight suppers and languid weekend dinners with friends. For the first time all year, time slows down, and fresh produce from the Saturday farmers' market inspires new dishes. The best become summer anthems that get plugged into a playlist of oldies but goodies, recipes like this Charred Bean Salad.

I first made it several summers ago for Scott Mowbray, a good cook who edited this magazine before me. We cooks aim to please, so I wanted to wow Scott and his wife, Kate, with something fresh, seasonal, and big on flavor. Something that could be made ahead and served at room temperature. No pressure.

So I charred onions and long beans over a hot fire until they surrendered, tossed the tender vegetables with a quick, all-purpose fish sauce dressing, and then showered them with handfuls of torn mint leaves and crunchy peanuts. It passed the test.

Quick & Easy • Kid Friendly
Make Ahead

Charred Bean Salad

Hands-on: 25 min. Total: 25 min.
The salad will keep for 2 days in the fridge.

2 tablespoons fresh lime juice
1 tablespoon toasted sesame oil
4 teaspoons fish sauce
2 teaspoons agave nectar
¹⁄₂ teaspoon crushed red pepper
2 garlic cloves, minced
1 pound long beans or green beans, trimmed
2 tablespoons canola oil, divided
1 large sweet onion, cut into ¹⁄₂-inch-thick rings
¹⁄₄ cup torn fresh mint leaves
¹⁄₂ cup dry-roasted unsalted peanuts

1. Heat grill to high (about 500°F). Combine first 6 ingredients in a bowl; stir with a whisk. Set aside.
2. Toss long beans with 1 tablespoon canola oil in a large bowl. Brush onion rings with remaining 1 tablespoon oil. Grill, turning occasionally, until vegetables are tender and charred in spots, about 8 minutes. Cut beans in half, and coarsely chop onions. Transfer beans and onions to a large bowl. Dress with prepared sauce. Add mint leaves and peanuts. Toss to combine, and serve warm, at room temperature, or cold on a platter. Serves 6

CALORIES 161; **FAT** 10.4g (sat 1.2g, mono 5.5g, poly 3g); **PROTEIN** 4g; **CARB** 15g; **FIBER** 1g; **SUGARS** 8g (est. added sugars 2g); **CHOL** 0mg; **IRON** 1mg; **SODIUM** 262mg; **CALC** 58mg

GAME PLAN

While water for ravioli comes to a boil:
- Assemble ravioli.

While ravioli cook:
- Sauté spinach.

Quick & Easy • Kid Friendly Vegetarian

Basil-Ricotta Ravioli with Spinach

With Blistered Balsamic Cherry Tomatoes

³/₄ cup whole-milk ricotta cheese
1 ounce Parmesan cheese, grated and divided (about ¹/₄ cup)
¹/₄ cup torn fresh basil, divided
¹/₂ teaspoon grated lemon rind
³/₈ teaspoon black pepper, divided
¹/₄ teaspoon kosher salt, divided
16 square wonton wrappers, divided
1 large egg, lightly beaten
4 teaspoons extra-virgin olive oil, divided
3 garlic cloves, sliced
10 ounces baby spinach (about 8 cups)
2 teaspoons fresh lemon juice

1. Combine ricotta, 3 tablespoons Parmesan, 2 tablespoons basil, rind, ⅛ teaspoon pepper, and ⅛ teaspoon salt in a bowl. Arrange 8 wonton wrappers on a work surface (cover remaining wrappers to prevent drying). Moisten edge of wrappers with egg. Place 1 tablespoon ricotta mixture in center of each wrapper. Fold each wrapper in half, pressing well to seal edge. Cover with a damp towel to prevent drying. Repeat procedure with remaining wonton wrappers, egg, and ricotta mixture.
2. Bring a large saucepan filled with water to a boil. Carefully add ravioli to pan; cook 3 minutes, stirring occasionally. Remove ravioli with a slotted spoon.
3. Heat 2 teaspoons oil in a large skillet over medium; add garlic, and sauté 2 minutes. Stir in remaining ⅛ teaspoon salt and spinach until wilted. Stir in juice. Divide spinach mixture among 4 plates; top with ravioli, remaining 1 tablespoon Parmesan, remaining 2 tablespoons basil, remaining ¼ teaspoon pepper, and remaining 2 teaspoons oil. Serves 4 (serving size: 4 ravioli and about ½ cup spinach)

CALORIES 245; **FAT** 13.5g (sat 5.8g, mono 5.8g, poly 1.1g); **PROTEIN** 12g; **CARB** 19g; **FIBER** 2g; **SUGARS** 1g (est. added sugars 0g); **CHOL** 57mg; **IRON** 3mg; **SODIUM** 499mg; **CALC** 245mg

Quick & Easy • Gluten Free Kid Friendly • Vegetarian

Blistered Balsamic Cherry Tomatoes

2 tablespoons olive oil
3 cups multicolored cherry tomatoes
²/₃ cup vertically sliced shallots (about 2 medium)
³/₈ teaspoon kosher salt
¹/₄ teaspoon black pepper
1 teaspoon balsamic glaze

1. Heat oil in a cast-iron skillet over medium-high. Add tomatoes; cook 3 minutes. Stir in shallots, salt, and pepper; cook 2 minutes. Remove pan from heat; drizzle with balsamic glaze. Serves 4 (serving size: about ½ cup)

CALORIES 108; **FAT** 7g (sat 1g, mono 5g, poly 0.8g); **PROTEIN** 2g; **CARB** 11g; **FIBER** 1g; **SUGARS** 5g (est. added sugars 2g); **CHOL** 0mg; **IRON** 1mg; **SODIUM** 186mg; **CALC** 12mg

GAME PLAN

While pepper mixture stands:
- Cook pork chops.

While pork chops cook:
- Make dressing for snap peas.

Quick & Easy • Gluten Free Make Ahead

Ancho Chile Pork Chops with Pickled Pepper Relish

With Charred Snap Peas with Creamy Tarragon Dressing

Multicolored mini or baby bell peppers keep their texture but take on a fantastic acidity with a quick pickling technique. Instead of adding salt to the pickling liquid, stir it into the finished relish so no flavor gets drained out.

¹/₄ cup white wine vinegar
¹/₄ cup water
2 tablespoons sugar
1¹/₄ cups thinly sliced sweet mini bell peppers (about 5 ounces)
¹/₄ cup packed fresh flat-leaf parsley leaves
2 tablespoons extra-virgin olive oil, divided
¹/₂ teaspoon kosher salt, divided
³/₄ teaspoon ancho chile powder
³/₄ teaspoon ground cumin
2 (6-ounce) bone-in, center-cut pork chops (about ³/₄ inch thick)

1. Bring vinegar, ¼ cup water, and sugar to a boil in a small saucepan, stirring until sugar dissolves. Remove pan from heat; add bell peppers. Let stand 15 minutes; drain. Combine peppers, parsley, 1 tablespoon oil, and ¼ teaspoon salt in a bowl.

2. Heat 1½ teaspoons oil in a large cast-iron skillet over medium-high. Combine remaining ¼ teaspoon salt, chile powder, and cumin in a small bowl. Rub pork chops with remaining 1½ teaspoons oil and spice mixture. Add pork to pan; cook 4 to 5 minutes on each side or until a thermometer inserted in the center registers 145°F. Top pork evenly with bell pepper mixture. Serves 2 (serving size: 1 pork chop and about ½ cup pepper mixture)

CALORIES 329; **FAT** 20.6g (sat 3.9g, mono 12.3g, poly 2.3g); **PROTEIN** 25g; **CARB** 10g; **FIBER** 3g; **SUGARS** 7g (est. added sugars 3g); **CHOL** 75mg; **IRON** 2mg; **SODIUM** 569mg; **CALC** 46mg

Quick & Easy • Gluten Free Vegetarian

Charred Snap Peas with Creamy Tarragon Dressing

Summer makes us crave the flavors of fire, though grilling out isn't always an option on a weeknight. Enter the cast-iron skillet. In less than 5 minutes, the snap peas become crisp-tender while taking on extra smoky char, a nice contrast to the creamy tarragon dressing.

2 tablespoons plain 2% reduced-fat Greek yogurt
2 tablespoons whole buttermilk
2 teaspoons chopped fresh tarragon
1 teaspoon fresh lemon juice
⅛ teaspoon kosher salt
1 tablespoon olive oil
1½ cups sugar snap peas, trimmed

1. Combine first 5 ingredients in a bowl, stirring with a whisk.

2. Heat oil in large cast-iron skillet over medium-high. Add snap peas; cook 3 minutes or until crisp-tender and lightly charred, stirring occasionally. Drizzle with yogurt mixture. Serves 2 (serving size: about ¾ cup)

CALORIES 100; **FAT** 7.7g (sat 1.4g, mono 5.1g, poly 1g); **PROTEIN** 3g; **CARB** 5g; **FIBER** 1g; **SUGARS** 3g (est. added sugars 0g); **CHOL** 3mg; **IRON** 1mg; **SODIUM** 143mg; **CALC** 51mg

READY IN 40 MINUTES

························

GAME PLAN

························

While steak grills:
- Cook bean mixture.
- Spiralize zucchini.

While steak rests:
- Finish zucchini mixture.

Quick & Easy • Gluten Free Kid Friendly

Coriander-Crusted Flank Steak with Cuban Black Beans

With Elote-Style Zucchini Noodles

Amp up canned black beans by simmering with sautéed bell pepper, onion, and cumin and finishing with a splash of vinegar.

2 teaspoons cracked coriander seeds
2 teaspoons cracked black pepper
1 teaspoon kosher salt, divided
1 (1-pound) flank steak
2 tablespoons olive oil, divided
Cooking spray
½ cup chopped yellow onion

½ cup chopped red bell pepper
2 tablespoons unsalted tomato paste
½ teaspoon ground cumin
½ cup unsalted chicken stock (such as Swanson)
1 teaspoon apple cider vinegar
1 (15-ounce) can unsalted black beans, drained and rinsed
3 tablespoons chopped fresh cilantro

1. Preheat grill to medium-high (about 450°F).

2. Combine coriander, black pepper, and ½ teaspoon salt in a bowl. Rub steak with 1 tablespoon oil and spice mixture. Coat grill grate with cooking spray. Add steak to grate; grill 5 minutes on each side for medium-rare or until desired degree of doneness. Place steak on a cutting board; let stand 5 minutes. Cut across the grain into thin slices.

3. Heat remaining 1 tablespoon oil in a medium skillet over medium-high. Add onion and bell pepper; sauté 3 minutes. Stir in tomato paste and cumin; cook 30 seconds. Add remaining ½ teaspoon salt, stock, vinegar, and beans; cook 3 minutes. Stir in cilantro. Serve with steak. Serves 4 (serving size: 3 ounces steak and ½ cup bean mixture)

CALORIES 330; **FAT** 13.4g (sat 3.3g, mono 7.3g, poly 1g); **PROTEIN** 32g; **CARB** 20g; **FIBER** 7g; **SUGARS** 3g (est. added sugars 0g); **CHOL** 70mg; **IRON** 4mg; **SODIUM** 577mg; **CALC** 91mg

continued

Elote-Style Zucchini Noodles

Elote, corn dressed with chile and a creamy drizzle, joins spiralized zucchini "noodles" for an addictive summer salad.

3/4 cup fresh corn kernels
2 tablespoons chopped fresh cilantro
1 1/2 tablespoons extra-virgin olive oil
1 tablespoon fresh lime juice
1/4 teaspoon kosher salt
1 large zucchini (about 8 ounces), trimmed and spiralized into thin noodles
2 tablespoons light sour cream
2 teaspoons water
2 tablespoons crumbled queso fresco cheese
1/8 teaspoon ground red pepper

1. Place first 6 ingredients in a large bowl; toss. Combine sour cream and 2 teaspoons water; drizzle over zucchini mixture. Top with cheese and ground red pepper. Serves 4 (serving size: about 1/2 cup)

CALORIES 100; **FAT** 7.5g (sat 1.9g, mono 4.3g, poly 1g); **PROTEIN** 3g; **CARB** 8g; **FIBER** 1g; **SUGARS** 3g (est. added sugars 0g); **CHOL** 5mg; **IRON** 0mg; **SODIUM** 162mg; **CALC** 42mg

READY IN 35 MINUTES

GAME PLAN

While eggs and beans cook:
- Cook salmon.
- Cook potatoes.

While potatoes dry:
- Assemble salads.

Summer Salmon Niçoise Salad

With Parsley-and-Dill Potatoes

A crisp, colorful main-dish salad is just the kind of simple, vibrant, hot-weather food we love. You can sub steak or chicken for salmon.

2 large eggs
1 (8-ounce) package haricots verts (French green beans)
3 tablespoons extra-virgin olive oil, divided
1 (12-ounce) salmon fillet, about 1 inch thick
1/2 teaspoon kosher salt, divided
1/4 teaspoon freshly ground black pepper, divided
2 tablespoons white wine vinegar
1 tablespoon chopped fresh flat-leaf parsley
3/4 teaspoon Dijon mustard
1 head butter lettuce, torn (about 6 cups)
3/4 cup chopped English cucumber
1/2 cup fresh yellow corn kernels
1 1/2 ounces pitted kalamata or Niçoise olives (about 1/4 cup)
4 small radishes, cut into 1/2-inch wedges

1. Bring a medium saucepan filled with water to a boil. Carefully add eggs to pan; cook 6 minutes. Add green beans; cook 2 minutes. Drain; plunge bean mixture into a bowl of ice water. Let stand 3 minutes; drain. Peel eggs, and cut into quarters.
2. Heat 1 1/2 teaspoons oil in a large nonstick skillet over medium-high. Sprinkle fish with 1/4 teaspoon salt and 1/8 teaspoon pepper. Add fish, skin side down, to pan; cook 7 minutes. Turn, and cook 3 minutes. Remove fish from pan; break into large flakes with a fork.
3. Combine remaining 2 1/2 tablespoons oil, remaining 1/4 teaspoon salt, remaining 1/8 teaspoon pepper, vinegar, parsley, and mustard in a bowl. Divide lettuce among 4 plates; top evenly with eggs, beans, cucumber, corn, olives, radishes, and fish. Drizzle with vinaigrette. Serves 4 (serving size: about 2 1/2 cups)

CALORIES 325; **FAT** 21.7g (sat 3.6g, mono 12.4g, poly 4.7g); **PROTEIN** 23g; **CARB** 11g; **FIBER** 3g; **SUGARS** 4g (est. added sugars 0g); **CHOL** 140mg; **IRON** 3mg; **SODIUM** 521mg; **CALC** 84mg

Parsley-and-Dill Potatoes

Give the potatoes a head start by microwaving them until just shy of tender. The secret to supercrispy spuds isn't extra oil or a searing-hot pan; it's letting them dry out on paper towels before sautéing.

1 tablespoon water
1 pound baby golden potatoes, quartered
1 tablespoon olive oil
1 garlic clove, grated
3 tablespoons chopped fresh flat-leaf parsley
1 tablespoon chopped fresh dill
1/2 teaspoon kosher salt
1/4 teaspoon black pepper

1. Place 1 tablespoon water and quartered potatoes in a microwave-safe bowl; cover with plastic wrap. Microwave at HIGH 4 minutes or until tender. Place potatoes on a paper towel–lined baking sheet; let potatoes dry for 5 minutes.
2. Heat oil in a large cast-iron skillet over medium-high. Add potatoes; cook 3 minutes or until browned and crisp. Combine potato mixture, garlic, and remaining ingredients; toss. Serves 4 (serving size: about ⅔ cup)

CALORIES 115; **FAT** 3.4g (sat 0.5g, mono 2.5g, poly 0.4g); **PROTEIN** 2g; **CARB** 21g; **FIBER** 2g; **SUGARS** 0g (est. added sugars 0g); **CHOL** 0mg; **IRON** 1mg; **SODIUM** 278mg; **CALC** 89mg

READY IN
40
MINUTES

GAME PLAN

While the oven preheats:
- Prepare dough.
- Prepare yogurt mixture.

While pizza bakes:
- Prepare salad.

Quick & Easy • Kid Friendly

Cobb Pizza

With Watermelon-Basil Salad

The classic salad is transformed brilliantly into a summer pizza here, thanks to fresh veggies and a dressing-inspired sauce of tangy yogurt, mayo, and buttermilk.

10 ounces refrigerated fresh whole-wheat pizza dough
¼ cup plain 2% reduced-fat Greek yogurt
2 tablespoons low-fat buttermilk
2 tablespoons canola mayonnaise

½ cup halved cherry tomatoes
¼ cup vertically sliced red onion
3 ounces skinless, boneless rotisserie chicken breast, shredded (about ¾ cup)
1½ ounces part-skim mozzarella cheese, shredded (about ⅓ cup)
½ cup packed arugula
1 teaspoon extra-virgin olive oil
1 ounce blue cheese, crumbled (about ¼ cup)
2 bacon slices, cooked and crumbled
1 medium-sized ripe avocado, chopped
¼ teaspoon black pepper

1. Preheat oven to 500°F. Place a pizza stone or heavy baking sheet in oven (keep pan in oven as it preheats).
2. Place dough in a microwave-safe bowl; microwave at HIGH 30 seconds or until room temperature. Roll dough into a 14- x 10-inch rectangle on a large piece of lightly floured parchment paper; pierce dough liberally with a fork. Carefully place parchment paper and dough on preheated pizza stone or baking sheet; bake at 500°F for 5 minutes or until crust is lightly browned.
3. Combine yogurt, buttermilk, and mayonnaise in a bowl; spread over crust, leaving a 1-inch border. Top evenly with tomatoes, onion, chicken, and mozzarella; bake at 500°F for 5 minutes. Place arugula and oil in a bowl; toss to coat. Sprinkle arugula mixture, blue cheese, bacon, avocado, and pepper over pizza. Cut into 8 slices. Serves 4 (serving size: 2 slices)

CALORIES 394; **FAT** 21.2g (sat 4.6g, mono 9.8g, poly 3g); **PROTEIN** 19g; **CARB** 36g; **FIBER** 5g; **SUGARS** 2g (est. added sugars 0g); **CHOL** 39mg; **IRON** 1mg; **SODIUM** 658mg; **CALC** 147mg

Quick & Easy • Gluten Free
Kid Friendly • Vegetarian

Watermelon-Basil Salad

You can substitute unseasoned rice vinegar or fresh lime juice for the white balsamic, adding a touch of honey if needed. Fresh mint can stand in for the basil.

2 cups cubed seedless watermelon
1 cup chopped English cucumber
1 tablespoon white balsamic vinegar
1½ teaspoons extra-virgin olive oil
¼ teaspoon kosher salt
2 tablespoons torn fresh basil
¼ teaspoon freshly ground black pepper

1. Combine watermelon, cucumber, vinegar, oil, and salt in a medium bowl; toss gently to coat. Sprinkle with basil and pepper. Serves 4 (serving size: about ⅔ cup)

CALORIES 46; **FAT** 1.9g (sat 0.3g, mono 1.3g, poly 0.3g); **PROTEIN** 1g; **CARB** 8g; **FIBER** 0g; **SUGARS** 6g (est. added sugars 0g); **CHOL** 0mg; **IRON** 0mg; **SODIUM** 122mg; **CALC** 13mg

FRESH FIX

Top any pizza with a pile of lightly dressed greens, like peppery arugula, for a bit of freshness in every bite.

SUPERFAST 20-MINUTE COOKING

Quick & Easy • Gluten Free

Pork Medallions with Red Wine–Cherry Sauce

The pan sauce gets its concentrated fruit flavor, body, and thickness from tart-sweet cherry preserves, a great complement to the pork and red wine. Try a Merlot or Cabernet for the wine, or sub in unsalted chicken stock.

1 tablespoon olive oil
1 (1-pound) pork tenderloin, trimmed and cut into 12 slices
1 tablespoon chopped fresh thyme, divided
½ cup dry red wine
¾ teaspoon kosher salt
½ teaspoon black pepper
1 cup unsalted chicken stock
⅓ cup cherry preserves

1. Heat oil in a large skillet over medium-high. Add pork slices; cook 2 minutes on each side. Remove pork from pan; keep warm.
2. Increase heat to high. Add 2 teaspoons thyme to drippings in pan; cook 30 seconds. Add wine, salt, and pepper; cook 2 minutes or until liquid almost evaporates, scraping pan to loosen browned bits. Add stock and preserves; cook 8 minutes or until reduced to about ½ cup, stirring occasionally. Spoon cherry mixture evenly over pork; sprinkle with remaining 1 teaspoon thyme. Serves 4 (serving size: 3 pork medallions and about 2 tablespoons sauce)

CALORIES 251; FAT 7.4g (sat 1.8g, mono 4g, poly 1g); PROTEIN 24g; CARB 18g; FIBER 0g; SUGARS 16g (est. added sugars 16g); CHOL 74mg; IRON 1mg; SODIUM 452mg; CALC 12mg

---

*Staff Favorite • Quick & Easy
Gluten Free • Kid Friendly*

Chicken Breasts with Brown Butter–Garlic Tomato Sauce

Browned butter is the quick cook's best-kept secret: It takes less than 2 minutes and provides a fragrant, nutty note in any dish.

4 (6-ounce) skinless, boneless chicken breasts
¾ teaspoon kosher salt, divided
¾ teaspoon black pepper, divided
2 tablespoons olive oil, divided
2 tablespoons unsalted butter
6 garlic cloves, sliced
2 cups halved grape tomatoes
3 tablespoons fresh flat-leaf parsley leaves

1. Place chicken breasts on a cutting board; pound to a ½-inch-thickness using a meat mallet or small, heavy skillet (all four breasts should fit in one large skillet). Sprinkle chicken with ½ teaspoon salt and ½ teaspoon pepper.
2. Heat 1 tablespoon oil in a large skillet over medium-high. Add chicken to pan; cook 4 to 5 minutes on each side or until done. Remove from pan; keep warm. Do not wipe pan clean.
3. Reduce heat to medium. Add remaining 1 tablespoon oil, remaining ¼ teaspoon salt, remaining ¼ teaspoon pepper, butter, and garlic to drippings in pan; cook 2 minutes or until butter just begins to brown, stirring frequently. Stir in tomatoes; cook 2 minutes or until tomatoes are wilted. Spoon tomato mixture over chicken; sprinkle with parsley. Serves 4 (serving size: 1 chicken breast and about ⅓ cup tomato mixture)

CALORIES 341; FAT 17.3g (sat 5.6g, mono 8.1g, poly 1.6g); PROTEIN 39g; CARB 5g; FIBER 1g; SUGARS 4g (est. added sugars 0g); CHOL 139mg; IRON 1mg; SODIUM 443mg; CALC 36mg

---

*Quick & Easy • Gluten Free
Kid Friendly • Make Ahead*

Seared Cajun-Style Steak with Green Tomato Relish

Many seasoning blends now offer low- or no-salt options, making spice rubs an easy, instant way to spruce up quickly seared chicken, seafood, or steak without overdoing the sodium.

2 (8-ounce) sirloin steaks, trimmed
1 teaspoon unsalted Cajun seasoning (such as Tony Chachere's)
½ teaspoon kosher salt, divided
2 cups chopped green tomatoes (about 3 medium)
1 cup canned white hominy, drained
½ cup chopped red onion
½ cup chopped green bell pepper
2 tablespoons torn fresh basil
1 tablespoon fresh lime juice
1 tablespoon extra-virgin olive oil
1 tablespoon honey

1. Heat a large nonstick skillet over medium-high. Sprinkle steaks evenly with Cajun seasoning and ¼ teaspoon salt. Add steaks to pan; cook 5 minutes on each side for medium-rare or until desired degree of doneness. Place steaks on a cutting board; let stand 5 minutes. Cut across the grain into thin slices.
2. Combine remaining ¼ teaspoon salt, tomatoes, and remaining ingredients in a bowl; toss well to combine. Spoon tomato mixture over steak. Serves 4 (serving size: about 3 ounces steak and ¾ cup tomato mixture)

CALORIES 290; FAT 13.1g (sat 4.2g, mono 6.9g, poly 1g); PROTEIN 25g; CARB 18g; FIBER 3g; SUGARS 10g (est. added sugars 4g); CHOL 76mg; IRON 4mg; SODIUM 443mg; CALC 37mg

Sesame Shrimp with Smashed Cucumber Salad

Gently smashing fresh cucumber slices helps them absorb more vinaigrette, almost as if they've been marinating overnight. Serve over hot cooked brown rice.

1/4 cup toasted sesame oil, divided
1 pound medium shrimp, peeled and deveined
5 teaspoons reduced-sodium soy sauce, divided
2 cups thinly sliced (1/8-inch-thick) cucumbers
2 tablespoons chopped fresh flat-leaf parsley
2 tablespoons unseasoned rice vinegar
1 tablespoon honey
1 tablespoon minced peeled fresh ginger
1 teaspoon crushed red pepper
1 garlic clove, minced

1. Heat 2 tablespoons oil in a large nonstick skillet over medium-high. Add shrimp; cook 3 minutes on each side. Add 1 tablespoon soy sauce; cook 30 seconds.
2. Place remaining 2 tablespoons oil, remaining 2 teaspoons soy sauce, and remaining ingredients in a large ziplock bag; seal and shake. Lay bag flat on a cutting board. Use a rolling pin or the side of a knife to gently smash cucumber mixture a few times so that slices just begin to break into large pieces. Serve cucumber mixture with shrimp. Serves 4 (serving size: 4 ounces shrimp and about ½ cup cucumber mixture)

CALORIES 233; FAT 15.3g (sat 2.2g, mono 6.1g, poly 6.2g); PROTEIN 16g; CARB 9g; FIBER 1g; SUGARS 5g (est. added sugars 4g); CHOL 143mg; IRON 1mg; SODIUM 410mg; CALC 75mg

Turkey Sliders with Crunchy Green Apple Slaw

Sliders make any burger night more fun, especially since you get double the patties and double the creamy, crunchy slaw. Look for ground turkey rather than ground turkey breast—the former has a bit more fat and flavor from dark meat while still keeping a lean profile.

1/2 teaspoon ground cumin
1/2 teaspoon kosher salt
1/4 teaspoon ground red pepper
1 pound ground turkey
1 cup shredded coleslaw mix
1/2 cup chopped Granny Smith apple
1/4 cup canola mayonnaise
2 tablespoons fresh lime juice
1 small cucumber, cut into 1/4-inch-thick slices
8 (1¼-ounce) whole-wheat slider buns, toasted

1. Preheat broiler with oven rack in upper middle position.
2. Combine first 4 ingredients in a medium bowl. Divide and shape turkey mixture into 8 (2-inch) patties. Arrange patties on a baking sheet; broil 2 to 3 minutes on each side or until done.
3. Combine coleslaw, apple, mayonnaise, and juice in a bowl. Divide cucumber slices over bottom halves of buns. Top evenly with turkey burgers, coleslaw mixture, and top halves of buns. Serves 4 (serving size: 2 sliders)

CALORIES 430; FAT 16.5g (sat 2.3g, mono 5.3g, poly 5.9g); PROTEIN 33g; CARB 40g; FIBER 4g; SUGARS 10g (est. added sugars 4g); CHOL 78mg; IRON 1mg; SODIUM 687mg; CALC 107mg

PB&J Smoothie

Blend up the flavors of this kid-friendly duo into a cool, creamy smoothie. Add the ingredients to the blender as listed in the recipe for the smoothest results. You can use frozen fruit instead of fresh fruit and ice, adding water as needed to thin it out.

1 cup ice
6 ounces strawberries, hulled (about 1¼ cups)
6 ounces raspberries (about 1 cup)
1/2 cup plain 2% reduced-fat Greek yogurt
3 tablespoons honey
2 tablespoons creamy peanut butter
1/4 teaspoon kosher salt
2 teaspoons coarsely chopped unsalted dry-roasted peanuts

1. Place all ingredients except peanuts in a blender; blend until smooth. Divide smoothie among 4 glasses; sprinkle evenly with peanuts. Serve immediately. Serves 4 (serving size: about ⅔ cup)

CALORIES 159; FAT 5.8g (sat 1.3g, mono 2.5g, poly 1.4g); PROTEIN 5g; CARB 25g; FIBER 4g; SUGARS 19g (est. added sugars 13g); CHOL 2mg; IRON 1mg; SODIUM 165mg; CALC 42mg

**Quick & Easy • Gluten Free
Kid Friendly • Make Ahead
Vegetarian**

Sweet Corn Oatmeal with Peaches

Try substituting unsweetened almond milk (we like Almond Breeze) for the whole milk for a rich, slightly nutty flavor.

**1 tablespoon unsalted butter
2 cups fresh corn kernels
1 tablespoon maple syrup
2 cups old-fashioned rolled oats
1 teaspoon kosher salt
3 cups water
1 cup whole milk
⅛ teaspoon ground nutmeg
¼ cup plain 2% reduced-fat
   Greek yogurt
¼ teaspoon vanilla extract
1 cup sliced peaches**

1. Melt butter in a medium saucepan over medium. Add corn and syrup; cook 3 minutes. Stir in oats and salt; cook 2 minutes. Add 3 cups water, milk, and nutmeg; cover, and simmer 5 minutes.
2. Combine yogurt and vanilla in a small bowl. Divide oatmeal among 4 bowls. Top each serving evenly with yogurt mixture and peaches. Serves 4 (serving size: about 1 cup)

CALORIES 314; **FAT** 9.3g (sat 3.9g, mono 2.6g, poly 1.6g); **PROTEIN** 11g; **CARB** 51g; **FIBER** 6g; **SUGARS** 15g (est. added sugars 3g); **CHOL** 15mg; **IRON** 2mg; **SODIUM** 523mg; **CALC** 88mg

Quick & Easy • Kid Friendly

Egg-in-a-Nest BLT Sandwiches

(pictured on page 226)

These toasty handfuls may just be the ultimate combo in the world of sandwiches. The recipe combines some of our favorite things: It's a delicious mash-up of egg-in-a-hole, avocado toast, and a classic BLT.

**8 (1-ounce) whole-wheat sourdough
   bread slices, lightly toasted
2 center-cut bacon slices, diced
1 medium-sized ripe avocado
1 tablespoon canola mayonnaise
¼ teaspoon kosher salt
4 large eggs
½ teaspoon black pepper, divided
8 Bibb lettuce leaves (about 2
   ounces)
8 tomato slices**

1. Using a 2½-inch round cookie cutter, cut a hole from the center of 4 bread slices. Discard bread rounds or reserve for another use.
2. Heat a large skillet over medium. Add bacon; cook 6 minutes. Increase heat to medium-high; cook 2 minutes or until crisp. Place bacon on a paper towel–lined plate. Pour bacon drippings into a bowl and reserve.
3. Combine avocado, mayonnaise, and salt in a small bowl; mash to combine. Stir in bacon.
4. Add half of reserved bacon drippings to pan over medium-high. Place 2 cut bread slices in skillet; break 1 egg into each hole. Sprinkle ⅛ teaspoon pepper on each egg. Cook 2 minutes or until eggs begin to set. Carefully turn bread; cook 2 minutes or until eggs are set. Remove from pan. Repeat procedure with remaining half of bacon drippings, cut bread slices, eggs, and pepper.
5. Spread avocado mixture evenly over 4 uncut bread slices. Top each with 2 lettuce leaves, 2 tomato slices, and 1 egg-in-a-nest bread slice. Serves 4 (serving size: 1 sandwich)

CALORIES 297; **FAT** 14.9g (sat 2.8g, mono 6.7g, poly 2.4g); **PROTEIN** 13g; **CARB** 26g; **FIBER** 6g; **SUGARS** 4g (est. added sugars 0g); **CHOL** 190mg; **IRON** 3mg; **SODIUM** 468mg; **CALC** 72mg

**Quick & Easy • Gluten Free
Kid Friendly • Vegetarian**

Shaved Honeydew-and-Cucumber Salad

Use the remaining honeydew melon for smoothies, or try blending it with cucumber, mint, onion, and a seeded jalapeño for a green gazpacho.

**1 firm honeydew melon, quartered
   and seeded
1 medium cucumber
½ cup thinly sliced red onion
2 tablespoons fresh lime juice
2 tablespoons extra-virgin olive oil
1 teaspoon chopped fresh oregano
1 teaspoon ground cumin
½ teaspoon kosher salt
⅛ teaspoon ground red pepper**

1. Using a vegetable peeler, shave 1 quarter honeydew into long strips to yield 1 cup (reserve remaining honeydew for another use). Shave cucumber into large strips to yield about 1 cup.
2. Combine shaved honeydew, shaved cucumber, and remaining ingredients in a bowl; toss gently to combine. Serve immediately. Serves 4 (serving size: ½ cup)

CALORIES 92; **FAT** 7.2g (sat 1g, mono 5.4g, poly 0.7g); **PROTEIN** 1g; **CARB** 7g; **FIBER** 1g; **SUGARS** 5g (est. added sugars 0g); **CHOL** 0mg; **IRON** 0mg; **SODIUM** 250mg; **CALC** 16mg

**Quick & Easy • Gluten Free
Vegetarian**

Shaved Mango-and-Cabbage Salad

A slightly firm, underripe mango will shave more easily.

**1 medium-sized firm mango, peeled
1 cup thinly sliced red cabbage
2 tablespoons thinly sliced shallots
2 tablespoons fresh cilantro leaves
2 tablespoons fresh lime juice
2 tablespoons extra-virgin olive oil
1 tablespoon thinly sliced seeded
  jalapeño
¹/₂ teaspoon kosher salt
¹/₂ teaspoon ground allspice**

1. Using a vegetable peeler, shave mango crosswise into long strips, turning mango slightly after removing each strip. Discard pit.
2. Combine mango and remaining ingredients in a bowl; toss to combine. Serve immediately.
Serves 4 (serving size: ½ cup)

CALORIES 122; **FAT** 7.1g (sat 1g, mono 5.1g, poly 0.8g); **PROTEIN** 1g; **CARB** 16g; **FIBER** 2g; **SUGARS** 13g (est. added sugars 0g); **CHOL** 0mg; **IRON** 0mg; **SODIUM** 247mg; **CALC** 22mg

**Quick & Easy • Gluten Free
Vegetarian**

Shaved Squash-and-Radish Salad

You can use white balsamic or red or white wine vinegar combined with a dash of sugar in place of the Champagne vinegar.

**1 medium zucchini
1 medium-sized yellow squash
¹/₂ cup thinly sliced radishes
2 tablespoons chopped fresh dill
2 tablespoons Champagne vinegar**

**2 tablespoons extra-virgin olive oil
¹/₂ teaspoon kosher salt
¹/₂ teaspoon black pepper**

1. Using a vegetable peeler, shave zucchini and yellow squash into strips (about 1 cup zucchini and 1 cup yellow squash).
2. Combine zucchini, squash, radishes, and remaining ingredients in a bowl; toss gently to coat. Serve immediately. Serves 4 (serving size: ½ cup)

CALORIES 77; **FAT** 7.2g (sat 1g, mono 5.4g, poly 0.7g); **PROTEIN** 1g; **CARB** 3g; **FIBER** 1g; **SUGARS** 2g (est. added sugars 0g); **CHOL** 0mg; **IRON** 0mg; **SODIUM** 249mg; **CALC** 14mg

SLOW COOKER

TANGY SPIKED BAKED BEANS

Round out your summer cookout with this scene-stealing side dish.

**Quick & Easy • Make Ahead
Freezable**

Slow Cooker Bourbon-Peach Baked Beans

Hands-on: 15 min. Total: 4 hr. 15 min.
Skip the canned baked beans in favor of our fuss-free version, which saves up to 300mg sodium per serving. Adobo sauce and bacon build a smoky backbone, while peak-season peaches offer sweet contrast. Bonus: The beans will stay warm in a covered slow cooker for up to 2 hours after being unplugged.

**3 center-cut bacon slices, chopped
Cooking spray
2 (15-ounce) cans unsalted cannellini
  beans, drained and rinsed
2 (15-ounce) cans unsalted pinto
  beans, drained and rinsed
2 ripe peaches (about 1 pound),
  peeled and finely diced (about
  2 cups)
2 garlic cloves, minced
¹/₂ cup organic ketchup
¹/₂ cup bourbon
¹/₄ cup pure maple syrup
2 tablespoons balsamic vinegar
1 tablespoon Dijon mustard
2 teaspoons chopped canned chipotle
  chiles in adobo sauce
2 teaspoons chili powder
1 teaspoon smoked paprika
¹/₄ teaspoon kosher salt
¹/₄ teaspoon freshly ground black
  pepper**

1. Heat a large nonstick skillet over medium-high. Add bacon, and cook, stirring occasionally, until crisp, 4 to 5 minutes. Remove bacon from skillet.
2. Coat inside of a 4-quart slow cooker with cooking spray. Add bacon, beans, and remaining ingredients. Stir well.
3. Cover, and cook on LOW 4 to 6 hours. Keep covered until beans are ready to serve. Serves 12 (serving size: about ½ cup)

CALORIES 181; **FAT** 1g (sat 0.1g, mono 0.2g, poly 0.4g); **PROTEIN** 7g; **CARB** 30g; **FIBER** 6g; **SUGARS** 7g (est. added sugars 4g); **CHOL** 1mg; **IRON** 2mg; **SODIUM** 267mg; **CALC** 64mg

SWEET AND SPICY CORN CAKES

Enjoy amped-up whole-grain pancakes on the fly with this freezer-friendly recipe.

Staff Favorite • Quick & Easy Kid Friendly • Make Ahead Freezable

Spanish Chorizo Corn Cakes

Hands-on: 25 min. Total: 25 min.
Is there any time of day when a pancake isn't welcome at the table? These sweet and savory cakes are a scrumptious choice for breakfast, dinner, or a quick snack on the go. Keep warm and toasty by placing them in a single layer on a baking sheet in a 200°F oven for up to 30 minutes. Reheating is as easy as popping frozen cakes in the toaster.

2 ounces dry-cured Spanish chorizo, diced
1 cup fresh yellow corn kernels (about 2 ears)
1 tablespoon diced seeded jalapeño
4 ounces white whole-wheat flour (about 1 cup)
1 teaspoon granulated sugar
3/4 teaspoon baking powder
1/2 teaspoon baking soda
1 cup low-fat buttermilk
9 large eggs, divided
2 tablespoons salted butter, melted
Cooking spray
1/4 cup pure maple syrup
1 1/2 teaspoons adobo sauce from canned chipotle peppers
1/4 teaspoon freshly ground black pepper
Fresh cilantro leaves

1. Place chorizo, corn, and jalapeño in a medium nonstick skillet over medium-high. Cook, stirring often, until corn is crisp-tender, about 3 minutes. Remove from heat.
2. Combine flour, sugar, baking powder, and baking soda in a bowl, stirring with a whisk. In a separate bowl, whisk together buttermilk and 1 egg. Add buttermilk mixture and chorizo mixture to flour mixture, mixing until just incorporated. Gently stir in butter. Let stand 5 minutes.
3. Preheat an electric griddle to 350°F, or heat a nonstick skillet over medium-high. Lightly grease griddle or skillet with cooking spray. Spoon about 2½ tablespoons batter for each of 16 cakes onto griddle; gently spread into 3-inch rounds using back of spoon. Cook until golden brown, 2 to 3 minutes on each side. Remove from pan and keep warm, or follow freezing instructions.
4. Crack remaining 8 eggs on lightly greased griddle; cover, and cook 3 minutes or until whites are set and yolks are cooked to desired degree of doneness.
5. In a small bowl, whisk together maple syrup and adobo sauce. Place cakes on each of 8 plates; top each serving with egg. Drizzle syrup over eggs and corn cakes. Sprinkle with black pepper and cilantro. Serves 8 (serving size: 2 cakes, 1 egg, and about ½ teaspoon syrup mixture)

CALORIES 249; **FAT** 11.9g (sat 4.8g, mono 4.4, poly 1.7g); **PROTEIN** 12g; **CARB** 22g; **FIBER** 2g; **SUGARS** 9g (est. added sugars 7g); **CHOL** 224mg; **IRON** 2mg; **SODIUM** 392mg; **CALC** 102mg

HOW TO

FREEZE
Cool cooked corn cakes completely. Wrap corn cakes tightly in plastic wrap in stacks of 4 with parchment paper or plastic wrap between each cake. Place in a large ziplock plastic freezer bag; seal and freeze up to 2 months.

REHEAT
Toast frozen corn cakes in a toaster or in a toaster oven on medium until heated through, 4 to 5 minutes.

SUMMER CANDY

Know how you can't eat just one grape? Bite-sized, bumblebee-yellow Sun Gold tomatoes are the same way—so sweet and juicy they remind you that tomatoes are indeed fruits. Find them at farmers' markets, or grow your own for garden-fresh treats that'll turn picky kids into tomato fans and adults into fiends.

Quick & Easy • Gluten Free Kid Friendly • Vegetarian

Sun Gold Tomato Caprese Salad
(pictured on page 226)

Hands-on: 12 min. Total: 12 min.
We use young heirloom Cherokee Purple tomatoes to balance the intense sweetness of Sun Golds with a little acid and umami depth, but other red cherry tomatoes will work well also.

3 cups halved Sun Gold cherry tomatoes
1 cup halved young Cherokee Purple tomatoes
2 tablespoons extra-virgin olive oil
3 ounces small fresh mozzarella balls
1/2 teaspoon kosher salt
1/4 teaspoon black pepper
1/3 cup torn fresh basil

1. Combine all ingredients except basil in a large bowl; toss gently. Top with basil. Serves 6 (serving size: ¾ cup)

CALORIES 100; **FAT** 8.2g (sat 2.7g, mono 3.6g, poly 0.5g); **PROTEIN** 3g; **CARB** 4g; **FIBER** 1g; **SUGARS** 3g (est. added sugars 0g); **CHOL** 12mg; **IRON** 0mg; **SODIUM** 173mg; **CALC** 14mg

COOK ONCE, EAT 3X

Toss some extra veggies on the grill at your next cookout for summery panini, farro bowls, and a frittata during the week.

Quick & Easy • Kid Friendly Make Ahead • Vegetarian

Grilled Caponata Panini

Hands-on: 40 min. Total: 40 min.
We deconstruct classic caponata, a Sicilian dish with eggplant, capers, garlic, and basil, and turn it into robust grilled vegetable sandwiches with a smoky red bell pepper and olive spread. For toasty bread, let the cast-iron skillet heat on the grill while the vegetables cook, and then use it to press the sandwiches on the grill.

Vegetables:
2 medium zucchini, cut lengthwise into $1/2$-inch-thick slices
2 medium-sized yellow squash, cut lengthwise into $1/2$-inch-thick slices
1 medium eggplant, cut lengthwise into $1/2$-inch-thick slices
1 medium-sized red onion, cut into $3/4$-inch wedges
4 ounces mini bell peppers (about 8)
3 green onions
Cooking spray
3 tablespoons extra-virgin olive oil
2 tablespoons fresh lemon juice
1 tablespoon water
$1/2$ teaspoon kosher salt
$1/4$ teaspoon freshly ground black pepper
2 garlic cloves, coarsely chopped

Panini:
$1/4$ cup pitted kalamata olives
$1 1/2$ teaspoons capers, drained
$1/2$ teaspoon freshly ground black pepper
$1/4$ teaspoon ground red pepper
4 ($3 1/2$-ounce) ciabatta rolls, halved lengthwise
3 ounces fresh mozzarella, sliced
$1/4$ cup chopped fresh basil

1. To prepare vegetables, preheat grill to medium-high (about 450°F). Coat first 6 ingredients with cooking spray; arrange on grill grate. Grill green onions 2 minutes; remove from grill and chop. Grill remaining vegetables 5 more minutes, turning occasionally. Remove stems and seeds from bell peppers; discard. Reserve 4 bell peppers and 4 red onion wedges; cut remaining vegetables into 2-inch pieces.
2. Place chopped green onions, oil, juice, 1 tablespoon water, salt, $1/4$ teaspoon black pepper, and garlic in a food processor; process until smooth. Combine grilled vegetables and green onion mixture in a bowl. Reserve 4 cups vegetable mixture for Recipes 2 and 3.
3. To prepare panini, place reserved 4 bell peppers and 4 red onion wedges in food processor with olives, capers, $1/2$ teaspoon black pepper, and ground red pepper; process until smooth. Hollow out top and bottom halves of rolls, leaving a $1/2$-inch-thick shell. Spread bell pepper mixture over bottom halves of rolls; top with grilled vegetables, mozzarella, basil, and top halves of rolls.
4. Coat grill grate with cooking spray. Place 2 sandwiches on grate; top with a cast-iron skillet. Grill 2 minutes on each side or until cheese melts. Repeat procedure with remaining 2 sandwiches. Serves 4 (serving size: 1 sandwich)

CALORIES 358; **FAT** 15.6g (sat 4.2g, mono 8.7g, poly 1.5g); **PROTEIN** 12g; **CARB** 43g; **FIBER** 4g; **SUGARS** 6g (est. added sugars 0g); **CHOL** 17mg; **IRON** 3mg; **SODIUM** 727mg; **CALC** 44mg

Quick & Easy • Kid Friendly Make Ahead • Vegetarian

Farro Burrito Bowls

Hands-on: 15 min. Total: 25 min.
Enjoy these make-ahead grain bowls for lunch or as a no-cook dinner on hot days.

3 tablespoons extra-virgin olive oil
2 tablespoons chopped fresh cilantro
2 tablespoons fresh lime juice
2 teaspoons honey
$3/4$ teaspoon ancho chile powder
$3/4$ teaspoon kosher salt
$1/2$ teaspoon black pepper
2 cups cooked farro
2 cups grilled vegetable mixture (from Recipe 1), coarsely chopped
1 (15-ounce) can unsalted black beans, rinsed and drained
3 ounces queso fresco, crumbled (about $3/4$ cup)
1 medium-sized avocado, sliced
Lime wedges

1. Combine first 7 ingredients in a medium bowl, stirring with a whisk. Reserve $1 1/2$ tablespoons cilantro mixture. Add farro to remaining cilantro mixture; toss to coat.
2. Divide farro mixture, chopped grilled vegetables, beans, cheese, and avocado among 4 shallow bowls. Drizzle with reserved $1 1/2$ tablespoons cilantro mixture. Serve with lime wedges. Serves 4 (serving size: 2 cups)

CALORIES 452; **FAT** 24.8g (sat 5.4g, mono 14g, poly 2.9g); **PROTEIN** 16g; **CARB** 53g; **FIBER** 13g; **SUGARS** 7g (est. added sugars 3g); **CHOL** 15mg; **IRON** 2mg; **SODIUM** 614mg; **CALC** 195mg

Quick & Easy • Gluten Free
Kid Friendly • Make Ahead
Vegetarian

Grilled Vegetable Frittata

Hands-on: 15 min. Total: 25 min.
Frittatas are great canvases for leftovers, especially grilled summer vegetables. Add the vegetables to the egg mixture just before it sets so the veggies don't release too much moisture into the frittata.

1½ tablespoons olive oil, divided
2 medium Yukon Gold potatoes, peeled and diced (about 10 ounces)
2 tablespoons 2% reduced-fat milk
2 teaspoons chopped fresh oregano
½ teaspoon kosher salt
¼ teaspoon black pepper
¼ teaspoon crushed red pepper
1 ounce Parmesan cheese, finely grated (about ⅓ cup)
6 large eggs
2 large egg whites
2 cups grilled vegetable mixture (from Recipe 1), coarsely chopped

1. Preheat broiler with oven rack in upper middle position.
2. Combine 1½ teaspoons oil and potatoes in a microwave-safe bowl; cover with plastic wrap. Microwave at HIGH 3 minutes or until just tender. Uncover; cool slightly.
3. Combine milk and next 7 ingredients in a bowl, stirring with a whisk.
4. Heat remaining 1 tablespoon oil in a nonstick ovenproof skillet over medium-high. Add potatoes; sauté 6 minutes or until browned. Reduce heat to medium-low; add egg mixture, and cook 5 minutes. Top evenly with grilled vegetable mixture. Place pan in oven, and broil 3 minutes or until egg is set. Cut into 8 wedges. Serves 4 (serving size: 2 wedges)

CALORIES 293; **FAT** 17.2g (sat 4.8g, mono 9g, poly 2.5g); **PROTEIN** 17g; **CARB** 19g; **FIBER** 3g; **SUGARS** 4g (est. added sugars 0g); **CHOL** 285mg; **IRON** 3mg; **SODIUM** 584mg; **CALC** 213mg

BACK POCKET PASTA

A NEW WAY TO LOVE BROCCOLI

Roasted until lightly charred, this everyday vegetable becomes a surprising pasta star.

Quick & Easy • Kid Friendly
Make Ahead • Vegetarian

Pasta with Charred Broccoli, Feta, and Lemon

Hands-on: 20 min. Total: 35 min.
The feta cheese emulsifies in the pasta water, creating a velvety sauce for the pasta.

4 cups small broccoli florets
3 tablespoons olive oil, divided
2¼ teaspoons kosher salt, divided
½ teaspoon crushed red pepper
8 ounces uncooked strozzapreti or mezze penne pasta
2 garlic cloves, thinly sliced
1½ tablespoons all-purpose flour
½ cup whole milk
3 ounces feta cheese, crumbled (about ¾ cup)
1 tablespoon grated lemon rind
¼ teaspoon freshly ground black pepper
¼ teaspoon flaked sea salt (such as Maldon)

1. Preheat oven to 425°F.
2. Combine broccoli, 1½ tablespoons oil, ¼ teaspoon kosher salt, and crushed red pepper on a baking sheet; spread in a single layer. Bake at 425°F for 20 to 25 minutes or until broccoli is charred and browned in spots, stirring after 15 minutes.
3. Bring a large saucepan filled with water and remaining 2 teaspoons

kosher salt to a boil. Add pasta, and cook 7 to 8 minutes or until al dente. Drain in a colander over a bowl, reserving ¾ cup cooking liquid.
4. Heat remaining 1½ tablespoons oil and garlic in a large skillet over medium-low. Cook 2 minutes or until garlic is golden, stirring occasionally. Sprinkle flour over pan; cook 30 seconds, stirring constantly. Gradually add reserved ¾ cup pasta cooking liquid and milk to pan, stirring constantly with a whisk. Stir in feta; cook 3 minutes or until feta begins to melt and sauce is slightly thickened. Add broccoli, pasta, and lemon rind; toss. Divide pasta mixture among 4 bowls; sprinkle evenly with black pepper and ¼ teaspoon flaked salt. Serves 4 (serving size: about 1¼ cups)

CALORIES 408; **FAT** 17g (sat 5.2g, mono 8.6g, poly 1.4g); **PROTEIN** 14g; **CARB** 50g; **FIBER** 3g; **SUGARS** 4g (est. added sugars 0g); **CHOL** 22mg; **IRON** 2mg; **SODIUM** 637mg; **CALC** 180mg

THE COOKING LIGHT DIET

PICNIC-PERFECT CHICKEN SALAD

Light yet satisfying, this make-ahead lunch comes together in just 10 minutes.

When we sent this chicken salad recipe to Cooking Light Diet community member Patrick Moore to preview, he was skeptical about its ½-cup serving size. The Indiana native is someone who described his eating style before the Cooking Light Diet as "anything that got in my way," so Patrick was unsure that the suggested portion would work for him.

"I was surprisingly satisfied with the serving size, and the flavor was out of this world," Patrick describes. "Even consistency-wise, it was perfect. Not too dry, not too creamy. My wife, Becky, put this on a bed of greens, and it was just excellent. We've already determined it's going in the regular rotation for us."

But don't just take Patrick's word for it. Try this recipe yourself for an easy make-ahead lunch, or pack it up for your next summer outing.

Quick & Easy • Gluten Free
Kid Friendly • Make Ahead

Tart Apple-Hazelnut Chicken Salad

Hands-on: 10 min. Total: 10 min.
Here's a sumptuous new spin on the classic. This quick, make-ahead salad comes from Cooking That Counts: 1,200- to 1,500-Calorie Meal Plans to Lose Weight Deliciously ($22, Oxmoor House). Serve it over a bed of greens or with a side of veggies and multigrain crackers.

1/4 cup canola mayonnaise
　(such as Hellmann's)
1 1/2 tablespoons chopped fresh
　tarragon
2 teaspoons water
1/8 teaspoon black pepper
2 cups chopped skinless, boneless
　rotisserie chicken breast
1/2 cup chopped Granny Smith apple
3 tablespoons chopped toasted
　hazelnuts

1. Stir together mayonnaise, tarragon, 2 teaspoons water, and black pepper in a large bowl. Add the chicken, apple, and hazelnuts to dressing; toss gently to combine. Cover and chill until ready to serve. Serves 4 (serving size: 1/2 cup)

CALORIES 198; FAT 9.7g (sat 0.9g, mono 5.8g, poly 2.2g); PROTEIN 23g; CARB 5g; FIBER 1g; SUGARS 4g (est. added sugars 0g); CHOL 66mg; IRON 1mg; SODIUM 361mg; CALC 22mg

THE SHORTCUT

FLAME-KISSED ROMAINE SALAD

Capture the essence of seasonal produce in this speedy summertime main.

Quick & Easy • Vegetarian
Kid Friendly • Make Ahead

Grilled Romaine Salad with Crab

Hands-on: 20 min. Total: 25 min.
Welcome to grilled salad season. A quick char adds smoky depth and a glossy finish to crisp romaine hearts, making them the perfect base for fresh fixings. You'll get smokier results on an outdoor grill, but a stovetop grill pan will give a subtler effect. Our guacamole dressing is a simple riff on green goddess, mastering the less-is-more summer motif. If you can't find crab, use frozen, thawed shrimp instead.

2 ears fresh yellow corn, shucked
Cooking spray
12 ounces fresh lump crabmeat,
　drained and picked
1/4 teaspoon black pepper
6 tablespoons fresh lemon juice,
　(from 3 lemons) divided
1/2 teaspoon kosher salt, divided
1/4 cup canola oil
6 large romaine lettuce hearts
　(about 2 1/2 pounds), halved
　lengthwise
3/4 cup prepared guacamole
2 cups halved cherry tomatoes

1. Heat outdoor grill or a grill pan over medium-high. Coat corn with cooking spray, and place on grill grate (or pan). Grill, turning until charred on all sides, 12 to 14 minutes. Place on a cutting board; let stand 5 minutes or until slightly cooled. Cut kernels from corn into a bowl.
2. Place crabmeat, pepper, 2 tablespoons lemon juice, and 1/4 teaspoon salt in a large bowl. Toss to combine.
3. Brush oil evenly over cut sides of lettuce hearts; place 3 lettuce halves, cut sides down, on hot grill or grill pan. Grill until charred, about 1 minute, watching closely to prevent burning. Repeat procedure with remaining romaine hearts.
4. Stir together guacamole, remaining 1/4 cup lemon juice, and remaining 1/4 teaspoon salt.
5. Place romaine halves, charred side up, on each of 6 plates. Spoon crabmeat mixture over top. Top with corn and tomatoes. Spoon guacamole dressing over salads. Serves 6 (serving size: 2 romaine halves, 2 ounces crabmeat mixture, 1/4 cup corn, 1/3 cup tomatoes, and 2 tablespoons dressing)

CALORIES 264; FAT 13.6g (sat 2.3g, mono 7.6g, poly 2.8g); PROTEIN 18g; CARB 19g; FIBER 5g; SUGARS 9g (est. added sugars 0g); CHOL 65mg; IRON 3mg; SODIUM 532mg; CALC 149mg

CRABMEAT

SHOP
Look to your local seafood market for the freshest lump crabmeat, free of fillers and binders.

GRADE
Anything marked "jumbo lump" or "backfin" contains the largest chunks from the crab. "Special" consists of smaller pieces of white meat, ideal for salads or cakes. "Claw meat" is brown and has a stronger flavor profile.

PREPARE
Fresh crabmeat may contain tiny bits of shell. Rather than picking through the meat, you can spread it out on a baking sheet and broil it for one minute. The heat will turn the shells red, making them easier to spot.

FIRED UP FOR MELON

Texas chef Tim Love shows how hot flames and a touch of seasoning take watermelon's natural sweetness to the next level.

CL: It's a bold move, tinkering with a slice of cold watermelon, arguably the perfect summer snack as is. How do you improve upon it?

TL: While it's extremely tasty on its own, a few other ingredients make it even better. Salt brings the sweetness out even more, and a little chile powder brings nice roasty heat. Then the acidity you get from the char as the watermelon grills—it's a great flavor with sweet fruit. It kind of plays a mind game with you.

CL: Nothing extraneous is in this dish—seems like a master class in the less-is-more approach. It's one of those recipes that when you're writing it down, you think, wow, that looks really simple. And the cooking part is easy. It's the ideas that are hard. Do you want to get fancy with this?

CL: We just may.

TL: Then you can slice up the lemon and char it on the grill, and then squeeze it on the melon when it's done—it gives it real depth.

CL: Help us solve the annual mystery: What's the best way to pick a winner with whole watermelons?

TL: On the outside, you've got waves of dark green and lighter green. Look for really dark green waves—the darker they are, the riper the watermelon is going to be.

Quick & Easy • Gluten Free
Kid Friendly • Vegetarian

Hot-Sweet Grilled Watermelon

Hands-on: 17 min. Total: 37 min.
Tim Love likes to use guajillo chile powder here, which provides moderate heat. Cayenne or chipotle powder would also work.

1 small seedless red watermelon (about 5 pounds)
2 lemons
¾ teaspoon kosher salt
1 teaspoon guajillo chile powder or ground red chile powder

1. Preheat grill to high (about 500°F).
2. Slice watermelon crosswise into 5 (1½-inch-thick) slices. Cut each slice into quarters to make 20 wedges. Grate 2 tablespoons lemon rind from lemons; set aside. Slice lemons into ½-inch-thick slices.
3. Add watermelon wedges and lemon slices to grill grate; grill 1 minute on each side or until nicely charred. Place watermelon on a serving platter. Squeeze juice from a few charred lemon slices over watermelon; add remaining slices to platter. Sprinkle watermelon evenly with salt, chile powder, and lemon rind. Serves 10 (serving size: 2 wedges)

CALORIES 71; **FAT** 0.7g (sat 0.2g, mono 0.2g, poly 0.3g); **PROTEIN** 1g; **CARB** 0g; **FIBER** 0g; **SUGARS** 16g (est. added sugars 0g); **CHOL** 0mg; **IRON** 1mg; **SODIUM** 156mg; **CALC** 17mg

---

TRUE NOPAL CACTUS WATER

Unlike other brands, True Nopal has no added sugar, so you can taste the prickly pear—it's like mild grape juice, pleasant on its own, and a great mixer that won't step on other flavors. It has half the calories and sugar of many coconut waters. Available at grocery stores nationwide.

LET'S GET SIPPING

CACTUS WATER COCKTAIL

In the new wave of plant waters, cactus water is among the most nutritionally stacked. It's loaded with antioxidants and amino acids, and it may even help to reduce some hangover symptoms—a pretty perfect mixer if you ask us.

Quick & Easy • Gluten Free
Vegetarian

Prickly Pear Punch

Hands-on: 7 min. Total: 7 min.
We like the clean flavor and mixability of silver tequila here. For a nonalcoholic drink, omit it and top with sparkling water.

1 teaspoon sugar
1 (1-inch) lemon rind strip
1 cup cactus water (see box at left)
½ cup silver tequila
2 tablespoons honey
½ cup ice cubes
¼ cup prosecco or other dry sparkling wine

1. Muddle together sugar and lemon rind in a large glass. Stir in cactus water, tequila, and honey. Add ice cubes; cover, and shake well. Strain tequila mixture evenly into 4 glasses. Top each serving with 1 tablespoon prosecco. Serves 4 (serving size: about ½ cup)

CALORIES 121; **FAT** 0g; **PROTEIN** 0g; **CARB** 11g; **FIBER** 0g; **SUGARS** 11g (est. added sugars 8g); **CHOL** 0mg; **IRON** 0mg; **SODIUM** 1mg; **CALC** 8mg

Quick & Easy • Kid Friendly
Make Ahead

Summer Chicken Parmesan

Hands-on: 20 min. Total: 20 min.
This dish is inspired by chicken Parmesan with the same crispy chicken and melty cheese only we finish it with a fresh summer vegetable topping. Sprinkle it with a little Parmesan, if you like.

1 ounce white whole-wheat flour (about ¼ cup)
1 large egg, lightly beaten
⅔ cup plain whole-wheat breadcrumbs
4 (4-ounce) chicken breast cutlets
⅝ teaspoon kosher salt, divided
½ teaspoon black pepper
2 tablespoons olive oil, divided
Cooking spray
3 ounces part-skim mozzarella cheese, shredded (about ¾ cup)
1½ cups chopped zucchini (about 1 medium)
1½ cups cherry tomatoes, halved
2 garlic cloves, thinly sliced
¼ cup chopped fresh basil

1. Preheat broiler with oven rack in middle position. Place flour, egg, and breadcrumbs in separate shallow dishes. Sprinkle chicken with ½ teaspoon salt and pepper. Dredge chicken in flour; dip in egg, and dredge in breadcrumbs.
2. Heat 1½ teaspoons oil in a large skillet over medium-high. Add 2 cutlets; cook 1 minute on each side. Place on a baking sheet coated with cooking spray. Repeat procedure with 1½ teaspoons oil and remaining cutlets.
3. Top cutlets with cheese; broil 1½ minutes. Heat remaining oil in skillet. Add zucchini; sauté 1 minute. Add remaining ⅛ teaspoon salt, tomatoes, and garlic; sauté 4 minutes. Serve with chicken, and top with basil. Serves 4 (serving size: 1 cutlet and about ¾ cup vegetables)

CALORIES 398; **FAT** 16.2g (sat 4.5g, mono 7.4g, poly 2g); **PROTEIN** 37g; **CARB** 25g; **FIBER** 4g; **SUGARS** 3g (est. added sugars 0g); **CHOL** 143mg; **IRON** 1mg; **SODIUM** 521mg; **CALC** 191mg

USE IT UP

CANNED CHICKPEAS

Whether you call them chickpeas or garbanzo beans, they're deliciously versatile.

Quick & Easy • Gluten Free
Kid Friendly • Make Ahead
Vegetarian
Chili-Lime Roasted Chickpeas
Preheat oven to 400°F. Arrange 1 (15-ounce) can unsalted chickpeas, drained and rinsed, on paper towels; pat dry. Combine chickpeas and 1½ tablespoons olive oil on a foil-lined baking sheet coated with cooking spray. Bake at 400°F for 30 minutes or until crisp, stirring after 15 minutes. Sprinkle with 1½ teaspoons chili powder, 1½ teaspoons grated lime rind, and ¼ teaspoon kosher salt; toss to combine. Serves 4 (serving size: about ¼ cup)

CALORIES 151; **FAT** 5.9g (sat 0.7g, mono 3.4g, poly 0.5g); **PROTEIN** 6g; **CARB** 19g; **FIBER** 4g; **SUGARS** 1g (est. added sugars 0g); **CHOL** 0mg; **IRON** 1mg; **SODIUM** 175mg; **CALC** 43mg

Quick & Easy • Kid Friendly
Vegetarian
Pasta with Chickpea Sauce
Heat 3 tablespoons olive oil in a skillet over medium. Add 1 cup chopped onion, 1 cup chopped carrot, and 4 minced garlic cloves; cook 8 minutes. Place onion mixture, 1 cup drained canned unsalted chickpeas, ¾ cup water, 1 teaspoon kosher salt, and ½ teaspoon black pepper in a blender; process until smooth. Toss with 4 cups hot cooked whole-grain penne (8 ounces uncooked); sprinkle with ¼ cup each chopped fresh parsley and basil. Serves 4 (serving size: about 1 cup)

CALORIES 393; **FAT** 12.3g (sat 1.7g, mono 7.6g, poly 1.7g); **PROTEIN** 12g; **CARB** 61g; **FIBER** 10g; **SUGARS** 4g (est. added sugars 0g); **CHOL** 0mg; **IRON** 3mg; **SODIUM** 532mg; **CALC** 62mg

Quick & Easy • Kid Friendly
Mske Ahead • Vegetarian
Smashed Chickpea Salad Toasts
Place 1 (15-ounce) can unsalted chickpeas, drained and rinsed, in a bowl; coarsely mash. Stir in ¼ cup diced celery, ¼ cup diced dill pickle, ¼ cup canola mayonnaise, 2 tablespoons minced red onion, 1½ teaspoons fresh lemon juice, ¼ teaspoon kosher salt, and ¼ teaspoon black pepper. Spread about ⅔ cup chickpea salad onto each of 3 (1½-ounce) slices whole-grain bakery bread, toasted. Serves 3 (serving size: 1 topped toast)

CALORIES 305; **FAT** 7.6g (sat 0.3g, mono 3.4g, poly 2.6g); **PROTEIN** 13g; **CARB** 45g; **FIBER** 8g; **SUGARS** 4g (est. added sugars 1g); **CHOL** 0mg; **IRON** 3mg; **SODIUM** 632mg; **CALC** 136mg

Quick & Easy • Gluten Free
Kid Friendly • Make Ahead
Vegetarian
Summery Chickpea Salad
Combine 1½ cups halved multi-colored cherry tomatoes; 1 cup canned unsalted chickpeas, drained and rinsed; 1 cup half-moon English cucumber slices; ⅓ cup coarsely chopped fresh flat-leaf parsley; ¼ cup slivered red onion; 2 tablespoons extra-virgin olive oil; 1½ tablespoons fresh lemon juice; ½ teaspoon black pepper; and ⅜ teaspoon kosher salt. Toss gently to combine. Serves 4 (serving size: ¾ cup)

CALORIES 145; **FAT** 7.5g (sat 1g, mono 5g, poly 0.8g); **PROTEIN** 4g; **CARB** 16g; **FIBER** 4g; **SUGARS** 3g (est. added sugars 0g); **CHOL** 0mg; **IRON** 1mg; **SODIUM** 202mg; **CALC** 45mg

Gluten Free • Make Ahead
Vegetarian

Grill-Smoked Baba Ghanoush

Hands-on: 47 min. Total: 1 hr. 7 min.

4 medium eggplants (about 3 pounds)
3 green onions, trimmed
4 unpeeled garlic cloves, removed from head in a bundle
1/4 cup fresh lemon juice
3 tablespoons tahini (sesame seed paste)
1 1/2 teaspoons kosher salt
3/4 teaspoon black pepper
1/4 cup extra-virgin olive oil
1/2 teaspoon smoked paprika
1/4 cup chopped fresh flat-leaf parsley

1. Preheat a gas grill to medium-high (about 450°F) on one side, or push hot coals to one side of a charcoal grill. Place eggplants, green onions, and garlic on grate over hot side of grill. Grill onions 3 minutes or until well marked and just tender, turning occasionally. Remove from grill; chop into 1/2-inch pieces. Grill garlic 4 minutes or until mostly blackened, turning occasionally. Remove from grill; cool 10 minutes. Peel. Grill eggplants over direct heat for 10 minutes or until skin is well charred, turning occasionally; move to cool side of grill. Cover grill; cook eggplant 20 minutes or until completely tender. Cool 10 minutes.
2. Remove eggplant skin and scoop flesh into a medium saucepan; discard skin. Place pan over medium heat; cook eggplant 10 minutes or until liquid has evaporated, stirring occasionally. Place eggplant and garlic in a food processor or blender. Add juice, tahini, salt, and pepper; process until smooth. With processor on, slowly add oil; process until well blended and creamy. Place eggplant mixture in a serving bowl. Top with, or stir in, chopped green onions. Sprinkle with paprika and parsley. Serves 12 (serving size: about 1/4 cup)

CALORIES 98; **FAT** 6.9g (sat 1g, mono 4.4g, poly 1.4g); **PROTEIN** 2g; **CARB** 9g; **FIBER** 4g; **SUGARS** 4g (est. added sugars 0g); **CHOL** 0mg; **IRON** 1mg; **SODIUM** 246mg; **CALC** 25mg

---

HOW TO PERFECTLY CHAR VEGGIES

A little bit of blackening is part of what makes grilled food so delicious. Char adds a touch of tangy bitterness and ultracrisp texture that you can't get as easily with other cooking methods. Fresh vegetables take on char like a dream as their natural sugars first caramelize, and then lightly scorch, like the crust of a crème brûlée. The trick, as with much of cooking, is heat control. Here's what you need to know.

START HOT, FINISH COOLER The eggplant needs to cook through completely. Set over hot flames first to char the skin, and then move to the cooler side of the grill to finish roasting.

FLAMES WORK FAST Thin green onions cook in a flash. To retain a little texture, char them over the hottest part of the grill, and remove as soon as they're marked.

CHAR THE UNEXPECTED Toasting garlic on the grill is a smart way to make it sweet, tender, and slightly smoky. Leave the papery skin on the clove bundle and remove from the grill once the outside is mostly blackened.

Gluten Free • Kid Friendly

Brined Shrimp with Charred Corn Salad

Hands-on: 13 min. Total: 43 min.
Seared shrimp with a quick spice mix pairs with pan-charred summer vegetables in this simple dish that pops with fresh flavor. A little white wine vinegar balances the sweetness of the caramelized veggies and also complements the shrimp.

1 tablespoon kosher salt
1 quart water
1 pound large raw shrimp, peeled and deveined
3 cups fresh yellow corn kernels (from about 4 ears)
1 cup thinly sliced baby red bell pepper rings
1 cup vertically sliced red onion
2 tablespoons chopped fresh chives
2 tablespoons white wine vinegar
1 tablespoon extra-virgin olive oil
1/2 teaspoon chili powder

1. Combine salt and 1 quart water in a medium bowl, stirring until the salt dissolves. Add shrimp to brine; cover bowl with plastic wrap. Place in refrigerator for 30 minutes.
2. Heat a large cast-iron skillet over medium-high. Add corn, bell pepper, and onion; cook 5 minutes or until vegetables are lightly charred and tender. Place corn mixture in a large bowl. Stir in chives, vinegar, and oil.
3. Wipe skillet clean; return to medium-high. Remove shrimp from brine; pat dry between paper towels. Sprinkle shrimp with chili powder. Add shrimp to pan; cook 1 minute on each side or until done. Serve shrimp with salad. Serves 4 (serving size: about 5 shrimp and 1 cup salad)

CALORIES 232; **FAT** 6g (sat 1g, mono 3g, poly 1.1g); **PROTEIN** 20g; **CARB** 27g; **FIBER** 4g; **SUGARS** 10g (est. added sugars 0g); **CHOL** 143mg; **IRON** 1mg; **SODIUM** 557mg; **CALC** 77mg

HOW TO SPATCHCOCK

A butterflied bird cooks quickly and browns evenly—use this method for any poultry.

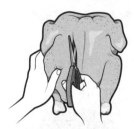

1 FLIP THE CHICKEN OVER
so it rests breast-side down. Use kitchen shears to cut along one side of the back-bone from tail to neck.

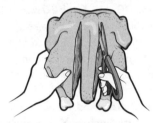

2 CUT ALONG THE OTHER SIDE
of the backbone to completely remove it. Save the bone in a ziplock plastic bag in the freezer for making chicken stock.

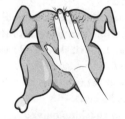

3 TURN CHICKEN OVER
with leg quarters splayed out. Press down on the breasts until you hear and feel the breastbone crack and the bird lies flat.

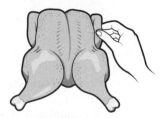

4 TUCK WING TIPS UNDER
the front end of the breasts to prevent burning and make the chicken easier to maneuver in the pan and carve once cooked.

WOW! A NEW TWIST ON MARGARITAS

Staff Favorite • Gluten Free Vegetarian

Roasted Strawberry Margaritas with Aquafaba Whip

Hands-on: 25 min. Total: 50 min.
Aquafaba, the viscous fluid from canned chickpeas, is the surprising key to making a plant-based whipped topping. The process is pretty miraculous: The liquid whips up to a thick, fluffy foam that mimics whipped cream. Just be sure to use the liquid from unsalted chickpeas for the best results (we like Eden brand).

2 pounds fresh strawberries, hulled and halved
1/2 teaspoon kosher salt
1/4 cup granulated sugar, divided
1 (15-ounce) can unsalted chickpeas, undrained
1/2 teaspoon vanilla extract
1/8 teaspoon cream of tartar
6 cups ice
1 1/4 cups (10 ounces) silver tequila
2/3 cup fresh lime juice (from about 5 limes)
1/3 cup loosely packed fresh mint leaves, plus sprigs for garnish
3 tablespoons light agave nectar
1/2 cup fresh blueberries (optional)

1. Preheat oven to 375°F. Line a rimmed baking sheet with parchment paper. Place strawberry halves, salt, and 2 tablespoons sugar in a medium bowl; toss to coat. Spread strawberries in a single layer on prepared baking sheet. Bake at 375°F for 25 minutes. Let strawberries cool slightly, about 20 minutes.
2. Drain liquid from can of chickpeas into bowl of a heavy-duty stand mixer fitted with whisk attachment (reserve chickpeas for another use). Add vanilla and cream of tartar to chickpea liquid, and beat on medium-high speed, gradually adding remaining 2 tablespoons sugar, until soft peaks form, 6 to 8 minutes.
3. Transfer roasted strawberries and juice from pan to a high-powered blender. Add ice, tequila, lime juice, mint leaves, and agave nectar. Process on high speed until creamy, about 1 minute. Pour evenly into each of 8 glasses; top each with about 1/3 cup aquafaba whip.
4. If desired, thread blueberries onto each of 8 small skewers, and add to each glass with a mint sprig. Serves 8 (serving size: about 1 cup)

CALORIES 175; **FAT** 0.4g (sat 0g, mono 0.1g, poly 0.2g); **PROTEIN** 1g; **CARB** 24g; **FIBER** 2g; **SUGARS** 18g (est. added sugars 12g); **CHOL** 0mg; **IRON** 1mg; **SODIUM** 123mg; **CALC** 25mg

FAST 5-INGREDIENT DINNERS

A handful of fresh ingredients and 25 minutes (or less!) are all you need to make fantastic summer meals.

---

1. BEEF TENDERLOIN
2. SUMMER SQUASH
3. POTATOES
4. GARLIC
5. CILANTRO

---

*Quick & Easy • Gluten Free
Kid Friendly*

Steak and Veggies with Zesty Chimichurri

Hands-on: 10 min. Total: 20 min.
Beef tenderloin fillets make this quick summer dish a little special. You can also use 2 (8-ounce) sirloin steaks, grilled for 4 minutes on each side.

1¼ pounds Yukon Gold potatoes, cut into wedges
Cooking spray
4 (4-ounce) beef tenderloin fillets
1 teaspoon kosher salt, divided
1 teaspoon black pepper, divided
1 pound yellow squash, cut diagonally into (¼-inch-thick) slices (about 3 cups)
2 cups loosely packed fresh cilantro leaves
1½ tablespoons chopped garlic
¼ cup olive oil

1. Preheat grill to medium (350°F to 400°F).
2. Place potatoes in a microwave-safe dish; cover tightly with plastic wrap. Cut a ½-inch slit in plastic. Microwave at HIGH 6 minutes or until almost tender. Coat grill grate with cooking spray. Add potatoes to grill (skewer if necessary); cook 5 minutes or until tender and well marked, turning after 3 minutes.
3. Coat fillets with cooking spray; sprinkle evenly with ¼ teaspoon salt and ¼ teaspoon pepper. Add fillets to grill; cook 3 to 5 minutes on each side or until desired degree of doneness. Remove fillets from pan; cover, and keep warm.
4. Coat squash with cooking spray; sprinkle with ¼ teaspoon salt and ¼ teaspoon pepper. Add squash to grill; cook 3 minutes or until tender and lightly charred.
5. Place remaining ½ teaspoon salt, remaining ½ teaspoon pepper, cilantro, and garlic in a food processor; pulse until finely chopped. Add oil; process 30 seconds or until smooth. Serve cilantro mixture with potatoes, fillets, and squash. Serves 4 (serving size: 1 fillet, about ½ cup potatoes, ½ cup squash, and 2 tablespoons cilantro mixture)

CALORIES 391; FAT 20.2g (sat 4.4g, mono 12.6g, poly 2.1g); PROTEIN 27g; CARB 28g; FIBER 4g; SUGARS 4g (added sugars 0g); CHOL 68mg; IRON 4mg; SODIUM 555mg; CALC 56mg

---

1. ROTISSERIE CHICKEN
2. PIZZA CRUST
3. ZUCCHINI
4. CORIANDER
5. FETA CHEESE

Quick & Easy • Kid Friendly

Zucchini-Ribbon Pizza with Chicken

Hands-on: 10 min. Total: 20 min.
If we could make a crisp, fresh salad a mandatory pizza topper, we would. Use a vegetable peeler to ribbon zucchini. Ground coriander adds lemony flavor.

1 (12-inch) prebaked whole-grain pizza crust (such as Mama Mary's)
Cooking spray
2 tablespoons olive oil, divided
5 teaspoons ground coriander, divided
1 teaspoon black pepper, divided
8 ounces skinless, boneless rotisserie chicken breast, shredded (about 2 cups)
1½ ounces feta cheese, crumbled (about ⅓ cup)
1 medium zucchini, halved lengthwise, seeded, and shaved into long ribbons (about 2 cups)
¼ cup fresh cilantro leaves (optional)

1. Preheat oven to 450°F with oven rack in middle.
2. Place crust on a baking sheet; coat both sides of crust with cooking spray. Place pan in oven; immediately reduce temperature to 425°F. Bake at 425°F for 14 minutes, flipping the crust halfway through cooking. Remove pan from oven.
3. Preheat broiler to high.
4. Combine 1 tablespoon oil, 1 tablespoon coriander, ½ teaspoon

pepper, and chicken in a bowl; toss to coat. Top crust with chicken mixture, leaving a ¼-inch border. Sprinkle feta evenly over pizza. Broil 2 minutes or until the crust is golden and crisp.

5. Combine remaining 1 tablespoon oil, remaining 2 teaspoons coriander, remaining ½ teaspoon pepper, and zucchini in a bowl; toss to coat. Top pizza with zucchini mixture; cut pizza into 8 slices. Sprinkle with cilantro, if desired. Serves 4 (serving size: 2 slices)

CALORIES 338; FAT 16.1g (sat 3.6g, mono 7.1g, poly 4.1g); PROTEIN 23g; CARB 32g; FIBER 5g; SUGARS 5g (added sugars 0g); CHOL 58mg; IRON 3mg; SODIUM 646mg; CALC 127mg

---

1. HALIBUT

2. CHERRY TOMATOES

3. CORN

4. BALSAMIC GLAZE

5. SHALLOTS

Staff Favorite • Quick & Easy Gluten Free • Kid Friendly

Fish with Fire-Roasted Summer Veggies

Hands-on: 20 min. Total: 25 min.
If you haven't tried halibut yet, this simple recipe is a great place to splurge. The fish is mild with a texture that's just firm enough to do well on the grill. If you can't find it, try sustainably caught flounder or snapper.

4 ears shucked corn
Cooking spray
3 cups cherry tomatoes, divided
2 tablespoons canola oil, divided
4 ounces shallots, peeled and halved lengthwise
1 teaspoon kosher salt, divided
3/4 teaspoon black pepper, divided

4 (6-ounce) halibut fillets, skinned
2 teaspoons balsamic glaze
2 tablespoons chopped fresh basil (optional)

1. Preheat grill to medium (350°F to 400°F).
2. Coat corn ears with cooking spray. Place 1 cup tomatoes, 1 tablespoon oil, and shallots in a bowl; toss to coat. Place tomato mixture in a grill basket. Add corn to grill; cook 6 minutes or until lightly charred, turning occasionally. Add tomato mixture to grill; cook 4 minutes or until tomatoes blister and turn lightly brown. Remove corn kernels from ears; discard cobs. Coarsely chop shallots; set aside. Place grilled tomatoes, remaining 1 tablespoon oil, ¼ teaspoon salt, and ¼ teaspoon pepper in a food processor; process until smooth.
3. Coat fillets with cooking spray; sprinkle with ½ teaspoon salt and ¼ teaspoon pepper. Add fillets to grill; cook 3 minutes on each side or until desired doneness. Remove; keep warm.
4. Slice remaining 2 cups tomatoes in half. Combine corn, shallots, fresh tomatoes, 2 tablespoons pureed tomato mixture, remaining ¼ teaspoon salt, and remaining ¼ teaspoon pepper in a bowl. Place 1 cup corn mixture on each of 4 plates. Top each serving with 1 fillet, 1 tablespoon pureed tomato mixture, and ½ teaspoon balsamic glaze. Top with basil, if desired. Serves 4

CALORIES 351; FAT 11.1g (sat 1.4g, mono 5.7g, poly 3.1g); PROTEIN 37g; CARB 29g; FIBER 4g; SUGARS 12g (added sugars 1g); CHOL 83mg; IRON 2mg; SODIUM 620mg; CALC 41mg

---

1. SHRIMP

2. SHIITAKE MUSHROOMS

3. BROWN RICE

4. SHISHITO PEPPERS

5. SRIRACHA

Quick & Easy • Gluten Free

Shrimp-Chile Skewers

Hands-on: 20 min. Total: 25 min.
Look for shishito peppers at Asian markets and gourmet grocers. They're mostly mild, but bear in mind that roughly 1 in 10 is about as hot as a jalapeño.

24 large fresh shrimp, peeled and deveined (about 1 pound)
24 shishito peppers (about 6 ounces)
16 shiitake mushrooms, stemmed and halved
Cooking spray
1/2 teaspoon kosher salt
1/4 teaspoon black pepper
2 (8.8-ounce) packages precooked brown rice (such as Uncle Ben's)
1/4 cup canola mayonnaise (optional)
1 tablespoon Sriracha chili sauce
1 lime, cut into wedges (optional)

1. Preheat grill to medium (350°F to 400°F).
2. Thread 3 shrimp, 3 peppers, and 4 mushroom halves alternately onto each of 8 (8-inch) skewers; coat skewers with cooking spray, and sprinkle with salt and black pepper. Add skewers to grill; cook 2 to 3 minutes on each side or until shrimp are pink and peppers are lightly charred. Place skewers on a platter.
3. Heat rice according to package directions. Combine mayonnaise (if using) and Sriracha in a small bowl. Serve sauce with skewers, rice, and lime wedges, if desired. Serves 4 (serving size: 2 skewers and about ½ cup rice)

CALORIES 308; FAT 7.8g (sat .07g, mono 3.3g, poly 2.6g); PROTEIN 22g; CARB 40g; FIBER 5g; SUGARS 2g (added sugars 0g); CHOL 143mg; IRON 2mg; SODIUM 610mg; CALC 69mg

Quick & Easy • Kid Friendly

Chicken Thighs with Peach Salad

Hands-on: 15 min. Total: 25 min.
Sweet peaches and tart green tomatoes gain depth from a bit of char on the grill. Look for peaches that are still slightly firm so they hold up to the heat.

1 cup plus 1 tablespoon water, divided
¾ teaspoon kosher salt, divided
½ cup uncooked whole-wheat couscous
4 (6-ounce) skinless, boneless chicken thighs
Cooking spray
¾ teaspoon black pepper, divided
8 (¼-inch-thick) round green tomato slices
8 (¼-inch-thick) round pitted peach slices
¼ cup sour cream
2 tablespoons fresh flat-leaf parsley leaves (optional)

1. Preheat grill to high (450°F to 550°F).
2. Bring 1 cup water and ¼ teaspoon salt to a boil in a small saucepan over medium-high. Stir in couscous. Cover, remove pan from heat, and let stand 10 minutes. Uncover pan; fluff with a fork.
3. Coat chicken thighs with cooking spray; sprinkle evenly with ¼ teaspoon salt and ½ teaspoon pepper. Coat tomato and peach slices with cooking spray. Add chicken to grill; cook 4 minutes on each side or until done. Add tomato and peach slices to grill; cook 1 to 2 minutes on each side or until just slightly tender.
4. Combine remaining 1 tablespoon water, remaining ¼ teaspoon salt, remaining ¼ teaspoon pepper, and sour cream in a small bowl, stirring with a whisk.
5. Cut peach slices into wedges. Place ½ cup couscous and 1 chicken thigh on each of 4 plates; top evenly with peaches and tomatoes. Drizzle each serving with 1 tablespoon sour cream mixture. Sprinkle with parsley, if desired. Serves 4

CALORIES 372; FAT 10.4g (sat 3.7g, mono 2.6g, poly 1.7g); PROTEIN 39g; CARB 29g; FIBER 5g; SUGARS 12g (added sugars 0g); CHOL 170mg; IRON 3mg; SODIUM 539mg; CALC 49mg

Quick & Easy • Gluten Free
Kid Friendly

Summery Pork and Beans

Hands-on: 18 min. Total: 25 min.
This one-skillet meal can work on a busy weeknight or for casual weekend entertaining. Butter deglazes the pan, melding flavors.

Cooking spray
4 (6-ounce) bone-in, center-cut pork chops
1 teaspoon kosher salt, divided
1 teaspoon black pepper, divided
1 pound fresh green beans, trimmed
1 pint cherry tomatoes
2 tablespoons unsalted butter
2 tablespoons torn fresh basil

1. Heat a large cast-iron skillet over medium-high. Coat pan with cooking spray. Sprinkle pork evenly with ½ teaspoon salt and ½ teaspoon pepper. Add pork to pan; cook 3 minutes on each side or until desired degree of doneness. Remove the pork from pan; cover, and keep warm.
2. Add beans, ¼ teaspoon salt, and ¼ teaspoon pepper to pan; cook 5 minutes or until blistered and lightly browned, stirring occasionally. Remove from pan. Add tomatoes to pan; cook 3 minutes or until blistered and beginning to pop. Remove from pan.
3. Add remaining ¼ teaspoon salt, remaining ¼ teaspoon pepper, butter, and basil to pan, swirling until butter melts. Divide pork, beans, and tomatoes among 4 plates; top evenly with butter mixture. Serves 4 (serving size: 1 pork chop, about ½ cup beans, 2 tablespoons tomatoes, and 2 teaspoons butter mixture)

CALORIES 259; FAT 12.8g (sat 5.7g, mono 3.9g, poly 1.1g); PROTEIN 27g; CARB 10g; FIBER 4g; SUGARS 5g (added sugars 0g); CHOL 90mg; IRON 2mg; SODIUM 540mg; CALC 74mg

SUPERMARKET SHORTCUT DINNERS

Grocery stores abound with convenience products you can feel good about. Combine them with a few fresh ingredients for speedy, impressive mains that don't let on just how easy they are to make.

SHORTCUTS

BROCCOLI SLAW
Washed and julienned, this heartier version of cabbage slaw can be sautéed, folded into batters, or simply dressed.

PRESLICED MUSHROOMS
Cleaned and sliced mushrooms save valuable prep time on busy nights.

PRECOOKED BROWN RICE
Microwave or reheat on the stove for 90 seconds and save about 45 minutes. The math couldn't be better.

Quick & Easy • Kid Friendly
Vegetarian

Egg Foo Yong with Mushroom Sauce

(pictured on page 230)

Hands-on: 20 min. Total: 20 min.

2 tablespoons sesame oil, divided
³⁄₄ cup matchstick-cut carrots
1 bunch green onions, thinly sliced, white and green parts divided
2 cups packaged broccoli slaw
1 teaspoon minced peeled fresh ginger
3 garlic cloves, grated
1 tablespoon unseasoned rice vinegar
1¹⁄₂ tablespoons tamari sauce or reduced-sodium soy sauce, divided
³⁄₄ teaspoon freshly ground black pepper, divided
6 large eggs, lightly beaten
1 cup unsalted vegetable stock
1 tablespoon all-purpose flour
1 (8-ounce) package presliced cremini mushrooms
2 (8.8-ounce) packages precooked brown rice (such as Uncle Ben's)
1 tablespoon toasted sesame seeds

1. Preheat broiler; place rack in upper middle position.
2. Heat a 10-inch oven-safe skillet over medium-high. Add 1 tablespoon oil, carrots, and white parts of green onions; sauté 3 minutes. Add slaw, ginger, and garlic; cook 3 minutes, stirring occasionally. Add vinegar; cook 1 minute or until liquid evaporates.
3. Combine 1¹⁄₂ teaspoons tamari, ¹⁄₄ teaspoon pepper, and eggs in a bowl, stirring with a whisk. Add egg mixture to slaw mixture in pan, tilting pan to spread mixture evenly. Cook 3 to 4 minutes or until egg is set on the bottom. Place pan in oven; broil 2 minutes or until top is set and golden. Cut into quarters.
4. Combine stock and flour in a bowl, stirring with a whisk. Heat remaining 1 tablespoon oil in a skillet over medium-high. Add mushrooms; cook 5 minutes or until browned. Add flour mixture; bring to a boil, and cook 1 minute or until mixture is slightly thickened. Stir in remaining 1 tablespoon tamari and ¹⁄₄ teaspoon pepper.
5. Heat rice according to package directions; divide evenly among 4 plates. Top each serving with 1 wedge of the pancake and ¹⁄₄ cup mushroom mixture; top evenly with green parts of onions, remaining ¹⁄₄ teaspoon pepper, and sesame seeds. Serves 4

CALORIES 390; FAT 17.6g (sat 3.5g, mono 5.8g, poly 4.8g); PROTEIN 18g; CARB 44g; FIBER 5g; SUGARS 4g (est. added sugars 0g); CHOL 279mg; IRON 4mg; SODIUM 658mg; CALC 90mg

Quick & Easy

Tuna-and-Pickled-Vegetable Pita Pockets

Hands-on: 15 min. Total: 15 min.

1 (8-ounce) package microwave-in-bag haricots verts (French green beans)
1 cup chopped pickled vegetable salad (such as cauliflower, red peppers, and onions)
2 tablespoons olive oil
2 tablespoons fresh lemon juice
¼ teaspoon kosher salt
¼ teaspoon black pepper
1 (6-ounce) can albacore tuna, flaked
6 pitted kalamata olives, sliced
¼ cup prepared plain hummus
2 (6-inch) whole-wheat pitas, halved and toasted
1 cup baby spinach leaves
2 large hard-cooked eggs, sliced

1. Cook haricots verts per package directions. Remove from the package, and plunge into ice water. Drain and pat dry. Cut half of haricots verts into 1½-inch pieces. Reserve remaining half for another use.
2. Gently toss together chopped haricots verts, pickled vegetables, oil, juice, salt, black pepper, tuna, and olives in a large bowl.
3. Spread 1 tablespoon hummus inside each pita half; fill each with about ¼ cup spinach and ½ cup tuna mixture. Top with egg slices. Serves 4 (serving size: 1 filled pita half)

CALORIES 296; FAT 14.2g (sat 2.6g, mono 8g, poly 2.7g); PROTEIN 18g; CARB 26g; FIBER 4g; SUGARS 5g (est. added sugars 0g); CHOL 111mg; IRON 3mg; SODIUM 643mg; CALC 62mg

Quick & Easy • Kid Friendly
Make Ahead • Vegetarian

Feta-Quinoa Cakes with Spinach

Hands-on: 30 min. Total: 30 min.

1 cup frozen green peas, thawed
⅓ cup whole-wheat panko (Japanese breadcrumbs)
⅓ cup grated yellow onion
3 tablespoons chopped fresh flat-leaf parsley
2 garlic cloves, grated
1 teaspoon grated lemon rind
2 teaspoons fresh lemon juice
3 ounces feta cheese crumbles (about ¾ cup)
3 large eggs, lightly beaten
2 (8-ounce) packages precooked plain quinoa (such as Simply Balanced)
⅜ teaspoon kosher salt, divided
½ teaspoon black pepper, divided
1½ tablespoons olive oil, divided
6 cups fresh baby spinach or watercress
2 tablespoons canola mayonnaise
2 tablespoons light sour cream
¼ teaspoon smoked paprika

1. Combine first 10 ingredients in a large bowl. Stir in ¼ teaspoon salt and ¼ teaspoon pepper. Divide and shape mixture into 8 (1-inch-thick) patties (about ½ cup each).
2. Heat a large nonstick skillet over medium-high. Add 1 tablespoon oil to pan; swirl to coat. Add patties to pan; cook 4 minutes on each side or until browned and crisp. Remove from heat.
3. Combine remaining 1½ teaspoons oil and spinach in a medium bowl; toss gently to combine.
4. Combine remaining ⅛ teaspoon salt, remaining ¼ teaspoon pepper, mayonnaise, sour cream, and paprika in a bowl, stirring with a whisk. Divide spinach among 4 plates; top evenly with patties and mayonnaise mixture. Serve immediately. Serves 4 (serving size: about 1½ cups spinach, 2 patties, and 1 tablespoon mayonnaise mixture)

CALORIES 429; FAT 22.1g (sat 6.4g, mono 9.7g, poly 4.2g); PROTEIN 18g; CARB 40g; FIBER 8g; SUGARS 5g (est. added sugars 0g); CHOL 165mg; IRON 6mg; SODIUM 591mg; CALC 244mg

Curried Lentil-and-Vegetable Stew

Quick & Easy • Kid Friendly
Make Ahead • Vegetarian

Hands-on: 20 min. Total: 20 min.

2 teaspoons olive oil
1 (8-ounce) package prechopped
 yellow onion
2 cups chopped zucchini
2 garlic cloves, thinly sliced
1 cup chopped seeded tomato
2 tablespoons curry powder
2 tablespoons unsalted ketchup
2 cups unsalted vegetable stock
2 tablespoons all-purpose flour
1/2 teaspoon kosher salt
1 (17.6-ounce) package steamed
 cooked lentils (about 2 1/2 cups)
2 tablespoons fresh lime juice
2 tablespoons plain whole-milk
 yogurt (not Greek-style)
1/4 cup chopped fresh cilantro

1. Heat oil in a large saucepan over medium-high. Add onion; sauté 4 minutes. Add zucchini and garlic; cook 3 minutes. Add tomato, curry powder, and ketchup; cook 1 minute, stirring constantly.
2. Combine stock and flour in a small bowl. Add stock mixture to pan; bring to a boil. Stir in salt and lentils; cook 3 minutes. Remove pan from heat; stir in lime juice. Divide lentil mixture among 4 bowls; top evenly with yogurt and cilantro. Serves 4 (serving size: about 1 1/2 cups)

CALORIES 321; FAT 4.5g (sat 0.7g, mono 2.1g, poly 0.7g); PROTEIN 17g; CARB 57g; FIBER 15g; SUGARS 10g (est. added sugars 2g); CHOL 1mg; IRON 5mg; SODIUM 418mg; CALC 81mg

---

SHORTCUTS

FAJITA STEAK
Thinly sliced flank steak is ready for the skillet, the broiler, the grill, or the wok.

PRESLICED BELL PEPPERS
Use for hoagies or sautés, or whiz up in the food processor as a base for salsa or relish.

CORN TORTILLAS
We call these convenient because they keep well, warm quickly, and can turn just about anything into a meal.

Quick & Easy • Gluten Free
Kid Friendly

Sheet Pan Steak Fajitas

Hands-on: 22 min. Total: 22 min.
Look in the refrigerated precut produce section for a blend of sliced multicolored peppers. If starting from whole peppers, use about 2 medium peppers of each color (this step can also be done ahead).

2 tablespoons olive oil
1 teaspoon ground cumin
3/4 teaspoon kosher salt, divided
1/2 teaspoon ground chipotle
 chile powder
1/2 teaspoon black pepper
12 ounces fajita steak (thinly sliced
 uncooked, unseasoned flank steak)
2 (8-ounce) packages presliced
 multicolored bell peppers
1 1/2 cups sliced yellow onion
Cooking spray
1/4 cup cilantro leaves
1 lime, cut into wedges
1/2 cup light sour cream
1 tablespoon fresh lime juice
1/4 teaspoon ground red pepper
8 (6-inch) corn tortillas

1. Preheat broiler with oven rack in the top position. Place a rimmed baking sheet in oven (leave pan in oven as it preheats).
2. Combine oil, cumin, 1/2 teaspoon salt, chile powder, and black pepper in a bowl, stirring with a whisk. Place steak in a bowl. Place bell peppers and onion in a bowl. Add half of oil mixture to steak; toss. Add remaining half of oil mixture to pepper mixture; toss.
3. Carefully remove baking sheet from oven. Coat pan with cooking spray. Add pepper mixture to pan; broil 10 minutes or until almost tender. Remove pan from oven. Move pepper mixture to sides of pan; arrange steak in center of pan. Broil 3 minutes or until steak reaches desired degree of doneness. Sprinkle cilantro and lime wedges over pan.
4. Combine remaining 1/4 teaspoon salt, sour cream, lime juice, and ground red pepper in a small bowl, stirring with a whisk. Heat tortillas according to package directions. Serve sour cream mixture and tortillas with steak and pepper mixture. Serves 4 (serving size: 2 filled tortillas)

CALORIES 424; FAT 17.5g (sat 5.1g, mono 6.6g, poly 1.9g); PROTEIN 25g; CARB 46g, FIBER 7g; SUGARS 10g (est. added sugars 0g); CHOL 68mg; IRON 2mg; SODIUM 450mg; CALC 129mg

---

SHORTCUTS

ROTISSERIE CHICKEN
Look for a plain rotisserie chicken or one with a neutral flavor (like lemon and herb) that won't clash with other ingredients.

FROZEN EDAMAME
Like peas, these precooked soybeans need only a minute or two to cook and add a pop of green to any dish.

FRESH GINGER PASTE
A squeeze is all you need for a hit of spicy flavor. Look for this time-saver in tubes near the herbs.

continued

Crunchy Sesame-Ginger Chicken Salad

Hands-on: 15 min. Total: 15 min.
We like plain, sesame, and nori flavors for the rice crackers.

6 tablespoons fresh lime juice
¼ cup toasted sesame oil
2 tablespoons honey
**2 teaspoons fresh ginger paste
 (such as Gourmet Garden)**
½ teaspoon kosher salt
**2 cups shredded rotisserie chicken
 breast (8 ounces)**
**1 cup frozen shelled edamame,
 thawed**
1 cup thinly sliced red bell pepper
½ cup diagonally sliced green onions
**6 tablespoons chopped fresh cilantro,
 divided**
**1 (14-ounce) package shredded
 tricolor coleslaw mix**
**15 rice crackers, broken in half
 (about 2 ounces)**
**2 tablespoons toasted sesame seeds,
 divided**

1. Stir together juice, oil, honey, ginger, and salt in a large bowl with a whisk. Add chicken, edamame, bell pepper, green onions, ¼ cup cilantro, and coleslaw to juice mixture; toss to coat. Add crackers and 1 tablespoon sesame seeds; toss. Divide cabbage mixture among 4 plates; sprinkle with remaining 2 tablespoons cilantro and 1 tablespoon sesame seeds. Serves 4 (serving size: about 2 cups)

CALORIES 393; **FAT** 18.9g (sat 2.7g, mono 6.7g, poly 6.9g); **PROTEIN** 22g; **CARB** 35g; **FIBER** 5g; **SUGARS** 15g (est. added sugars 9g); **CHOL** 49mg; **IRON** 2mg; **SODIUM** 479mg; **CALC** 93mg

TOO MUCH OF A GOOD THING

This is a time of plenty, when backyard gardens and farmers' markets spill over with corn, basil, tomatoes, peaches, and zucchini. So maybe you've found yourself over-inspired...to the tune of 6 pounds of tomatoes and double that of peaches. The recipes here will help you use up that glut deliciously. For each ingredient, we include one "put-up" recipe—a save-it-for-later condiment that keeps well and has multiple uses. We also have an eat-it-now dish to enjoy for dinner or share with company. Six pounds of zucchini? Pshaw, we've got you covered.

Basil, Blackberry, and Grilled Chicken Salad

Hands-on: 25 min. Total: 25 min.

**2 (8-ounce) boneless, skinless
 chicken breasts, trimmed**
¼ cup extra-virgin olive oil, divided
¾ teaspoon kosher salt, divided
½ teaspoon black pepper, divided
Cooking spray
2 tablespoons white balsamic vinegar
1½ teaspoons honey
1½ teaspoons Dijon mustard

4 cups packed baby arugula
**3 ounces fresh basil, stems removed
 and large leaves torn in half
 (about 2 packed cups)**
¼ cup slivered red onion
6 ounces fresh blackberries
**2 ounces goat cheese, crumbled
 (about ½ cup)**

1. Preheat grill to medium-high (about 450°F). Brush chicken with 1 tablespoon oil; sprinkle evenly with ¼ teaspoon salt and ¼ teaspoon pepper. Place chicken on grill grate coated with cooking spray. Grill, uncovered, until a meat thermometer inserted in thickest portion registers 160°F, 5 to 6 minutes per side. Let stand 5 minutes; cut into slices.

2. Whisk together remaining 3 tablespoons oil, vinegar, honey, mustard, remaining ½ teaspoon salt, and remaining ¼ teaspoon pepper in a large bowl. Add arugula, basil, and onion; toss gently to coat. Divide salad among 4 plates; top with chicken, blackberries, and cheese. Serves 4 (serving size: 1½ cups salad mixture, 3 ounces chicken, and 2 tablespoons cheese)

CALORIES 342; **FAT** 20g (sat 4.6g, mono 11.4g, poly 2.2g); **PROTEIN** 30g; **CARB** 10g; **FIBER** 3g; **SUGARS** 6g (est. added sugars 2g); **CHOL** 89mg; **IRON** 2mg; **SODIUM** 530mg; **CALC** 113mg

Quick & Easy • Make Ahead
Freezable

Miso-Sesame Pesto

Hands-on: 10 min. Total: 10 min.
Traditional pesto takes a detour through the continent of Asia, swapping in peanuts for pine nuts, toasted sesame oil for olive oil, and miso and fish sauce for Parmesan.

⅓ cup unsalted dry-roasted peanuts
3 medium garlic cloves
3 ounces fresh basil, large stems removed (2 packed cups)
¼ cup canola oil
2 tablespoons toasted sesame oil
2 tablespoons white miso
1 tablespoon rice vinegar
2 teaspoons fish sauce
½ teaspoon crushed red pepper

1. Pulse peanuts and garlic in a food processor until finely chopped, 4 to 5 times. Add basil; pulse until finely chopped, 4 to 5 times. Add oils, miso, vinegar, fish sauce, and red pepper; process until almost smooth. Store in an airtight container in refrigerator up to 1 week, or freeze up to 2 months. Serves 12 (serving size: about 1½ tablespoons)

CALORIES 93; **FAT** 9.1g (sat 1g, mono 5g, poly 2.8g); **PROTEIN** 2g; **CARB** 2g; **FIBER** 1g; **SUGARS** 1g (est. added sugars 0g); **CHOL** 0mg; **IRON** 1mg; **SODIUM** 169mg; **CALC** 17mg

Staff Favorite • Quick & Easy
Gluten Free • Kid Friendly

Creole Shrimp and Creamed Corn

Hands-on: 30 min. Total: 30 min.
This dish is a fresh, tasty twist on shrimp and grits.

7 ears fresh shucked corn
1½ cups 1% low-fat milk
2 tablespoons cornstarch
2 tablespoons butter, divided
¾ teaspoon kosher salt, divided
1 pound raw large shrimp, peeled and deveined
1 teaspoon salt-free Creole seasoning (such as Tony Chachere's)
¾ teaspoon smoked paprika
½ teaspoon black pepper
2 tablespoons olive oil
1 cup halved grape tomatoes
1 tablespoon fresh thyme leaves
5 garlic cloves, minced
½ cup sliced green onions
¼ cup dry white wine or chicken stock

1. Cut kernels from corn to equal 3½ cups; reserve cobs. Set aside ½ cup kernels. Pulse remaining 3 cups kernels in a food processor until almost creamy, 5 or 6 times. Using dull side of a knife, scrape milk and pulp from cobs into a medium saucepan; discard cobs. Add processed kernels, milk, and cornstarch to pan. Bring to a simmer over medium heat, stirring often. Reduce heat to low; simmer, stirring occasionally, until thickened, about 5 minutes. Stir in 1½ tablespoons butter and ½ teaspoon salt. Remove from heat; cover and keep warm.
2. Combine shrimp, Creole seasoning, paprika, and pepper. Heat a large skillet over medium-high. Add oil and remaining 1½ teaspoons butter to pan; cook until butter melts. Add

shrimp; cook, without stirring, 1 minute. Add tomatoes, thyme, garlic, and remaining ¼ teaspoon salt; cook, stirring occasioally, 3 minutes. Add onions and reserved ½ cup corn; cook, stirring occasionally, until shrimp are done, 1 to 2 minutes. Add wine; cook, stirring and scraping pan to loosen browned bits, 30 seconds. Serve shrimp mixture over creamed corn. Serves 4 (serving size: about 1 cup corn mixture and ½ cup shrimp mixture)

CALORIES 430; **FAT** 17.1g (sat 5.9g, mono 7.5g, poly 2g); **PROTEIN** 25g; **CARB** 47g; **FIBER** 5g; **SUGARS** 17g (est. added sugars 0g); **CHOL** 163mg; **IRON** 2mg; **SODIUM** 649mg; **CALC** 209mg

Quick & Easy • Gluten Free
Kid Friendly • Make Ahead
Vegetarian

Grilled Corn Salsa

Hands-on: 25 min. Total: 25 min.
Use this crunchy combo as a dip with tortilla chips, tuck into tacos, stuff into omelets, or serve over blackened fish or chicken.

6 ears fresh shucked corn
3 tablespoons. olive oil, divided
½ cup minced red onion
½ cup chopped fresh cilantro
1 teaspoon grated lime rind
2 tablespoons fresh lime juice
1 teaspoon kosher salt
2 red jalapeños, seeded and minced

1. Preheat grill to medium-high (about 450°F). Brush corn with 1 tablespoon oil. Grill, uncovered, turning often, until charred, 15 to 20 minutes. Cut kernels from cobs.
2. Combine corn, remaining 2 tablespoons oil, onion, and remaining ingredients. Store in refrigerator up to 1 week. Serves 12 (serving size: about ⅓ cup)

CALORIES 78; **FAT** 4.1g (sat 0.6g, mono 2.7g, poly 0.6g); **PROTEIN** 2g; **CARB** 11g; **FIBER** 1g; **SUGARS** 4g (est. added sugars 0g); **CHOL** 0mg; **IRON** 0mg; **SODIUM** 168mg; **CALC** 4mg

Tomato Gratin Lasagna

Hands-on: 30 min. Total: 1 hr.
This is a fresh, summery take on lasagna.
We call for seeding one-third of the
tomatoes to get just the right amount
of juiciness.

1 (15-ounce) container part-skim
ricotta cheese
2 large eggs, lightly beaten
1/2 cup chopped fresh basil, divided
4 teaspoons grated garlic, divided
1 1/4 teaspoons kosher salt, divided
3/4 teaspoon black pepper, divided
4 pounds firm globe and beefsteak
heirloom tomatoes (about 5 large),
cored and cut into 1/2-inch-thick
slices
6 tablespooons extra-virgin olive oil,
divided
1 tablespoon white wine vinegar or
red wine vinegar
Cooking spray
9 no-boil lasagna noodles
(such as Barilla), divided
2 ounces whole-grain bread, torn
into pieces
2 ounces Parmigiano-Reggiano
cheese, grated (1/2 cup)

1. Preheat oven to 375°F. Stir
together ricotta, eggs, ¼ cup basil,
2 teaspoons garlic, ¼ teaspoon salt,
and ¼ teaspoon pepper.
2. Remove and discard seeds from
one-third of the tomato slices.
(If tomatoes are particular seedy or
juicy, remove seeds from one-half
of the tomatoes.) Combine all
tomato slices, ¼ cup oil, vinegar,
remaining 2 teaspoons garlic,
remaining 1 teaspoon salt, and
remaining ½ teaspoon pepper in a
large bowl; toss gently to combine.
3. Coat a 13- x 9-inch glass or
ceramic baking dish with cooking

spray. Arrange one-third of the
tomato slices in a single layer on
bottom of baking dish; top with
3 lasagna noodles. Spread ricotta
mixture evenly over noodles; top
with 3 lasagna noodles. Arrange
one-third of the tomato slices in a
single layer over noodles, and top
with remaining 3 noodles. Arrange
remaining tomatoes over top, shin-
gling if necessary. Pour any tomato
juices from bowl evenly over lasagna.
Cover baking dish with foil, and
bake at 375°F for 15 minutes.
4. Meanwhile, place bread in a food
processor; pulse until coarse crumbs
form, 4 to 5 times. Heat remaining
2 tablespoons oil in a large skillet
over medium. Add breadcrumbs;
cook, stirring often, until toasted,
3 to 4 minutes. Transfer to a medium
bowl; cool 5 minutes. Add cheese
and remaining ¼ cup basil; toss.
5. Remove lasagna from oven;
remove foil. Sprinkle breadcrumb
mixture over lasagna. Return dish
to oven; bake at 375°F until top is
browned, about 10 minutes. Serves 8
(serving size: 1 piece)

CALORIES 347; **FAT** 18.5g (sat 5.7g, mono 9.9g,
poly 1.8g); **PROTEIN** 16g; **CARB** 31g; **FIBER** 4g;
SUGARS 7g (est. added sugars 0g); **CHOL** 68mg;
IRON 2mg; **SODIUM** 507mg; **CALC** 274mg

Zucchini Pie

Hands-on: 35 min. Total: 2 hr.
In this riff on spaghetti pie, zucchini
"noodles" stand in for pasta.

3 pounds zucchini
1 1/2 teaspoons kosher salt, divided
1 1/2 tablespoons olive oil
1 pint grape tomatoes, halved
2 tablespoons chopped fresh oregano
5 garlic cloves, minced
7 large eggs
2/3 cup 1% low-fat milk
1/4 cup all-purpose flour

1/2 teaspoon black pepper
2 1/2 ounces preshredded part-skim
mozzarella cheese (about 2/3 cup)
2 ounces Parmigiano-Reggiano
cheese, grated (1/2 cup)
Cooking spray

1. Using the large holes of a spiralizer, cut zucchini into noodles, or
cut zucchini into long noodles using
a julienne peeler. Place zucchini
in a colander in sink. Toss zucchini
with 1 teaspoon salt. Let stand
20 minutes.
2. Heat oil in a large skillet over
medium-high. Add tomatoes,
oregano, and garlic; cook, stirring
often, until tomatoes are wilted,
3 to 4 minutes. Remove mixture
from pan; cool slightly.
3. Preheat oven to 375°F. Place
half of zucchini noodles on a clean
kitchen towel. Wrap towel around
zucchini; twist and squeeze until
all liquid is extracted. Repeat with
remaining zucchini. Cut zucchini
into manageable lengths.
4. Whisk eggs in a large bowl until
lightly beaten. Whisk in milk, flour,
pepper, and remaining ½ teaspoon
salt. Add tomato mixture, cheeses,
and zucchini; toss.
5. Wrap bottom plate of a 9-inch
springform pan tightly with foil.
Assemble pan; coat bottom and sides
with cooking spray. Pour egg mixture
into pan. Bake at 375°F until set in
the middle, 50 minutes to 1 hour.
Cool 10 to 15 minutes. Remove
sides from pan; cut zucchini pie
into 6 wedges. Serves 6 (serving size:
1 wedge)

CALORIES 267; **FAT** 14.8g (sat 5.6g, mono 6g,
poly 1.9g); **PROTEIN** 18g; **CARB** 17g; **FIBER** 3g;
SUGARS 8g (est. added sugars 0g); **CHOL** 232mg;
IRON 2mg; **SODIUM** 614mg; **CALC** 318mg

Peach-Vanilla Slab Pie

Hands-on: 1 hr. 30 min.
Total: 3 hr. 50 min.
The next time you need a dessert for a crowd—backyard barbecue, picnic, block party—think slab pie. You'll need to roll the dough out so that it's very thin; to make this easier, you can roll it out on parchment paper and place the whole thing, including the paper, in the pan.

12 ounces whole-wheat pastry flour (about 3⅓ cups)
4¼ ounces unbleached all-purpose flour (1 cup)
1¼ teaspoons kosher salt, divided
½ cup cold unsalted butter, cut into small pieces
¼ cup olive oil
1 tablespoon fresh lemon juice
⅔ cup plus 1 to 2 tablespoons cold water, divided
6 pounds ripe peaches, peeled and sliced (about 12 cups)
1⅓ cups packed brown sugar
3 tablespoons cornstarch
1 tablespoon vanilla bean paste or vanilla extract
1 teaspoon ground cinnamon
1 large egg yolk, lightly beaten
1 teaspoon room-temperature water

1. Pulse flours and 1 teaspoon salt in a food processor 2 times. Add butter; pulse until mixture resembles coarse meal, 4 to 5 times. Stir together oil, lemon juice, and ⅔ cup cold water in a small bowl. While pulsing, pour oil mixture through food chute. Process just until dough comes together and starts to form a shaggy ball. Add an additional 2 tablespoons cold water, 1 tablespoon at a time, if necessary to bring dough together. (Be careful not to overprocess.)
2. Turn dough out onto a work surface; knead until dough just comes together, about 2 times. Divide dough into 2 pieces, one roughly 60% of the dough and the other 40%. Flatten each into a 1-inch-thick disk; wrap each in plastic wrap. Chill 2 hours or up to overnight.
3. Preheat oven to 375°F. Combine peaches, brown sugar, cornstarch, vanilla bean paste, cinnamon, and remaining ¼ teaspoon salt in a large bowl; toss well to combine. Set aside.
4. Remove dough disks from refrigerator, and unwrap. Place larger dough disk between 2 lightly floured sheets of plastic wrap; roll into a very thin 20- x 15-inch rectangle. Using a thin pan or cutting board for support, carefully slide dough from plastic wrap onto a 13- x 18-inch rimmed baking sheet. Remove plastic wrap, and press dough into corners of baking sheet. Spoon peach mixture evenly over dough. Place second dough disk between 2 lightly floured sheets of plastic wrap; roll into a very thin 13- x 18-inch rectangle. Cut dough lengthwise into ¾-inch-thick strips. Arrange strips in a lattice pattern over peach mixture; crimp edges to seal. Whisk together egg yolk and 1 teaspoon room-temperature water in a small bowl. Brush dough lattice evenly with egg yolk mixture.
5. Bake at 375°F until filling is thick and bubbly and crust is browned, about 50 to 55 minutes. Cool at least 20 minutes before serving. Serves 18 (serving size: 1 piece)

CALORIES 278; **FAT** 9g (sat 3.8g, mono 3.7g, poly 0.7g); **PROTEIN** 4g; **CARB** 47g; **FIBER** 4g; **SUGARS** 25g (est. added sugars 16g); **CHOL** 24mg; **IRON** 2mg; **SODIUM** 140mg; **CALC** 38mg

Zucchini Butter

Hands-on: 15 min. Total: 45 min.
Zucchini's mild flavor concentrates into something much richer when you cook it until most of its liquid evaporates.

2½ pounds zucchini (3 to 4 large zucchini)
3 tablespoons butter
2 tablespoons olive oil
4 garlic cloves, minced
1 teaspoon kosher salt
½ teaspoon black pepper

1. Shred zucchini on the large holes of a box grater to equal about 6 cups. Spread zucchini on a clean kitchen towel; squeeze well to extract most of the liquid.
2. Heat butter and oil in a large skillet over medium until butter melts. Add zucchini and garlic. Reduce heat to medium-low, and cook, stirring occasionally, until liquid evaporates and mixture is silky and tender, 30 to 35 minutes. Remove from heat, and stir in salt and pepper. Store in an airtight container in refrigerator up to 1 week, or freeze up to 2 months. Serves 10 (serving size: about ¼ cup)

CALORIES 75; **FAT** 6.5g (sat 2.7g, mono 2.9g, poly 0.5g); **PROTEIN** 1g; **CARB** 4g; **FIBER** 1g; **SUGARS** 2g (est. added sugars 0g); **CHOL** 9mg; **IRON** 0mg; **SODIUM** 228mg; **CALC** 21mg

Cherry Tomato Confit

Hands-on: 10 min. Total: 2 hr.

3 pounds cherry tomatoes
3/4 cup olive oil
1 1/2 teaspoons kosher salt
1 teaspoon black pepper
10 garlic cloves, sliced
8 large thyme sprigs

1. Preheat oven to 275°F. Spread tomatoes onto a large rimmed baking sheet. Add oil, salt, pepper, and garlic; toss gently to coat. Tuck thyme sprigs into mixture. Bake at 275°F until tomatoes are wilted but not all have burst, 1 1/2 to 2 hours.
2. Cool tomato mixture to room temperature; discard thyme. Store tomatoes with oil and accumulated pan juices in an airtight container in refrigerator up to 2 weeks, or freeze up to 2 months. Serves 15 (serving size: about 1/3 cup)

CALORIES 116; **FAT** 11g (sat 1.5g, mono 7.9g, poly 1.2g); **PROTEIN** 1g; **CARB** 4g; **FIBER** 1g; **SUGARS** 2g (est. added sugars 0g); **CHOL** 0mg; **IRON** 0mg; **SODIUM** 197mg; **CALC** 16mg

Honey-Bourbon Peach Preserves

Hands-on: 35 min. Total: 1 hr. 40 min.
Don't be tempted to use a higher-proof whiskey; the flavor will be too "hot."

7 cups coarsely chopped peeled ripe peaches (about 3 1/2 pounds)
1 cup mild honey
1/2 cup (80- to 90-proof) bourbon
1 tablespoon fresh thyme leaves
1/2 teaspoon kosher salt

1. Pulse peaches in a food processor until finely chopped and chunky but not pureed, 5 or 6 times, stopping to stir occasionally to ensure they are evenly chopped. Transfer to a Dutch oven. Add honey, bourbon, thyme, and salt. Bring to a boil over medium. Reduce heat to low, and simmer, stirring occasionally, until mixture is thick and reduced to about 4 1/2 cups, about 1 hour to 1 hour and 20 minutes. Cool completely. Store in airtight containers in refrigerator up to 1 month, or freeze for up to 4 months. Makes 4 1/2 cups (serving size: 2 tablespoons)

CALORIES 44; **FAT** 0.1g (sat 0g, mono 0g, poly 0.1g); **PROTEIN** 0g; **CARB** 11g; **FIBER** 0g; **SUGARS** 10g (est. added sugars 8g); **CHOL** 0mg; **IRON** 0mg; **SODIUM** 27mg; **CALC** 3mg

GROW. HARVEST. COOK.

GARDEN SCHOOL: BOK CHOY BASICS

Student gardener Devine Nwosu shares her know-how with this crunchy, fast-growing Asian green. Shopping, growing, and cooking tips follow on page 197.

Sweet-and-Sour Sesame Bok Choy with Pork

Hands-on: 20 min. Total: 20 min.

1/2 cup unsalted chicken stock
3 tablespoons reduced-sodium soy sauce
2 tablespoons honey
2 tablespoons rice vinegar
1 tablespoon Chinese hot mustard
2 teaspoons cornstarch
1/2 teaspoon crushed red pepper
12 ounces ground pork
1 pound baby or small bok choy, quartered lengthwise
1 cup matchstick-cut carrots
2 tablespoons toasted sesame oil
3 cups hot cooked brown rice
2 teaspoons black or white sesame seeds (optional)

1. Whisk together stock, soy sauce, honey, vinegar, mustard, cornstarch, and crushed red pepper in a bowl. Set aside.
2. Heat a wok or large skillet over medium-high. Add pork; cook, stirring often and scraping bottom of pan with a wooden spoon to loosen browned bits, until pork is browned and crumbled, 4 to 5 minutes. Remove pork from pan with a slotted spoon.
3. Add bok choy and carrots to drippings in pan; cook over medium-high until slightly wilted, 2 to 3 minutes. Add stock mixture and pork. Bring to a boil; cook until thickened, 1 to 2 minutes. Remove from heat. Stir in sesame oil.
4. Serve over rice, and sprinkle with sesame seeds, if desired. Serves 4 (serving size: 3/4 cup rice and 1 cup bok choy mixture)

CALORIES 445; **FAT** 16.8g (sat 4.4g, mono 7.1g, poly 4.7g); **PROTEIN** 24g; **CARB** 51g; **FIBER** 5g; **SUGARS** 12g (est. added sugars 9g); **CHOL** 64mg; **IRON** 2mg; **SODIUM** 684mg; **CALC** 158mg

Grilled Bok Choy "Wedge" with Blue Cheese-Buttermilk Dressing

Hands-on: 15 min. Total: 15 min.
Bok choy adds a funky edge to our riff on a classic steak house salad, with far deeper flavor than lettuce.

Cooking spray
4 (4-ounce) bok choy heads, halved lengthwise
1/4 cup low-fat buttermilk
1 ounce blue cheese, crumbled (about 1/4 cup)
1 tablespoon apple cider vinegar
1 teaspoon granulated sugar
1/4 teaspoon freshly ground black pepper
1 cup halved grape tomatoes (about 6 ounces)
1/4 cup crispy fried onions (such as French's)

1. Heat a grill pan over high. Coat pan with cooking spray. Place bok choy halves, cut sides down, on pan. Cook 2 minutes per side, until both sides are marked and lightly charred. Remove from pan.
2. Stir together buttermilk, blue cheese, vinegar, sugar, and pepper in a bowl. Place bok choy halves, cut sides up, on a serving platter. Top with buttermilk dressing, and sprinkle with tomatoes and fried onions. Serves 4 (serving size: 2 bok choy halves, 2 tablespoons dressing, 1/4 cup tomatoes, and 1 tablespoon onions)

CALORIES 80; FAT 4.2g (sat 19g, mono 1.6g, poly 0.5g); PROTEIN 4g; CARB 7g; FIBER 2g; SUGARS 4g (est. added sugars 1g); CHOL 6mg; IRON 1mg; SODIUM 196mg; CALC 179mg

HOW TO SHOP

Stock up by the bunch for stir-fries, soups, crunchy salads, and slaws.

1. KNOW WHERE TO LOOK
You'll find bok choy at supermarkets and farmers' markets, but for the best selection, visit an Asian market. There, you'll find more variety—from tiny thumb-size babies to mature foot-long heads.

2. GAUGE FRESHNESS
Seek firm, thick stems with bright green leaves. A telltale sign of freshness is greens that are vibrant and not wilted. These fresh bundles pack a heap of vitamins A and C and many minerals.

3. PICK BOK, PAK, OR PAC
Whether called bok choy, pak choi, or pac choi, seeds and harvests of the Chinese cabbage family of greens are great buys. Size and shape vary, from towering tall stems of Joi Choi to compact, tender stems of Shanghai Green.

HOW TO GROW

Expect fast-growing, cold-tolerant bok choy to show up in your garden when cooler weather hits.

1. PLANT WHEN COOL
A cool-season green in the same family as cabbage, bok choy loves crisp weather, thriving even as temps flirt near freezing. Plant seeds or transplants 6–10 weeks before your area's first expected frost.

2. GIVE PLANTS SOME SPACE
Choose light, nutrient-rich soil. Scratch shallow rows 1/4 inch deep, placing seeds every 3 inches. "Don't just throw seeds in the soil!" warns Devine. "Make the hole two times bigger than the seed. Give the plants enough space." Allow 18 inches between rows, as the vase-shaped tops can grow 12–18 inches high.

3. SNACK ON TRIMMINGS
Great for curious classmates, bok choy seedlings are people pleasers that quickly pop up in five to seven days. Enjoy baby bok choy by plucking every other seedling when 2 to 3 weeks old, making room for growth. Harvest mature plants by clipping them at the base in 40–50 days.

NUTRITION MADE EASY

HOW TO TAME INFLAMMATION

The right food choices can help control and prevent chronic inflammation.

Occasional inflammation, like a swollen sprained ankle or painful cut, is healthy. It's a sign that the body's immune system is healing injuries and fighting off bacteria. While a little bothersome, the inflammation is acute and goes away in a few days. But there's another type of inflammation that's not so healthy: chronic inflammation. It's triggered by the immune system responding to irritants or foreign compounds, often in food or the environment. With no overt symptoms, chronic inflammation is a little harder to understand or even recognize. However, research has linked it with obesity, metabolic syndrome, heart disease, type 2 diabetes, cancer, Alzheimer's disease, and autoimmune diseases like rheumatoid arthritis. Read on for the scoop on what to eat and what to skip.

THE TOP INFLAMERS

These foods and habits fan the flames of inflammation. Try to limit or eliminate them as much as possible.

Refined carbs like white bread, white rice, etc.

Added sugars

Artificial sweeteners

High-fat meats and processed meats

Excessive alcohol

Regularly eating more calories than your body needs

Trans and saturated fats

Fried foods

A DAY OF ANTI-INFLAMMATORY EATING

We've taken the guesswork out of eating to beat inflammation and loaded breakfast, lunch, and dinner with flame-fighting foods. All you have to do is cook and enjoy!

BREAKFAST

Quick & Easy • Gluten Free
Kid Friendly • Vegetarian

Quinoa Bowls with Avocado and Egg

Hands-on: 15 min. Total: 15 min.
This satisfying breakfast is loaded with anti-inflammatory foods: extra-virgin olive oil, avocado, tomatoes, quinoa, and omega-3 eggs. For even more anti-inflammatory benefit, serve with an orange or grapefruit.

2 teaspoons extra-virgin olive oil, divided
1 teaspoon red wine vinegar
1/4 teaspoon kosher salt, divided
1 cup hot cooked tricolor quinoa
1 cup grape tomatoes, halved
1/2 cup canned unsalted black beans, rinsed, drained, and warmed
2 tablespoons chopped fresh cilantro, plus more for garnish
2 large omega-3 eggs
1/2 ripe avocado, sliced

1. Whisk together 1½ teaspoons of the oil, vinegar, and dash of salt.
2. Combine quinoa, tomatoes, beans, cilantro, and ⅛ teaspoon salt; toss gently to combine. Place mixture in each of 2 bowls.
3. Heat a medium nonstick skillet over medium. Add remaining ½ teaspoon oil; swirl to coat. Crack eggs, 1 at a time, into pan. Cover; cook until whites are set and yolk is still runny, 2 to 3 minutes. Drizzle dressing evenly over quinoa mixture; top with eggs and avocado. Sprinkle with remaining dash of salt. Garnish with

additional cilantro, if desired. Serves 2 (serving size: about ⅔ cup quinoa mixture, 1 egg, and ¼ avocado)

CALORIES 343; **FAT** 16.4g (sat 3.1g, mono 9g, poly 3.1g); **PROTEIN** 15g; **CARB** 35g; **FIBER** 9g; **SUGARS** 3g (est. added sugars 0g); **CHOL** 186mg; **IRON** 4mg; **SODIUM** 332mg; **CALC** 86mg

LUNCH

Quick & Easy • Gluten Free
Make Ahead

Salmon Salad with Cherry Vinaigrette

Hands-on: 15 min. Total: 15 min.
Cherry juice is a year-round alternative with the same anti-inflammatory benefits as fresh cherries. If you're taking this salad to work, store the dressing separately and drizzle over the salad just before eating.

2 tablespoons tart cherry juice
4 teaspoons extra-virgin olive oil
1 teaspoon toasted sesame oil
1 teaspoon rice vinegar
1 teaspoon Dijon mustard
1/2 teaspoon honey
1/2 teaspoon grated peeled fresh ginger
1/4 teaspoon kosher salt
4 cups dark baby greens mix (such as Dole Power Up Greens Baby Kale and Greens)
2 tablespoons very thinly sliced red onion
1 (6-ounce) can pink or red skinless, boneless salmon, drained and flaked
1/2 cup frozen shelled edamame, thawed
1/3 cup diced cucumber
2 tablespoons toasted slivered almonds

1. Combine first 8 ingredients (through salt) in a large bowl; whisk until well combined. Add greens and red onion; toss gently to combine. Divide salad mixture evenly between 2 plates; top evenly with flaked salmon, edamame, cucumber, and almonds. Serves 2 (serving size: 2 cups)

CALORIES 334; **FAT** 20.4g (sat 2.8g, mono 11g, poly 4.8g); **PROTEIN** 25g; **CARB** 15g; **FIBER** 6g; **SUGARS** 5g (est. added sugars 1g); **CHOL** 53mg; **IRON** 3mg; **SODIUM** 609mg; **CALC** 219mg

DINNER

Quick & Easy • Gluten Free
Kid Friendly • Make Ahead

Black Pepper-Curry Chicken Sauté

Hands-on: 25 min. Total: 25 min.
Black pepper adds a subtle spiciness and enhances your body's absorption of turmeric in the curry. For the boldest flavor, use 1 teaspoon peppercorns. Serve with roasted cauliflower or broccoli for an extra anti-inflammatory boost.

1 pound skinless, boneless chicken breasts, cut into 1-inch pieces
3/4 teaspoon kosher salt, divided
1/4 teaspoon freshly ground black pepper
1 tablespoon canola oil, divided
1½ cups vertically sliced onion
2 teaspoons minced peeled fresh ginger
3 garlic cloves, minced
2 teaspoons curry powder
1 cup canned light coconut milk
2 teaspoons fresh lime juice
1/2 to 1 teaspoon peppercorns, crushed
2 tablespoons chopped fresh cilantro or basil
2 cups hot cooked brown rice

1. Sprinkle chicken with ¼ teaspoon salt and ¼ teaspoon ground pepper. Heat 1½ teaspoons oil in a large nonstick skillet over medium-high. Add chicken to pan; cook, stirring frequently, 5 to 6 minutes or until chicken is lightly browned and almost cooked through. Remove chicken from pan.
2. Reduce heat to medium. Add remaining 1½ teaspoons oil to pan; swirl to coat. Add onion; cook 4 minutes or until tender, stirring occasionally. Add ginger and garlic; cook until softened, about 1 minute. Add curry powder; cook 15 to 30 seconds or until fragrant, stirring constantly. Stir in coconut milk, lime juice, crushed peppercorns, and remaining ½ teaspoon salt. Return chicken to pan. Cover, and cook over medium-low until sauce is slightly thickened and chicken is done, about 5 minutes. Remove from heat; stir in cilantro or basil. Serve over rice. Serves 4 (serving size: ½ cup rice and ¾ cup chicken mixture)

CALORIES 336; FAT 10.6g (sat 4g, mono 3.4g, poly 1.8g); PROTEIN 30g; CARB 31g; FIBER 3g; SUGARS 2g (est. added sugar 0g); CHOL 83mg; IRON 1mg; SODIUM 434mg; CALC 37mg

continued

EAT TO BEAT INFLAMMATION

Ongoing inflammation is problematic because it alters normal body processes and cells, which can cause long-term damage and increase your likelihood of developing a chronic condition.

Food plays a pivotal role—it can either help reduce or promote chronic inflammation. While there's still more research to be done, we know that filling your plate with more anti-inflammatory foods while dialing back on those that cause inflammation may have a powerful effect on your body's ability to ward off future diseases and even slow aging.

10 TOP ANTI-INFLAMMATORY FOODS

Lots of foods have anti-inflammatory qualities; these are a few of our favorites. Aim to work them into your diet as often as possible.

1. CHERRIES
Both sweet and tart varieties lower C-reactive protein, one of the key blood indicators used to test for inflammation. Cherries may even offer pain relief comparable to ibuprofen. When cherries aren't in season, try tart cherry juice in smoothies and salad dressings.

2. SALMON
The omega-3 fats DHA and EPA in salmon and other oily fish play key roles in suppressing inflammation and boosting production of anti-inflammatory compounds. Aim to eat fish or sea vegetables like algae several times per week.

3. BROCCOLI
This cruciferous veggie offers healthy doses of phytochemicals that quell inflammatory compounds associated with cancer development. Try to eat at least five weekly servings of cruciferous vegetables. These include broccoli, Brussels sprouts, cauliflower, cabbage, kale, mustard greens, watercress, and kohlrabi.

4. SHIITAKE MUSHROOMS
Research suggests that eating shiitake mushrooms daily lowers inflammatory markers and improves immune system function. Oyster and enoki mushrooms also have anti-inflammatory powers. Make sure you eat them raw or cook at low to moderate temps for the most impact.

5. EXTRA-VIRGIN OLIVE OIL
This pantry staple delivers the inflammation-suppressing compound oleocanthal, plus a small amount of omega-3s. Try other oils, too, such as flaxseed and canola, for a stronger dose of omega-3s.

6. AVOCADO
The creamy fruit works twofold thanks to monounsaturated fats and antioxidants. Avocado may even counteract eating some inflammatory foods: In one study, people who topped their hamburger with avocado had lower inflammatory markers than those who ate just the burger.

7. TURMERIC
Curcumin is the powerful compound in turmeric that eases symptoms in almost all inflammation-related conditions. Research varies on how much you need, but aim to cook with turmeric several times a week (curry powder is a good source).

8. TOMATOES
Tomatoes' lycopene propels them to the next nutritional level. Studies show lycopene reduces and suppresses inflammation—which is why tomatoes help lower cancer and cardiovascular incident risks.

9. SPINACH
While all leafy greens are recommended, spinach offers a mix of antioxidants that boost the immune system and suppress inflammation. It also helps that the leafy green is one of the most versatile veggies for quick meal prep.

10. STRAWBERRIES
These berries are loaded with anthocyanins and antioxidants called ellagitannins, which sweep up harmful free radicals that promote inflammation. In fact, all berries are good sources.

DOES DAIRY PROMOTE INFLAMMATION?

Contrary to popular belief, dairy products like yogurt actually have an anti-inflammatory effect in most people. Yogurt reduces inflammation by supporting gut health. But saturated fat can promote inflammation, so choose lower-fat versions.

However, if you have a dairy allergy or sensitivity, continue to avoid dairy, as it will trigger an inflammatory response.

SHOULD I AVOID NIGHTSHADE VEGETABLES?

Nightshade vegetables, such as tomatoes, eggplant, peppers, and potatoes, are often blamed for arthritis inflammation due to their compound solanine. However, there's no conclusive research that they do trigger inflammation. Nightshades are full of anti-inflammatory nutrients, such as lycopene and beta-carotene, so don't avoid them. However, if eating a specific one triggers pain or inflammation symptoms, it likely isn't the entire nightshade family, but rather a sensitivity to one that can be eliminated.

THE COOKING LIGHT DIET

A FAST AND FRESH FAMILY FAVORITE

Better-than-takeout homemade pizza in less than 30 minutes

COMMUNITY MEMBER
Katie Anderson, 46

LOCATION
Newnan, GA

SUCCESS STORY
Whole family eating healthier, together, for 2-plus years

Every Friday, the Anderson family has pizza night. It's a chance for them to get together and indulge while giving Katie, the matriarch, a chance to reset. We sent her this recipe to shake things up, and it was an instant hit. "The pizza was fabulous," Katie says. "You can't beat fresh mozzarella, and the veggies were very kid-friendly." Katie and her crew found that making pizza together as a family instead of ordering in made dinner more of a fun event. Her only concern was how involved the recipe would be. "It has to be easy," she says, and thankfully this recipe is: "We'll definitely be making this again on another summer pizza night."

Just let us know what time to come over, Katie!

Quick & Easy • Kid Friendly
Make Ahead • Vegetarian

Tomato, Basil, and Corn Pizza

Hands-on: 15 min. Total: 25 min.
A sprinkling of cornmeal keeps the dough from sticking to the pizza stone and gets the bottom of the crust extra crispy. If you don't have a rectangular pizza stone, use a heavy baking sheet instead. Serve with a green side salad for a winning weeknight combination.

1 pound refrigerated fresh pizza dough
1 tablespoon plain yellow cornmeal
$\frac{1}{2}$ cup lower-sodium marinara sauce (such as Rao's)
1 large tomato, thinly sliced
$\frac{2}{3}$ cup fresh corn kernels (from 2 ears)
$3\frac{1}{2}$ ounces fresh mozzarella cheese, torn (about 1 cup)
2 garlic cloves, thinly sliced
$\frac{1}{2}$ teaspoon kosher salt
$\frac{1}{2}$ teaspoon freshly ground black pepper
$\frac{1}{4}$ cup loosely packed fresh basil leaves, torn
$\frac{1}{4}$ teaspoon crushed red pepper
1 teaspoon olive oil
1 tablespoon balsamic glaze

1. Place a rectangular pizza stone in the oven, and preheat to 500°F. (Do not remove the pizza stone while the oven preheats.)
2. Place the dough in a microwave-safe bowl. Cover with plastic wrap, and microwave at HIGH 30 seconds, until the dough is slightly warmed. Place the dough on a lightly floured surface, and roll out into a 15- x 12-inch rectangle. Sprinkle cornmeal on a large piece of parchment paper; place the dough rectangle on the cornmeal. Let stand 5 minutes.
3. Place the parchment and dough on a flat baking sheet. Bake at 500°F for 3 minutes. Spread marinara sauce on crust. Top evenly with tomato, corn, cheese, and garlic. Sprinkle with salt and black pepper. Gently slide the pizza onto the preheated pizza stone. Bake at 500°F for 12 minutes or until crust is browned and edges are crispy. Sprinkle basil and crushed red pepper evenly over top; drizzle with oil and balsamic glaze. Cut into 6 slices. Serves 6 (serving size: 1 slice)

CALORIES 285; **FAT** 7.3g (sat 3.1g, mono 1.9g, poly 1.1g); **PROTEIN** 10g; **CARB** 43g; **FIBER** 6g; **SUGARS** 5g (est. added sugars 2g); **CHOL** 12mg; **IRON** 1mg; **SODIUM** 552mg; **CALC** 12mg

THE RITUAL

SWEET SUMMER SNOW

by Karen Hatfield

LA pastry chef Karen Hatfield rediscovers the simple frosty pleasures of fluffy granita.

I first fell in love with the granita as a palate cleanser. It was the 1980s, and I was a young girl eating my way through the top Zagat-rated restaurants of Los Angeles. It was the pinnacle of elegance, although admittedly I remember the taste less than the drama: the perfectly timed dance of finely dressed servers placing chilled, stemmed crystal glasses with what seemed to be an early dessert course. In these moments, restaurants cast their spell on me, and I knew instantly this was my true calling.

Years later, in the late '90s, I learned to make a "great" granita. I was working at Gramercy Tavern in New York for esteemed pastry chef Claudia Fleming. There was always a granita on the menu: almond, peach, raspberry—just about anything as long as there was tons of flavor. Most days, crates of amazing produce from the Greenmarket showed up, so there was always plenty of inspiration. I learned how to coax all the flavor from the fruit but still retain the light, fluffy, snowlike texture that is key to the best granita. And, more important, I learned that it was all about the taste and not so much the theatrics of yesteryear.

I served granita on and off as part of a first-course tasting dessert at our Michelin-starred restaurant, but I found less of a use for it over time. A few years ago, my family started visiting Hawaii during the summer, and we became obsessed with the shaved ice at Ululani's on Maui. Shaved ice and granita are pretty much the same thing, after all. Root beer and condensed milk may not have been the flavors I was used to, but on hot summer days, it's hard to find something more refreshing. My kids loved it so much that it inspired me to start making it again, but at home. Granita and summertime really go hand in hand.

My son loves watermelon and my daughter loves to cook, so the watermelon granita pulls everyone in. My son always selects just the right watermelon with the sweetest, strongest aroma, and then he carries the giant thing around to show how strong he is for a little guy. My daughter is patient and grates the granita with expert precision. So just like 20 years ago, it's off to the farmers' market to get the best melons from Weiser Family Farms and the sweetest strawberries from Harry's Berries to make our family's favorite summer treat.

Gluten Free • Kid Friendly Make Ahead • Freezable Vegetarian

Watermelon Granita with Hibiscus Syrup and Yogurt

(pictured on page 226)

Hands-on: 16 min. Total: 3 hr. 16 min.
Karen Hatfield serves this sophisticated granita at her LA restaurant, Odys + Penelope. Dried hibiscus flowers can be found at specialty markets, Latin markets, and health food stores. You can substitute grenadine syrup to good effect, but Hatfield asserts that hibiscus syrup best complements the fruit in this dish.

6 cups diced seedless yellow watermelon
7 tablespoons sugar, divided
¼ cup dried hibiscus flowers
¼ cup water
2 cups plain whole-milk Greek yogurt
2 cups strawberries, hulled and quartered
3 large fresh basil leaves, torn

1. Combine watermelon and ¼ cup sugar in a large bowl; toss well. Let stand 15 minutes. Place watermelon mixture in a blender, in batches if needed; blend until smooth. Pour puree through a fine-mesh strainer into a 13- x 9-inch glass or ceramic baking dish; discard solids. Place watermelon mixture in freezer for 45 minutes. Scrape with a fork, and stir; return to freezer. Repeat procedure every 30 minutes until granita is completely frozen.
2. Combine flowers, ¼ cup water, and remaining 3 tablespoons sugar in a small saucepan over medium heat. Bring to a boil; simmer 3 minutes or until syrup just coats a spoon, stirring well. Strain syrup through a fine-mesh strainer into a small bowl; discard solids.
3. Place ¼ cup yogurt in each of 8 chilled parfait glasses. Top each serving with ¼ cup strawberries. Drizzle about 1 teaspoon hibiscus syrup over strawberries. Scrape and fluff granita with a fork; top each serving with ½ cup granita. Top servings evenly with basil. Serve immediately. Serves 8

CALORIES 148; FAT 2.3g (sat 1.3g, mono 0.6g, poly 0.2g); PROTEIN 3g; CARB 31g; FIBER 1g; SUGARS 26g (est. added sugars 16g); CHOL 8mg; IRON 1mg; SODIUM 32mg; CALC 92mg

....
GAME PLAN
....

While broiler preheats:

- Sauté vegetables.

While ratatouille simmers:

- Toast bread.
- Make pesto.

**Quick & Easy • Gluten Free
Kid Friendly • Make Ahead
Vegetarian**

Skillet Ratatouille

With Pesto Toasts

**2 (15-ounce) cans unsalted diced
   tomatoes, divided**
**2 (15-ounce) cans unsalted
   chickpeas, rinsed and drained**
1½ tablespoons extra-virgin olive oil
1 tablespoon minced fresh garlic
1 teaspoon kosher salt, divided
1 cup chopped red onion
1 cup chopped red bell pepper
**1 large zucchini, cut into 1-inch pieces
   (about 8 ounces)**
**1 large yellow squash, cut into 1-inch
   pieces (about 8 ounces)**
**1 small eggplant, peeled and cut into
   1-inch pieces (about 5 ounces)**
1 tablespoon red wine vinegar
½ teaspoon smoked paprika
½ teaspoon black pepper
**2 tablespoons fresh basil leaves
   (optional)**

1. Drain 1 can tomatoes in a colander over a bowl, reserving ½ cup liquid. Drain remaining 1 can tomatoes; discard liquid. Combine tomatoes, reserved ½ cup liquid, and chickpeas in a bowl.

2. Heat 1 tablespoon oil in a large skillet over medium-high. Add garlic, ½ teaspoon salt, and next 5 ingredients (through eggplant); sauté 7 to 8 minutes or until slightly tender. Stir in tomato mixture and remaining ½ teaspoon salt; cover, and cook 5 minutes.
3. Uncover pan; stir in vinegar, paprika, and black pepper. Cook 5 minutes or until vegetable mixture is slightly thickened. Divide vegetable mixture among 4 shallow bowls; drizzle servings evenly with remaining 1½ teaspoons oil. Sprinkle with basil leaves, if desired. Serves 4 (serving size: about 1¾ cups)

CALORIES 354; **FAT** 7.3g (sat 0.8g, mono 3.7g, poly 0.7g); **PROTEIN** 15g; **CARB** 58g; **FIBER** 13g; **SUGARS** 13g (est. added sugars 1g); **CHOL** 4mg; **IRON** 4mg; **SODIUM** 558mg; **CALC** 148mg

**Quick & Easy • Kid Friendly
Vegetarian**

Pesto Toasts

**1 (4-ounce) whole-wheat French
   bread baguette, split lengthwise**
1 cup packed baby spinach
½ cup packed fresh basil leaves
1 tablespoon toasted pine nuts
1 teaspoon fresh minced garlic
**1 ounce Parmesan cheese, grated
   (about ¼ cup)**
2½ tablespoons extra-virgin olive oil

1. Preheat broiler with oven rack in upper middle position.
2. Place bread, cut sides up, on a baking sheet; broil 2 minutes or until toasted.
3. Place spinach, basil, pine nuts, garlic, and cheese in a mini food processor; pulse until finely chopped. With processor running, gradually add oil; process until smooth. Spread evenly over bread; cut into quarters. Serves 4 (serving size: 1 piece)

CALORIES 194; **FAT** 13g (sat 2.6g, mono 7.2g, poly 2.2g); **PROTEIN** 6g; **CARB** 14g; **FIBER** 2g; **SUGARS** 1g (est. added sugars 0g); **CHOL** 6mg; **IRON** 1mg; **SODIUM** 263mg; **CALC** 125mg

....
GAME PLAN
....

While chicken grills:

- Prepare salsa.

While chicken stands:

- Prepare salad.

**Quick & Easy • Gluten Free
Kid Friendly**

Pan-Grilled Chicken with Peach Salsa

With Tomato, Herb, and Baby Lettuce Salad

Fresh peaches are turned into a quick salsa that wakes up chicken breasts. Taste the peaches first, and omit the sugar if the peaches are especially ripe and juicy.

2 tablespoons olive oil
1 teaspoon ground cumin
½ teaspoon kosher salt
**½ teaspoon freshly ground
   black pepper**
2 garlic cloves, grated
**4 (6-ounce) skinless, boneless
   chicken breasts**
Cooking spray
**2¼ cups chopped peeled fresh
   peaches (about 2 large)**
**1 tablespoon finely chopped red
   Fresno chile**
1 tablespoon sugar
**1 tablespoon finely chopped
   fresh mint**
2 teaspoons fresh lemon juice

1. Combine first 5 ingredients in a large bowl; add chicken, turning to coat. Heat a grill pan over medium-high. Coat pan with cooking spray. Add chicken to pan; grill 6 minutes on each side or until done. Remove from pan; let stand 5 minutes.

2. Combine peaches and remaining ingredients in a bowl; serve with chicken. Serves 4 (serving size: 1 chicken breast and about ½ cup relish)

CALORIES 296; FAT 11.1g (sat 2.1g, mono 6.4g, poly 1.7g); PROTEIN 35g; CARB 13g; FIBER 2g; SUGARS 11g (est. added sugars 3g); CHOL 94mg; IRON 2mg; SODIUM 324mg; CALC 31mg

Quick & Easy • Gluten Free
Vegetarian

Tomato, Herb, and Baby Lettuce Salad

Fresh, crunchy, herby, juicy—this salad gets high marks for hitting all kinds of pleasure points. Feel free to use any types of tomatoes you find at your farmers' market.

2 tablespoons extra-virgin olive oil
1½ tablespoons white wine vinegar or fresh lemon juice
1½ teaspoons minced shallot
1 teaspoon Dijon mustard
¼ teaspoon kosher salt
¼ teaspoon black pepper
2 cups halved red cherry tomatoes
1 medium-sized ripe green tomato, sliced
2 cups torn hearts of romaine or Little Gem lettuce leaves
1 cup fresh basil leaves

1. Combine first 6 ingredients in a large bowl, stirring with a whisk. Add cherry tomatoes and green tomato; toss gently to coat. Let stand 5 minutes. Add lettuce and basil; toss gently to combine. Serves 4 (serving size: about 1 cup)

CALORIES 89; FAT 7.1g (sat 1g, mono 6g, poly 0.9g); PROTEIN 2g; CARB 6g; FIBER 2g; SUGARS 4g (est. added sugars 0g); CHOL 0mg; IRON 1mg; SODIUM 160mg; CALC 39mg

READY IN
25
MINUTES

GAME PLAN

While fish and vegetables grill:
- Microwave potatoes.

While potatoes grill:
- Make parsley mixture.

Quick & Easy • Gluten Free
Kid Friendly

Grilled Mahi-Mahi with Lemon-Parsley Potatoes

With Grilled Tomato, Onion, and Olive Salad

Cooking spray
¼ cup extra-virgin olive oil, divided
4 (6-ounce) mahi-mahi fillets, skinned
¾ teaspoon kosher salt, divided
½ teaspoon black pepper
8 medium red potatoes, cut into wedges (about 1 pound)
2 tablespoons water
½ cup chopped green onions
½ cup chopped fresh flat-leaf parsley
1½ tablespoons fresh lemon juice

1. Heat a grill pan over medium-high. Coat pan with cooking spray. Drizzle 1½ teaspoons oil over fish; sprinkle evenly with ½ teaspoon salt and pepper. Add fish to pan; cook 5 minutes on each side or until fish flakes easily when tested with a fork.

2. Place potatoes in a microwave-safe bowl with 2 tablespoons water; cover and microwave at HIGH 2 minutes or until crisp-tender. Combine potatoes, 1½ teaspoons oil, and ¼ teaspoon salt in a bowl; toss. Add

potatoes to grill pan; cook 5 minutes on each side or until tender and grill marks appear. Place in a bowl.

3. Place 3 tablespoons oil, green onions, parsley, and juice in a mini food processor; process until smooth. Add half of parsley mixture to potatoes; toss. Spoon remaining parsley mixture over fish. Serves 4 (serving size: 1 fillet and about ½ cup potatoes)

CALORIES 360; FAT 15.6g (sat 2.3g, mono 11g, poly 1.6g); PROTEIN 34g; CARB 20g; FIBER 3g; SUGARS 2g (est. added sugars 0g); CHOL 124mg; IRON 3mg; SODIUM 536mg; CALC 58mg

Quick & Easy • Gluten Free
Vegetarian

Grilled Tomato, Onion, and Olive Salad

Cooking spray
2 cups cherry tomatoes
2 tablespoons extra-virgin olive oil, divided
1 medium red onion, cut into 1-inch wedges
8 pitted kalamata olives, halved
¼ cup chopped fresh flat-leaf parsley
2 teaspoons red wine vinegar
¼ teaspoon kosher salt
¼ teaspoon black pepper

1. Heat a grill pan over medium-high. Coat pan with cooking spray. Thread tomatoes onto 2 (8-inch) skewers. Drizzle 1 tablespoon oil over tomatoes and onion wedges; add to pan. Cook 4 to 5 minutes on each side or until tomatoes are blistered and onions are lightly charred.

2. Remove tomatoes from skewers; place in a medium bowl. Add onion wedges, remaining 1 tablespoon oil, olives, and remaining ingredients; toss. Serves 4 (serving size: about ¾ cup)

CALORIES 109; FAT 9.1g (sat 1.2g, mono 6.5g, poly 1g); PROTEIN 1g; CARB 7g; FIBER 2g; SUGARS 2g (est. added sugars 0g); CHOL 0mg; IRON 1mg; SODIUM 250mg; CALC 22mg

GAME PLAN

While chicken stands:
- Make dressing for slaw.

While chicken grills:
- Heat potatoes. Finish slaw.

Staff Favorite • Quick & Easy
Gluten Free • Kid Friendly
Make Ahead

Quick BBQ Chicken Thighs with Mashed Potatoes

With Creamy Carrot-and-Broccoli Slaw

A homemade barbecue sauce comes together surprisingly quickly and is a great way to control sodium and added sugar.

1 cup unsalted ketchup
2½ tablespoons light brown sugar
1 tablespoon apple cider vinegar
½ teaspoon black pepper
½ teaspoon dry mustard
¼ teaspoon onion powder
¼ teaspoon garlic powder
1½ pounds skinless, boneless chicken thighs (about 8)
Cooking spray
½ teaspoon kosher salt
2 cups refrigerated prepared mashed potatoes (such as Simply Potatoes)

1. Combine first 7 ingredients in a bowl, stirring with a whisk. Place ½ cup ketchup mixture in a small bowl. Add chicken to remaining ketchup mixture; toss. Let stand 5 minutes.

2. Heat a grill pan over medium-high. Coat pan with cooking spray. Remove chicken from ketchup mixture; discard ketchup mixture. Add chicken to pan; grill 5 minutes on each side or until done, brushing occasionally with reserved ½ cup ketchup mixture. Remove chicken from pan; sprinkle with salt.

3. Heat potatoes according to package directions. Serve with chicken. Serves 4 (serving size: 6 ounces chicken and ½ cup potatoes)

CALORIES 439; FAT 10.8g (sat 4.4g, mono 2.6g, poly 1.6g); PROTEIN 36g; CARB 48g; FIBER 2g; SUGARS 19g (est. added sugars 17g); CHOL 170mg; IRON 2mg; SODIUM 592mg; CALC 39mg

Quick & Easy • Gluten Free
Kid Friendly • Make Ahead
Vegetarian

Creamy Carrot-and-Broccoli Slaw

Prepared slaw mix has gone beyond traditional cabbage to include shaved broccoli and even Brussels sprouts as the base. Broccoli slaw is as endlessly adaptable as any package of mixed greens: Try a creamy yogurt dressing, or opt for a vinaigrette, like sesame-ginger, warm bacon-and-shallot, or curry-and-cumin.

⅓ cup light sour cream
3 tablespoons non-fat buttermilk
2 tablespoons canola mayonnaise
1 tablespoon finely chopped fresh dill
1 tablespoon apple cider vinegar
½ teaspoon black pepper
⅛ teaspoon kosher salt
2 cups matchstick-cut carrots
1 (12-ounce) package broccoli slaw

1. Combine first 7 ingredients in a large bowl, stirring with a whisk. Add carrots and broccoli slaw to sour cream mixture; toss to coat. Serves 4 (serving size: about 1¼ cups)

CALORIES 102; FAT 4.2g (sat 1.4g, mono 1.8g, poly 0.9g); PROTEIN 4g; CARB 13g; FIBER 4g; SUGARS 5g (est. added sugars 0g); CHOL 7mg; IRON 1mg; SODIUM 209mg; CALC 105mg

GAME PLAN

While red onion soaks:
- Cook steak mixture.

While quesadillas cook:
- Make salad.

Quick & Easy • Kid Friendly

Steak, Feta, and Olive Quesadillas

With Cucumber, Onion, and Tomato Salad
(pictured on page 229)

We've given the steak quesadilla a Mediterranean spin with feta cheese, olives, and a dollop of creamy Greek yogurt. Meaty, slightly fruity Castelvetrano olives have less sodium than other olives and add a pretty pop of green. If you can't find them, try swapping in rich kalamata olives.

2 tablespoons extra-virgin olive oil, divided
12 ounces sirloin steak, thinly sliced
1 cup chopped fresh spinach (about 1½ ounces)
1½ ounces ⅓-less-fat cream cheese
1 ounce feta cheese, crumbled (about ¼ cup)
12 Castelvetrano olives, chopped
4 (8-inch) whole-wheat tortillas
¼ cup plain 2% reduced-fat Greek yogurt

1. Heat 1 tablespoon oil in a large skillet over medium-high. Add steak; cook 5 minutes or until browned. Add spinach, cream cheese, feta, and olives; cook 2 minutes. Remove steak mixture from pan.

2. Wipe pan clean with paper towels. Spoon about ⅓ cup steak mixture evenly over half of each tortilla. Fold tortillas in half over filling. Add 1½ teaspoons oil to pan. Place 2 quesadillas in pan; cook 3 minutes on each side or until browned. Repeat procedure with remaining 1½ teaspoons oil and remaining 2 quesadillas. Cut each quesadilla into 4 wedges. Serve with yogurt. Serves 4 (serving size: 4 wedges and 1 tablespoon yogurt)

CALORIES 346; FAT 18.2g (sat 5.4g, mono 10.2g, poly 1.3g); PROTEIN 23g; CARB 20g; FIBER 1g; SUGARS 1g (est. added sugars 0g); CHOL 59mg; IRON 2mg; SODIUM 672mg; CALC 118mg

Quick & Easy • Gluten Free
Kid Friendly • Vegetarian

Cucumber, Onion, and Tomato Salad

This simple, refreshing combo will never go out of style. Soaking the sliced red onion in cold water mellows its pungent bite.

1 cup thinly sliced red onion
2 cups cherry tomatoes, halved
2 cups English cucumber, sliced and seeded
2 tablespoons red wine vinegar
2 tablespoons extra-virgin olive oil
¼ cup chopped fresh parsley
¼ teaspoon kosher salt

1. Place sliced onion in a bowl; cover with cold water. Let stand 10 minutes; drain. Place onion in a medium bowl. Add tomatoes and remaining ingredients; toss. Serves 4 (serving size: 1 cup)

CALORIES 95; FAT 7g (sat 1g, mono 5g, poly 0.8g); PROTEIN 1g; CARB 8g; FIBER 2g; SUGARS 4g (est. added sugars 0g); CHOL 0mg; IRON 1mg; SODIUM 129mg; CALC 28mg

SUPERFAST 20-MINUTE COOKING

Staff Favorite • Quick & Easy
Kid Friendly • Make Ahead

Green Gazpacho with Shrimp

1½ cups plain low-fat yogurt (not Greek-style)
¼ cup olive oil, divided
2 tablespoons fresh lime juice
¾ cup coarsely chopped seeded poblano chile
½ cup coarsely chopped green onions
3 ounces whole-wheat bread, crusts removed and torn into bite-sized pieces (about 2 cups)
2 cups chopped seeded English cucumber
½ teaspoon sugar
½ teaspoon kosher salt
½ teaspoon black pepper
4 large tomatillos, husks removed, rinsed, and quartered (about 1 pound)
1 pound medium shrimp, peeled and deveined

1. Combine yogurt, 3 tablespoons oil, and juice in a large bowl, stirring with a whisk. Stir in poblano, green onions, and bread; let stand 10 minutes, stirring occasionally. Place yogurt mixture in a blender with cucumber, sugar, salt, black pepper, and tomatillos; blend until smooth.
2. Heat 1 teaspoon oil in a large nonstick skillet over medium-high. Add shrimp to pan; cook 3 to 5 minutes or until done. Place 1¾ cups cucumber mixture in each of 4 bowls; top evenly with shrimp and remaining 2 teaspoons oil. Serves 4

CALORIES 352; FAT 18g (sat 3.2g, mono 10.6g, poly 2.3g); PROTEIN 24g; CARB 26g; FIBER 4g; SUGARS 13g (est. added sugars 1g); CHOL 148mg; IRON 2mg; SODIUM 542mg; CALC 280mg

Quick & Easy • Gluten Free
Kid Friendly • Make Ahead

Chicken Thighs with Peperonata and Roasted Broccoli

1 tablespoon olive oil, divided
4 (6-ounce) bone-in, skin-on chicken thighs
¾ teaspoon kosher salt, divided
¾ teaspoon black pepper, divided
1 (12-ounce) package fresh broccoli florets
1½ cups thinly sliced yellow onion
1 cup thinly sliced red bell pepper
1 cup thinly sliced yellow bell pepper
1 tablespoon thinly sliced garlic
1 tablespoon chopped fresh thyme
1 teaspoon anchovy paste
¼ cup unsalted chicken stock
1 tablespoon balsamic vinegar

1. Preheat oven to 425°F.
2. Heat 1½ teaspoons oil in a large skillet over medium-high. Sprinkle chicken with ½ teaspoon salt and ½ teaspoon black pepper. Add chicken to pan; cook 3 minutes on each side or until browned. Place, skin side up, on one side of a rimmed baking sheet.
3. Combine remaining 1½ teaspoons oil, remaining ¼ teaspoon salt, remaining ¼ teaspoon pepper, and broccoli; add to other side of pan with chicken. Bake at 425°F for 10 minutes or until chicken is done.
4. Return skillet to medium-high. Add onion and bell peppers; sauté 3 minutes. Stir in garlic, thyme, and anchovy paste; cook 1 minute. Stir in stock, scraping pan to loosen browned bits. Stir in vinegar. Serve with chicken and broccoli. Serves 4 (serving size: 1 chicken thigh, ½ cup broccoli, and ⅓ cup pepper mixture)

CALORIES 434; FAT 20.3g (sat 7.1g, mono 12.5g, poly 5.6g); PROTEIN 29g; CARB 17g; FIBER 5g; SUGARS 6g (est. added sugars 0g); CHOL 142mg; IRON 2mg; SODIUM 604mg; CALC 81mg

Peach-Glazed Pork Tenderloin

A sweet and savory peach glaze caramelizes on the pork as it cooks to perfection in a grill pan. We cut the tenderloin in half crosswise for easier maneuvering and faster cooking, and we tent the pork with foil to hold in more heat while it's in the pan. You could also use a cast-iron skillet if you don't have a grill pan.

Cooking spray
1 tablespoon olive oil
1 (1-pound) pork tenderloin, trimmed and cut in half crosswise
3 tablespoons peach preserves
1 tablespoon reduced-sodium soy sauce
1½ teaspoons white wine vinegar
1 garlic clove, grated
½ teaspoon sea salt or flaked salt
½ teaspoon freshly ground black pepper

1. Heat a grill pan over medium-high. Coat pan with cooking spray. Rub oil over pork. Add pork to pan; loosely tent pork with foil. Grill 10 minutes, turning occasionally.
2. While pork cooks, combine peach preserves, soy sauce, vinegar, and garlic in a microwave-safe bowl. Microwave at HIGH 30 seconds or until preserves melt. Grill pork 6 minutes more, or until thermometer registers 145°F, turning and brushing frequently with peach glaze. Remove pork from pan; let stand 3 minutes. Cut pork crosswise into slices. Sprinkle evenly with salt and pepper. Serves 4 (serving size: 3 ounces)

CALORIES 237; FAT 10.1g (sat 2.9g, mono 5.2g, poly 1g); PROTEIN 25g; CARB 10g; FIBER 0g; SUGARS 9g (est. added sugars 7g); CHOL 78mg; IRON 1mg; SODIUM 487mg; CALC 8mg

Breakfast Bowl with Tomato, Avocado, and Egg

This is the kind of breakfast that's worth waking up for—and enjoying again for lunch or dinner. If you want a starchy component, add precooked farro or quinoa.

3 bacon slices
3 tablespoons apple cider vinegar
2 tablespoons extra-virgin olive oil, divided
1 tablespoon water
¼ cup whole-wheat panko (Japanese breadcrumbs)
2 teaspoons chopped fresh basil
½ teaspoon kosher salt, divided
2 (8-ounce) tomatoes, halved
4 large eggs
4 cups packed baby spinach leaves
2 ripe avocados, halved and sliced
¼ teaspoon black pepper

1. Preheat broiler to high with oven rack in middle position.
2. Cook bacon in a nonstick skillet over medium-high 5 minutes or until crisp. Remove from pan; crumble. Add vinegar, 1 teaspoon oil, and 1 tablespoon water to drippings in pan. Cook 30 seconds, scraping pan to loosen browned bits. Place vinegar mixture in a small bowl (do not wipe out pan).
3. Combine 2 teaspoons oil, panko, basil, and ¼ teaspoon salt in a bowl. Place tomato halves, cut side up, on a rimmed baking sheet; top with panko mixture. Broil 2 minutes or until surface is browned.
4. Heat remaining 1 tablespoon oil in skillet over medium-high. Crack eggs over pan; cook 2 minutes or until whites are set.
5. Divide spinach among 4 shallow bowls; top evenly with tomato halves, avocado slices, eggs, and bacon. Drizzle vinegar mixture over top.

Sprinkle remaining ¼ teaspoon salt and pepper over eggs. Serves 4

CALORIES 383; FAT 31.1g (sat 6.8g, mono 17.6g, poly 4.3g); PROTEIN 13g; CARB 16g; FIBER 7g; SUGARS 4g (est. added sugars 0g); CHOL 200mg; IRON 3mg; SODIUM 491mg; CALC 81mg

Watermelon-Tomato Salad

1 tablespoon white balsamic vinegar
1 tablespoon extra-virgin olive oil
¼ teaspoon kosher salt
¼ teaspoon black pepper
1 cup halved cherry tomatoes
1 cup baby arugula
¼ cup thinly vertically sliced red onion
¼ cup fresh mint leaves
12 ounces seedless watermelon, cut into thin triangle slices
1 ounce pecorino Romano cheese, shaved

1. Whisk together first 4 ingredients in a large bowl. Add tomatoes and remaining ingredients; toss gently. Serves 4 (serving size: 1 cup)

CALORIES 99; FAT 5.5g (sat 1.7g, mono 3.1g, poly 0.5g); PROTEIN 3g; CARB 10g; FIBER 1g; SUGARS 8g (est. added sugars 0g); CHOL 7mg; IRON 0mg; SODIUM 226mg; CALC 95mg

Cornmeal Waffles with Fresh Blueberry Compote

Whole buttermilk is the key to fluffy, tender cornmeal waffles. For an even quicker a.m. meal, make the batter the night before.

1 cup fresh blueberries
3 tablespoons sugar, divided
1 tablespoon water
1 tablespoon thinly sliced fresh basil
3 ounces white whole-wheat flour (about ¾ cup)
¾ cup finely ground yellow cornmeal
2 teaspoons baking powder
1½ cups whole buttermilk
2 large eggs, lightly beaten
Cooking spray

1. Bring blueberries, 2 tablespoons sugar, and 1 tablespoon water to a simmer in a small saucepan over medium-high; cook 8 minutes or until thickened. Stir in basil.
2. Heat waffle iron to medium-high. Weigh or lightly spoon flour into a dry measuring cup; level with a knife. Combine flour, cornmeal, and baking powder in a bowl. Combine remaining 1 tablespoon sugar, buttermilk, and eggs in a bowl. Add flour mixture to buttermilk mixture, stirring until just combined.
3. Coat waffle iron with cooking spray. Spoon ⅓ cup batter per waffle onto iron. Cook 4 minutes or until lightly browned; repeat with remaining batter. Serve with compote. Serves 4 (serving size: 2 waffles and about 2 tablespoons compote)

CALORIES 305; **FAT** 6.7g (sat 2.7g, mono 1.9g, poly 1.1g); **PROTEIN** 11g; **CARB** 50g; **FIBER** 5g; **SUGARS** 18g (est. added sugars 9g); **CHOL** 103mg; **IRON** 3mg; **SODIUM** 385mg; **CALC** 274mg

Seared Salmon Salad with Beets and Blackberries

3 tablespoons olive oil, divided
4 (6-ounce) salmon fillets
¾ teaspoon kosher salt, divided
½ teaspoon black pepper, divided
2 (6-ounce) golden beets, peeled and cut into ½-inch wedges
¼ cup water
1 tablespoon white balsamic vinegar
½ teaspoon grated lime rind
2 teaspoons fresh lime juice
1 (5-ounce) package mixed baby greens
1 cup fresh blackberries, halved
¼ cup torn fresh mint

1. Heat 1½ teaspoons oil in a large nonstick skillet over medium. Sprinkle fillets with ½ teaspoon salt and ¼ teaspoon pepper. Add fillets, skin side down, to pan; cook 4 minutes on each side or until done. Remove from pan.
2. Place beets and ¼ cup water in a microwave-safe bowl; cover with plastic wrap. Microwave at HIGH 6 minutes or until tender. Drain.
3. Whisk together remaining 2½ tablespoons of the oil, remaining ¼ teaspoon of the salt, remaining ¼ teaspoon of the pepper, vinegar, rind, and juice in a small bowl. Combine beets, greens, blackberries, and mint in a large bowl. Add vinegar mixture; toss. Place 2 cups salad on each of 4 plates; top each serving with 1 fillet. Serves 4

CALORIES 397; **FAT** 20g (sat 3.5g, mono 10.6g, poly 4.6g); **PROTEIN** 39g; **CARB** 15g; **FIBER** 5g; **SUGARS** 8g (est. added sugars 0g); **CHOL** 90mg; **IRON** 4mg; **SODIUM** 539mg; **CALC** 80mg

Quick Mongolian Beef Stir-Fry

Hands-on: 15 min. Total: 20 min.
Make this version of the takeout classic in a flash—no special equipment required.

2 tablespooons canola oil, divided
12-ounce flank steak, thinly sliced
½ teaspoon black pepper
¼ teaspoon kosher salt
¼ cup dark brown sugar
3 tablespoons reduced-sodium soy sauce
2 tablespoons unseasoned rice vinegar
3 cups fresh broccoli florets
3 cups sliced red bell peppers (about 2 medium)
2 cups hot cooked brown rice
½ cup chopped green onions (green parts only)

1. Heat 1 tablespoon oil in a large skillet over high. Sprinkle steak with black pepper and salt. Add steak to pan; cook 5 minutes or until browned, stirring occasionally. Remove steak from pan (do not wipe out pan).
2. Combine sugar, soy sauce, and vinegar in a small bowl. Add remaining 1 tablespoon oil, broccoli, and bell peppers to pan; cover, and cook 2 minutes. Uncover pan; add soy sauce mixture.
3. Cook 6 minutes or until vegetables are crisp-tender and liquid reduces by about half. Add steak; cook 1 minute. Place rice on each of 4 plates; top with beef mixture and green onions. Serves 4 (serving size: about 1¼ cups beef mixture and ½ cup rice)

CALORIES 394; **FAT** 13g (sat 2.5g, mono 6.4g, poly 2.6g); **PROTEIN** 25g; **CARB** 45g; **FIBER** 6g; **SUGARS** 16g (est. added sugars 12g); **CHOL** 53mg; **IRON** 3mg; **SODIUM** 634mg; **CALC** 87mg

SIMPLE, ELEGANT CRAB PASTA

Sweet crabmeat, sautéed fennel, and lots of herbs create a fresh and easy dish.

Quick & Easy • Kid Friendly

Crab, Fennel, and Basil Spaghetti

Hands-on: 20 min. Total: 20 min.
Because this is light and delicately flavored, it's perfect for warm weather. Feel free to "back pocket" your way with it, subbing shrimp or flaky white fish for the crab and using tarragon, chives, or chervil.

8 ounces uncooked spaghetti
2 tablespoons olive oil
1½ cups sliced cored fennel bulb (about 1 medium)
1 teaspoon crushed red pepper
¼ teaspoon kosher salt
2 garlic cloves, thinly sliced
12 ounces fresh lump crabmeat, picked
5 tablespoons chopped fresh flat-leaf parsley, divided
2 tablespoons thinly sliced fresh basil
2 tablespoons chopped fresh mint
4 lemon wedges

1. Cook pasta according to package directions, omitting fat and salt. Drain pasta over a bowl, reserving ¾ cup pasta cooking liquid for the sauce.
2. Heat oil in a large skillet over medium. Add fennel; sauté 7 minutes. Add crushed red pepper, salt, and garlic; cook 1 minute. Add crab; cook 2 minutes, stirring occasionally. Add pasta and reserved ¾ cup pasta cooking liquid; toss to coat. Stir in 3 tablespoons parsley.
3. Divide pasta mixture among 4 bowls; top evenly with remaining 2

tablespoons parsley, basil, and mint. Serve with lemon wedges. Serves 4 (serving size: 1¾ cups)

CALORIES 354; **FAT** 9.4g (sat 1.1g, mono 5.1g, poly 1.1g); **PROTEIN** 20g; **CARB** 48g; **FIBER** 4g; **SUGARS** 4g (est. added sugars 0g); **CHOL** 76mg; **IRON** 3mg; **SODIUM** 605mg; **CALC** 82mg

10-MINUTE SALMON TARTINES

Elevate your avocado toast with silky smoked salmon for a brag-worthy lunch.

Quick & Easy • Kid Friendly

Avocado-and-Pea Salmon Tartines

Hands-on: 10 min. Total: 10 min.
This recipe delivers a double dose of heart-healthy unsaturated fats from both salmon and avocado, plus 35% of your daily fiber goal. Look for salmon that's labeled "wild Alaskan" to be sure you're getting sustainable seafood.

2 ripe avocados, peeled and seeded
¾ cup frozen green peas, thawed
1 tablespoon fresh lemon juice
1 tablespoon chopped fresh mint
¼ teaspoon kosher salt
¼ teaspoon black pepper
8 (1½-ounce) whole-grain bread slices, toasted
8 thin smoked salmon slices (about 8 ounces)
⅓ cup very thinly sliced radishes (about 4 radishes)
1 tablespoon olive oil
Fresh mint leaves

1. Place avocados and peas in a bowl. Using a fork, thoroughly mash. Add lemon juice, chopped mint, salt, and pepper; stir well.

2. Spread ¼ cup avocado mixture on one side of each bread slice; top each with 1 smoked salmon slice. Arrange radish slices evenly over salmon slices; drizzle with olive oil. Garnish with fresh mint leaves. Serves 4 (serving size: 2 tartines)

CALORIES 399; **FAT** 20.5g (sat 3.3g, mono 11.5g, poly 4.5g); **PROTEIN** 23g; **CARB** 33g; **FIBER** 10g; **SUGARS** 5g (est. added sugars 0g); **CHOL** 0mg; **IRON** 3mg; **SODIUM** 355mg; **CALC** 106mg

THE GOLDEN RUM RATIO

Barbados, the Caribbean birthplace of rum, has a rum punch recipe as foolproof as it is versatile: "One of sour, two of sweet, three of strong, and four of weak." In our take, fruit juice and ginger ale serve as both sweet and weak.

Quick & Easy • Gluten Free
Make Ahead • Vegetarian

Barbados Rum Punch

Hands-on: 5 min. Total: 5 min.

¼ cup gold rum (such as Mount Gay)
⅔ cup pineapple-coconut juice (such as R. W. Knudsen)
¼ cup fresh lime juice
6 tablespoons ginger ale
Fresh lime or pineapple slices (optional)

1. Combine first 3 ingredients in a pitcher, stirring until sugar dissolves. Cover, and chill until ready to serve.
2. Divide rum mixture among 4 ice-filled glasses. Stir 1½ tablespoons ginger ale into each serving. Garnish with fresh lime or pineapple slices, if desired. Serves 4 (serving size: about ⅔ cup)

CALORIES 137; **FAT** 0.2g (sat 0.1g, mono 0g, poly 0g); **PROTEIN** 0g; **CARB** 10g; **FIBER** 0g; **SUGARS** 9g (est. added sugars 4g); **CHOL** 0mg; **IRON** 0mg; **SODIUM** 6mg; **CALC** 9mg

Maple-Mustard
Roasted Chicken
With Squash and
Brussels Sprouts,
page 36

**Creamy Carrot
and Herb Linguine,**
page 40

**Wilted Chard
with Red Onion
and Pine Nuts,**
page 41

Turkey and Swiss Sloppy Joes,
page 46

BBQ Beef-Stuffed Potatoes,
page 47

Pumpkin Soup with Almonds and Sage,
page 44

Caesar-Crusted Chicken Salad,
page 71

Sausage and
Broccoli Rabe
Flatbreads,
page 70

**Rich Dark Chocolate
Smoothie,**
page 62

Chicken Piccata with Crispy Garlic, *page 73*

Matcha-Glazed Donuts,
page 56

Broccoli, Cheddar, and Brown Rice Cakes,
page 87

Spinach, Cheese, and Bacon Bread Puddings,
page 88

Banana-Bacon-Nut Toast,
page 52

Herbed Ricotta, Asparagus, and Phyllo Tart, *page 82*

**Browned Butter
Carrot Cake with
Toasted Pecans,**
page 82

Honey-Baked Pork Roast,
page 81

Beer-Brushed Tofu Skewers with Barley,
page 114

Chicken-and-Vegetable Hand Pies,
page 94

Honey-Dijon Chicken Paillards with Zucchini Slaw,
page 122

Lentil-Tahini Burgers with Pickled Cabbage,
page 102

**Esquites
(Corn Salad),**
page 99

**Creamy
Poblano Tacos,**
page 100

Pork Loin Stuffed with Spinach and Goat Cheese, *page 124*

Peach-Thyme Galette,
page 133

Mini Mozzarella-and-Kale Pita Pizzas,
page 122

Cantaloupe-White Balsamic Sorbet,
page 134

Minestrone Verde,
page 128

Blackened Grouper Sandwiches with Rémoulade,
page 149

**BBQ Chicken-and-
Black Bean Tacos,**
page 150

Honeydew–
Jalapeño
Margaritas,
page 129

225

Egg-in-a-Nest BLT Sandwiches,
page 176

Sweet-and-Sour Cherry Tartlets,
page 167

Sun Gold Tomato Caprese Salad,
page 178

Watermelon Granita with Hibiscus Syrup and Yogurt,
page 201

**Grill-Steamed
Corn with Cilantro
and Chile Powder**
page 157

**Grilled Chicken Drumsticks
with Bourbon-Cherry BBQ
Sauce,**
page 167

**Steak, Feta, and
Olive Quesadillas,**
page 204

Egg Foo Yong with Mushroom Sauce, *page 189*

**Triple Melon
Cream Pops,**
page 241

**Family-Style
Meatball "Fondue,"**
page 256

Cheesy Chicken-
and-Spinach
Stromboli Ring,
page 253

Chicken Potpie Skillet Pizza,
page 348

Maple-Bacon Baked Beans,
page 283

Slow-Cooked BBQ Pork Roast,
page 294

Celery, Apple, and Almond Salad,
page 296

Mummy
Buckeyes,
page 281

**Apple Spice
Bundt Cake with
Cider Glaze,**

page 318

Mussels with Buttery Turmeric Broth,
page 316

Herbed Whole-Grain Yeast Rolls,
page 309

Acorn Squash with Wild Rice Stuffing,
page 307

Maple-Caraway Brussels Sprouts,
page 312

Herb, Lemon, and Garlic Turkey,
page 308

Tricolor Beet-and-
Carrot Salad,
page 313

Salted Caramel
Apple Pie,
page 315

USE YOUR MELON

Turn the bumper crop of peak-season melon into crowd-pleasing cream pops. Floral honeydew, musky cantaloupe, and candy-sweet watermelon provide dazzling pastel colors, while a bit of yogurt lends creamy appeal.

Gluten Free • Kid Friendly Make Ahead • Freezable Vegetarian

Triple Melon Cream Pops

(pictured on page 231)

Hands-on: 17 min. Total: 6 hr. 17 min.

2 cups cubed seedless red watermelon
1 tablespoon sugar
6 tablespoons plain whole-milk Greek yogurt
1 tablespoon fresh lemon juice
3 dashes kosher salt
2 cups cubed honeydew melon
2 cups cubed cantaloupe melon
16 craft sticks

1. Process watermelon, 1 teaspoon sugar, 2 tablespoons yogurt, 1 teaspoon juice, and 1 dash salt in a blender until smooth. Pour into a pitcher; rinse blender. Repeat with honeydew; the same amounts of sugar, yogurt, juice, and salt; and a separate pitcher. Repeat with cantaloupe; remaining sugar, yogurt, juice, and salt; and a third pitcher.
2. Fill bottom third of 16 ice-pop molds with watermelon mixture. Freeze 2 hours or until solid. Fill middle third of molds with honeydew mixture. Freeze 1 hour or until surface is frozen. Insert craft sticks in molds through honeydew layer; freeze 1 hour or until solid. Fill top third with cantaloupe mixture. Freeze until solid. Serves 16 (serving size: 1 ice pop)

CALORIES 30; FAT 0.6g (sat 0.4g, mono 0g, poly 0g); PROTEIN 1g; CARB 6g; FIBER 0g; SUGARS 5g (est. added sugars 1g); CHOL 1mg; IRON 0mg; SODIUM 31mg; CALC 9mg

PESTO PASTA, PRESTO!

Bay Area über-chef Chris Cosentino makes hearty, healthy kale pesto the star of a quick and simple dinner fave.

CL: What makes this dish a home-cooked staple for you?
CC: This dish is very quick and easy to make, and it resonates with everybody. I chose kale here because I wanted something healthy in the pesto but super-flavorful. When you have beautiful lacinato kale available, it's a great gift. It's nutrient-dense, and holds up to high-heat cooking.

CL: Why do you blanch the kale first instead of using the raw leaves?
CC: Blanching helps tenderize it so you don't get fibrous pesto. It also allows the flavor to be really clean so the pesto keeps its integrity.

CL: Why add cheese at the end?
CC: At the restaurant, we actually keep both the cheese and nuts out of the pesto until the end so we can make the dish nut- and dairy-free if needed. You can do the same at home and customize it to anyone's needs or tastes.

Vegetarian

Rigatoni with Kale Pesto

Hands-on: 22 min. Total: 34 min.
Whole-wheat pasta would be a tasty option here.

2 bunches lacinato kale, stemmed
2 tablespoons pine nuts, toasted
2 garlic cloves, chopped
½ cup extra-virgin olive oil
1 tablespoon freshly grated lemon rind
2 ounces fresh pecorino Romano cheese, finely grated (about ½ cup)
½ teaspoon kosher salt
½ teaspoon freshly ground black pepper
Dash of Aleppo pepper (optional)
1 pound rigatoni pasta

1. Bring a large pot of water to a boil. Fill a large bowl with ice water. Working in two or three batches, submerge kale in boiling water for 15 seconds until wilted and deep green; remove, and immediately plunge into ice water for 15 seconds. Drain kale well; place on layers of paper towels, and press to remove excess liquid. Place kale, pine nuts, and garlic in a food processor or blender. Pulse until coarsely chopped. Slowly add oil with motor running; blend until pesto is smooth. Place pesto in a medium bowl; stir in rind, cheese, salt, and peppers.
2. Cook pasta according to package instructions, omitting salt and fat. When pasta is al dente, drain, reserving 1 cup pasta cooking liquid. Return pasta to pan over medium-low heat; stir in pesto. Add pasta cooking liquid, 1 tablespoon at a time, until sauce reaches desired consistency. Serves 8 (serving size: about 1 cup)

CALORIES 424; FAT 23.2g (sat 4.7g, mono 14.4g, poly 1.7g); PROTEIN 10g; CARB 44g; FIBER 3g; SUGARS 3g (added sugars 0g); CHOL 8mg; IRON 2mg; SODIUM 508mg; CALC 100mg

OUR FRESHEST SUMMER SOUP

Put your farmers' market haul to delicious use in this satisfying vegetarian main.

Quick & Easy • Gluten Free
Kid Friendly • Vegetarian
Freezable

Silky Tomato-Basil Soup with Fresh Corn

Hands-on: 25 min. Total: 25 min.
Silken tofu stands in for traditional heavy cream, lending rich body and a hit of quality protein.

- **¹/₂ cup plus 3 tablespoons extra-virgin olive oil, divided**
- **2 (8-ounce) containers prechopped onion**
- **3 garlic cloves, smashed**
- **¹/₂ cup unsalted tomato paste**
- **2¹/₂ pounds chopped fresh tomatoes**
- **³/₄ cup unsalted vegetable stock (such as Swanson)**
- **2 teaspoons kosher salt**
- **1¹/₄ teaspoons black pepper**
- **1 cup chopped fresh basil leaves, divided**
- **1 (16-ounce) package silken tofu, drained**
- **2¹/₂ cups chopped heirloom tomatoes (about 1¹/₄ pounds)**
- **1¹/₂ cups fresh corn kernels (about 3 ears)**
- **6 tablespoons red wine vinegar**

1. Heat 3 tablespoons oil in a large saucepan over medium-high. Add onion and garlic; cook 5 minutes, stirring frequently, until softened. Add tomato paste; cook 1 minute, stirring constantly. Remove from heat; stir in 2½ pounds chopped tomatoes, stock, salt, pepper, and ½ cup basil.
2. Transfer half of tomato mixture to a blender. Process 1 minute or until smooth. Pour pureed tomato mixture into a bowl. Transfer remaining tomato mixture to blender; process 1 minute or until smooth. With blender running, add ¼ cup oil in a slow, steady stream, processing until smooth. If freezing, follow freezing instructions. If using immediately, add tofu to tomato mixture in blender; process until smooth.
3. Return pureed tomato mixture and pureed tomato-tofu mixture to pan; bring to a simmer, and cook, stirring often, until heated through.
4. Combine heirloom tomatoes, corn, vinegar, and remaining ½ cup basil in a bowl. Ladle soup into each of 8 bowls. Top with corn mixture; drizzle remaining ¼ cup olive oil evenly over top. Serves 8 (serving size: 1 cup soup, ⅓ cup corn mixture, and about 1½ teaspoons oil)

CALORIES 305; **FAT** 21.4g (sat 2.9g, mono 15g, poly 2.1g); **PROTEIN** 7g; **CARB** 23g; **FIBER** 5g; **SUGARS** 12g (est. added sugars 0g); **CHOL** 0mg; **IRON** 2mg; **SODIUM** 518mg; **CALC** 85mg

HOW TO

FREEZE
Combine pureed tomato mixtures. Freeze in a large ziplock plastic freezer bag up to 2 months.

THAW
Microwave soup in freezer bag on MEDIUM (50% power) 8 minutes or until thawed.

REHEAT
Place half of soup in a blender. Add tofu; process until smooth. Combine with remaining soup in a saucepan; simmer until heated through. Proceed with step 4.

COOK ONCE, EAT 3X

Grill a few extra patties tonight, and then crumble them over a crisp salad and fold into a cheesy nacho dip during the week.

Kid Friendly • Make Ahead

Smoky Caramelized Onion Burgers

Hands-on: 25 min. Total: 45 min.
Sometimes we want our grilled beef patties to have just a little more oomph. These burgers deliver exactly that and more. Caramelized onions and garlic go into the ground sirloin mixture to keep the burgers moist, followed by a bold hit of ground cumin and smoked paprika for a jolt of flavor.

Patties:
- **1 tablespoon olive oil**
- **3 cups thinly sliced yellow onion**
- **2¹/₂ tablespoons minced fresh garlic**
- **1 tablespoon ground cumin**
- **2 teaspoons smoked paprika**
- **1¹/₂ teaspoons kosher salt**
- **1 teaspoon freshly ground black pepper**
- **2 pounds 90% lean ground sirloin**
- **Cooking spray**

Burgers:
- **2 tablespoons canola mayonnaise**
- **2 tablespoons finely chopped bottled roasted red bell pepper**
- **1 tablespoon minced fresh chives**
- **4 (1¹/₄-ounce) whole-wheat hamburger buns, split and toasted**
- **4 (¹/₂-inch-thick) tomato slices**
- **2 red onion slices, separated into rings**
- **1 cup baby arugula leaves (1 ounce)**

1. To prepare patties, preheat grill to medium-high (about 450°F). **2.** Heat oil in large nonstick skillet over medium. Add yellow onion; sauté 8 minutes or until deep golden-brown. Stir in garlic; cook 1 to 2 minutes or until fragrant. Remove pan from heat; let cool, and then chop onion mixture. **3.** Combine onion mixture, cumin, paprika, salt, black pepper, and beef in a large bowl. Divide and shape beef mixture into 8 (1-inch-thick) patties. Press an indentation into the center of each patty with your thumb. **4.** Coat grill grate with cooking spray; place on grill. Place patties on grill grate; cook 3 to 4 minutes on each side for medium-rare or until desired degree of doneness. Reserve 4 cooked patties for Recipes 2 and 3. **5.** To prepare burgers, combine mayonnaise, bell pepper, and chives in a bowl. Place remaining 4 patties on bottom halves of buns; top evenly with tomato, red onion, arugula, mayonnaise mixture, and top halves of buns. Serves 4 (serving size: 1 burger)

CALORIES 385; **FAT** 17.4g (sat 5.1g, mono 7.7g, poly 2.3g); **PROTEIN** 28g; **CARB** 30g; **FIBER** 5g; **SUGARS** 7g (est. added sugars 2g); **CHOL** 74mg; **IRON** 4mg; **SODIUM** 728mg; **CALC** 99mg

SHOP SMARTER

Know your beef: Affordable, versatile, and nutritious (delivering key nutrients like iron, phosphorus, and zinc), ground beef has truly earned its coveted spot in our kitchens and on our grills. But if you're shopping with nutrition in mind, beef labels at the meat counter can be confusing. Let's decode them.

LEAN GROUND SIRLOIN Contains 10% fat by weight (51% of calories come from fat) and is what we suggest for the recipes on this page.

GROUND ROUND This cut weighs in at about 10% to 15% fat.

GROUND CHUCK Delivers anywhere from 15% to 30% fat.

Quick & Easy

Thai Beef-and-Cabbage Salad

Hands-on: 20 min. Total: 20 min.
This refreshing Southeast Asian salad, also called larb, is a great use for leftover burgers.

½ cup fresh lime juice
2 tablespoons light brown sugar
2 teaspoons fish sauce
1½ teaspoons Sriracha chili sauce
2 tablespoons olive oil, divided
2 cooked ground beef patties (from Recipe 1), finely crumbled
1 (8-ounce) package microwave-in-bag haricots verts (French green beans)
6 cups thinly sliced napa cabbage
¼ cup thinly sliced green onions
1 red Fresno chile, thinly sliced
¼ cup chopped roasted unsalted peanuts
4 lime wedges

1. Combine first 4 ingredients in a small bowl, stirring with a whisk. Place 6 tablespoons juice mixture in a small bowl; reserve. **2.** Heat 1 tablespoon oil in a large skillet over high. Add crumbled patties to pan; cook 2 to 3 minutes or until thoroughly heated and slightly crisp. Add remaining juice mixture to pan; cook 1 to 2 minutes or until liquid is absorbed. **3.** Cook haricots verts according to package directions; cut into 1-inch pieces. Combine haricots verts, cabbage, and green onions in a bowl. Add remaining 1 tablespoon oil to reserved 6 tablespoons juice mixture. Divide cabbage mixture among 4 plates; top evenly with beef, Fresno chile, peanuts, and juice mixture. Serve with lime wedges. Serves 4 (serving size: about 2 cups)

CALORIES 322; **FAT** 18.2g (sat 4g, mono 10.3g, poly 2g); **PROTEIN** 17g; **CARB** 25g; **FIBER** 5g; **SUGARS** 13g (est. added sugars 6g); **CHOL** 37mg; **IRON** 3mg; **SODIUM** 516mg; **CALC** 122mg

---

Staff Favorite • Quick & Easy
Kid Friendly

Skillet Nacho Dip

Hands-on: 20 min. Total: 20 min.
Our favorite parts of cheesy queso dip and loaded beef nachos meld into an epic dish.

1 teaspoon olive oil
¾ cup chopped red onion, divided
2 tablespoons seeded minced jalapeño
1½ tablespoons all-purpose flour
2 teaspoons ground cumin
2 teaspoons chili powder
⅔ cup unsalted beef stock
2 cooked ground beef patties (from Recipe 1), finely crumbled
1 cup drained unsalted canned pinto beans
2 ounces preshredded part-skim mozzarella cheese (about ½ cup)
2 ounces preshredded 2% reduced-fat Mexican-blend cheese (about ½ cup)
½ cup chopped tomato
½ cup chopped avocado
2½ cups baked tortilla chips

1. Preheat broiler with oven rack in upper middle position. **2.** Heat oil in a large cast-iron skillet over medium-high. Add ½ cup onion and jalapeño to pan; sauté 4 minutes or until tender. Add flour, cumin, and chili powder; cook 1 minute, stirring constantly. Add stock; bring to a boil. Reduce heat to medium, and stir in crumbled beef patties and beans; cook 2 minutes. Stir in mozzarella; cook 1 minute or until cheese is melted. Remove pan from heat. **3.** Sprinkle Mexican-blend cheese over pan; broil 1 minute or until cheese is melted. Sprinkle remaining ¼ cup red onion, tomato, and avocado over pan. Serve with chips. Serves 4 (serving size: ½ cup dip and about ⅔ cup chips)

CALORIES 385; **FAT** 18.2g (sat 6.5g, mono 8g, poly 1.7g); **PROTEIN** 25g; **CARB** 31g; **FIBER** 7g; **SUGARS** 3g (est. added sugars 0g); **CHOL** 54mg; **IRON** 3mg; **SODIUM** 561mg; **CALC** 327mg

SWEET AND SAUCY CHICKEN SANDWICHES

For slow-simmered flavor without the hassle, reach for your handy slow cooker.

Kid Friendly • Make Ahead

Habanero-Apricot Chicken Sandwiches

Hands-on: 20 min.
Total: 5 hr. 20 min.
Habaneros contain more capsaicin (the compound that contributes spicy heat) than jalapeños, but removing the seeds and membranes lessens that heat considerably.

Cooking spray
2 pounds boneless, skinless chicken thighs
1/3 cup apricot preserves
1 tablespoon Dijon mustard
2 teaspoons reduced-sodium Worcestershire sauce
2 tablespoons plus 1 teaspoon minced habanero chiles (seeds and membranes removed), divided
1 tablespoon apple cider vinegar, divided
1/2 teaspoon kosher salt, divided
1/2 teaspoon black pepper, divided
2 garlic cloves, minced
2 cups very thinly sliced cored red cabbage
1 cup matchstick-cut carrots
1/2 cup thinly sliced radishes
1/3 cup chopped fresh basil
1 tablespoon raw sunflower seeds
2 tablespoons fresh lime juice
1 tablespoon olive oil
1 tablespoon cornstarch
1 tablespoon water
6 whole-wheat hamburger buns, lightly toasted

1. Coat a 5- to 6-quart slow cooker with cooking spray; place chicken in bottom of slow cooker.
2. Combine apricot preserves, mustard, Worcestershire sauce, 2 tablespoons habanero chile, 2 teaspoons vinegar, 1/4 teaspoon salt, 1/4 teaspoon black pepper, and garlic in a bowl; stir with a whisk. Pour apricot mixture over chicken in slow cooker. Toss to coat. Cover and cook on LOW 5 hours.
3. Combine cabbage, carrots, radishes, basil, and sunflower seeds in a large bowl. Stir together lime juice, oil, remaining 1 teaspoon vinegar, remaining 1 teaspoon habanero, remaining 1/4 teaspoon salt, and remaining 1/4 teaspoon black pepper in a separate smaller bowl. Add to cabbage mixture; toss to combine. Let stand at room temperature 15 minutes.
4. Transfer chicken to a cutting board. Shred with 2 forks; place in a large bowl. Skim fat from juices in slow cooker; discard fat. Combine cornstarch and 1 tablespoon water in a small bowl; stir until smooth. Stir cornstarch mixture into juices in slow cooker. Cover and cook on HIGH 5 minutes or until thickened. Add chicken back to slow cooker; toss to combine.
5. Place 5 ounces chicken mixture on bottom halves of each bun. Top each with 1/2 cup slaw and top halves of buns. Serves 6 (serving size: 1 sandwich)

CALORIES 385; **FAT** 11.5g (sat 3.1g, mono 5.2g, poly 2.2g); **PROTEIN** 38g; **CARB** 41g; **FIBER** 7g; **SUGARS** 12g (est. added sugars 6g); **CHOL** 120mg; **IRON** 2mg; **SODIUM** 624mg; **CALC** 355mg

Kid Friendly

Crispy Salmon Fillets with Sesame-Soy Drizzle

Hands-on: 14 min. Total: 45 min.
Drying the skin as thoroughly as possible ensures it will crisp up instead of steaming and becoming soggy in the pan. To get the absolute last bit of moisture out, try this trick: After patting the whole fillet dry with towels, run the dull back edge of a knife along the skin like a squeegee—wipe off any liquid this pulls out onto the knife, and pat the skin dry again.

4 (6-ounce) skin-on salmon fillets
1/2 teaspoon kosher salt
1 tablespoon canola oil
2 tablespoons toasted sesame oil
2 tablespoons reduced-sodium soy sauce
1 tablespoon rice vinegar
1/4 teaspoon crushed red pepper
1/4 cup thinly sliced green onions

1. Pat salmon and skin thoroughly dry with paper towels. Place fillets, skin sides up, on a large plate. Place plate, uncovered, in refrigerator; chill salmon 30 minutes to air-dry the skin.
2. Remove salmon from refrigerator. Sprinkle evenly with salt. Heat a large nonstick skillet over medium-high. Add canola oil to pan. When oil is very hot, add salmon fillets, skin sides down. Press fillets gently with a spatula 30 seconds or until skin stays flat in pan. Reduce heat to medium. Cook salmon 7 minutes or until skin is browned and crisp and flesh is cooked almost to medium. Flip fillets; cook 1 minute or until tops are light brown. Place fillets, skin sides up, on a serving platter.

3. Combine sesame oil, soy sauce, vinegar, and crushed red pepper in a small bowl; drizzle mixture over salmon fillets. Sprinkle salmon evenly with green onions. Serve immediately. Serves 4 (serving size: 1 salmon fillet and about 1 tablespoon sauce)

CALORIES 337; FAT 19.8g (sat 2.8g, mono 8g, poly 7.9g); PROTEIN 39g; CARB 1g; FIBER 0g; SUGARS 0g; CHOL 99mg; IRON 1mg; SODIUM 630mg; CALC 14mg

5 FISH TO PAN-SEAR

These sustainable picks have thin, sturdy skins that cook deliciously crisp.

1. BLACK SEA BASS
Mild and meaty with buttery texture, this is a great gateway choice for reluctant seafood eaters. Look for Atlantic wild-caught (not otter-trawled) or farmed black sea bass from fisheries worldwide.

2. ROCKFISH
Sweet and flaky rockfish (sometimes sold as Pacific snapper) has made a big comeback in recent years since being overfished on the West Coast for decades. Wild-caught U.S. rockfish are fully sustainable options.

3. STRIPED BASS
Firm and rich-flavored, this is a favorite among the seafood savvy. The flesh holds up well in a hot pan, and its healthy fat keeps it wonderfully moist. Atlantic stripers caught with hooks and lines are the most sustainable choice.

4. RAINBOW TROUT
Mild, sweet, delicate trout is tilapia-like in its ability to win over seafood-sensitive palates. Farm-raised in the U.S., it's an environmentally sound pick, widely available in fish markets nationwide, and pretty cheap to boot.

5. ARCTIC CHAR
Pink-fleshed with flavor like a cross between salmon and trout, arctic char has become more common at seafood markets nationwide as consumers have come to crave it. Whether farmed or wild-caught, it's a sustainable option.

HOW TO BUILD A PAN BAGNAT, THE PICNIC-PERFECT SANDWICH

1. HOLLOW OUT THE LOAF. Tear the crumb out of the top and bottom halves of the boule to make shells about 1 inch thick. Save the torn crumb for other uses, such as a fresh breadcrumb topping or rustic croutons. Then toast the hollowed halves to help them stand up to the oil dressing, giving the bread texture like a good Thanksgiving stuffing: crisp yet moist.

2. BATHE THE BREAD. Pan bagnat roughly translates to "bathed bread" in French; the loaf gets a light soaking in fruity oil then absorbs flavors from the fillings as it stands. Spoon the tuna mixture into the bottom loaf half, mounding and pressing as needed to make it fit. Drizzle the top half of the loaf with oil and lemon juice, and then layer the filling with the traditional toppers: fresh lettuce, tomato, and hard-boiled egg.

3 WRAP IT UP. It'd be fine to eat at this point, but pan bagnat gets even better with a little patience. Seal it snugly in plastic wrap and refrigerate two hours or overnight. This is when the magic happens: The layers press together, flavors marry, and textures grow more interesting. A tight wrap also helps the layers hold together so the thick sandwich is easier to slice.

4. ET VOILÀ! After resting in the fridge for hours, the sandwich hangs together nicely now, slicing into four impressively tall yet neat quarters. The bread shells have also taken on the flavors of olive oil and tart lemon, briny capers and olives, and pungent onion. If you take your pan bagnat to a picnic, leave it whole and wrapped. When ready to eat, just unwrap and slice to serve.

Kid Friendly • Make Ahead

Pan Bagnat Tuna Sandwich

Hands-on: 19 min. Total: 2 hr. 19 min.

1 (8-ounce) whole-wheat sourdough loaf
¼ cup chopped Niçoise or kalamata olives
3 tablespoons chopped red onion
2 tablespoons capers, drained
3 tablespoons extra-virgin olive oil, divided
5 teaspoons fresh lemon juice, divided
2 (5-ounce) cans water-packed premium white tuna, drained
2 medium-sized green leaf lettuce leaves
3 tomato slices
1 large hard-boiled egg, thinly sliced

1. Preheat broiler (to toast bread).
2. Halve loaf horizontally. Scoop out halves to make 1-inch bread shells. Toast shells until golden.
3. Combine olives, onion, capers, 2 tablespoons oil, 1 tablespoon lemon juice, and tuna; place mixture in bottom shell. Drizzle top shell with remaining oil and juice. Top tuna mixture with lettuce, tomato, egg slices, and top shell. Wrap in plastic wrap; refrigerate 2 hours or up to overnight. Cut into quarters. Serves 4 (serving size: ¼ sandwich)

CALORIES 298; FAT 15.5g (sat 2.3g, mono 9.6g, poly 2.1g); PROTEIN 19g; CARB 18g; FIBER 3g; SUGARS 3g (added sugars 1g); CHOL 70mg; IRON 2mg; SODIUM 607mg; CALC 55mg

WOW! TRY THIS: CANDIED PANCETTA

Gluten Free • Kid Friendly Make Ahead

Candied Pancetta Stacks

Hands-on: 20 min. Total: 45 min.
Here's a fresh take on caprese that invites a meaty, umami burst from pancetta. Serve as an appetizer or dessert (think cheese-and-charcuterie board reinvented) at your next summer soiree for a crowd-pleasing treat.

1 tablespoon light brown sugar
¼ teaspoon ground fennel seeds
6 (¾-ounce) round pancetta slices
½ cup white balsamic vinegar
2 teaspoons honey
2 teaspoons fresh lemon juice
   (from 1 lemon)
3 medium peaches (about 1 pound)
6 (½-ounce) fresh mozzarella slices
½ cup fresh basil leaves

1. Preheat oven to 300°F. Line a baking sheet with parchment paper or a silicone baking mat.
2. Combine sugar and fennel seeds. Place pancetta in a single layer on prepared baking sheet; rub spice mixture evenly on each side. Bake at 300°F for 25 minutes or until crisp.
3. Combine vinegar, honey, and juice in a small saucepan; bring to a boil over medium-high. Cook, stirring often, 6 to 8 minutes or until mixture thickens and reduces by half.
4. Cut each peach in half horizontally; discard pits. Cut peach halves in half horizontally. (You should have 4 round, flat slices from each peach.)
5. To assemble, place 6 peach slices on a serving platter. Layer each with 1 mozzarella slice, 1 additional peach slice, and 1 pancetta slice. Drizzle vinegar mixture evenly over stacks. Sprinkle with basil. Serves 6 (serving size: 1 stack)

CALORIES 156; **FAT** 9.5g (sat 4.8g, mono 2.4g, poly 0.2g); **PROTEIN** 4g; **CARB** 14g; **FIBER** 1g; **SUGARS** 10g (est. added sugars 3g); **CHOL** 25mg; **IRON** 1mg; **SODIUM** 223mg; **CALC** 13mg

USE IT UP

ANCHOVY PASTE

The secret ingredient for savory depth

Quick & Easy • Gluten Free
Broccoli Rabe with Anchovy Butter
Cook 1 pound trimmed broccoli rabe in a large pot of boiling water for 2 minutes; drain and rinse with cold water. Heat 1 tablespoon unsalted butter and 1 tablespoon canola oil in a large skillet over medium. Add ½ teaspoon crushed red pepper and 2 thinly sliced garlic cloves; cook 2 minutes. Stir in 1 teaspoon anchovy paste. Add broccoli rabe; toss to coat. Sprinkle with ¼ teaspoon kosher salt. Serves 4 (serving size: about 1 cup)

CALORIES 87; **FAT** 7.2g (sat 2.2g, mono 3g, poly 1.3g); **PROTEIN** 4g; **CARB** 4g; **FIBER** 3g; **SUGARS** 0g; **CHOL** 12mg; **IRON** 2mg; **SODIUM** 236mg; **CALC** 126mg

Quick & Easy • Gluten Free
Kid Friendly • Make Ahead
Umami Popcorn
Heat 1 tablespoon olive oil in a Dutch oven over medium-high. Add ⅓ cup unpopped popcorn; cover, and cook 3 minutes or until kernels pop (about 8 cups), shaking pan often. Pour popcorn into a bowl. Add 3 tablespoons olive oil to pan. Add 1½ tablespoons chopped fresh thyme, 2½ teaspoons anchovy paste, and 3 minced garlic cloves; cook 1 minute, stirring constantly. Add popcorn; toss to coat. Serves 4 (serving size: about 2 cups)

CALORIES 187; **FAT** 14.7g (sat 2.1g, mono 10g, poly 1.8g); **PROTEIN** 2g; **CARB** 12g; **FIBER** 2g; **SUGARS** 0g; **CHOL** 11mg; **IRON** 1mg; **SODIUM** 198mg; **CALC** 9mg

Quick & Easy • Gluten Free
Kid Friendly • Make Ahead
Savory Potato Salad
Place 2 pounds halved small red potatoes in a Dutch oven; cover with water. Bring to a boil; reduce heat, and simmer 12 minutes or until tender. Drain. Combine ¼ cup extra-virgin olive oil, 2 tablespoons fresh lemon juice, 1 teaspoon black pepper, 2 teaspoons anchovy paste, ¾ teaspoon kosher salt, and 1 grated garlic clove in a large bowl. Stir in potatoes, ⅓ cup slivered red onion, and ⅓ cup chopped fresh parsley. Serves 6 (serving size: about 1 cup)

CALORIES 214; **FAT** 9.3g (sat 1.3g, mono 6.6g, poly 1g); **PROTEIN** 4g; **CARB** 28g; **FIBER** 2g; **SUGARS** 0g; **CHOL** 6mg; **IRON** 2mg; **SODIUM** 356mg; **CALC** 9mg

Staff Favorite • Quick & Easy
Kid Friendly • Make Ahead
Caesar Bagels
Combine 3 ounces softened ⅓-less-fat cream cheese, 1½ teaspoons fresh lemon juice, 1½ teaspoons anchovy paste, 1 grated garlic clove, and ¾ ounce grated Parmesan cheese in a bowl, stirring well. Combine 2⅔ cups torn romaine lettuce, 2 teaspoons olive oil, and 1½ teaspoons fresh lemon juice, tossing gently. Divide cream cheese and lettuce mixtures among 4 (3.4-ounce) whole-wheat bagels. Serves 4 (serving size: 1 sandwich)

CALORIES 346; **FAT** 11g (sat 4.4g, mono 4.4g, poly 0.8g); **PROTEIN** 14g; **CARB** 52g; **FIBER** 8g; **SUGARS** 8g (est. added sugars 6g); **CHOL** 27mg; **IRON** 2mg; **SODIUM** 687mg; **CALC** 181mg

FAMILY FAVORITES IN HALF THE TIME

Think you don't have time to cook chili tonight? Think again: Our speedy kitchen hacks bring comfort food classics to your table in record time.

THE FLAVOR SHORTCUT

TIME SAVED: 1 HR. 35 MIN.
Instant umami boosters like Worcestershire sauce and tomato paste build savory depth in minutes. Flank steak cooks quickly yet has the beefiness of tougher cuts like brisket. Coating the meat in flour before searing allows for more browning and helps add body to the chili.

Staff Favorite • Make Ahead

Quick Texas Chili

Hands-on: 25 min. Total: 1 hr.

3 tablespoons olive oil, divided
2 teaspoons chili powder
1 teaspoon ground cumin
1 teaspoon paprika
1 teaspoon unsweetened cocoa
1/4 teaspoon ground red pepper
1/4 teaspoon dried oregano
12 ounces flank steak, cut into
  3/4-inch pieces
3/4 teaspoon kosher salt, divided
3 tablespoons all-purpose flour
2 tablespoons unsalted tomato paste
1 tablespoon molasses
2 cups unsalted beef stock
1/2 cup dark beer
1 tablespoon reduced-sodium
  Worcestershire sauce
2 cups hot cooked brown rice
1/4 cup light sour cream
1/4 cup chopped green onions
1/4 cup sliced radishes
4 lime wedges

1. Combine 2 tablespoons oil and the next 6 ingredients in a microwave-safe bowl; microwave at HIGH 1 minute, stirring after 30 seconds.
2. Sprinkle steak with 1/4 teaspoon salt; toss with flour. Heat remaining 1 tablespoon oil in a Dutch oven over medium-high. Add steak; cook 6 minutes. Add spice mixture; cook 1 minute. Stir in tomato paste and molasses; cook 3 minutes. Add remaining 1/2 teaspoon salt, stock, beer, and Worcestershire. Bring to a boil; reduce heat, and simmer 30 minutes.
3. Divide rice and chili among 4 bowls. Top evenly with sour cream, onions, and radishes; serve with lime wedges. Serves 4 (serving size: about 3/4 cup chili and 1/2 cup rice)

CALORIES 439; **FAT** 18g (sat 5g, unsat 13g); **PROTEIN** 24g; **CARB** 43g; **FIBER** 4g; **SUGARS** 6g (added sugars 4g); **SODIUM** 582mg; **CALC** 8% DV; **POTASSIUM** 18% DV

THE THIN SLICES SHORTCUT

TIME SAVED: 40 MIN.
Thin foods cook faster. Pork medallions get better browning than a whole tenderloin; potato slices get crispier than wedges. Thinly sliced apple, fennel, and shallots absorb more vinaigrette without losing crunch.

Staff Favorite • Gluten Free

Pork Medallions with Fennel-Apple Slaw

Hands-on: 25 min. Total: 35 min.

1 (6-ounce) sweet potato, halved
  lengthwise and thinly sliced
1/4 cup olive oil, divided
1 (1-pound) pork tenderloin, trimmed
  and cut into 1/2-inch-thick slices
1/2 teaspoon kosher salt, divided
1/2 teaspoon black pepper
1/2 cup hard apple cider or regular
  cider
2 tablespoons grainy mustard
2 tablespoons Dijon mustard
2 tablespoons unsalted butter
2 cups thinly sliced apple
1 cup thinly sliced fennel bulb, plus
  fennel fronds for garnish
2 tablespoons sliced shallots
2 tablespoons minced fresh parsley
2 tablespoons fresh lemon juice

1. Preheat oven to 450°F.
2. Combine potato and 1 tablespoon oil on a rimmed baking sheet lined with parchment paper. Bake at 450°F for 10 minutes or until tender.
3. Heat 1 tablespoon oil in a skillet over medium-high. Sprinkle pork slices with 1/4 teaspoon salt and pepper. Add to pan; cook 5 minutes on one side. Remove from pan; add cider, and cook 1 minute. Stir in mustards. Remove pan from heat; stir in butter. Add pork to pan; let stand 3 minutes.
4. Combine potatoes, remaining 2 tablespoons oil, remaining 1/4 teaspoon salt, apple, fennel bulb, and remaining ingredients in a bowl. Serve slaw with pork and pan sauce. Garnish with fennel fronds. Serves 4 (serving size: 3 ounces pork, 1 1/2 cups slaw, and 2 tablespoons sauce)

CALORIES 406; **FAT** 22g (sat 6g, unsat 15g); **PROTEIN** 25g; **CARB** 23g; **FIBER** 4g; **SUGARS** 12g (added sugars 0g); **SODIUM** 615mg; **CALC** 4% DV; **POTASSIUM** 23% DV

Fast • Make Ahead

Meatloaf Burger Steaks with Tomato Gravy

Hands-on: 20 min. Total: 30 min.
These burger steaks deliver classic meatloaf flavor with more glazy, crispy crust. A quick tomato gravy mimics a savory ketchup topping.

4 ounces cremini mushrooms, cut in half (about 1 cup)
3 garlic cloves, peeled
1 small carrot, trimmed and cut into 1-inch pieces
1 celery stalk, trimmed and cut into 1-inch pieces
1/2 small onion, peeled and cut into 1-inch pieces
1/3 cup whole-wheat panko
2 large eggs, lightly beaten
1 pound 90% lean ground sirloin
1 tablespoon canola oil
1 teaspoon kosher salt, divided
3/4 teaspoon freshly ground black pepper, divided
1/4 cup dry red wine
1/2 cup unsalted ketchup
2 tablespoons honey
1 tablespoon reduced-sodium Worcestershire sauce
1 tablespoon water
1 pound Yukon Gold potatoes, cut into 2-inch pieces
1/2 cup 1% low-fat milk
1 tablespoon unsalted butter
1 (12-ounce) package fresh microwave-in-bag broccoli florets

1. Place first 5 ingredients in a food processor; pulse 3 to 4 times or until chopped.
2. Combine panko, eggs, and beef; divide and shape into 4 (1½-inch-thick) patties. Heat oil in a large nonstick skillet over medium-high. Sprinkle patties with ½ teaspoon salt and ½ teaspoon pepper. Add to pan; cook 4 minutes on each side (patties will not be cooked through). Remove patties from pan (do not wipe out pan).
3. Add mushroom mixture to pan; cook 6 minutes. Add wine; cook 2 minutes or until liquid almost evaporates, scraping to loosen browned bits. Stir in ketchup, honey, and Worcestershire; cook 3 minutes or until slightly thickened. Reduce heat to low. Add patties; cook 6 minutes or until done, turning to coat.
4. Place 1 tablespoon water and potatoes in a medium microwave-safe bowl; cover with plastic wrap. Microwave at HIGH 6 minutes or until tender. Add ¼ teaspoon salt, remaining ¼ teaspoon pepper, milk, and butter to potatoes; mash to desired consistency.
5. Cook broccoli according to package directions; sprinkle with remaining ¼ teaspoon salt. Serve with patties, sauce, and mashed potatoes. Serves 4 (serving size: 1 meatloaf patty, ½ cup potatoes, and ½ cup broccoli)

CALORIES 538; FAT 21g (sat 8g, unsat 11g); PROTEIN 34g; CARB 54g; FIBER 6g; SUGARS 21g (added sugars 14g); SODIUM 702mg; CALC 13% DV; POTASSIUM 50% DV

Gluten Free • Make Ahead

Crispy Chicken Thighs with Schmaltzy Vinaigrette

Hands-on: 35 min. Total: 45 min.
You'll get all the deliciousness of a roast chicken in a fraction of the time when you opt for bone-in thighs as opposed to a whole bird. Schmaltz, a Yiddish word for chicken fat, is the base for a bright pan sauce that's drizzled over the vegetables and crispy chicken thighs. A cast-iron skillet will maintain an even heat so the hot drippings don't smoke or scorch.

1/3 cup extra-virgin olive oil, divided
3/4 teaspoon kosher salt, divided
1 pound small Yukon Gold potatoes, quartered
4 (6-ounce) skin-on, bone-in chicken thighs (about 1½ pounds)
1/2 teaspoon freshly ground black pepper, divided
2 cups halved Brussels sprouts
1½ cups chopped carrots
3 tablespoons finely chopped shallots
3 tablespoons sherry vinegar
1 tablespoon light brown sugar

1. Preheat oven to 450°F.
2. Line a baking sheet with parchment paper. Combine 1 tablespoon oil, ¼ teaspoon salt, and potatoes in

a bowl; toss to coat. Spread potato mixture on prepared pan; bake at 450°F for 15 minutes or until potatoes are tender when pierced with a fork. Remove pan from oven; keep warm.

3. Meanwhile, place a wire rack on a baking sheet. Heat 1 tablespoon oil in a large cast-iron skillet over medium-high. Sprinkle the chicken with ¼ teaspoon salt and ¼ teaspoon pepper. Add chicken to skillet, skin side down; cook 8 minutes. Flip, and cook 2 minutes (chicken will not be cooked through). Place chicken on a wire rack (reserve drippings in skillet). Bake chicken at 450°F for 10 minutes or until done.

4. Return skillet to medium-high heat. Add remaining ¼ teaspoon salt, remaining ¼ teaspoon black pepper, halved Brussels sprouts, and carrots to drippings in pan; cook 8 minutes. Remove pan from heat. Remove vegetables from pan with a slotted spoon; set aside (do not wipe out pan).

5. Place shallots in a small bowl. Add vinegar to skillet, scraping to loosen browned bits. Add vinegar mixture, remaining oil, and brown sugar to shallots, stirring to combine. Place 1 cup potatoes and ½ cup vegetable mixture on each of 4 plates; top each serving with 1 chicken thigh and about 1½ tablespoons shallot mixture. Serves 4

CALORIES 420; **FAT** 23g (sat 4g, unsat 19g); **PROTEIN** 24g; **CARB** 30g; **FIBER** 5g; **SUGARS** 7g (added sugars 2g); **SODIUM** 523mg; **CALC** 6% DV; **POTASSIUM** 32% DV

THE ONE-PAN SHORTCUT

TIME SAVED: 1 HR. 20 MIN.
Vegetables take turns cooking in a single pan, not several. A stovetop simmer quickly cooks the noodles through; no need for a separate boil. The pan shifts easily to the oven for a last-minute broil to melt and meld the cheeses.

Make Ahead • Vegetarian

Skillet Vegetable Lasagna

Hands-on: 20 min. Total: 40 min.

2 tablespoons olive oil, divided
12 ounces zucchini, cut lengthwise into ¼-inch-thick slices, divided
1½ cups thinly sliced yellow onion
1 (8-ounce) package presliced cremini mushrooms
4 cups baby spinach
3 garlic cloves, thinly sliced
1 (28-ounce) can unsalted crushed tomatoes, divided
½ teaspoon kosher salt
4½ no-boil lasagna noodles
4 ounces part-skim ricotta cheese (about 1 cup)
4 ounces preshredded low-moisture part-skim mozzarella cheese (about 1 cup)

1. Heat 1½ teaspoons oil in a large cast-iron skillet over medium-high. Add half of zucchini; cook 3 minutes on each side or until browned. Remove from pan. Repeat procedure with 1½ teaspoons oil and remaining zucchini. Add remaining 1 tablespoon oil to pan. Add onion and mushrooms; cook 6 minutes. Stir in spinach and garlic; cook 1 minute. Remove pan from heat.

2. Spread mushroom mixture in bottom of pan; top with cooked zucchini. Pour 2 cups tomatoes over zucchini; sprinkle with salt. Arrange noodles over top, breaking ends as needed to fit in pan. Spread remaining tomatoes over pan; top with ricotta. Cover, and simmer 20 minutes over medium-low or until noodles are done.

3. Remove pan from heat. Preheat broiler with oven rack in the top position.

4. Sprinkle mozzarella over pan; broil 3 minutes or until melted and lightly browned. Serves 4 (serving size: about 1½ cups)

CALORIES 384; **FAT** 15g (sat 5g, unsat 9g); **PROTEIN** 21g; **CARB** 44g; **FIBER** 7g; **SUGARS** 5g (added sugars 0g); **SODIUM** 548mg; **CALC** 39% DV; **POTASSIUM** 17% DV

MUFFIN-TIN MAINS

Use your muffin tins to make tidy breakfast bundles. They're simple to assemble, individually portioned, and perfect for families who need breakfast on the go.

Soft-Yolk Muffins with Sausage and Cheese

Hands-on: 20 min. Total: 50 min.
Dazzle family and friends with these meaty muffins that break open to reveal medium-boiled eggs with creamy yolks in the middle. You need two sizes of egg here—the mediums fit in the muffin tins, while the larges go in the batter.

Cooking spray
12 medium eggs
6 ounces ground turkey sausage, casings removed
8 ounces whole-wheat flour (about 2 cups)
4.25 ounces all-purpose flour (about 1 cup)
1 tablespoon baking powder
1 teaspoon granulated sugar
1/2 teaspoon baking soda
1/2 teaspoon ground black pepper
2 cups reduced-fat buttermilk
3 tablespoons canola oil
3 large eggs, lightly beaten
4 ounces cheddar cheese, grated and divided (about 1 cup)

1. Preheat oven to 400°F. Coat a 12-cup muffin pan with cooking spray.
2. Bring a large saucepan of water to a boil over high. Carefully lower 12 medium eggs into water with a strainer or slotted spoon. Boil 4 minutes and 30 seconds; immediately plunge into a bowl of ice water. Cool 10 minutes. Peel eggs.
3. Heat a small nonstick skillet over medium-high. Add sausage to pan; cook 4 minutes or until browned, stirring occasionally to crumble. Drain on paper towels.
4. Whisk together flours, baking powder, sugar, baking soda, and pepper in a bowl. Whisk together buttermilk, oil, and large eggs in a separate bowl until smooth. Add flour mixture to buttermilk mixture; stir with a wooden spoon or rubber spatula until smooth. Fold in two-thirds of sausage and 2 ounces cheese.
5. Divide half of batter evenly among cups of prepared muffin pan. Nestle 1 peeled cooked egg vertically into batter in each cup. Top with remaining batter. Sprinkle muffins with remaining sausage and remaining 2 ounces cheese.
6. Bake at 400°F on bottom rack until cheese melts and a wooden pick inserted in center comes out with moist crumbs, about 17 minutes. Remove from oven; cool on a wire rack 10 minutes. Carefully run an offset spatula or butter knife around edges to loosen muffins. Serves 12 (serving size: 1 soft-yolk muffin)

CALORIES 298; **FAT** 15g (sat 5g, unsat 8g); **PROTEIN** 18g; **CARB** 24g; **FIBER** 2g; **SUGARS** 3g (added sugars 1g); **SODIUM** 516mg; **CALC** 22% DV; **POTASSIUM** 6% DV

Granola Cups with Yogurt and Berries

Hands-on: 13 min. Total: 28 min.

1 1/2 cups old-fashioned rolled oats
1/4 cup chopped walnuts, toasted
1/4 teaspoon ground cinnamon
1/8 teaspoon kosher salt
3 tablespoons honey
2 tablespoons creamy almond butter
1 large egg white
Cooking spray
2 cups plain 2% reduced-fat Greek yogurt
2 cups fresh blueberries
Grated lemon rind (optional)

1. Preheat oven to 325°F.
2. Combine oats, walnuts, cinnamon, and salt in a large bowl. Combine honey and almond butter in a small microwave-safe bowl. Microwave at HIGH 20 to 30 seconds; stir until smooth. Add honey mixture and egg white to oat mixture; toss to coat. Divide oat mixture evenly among 8 muffin cups coated with cooking spray. Using a piece of parchment paper (to prevent sticking), press oat mixture into bottom and up sides of each muffin cup. Bake at 325°F for 15 minutes or until edges are browned and crisp; cool completely in pan.
3. Carefully run an offset spatula or butter knife around edges to loosen granola cups; remove from pan. Fill each cup with about 1/4 cup yogurt, and top with about 1/4 cup berries. Sprinkle with grated lemon rind, if desired. Serves 8 (serving size: 1 filled granola cup)

CALORIES 191; **FAT** 7g (sat 1g, unsat 5g); **PROTEIN** 9g; **CARB** 26g; **FIBER** 3g; **SUGARS** 13g (added sugars 6g); **SODIUM** 57mg; **CALC** 6% DV; **POTASSIUM** 2% DV

Corn Muffins with Prosciutto, Sun-Dried Tomatoes, and Goat Cheese

Hands-on: 20 min. Total: 50 min.
Salty, umami-packed prosciutto and creamy, tangy goat cheese lend loads of flavor to the tender corn muffin base. You can use domestic ham instead of prosciutto, if you prefer. We find oil-packed sun-dried tomatoes to be softer than those without oil, so they're better in this dish.

Cooking spray
6.38 ounces all-purpose flour (about 1½ cups)
6.38 ounces whole-grain cornmeal (about 1½ cups)
2 tablespoons sugar
1½ tablespoons baking powder
¾ teaspoon freshly ground black pepper
1½ cups whole buttermilk
¼ cup unsalted butter, melted and cooled slightly
3 large eggs, lightly beaten
¼ cup chopped fresh chives
4 ounces finely chopped prosciutto, divided
½ cup sliced sun-dried tomatoes in oil, drained and divided
4 ounces goat cheese, crumbled and divided (about 1 cup)

1. Preheat oven to 375°F. Coat a 12-cup muffin pan with cooking spray.
2. Whisk together flour, cornmeal, sugar, baking powder, and pepper in a large bowl. Whisk together buttermilk, butter, and eggs in a large bowl until smooth. Add flour mixture to buttermilk mixture; stir with a wooden spoon or rubber spatula until smooth. Fold in chives, two-thirds (about 2½ ounces) of prosciutto, ¼ cup tomatoes, and 2 ounces cheese.
3. Divide batter evenly among cups of prepared muffin pan. Sprinkle muffins with remaining prosciutto, remaining ¼ cup tomatoes, and remaining 2 ounces cheese.
4. Bake at 375°F for 20 minutes or until cheese melts and a wooden pick inserted in center of muffin comes out with moist crumbs. Remove from oven; cool on a wire rack 10 minutes. Carefully run an offset spatula or butter knife around edges to loosen muffins. Serves 12 (serving size: 1 corn muffin)

CALORIES 256; **FAT** 11g (sat 6g, unsat 4g); **PROTEIN** 10g; **CARB** 28g; **FIBER** 2g; **SUGARS** 4g (added sugars 2g); **SODIUM** 511mg; **CALC** 17% DV; **POTASSIUM** 6% DV

Muffin-Tin Pumpkin-and-Pear Stratas

Hands-on: 10 min. Total: 45 min.
Bosc or Anjou pears will also work here, as long as they're ripe. Your bare hands do the best job of mixing the bread into the egg.

Cooking spray
1½ cups vanilla whole-milk yogurt (not Greek-style)
1 cup canned pumpkin
¼ cup light brown sugar
½ teaspoon ground ginger
½ teaspoon ground nutmeg
½ teaspoon kosher salt
5 large eggs, lightly beaten
1 (1-pound) French bread loaf, torn into 2-inch pieces
2 cups chopped ripe Bartlett pears (about 2 large)
¾ cup dried cranberries
2 tablespoons powdered sugar

1. Preheat oven to 375°F. Coat a 12-cup muffin pan with cooking spray.
2. Combine yogurt, pumpkin, brown sugar, ginger, nutmeg, salt, and eggs in a large bowl; whisk until smooth. Add bread; stir until liquid is absorbed. Fold in pears and cranberries.
3. Divide pumpkin mixture evenly among cups of prepared muffin pan; lightly press to remove air pockets. (They will mound up.) Bake at 375°F for 25 minutes or until batter is set and tops are lightly browned. Remove from oven to a wire rack; cool 10 minutes. Carefully run an offset spatula or butter knife around edges to loosen muffins. Place muffins on a plate; sift powdered sugar over top. Serves 12 (serving size: 1 strata muffin)

CALORIES 241; **FAT** 4g (sat 2g, unsat 2g); **PROTEIN** 8g; **CARB** 44g; **FIBER** 3g; **SUGARS** 18g (added sugars 10g); **SODIUM** 355mg; **CALC** 9% DV; **POTASSIUM** 4% DV

Broccoli-and-Bacon Muffin-Tin Frittatas

Hands-on: 10 min. Total: 35 min.
This easy make-ahead breakfast will have you set for the week. You get two mini frittatas per serving for only 168 calories; pair with a piece of fruit for a satisfying breakfast. Store cooked frittatas in the fridge for up to four days.

Cooking spray
2 cups small broccoli florets, cooked until crisp-tender
3 bacon slices, cooked and crumbled
8 large eggs
¼ cup 2% reduced-fat milk
½ teaspoon kosher salt
½ teaspoon freshly ground black pepper
2 ounces sharp cheddar cheese, shredded (about ½ packed cup)

1. Preheat oven to 350°F.
2. Coat a 12-cup muffin pan with cooking spray. Divide broccoli and bacon evenly among muffin cups.
3. Crack eggs into a large bowl. Add milk, salt, and pepper; stir with a whisk until well combined. Divide egg mixture evenly among muffin cups. Sprinkle cheese evenly on top. Bake at 350°F for 18 minutes or until just set. Cool on a wire rack 2 to 3 minutes. Carefully run an offset spatula or butter knife around edges to loosen frittatas. Serves 12 (serving size: 2 mini frittatas)

CALORIES 168; **FAT** 12g (sat 5g, unsat 6g); **PROTEIN** 13g; **CARB** 3g; **FIBER** 1g; **SUGARS** 1g (added sugars 0g); **SODIUM** 395mg; **CALC** 13% DV; **POTASSIUM** 6% DV

THE NEW MOVEABLE FEASTS

Bring your crew together over eat-anywhere dishes that are meant to be shared—whether that's at the dining table, on the patio, or in the living room.

With hectic afternoon and evening schedules, sometimes a meal around the family dinner table just isn't possible. Instead, focus on gathering somewhere as a family, even if it's around the coffee table. Make your peace with this, because, well, life is too short.

No matter the setting, it's good to gather at the same time to enjoy the same good food. It's even more intimate when serving more communal dishes, food eaten from a common pot, so to speak. These recipes get you to that place; they bring the family together in the midst of all the hectic push and pull of life to commune over a shared experience. And that quality time is something to cherish in whatever form it takes.

Pesto Yogurt Dip

Hands-on: 8 min. Total: 8 min.
Use this herby dip to anchor a tray of what we call Snack Dinner. Surround it with lots of fresh vegetable dippers, seasonal fruit, sliced cheese, olives, nuts, and a little meat.

1 large garlic clove
2 cups loosely packed basil leaves (about 1½ ounces stemmed basil)
1⅓ cups plain 2% reduced-fat Greek yogurt
½ cup whole buttermilk
¼ teaspoon kosher salt
2 ounces Parmigiano-Reggiano cheese, finely grated (about ½ cup)
Finely chopped chives (optional)

1. Place garlic clove in a mini food processor; process until finely chopped. Add basil; pulse until finely chopped. Add yogurt, buttermilk, and salt; pulse until well combined. Add cheese; pulse just until combined. Sprinkle dip evenly with chives, if desired. Serves 8 (serving size: ¼ cup)

CALORIES 68; **FAT** 3g (sat 2g, unsat 1g); **PROTEIN** 7g; **CARB** 3g; **FIBER** 0g; **SUGARS** 3g (added sugars 0g); **SODIUM** 188mg; **CALC** 15% DV; **POTASSIUM** 1% DV

Cheesy Chicken-and-Spinach Stromboli Ring

(pictured on page 233)

Hands-on: 30 min. Total: 50 min.
Shake up dinner with a gorgeous stromboli ring. Though it may look difficult, it's actually an easy process (see instructions below). Most store-bought pizza dough comes in 1- or 1½-pound portions, but you only need 12 ounces here. Use the leftovers to make breadsticks or flatbread the next day.

12 ounces fresh prepared whole-wheat pizza dough
1 tablespoon olive oil
4 garlic cloves, thinly sliced
8 ounces fresh spinach
1 cup part-skim ricotta cheese
1 ounce Parmesan cheese, grated (about ¼ cup)
6 ounces shredded skinless rotisserie chicken breast (about 1½ cups)

1. Let pizza dough stand at room temperature 15 minutes. Preheat oven to 450°F.

2. Heat a large skillet over medium-low. Add oil and garlic; cook, swirling occasionally, until garlic is golden, about 2 to 4 minutes. Drain oil from pan into a small bowl to reserve, keeping garlic in pan. Add spinach to pan; increase heat to medium-high, and cook, tossing constantly, until spinach is wilted, about 2 minutes. Let stand 10 minutes to cool.

3. Stir together ricotta and Parmesan in a medium bowl. Add spinach mixture and chicken; stir well to combine.

4. Place dough on a large piece of parchment paper, and roll dough into a 20- x 6-inch rectangle. Spoon chicken mixture down center of dough to make an approximately 20- x 3-inch strip. Using a pizza cutter or sharp knife, create tabs in dough on both sides of filling: Starting at the edge of dough, cut 1½-inch-long diagonal slits (½ inch to ¾ inch apart) in toward filling. Fold tabs over filling, and pinch tabs together to seal. Carefully shape stuffed dough into a ring; pinch ends of dough together to seal.

5. Transfer stromboli ring on parchment to a baking sheet; fold or cut away excess parchment to fit baking sheet. Brush half of reserved garlic-infused oil over dough. Bake stromboli at 450°F until dough is browned, about 18 minutes. Remove from oven; brush with remaining garlic oil. Let stand 5 minutes before serving. Serves 4 (serving size: ¼ stromboli)

CALORIES 399; **FAT** 15g (sat 5g, unsat 8g); **PROTEIN** 29g; **CARB** 42g; **FIBER** 4g; **SUGARS** 1g (added sugars 0g); **SODIUM** 697mg; **CALC** 32% DV; **POTASSIUM** 21% DV

STROMBOLI RING STEP-BY-STEP

1. Spoon the filling down the center of the dough; create tabs by cutting diagonal slits about ½ to ¾ inch apart on either side.

2. Fold the dough tabs over the filling. Pinch the tabs together over the center of the filling to seal and hold the dough in place as it bakes.

3. Carefully and slowly bring the ends of the dough together to form a circle.

4. Once the dough comes together into a circle, pinch the ends together to seal the ring and hide the seam.

HOW TO BUILD A SNACK DINNER

Snack Dinners are inspired by classic antipasti platters, but with less meat and cheese and more vegetables and fruit. It's quick to assemble, gets everyone eating more produce, and is always a home run. Here are some tips for building your own; snap a photo of your creations, and share on Instagram using #snackdinner.

THE PLATTER
You don't need anything fancy. You can use a half sheet pan.

THE DIP
Something family-friendly will encourage extra veggie noshing. Hummus, guacamole, and our Pesto Yogurt Dip (recipe on page 252) are winners.

THE PRODUCE
Pile on as much as the platter will hold: blanched Broccolini, Little Gem lettuce, baby carrots, mini bell peppers, watermelon radishes, pears, grape or cherry tomatoes, and red grapes. Go for whatever is in season, and cut veggies into dippable pieces.

THE CHEESE
One type of cheese is fine; just go with something your family will enjoy. Creamy Havarti always wins.

THE MEAT
Aim for 1 ounce per person of something rich and indulgent—prosciutto, salami or soppressata, or smoked salmon.

THE NIBBLES
Nestle little bowls of olives and nuts onto the platter. "Little" is the key word; too much of these can pack on the calories and sodium.

Staff Favorite • Fast
Gluten Free • Make Ahead

Creamy Hummus with Spiced Ground Beef

Hands-on: 20 min. Total: 20 min.
Typically, this style of supersmooth hummus starts with dried chickpeas; we discovered a shortcut with canned chickpeas where a little baking soda softens or dissolves the peas' skins. Be sure to use a blender; a food processor will not get the hummus this smooth. Serve with soft whole-wheat pita and crudités.

1 (15-ounce) can unsalted chickpeas
1½ teaspoons baking soda
⅓ cup tahini (sesame seed paste)
5 tablespoons fresh lemon juice (about 2 lemons), divided
¼ cup to ½ cup water
¾ teaspoon kosher salt, divided
5 garlic cloves, minced and divided
1 tablespoon olive oil
⅔ cup finely chopped yellow onion
8 ounces 93% lean ground beef
½ teaspoon ground cumin
½ teaspoon ground coriander
¼ teaspoon crushed red pepper
⅓ cup golden raisins
¼ cup chopped fresh flat-leaf parsley

1. Pour chickpeas and liquid from can into a small saucepan; stir in baking soda. Bring to a simmer over medium; cook, stirring occasionally, 3 to 5 minutes or until heated through. Drain and rinse in saucepan with cold water until chickpeas are room temperature; discard any skins that float to the top. Drain well.
2. Place chickpeas, tahini, ¼ cup lemon juice, ¼ cup water, ½ teaspoon salt, and 1 minced garlic clove in a blender; process until completely smooth and creamy, about 2 minutes, stopping to scrape sides as needed. Add up to ¼ cup more water, 1 tablespoon at a time, as needed. Let stand 5 minutes.
3. Heat a large skillet over medium. Add oil; swirl to coat. Add onion and remaining 4 minced garlic cloves; cook 2 minutes, stirring often. Add beef, cumin, coriander, crushed red pepper, and remaining ¼ teaspoon salt; cook, stirring occasionally to crumble, until beef is browned, about 5 minutes. Stir in raisins; cook 1 minute. Remove from heat; stir in parsley and remaining 1 tablespoon lemon juice.
4. Spread hummus in a thin layer on a large plate or platter; top evenly with beef mixture. Serves 4 (serving size: ½ cup hummus and a scant ½ cup beef topping)

CALORIES 399; FAT 19g (sat 4g, unsat 13g); PROTEIN 22g; CARB 39g; FIBER 6g; SUGARS 10g (added sugars 0g); SODIUM 553mg; CALC 10% DV; POTASSIUM 19% DV

Gluten Free • Make Ahead

Slow Cooker Korean Pork Lettuce Wraps

Hands-on: 30 min. Total: 8 hr.
This dish is great for a casual get-together or a weeknight meal (with leftovers). The seasoning paste is modeled after Korean ssamjang—a concentrated, salty, slightly spicy concoction. Unlike traditional versions, though, ours is made with grocery store ingredients for ease and convenience.

1 teaspoon ground ginger
3 tablespoons light brown sugar, divided
1 (2-pound) trimmed boneless pork shoulder roast (about 2½ to 3 pounds before trimming)
2½ tablespoons toasted sesame oil, divided
½ cup unsalted chicken stock
6 garlic cloves, crushed
1½ teaspoons kosher salt, divided

1¼ cups rice vinegar
1¼ cups water
1½ cups precut matchstick-cut
  carrots
1½ cups matchstick-cut daikon
  radish
6 tablespoons white miso
1 tablespoon Sriracha chili sauce
24 red leaf lettuce leaves
4 cups hot cooked short-grain
  brown rice or 2 (8.5-ounce)
  pouches microwavable
  whole-grain brown rice

1. Heat a medium skillet over medium-high. Combine ginger and 1 tablespoon sugar; rub evenly over all sides of pork. Add 1 tablespoon oil to pan; swirl to coat. Add pork; cook, turning until charred on all sides, about 8 minutes. Place pork in a 5- to 6-quart slow cooker; add stock and garlic. Cover and cook on low until pork shreds easily with a fork, 7 ½ to 8 hours. Remove pork from slow cooker, reserving ¼ cup cooking liquid. Shred meat with 2 forks, and place in a large bowl. Add reserved ¼ cup cooking liquid and ¾ teaspoon salt; toss well to combine.
2. Meanwhile, combine vinegar, 1¼ cups water, remaining 2 tablespoons sugar, and remaining ¾ teaspoon salt in a saucepan; bring to a boil over medium-high, stirring to dissolve sugar. Add carrots and radish. Remove from heat; cool completely, about 30 minutes or up to 7 hours. Drain well.
3. Combine miso, Sriracha, and remaining 1½ tablespoons oil. Spread about 1 teaspoon sauce over each lettuce leaf; top each with about 1 ounce pork and 2 tablespoons pickled vegetables. Serve with rice. Serves 8 (serving size: 3 lettuce wraps and ½ cup rice)

CALORIES 368; **FAT** 13g (sat 4g, unsat 9g);
PROTEIN 28g; **CARB** 34g; **FIBER** 5g; **SUGARS** 6g
(added sugars 3g); **SODIUM** 790mg; **CALC** 5% DV;
POTASSIUM 18% DV

Chicken-and-Mushroom Dumplings with Bok Choy

Hands-on: 30 min. Total: 40 min.
We keep these dumplings weeknight-doable by using easy-to-find wonton wrappers (look for them near the tofu) and the simplest folding method. To make this a communal meal, set out the steamer baskets on a towel so your family can help themselves. If your bok choy is larger than what we call for, cut it into quarters so it will fit in the baskets.

8 ounces fresh shiitake mushrooms
1 tablespoon toasted sesame oil
1 cup chopped leek (about 1 leek)
¾ teaspoon grated peeled fresh
  ginger
2 garlic cloves, minced
Cooking spray
6 ounces ground chicken
2 tablespoons plus ½ teaspoon
  reduced-sodium soy sauce, divided
24 square wonton wrappers
4 (3-ounce) baby bok choy, halved
3 tablespoons fresh lemon juice
2 tablespoons mirin
1 teaspoon granulated sugar

1. Remove stems from mushrooms; discard or reserve for making stock. Finely chop mushroom caps.
2. Heat a large skillet over medium-high. Add oil; swirl to coat. Add mushrooms, leek, ginger, and garlic; cook until leek is tender and mushroom liquid has evaporated, about 7 minutes. Cool 10 minutes.
3. Line a baking sheet with plastic wrap, and coat with cooking spray. Combine chicken, mushroom mixture, and ½ teaspoon soy sauce. Working with 1 wonton wrapper at a time (cover remaining wrappers with a damp towel to prevent drying),

place wrapper on a work surface, starchy side up. Moisten edges of wrapper with water. Spoon about 2 teaspoons filling into center of each wrapper. Bring 2 opposite corners together; pinch points together to seal. Bring remaining 2 corners to center; pinch to seal. Pinch 4 edges together to seal. Place on prepared baking sheet; cover with a damp towel or paper towels to prevent drying. Repeat procedure with remaining wrappers and filling.
4. Line both tiers of a 2-tiered bamboo steamer with parchment paper. Divide dumplings and bok choy between baskets. Stack baskets; cover with steamer lid. Add water to a skillet to a depth of 1 inch; bring to a boil over high. Place steamer in pan; steam dumplings 8 minutes or until done.
5. Meanwhile, combine lemon juice, mirin, sugar, and remaining 2 tablespoons soy sauce in a small bowl, stirring until sugar dissolves. Serve dumplings and bok choy with sauce. Serves 4 (serving size: 6 dumplings, 2 bok choy halves, and about 5 teaspoons sauce)

CALORIES 298; **FAT** 8g (sat 2g, unsat 6g);
PROTEIN 15g; **CARB** 42g; **FIBER** 3g; **SUGARS** 6g
(added sugars 3g); **SODIUM** 655mg; **CALC** 12% DV;
POTASSIUM 21% DV

Fast • Gluten Free

Sheet Pan Beefy Nachos

Hands-on: 30 min. Total: 30 min.
If you have young kids serving themselves, lift the nachos off the pan with the parchment paper (and remove the hot pan from the table). For the creamiest nacho sauce, start with a block of cheese and shred it yourself.

Cooking spray
6 ounces 93% lean ground beef
1 teaspoon garlic powder
3/4 teaspoon ground cumin
1/2 teaspoon chipotle chile powder
1 1/2 teaspoons cornstarch, divided
1/4 teaspoon kosher salt
5 tablespoons water, divided
3 ounces 2% reduced-fat sharp cheddar cheese, shredded (about 3/4 cup)
1/2 cup fat-free evaporated milk
1 teaspoon hot sauce (such as Cholula)
6 ounces multigrain tortilla chips (such as Tostitos)
1 cup chopped tomatoes
1/2 cup chopped green onions
1 red or green jalapeño, thinly sliced (about 1/3 cup)
1/4 cup plain nonfat Greek yogurt
1/4 cup roughly chopped fresh cilantro
1/4 cup thinly sliced radishes (optional)
Lime wedges (optional)

1. Heat a medium skillet over medium. Coat pan with cooking spray. Add beef, garlic powder, cumin, chile powder, 1/2 teaspoon cornstarch, and salt; cook, stirring to crumble, until beef is browned, about 4 minutes. Add 1/4 cup water; reduce heat to medium, and simmer until saucy and thickened, about 2 minutes.
2. Preheat broiler to high with oven rack in top position.

3. Place cheese and remaining 1 teaspoon cornstarch in a small saucepan; toss to coat. Add evaporated milk. Cook over medium-low, stirring often, until thickened and smooth, about 5 minutes. Remove from heat; stir in hot sauce.
4. Line a sheet pan with parchment paper. Arrange chips on prepared pan. Spoon beef mixture evenly over chips; drizzle with cheese sauce. Top evenly with tomatoes, onions, and jalapeño; broil just until toppings are warmed, 1 to 2 minutes. Stir together yogurt and remaining 1 tablespoon water. Drizzle yogurt mixture over nachos; sprinkle with cilantro. Top with radishes and lime wedges, if desired. Serves 4

CALORIES 417; FAT 20g (sat 6g, unsat 14g); PROTEIN 22g; CARB 36g; FIBER 4g; SUGARS 8g (added sugars 0g); SODIUM 615mg; CALC 31% DV; POTASSIUM 15% DV

Fast • Make Ahead

Family-Style Meatball "Fondue"
(pictured on page 232)

Hands-on: 30 min. Total: 30 min.
We're using the term "fondue" loosely; the idea is that everyone scoops into a skillet of cheesy meatballs with hearty bread slices. The meatballs are more tender than traditional versions because they don't include breadcrumbs; we like the softer texture for this type of dish, where you want them to give way easily on the bread.

Cooking spray
3/4 cup shredded zucchini (about 1 small zucchini)
12 ounces ground turkey
1/3 cup shredded yellow onion (from 1 small onion)
1/2 teaspoon dried oregano
1/4 teaspoon kosher salt

1/4 teaspoon freshly ground black pepper
1 large egg
1 tablespoon olive oil
8 ounces sliced cremini mushrooms
2 garlic cloves, minced
1 1/2 cups lower-sodium marinara sauce (such as Rao's or Dell'Amore)
1/4 cup water
4 ounces part-skim mozzarella cheese, shredded (about 1 cup)
4 ounces whole-wheat baguette, cut into 24 thin slices and toasted

1. Preheat oven to 400°F. Line a baking sheet with aluminum foil; coat with cooking spray.
2. Place zucchini between a double layer of paper towels; squeeze to extract excess moisture. Stir together zucchini, turkey, onion, oregano, salt, pepper, and egg in a bowl. Form 24 meatballs with turkey mixture, about 1 tablespoon each; arrange on prepared baking sheet. (Turkey mixture will be very soft, but it firms up as meatballs cook.) Bake at 400°F until fully cooked, about 12 minutes.
3. Meanwhile, heat a large ovenproof skillet over medium-high. Add oil to pan; swirl to coat. Add mushrooms and garlic; cook, stirring occasionally, until mushroom liquid is mostly evaporated, about 5 minutes. Stir in marinara sauce and 1/4 cup water; reduce heat to medium, and simmer 5 minutes. Add meatballs to skillet (leave behind cooked-out proteins); gently stir to coat with sauce. Sprinkle evenly with cheese.
4. Preheat broiler with oven rack in top position. Broil meatball mixture just until cheese is melted and bubbly, about 2 minutes. Serve with toasted baguette. Serves 4 (serving size: 6 bread slices, 6 meatballs, and about 1/2 cup sauce)

CALORIES 403; FAT 21g (sat 6g, unsat 12g); PROTEIN 31g; CARB 26g; FIBER 3g; SUGARS 7g (added sugars 0g); SODIUM 693mg; CALC 26% DV; POTASSIUM 15% DV

MAKE-AHEAD LUNCH BOXES

Treat yourself to a fun midday meal with easy, produce-packed, portable lunches that are anything but boring.

Smoked Salmon Sushi Sandwiches

Hands-on: 10 min. Total: 10 min.
Love sushi rolls, but feel intimidated by the rolling technique? Try sushi sandwiches. Simply layer ingredients onto nori (seaweed), and then fold the nori to form a packet.

1 (6.3-ounce) package cooked brown sticky rice (such as Annie Chun's) or 1 packed cup cooked brown sticky rice
2 (8-inch) nori sheets
¼ cup tub-style ⅓-less-fat cream cheese
2 tablespoons thinly sliced green onions
2 ounces thinly sliced lox or other cold-smoked salmon
½ cup very thinly sliced cucumber
½ cup matchstick-cut carrots

1. Heat rice according to package directions.
2. Arrange nori sheets, rough side up, on a work surface so they're diamond-shaped. Pat ¼ cup rice into a 3½-inch square in center of each nori sheet. Spread 2 tablespoons cream cheese onto each rice square; sprinkle each with 1 tablespoon onions. Top each with even layers of 1 ounce salmon, ¼ cup cucumber, and ¼ cup carrots; pat ¼ cup rice over each stack. Bring 2 side corners of nori over filling; press gently to seal. Fold top and bottom corners over filling; press gently to seal.
3. Wrap sandwiches in wax paper or parchment paper; cut in half. Serves 2 (serving size: 1 sandwich)

CALORIES 246; **FAT** 8g (sat 4g, unsat 3g); **PROTEIN** 11g; **CARB** 34g; **FIBER** 2g; **SUGARS** 3g (added sugars 0g); **SODIUM** 699mg; **CALC** 6% DV; **POTASSIUM** 3% DV

Sushi Sandwich Lunch Box

1 Smoked Salmon Sushi Sandwich (recipe at left)
4 ounces cooked Broccolini tossed with ⅛ teaspoon reduced-sodium soy sauce
½ cup steamed edamame in pods tossed with ½ teaspoon toasted sesame oil

Serves 1

CALORIES 413; **FAT** 13g (sat 4g, unsat 8g); **PROTEIN** 23g; **CARB** 51g; **FIBER** 8g; **SUGARS** 7g (added sugars 0g); **SODIUM** 787mg; **CALC** 20% DV; **POTASSIUM** 14% DV

Lemon-Thyme Chicken Salad

Hands-on: 10 min. Total: 25 min.

4 cups water
2 bay leaves
9 ounces skinless, boneless chicken breast
¼ cup plain 2% reduced-fat Greek yogurt
1 tablespoon olive oil
1½ teaspoons fresh thyme leaves
1 teaspoon grated lemon rind
¼ teaspoon kosher salt
¼ teaspoon freshly ground black pepper
2 tablespoons slivered red onion

1. Bring 4 cups water and bay leaves to a simmer in a saucepan. Add chicken; simmer 15 minutes or until done. Drain; discard bay leaves. Cool chicken slightly; shred.
2. Combine yogurt, oil, thyme, rind, salt, and pepper in a medium bowl, stirring with a whisk. Add chicken and onion; toss well to combine. Serves 2 (serving size: about 1 cup)

CALORIES 236; **FAT** 11g (sat 2g, unsat 7g); **PROTEIN** 31g; **CARB** 2g; **FIBER** 0g; **SUGARS** 1g (added sugars 0g); **SODIUM** 307mg; **CALC** 3% DV; **POTASSIUM** 13% DV

continued

Chicken Salad Lunch Box

3 Bibb lettuce leaves
1 cup Lemon-Thyme Chicken Salad (recipe on page 257)
1 celery stalk, cut into 4 pieces
4 Peppadew peppers stuffed with 1 ounce goat cheese and sprinkled with fresh thyme
²/₃ cup cantaloupe cubes or slices

Serves 1

CALORIES 392; FAT 17g (sat 6g, unsat 9g);
PROTEIN 38g; CARB 21g; FIBER 2g; SUGARS 16g
(added sugars 4g); SODIUM 553mg; CALC 11% DV;
POTASSIUM 26% DV

Fast • Gluten Free
Make Ahead • Vegetarian

Spiced Apple Chutney

Hands-on: 10 min. Total: 20 min.
Here's an easy homemade condiment that's tangy and sweet with a little spicy kick. It's delicious as part of a cheese board, on a burger or sandwich, with pork chops or pork tenderloin, or tucked into the ultimate snack lunch, as we've done here.

1 tablespoon olive oil
¼ cup finely chopped shallots
1½ cups diced peeled Honeycrisp apple
1 tablespoon yellow mustard seeds
1 tablespoon brown sugar
⅛ teaspoon crushed red pepper
⅛ teaspoon ground cloves
Dash of kosher salt
2 tablespoons apple cider vinegar
2 tablespoons water

1. Heat a small saucepan over medium-high. Add oil; swirl to coat. Add shallots; cook 1 minute, stirring constantly. Add apple; cook 3 minutes, stirring frequently. Stir in mustard seeds, sugar, pepper, cloves, and salt. Add vinegar and 2 tablespoons water; bring to a boil. Cover, reduce heat, and simmer 10 minutes or until apples are tender and most of liquid is absorbed. Serves 4 (serving size: about 3 tablespoons)

CALORIES 83; FAT 4g (sat 1g, unsat 3g);
PROTEIN 0g; CARB 11g; FIBER 1g; SUGARS 8g
(added sugars 3g); SODIUM 33mg; CALC 3% DV;
POTASSIUM 2% DV

Fast • Make Ahead

Ploughman's Lunch Box

3 tablespoons Spiced Apple Chutney (recipe at left)
2 tablespoons Marcona almonds
½ cup seedless red or green grapes
1 ounce thinly sliced whole-wheat baguette, toasted or grilled
¾ ounce soppressata, thinly sliced
1 ounce aged Gruyère cheese, thinly sliced
4 radishes (such as red and watermelon)

Serves 1

CALORIES 498; FAT 29g (sat 9g, unsat 17g);
PROTEIN 21g; CARB 41g; FIBER 5g; SUGARS 21g
(added sugars 3g); SODIUM 746mg; CALC 37% DV;
POTASSIUM 12% DV

Fast • Make Ahead
Vegetarian

Farro, Green Bean, and Kale Salad

Hands-on: 6 min. Total: 12 min.

4 cups water
1 cup halved haricots verts or green beans
2 tablespoons red wine vinegar
1½ tablespoons extra-virgin olive oil
1 teaspoon Dijon mustard
¼ teaspoon kosher salt
¼ teaspoon freshly ground black pepper
1 (8.5-ounce) package precooked farro (2 cups)
2 cups thinly sliced lacinato kale
1 cup halved cherry or grape tomatoes
1 ounce feta cheese, crumbled (about ¼ cup)

1. Bring 4 cups water to a boil in a small saucepan. Add green beans; cook 3 to 5 minutes or until crisp-tender. Drain, and rinse well with cold water; drain.
2. Combine vinegar, oil, mustard, salt, and pepper in a medium bowl, stirring with a whisk. Heat farro according to package directions. Add farro, kale, tomatoes, and green beans to dressing; toss well. Sprinkle with cheese. Serves 2 (serving size: about 2 cups)

CALORIES 321; FAT 14g (sat 4g, unsat 9g);
PROTEIN 8g; CARB 42g; FIBER 6g; SUGARS 5g
(added sugars 0g); SODIUM 459mg; CALC 14% DV;
POTASSIUM 11% DV

Fast • Make Ahead

Farro Salad Lunch Box

2 cups Farro, Green Bean, and Kale Salad (recipe at left)
1 hard-cooked large egg, halved and wrapped with 2 dill sprigs and ¼ ounce prosciutto
1 clementine or small orange

Serves 1

CALORIES 440; FAT 20g (sat 5g, unsat 13g);
PROTEIN 17g; CARB 52g; FIBER 7g; SUGARS 12g
(added sugars 0g); SODIUM 638mg; CALC 19% DV;
POTASSIUM 17% DV

20-MINUTE MAINS

Fast • Make Ahead

Quick Green Chicken Chili

Hands-on: 20 min. Total: 20 min.
Rotisserie chicken and canned green chiles save major time.

1½ cups unsalted chicken stock, divided
2 (15-ounce) cans unsalted Great Northern beans, rinsed, drained, and divided
2 tablespoons olive oil
1 cup chopped yellow onion
1 tablespoon minced fresh garlic
1½ teaspoons all-purpose flour
1 tablespoon ground cumin
2 (4-ounce) cans mild chopped green chiles, drained
½ teaspoon black pepper, divided
¼ teaspoon kosher salt
8 ounces boneless, skinless rotisserie chicken breast, shredded (about 1 cup)
2 tablespoons fresh lime juice
¼ cup sliced radishes
2 tablespoons light sour cream
2 tablespoons fresh cilantro leaves
1 ripe avocado, sliced

1. Place ½ cup stock and 1 can beans in a blender, and blend until smooth. Heat olive oil in a large Dutch oven over medium-high. Add onion; sauté 4 minutes. Add garlic; sauté 2 minutes. Sprinkle flour over pan; cook 1 minute. Stir in cumin and chiles; cook 1 minute. Add bean mixture, remaining 1 cup stock, remaining 1 can beans, ¼ teaspoon pepper, and salt; bring to a boil.

2. Reduce heat to medium; simmer 5 minutes or until slightly thickened. Add chicken; cook 2 minutes. Stir in juice. Divide chili among 4 bowls; top evenly with radishes, sour cream, cilantro, avocado, and remaining ¼ teaspoon pepper. Serves 4 (serving size: about 1¼ cups)

CALORIES 376; FAT 16g (sat 3g, unsat 11g); PROTEIN 27g; CARB 34g; FIBER 11g; SUGARS 4g (added sugars 0g); SODIUM 636mg; CALC 12% DV; POTASSIUM 23% DV

ORANGE PREP

After zesting, remove the orange peel and pith with a paring knife. Hold the orange in one hand; use the knife to cut on both sides of each orange section, and remove.

Fast

Five-Spice Chicken Breasts with Sesame-Orange Beans

Hands-on: 20 min. Total: 20 min.
Five-spice powder packs some serious aromatic punch; it's all you need to season the chicken breasts here. You can sub broccoli florets or chopped kale for the green beans.

2 tablespoons canola oil, divided
4 (6-ounce) skinless, boneless chicken breasts
2 teaspoons five-spice powder
½ teaspoon kosher salt
¾ cup thinly sliced red onion
1½ teaspoons grated orange rind
2 garlic cloves, thinly sliced
1 (12-ounce) package haricots verts (French green beans)
1½ tablespoons reduced-sodium soy sauce
½ cup orange sections
4 teaspoons toasted sesame oil

1. Heat 1 tablespoon canola oil in an oven-safe skillet over medium-high. Sprinkle chicken with five-spice powder and salt. Add chicken to pan; cook 5 minutes on each side or until done. Remove from pan. Let stand 5 minutes. Cut across the grain into slices.

2. Add remaining 1 tablespoon canola oil to pan. Add onion; sauté 4 to 5 minutes or until browned. Add orange rind and garlic; cook 30 seconds, stirring constantly. Add haricots verts; cook 4 minutes or until lightly browned and crisp-tender. Stir in soy sauce. Top with orange sections, and drizzle with sesame oil. Serve with chicken. Serves 4 (serving size: 1 breast and about ½ cup green bean mixture)

CALORIES 363; FAT 17g (sat 2g, unsat 12g); PROTEIN 41g; CARB 13g; FIBER 3g; SUGARS 6g (added sugars 0g); SODIUM 538mg; CALC 7% DV; POTASSIUM 8% DV

FIVE-SPICE POWDER BACKS SOME SERIOUS AROMATIC PUNCH. FOR MORE IDEAS ABOUT HOW TO USE IT, SEE PAGE 261.

Fast • Gluten Free
Make Ahead

Skillet Red Beans and Rice

Hands-on: 20 min. Total: 20 min.
Look for trinity blend (a mix of onion, bell pepper, and celery) with the prepared produce. Or make your own with 3/4 cup onion, 3/4 cup celery, and 1/2 cup bell pepper.

4 ounces chopped andouille sausage
3 garlic cloves, chopped
1 (8-ounce) package fresh trinity
**   blend**
1/2 cup chopped red bell pepper
1 (15-ounce) can unsalted kidney
**   beans, rinsed and drained**
2/3 cup unsalted chicken stock
1 tablespoon red wine vinegar
1/2 teaspoon kosher salt
1/4 teaspoon ground red pepper
2 (8.8-ounce) packages precooked
**   brown rice (such as Uncle Ben's)**
1/3 cup chopped green onions

1. Heat a large nonstick skillet over medium-high. Add sausage; cook 4 minutes or until browned, stirring occasionally. Add garlic, trinity blend, and red bell pepper; sauté 3 minutes or until tender. Stir in beans and next 4 ingredients (through ground red pepper). Cover, bring to a simmer, and cook 4 minutes. Mash half of bean mixture in pan. Stir in rice; cover, and cook 4 minutes. Sprinkle with green onions. Serves 4 (serving size: about 2 cups rice mixture)

CALORIES 329; **FAT** 6g (sat 1g, unsat 5g); **PROTEIN** 17g; **CARB** 54g; **FIBER** 12g; **SUGARS** 3g (added sugars 2g); **SODIUM** 505mg; **CALC** 7% DV; **POTASSIUM** 14% DV

Fast • Gluten Free

Shrimp Fried Cauliflower Rice

Hands-on: 20 min. Total: 20 min.
This five-ingredient main is a great way to get more seafood into your weeknight rotation. Seek out shrimp that's free of sodium tripolyphosphate (STP), a common preservative that significantly boosts the sodium in your shrimp. Can't find riced cauliflower? Make your own by pulsing cauliflower florets in a food processor until crumbled. Easy!

3 tablespoons toasted sesame oil,
**   divided**
10 ounces medium shrimp, peeled
**   and deveined**
5 large eggs, lightly beaten
1 cup sliced green onions, divided
16 ounces fresh or frozen riced
**   cauliflower (such as Green Giant)**
1/2 teaspoon freshly ground black
**   pepper**
1/4 teaspoon kosher salt

1. Heat 1½ teaspoons sesame oil in a large nonstick skillet over medium-high. Add shrimp; cook 3 minutes. Remove shrimp from pan.
2. Return pan to medium-high. Add 1½ teaspoons oil. Add eggs; cook 2 minutes or until almost set, stirring once. Fold cooked eggs in half; remove from pan. Cool, and cut into ½-inch pieces.
3. Heat remaining 2 tablespoons oil in pan over medium-high. Add ¾ cup green onions and cauliflower; cook 5 minutes, without stirring, or until browned. Stir in shrimp, eggs, pepper, and salt. Top with remaining ¼ cup green onions. Serves 4 (serving size: about 1 cup)

CALORIES 269; **FAT** 17g (sat 4g, unsat 12g); **PROTEIN** 20g; **CARB** 9g; **FIBER** 3g; **SUGARS** 3g (added sugars 0g); **SODIUM** 358mg; **CALC** 12% DV; **POTASSIUM** 16% DV

THE SHORTCUT

SHORTCUT INGREDIENTS

Rotisserie chicken, canned chickpeas, and fresh vegetables bulk up these bowls for a meal that's practically no-cook. You'll find microwave-in-bag farro in the grain aisle.

Staff Favorite • Fast
Make Ahead

15-Minute Chicken Shawarma Bowls

Hands-on: 15 min. Total: 15 min.
This Middle Eastern–inspired bowl is all about big flavor with minimal effort. A garlicky, tahini-spiked yogurt brings all the elements together and takes just minutes to make. Assemble a few bowls at the beginning of the week for easy make-ahead lunches.

12 ounces skinless, boneless rotisserie
**   chicken breast, shredded (about**
**   3 cups)**
2 teaspoons olive oil
3/4 teaspoon kosher salt, divided
1/2 teaspoon cumin, divided
1/8 teaspoon paprika
1/2 cup plain 2% reduced-fat
**   Greek yogurt**
1 tablespoon fresh lemon juice
1 tablespoon tahini (sesame seed
**   paste)**
1 teaspoon minced fresh garlic
1 (8.5-ounce) package precooked
**   farro**
2 cups chopped English cucumber
2 cups halved cherry tomatoes
1 (15-ounce) can unsalted chickpeas,
**   rinsed and drained**
2 tablespoons chopped fresh parsley
1/4 teaspoon freshly ground black
**   pepper**

1. Place chicken and oil in a large bowl; toss to coat. Combine ½ teaspoon salt, ¼ teaspoon cumin, and paprika in a bowl. Add spice mixture to chicken mixture; toss to coat.
2. Combine remaining ¼ teaspoon salt, remaining ¼ teaspoon cumin, yogurt, lemon juice, tahini, and garlic in a small bowl. Set aside.
3. Heat farro according to package directions. Place ½ cup farro in each of 4 bowls. Top each serving with about ¾ cup chicken mixture, ½ cup cucumber, ½ cup tomatoes, about ⅓ cup chickpeas, and 2½ tablespoons Greek yogurt mixture. Top with parsley and black pepper. Serves 4 (serving size: 1 bowl)

CALORIES 395; **FAT** 9g (sat 2g, unsat 5g); **PROTEIN** 36g; **CARB** 42g; **FIBER** 7g; **SUGARS** 5g (added sugars 0g); **SODIUM** 677mg; **CALC** 12% DV; **POTASSIUM** 21% DV

USE IT UP

WAYS TO USE FIVE-SPICE POWDER

This fragrant spice blend—made from cumin, star anise, cinnamon, peppercorns, and cloves—gives the chicken on page 259 its distinctive flavor. Look for it on the spice aisle, and use it to lend sweet depth to your everyday cooking.

Fast • Vegetarian
Spiced Whiskey Sour
Five-spice powder turns the classic whiskey sour into something special. You can double, triple, or quadruple the spiced sugar syrup and refrigerate for up to two weeks. Use in cocktails, or drizzle over hot oatmeal.

1. Combine 2 tablespoons water and 1½ tablespoons sugar in a small microwave-safe bowl; microwave at HIGH for 20 seconds

or until sugar dissolves. Stir in ½ teaspoon five-spice powder; cool to room temperature.
2. Place sugar syrup, 3 tablespoons fresh lemon juice, and 3 ounces bourbon in a cocktail shaker filled with ice; shake mixture for 10 seconds. Strain into 2 glasses filled with ice. Garnish each drink with a lemon rind strip, if desired. Serves 2 (serving size: about ½ cup)

CALORIES 140; **FAT** 0g; **PROTEIN** 0g; **CARB** 11g; **FIBER** 0g; **SUGARS** 10g (added sugars 9g); **SODIUM** 1mg; **CALC** 0% DV; **POTASSIUM** 1% DV

Gluten Free • Vegetarian
Spicy Sweet Potato Wedges
Smoky, fiery chipotle powder counters the warm, sweet five-spice powder and naturally sweet spuds. For less kick, use ¼ teaspoon chipotle. Be sure to line the pan with parchment paper to help prevent burning.

1. Preheat oven to 500°F.
2. Cut 1½ pounds unpeeled sweet potatoes lengthwise into ½- to ⅔-inch wedges; place in a bowl. Drizzle with 2 tablespoons olive oil; toss to coat. Sprinkle with ½ teaspoon kosher salt, ½ teaspoon five-spice powder, and ½ teaspoon chipotle chile powder; toss well.
3. Arrange wedges in a single layer on a baking sheet lined with parchment paper. Bake at 500°F for 20 minutes or until tender, turning after 10 minutes. Serves 4 (serving size: 6 ounces)

CALORIES 207; **FAT** 7g (sat 1g, unsat 6g); **PROTEIN** 3g; **CARB** 34g; **FIBER** 5g; **SUGARS** 7g (added sugars 0g); **SODIUM** 343mg; **CALC** 5% DV; **POTASSIUM** 17% DV

Fast • Make Ahead
Five-Spice Flank Steak
This quick spice rub lends robust flavor and helps achieve delicious charring on the surface of the meat. Flank steak is a lean cut that's relatively inexpensive; be sure to slice thinly across the grain for tender bites.

1. Combine 1 teaspoon five-spice powder, 1 teaspoon light brown sugar, ¾ teaspoon kosher salt, ¾ teaspoon garlic powder, and ¼ teaspoon ground red pepper in a small bowl. Rub spice mixture over both sides of a 1-pound flank steak.
2. Heat a large cast-iron skillet over medium-high. Add 1 tablespoon olive oil to pan; swirl to coat. Add steak to pan; cook 4 minutes on each side or until desired degree of doneness. Remove steak from pan; let stand 5 to 10 minutes. Cut steak across the grain into thin slices. Serves 4 (serving size: 3 ounces)

CALORIES 266; **FAT** 14g (sat 5g, unsat 8g); **PROTEIN** 31g; **CARB** 2g; **FIBER** 0g; **SUGARS** 1g (added sugars 1g); **SODIUM** 421mg; **CALC** 2% DV; **POTASSIUM** 11% DV

4 GO-WITH-ANYTHING SIDES

Fast • Gluten Free
Make Ahead • Vegetarian
Almond-Garlic Swiss Chard
Don't toss those stems! They have a lovely texture when sautéed. Use rainbow chard for stems that will add a vibrant pop of color.

Heat 2 tablespoons extra-virgin olive oil in a large skillet over medium-high. Add 3 thinly sliced garlic cloves; cook 2 minutes or until aromatic and golden-brown. Add 8 cups chopped Swiss chard, including stems (about 8 ounces), and ¼ teaspoon kosher salt; cook 3 minutes or until chard is slightly wilted and bright green. Stir in ⅓ cup toasted sliced almonds. Serves 4 (serving size: about ⅔ cup)

CALORIES 118; **FAT** 11g (sat 1g, unsat 9g); **PROTEIN** 3g; **CARB** 5g; **FIBER** 2g; **SUGARS** 1g (added sugars 0g); **SODIUM** 241mg; **CALC** 5% DV; **POTASSIUM** 0% DV

continued

Fast • Make Ahead
Vegetarian
Cauliflower-Couscous Toss
Use this recipe as a template for any hearty vegetables and grains you have, like broccoli and green beans or quinoa and farro.

Preheat oven to 450°F. Cook ⅔ cup Israeli couscous according to package directions; cool. Arrange 2 cups cauliflower florets on a sheet pan; bake at 450°F for 11 minutes. Combine couscous, cauliflower, ¼ cup chopped parsley, 3 tablespoons chopped green onions, 2 tablespoons chopped fresh dill, 2 tablespoons pine nuts, 2 tablespoons fresh lemon juice, 2 tablespoons olive oil, and ⅝ teaspoon kosher salt. Serves 4 (serving size: about ⅔ cup)

CALORIES 192; FAT 10g (sat 1g, unsat 8g); PROTEIN 4g; CARB 23g; FIBER 3g; SUGARS 2g (added sugars 0g); SODIUM 321mg; CALC 2% DV; POTASSIUM 7% DV

Fast • Gluten Free
Make Ahead • Vegetarian
Roasted Butternut with Sage and Thyme
Sometimes the simplest dishes are the best. In this one, butternut squash combines with oil, sage, and thyme for a can't-be-beat weeknight side.

Preheat oven to 425°F. Peel and seed 1 (2-pound) butternut squash; halve lengthwise. Cut crosswise into ¾-inch slices. Toss with 2 tablespoons olive oil, 1 tablespoon chopped fresh sage, 1½ teaspoons chopped fresh thyme, ½ teaspoon kosher salt, and ¼ teaspoon black pepper. Arrange on a baking sheet. Bake at 425°F for 20 minutes. Serves 4 (serving size: about ⅔ cup)

CALORIES 147; FAT 7g (sat 1g, unsat 6g); PROTEIN 2g; CARB 23g; FIBER 4g; SUGARS 4g (added sugars 0g); SODIUM 248mg; CALC 10% DV; POTASSIUM 19% DV

Fast • Gluten Free
Vegetarian
Broccoli-and-Arugula Salad
Packaged broccoli slaw adds instant crunch and color to this salad. You can also toss it into stir-fries, use it to bulk up chili, or add it to quiche or casseroles for a veggie boost.

Combine 3 tablespoons extra-virgin olive oil, 2 tablespoons sherry or apple cider vinegar, ½ teaspoon black pepper, and ⅜ teaspoon kosher salt in a large bowl, stirring with a whisk. Add 3 cups baby arugula (about 3 ounces), 1½ cups broccoli slaw mix, and 1 cup shredded carrot; toss gently to combine. Serves 4 (serving size: about ⅔ cup)

CALORIES 120; FAT 10g (sat 1g, unsat 9g); PROTEIN 1g; CARB 7g; FIBER 2g; SUGARS 5g (added sugars 0g); SODIUM 214mg; CALC 6% DV; POTASSIUM 5% DV

4 SAUCES FOR ANY PROTEIN

Fast • Gluten Free
Vegetarian
End-of-Summer Tomato Salsa
Late-season cherry tomatoes and woodsy thyme bridge the seasons in this versatile condiment. Try it on everything from grilled chicken breasts to sautéed salmon and roasted pork tenderloin.

Combine 2 tablespoons extra-virgin olive oil, 1 tablespoon balsamic vinegar, ½ teaspoon freshly ground black pepper, ⅜ teaspoon kosher salt, and 1 grated garlic clove in a medium bowl; whisk until well blended. Stir in 1½ cups halved or quartered cherry tomatoes, ¼ cup slivered shallots, and 2 teaspoons fresh thyme leaves. Serves 4 (serving size: about ⅓ cup)

CALORIES 83; FAT 7g (sat 1g, unsat 6g); PROTEIN 1g; CARB 5g; FIBER 1g; SUGARS 3g (added sugars 0g); SODIUM 185mg; CALC 2% DV; POTASSIUM 5% DV

Fast • Make Ahead
Miso-Chili-Garlic Sauce
Just four ingredients deliver big umami flavor with a hint of heat thanks to the chili garlic sauce. It pairs well with most proteins— we like it with shrimp, chicken, or tofu. Thin leftover sauce with a little sesame oil for a quick salad dressing.

Combine 2 tablespoons white or yellow miso paste, 1 tablespoon chili garlic sauce, and 1 teaspoon fish sauce in a medium bowl; stir with a whisk until well blended. Slowly whisk in 6 tablespoons toasted sesame oil until blended. Serves 8 (serving size: 1 tablespoon)

CALORIES 98; FAT 10g (sat 1g, unsat 8g); PROTEIN 1g; CARB 2g; FIBER 1g; SUGARS 1g (added sugars 0g); SODIUM 220mg; CALC 0% DV; POTASSIUM 0% DV

Fast • Gluten Free
Vegetarian
Cilantro-Caper Sauce
Herby, garlicky, and briny, this easy food processor sauce is a loose combination of classic Italian salsa verde and Argentinian chimichurri. Use it to brighten up seared pork chops, grilled steak, or grilled chicken skewers.

Place 1 cup coarsely chopped fresh cilantro leaves and stems, ¼ cup chopped green onions, 2 tablespoons drained capers, and 1 garlic clove in a mini food processor; pulse until finely chopped. Add ¼ cup extra-virgin olive oil, 2 tablespoons water, 1½ tablespoons red wine vinegar, ¼ teaspoons kosher salt, and ¼ teaspoon crushed red pepper; process until well blended. Serves 4 (serving size: about 3 tablespoons)

CALORIES 126; FAT 14g (sat 2g, unsat 11g); PROTEIN 0g; CARB 1g; FIBER 1g; SUGARS 0g; SODIUM 226mg; CALC 1% dv; POTASSIUM 1% DV

Fast • Gluten Free
Make Ahead • Vegetarian
Quick Roasted Red Pepper Sauce
A quick whir in the food processor brings this romesco-style sauce together in seconds. The ingredients are also easy to keep on hand for a last-minute sauce that's delicious on mild fish fillets or simple baked chicken breasts.

Pulse ⅓ cup whole unsalted almonds in a mini food processor until chopped. Add 12 ounces bottled drained roasted red peppers, and blend into a chunky paste. Add 1 tablespoon extra-virgin olive oil, 2 teaspoons smoked paprika, and 1 ounce grated Parmesan cheese; process until just combined. Serves 12 (serving size: 2 tablespoons)

CALORIES 54; FAT 4g (sat 1g, unsat 3g); PROTEIN 2g; CARB 3g; FIBER 2g; SUGARS 0g (added sugars 0g); SODIUM 101mg; CALC 6% DV; POTASSIUM 1% DV

WEEKNIGHT MAINS

Quick Chicken Picatta with Parslied Orzo

Hands-on: 35 min. Total: 35 min.
Cook the orzo while you bread the chicken; while the chicken cooks, spread the orzo on a baking sheet to cool and to keep the grains from sticking together.

1 cup uncooked whole-wheat orzo
3 tablespoons lemon juice, divided
2½ tablespoons extra-virgin olive oil, divided
½ cup finely chopped flat-leaf parsley
½ teaspoon kosher salt, divided
½ teaspoon freshly ground black pepper, divided
½ cup all-purpose flour
4 (4-ounce) chicken breast cutlets

¼ cup finely chopped shallot
2 teaspoons minced fresh garlic
8 thin lemon slices, seeds removed
1 tablespoon capers, drained
1 tablespoon unsalted butter

1. Cook orzo according to package directions, omitting salt and fat; drain. Spread orzo on a baking sheet; cool 10 minutes. Place orzo in a bowl; add 1 tablespoon juice, 1½ tablespoons oil, parsley, ¼ teaspoon salt, and ¼ teaspoon pepper, stirring to combine.
2. Place flour in a shallow dish. Sprinkle chicken with remaining ¼ teaspoon salt and remaining ¼ teaspoon pepper. Dredge chicken in flour, shaking off excess. Heat remaining 1 tablespoon oil in a large skillet over medium-high. Add chicken; cook 3 minutes on each side or until done. Place chicken on a platter (do not wipe out pan).
3. Add shallot and garlic to pan; cook 2 minutes, stirring frequently. Stir in remaining 2 tablespoons juice and lemon slices, scraping pan to loosen browned bits. Reduce heat to low; add capers and butter, stirring until butter melts. Spoon lemon mixture over chicken. Serve with orzo. Serves 4 (serving size: 1 cutlet and about ½ cup orzo mixture)

CALORIES 459; FAT 15g (sat 4g, unsat 9g); PROTEIN 33g; CARB 45g; FIBER 8g; SUGARS 1g (added sugars 0g); SODIUM 348mg; CALC 3% DV; POTASSIUM 14% DV

Gluten Free

Steak Salad with Butternut Squash and Cranberries

Hands-on: 20 min. Total: 35 min.
A summer classic leans into fall with roasted butternut squash, tart-sweet dried cranberries, and fresh rosemary. Find peeled, diced fresh butternut squash in the produce section. You can sub crumbled

goat cheese or feta for the blue cheese and walnuts or pecans for the hazelnuts.

1 (11-ounce) package peeled diced butternut squash
Cooking spray
¾ teaspoon kosher salt, divided
½ teaspoon freshly ground black pepper, divided
1 (8-ounce) sirloin steak
3 tablespoons olive oil
1 tablespoon white wine vinegar
1 teaspoon minced fresh rosemary
1 (5-ounce) package baby spinach
¼ cup dried cranberries
¼ cup toasted hazelnuts, chopped
1 small shallot, thinly sliced
1 ounce blue cheese, crumbled (about ¼ cup)

1. Preheat oven to 425°F.
2. Arrange butternut squash in a single layer on a rimmed baking sheet; coat with cooking spray. Sprinkle evenly with ¼ teaspoon salt and ¼ teaspoon pepper. Bake at 425°F for 15 minutes or until browned, stirring once halfway through cooking.
3. Heat a medium skillet over medium-high. Coat pan with cooking spray. Sprinkle steak with ¼ teaspoon salt and remaining ¼ teaspoon pepper. Add steak to pan; cook 4 minutes on each side or until desired degree of doneness. Place steak on a cutting board; let stand 10 minutes. Cut steak across the grain into thin slices.
4. Combine remaining ¼ teaspoon salt, olive oil, vinegar, and rosemary in a small bowl, stirring with a whisk. Arrange spinach on a platter; top with butternut squash, cranberries, and steak. Sprinkle with hazelnuts and shallot. Drizzle vinegar mixture over top. Sprinkle with cheese. Serves 4 (serving size: 2 ounces steak and about 1½ cups salad)

CALORIES 350; FAT 24g (sat 6g, unsat 16g); PROTEIN 16g; CARB 20g; FIBER 4g; SUGARS 8g (added sugars 4g); SODIUM 503mg; CALC 14% DV; POTASSIUM 16% DV

Fast • Make Ahead

Garlicky Kale, Sausage, and Tomato Pasta

Hands-on: 30 min. Total: 30 min.
Just in time for fall, this dish combines juicy tomatoes with hearty whole-wheat pasta, sausage, and kale. Try Bionaturae or Barilla whole-wheat spaghetti; both have a light color and mild wheat flavor.

8 ounces uncooked whole-wheat or multigrain spaghetti
Cooking spray
6 ounces mild pork Italian sausage
2 1/2 tablespoons olive oil
1/4 teaspoons crushed red pepper
5 garlic cloves, thinly sliced
4 cups coarsely chopped stemmed curly kale
1 pint small cherry tomatoes or grape tomatoes
2 tablespoons unsalted tomato paste
3/8 teaspoon kosher salt
1 ounce Parmigiano-Reggiano cheese, shaved

1. Cook pasta according to package directions, omitting salt and fat. Drain in a colander over a bowl, reserving 1 cup pasta cooking liquid.

2. Heat a large skillet over medium-high. Coat pan with cooking spray. Add sausage; cook 5 minutes or until browned, stirring to crumble. Remove sausage from pan.
3. Add oil to pan; swirl to coat. Add pepper and garlic; cook 30 seconds. Stir in kale and tomatoes; cover, and cook 6 minutes or until tomatoes soften and wilt, stirring occasionally. Push kale and tomatoes to outer edges of pan. Add tomato paste to center of pan; cook 1 minute, stirring constantly. Gradually add reserved 1 cup pasta cooking liquid, stirring constantly. Stir in sausage and salt. Add pasta to pan; cook 3 minutes, stirring to coat. Top with cheese. Serves 4 (serving size: about 1 1/3 cups pasta mixture and 1 tablespoon cheese)

CALORIES 426; **FAT** 19g (sat 4g, unsat 12g); **PROTEIN** 19g; **CARB** 47g; **FIBER** 6g; **SUGARS** 6g (added sugars 0g); **SODIUM** 478mg; **CALC** 13% DV; **POTASSIUM** 12% DV

Vegetarian

Skillet Mushroom Mac and Cheese

Hands-on: 40 min. Total: 40 min.
Mushrooms and aged Gruyère cheese add heft and depth to this vegetarian main.

8 ounces uncooked whole-wheat elbow pasta (such as Bionaturae)
1 tablespoon extra-virgin olive oil
1 (8-ounce) package cremini mushrooms, cut into quarters
4 ounces shiitake mushroom caps, cut into halves
5 teaspoons chopped fresh thyme
1/2 teaspoon kosher salt
2 tablespoons all-purpose flour
1 1/2 cups 2% reduced-fat milk
2 ounces Gruyère cheese, shredded (about 1/2 cup)
2 ounces low-moisture part-skim mozzarella cheese, shredded and divided (about 1/2 cup)

3 cups baby spinach
2 tablespoons whole-wheat panko (Japanese breadcrumbs)

1. Preheat oven to 375°F.
2. Cook pasta according to package directions, omitting salt and fat; drain.
3. Heat oil in a large oven-safe skillet over medium-high. Add mushrooms; cook 4 minutes or until lightly browned. Stir in 1 tablespoon thyme and salt; cook 2 minutes. Sprinkle flour over pan; cook 1 minute. Add milk; bring to a simmer. Add pasta, Gruyère cheese, and 1 ounce mozzarella cheese, stirring until cheese melts. Stir in spinach. Spread pasta mixture in an even layer in pan; sprinkle with remaining 1 ounce mozzarella cheese and panko.
4. Bake at 375°F for 10 minutes. Carefully remove pan from oven; sprinkle with remaining 2 teaspoons thyme. Serves 4 (serving size: about 1 1/2 cups)

CALORIES 442; **FAT** 15g (sat 6g, unsat 6g); **PROTEIN** 21g; **CARB** 57g; **FIBER** 7g; **SUGARS** 9g (added sugars 0g); **SODIUM** 505mg; **CALC** 41% DV; **POTASSIUM** 18% DV

Ham and Sweet Potato Hash

Hands-on: 40 min. Total: 40 min.
This colorful breakfast-for-dinner dish uses sweet potatoes and red bell peppers for a double hit of beta-carotene, a carotenoid that most recently was shown to potentially lower breast cancer risk.

2¹/₂ cups (¹/₂-inch) diced peeled sweet potatoes
4 tablespoons water, divided
2¹/₂ tablespoons extra-virgin olive oil, divided
5 ounces reduced-sodium ham (such as Boar's Head), diced
1¹/₂ cups finely chopped leeks
1 cup chopped red bell pepper
¹/₂ teaspoon freshly ground black pepper, divided
¹/₄ teaspoon kosher salt, divided
¹/₃ cup chopped fresh flat-leaf parsley
4 large eggs (in shells)
¹/₂ teaspoon hot sauce (optional)

1. Place potatoes and 2 tablespoons water in a microwave-safe dish; cover with plastic wrap. Microwave at HIGH 5 minutes or until tender. Place potatoes on a paper towel–lined plate. Let stand 5 minutes.
2. Heat 1 teaspoon oil in a cast-iron skillet over medium. Add ham; cook 8 minutes or until browned and crisp, stirring occasionally. Remove ham to a paper towel–lined plate.
3. Increase heat to medium-high. Add 1 tablespoon oil to drippings in pan. Add leeks; sauté 1¹/₂ minutes. Add remaining 2 tablespoons water to leek mixture; cook 1¹/₂ minutes. Add 2 teaspoons oil, potatoes, bell pepper, ¹/₄ teaspoon black pepper, and ¹/₈ teaspoon salt; cook 6 to 8 minutes or until potatoes are crisp. Stir in ham and parsley. Divide potato mixture evenly among 4 plates.
4. Reduce heat to medium. Add remaining 1¹/₂ teaspoons oil to pan.

Crack eggs into pan; cook 3 to 4 minutes or until whites are set. Place 1 egg over each serving; sprinkle evenly with remaining ¹/₄ teaspoon black pepper and remaining ¹/₈ teaspoon salt. Drizzle with hot sauce, if desired. Serves 4 (serving size: about 1¹/₂ cups potato mixture and 1 egg)

CALORIES 308; FAT 16g (sat 4g, unsat 12g); PROTEIN 16g; CARB 25g; FIBER 4g; SUGARS 7g (added sugars 0g); SODIUM 661mg; CALC 7% DV; POTASSIUM 18% DV

SLOW COOKER

GO MEATLESS

The tricks to a fantastic vegetarian main in the slow cooker are to start with hearty vegetables, go bold with spices, and keep liquid to a minimum so that the result is rich and complex, not soupy and bland.

**Staff Favorite • Gluten Free
Make Ahead • Vegetarian**

Sweet Potato-and-Red Lentil Curry

Hands-on: 15 min. Total: 8 hr. 15 min.
This fragrant, Indian-style stew hits all the right notes with aromatic garam masala, fresh ginger, and concentrated red curry paste. The coconut milk mellows and loosens the potato and lentil mixture just enough so that it can be spooned over rice.

4 cups cubed peeled sweet potato (about 2 medium)
3¹/₂ cups water, divided
2 cups dried red lentils
2 cups low-sodium fat-free vegetable broth
³/₄ cup finely chopped white onion
3 tablespoons Thai red curry paste (such as Thai Kitchen)
2 teaspoons garam masala

2 teaspoons grated peeled fresh ginger
2 teaspoons ground turmeric
Cooking spray
1 tablespoon sugar, divided
³/₄ teaspoon kosher salt
3 garlic cloves, minced
1 (6-ounce) can tomato paste
1 cup canned light coconut milk
¹/₂ cup apple cider vinegar
1 cup very thinly sliced red onion
4 cups hot cooked brown rice
1 cup fresh cilantro leaves

1. Place sweet potato, 3 cups water, and next 7 ingredients (through turmeric) in a 5- to 6-quart electric slow cooker coated with cooking spray. Add 1 teaspoon sugar, salt, garlic, and tomato paste; stir well to combine. Cover and cook on low 8 hours. Turn off heat; stir in coconut milk. Let stand, covered, 5 minutes.
2. Combine remaining ¹/₂ cup water, remaining 2 teaspoons sugar, and vinegar in a microwave-safe bowl; microwave at HIGH 2 minutes or until boiling. Add onion to vinegar mixture; let stand 20 minutes at room temperature. Drain.
3. Place ¹/₂ cup rice in each of 8 shallow bowls. Top each serving with 1¹/₄ cups lentil mixture, 2 tablespoons red onion mixture, and 2 tablespoons cilantro. Serves 8

CALORIES 395; FAT 3g (sat 2g, unsat 1g); PROTEIN 17g; CARB 75g; FIBER 8g; SUGARS 11g (added sugars 2g); SODIUM 548mg; CALC 6% DV; POTASSIUM 16% DV

1 LIST
3 DINNERS

Shop this list to feed four for three nights, all for about $30. Read the recipes first to see what staples you already have on hand.

1 large onion

1 package fresh basil

2 (12-ounce) packages steam-in-bag fresh broccoli florets

1 lemon

Garlic

2 limes

4 carrots

4 radishes

1 avocado

1 loaf whole-wheat sourdough bread

8 (6-inch) corn tortillas

1 tube unsalted tomato paste

2 (14.5-ounce) cans unsalted fire-roasted tomatoes

1 (32-ounce) container unsalted chicken stock

1 (7-ounce) container plain whole-milk Greek yogurt

6 (6-ounce) fresh or frozen tilapia fillets, thawed

**Fast • Gluten Free
Make Ahead**

Fire-Roasted Tomato-Basil Soup

Hands-on: 20 min. Total: 25 min.
Start with canned fire-roasted tomatoes to give the soup some smoky depth. Serve with sliced toasted sourdough and steamed broccoli from your list.

1 tablespoon olive oil
1 1/2 cups chopped onion
1/2 teaspoon kosher salt, divided
1/4 teaspoon crushed red pepper
2 teaspoons minced garlic
1 tablespoon unsalted tomato paste
2 cups unsalted chicken stock
1/2 cup torn basil leaves
2 (14.5-ounce) cans unsalted fire-roasted tomatoes
1/2 teaspoon sugar
1/4 teaspoon freshly ground black pepper
1/2 cup plain whole-milk Greek yogurt
2 tablespoons chopped fresh basil

1. Heat oil in a large Dutch oven over medium-high. Add onion; sauté 3 minutes. Add 1/4 teaspoon salt, crushed red pepper, and garlic; cook 1 minute. Stir in tomato paste; cook 1 minute. Add stock, torn basil leaves, and tomatoes; bring to a simmer. Cook 8 minutes. Stir in remaining 1/4 teaspoon salt, sugar, and freshly ground black pepper.
2. Place tomato mixture in a blender. Remove center piece from blender lid (to allow steam to escape); secure lid on blender. Place a clean towel over opening (to avoid splatters); blend until smooth. Place 1/4 cup soup and yogurt in a small bowl; stir until smooth. Stir yogurt mixture into remaining soup. Divide soup among 4 bowls; top evenly with

---

chopped basil. Serves 4 (serving size: about 1 1/4 cups soup)

CALORIES 155; **FAT** 5g (sat 1g, unsat 4g); **PROTEIN** 8g; **CARB** 20g; **FIBER** 3g; **SUGARS** 12g (added sugars 2g); **SODIUM** 346mg; **CALC** 6% DV; **POTASSIUM** 6% DV

Fast • Gluten Free

Blackened Tilapia Tacos with Basil-Lime Mayo

Hands-on: 20 min. Total: 20 min.
Firm tilapia can stand up to the simple yet robust spice rub here. Double the basil-mayo mixture and use as a veggie dip or sandwich spread for lunch.

3/4 teaspoon ground paprika
3/4 teaspoon kosher salt, divided
1/2 teaspoon ground cumin
1/4 teaspoon ground red pepper
2 (6-ounce) tilapia fillets, cut crosswise into 1/2-inch-thick pieces
1 tablespoon canola oil
2 tablespoons canola mayonnaise
2 tablespoons plain whole-milk Greek yogurt
2 tablespoons finely chopped fresh basil
1 tablespoon fresh lime juice
1/2 teaspoon water
8 (6-inch) corn tortillas, warmed
1 cup shaved carrot ribbons
1/2 cup thinly sliced radishes
1 avocado, peeled and sliced
4 lime wedges

1. Combine paprika, 1/2 teaspoon salt, cumin, and ground red pepper in a bowl. Rub spice mixture evenly over fish pieces. Heat oil in a large non-stick skillet over medium-high. Add fish; cook 2 minutes on each side or until done.

2. Combine remaining ¼ teaspoon salt, mayonnaise, yogurt, basil, juice, and ½ teaspoon water in a bowl. Top tortillas evenly with carrot ribbons, radishes, avocado, fish, and mayonnaise mixture. Serve with lime wedges. Serves 4 (serving size: 2 tacos)

CALORIES 354; FAT 15g (sat 2g, unsat 11g); PROTEIN 22g; CARB 39g; FIBER 8g; SUGARS 4g (added sugars 0g); SODIUM 507mg; CALC 7% DV; POTASSIUM 17% DV

Fast

Sheet Pan Baked Tilapia with Roasted Vegetables

Hands-on: 15 min. Total: 30 min.
Arrange the fish and the broccoli-carrot mixture on the same pan for quick cleanup. Add lemon wedges and bring to the table for a gorgeous presentation.

1 tablespoon butter
1 garlic clove, minced
2 ounces whole-wheat sourdough bread, finely ground
2.25 ounces all-purpose flour (about ½ cup)
1 egg, lightly beaten
4 (6-ounce) tilapia fillets
¾ teaspoon kosher salt, divided
½ teaspoon freshly ground black pepper, divided
1½ tablespoons olive oil
1 (12-ounce) package steam-in-bag fresh broccoli florets
2 medium carrots, peeled and diagonally sliced
Cooking spray
1 lemon, cut into wedges

1. Preheat oven to 400°F.
2. Melt butter in a skillet over medium-high. Add garlic; cook 30 seconds. Add breadcrumbs; cook 5 minutes.
3. Place breadcrumb mixture, flour, and egg in three shallow dishes. Sprinkle fish with ½ teaspoon salt and ¼ teaspoon pepper. Dredge fish in flour; dip in egg. Coat in breadcrumb mixture.
4. Combine remaining ¼ teaspoon salt, remaining ¼ teaspoon pepper, oil, broccoli, and carrots on a sheet pan coated with cooking spray; add fish to pan. Bake at 400°F for 15 minutes or until done. Serve with lemon wedges. Serves 4 (serving size: 1 fillet and about 1 cup vegetables)

CALORIES 389; FAT 13g (sat 4g, unsat 8g); PROTEIN 42g; CARB 27g; FIBER 5g; SUGARS 3g (added sugars 0g); SODIUM 598mg; CALC 11% DV; POTASSIUM 28% DV

1 INGREDIENT, 3 SIDES

3 WAYS TO USE PARSNIPS

Parsnips are the carrot's sweeter, starchier cousin, perfect for roasting. Be sure to trim the tops and remove their tough skins before cooking.

Fast • Gluten Free
Make Ahead • Vegetarian
Pecan-and-Raisin Parsnips
Parsnips pair beautifully with piney rosemary and toasted pecans for a taste of early fall. A splash of red wine vinegar lifts the dish.

1. Combine 2 cups peeled parsnips, cut diagonally into ½-inch pieces, and 3 tablespoons water in a non-stick skillet over medium-high; bring to a simmer. Cover, and cook 2 minutes or until water evaporates.

2. Uncover; stir in 1 tablespoon olive oil, 1 teaspoon chopped fresh rosemary, ½ teaspoon kosher salt, and ¼ teaspoon black pepper. Cook 3 minutes or until parsnips are browned and tender. Stir in 1 teaspoon red wine vinegar; remove from heat. Stir in 2 tablespoons chopped toasted pecans and 1 tablespoon raisins. Serves 4 (serving size: about ½ cup)

CALORIES 124; FAT 6g (sat 1g, unsat 5g); PROTEIN 1g; CARB 13g; FIBER 4g; SUGARS 9g (added sugars 0g); SODIUM 251mg; CALC 3% DV; POTASSIUM 10% DV

Fast • Gluten Free
Make Ahead • Vegetarian
Moroccan-Spiced Parsnips
Earthy cumin and lemony coriander counter and complement parsnips' sweet edge. Serve with roasted lamb, pot roast, or seared steaks.

1. Combine 2 cups peeled parsnips, cut diagonally into ½-inch pieces, and 3 tablespoons water in a non-stick skillet over medium-high; bring to a simmer. Cover, and cook 2 minutes or until water evaporates.
2. Uncover; stir in 1 tablespoon olive oil, ½ teaspoon ground cumin, ½ teaspoon ground coriander, ⅜ teaspoon kosher salt, and ¼ teaspoon paprika. Cook 3 minutes or until parsnips are browned and tender. Remove from heat; stir in 1 teaspoon fresh lemon juice and 2 tablespoons chopped fresh parsley. Sprinkle with 1 ounce crumbled feta cheese. Serves 4 (serving size: about ½ cup)

CALORIES 101; FAT 5g (sat 2g, unsat 3g); PROTEIN 2g; CARB 13g; FIBER 4g; SUGARS 4g (added sugars 0g); SODIUM 253mg; CALC 7% DV; POTASSIUM 7% DV

continued

Pan-Roasted Parsnips and Pears
This lovely side dish leans to the sweet side, making it a brilliant pairing for pork. Use slightly firm pears for the best texture.

1. Combine 2 cups peeled parsnips, cut diagonally into ½-inch pieces, and 3 tablespoons water in a non-stick skillet over medium-high; bring to a simmer. Cover, and cook 2 minutes or until water evaporates.
2. Uncover; stir in 1 tablespoon olive oil, 1½ cups chopped red Anjou pear (about 1 medium), 1 teaspoon chopped fresh thyme, and ¼ teaspoon kosher salt. Cook 3 minutes or until parsnips are browned and tender. Remove from heat. Combine 1 tablespoon grainy Dijon mustard and 2 teaspoons apple cider vinegar; stir into parsnip mixture. Serves 4 (serving size: about ¾ cup)

CALORIES 116; **FAT** 4g (sat 1g, unsat 3g); **PROTEIN** 1g; **CARB** 20g; **FIBER** 5g; **SUGARS** 8g (added sugars 0g); **SODIUM** 204mg; **CALC** 3% DV; **POTASSIUM** 9% DV

COOKING LIGHT DIET

Fast • Gluten Free
Make Ahead

Peanut, Shrimp, and Broccoli Rolls

Hands-on: 15 min. Total: 15 min.
We turned this popular appetizer into a quick, diet-friendly dinner solution for two. It's a fresh, low-calorie alternative to takeout. In place of bottled peanut sauce, you can instead try our Miso-Chili-Garlic Sauce on page 262.

1½ cups packaged broccoli slaw
¼ cup torn fresh cilantro leaves
¼ cup diagonally sliced green onions (optional)

Hot water
4 (8-inch) round rice paper sheets
4 ounces cooked shrimp, peeled and deveined (tails removed)
2 tablespoons bottled peanut sauce
1 tablespoon water

1. Combine broccoli slaw, cilantro, and green onions, if using.
2. Fill a large, shallow dish with hot water to a depth of 1 inch. Place 1 rice paper sheet in dish; let stand 30 seconds or just until soft. Place sheet on a flat surface. Place about one-fourth of shrimp on half of the sheet, leaving a ½-inch border; top shrimp with about ½ cup broccoli slaw mixture. Fold in sides of sheet toward center over filling. Starting with the filled side, roll up tightly, pressing seam to seal. Place roll, seam side down, on a serving platter; cover to keep from drying. Repeat procedure 3 times with remaining 3 rice paper sheets, remaining shrimp, and remaining 1½ cups broccoli mixture.
3. Combine peanut sauce and 1 tablespoon water in a bowl. Serve with rolls. Serves 2 (serving size: 2 rolls and ½ tablespoon dipping sauce)

CALORIES 198; **FAT** 3g (sat 0g, unsat 1g); **PROTEIN** 20g; **CARB** 23g; **FIBER** 4g; **SUGARS** 5g (added sugars 1g); **SODIUM** 564mg; **CALC** 9% DV; **POTASSIUM** 6% DV

DINNER IN AMERICA

Get the family involved! One can crumble the bacon, one can grate the cheese, and everyone can help stir the risotto. With a flavor reminiscent of loaded potatoes, this risotto is bound to be a kid-friendly favorite. Frozen peas cook in just two minutes and add a sweet, fresh pop to the dish.

White Cheddar and Bacon Risotto

Hands-on: 29 min. Total: 29 min.

4 cups unsalted chicken stock
2 fresh thyme sprigs
2 bacon slices
1¼ cups diced onion
1 cup Arborio rice
½ cup dry white wine
¼ teaspoon kosher salt
½ teaspoon black pepper
1 cup frozen green peas, thawed
1 teaspoon finely chopped fresh thyme
3 ounces white cheddar cheese, shredded (¾ cup)
¼ cup thinly sliced green onions

1. Bring stock and thyme sprigs to a simmer in a saucepan over medium; keep warm over low.
2. Cook bacon in a Dutch oven over medium for 4 minutes or until crisp. Remove from pan; crumble. Add onion to pan; sauté 4 minutes. Add rice; cook 1 minute, stirring to coat. Add wine; cook 2 minutes or until liquid is absorbed, stirring frequently. Stir in 1½ cups stock; cook 4 minutes or until liquid is nearly absorbed, stirring frequently. Add 2¼ cups stock, ¾ cup at a time, stirring frequently until each portion is absorbed before adding more. Reserve remaining ¼ cup stock; discard thyme sprigs. Stir in salt and pepper.
3. Stir in peas, chopped thyme, and cheese; cook 2 minutes. Remove pan from heat; stir in reserved ¼ cup stock. Divide rice mixture among 4 bowls; top with green onions and bacon. Serves 4 (serving size: 1 cup)

CALORIES 408; **FAT** 14g (sat 6g, unsat 6g); **PROTEIN** 17g; **CARB** 50g; **FIBER** 5g; **SUGARS** 5g (added sugars 0g); **SODIUM** 519mg; **CALC** 17% DV; **POTASSIUM** 5% DV

WHY INGREDIENTS MATTER

RED SAUCE ROSTER

A blend of traditional and new-school items delivers killer marinara with rich, deep flavor.

Make Ahead • Vegetarian

Essential Marinara

Hands-on: 46 min. Total: 7 hr. 16 min.
Quick hack: Sub 3 (28-ounce) cans undrained whole tomatoes, crushed, for fresh; use rest of ingredients as directed. Bake uncovered 50 minutes at 425°F.

¼ cup extra-virgin olive oil
1 cup finely chopped sweet onion
5 garlic cloves, minced
7 pounds fresh tomatoes, cored and lightly scored on bottom
1 tablespoon sugar
2 teaspoons kosher salt
½ teaspoon dried oregano
2 teaspoons reduced-sodium soy sauce
1 tablespoon butter
2 sprigs fresh basil

1. Heat oil in a large Dutch oven or large ovensafe saucepan over medium-low. Add onion and garlic; cook 20 minutes or until translucent and tender, stirring occasionally.
2. Preheat oven to 300°F. Bring a large pot of water to a boil. Working in batches, plunge tomatoes into water; blanch 15 seconds or until peels loosen at scored edges. Remove from water; drain. Remove peels; discard. Chop tomatoes.
3. Add tomatoes to onion mixture. Stir in sugar, salt, oregano, and soy sauce. Bring mixture to a simmer. Place in oven; bake, uncovered, at 300°F for 6 hours. Remove from oven. Stir in butter, lapping sauce around sides of pot to deglaze browned splatters. Stir in basil; let sauce stand 20 minutes. Remove basil sprigs. Serves 12 (serving size: about ½ cup)

CALORIES 109; **FAT** 6g (sat 1g, unsat 5g); **PROTEIN** 3g; **CARB** 13g; **FIBER** 3g; **SUGARS** 9g (added sugars 3g); **SODIUM** 374mg; **CALC** 3% DV; **POTASSIUM** 2% DV

 +  +

SOY SAUCE
Just a little bit gives marinara what it needs most: meaty, savory, umami taste that makes it craveable.

SWEET ONION
The natural sweetness in Vidalias and Walla Wallas balances acidic tomatoes, so you don't need to lean so much on added sugar.

BUTTER
Savvy chefs know this secret to amazing marinara. Stir in at the end to magically round out flavor and add velvety texture.

 +  +

FRESH BASIL
Timing is key with fresh herbs in long-simmered sauce. Add sprigs at the end so the essential oils stay potent.

FRESH TOMATOES
Ripe (and local, ideally), they're loaded with nutrents and free of tinny canned taste. Use a variety for complex flavor.

SUGAR
There's really no way around that pinch of sugar every Italian Nonna adds to her sauce for the perfect flavor balance.

HOW TO MASTER THE METHOD

ROAST CHICKEN REVELATION

This technique for dry-brined, slow-roasted chicken keeps the meat tender and lets you crisp the skin.

Gluten Free • Make Ahead

Slow-Roasted Chicken

Hands-on: 18 min. Total: 11 hr. 13 min.

1 (4-pound) whole chicken, backbone removed and flattened (at right)
1½ teaspoons kosher salt
1 tablespoon olive oil

1. Use fingers to loosen skin under chicken breasts and legs. Rub meat beneath skin evenly with salt. Pat skin completely dry. Place chicken, skin side up, in a 13- x 9-inch glass or ceramic baking dish. Place dish, uncovered, on bottom shelf of refrigerator; chill 8 hours or overnight.
2. Remove chicken dish from refrigerator; let stand at room temperature 1 hour. Preheat oven to 200°F. Place dish in oven; roast chicken, skin side up, 2 hours and 45 minutes or until a meat thermometer registers 155°F in meatiest part of breast and at least 165°F in meatiest part of thigh.
3. Heat a large skillet over medium-high. Add oil to pan. Add chicken, skin side down; cook 3 minutes or until skin is browned and crispy. Remove from pan; let stand 30 minutes before carving. Serves 6 (serving size: about 3 ounces chicken with skin)

CALORIES 174; **FAT** 12g (sat 3g, unsat 8g); **PROTEIN** 16g; **CARB** 0g; **FIBER** 0g; **SUGARS** 0g; **SODIUM** 536mg; **CALC** 0% DV; **POTASSIUM** 5% DV

1. SPATCHCOCK THE BIRD With the chicken breast-side down, use kitchen shears to cut along both sides of the backbone, and remove it. Flip the chicken breast-side up, and then press down on the breasts until the bones crack and the bird lays flat.

2. SALT & AIR-CHILL Rub salt into the meat under the skin. The salt penetrates deeply into the meat and seasons the chicken over several hours, as with a wet brine. The advantage here: The chicken isn't underwater, so the skin dries as it chills, making it easier to brown and crisp in a pan later.

3. ROAST LOW & SLOW Roasting at 200°F keeps the meat from seizing up and squeezing out lots of juice, a risk you run with high oven temps. The chicken's temperature rises slowly, so you're less likely to overcook it. And roasting it skin-side up dries the skin even more before the pan-browning.

4. BROWN & CRISP Unlike with whole chickens, it's easy to sear the skin on a spatchcocked bird. Just a few minutes sizzling in a hot pan will yield crunchy, golden skin without overcooking the meat.

RECIPE MAKEOVER

LIGHTEN UP SPAGHETTI AND MEATBALLS

Our veggie-packed makeover of a comforting classic slashes 450 calories and more than half a day's sodium.

A bowl of slurp-worthy spaghetti and meatballs is as ubiquitous as it is timeless, though this Sunday supper can pack nearly a day's worth of sodium (over 2,000mg) and 60% of your daily recommended limit for saturated fat (12g) in just one serving. The challenge: Re-create this family favorite to highlight the whole grains and add vegetables, while still keeping plenty of meaty, saucy goodness. Our solution: a version that boasts almost 1½ cups of vegetables in each serving and delivers your daily quota for whole grains, while saving 450 calories, 8g sat fat, and a whopping 1,400mg sodium over most traditional recipes. This is pasta night reinvented.

PASTA NIGHT MAKEOVER

MEATBALLS
Shiitake mushrooms amp up beef's meaty texture and savory flavor while stretching 1 pound of meat across eight servings for robust meatballs.

SPAGHETTI
Whole-wheat spaghetti is intertwined with zucchini noodles to punch up fiber, add nutrients, and save 40 calories per ounce of noodles.

SAUCE
Homemade tomato-basil sauce can slash up to 200mg sodium per serving— that's 9% of your daily limit—over jarred pasta sauce.

Make Ahead

Spaghetti and Meatballs

Hands-on: 40 min. Total: 1 hr. 40 min.

¼ cup olive oil, divided
1 cup finely chopped yellow onion, divided
4 minced garlic cloves, divided
1½ teaspoons kosher salt, divided
¼ teaspoon red pepper flakes
2 (28-ounce) cans unsalted whole peeled tomatoes, undrained
½ cup finely torn fresh basil leaves
1 teaspoon sugar
½ teaspoon freshly ground black pepper, divided
½ teaspoon dried oregano
2 ounces whole-wheat bread, crusts removed
2 tablespoons 2% reduced-fat milk
4 ounces shiitake mushroom caps, finely chopped
1 pound 90% lean ground beef
1 egg, lightly beaten
¼ teaspoon ground fennel seeds
¼ cup finely chopped fresh parsley, plus more for garnish
Cooking spray
1 pound zucchini (about 3 medium)
1 (13.25-ounce) box whole-grain spaghetti (such as Barilla)
1½ ounces freshly grated Parmesan cheese (about ⅓ cup)

1. Heat 3 tablespoons oil in a Dutch oven over medium. Add ½ cup onion, 2 garlic cloves, and ½ teaspoon salt; cook 3 minutes. Add red pepper flakes; cook 30 seconds. Add tomatoes, basil, sugar, ¼ teaspoon black pepper, and oregano. Bring to a simmer; cook 1 hour, stirring occasionally, using a slotted spoon to break up tomatoes into smaller pieces.
2. Preheat oven to 350°F.
3. Tear bread into small pieces, and combine with milk in a bowl; stir until bread is moistened. Let stand 10 minutes.

4. Heat remaining 1 tablespoon oil in a large skillet over medium. Add remaining ½ cup onion, mushrooms, ½ teaspoon salt, and remaining ¼ teaspoon black pepper; cook 3 minutes. Add remaining 2 cloves garlic; cook 1 minute. Remove from heat; let cool slightly. Combine beef, bread mixture, egg, fennel seeds, and parsley in a bowl. Add mushroom mixture; combine with hands. Shape into 24 meatballs. Arrange on 2 foil-lined baking sheets coated with cooking spray. Bake at 350°F for 18 to 20 minutes. Place meatballs in tomato sauce; reduce heat to low.
5. Run zucchini through a spiralizer to create noodles, or cut into ribbons with a vegetable peeler. Set aside.
6. Bring 6 quarts water to a boil in an 8-quart pot. Add pasta and remaining ½ teaspoon salt; cook 8 to 9 minutes or until al dente. Reserve ½ cup cooking liquid, and then drain pasta. Return pasta to pot; add zucchini and reserved ½ cup cooking liquid; stir 1 to 2 minutes, until zucchini noodles soften.
7. Place 1½ cups noodles into each of 8 bowls. Top each with 3 meatballs, ½ cup sauce, 2 teaspoons cheese, and parsley. Serves 8 (serving size: 1 bowl spaghetti and meatballs)

CALORIES 427; **FAT** 15g (sat 4g, unsat 9g); **PROTEIN** 26g; **CARB** 52g; **FIBER** 9g; **SUGARS** 10g (added sugars 1g); **SODIUM** 571mg; **CALC** 10% DV; **POASSIUM** 21% DV

HEALTHY SUPERMARKET PICK

RAO'S HOMEMADE ITALIAN PEELED TOMATOES: Most canned tomatoes are loaded with sodium. (Some have over 200mg per serving!) We like Rao's, which have only 10mg sodium per serving. Can't find Rao's? Pick a variety with salt as one of the last items on the ingredients list.

THE PICKY EATER GURU

MAKE BETTER SLOW COOKER MEATLOAF

By Gina Homolka

Satisfy everyone in your house with a set-and-forget main from this full-time working mom of two.

Hi, I'm Gina Homolka, a wife; mother of two girls, Madison and Karina; creator of skinnytaste.com; and author of the New York Times best-selling books *Skinnytaste Fast and Slow* and *The Skinnytaste Cookbook*.

In this new column, I'll show you that cooking healthy, nutritious, and tasty meals for my two girls and my picky husband, Tommy, can be quick and painless—as a mom with a full-time job, it has to be.

With my youngest daughter back in school (hello, homework!) and another book deadline looming, September is an extra-busy month for me. My solution? I let my slow cooker do the work while I'm away. I prep fun and easy twists on comfort classics, like this meatloaf, the night before or early in the morning, place it in the slow cooker, and go about my day. I make my version with lean turkey instead of beef; stud it with good-for-you black beans, corn, and green chiles; and smother it all with a mild enchilada sauce, Mexican cheese, and, for even more heat, jalapeños. Trust me, this is not your mother's meatloaf.

continued

Slow Cooker Santa Fe Meatloaf

Hands-on: 20 min. Total: 6 hr. 30 min.
Oven-baked meatloaf can turn dry, but the moisture-sealing magic of the slow cooker makes this one melt in your mouth.

1½ pounds 93% lean ground turkey
⅔ cup plus 2 tablespoons mild red
   enchilada sauce, divided
½ cup quick oats
½ cup chopped green onions
⅓ cup plus 1 tablespoon fresh or
   frozen corn kernels, divided
5 tablespoons canned unsalted black
   beans, rinsed, drained, and divided
½ cup chopped fresh cilantro
1½ teaspoons ground cumin
1 teaspoon kosher salt
1 teaspoon onion powder
1 (4-ounce) can mild chopped green
   chiles, drained well
1 large egg, lightly beaten
1 garlic clove, crushed or grated
1½ ounces preshredded Mexican
   cheese blend (about ⅓ cup)
1 jalapeño, thinly sliced (optional)
Cilantro leaves (optional)

1. Cut parchment paper to about 15 x 9½ inches to form a sling to allow you to easily insert and remove the meatloaf from your slow cooker.
2. Combine turkey, 2 tablespoons enchilada sauce, oats, onions, ⅓ cup corn, ¼ cup black beans, chopped cilantro, cumin, salt, onion powder, chiles, egg, and garlic. Mix everything well using clean hands, and then shape into a 9- x 5-inch oval loaf flattened slightly on top. Place loaf onto prepared parchment paper; while holding edges of paper, carefully insert into a 5- to 6-quart slow cooker (make sure lid closes well without the paper getting in the way). Cover, and cook on low for 6 hours or high for 3 hours.

3. Pull loaf out of slow cooker using parchment sling; set aside. Wipe parchment clean; drain liquid from bottom of slow cooker. Return loaf to slow cooker using parchment sling. Cover loaf with remaining ⅔ cup enchilada sauce, cheese, jalapeño (if using), remaining 1 tablespoon corn, and remaining 1 tablespoon black beans.
4. Cover and cook on high until cheese is melted, about 10 minutes. Garnish with cilantro leaves, if desired. Pull loaf out of slow cooker; cut into 12 slices. Serves 6 (serving size: 2 slices)

CALORIES 213; FAT 10g (sat 3g, unsat 6g); PROTEIN 23g; CARB 13g; FIBER 2g; SUGARS 1g (added sugars 0g); SODIUM 607mg; CALC 8% DV; POTASSIUM 4% DV

THE TEACHER

WHY YOU NEED A CARBON STEEL PAN

By Andrea Nguyen

Culinary heavyweight Andrea Nguyen invested in a carbon steel skillet. You should, too.

When it comes to nonstick skillets, people gravitate toward either high-tech coated or old-fashioned cast iron, but there's a third option to consider: carbon steel. The lighter-weight, smoother cousin of cast iron, carbon steel pans have been around for ages, but brands like Mauviel, de Buyer, and Matfer Bourgeat have been associated with toque-wearing chefs and fancy European kitchens.

The reality is this: Carbon steel skillets should be the nonstick workhorses in your home kitchen. Aside from searing food well, they are oven-safe, light enough to casually lift and toss ingredients around, and easy to clean, and they work on induction stoves. Moreover, they're tough enough to outlast you. After decades of using coated nonsticks for my work as a cookbook author and culinary instructor based in Santa Cruz, California, I was tired of periodically replacing worn-out skillets. Cast iron was a potential substitute, but its heft makes it unwieldy.

I settled on an 11-inch Mauviel M'steel skillet. At roughly 4 pounds, it's crafted from thicker metal than my carbon steel wok—a sign of good high-heat conduction. After removing the wax coating and seasoning it (see page 273 for tips), I test-drove the pan. I fried eggs and, with little oil involved, they developed crisp bottoms and released from the skillet handily. Fried rice danced on the hot metal. Potatoes achieved a beautiful golden shell. Steaks developed a delicate deep-brown crust. Broccoli picked up character while cooking to a tender crispness. My go-to weeknight salmon seared quickly and stayed moist.

The carbon steel skillet gave me greater control than other pans that I own. It heated up fast and held its temperature, but I could quickly and easily adjust that heat because it's a lot thinner than cast iron. About 2 teaspoons of oil poured into the pan visibly coated the entire surface; in a nonstick, that oil would have just beaded and pooled. Here, it shimmered.

This may sound California wavy-gravy, but I felt a greater connection with my food when preparing it in the carbon steel pan. Good cooking depends on monitoring and manipulating the transformation of ingredients. The skillet helped me do just that.

There are downsides: Carbon steel is not dishwasher safe. It will react to prolonged cooking of acidic or alkaline ingredients (don't simmer a tomato sauce in it). Each skillet is different and will mottle, darken, and age differently.

It cleans up best soon after being used. Let the pan cool briefly, and then wash with hot water and a soft scrub sponge before drying over medium-low to low heat. A little smudging of oil (use tongs and a paper towel) prevents rusting; over time it'll likely only need periodic oiling.

If this all seems fussy, consider it a routine to keep a loyal kitchen friend happy. A carbon steel skillet will repay you many times over, probably achieving family heirloom status.

Fast • Gluten Free

Fast Pan-Fried Salmon

Hands-on: 11 min. Total: 11 min.
Cutting fish into escalopes (thin slices)—as the famous Troisgros restaurant family in France does—facilitates fast cooking and delicate searing. Serve with sautéed veggies. Use white pepper on the fish for an earthy flavor with less heat. Black pepper adds specks of color and a hotter taste.

4 (6-ounce) center-cut salmon fillets, each about 1¼ inches at the thickest, 6 inches long, 2 inches wide
½ teaspoon fine sea salt
¼ teaspoon white or black pepper
1 tablespoon canola oil or other neutral oil, divided
1 lemon, cut into wedges

1. To skin each fillet, set it skin side down on a cutting board, long edge facing you. Run your finger along one of the shorter edges to separate the flesh from the skin and form a small gap. Slide a boning or fillet knife in the gap. Angle the blade downward to cut the skin away from the flesh. When there's enough detached skin, hold it to keep the fillet in place. Saw and push the knife all the way through to the other edge to finish.
2. Using a long knife with a very sharp, thin blade, slice each fillet horizontally into 2 thin pieces. Each piece will be about ⅓ inch thick; one will resemble a speed bump. If the longer piece seems potentially unwieldy to cook, cut it in half crosswise. Repeat the skinning and cutting with remaining fish. You'll have 8 or 12 pieces total.
3. Put the fish on a plate, handsome side down. Season the back side with salt and pepper. Set aside.
4. Heat a large (11- to 12-inch) carbon steel skillet over medium. Add 1½ teaspoons oil, swirling to coat the bottom. When oil shimmers, add half of the fish, handsome side down. Cook about 1 minute or until bottom half is opaque (cooked). Turn fish over; cook for about 30 seconds, until the pink rawness is only faintly visible. Transfer fish to a plate, and pour off excess oil. Repeat procedure with remaining 1½ teaspoons oil and remaining fish. Serve with lemon wedges. Serves 4 (serving size: about 4½ ounces fish)

CALORIES 271; **FAT** 13g (sat 2g, unsat 7g); **PROTEIN** 36g; **CARB** 0g; **FIBER** 0g; **SUGARS** 0g; **SODIUM** 373mg; **CALC** 2% DV; **POTASSIUM** 17% DV

HOW TO SEASON A CARBON STEEL SKILLET

FOLLOW THESE THREE STEPS, AND SEASONING THE SKILLET YOURSELF IS EASY, IF NOT RATHER FUN. HERE'S HOW ANDREA NGUYEN SEASONED HER 11-INCH MAUVIEL M'STEEL SKILLET.

STEP 1 Pour a kettle's worth of boiling hot water all over to remove the protective wax (gray stuff). Repeat as needed. Finish by scrubbing with dish soap and hot water.

STEP 2 Put ⅓ cup canola oil, ⅔ cup salt, and the peels of 2 potatoes into the pan, and cook over medium heat for 8 to 10 minutes. Stir and press the solids against the skillet walls all the way to the rim. When finished, the potato skins will be dark and crisp and the pan will be blotchy. The salt and potato get rid of excess wax, and the oil bonds with the metal to create a nonstick surface.

STEP 3 Let cool slightly. Dump out the solids, and then use a paper towel to wipe the skillet clean. Now it's ready to use!

TURN UP THE HEAT

Ditch the cold summer salads and crank up the oven for some serious cooking as you head into fall. We've got all you need to know about the season's star, Hatch chiles.

HATCH CHILE PEPPERS

PASSION FOR THE PRIZE CHILES FROM HATCH, NEW MEXICO—NOW IN PEAK SEASON—HAS SPREAD NATIONWIDE. FOLLOW THESE TIPS TO ENJOY THEIR EARTHY-SWEET FLAVOR.

BUY Hatch come in hot and mild varieties—the hot ones are about as spicy as jalapeños. Find them at green markets and specialty grocers, or online at hatch-green-chile.com. If you can't find them, Anaheim chiles are similar.

STORE Refrigerate fresh unwashed Hatch chiles in the veggie crisper for up to a week. For longer storage, roast, peel, and seed them, and freeze them for up to six months.

COOK Hatch chile skins are thick, so it's best to roast and peel them. Traditionally, they're fire-roasted for a little smoky flavor. Char on a grill or under the broiler until mostly black, and then peel, seed, and stem them.

SAVOR Stir roasted chiles into stews and chilis, toss with a stir-fry, add to casseroles, use for salsa verde, or bake into cornbread.

Staff Favorite • Fast
Vegetarian

Pepper-Only Pizza

Hands-on: 18 min. Total: 28 min.
Look for mild Sweety Drop peppers at specialty stores, or use chopped pickled sweet cherry peppers instead. A baking steel works great here if you preheat it for an hour.

1 Hatch or Anaheim chile (hot or mild)
6 ounces fresh refrigerated whole-wheat pizza dough, at room temperature
2 tablespoons lower-sodium marinara sauce
1 ounce crumbled queso fresco (about ¼ cup)
1 tablespoon pickled Sweety Drop peppers
1 tablespoon Mexican crema

1. Preheat broiler to high. Place Hatch chile on a piece of heavy-duty foil. Broil 10 minutes or until blackened, turning occasionally. Wrap chile in foil; let stand 10 minutes. Peel chile; discard skin, seeds, and stem. Slice into thin strips.
2. Preheat oven to 550°F with a large cast-iron pan inside; continue to heat pan an additional 10 minutes after oven has reached 550°F.
3. Press dough with fingers into a 9-inch circle on a floured surface. Carefully remove pan from oven. Place dough circle in pan. Spread sauce on dough, leaving a ¾-inch rim around outside. Sprinkle evenly with cheese. Top with sliced chile and Sweety Drop peppers. Place pan in oven; bake at 550°F for 7 minutes or until top is browned. Drizzle with crema. Cut into quarters. Serves 2 (serving size: 2 slices)

CALORIES 274; **FAT** 5g (sat 1g, unsat 2g); **PROTEIN** 10g; **CARB** 46g; **FIBER** 8g; **SUGARS** 3g (added sugars 2g); **SODIUM** 473mg; **CALC** 5% DV; **POTASSIUM** 4% DV

CHEERS TO YOUR HEALTH

Fast • Make Ahead • Vegetarian

Honeycrisp-Maple Sipper

Hands-on: 5 min. Total: 5 min.
Autumn's apple abundance is well worth raising a glass to. Honeycrisp apples are sweet with a touch of tartness that lends an invigorating crisp flavor, giving this boozy beverage plenty to buzz about. Maple syrup bolsters the warmth of the bourbon.

Process 14 ounces Honeycrisp apple slices (about 3 medium apples), 1 cup water, ½ cup unfiltered apple cider, 3 tablespoons fresh lemon juice, and 1½ tablespoons maple syrup in a blender until smooth, about 1½ minutes. Pour through a fine sieve into an ice-filled pitcher. Discard solids. Stir in 5 ounces bourbon. Garnish with additional apple slices and thyme springs, if desired. Serves 4 (serving size: about 1 cup)

CALORIES 154; **FAT** 0g; **PROTEIN** 0g; **CARB** 19g; **FIBER** 1g; **SUGARS** 16g (added sugars 7g); **SODIUM** 2mg; **CALC** 1% DV; **POTASSIUM** 3% DV

MAKE IT A MOCKTAIL

Swap out the bourbon for 5 ounces light ginger beer, such as Fever-Tree Naturally Light.

THE FOOD SNOB'S GUIDE TO THE SLOW COOKER

Like most of you, we're wild about our slow cookers. But some persnickety cooks—let's call them the vocal minority—refuse to plug in. We gathered their complaints and solved every one, proving that anyone can turn out company-worthy dinners with this simple machine.

THE CHALLENGE

"I know it's hands-free cooking, but why wouldn't I just make something in my Dutch oven in a fourth the time?"

OUR SOLUTION

Trust us—some food does fare better with even, gentle, long, low heat. Brisket is a prime example. It'll take you about three to four hours of oven or stovetop braising to get it tender, so why not go longer, lower, and unattended in the slow cooker for meat that's even more tender with less fuss?

Minimal seasonings combine with beef and onions so that the flavor focus is squarely on the brisket; a bright, pickled onion garnish balances all that beefiness.

Make Ahead

Brisket with Melted and Pickled Onions

Hands-on: 25 min. Total: 8 hr. 25 min.

3 tablespoons olive oil, divided
1 (2-pound) beef brisket, fat trimmed to ¼ inch
1 teaspoon black pepper
2½ teaspoons kosher salt, divided
2 bay leaves
2 tablespoons Worcestershire sauce
⅔ cup plus 2 tablespoons water, divided
1 pound sweet onions, cut into ½-inch-thick rings (about 2 onions)
⅔ cup red wine vinegar
2 tablespoons granulated sugar
2 whole cloves
1½ cups vertically sliced red onion (about 6 ounces)

1. Heat 1 tablespoon oil in a large skillet over medium-high. Sprinkle brisket evenly with pepper and ¾ teaspoon salt. Add brisket to skillet; cook until very well browned, about 4 minutes per side.
2. Place bay leaves in bottom of a 5- to 6-quart slow cooker; add Worcestershire sauce and 2 tablespoons water. Add brisket to slow cooker. Separate sweet onion into rings; toss with remaining 2 tablespoons oil. Arrange onion rings over brisket. Cover, and cook on low until brisket is tender, about 8 hours.
3. Meanwhile, bring vinegar, sugar, cloves, 1 teaspoon salt, and remaining ⅔ cup water to a boil in a saucepan over high. Add red onion; remove from heat, and cool to room temperature. Place in a bowl; refrigerate up to 8 hours.
4. Remove brisket from slow cooker; cut across grain into 16 slices. Arange on a platter. Top with sweet onion mixture and remaining ¾ teaspoon salt. Drain red onions; discard cloves. Arrange pickled red onions on platter. Serves 8 (serving size: 2 brisket slices, about ¼ cup melted onions, and about 2 tablespoons pickled onions)

CALORIES 254; FAT 14g (sat 4g, unsat 9g); PROTEIN 22g; CARB 8g; FIBER 1g; SUGARS 5g (added sugars 1g); SODIUM 538mg; CALC 3% DV; POTASSIUM 1% DV

MAKE-AHEAD MISTAKE

We know it's tempting to load food into the slow cooker's crock, refrigerate it overnight, and start the cooker in the morning—but manufacturers do not recommend this for food safety reasons. It keeps uncooked meat in the temperature danger zone for too long.

"I always end up with soup. Where does all that liquid come from?"

OUR SOLUTION

Anything you put in the slow cooker will release liquid as it cooks, and there's no way for that liquid to evaporate. If you're not careful, you will indeed end up with soup. Sometimes, it's best to add no liquid to the cooker.

Here, we toss onion wedges, baby potatoes, and large carrot chunks with oil and harissa (look for it with the hot sauces or in the global foods section). We then arrange seared chicken thighs on top and cook the mixture with no liquid added. Over the long cooking period, the chicken releases juices that baste the veggies underneath and create just enough sauce.

Gluten Free • Make Ahead

Chicken Thighs with Harissa Vegetables

Hands-on: 20 min. Total: 8 hr. 20 min.

1 medium-sized yellow onion (about 10 ounces)
¼ cup harissa paste or sauce (such as Mina)
2 tablespoons olive oil, divided
1½ pounds baby yellow potatoes (about 1½-inch diameter)
1 pound large carrots, peeled and cut diagonally into 2-inch-long pieces (about 4 large carrots)
1 teaspoon garlic powder
1 teaspoon smoked paprika
1 teaspoon black pepper
1 teaspoon kosher salt, divided
8 (5-ounce) bone-in chicken thighs, skinned
Lemon wedges(optional)
Finely chopped fresh flat-leaf parsley (optional)

1. Peel onion, and cut vertically into 8 wedges, keeping root end intact to hold wedges together. Combine harissa and 1 tablespoon oil in a 5- to 6-quart slow cooker. Add potatoes, carrots, and onion; toss gently to coat.
2. Combine garlic powder, paprika, pepper, and ¼ teaspoon salt in a small bowl. Sprinkle mixture evenly over meaty side of chicken thighs. Heat a large skillet over medium-high. Add remaining 1 tablespoon oil to skillet; swirl to coat. Add chicken thighs, meaty side down. Cook until well browned on one side, 5 to 6 minutes.
3. Arrange chicken thighs over vegetables in slow cooker, browned side up. Cover, and cook on low 8 hours. Remove chicken from slow cooker, and sprinkle vegetables with remaining ¾ teaspoon salt. Divide vegetables evenly among 4 bowls; top evenly with chicken. Spoon juices over chicken and vegetables. Serve with lemon wedges and garnish with parsley, if desired. Serves 4 (serving size: 2 thighs, about 2 cups vegetable mixture, and about ¼ cup juices)

CALORIES 462; FAT 15g (sat 3g, unsat 11g); PROTEIN 38g; CARB 47g; FIBER 8g; SUGARS 7g (added sugars 0g); SODIUM 786mg; CALC 19% DV; POTASSIUM 24% DV

THE CHALLENGE

"The flavors are always too bland."

OUR SOLUTION

It's true that the long, slow cooking period mellows flavors. But bold spices in bold amounts will hold their own over time. Here, we start with big flavor from a large amount of curry paste and fish sauce, and we finish with fresh touches of cilantro and lime juice that perk up the taste of the whole dish. Serve over a bed of brown rice or brown rice noodles to catch all the sauce.

Gluten Free • Make Ahead

Slow Cooker Thai Beef Curry

Hands-on: 30 min. Total: 8 hr. 45 min.

1 tablespoon canola oil
2 pounds beef stew meat
½ cup unsalted beef stock
¼ cup Thai red curry paste
2 tablespoons fish sauce
1 tablespoon light brown sugar
1 (10-ounce) yellow onion, sliced (about 2½ cups)
¾ cup well-shaken canned full-fat coconut milk
8 ounces haricots verts (French green beans), halved crosswise
½ cup loosely packed fresh cilantro leaves
9 ounces fresh spinach (about 9 cups)
3 tablepoons fresh lime juice
Cilantro sprigs (optional)

1. Heat a large skillet over medium-high. Add oil; swirl to coat. Add beef, and cook in 2 batches, turning occasionally, until browned on all sides, about 6 minutes. Place browned beef in a 5- to 6-quart slow cooker. Add stock to skillet, stirring and scraping to loosen browned bits from bottom of skillet; transfer mixture to slow cooker. Add curry paste, fish sauce, sugar, and onion; stir to loosely combine. Cover, and cook on low until beef is very tender, about 8 hours.
2. Add coconut milk and haricots verts to slow cooker. Increase heat to high; cook until haricots verts are tender, about 12 minutes. Turn off heat; add cilantro leaves, spinach, and lime juice. Stir gently until spinach starts to wilt. Garnish with cilantro sprigs, if desired. Serves 8 (serving size: about 1½ cups)

CALORIES 248; FAT 12g (sat 6g, unsat 5g); PROTEIN 27g; CARB 11g; FIBER 2g; SUGARS 5g (added sugars 2g); SODIUM 621mg; CALC 7% DV; POTASSIUM 22% DV

Gluten Free • Vegetarian

Acorn Squash with Sage-Cranberry Rice Stuffing

Hands-on: 10 min. Total: 7 hr. 50 min.

1 cup precooked microwavable brown rice (such as Uncle Ben's Ready Rice)
¼ cup sweetened dried cranberries
½ cup chopped green onions
1 tablespoon olive oil
2 teaspoons finely chopped fresh sage
⅝ teaspoon kosher salt
½ teaspoon freshly ground black pepper
1 (1½-pound) acorn squash
10 ounces ice cubes (about 2 cups)
¼ cup chopped hazelnuts, toasted
Fresh sage and thyme leaves (optional)

1. Knead the rice pouch to separate the grains. Combine rice, cranberries, green onions, oil, chopped sage, salt, and black pepper in a medium bowl, tossing well. Cut squash in half lengthwise; scoop out and discard seeds and membranes. Divide rice mixture evenly between squash halves.
2. Tightly twist a sheet of aluminum foil into 2 (6-inch) rings. Place foil rings side by side in bottom of slow cooker. Place each squash half, cut side up, on 1 foil ring. Place ice cubes on bottom of slow cooker around foil rings. Cover, and cook on low until squash is very tender, about 7 hours and 30 minutes. Sprinkle 2 tablespoons hazelnuts on each squash half before serving. Garnish with sage and thyme leaves, if desired. Serves 2 (serving size: 1 squash half)

CALORIES 459; **FAT** 18g (sat 2g, unsat 14g); **PROTEIN** 8g; **CARB** 76g; **FIBER** 10g; **SUGARS** 24g (added sugars 5g); **SODIUM** 629mg; **CALC** 16% DV; **POTASSIUM** 39% DV

Make Ahead

Lamb, Barley, and Apricot Tagine

Hands-on: 30 min. Total: 8 hr. 30 min.

3 cups unsalted beef stock
2½ cups chopped white onion (about 10½ ounces)
1 cup uncooked whole-grain hulled barley (not pearled) (about 7½ ounces)
1 cup dried apricot halves (about 6 ounces)
3 tablespoons tomato paste
2 teaspoons kosher salt
1½ teaspoons ground cumin
1 teaspoon ground coriander
½ teaspoon ground red pepper
8 garlic cloves, minced (about 2 tablespoons)
2 cinnamon sticks
2 pounds trimmed lamb shoulder or lamb leg, cut into 2-inch cubes
½ cup chopped fresh cilantro
½ cup golden raisins
1 tablespoon fresh lemon juice (from 1 lemon)

1. Combine stock, onion, barley, apricots, tomato paste, salt, cumin, coriander, red pepper, garlic, and cinnamon sticks in a 5- to 6-quart slow cooker.
2. Heat a large nonstick skillet over medium-high. Cook lamb in 2 batches, turning occasionally, until browned on all sides, about 8 minutes. Add browned lamb to slow cooker. Cover, and cook on low 8 hours. Discard cinnamon sticks.
3. Turn off slow cooker; stir in cilantro, raisins, and lemon juice just before serving. Serves 8 (serving size: about 1 cup)

CALORIES 436; **FAT** 18g (sat 7g, unsat 9g); **PROTEIN** 27g; **CARB** 43g; **FIBER** 8g; **SUGARS** 18g (added sugars 0g); **SODIUM** 647mg; **CALC** 7% DV; **POTASSIUM** 20% DV

"I'm not a morning person. I can't wake up early enough to do all the prep it takes to get the slow cooker going."

OUR SOLUTION

Make a recipe that gets better with age, such as chili or brisket, and cook it overnight while you sleep. In the morning, cool it slightly, get it in the fridge, and reheat it later for dinner. We keep prep to a minimum, but if you have more time, brown the meat for deeper flavor.

THE NEW GAME-DAY ESSENTIALS

Skip the crowded parking lot and huddle up with your home team to enjoy a homegating spread of healthier gridiron goodies—guaranteed!

Staff Favorite • Gluten Free
Make Ahead

Pork Chile Verde

Hands-on: 10 min. Total: 7 hr. 40 min.

4 cups unsalted chicken stock
2 cups dried Great Northern beans (unsoaked)
2 cups chopped white onion
1⅓ cups tomatillo salsa (such as Frontera)
½ cup water
2 teaspoons ground cumin
1 teaspoon dried oregano
1 teaspoon kosher salt
8 garlic cloves, minced
2 pounds trimmed boneless pork shoulder, cut into 1½-inch cubes
½ cup thinly sliced green onions
½ cup thinly sliced radishes (optional)

1. Combine chicken stock, beans, white onion, salsa, ½ cup water, cumin, oregano, salt, garlic, and pork in a 5- to 6-quart slow cooker. Cover, and cook on low 7 hours and 30 minutes to 8 hours. Sprinkle with green onions and radishes, if desired, before serving. Serves 8 (serving size: about 1¼ cups)

CALORIES 392; **FAT** 13g (sat 5g, unsat 8g); **PROTEIN** 30g; **CARB** 37g; **FIBER** 10g; **SUGARS** 4g (added sugars 0g); **SODIUM** 637mg; **CALC** 12% DV; **POTASSIUM** 27% DV

KEY PLAYS

For superior crunch, we use gluten-free pretzels; they're far crunchier than traditional.

Dry quinoa adds more crunch; the little beads disperse over every bite.

Whole almonds round out the effect with their firm texture.

Gluten Free • Make Ahead
Vegetarian

Spicy, Barely Sweet Supercrunch Granola

Hands-on: 10 min. Total: 2 hr. 10 min.
Our supremely crunchy, irresistible granola almost feels more like party mix (but still contains all those great whole grains). It stores well at room temperature in an airtight container for up to a week. Aside from eating out of hand, you can also try this on your morning bowl of yogurt, an ice cream parfait, or a hearty salad (think of it as a replacement for croutons). For folks with gluten allergies or sensitivities, be sure to use certified gluten-free oats.

2 cups uncooked old-fashioned rolled oats
½ cup unsalted roasted whole almonds
⅓ cup uncooked quinoa
2 ounces gluten-free pretzel sticks, broken in half (about 1 cup)
3 tablespoons smooth almond butter
3 tablespoons pure maple syrup
1 tablespoon olive oil
1 teaspoon ground cinnamon
¾ teaspoon kosher salt
½ teaspoon ground red pepper
1 large egg white

1. Preheat oven to 250°F. Combine oats, almonds, quinoa, and pretzels in a large bowl. Whisk together almond butter and remaining ingredients in a medium bowl until well combined. Add almond butter mixture to oat mixture; stir well to coat. Spread mixture in an even layer on a sheet pan lined with parchment paper, leaving some natural clumps. Bake at 250°F for 1 hour or until crisp, stirring after 30 minutes. Cool completely before serving, about 30 minutes. Serves 12 (serving size: about ½ cup)

CALORIES 169; **FAT** 8g (sat 1g, unsat 6g); **PROTEIN** 5g; **CARB** 22g; **FIBER** 3g; **SUGARS** 4g (added sugars 3g); **SODIUM** 176mg; **CALC** 4% DV; **POTASSIUM** 5% DV

Korean BBQ Buns

Hands-on: 30 min. Total: 35 min.
Chinese steamed buns are an unexpected treat; they're squishy, slightly chewy, and all-around wonderful. Look for them in the freezer section at Asian markets; aim for the folded buns, sometimes labeled lotus buns or Chinese hamburger buns. And if you can't find them, you can stuff the meatballs into standard slider buns.

⅓ cup rice vinegar
⅓ cup water
3 tablespoons light brown sugar, divided
¾ teaspoon crushed red pepper
3 garlic cloves, grated and divided
1 cup ⅛-inch-thick English cucumber slices
8 ounces 90% lean ground sirloin
¼ cup whole-wheat panko (Japanese breadcrumbs)
1 large egg white, beaten
2 tablespoons reduced-sodium soy sauce, divided
Cooking spray
2 teaspoons toasted sesame oil
8 frozen folded Chinese steamed buns
8 small red leaf lettuce leaves

1. Bring vinegar, ⅓ cup water, 1 tablespoon brown sugar, pepper, and 2 garlic cloves to a boil in a saucepan over medium-high. Remove from heat; add cucumber slices. Cool to room temperature, stirring occasionally, about 30 minutes. Drain.

2. Meanwhile, stir together sirloin, panko, egg white, 1½ teaspoons soy sauce, 1½ teaspoons brown sugar, and remaining grated garlic clove in a bowl until well blended. Shape mixture into 16 meatballs, a scant 1 tablespoon each.

3. Heat a large skillet over medium. Coat pan with cooking spray. Add meatballs to pan; cook, stirring occasionally, until browned and cooked through, 5 to 7 minutes. Move meatballs to side of skillet. Add oil, remaining 1½ tablespoons brown sugar, and remaining 1½ tablespoons soy sauce to center of skillet; cook until sugar dissolves and sauce is glazy, about 1 minute. Stir to coat meatballs.

4. Layer 3 well-moistened paper towels on a microwave-safe plate. Place frozen buns on prepared plate; cover with 3 more well-moistened paper towels. Microwave at HIGH until warmed, about 1 minute and 30 seconds, checking for doneness every 10 seconds after heating for 1 minute.

5. Divide cucumber slices, lettuce leaves, and meatballs evenly among buns. Serves 8 (serving size: 1 slider)

CALORIES 157; **FAT** 5g (sat 1g, unsat 3g); **PROTEIN** 10g; **CARB** 19g; **FIBER** 0g; **SUGARS** 5g (added sugars 5g); **SODIUM** 246mg; **CALC** 2% DV; **POTASSIUM** 4% DV

Gluten Free • Vegetarian

Garlic-Herb Shoestring Fries

Hands-on: 15 min. Total: 45 min.
These irresistible oven fries are inspired by April Bloomfield's iconic version at The Spotted Pig restaurant in New York City.

2 pounds russet potatoes
3½ tablespoons olive oil, divided
3 large garlic cloves, thinly sliced
2 tablespoons fresh rosemary leaves
1 teaspoon kosher salt

1. Preheat oven to 425°F. Run potatoes through a spiralizer using the fine blade just one size larger than angel hair size to make thin strands; cut strands into pieces no longer than about 6 inches.

2. Combine potatoes and 3 tablespoons olive oil in a large bowl; toss well to coat. Arrange potato mixture in a single layer on 2 rimmed baking sheets lined with parchment paper. Bake at 425°F until lightly browned, about 18 minutes.

3. Stir together garlic slices and remaining 1½ teaspoons oil. Divide garlic mixture evenly between the 2 pans; toss gently to combine and to ensure all potato pieces brown evenly. Rotate pans from top rack to bottom rack, and bake until browned and crispy, 10 to 12 minutes, gently stirring every 3 minutes.

4. Remove pans from oven; combine all potatoes and garlic on 1 pan. Sprinkle with rosemary and salt; toss gently to combine. Serve immediately. Serves 8 (serving size: about ½ cup)

CALORIES 144; **FAT** 6g (sat 1g, unsat 5g); **PROTEIN** 3g; **CARB** 21g; **FIBER** 2g; **SUGARS** 1g (added sugars 0g); **SODIUM** 246mg; **CALC** 2% DV; **POTASSIUM** 14% DV

KEY PLAYS

Cornflake breading cooks up crispy.

Malt vinegar lends complex savoriness that you won't find in most other vinegars.

The chicken soaks in buttermilk to boost the tang of the vinegar.

Salt-and-Vinegar Boneless "Wings"

Hands-on: 15 min. Total: 45 min.
The popular potato chip flavor translates fantastically to boneless "wings." OK, admittedly, they're basically chicken fingers, but for game day, we're calling them boneless wings. Be sure to line the baking sheet with parchment paper, as the chicken tends to stick to aluminum foil, even if it's coated with cooking spray.

1 pound boneless, skinless chicken breasts
1 cup whole buttermilk, divided
3 tablespoons malt vinegar, divided
1 1/2 cups crushed cornflakes
2 tablespoons plain yellow cornmeal
1 teaspoon garlic powder
3/4 teaspoon paprika
Cooking spray
3/8 teaspoon flaked sea salt
1/4 cup canola mayonnaise
2 teaspoons chopped fresh dill
1/2 teaspoon black pepper
1 small garlic clove, grated

1. Preheat oven to 450°F. Cut chicken breasts against the grain into 16 equal slices. Combine chicken slices, 3/4 cup buttermilk, and 1 tablespoon vinegar in a medium bowl; toss to coat. Let stand 10 minutes.
2. Stir together crushed cornflakes, cornmeal, garlic powder, and paprika in a shallow dish. Working with 1 chicken slice at a time, remove from buttermilk mixture, shaking off excess; dredge in cornflake mixture, and place on a baking sheet lined with parchment paper. Spray tops of breaded chicken with cooking spray. Bake at 450°F for 10 minutes. Turn chicken over, and spray tops with cooking spray. Bake until crisp, about 10 minutes. Sprinkle evenly with salt.
3. While chicken bakes, stir together mayonnaise, dill, pepper, grated garlic, and remaining 1/4 cup buttermilk in a bowl.
4. Drizzle remaining 2 tablespoons vinegar evenly over chicken "wings." Serve immediately with dipping sauce. Serves 8 (serving size: 2 "wings" and 1 tablespoon sauce)

CALORIES 142; FAT 5g (sat 1g, unsat 3g); PROTEIN 14g; CARB 9g; FIBER 0g; SUGARS 2g (added sugars 0g); SODIUM 232mg; CALC 4% DV; POTASSIUM 14% DV

KEY PLAYS

The silky texture of pureed pinto beans enhances creaminess.

Canola mayo helps stretch the cream cheese, providing similar richness with no saturated fat.

Broiler-charred jalapeños offer deeply earthy, toasty flavor.

Staff Favorite • Gluten Free

Jalapeño Popper Bean Dip

Hands-on: 20 min. Total: 1 hr.
Think beyond typical tortilla chips for this crowd-pleasing dip. You don't want to deny guests the deliciousness of chips, but those can get a little heavy; supplement with veggie dippers to keep things lighter overall. We suggest mini sweet peppers because their sweetness helps offset the heat of the jalapeños.

5 jalapeños
1 1/2 (15-ounce) cans unsalted pinto beans, rinsed and drained
4 ounces 1/3-less-fat cream cheese
1/2 cup canola mayonnaise
1 teaspoon ground cumin
1/4 teaspoon kosher salt
1 garlic clove, grated
2/3 cup chopped green onions (about 3)
Cooking spray
2 ounces Colby Jack cheese, shredded (about 1/2 cup)
4 bacon slices, cooked and crumbled
1 tablespoon chopped fresh cilantro (optional)

1. Preheat broiler with oven rack in top position. Arrange jalapeños on a foil-lined baking sheet. Broil, turning occasionally, until charred on all sides, about 8 minutes. Wrap jalapeños in foil from pan; let stand 10 minutes. Rub off skins; discard skins. Discard stems, membranes, and seeds. Finely chop jalapeños.
2. Reduce oven temperature to 350°F. Process beans, cream cheese, mayonnaise, cumin, salt, and garlic in a food processor until smooth, stopping to scrape down sides of bowl as necessary. Add jalapeños and onions; pulse just until combined. Spread mixture evenly in a 9-inch pie pan coated with cooking spray; top evenly with Colby Jack cheese. Bake at 350°F until cheese melts and dip is bubbly, about 20 minutes. Remove dip from oven; sprinkle with bacon and cilantro, if desired. Serves 12 (serving size: 1/3 cup)

CALORIES 96; FAT 6g (sat 2g, unsat 3g); PROTEIN 4g; CARB 7g; FIBER 2g; SUGARS 1g (added sugars 0g); SODIUM 169mg; CALC 6% DV; POTASSIUM 5% DV

KEY PLAYS

Fresh juice and a little simple syrup
replace margarita mix to cut
4 teaspoons (16g) added
sugars per serving.

Diluting tequila with juice and beer
makes for a gentler cocktail that'll keep
guests free from personal fouls.

Fast • Vegetarian

Grapefruit Beergaritas

Hands-on: 10 min. Total: 10 min.
*This fruity beer cocktail falls somewhere
between a shandy, a margarita, and a radler.
Serve with citrus slices and a half-salted rim,
if you'd like, or omit the salt for a straight-up
refreshing sipper.*

⅓ cup sugar
⅓ cup water
2 teaspoons grated lime rind
**2 (12-ounce) bottles pale lager beer
  (such as Corona), chilled**
**2 cups fresh pink grapefruit juice
  (from 2 grapefruits), chilled**
½ cup (4 ounces) tequila
¼ cup fresh lime juice (about 3 limes)

Combine first 3 ingredients in a
glass jar. Cover with lid; shake until
sugar dissolves. Pour mixture into a
pitcher. Add beer, grapefruit juice,
tequila, and lime juice; stir gently.
Serve over ice. Serves 8 (serving size:
about ¾ cup)

CALORIES 128; **FAT** 0g; **PROTEIN** 1g; **CARB** 18g;
FIBER 0g; **SUGARS** 14g (added sugars 8g);
SODIUM 4mg; **CALC** 1% DV; **POTASSIUM** 4% DV

SPOOKTACULAR SWEETS

Make healthier treats for your little goblins
on a holiday typically overloaded with
refined sugar.

**Gluten Free • Make Ahead
Vegetarian**

Mummy Buckeyes

(pictured on page 235)

Hands-on: 15 min. Total: 45 min.
*Our two-bite treats are scary-simple to
make and a ghoulishly good addition to your
spread of haunted sweets. When it comes
time to wrap the mummies in chocolate, let
the kids help out for a fun holiday craft.*

**1 (15.5-ounce) can unsalted
  chickpeas, rinsed and drained**
½ cup creamy peanut butter
2 tablespoons honey
½ teaspoon vanilla extract
¼ teaspoon kosher salt
⅓ cup white chocolate chips
**2 teaspoons semisweet chocolate
  minichips**

1. Place chickpeas in a food processor; pulse until smooth. Add peanut
butter, honey, vanilla, and salt. Pulse
until well combined. Turn mixture
out into a bowl; divide into 18 equal
portions. Roll each portion around
to form a ball; place on a parchment
paper–lined baking sheet. Chill until
firm, about 30 minutes.
2. Place white chocolate chips in
the top of a double boiler. Cook
over simmering water until white
chocolate melts, stirring occasionally.
Remove from heat, and let stand 1
minute. Alternatively, place chips in
a microwave-safe bowl. Microwave
at 20% power for 15 seconds; remove
bowl from microwave, and stir.
Repeat procedure about 4 or 5 times,
microwaving and stirring until most
of chocolate has melted. Let stand
1 minute or until chocolate is thoroughly melted and smooth, stirring
occasionally.
3. Dip the prongs of a fork into
melted white chocolate, and drizzle
over buckeyes, making crisscross
motions to resemble a mummy wrap.
4. Place 2 minichips over the white
chocolate to resemble eyes. Let stand
5 minutes at room temperature until
chocolate hardens. Serves 18 (serving size: 1 buckeye)

CALORIES 97; **FAT** 5g (sat 1g, unsat 3g); **PROTEIN** 3g;
CARB 10g; **FIBER** 1g; **SUGARS** 4g (added sugars 4g);
SODIUM 59mg; **CALC** 2% DV; **POTASSIUM** 2% DV

SNEAKY SUBSTITUTION

Traditional buckeye recipes call for up to
6 tablespoons butter, but we found that
protein-packed chickpeas lend the
same creamy texture and shave 42g sat
fat. Better yet: Your family will never
know these tasty treats are bean-based
and a great way to slip in extra fiber.

Make Ahead • Vegetarian

Black Sesame Cupcakes

Hands-on: 25 min. Total: 1 hr. 50 min.
There's nothing artificial about these dramatically hued treats. Supermoist (and whole-grain) chocolate cupcakes get their blackout color from black sesame seeds and antioxidant-rich dark cocoa powder. These desserts are delicious and better for you, with every bit of fun, festive flair you crave.

Frosting:
½ cup goji berries
⅓ cup warm water
6 ounces ⅓-less-fat cream cheese, softened
½ cup plain whole-milk Greek yogurt
½ cup powdered sugar

Cupcakes:
Baking spray with flour
½ cup black sesame seeds, plus more for garnish
2 eggs
⅔ cup granulated sugar
½ cup plain whole-milk Greek yogurt
¼ cup 2% reduced-fat milk
¼ cup canola oil
1 teaspoon vanilla extract
3.5 ounces whole-wheat pastry flour (about 1 cup)
3 tablespoons dark chocolate cocoa powder
1 teaspoon baking powder
½ teaspoon baking soda
½ teaspoon kosher salt

1. To prepare frosting, place goji berries and ⅓ cup warm water in a small bowl. Let stand 20 minutes.
2. Place goji berry mixture in a blender; process until smooth. Pour mixture through fine-mesh strainer; discard seeds. Set aside.
3. Place cream cheese and ½ cup yogurt in the bowl of a stand mixer.

Beat on high until smooth. Add powdered sugar; beat on low until combined. Add goji mixture; beat on medium until combined. Chill 30 minutes.
4. To prepare cupcakes, preheat oven to 350°F. Line 12 muffin cups with liners; coat with baking spray. Place sesame seeds in a mini food processor; process until seeds form a paste. Place in a bowl. Whisk in eggs, granulated sugar, ½ cup yogurt, milk, oil, and vanilla.
5. Whisk flour, cocoa, baking powder, baking soda, and salt in a medium bowl. Add sesame seed mixture to flour mixture; whisk to combine.
6. Divide batter among prepared muffin cups. Bake at 350°F for 17 to 19 minutes or until a wooden pick inserted in center comes out clean. Cool in pan on a wire rack for 10 minutes. Remove cupcakes from pan; cool completely on wire rack. Spread frosting evenly on cupcakes, and garnish with black sesame seeds. Serves 12 (serving size: 1 cupcake)

CALORIES 261; **FAT** 13g (sat 3g, unsat 8g); **PROTEIN** 6g; **CARB** 32g; **FIBER** 3g; **SUGARS** 21g (added sugars 16g); **SODIUM** 275mg; **CALC** 14% DV; **POTASSIUM** 2% DV

SNEAKY SUBSTITUTION

We skipped the artificial food dyes and instead used red-orange goji berries to achieve naturally colored frosting. Goji berries are packed with eye-healthy vitamin A and can be found at most well-stocked supermarkets in the dried fruit or bulk bin section.

CHEERS TO YOUR HEALTH

Staff Favorite • Fast
Gluten Free • Vegetarian

Grape-Kombucha Sipper

Hands-on: 15 min. Total: 30 min.
Juicy and pleasantly plump, grapes are at their peak now. This versatile fruit also packs a healthy punch: Black and red grapes are rich in anthocyanins—powerful antioxidants that may lower your risk of heart disease and cancer and boost brain power. By adding the kombucha last, we preserve its carbonation, making for a crisp and refreshing cocktail.

Combine 12 ounces seedless black grapes (about 2 cups), ¾ cup water, 3 tablespoons sugar, and 1 (2-inch) lemon rind strip in a small saucepan over medium-high. Bring to a boil; reduce heat, and simmer 14 minutes or until liquid is slightly syrupy, stirring occasionally. Cool completely. Discard rind. Place grape mixture in a blender; pulse until smooth. Strain through a fine sieve over a bowl, pressing gently to extract liquid; discard solids. To prepare each cocktail, fill each of 4 (8-ounce) glasses with ice and, if desired, frozen grapes. Pour ⅓ cup grape mixture into each glass. Add 1 ounce gin and 4 ounces kombucha. Garnish with fresh rosemary sprig. Serves 4 (serving size: about 1 cup)

CALORIES 165; **FAT** 0g; **PROTEIN** 1g; **CARB** 26g; **FIBER** 1g; **SUGARS** 21g (added sugars 10g); **SODIUM** 7mg; **CALC** 1% DV; **POTASSIUM** 4% DV

MAKE IT A MOCKTAIL

For an alcohol-free fall refresher, swap the 1 ounce gin in each drink for 2 ounces tonic water and 1 teaspoon fresh lemon juice.

---

1 POT OF BEANS 1,000 DINNERS

Nutrient-rich, cheap, and shelf-stable, dried beans will transform your cooking this fall. Follow our master method for the perfect batch every time.

Staff Favorite • Gluten Free Make Ahead

Red Beans and Rice

Hands-on: 25 min. Total: 35 min.
If you want stick-to-your-ribs fare, this dish is it: The beans and brown rice deliver complex carbohydrates and protein, both of which take longer to digest. We love the smoky heat of andouille sausage, but regular smoked turkey sausage links or hot Italian sausage also work.

8 ounces andouille chicken sausage links, halved lengthwise and sliced
2 cups chopped yellow onion
1½ cups chopped celery
1½ cups chopped green bell pepper
1 cup sliced carrot
10 garlic cloves, chopped
3 cups cooked red kidney beans, rinsed, drained, and divided (see Master Dried Beans, p. 285)
¾ cup unsalted chicken stock
⅜ teaspoon ground red pepper
½ cup chopped fresh flat-leaf parsley, divided
2 tablespoons red wine vinegar
3 cups hot cooked brown rice

1. Heat a large nonstick skillet over medium-high. Add sausage; cook 5 minutes or until lightly browned.

Stir in onion, celery, bell pepper, carrot, and garlic; cook 8 minutes.
2. Mash ½ cup beans with a fork. Add mashed beans, remaining 2½ cups beans, stock, and ground red pepper to sausage mixture in pan. Bring to a simmer; cook 8 to 10 minutes or until vegetables are tender, stirring occasionally. Stir in ¼ cup parsley and vinegar.
3. Divide rice evenly among 6 bowls; top evenly with bean mixture. Sprinkle with remaining ¼ cup parsley. Serves 6 (serving size: about 1½ cups)

CALORIES 382; **FAT** 8g (sat 2g, unsat 6g); **PROTEIN** 19g; **CARB** 58g; **FIBER** 11g; **SUGARS** 6g (added sugars 0g); **SODIUM** 436mg; **CALC** 13% DV; **POTASSIUM** 22% DV

Gluten Free • Make Ahead

Maple-Bacon Baked Beans
(pictured on page 234)

Hands-on: 10 min. Total: 55 min.
Think of this dish as classic baked beans turned all the way up to 11—sweet, smoky, and saucy, with extra richness from the slow-simmered beans. The starchiness from the cooked beans will help bind the casserole. Curry powder adds a hint of earthiness, but you can leave it out for a more straightforward flavor.

2 bacon slices, chopped
1 cup chopped yellow onion
6 cups cooked Great Northern beans, rinsed and drained (see Master Dried Beans, p. 285)
1 cup unsalted ketchup
3 tablespoons pure maple syrup
2 tablespoons dry mustard
½ teaspoon black pepper
1 teaspoon curry powder (optional)
Cooking spray

1. Preheat oven to 375°F.
2. Cook the bacon in a skillet over medium-high 5 minutes or until crisp, stirring occasionally. Add onion; cook 4 minutes or until softened, stirring occasionally.
3. Combine bacon mixture, beans, ketchup, syrup, dry mustard, pepper, and curry powder, if using, in a large bowl. Spoon bean mixture into a 2-quart glass or ceramic baking dish coated with cooking spray. Bake at 375°F for 45 to 50 minutes or until lightly browned and bubbly. Carefully remove dish from oven; let beans stand 5 minutes before serving. Serves 12 (serving size: about ½ cup)

CALORIES 201; **FAT** 5g (sat 1g, unsat 4g); **PROTEIN** 9g; **CARB** 32g; **FIBER** 7g; **SUGARS** 9g (added sugars 8g); **SODIUM** 101mg; **CALC** 8% DV; **POTASSIUM** 18% DV

HOW LONG TO SIMMER EACH BEAN VARIETY

Cook the beans with the aromatics and 1 teaspoon salt for the first 30 minutes. Add the second teaspoon of salt, and cook for the suggested time or until the beans are tender.

RED KIDNEY BEANS: 1 hr.
GREAT NORTHERN BEANS: 1 hr. 15 min.
BLACK BEANS: 1 hr. 15 min.
CANNELLINI BEANS: 1 hr. 45 min.
PINTO BEANS: 1 hr. 45 min.

THE MASTER METHOD

The path to a perfect pot of beans is precise but not at all fussy. The main ingredient is time: first to soak the beans, and then to slowly simmer them until tender and well seasoned. Each step is designed for the best end result, from salting throughout for the best flavor to storing in the cooled cooking liquid for the ideal texture. We break down the hows and whys of our method below. Find the Master Dried Beans recipe on page 285 and a chart for simmering each bean in the box on page 283.

1. THE SOAK
Pick out any small, shriveled beans—these aren't spoiled, just too hard to cook. An overnight soak rehydrates the beans for less simmering later.

2. THE LIQUID
Add just enough cold water to cover the beans before cooking; too much will dilute the flavor and make for less delicious beans.

3. THE FAT
Adding oil helps disperse other flavors from aromatics like thyme, bay leaves, and onion in the liquid. It also helps the beans become creamy.

4. THE SIMMER
Cook the beans at a slow simmer from start to finish, skimming the surface as needed. Boiling would damage the skins and cause the beans to fall apart.

5. THE SALT
Add salt before, during, and after cooking so the beans can gradually absorb it. Salt slows the softening of the beans so they don't lose their texture.

6. THE COOLDOWN
Cool and store the beans in their cooking liquid, draining only when ready to use. This way the beans stay plump and firm outside and tender inside.

Black Bean Dip

Hands-on: 15 min. Total: 15 min.

**3 cups cooked black beans, rinsed
and drained (see Master Dried
Beans, at right)**
**½ cup black bean cooking liquid,
divided**
2 tablespoons fresh lime juice
½ teaspoon kosher salt
**3 tablespoons chopped seeded
tomato**
**2 tablespoons thinly sliced green
onions**
**2 ounces queso fresco cheese,
crumbled (about ½ cup)**
6 ounces plantain chips

Place black beans, ¼ cup cooking
liquid, juice, and salt in a food
processor; process until smooth. Add
remaining ¼ cup cooking liquid to
processor, 1 tablespoon at a time,
pulsing after each addition until dip
reaches desired consistency. Place
black bean mixture in a bowl; top
with tomato, green onions, and
cheese. Serve with plantain chips.
Serves 12 (serving size: about 3
tablespoons dip and about 15 chips)

CALORIES 148; FAT 7g (sat 5g, unsat 2g);
PROTEIN 5g; CARB 19g; FIBER 5g; SUGARS 0g;
SODIUM 119mg; CALC 5% DV; POTASSIUM 8% DV

PRAISE FOR THE CAN

Canned beans will always have a place
in our pantry alongside the dried. We
love their convenience and versatility.
Look for unsalted or low-sodium beans
(rinsing and draining them will also cut
down on sodium). Another happy dis-
covery to come from the can? Aquafaba,
which is the liquid in a can of chickpeas
or beans that can be whipped to a me-
ringue-like consistency and used in
vegan cooking and baking.

Master Dried Beans

Hands-on: 10 min. Total: 9 hr. 10 min.
*Use this recipe as a template and the chart
on page 283 for suggested simmering
times. You can change up the aromatics
(try adding a dried chile or piece of smoked
bacon). Remember to cool and store the
beans in their cooking liquid so they retain
their flavor and texture.*

**1 pound dried beans, sorted and
rinsed**
**10 cups water, plus more for soaking
beans**
½ cup olive oil
1 tablespoon kosher salt, divided
4 thyme sprigs, tied with twine
2 bay leaves
**1 large yellow onion, quartered
lengthwise**

1. Place beans in a large bowl or
container; cover with cold water to
4 inches above beans. Let stand at
room temperature overnight; drain.
2. Bring drained beans and 10 cups
water to a boil in a large Dutch oven,
skimming surface occasionally. Add
oil, 1 teaspoon salt, thyme, bay leaves,
and onion to pan. Reduce heat to
low; cover, and simmer 30 minutes,
stirring occasionally.
3. Stir in 1 teaspoon salt. Cover,
and simmer another hour or more
depending on the bean (see chart,
page 283).
4. Remove thyme, bay leaves, and
onion; discard. Stir in remaining
1 teaspoon salt. Cool to room
temperature in cooking liquid. Place
beans and cooking liquid in an airtight container; refrigerate. Serves
12 (serving size: ½ cup)

CALORIES 132; FAT 3g (sat 0g, unsat 2g);
PROTEIN 8g; CARB 20g; FIBER 7g; SUGARS 0g;
SODIUM 62mg; CALC 7% DV; POTASSIUM 11% DV

Tuscan White Bean Salad with Shrimp

Hands-on: 15 min. Total: 30 min.
*Fragrant fresh rosemary and mild cannellini
beans are a fantastic duo. You can also mash
the two together for crostini or stir them
into soup. Add the rosemary to the dressing
rather than to the simmering pot of beans so
its flavor doesn't overpower.*

8 cups water
1 cup dry white wine
**1 pound (about 21) medium shrimp,
shells on**
1½ teaspoons grated lemon rind
3 tablespoons fresh lemon juice
**1½ teaspoons chopped fresh
rosemary**
1½ teaspoons Dijon mustard
½ teaspoon crushed red pepper
¼ cup extra-virgin olive oil
**3 cups cooked cannellini beans,
rinsed and drained (see Master
Dried Beans, at left)**
2 cups cherry tomatoes, halved
⅔ cup very thinly sliced red onion
**4 cups packed baby arugula
(about 5 ounces)**

1. Bring 8 cups water and wine to a
boil in a large saucepan. Add shrimp;
cook 4 minutes or just until opaque.
Drain; rinse under cold water. Drain.
Peel shrimp; discard shells.
2. Combine rind, juice, rosemary,
mustard, and red pepper in a bowl,
stirring with a whisk. Gradually add
oil, stirring constantly with a whisk.
Add shrimp, beans, tomatoes, and
onion to oil mixture; toss to coat.
Add arugula to shrimp mixture; toss
gently to combine. Serves 4 (serving
size: about 2 cups)

CALORIES 439; FAT 20g (sat 3g, unsat 16g);
PROTEIN 29g; CARB 38g; FIBER 12g; SUGARS 4g
(added sugars 0g), SODIUM 321mg; CALC 23% DV;
POTASSIUM 30% DV

Ham, Kale, and White Bean Soup

Hands-on: 25 min. Total: 11 hr.

1 pound dried cannellini beans
10 cups water, plus more for soaking beans
6 tablespoons olive oil, divided
4 thyme sprigs, tied with kitchen twine
2 bay leaves
1 large yellow onion, halved
2 pounds smoked ham hocks
1³/₄ teaspoons kosher salt, divided
2 cups sliced carrots
6 garlic cloves, sliced
4 cups sliced lacinato kale

1. Place beans in a large bowl or container; cover with cold water to 4 inches above beans. Let the beans stand at room temperature overnight; drain.
2. Bring drained beans and 10 cups water to a boil in a large Dutch oven, skimming surface occasionally. Add ¼ cup oil, thyme, bay leaves, onion, and ham hocks. Reduce heat to low; cover, and simmer 30 minutes, stirring occasionally. Stir in 1 teaspoon salt; cover, and simmer 1 hour and 45 minutes or until beans are tender.
3. Remove pan from heat. Remove thyme, bay leaves, and onion; discard. Place ham hocks on a cutting board. When cool enough to handle, remove meat from bones; discard bones and any fat and gristle. Shred ham into bite-sized pieces. Place 3 cups bean mixture in a bowl; mash with a fork. Stir ham, mashed beans, and remaining ¾ teaspoon salt into remaining bean mixture.
4. Heat remaining 2 tablespoons oil in a large skillet over medium-high. Add carrots; cook 4 minutes or until slightly tender. Add garlic; cook 1 minute. Add kale; cook 2 minutes or until wilted, stirring occasionally. Stir carrot mixture into soup. Serves 8 (serving size: about 1⅔ cups)

CALORIES 320; FAT 12g (sat 2g, unsat 8g); PROTEIN 15g; CARB 38g; FIBER 21g; SUGARS 3g (added sugars 0g); SODIUM 639mg; CALC 10% DV; POTASSIUM 27% DV

Texas Caviar

Hands-on: 20 min. Total: 20 min.
This colorful dip can double as a side salad or topper for seared fish. It tastes even better the next day.

1½ cups cooked pinto beans, rinsed and drained (see Master Dried Beans, p. 285)
1 cup chopped red bell pepper
1 cup chopped yellow bell pepper
½ cup chopped tomato
½ cup chopped poblano chile
½ cup chopped red onion
3 tablespoons olive oil
3 tablespoons red wine vinegar
2 tablespoons chopped fresh flat-leaf parsley
2 tablespoons chopped fresh oregano
½ teaspoon ground cumin
¼ teaspoon garlic powder
¼ teaspoon onion powder
4 ounces multigrain tortilla chips

Combine first 6 ingredients in a large bowl. Combine oil and next 6 ingredients (through onion powder) in a bowl. Add oil mixture to bean mixture; toss. Serve with chips. Serves 8 (serving size: about ½ cup dip and 5 chips)

CALORIES 197; FAT 11g (sat 1g, unsat 9g); PROTEIN 5g; CARB 21g; FIBER 5g; SUGARS 3g (added sugars 0g); SODIUM 97mg; CALC 5% DV; POTASSIUM 9% DV

20-MINUTE MAINS

Turmeric Lamb Chops with Crispy Potatoes and Broccoli

Hands-on: 20 min. Total: 20 min.
Lamb loin chops (shaped like mini T-bones) save about 11 grams sat fat per serving over rib or shoulder chops. You can also ask your butcher to cut "steaks" from a leg of lamb, also lean, or sub 2 (8-ounce) beef sirloin steaks.

1 tablespoon water
12 ounces baby Yukon Gold potatoes, quartered (about 2½ cups)
3 tablespoons olive oil, divided
2 teaspoons ground cumin
1 teaspoon ground turmeric
1¼ teaspoons kosher salt, divided
½ teaspoon black pepper, divided
8 (3-ounce) lamb loin chops
1 (12-ounce) package fresh steam-in-bag broccoli florets
1 tablespoon unsalted butter, softened
1 lemon, cut into wedges

1. Place 1 tablespoon water and potatoes in a medium microwave-safe bowl; cover with plastic wrap. Microwave at HIGH 4 minutes or until tender. Spread potatoes in a single layer on a paper towel–lined baking sheet; let dry 3 minutes.
2. Combine 1 tablespoon oil, cumin, turmeric, ½ teaspoon salt, and ¼ teaspoon pepper in a bowl. Rub spice mixture evenly over lamb chops.
3. Heat 1 tablespoon oil in a large cast-iron skillet over medium-high. Add lamb chops to pan; cook

3 minutes on each side for medium-rare or until desired degree of done-ness. Remove chops from pan; let stand 5 minutes.

4. Return pan to medium-high. Add the remaining 1 tablespoon oil. Add potatoes, ½ teaspoon salt, and remaining ¼ teaspoon pepper; cook 3 to 4 minutes or until crisp.

5. Cook broccoli according to package directions. Place broccoli, remaining ¼ teaspoon salt, and butter in a bowl; toss to coat. Serve with lamb, potato mixture, and lemon wedges. Serves 4 (serving size: 2 lamb chops, about ½ cup potatoes, and 1 cup broccoli)

CALORIES 453; FAT 24g (sat 7g, unsat 15g); PROTEIN 40g; CARB 22g; FIBER 5g; SUGARS 2g (added sugars 0g); SODIUM 766mg; CALC 15% DV; POTASSIUM 22% DV

Staff Favorite • Fast

Tahini Chicken with Bok Choy and Mango Salad

Hands-on: 15 min. Total: 20 min.
Tahini and honey create a beautifully charred crust on grilled chicken thighs in seconds. Sliced baby bok choy adds plenty of crunch and a faintly nutty flavor to the slaw. You can use fresh navel orange sections in place of the mango.

3 tablespoons tahini (sesame seed paste), well stirred
4 teaspoons honey, divided
4 (4-ounce) skinless, boneless chicken thighs
1 tablespoon canola oil
½ teaspoon kosher salt
¼ teaspoon black pepper
2 tablespoons toasted sesame oil
2 tablespoons unseasoned rice vinegar
1 tablespoon reduced-sodium soy sauce
4 cups thinly sliced baby bok choy
2 cups thinly sliced red cabbage

1½ cups chopped peeled mango
Fresh cilantro leaves

1. Combine tahini and 1 tablespoon honey in a small bowl, stirring with a whisk. Heat a grill pan over medium-high. Rub chicken thighs with canola oil; sprinkle with salt and pepper. Add chicken to pan; cook 4 to 5 minutes on each side or until done. Brush tahini mixture over both sides of chicken; cook 30 seconds on each side or until lightly charred. Remove chicken from pan; cut into 1-inch pieces.

2. Combine remaining 1 teaspoon honey, sesame oil, vinegar, and soy sauce in a large bowl. Add bok choy, cabbage, and mango; toss to coat. Divide salad evenly among 4 bowls; top with chicken. Sprinkle evenly with cilantro. Serves 4 (serving size: about 1½ cups bok choy mixture and ¾ cup chicken)

CALORIES 375; FAT 21g (sat 3g, unsat 17g); PROTEIN 26g; CARB 22g; FIBER 3g; SUGARS 16g (added sugars 6g); SODIUM 551mg; CALC 11% DV; POTASSIUM 15% DV

Staff Favorite • Fast
Make Ahead • Vegetarian

Black Bean and Mushroom Burgers

Hands-on: 20 min. Total: 20 min.
The food processor brings these meatless patties together in a flash. Another bonus? A new Harvard study found that those who regularly ate a healthy plant-based diet (like this burger) significantly lowered their risk of heart disease. Ground flaxseed adds body to the burgers; find more ways to use it on page 288.

1 tablespoon ground flaxseed
1 tablespoon Worcestershire sauce
½ teaspoon kosher salt, divided
½ teaspoon ground cumin
½ teaspoon black pepper

2 ounces cremini mushrooms
1 (15-ounce) can unsalted black beans, rinsed, drained, and divided
1 large egg, lightly beaten
1 garlic clove, smashed
⅓ cup whole-wheat panko (Japanese breadcrumbs)
1 tablespoon canola oil
1½ teaspoons fresh lime juice
1 ripe avocado, peeled and pitted
2 tablespoons plain 2% reduced-fat Greek yogurt
1 tablespoon water
4 whole-wheat hamburger buns, toasted
½ cup finely shredded red cabbage

1. Place flaxseed, Worcestershire sauce, ¼ teaspoon kosher salt, cumin, pepper, mushrooms, half of the beans, egg, and garlic in a food processor; process 1 minute or until almost smooth. Place bean mixture in a bowl; stir in remaining half of beans and panko.

2. Heat oil in a large cast-iron or nonstick skillet over medium-high. Fill a ½-cup measure with bean mixture; add to pan. Repeat procedure 3 times to form 4 patties. Flatten patties slightly with the back of a spatula. Cook 2 to 3 minutes on each side or until browned.

3. Combine remaining ¼ teaspoon salt, juice, and avocado in a bowl, mashing with a fork. Stir in yogurt and 1 tablespoon water. Divide patties among bottom halves of buns; top evenly with avocado mixture, cabbage, and top halves of buns. Serves 4 (serving size: 1 burger)

CALORIES 350; FAT 13g (sat 2g, unsat 10g); PROTEIN 14g; CARB 48g; FIBER 12g; SUGARS 5g (added sugars 3g); SODIUM 550mg; CALC 13% DV; POTASSIUM 19% DV

KID FRIENDLY

These quick burgers are a great way to work more meatless dishes into your week. Kids can help shape the patties, mix up the avocado spread, and build the sandwiches.

Fast
Creamy Chicken Quesadillas

Hands-on: 15 min. Total: 15 min.
A creamy base helps the cheese go further and keeps the chicken moist. For a crisp exterior, coat the filled tortillas with cooking spray instead of coating the pan.

1 tablespoon olive oil
4 teaspoons all-purpose flour
½ cup unsalted chicken stock
1 cup coarsely chopped spinach (about 1½ ounces)
1 tablespoon hot sauce (such as Cholula)
¼ teaspoon kosher salt
⅛ teaspoon black pepper
6 ounces skinless, boneless rotisserie chicken breast, shredded (about 1¼ cups)
4 ounces preshredded mozzarella cheese (about 1 cup)
4 (8-inch) whole-wheat flour tortillas
Cooking spray
1 ripe avocado, quartered

1. Heat oil in a small saucepan over medium. Sprinkle flour over pan; cook 30 seconds, stirring constantly. Slowly add stock; cook 2 minutes or until thickened, stirring frequently. Remove pan from heat; stir in spinach, hot sauce, salt, pepper, chicken, and cheese.
2. Heat a large skillet over medium. Divide chicken mixture evenly over half of each tortilla. Fold tortillas in half over filling. Carefully coat both sides of quesadillas with cooking spray. Add 2 quesadillas to pan; cook 2 minutes on each side or until browned and cheese is melted. Repeat with remaining quesadillas. Cut each into 4 wedges. Serve with avocado. Serves 4 (serving size: 4 wedges)

CALORIES 343; **FAT** 17g (sat 5g, unsat 10g); **PROTEIN** 23g; **CARB** 24g; **FIBER** 3g; **SUGARS** 1g (added sugars 0g); **SODIUM** 682mg; **CALC** 21% DV; **POTASSIUM** 9% DV

---

3 WAYS TO:
SPEED UP ANY DINNER

1. Gather all ingredients before you start. This way you won't need to dig through your fridge or pantry when you should be keeping an eye on the stove.

2. Stay busy. Rub the lamb while the potatoes cook; heat the skillet while they dry out. Cook the broccoli while the meat rests and the potatoes crisp (see page 286).

3. More moving parts make it easy to trip up, so get obstacles out of the way quickly. When a dish or utensil is no longer needed, move it to the sink.

Fast
Thai Turkey Lettuce Cups

Hands-on: 20 min. Total: 20 min.
A little sugar balances the vinegar tang in the turkey mixture and helps develop wonderful crispy bits in the pan. Delicate butter lettuce leaves have a nice cup shape for filling; you could also use romaine.

3 tablespoons canola oil, divided
3 tablespoons reduced-sodium soy sauce
2 tablespoons light brown sugar
2 tablespoons rice vinegar
1 pound ground turkey
12 butter lettuce leaves
1½ cups chopped English cucumber
1 cup matchstick-cut carrots
¼ cup chopped roasted unsalted peanuts
2 tablespoons chopped fresh mint

1. Combine 2 tablespoons oil, soy sauce, sugar, and vinegar in a bowl, stirring with a whisk.
2. Heat remaining 1 tablespoon oil in a nonstick skillet over medium. Add turkey; cook 7 minutes or until lightly browned, stirring to crumble. Add ¼ cup soy sauce mixture; cook

4 minutes or until liquid is absorbed.
3. Place about 3 tablespoons turkey mixture in each lettuce leaf; top evenly with cucumber, carrots, and peanuts. Drizzle evenly with remaining soy sauce mixture. Sprinkle with mint. Serves 4 (serving size: 3 filled lettuce cups)

CALORIES 426; **FAT** 26g (sat 4g, unsat 19g); **PROTEIN** 32g; **CARB** 24g; **FIBER** 7g; **SUGARS** 13g (added sugars 7g); **SODIUM** 538mg; **CALC** 22% DV; **POTASSIUM** 45% DV

USE IT UP

3 WAYS TO USE GROUND FLAXSEED

Add an omega-3 boost to a variety of dishes with this surprisingly versatile ingredient. Store-bought, preground flaxseed works as a thickener, binder, and gluten-free breadcrumb sub for breaded fish and meatloaf.

Fast • Gluten Free Vegetarian
Mocha-Flax Smoothie
This protein-packed sipper has only 6 grams of added sugars—far less than what you'll typically find at a smoothie shop. Look for shelf-stable cold-brew in the coffee aisle or refrigerated versions near the creamer or fresh juices.

Place 1 cup ice cubes, ⅔ cup plain 2% reduced-fat Greek yogurt, ¼ cup cold-brew coffee concentrate, 1½ tablespoons ground flaxseed, 1 tablespoon unsweetened cocoa, 1½ teaspoons maple syrup or honey, and ½ teaspoon vanilla extract in a blender; process until smooth. Serves 1 (serving size: about 1½ cups)

CALORIES 200; **FAT** 8g (sat 3g, unsat 5g); **PROTEIN** 16g; **CARB** 19g; **FIBER** 5g; **SUGARS** 13g (added sugars 6g); **SODIUM** 57mg; **CALC** 14% DV; **POTASSIUM** 6% DV

Fast • Gluten Free
Make Ahead
Flax-Boosted Meatloaf
We call for organic ketchup because it's usually sweetened with sugar, not high-fructose corn syrup.

1. Preheat oven to 375°F.
2. Combine ½ cup grated onion, ¼ cup ground flaxseed, ½ teaspoon kosher salt, ½ teaspoon black pepper, 1 pound 90% lean ground sirloin, 1 grated garlic clove, and 1 large egg in a large bowl. Shape into an 8- x 4-inch loaf on a foil-lined baking sheet coated with cooking spray. Spread ⅓ cup organic ketchup over loaf. Bake at 375°F for 40 minutes or until a thermometer registers 160°F. Cut meatloaf into 8 slices. Serves 4 (serving size: 2 slices)

CALORIES 291; **FAT** 16g (sat 5g, unsat 9g); **PROTEIN** 26g; **CARB** 11g; **FIBER** 2g; **SUGARS** 6g (added sugars 3g); **SODIUM** 589mg; **CALC** 5% DV; **POTASSIUM** 17% DV

Fast • Gluten Free
Almond-and-Flax-Crusted Fish
Earthy flaxseed and nutty-sweet almond meal are a delicious gluten-free breading for tilapia or chicken. Stick to medium heat so it doesn't burn.

1. Cut each of 4 (4-ounce) tilapia fillets in half lengthwise. Add to a large bowl with 1 beaten egg; toss to coat.
2. Combine ¼ cup ground flaxseed, ¼ cup almond meal, ¾ teaspoon kosher salt, ¾ teaspoon garlic powder, ½ teaspoon smoked paprika, and ¼ teaspoon ground red pepper in a large ziplock bag. Remove fish from egg, shaking off excess; place in bag, and shake to coat.
3. Heat a large nonstick skillet over medium. Add 3 tablespoons canola oil; swirl to coat. Add fish; cook 3 minutes on each side or until fish flakes easily when tested with a fork. Serves 4 (serving size: 2 pieces)

CALORIES 300; **FAT** 20g (sat 2g, unsat 16g); **PROTEIN** 27g; **CARB** 4g; **FIBER** 3g; **SUGARS** 0g; **SODIUM** 442mg; **CALC** 4% DV; **POTASSIUM** 14% DV

Fast • Make Ahead
Vegetarian

Greek Chopped Salad with Grilled Pita

Hands-on: 30 min. Total: 30 min.
We take the extra step of grilling the bell peppers along with the pita wedges to add a bit of char and smoky depth to the salad. You could also broil the peppers in the oven until blackened and peel them, and then toast the pita until browned.

Cooking spray
1 large red bell pepper
¼ cup olive oil, divided
2 teaspoons chopped fresh oregano, divided
½ teaspoon garlic powder
⅜ teaspoon kosher salt, divided
3 (6½-inch) whole-wheat pita rounds
1 tablespoon white wine vinegar
1 tablespoon fresh lemon juice
2 teaspoons Dijon mustard
¼ teaspoon black pepper
4 cups chopped romaine lettuce
2 cups chopped English cucumber
1 cup halved cherry tomatoes
2 tablespoons pitted kalamata olives, chopped
1 (15-ounce) can unsalted cannellini beans, rinsed and drained
1 ounce feta cheese, crumbled (about ¼ cup)

1. Heat a grill pan over medium-high. Coat pan with cooking spray. Remove the seeds and membranes from bell pepper; cut into quarters. Add the bell pepper to pan; cook 4 minutes on each side or until tender and charred. Remove bell pepper from pan; cut into bite-sized pieces.
2. Combine 1 tablespoon olive oil, 1 teaspoon oregano, garlic powder, and ⅛ teaspoon salt in a bowl. Brush oil mixture evenly over both sides of all pita rounds. Add pita rounds to pan; cook 2 minutes on each side or until well marked. Cut each pita into 6 wedges.
3. Combine remaining 3 tablespoons oil, vinegar, juice, and mustard in a large bowl, stirring with a whisk. Stir in remaining 1 teaspoon oregano, remaining ¼ teaspoon salt, and black pepper. Add charred red bell pepper, lettuce, cucumber, tomatoes, olives, and beans to bowl; toss well to combine. Divide salad among 4 plates; top evenly with cheese. Serve with grilled pita wedges. Serves 4 (serving size: about 2¼ cups salad and about 4 pita wedges)

CALORIES 396; **FAT** 19g (sat 3g, unsat 12g); **PROTEIN** 12g; **CARB** 48g; **FIBER** 10g; **SUGARS** 6g (added sugars 0g); **SODIUM** 684mg; **CALC** 12% DV; **POTASSIUM** 21% DV

GO MEATLESS

A chopped salad full of crunchy veggies and bound by a zingy vinaigrette is an easy last-minute meal. You can use any bean for protein such as navy beans or chickpeas.

Fast • Gluten Free

Spice-Roasted Salmon with Roasted Cauliflower

Hands-on: 20 min. Total: 30 min.
Moroccan spices blend earthy (cumin) with warm and fragrant (coriander and allspice). Salmon and cauliflower embrace these flavors well. Look for thicker salmon fillets from the upper portion of the fish rather than thinner tail pieces.

1 tablespoon olive oil
1 teaspoon ground cumin, divided
3/4 teaspoon kosher salt, divided
1/8 teaspoon freshly ground black pepper
4 cups cauliflower florets
1/4 cup chopped fresh cilantro
1/4 cup golden raisins
1 tablespoon fresh lemon juice
1/2 teaspoon ground coriander
1/8 teaspoon ground allspice
4 (4 1/2-ounce) skin-on salmon fillets (about 1 inch thick)
Cooking spray
4 lemon wedges

1. Preheat oven to 450°F.
2. Combine olive oil, 1/2 teaspoon ground cumin, 1/4 teaspoon salt, and black pepper in a large bowl. Add cauliflower florets; toss well to coat. Arrange cauliflower in a single layer on a rimmed baking sheet; bake at 450°F for 18 to 20 minutes or until cauliflower is browned and tender. Combine cauliflower mixture, cilantro, raisins, and lemon juice in a bowl; toss gently to combine.
3. Reduce oven temperature to 400°F.
4. Combine remaining 1/2 teaspoon cumin, remaining 1/2 teaspoon salt, coriander, and allspice in a small bowl. Rub spice mixture evenly over fillets. Arrange fillets, skin side down, on a foil-lined baking sheet coated with cooking spray; bake at 400°F for 10 minutes or until done. Serve with cauliflower mixture and lemon wedges. Serves 4 (serving size: 1 fillet and about 3/4 cup cauliflower)

CALORIES 270; FAT 11g (sat 2g, unsat 8g); PROTEIN 30g; CARB 13g; FIBER 3g; SUGARS 8g (added sugars 0g); SODIUM 455mg; CALC 5% DV; POTASSIUM 24% DV

Staff Favorite • Gluten Free

Pork Tenderloin with Mushrooms, Fennel, and Blue Cheese

Hands-on: 20 min. Total: 40 min.
This gorgeous main uses just one skillet—first to sear and roast the pork, and then to caramelize the fennel and mushrooms. Arugula isn't only for salads; it wilts nicely when sautéed in the pan juices from the pork tenderloin.

1 tablespoon olive oil
1 (1-pound) pork tenderloin
1/2 teaspoon kosher salt, divided
1/2 teaspoon black pepper, divided
3 cups thinly sliced fennel bulb
3 garlic cloves, thinly sliced
1 (8-ounce) package presliced cremini mushrooms
1/2 cup unsalted chicken stock (such as Swanson)
3 cups loosely packed arugula
2 ounces blue cheese, crumbled (about 1/2 cup)
2 tablespoons chopped fennel fronds

1. Preheat oven to 400°F.
2. Heat oil in a large ovenproof skillet over medium-high. Sprinkle pork with 1/4 teaspoon salt and 1/4 teaspoon pepper. Add pork to pan; cook 6 to 8 minutes, turning to brown on all sides. Place pan in oven; bake at 400°F for 18 minutes or until a thermometer inserted in the center registers 140°F. Place pork on a cutting board; let stand 5 minutes. Cut crosswise into slices.
3. Return pan to medium-high (use caution; the handle will be very hot). Add fennel, garlic, and mushrooms; cook 5 minutes or until golden, stirring occasionally. Add stock; bring to a boil. Cook 3 minutes or until liquid is reduced by half. Remove pan from heat; stir in remaining 1/4 teaspoon salt, remaining 1/4 teaspoon pepper, and arugula until wilted. Arrange pork on a platter; top evenly with fennel mixture, cheese, and fennel fronds. Serves 4 (serving size: 3 ounces pork and about 1 cup vegetables)

CALORIES 247; FAT 10g (sat 4g, unsat 6g); PROTEIN 30g; CARB 9g; FIBER 3g; SUGARS 4g (added sugars 0g); SODIUM 520mg; CALC 14% DV; POTASSIUM 29% DV

Chicken Fricassee with Browned Butter Noodles

Hands-on: 40 min. Total: 40 min.
This French-country-meets-retro classic gets a weeknight twist with quick-cooking chicken cutlets and egg noodles. Keep the sear on the chicken to a light golden color so it won't darken the delicate white wine sauce.

6 ounces uncooked whole-wheat egg noodles
1 tablespoon olive oil
1 pound skinless, boneless chicken breast cutlets
3/4 teaspoon kosher salt, divided
1/2 teaspoon black pepper, divided
1 1/2 cups 2% reduced-fat milk, divided
1 1/2 tablespoons all-purpose flour
2 cups chopped carrots
1 cup chopped yellow onion
1 cup chopped celery
1 tablespoon chopped fresh thyme
4 garlic cloves, chopped

1 (8-ounce) package cremini
  mushrooms, quartered
1/2 cup dry white wine
1 1/2 cups unsalted chicken stock
  (such as Swanson)
1 1/2 tablespoons unsalted butter
2 tablespoons chopped fresh
  flat-leaf parsley

1. Cook noodles according to package directions, omitting salt and fat;
drain.
2. Heat oil in a large skillet over
medium-high. Sprinkle chicken
with 1/4 teaspoon salt and 1/4 teaspoon
pepper. Add chicken to pan; cook
4 minutes on each side. Place
chicken on a plate (do not wipe
out pan).
3. Combine 1/4 cup milk and flour
in a bowl. Add carrots and next
5 ingredients (through mushrooms)
to pan; cook 6 minutes. Stir in wine;
cook 1 minute. Stir in 1/4 teaspoon
salt, remaining 1/4 teaspoon pepper,
remaining 1 1/4 cups milk, and stock;
bring to a boil. Stir in flour mixture.
Reduce heat, cover, and simmer
5 minutes. Return chicken to pan;
cook 3 minutes or until done.
4. Melt butter in a saucepan over
medium; cook 2 minutes or until
browned. Add cooked noodles and
remaining 1/4 teaspoon salt to pan;
toss. Divide noodle mixture among
4 plates; top with chicken, sauce,
and parsley. Serves 4 (serving size:
1 cup noodles, 4 ounces chicken,
and 1 cup sauce)

CALORIES 494; FAT 14g (sat 5g, unsat 6g);
PROTEIN 39g; CARB 53g; FIBER 8g; SUGARS 11g
(added sugars 0g); SODIUM 582mg; CALC 17% DV;
POTASSIUM 30% DV

3 WAYS TO

BRING IT ALL TOGETHER

1. Place a saucepan filled with water on
the back burner, and bring to a boil.
While you wait, cook the chicken and
vegetables on a front burner.

2. Leave the drained noodles in the colander while you add liquid to the skillet.
Heat the saucepan used to cook the
noodles on a front burner.

3. Finish the fricassee before melting
the butter in the empty saucepan. Do
this last so the butter doesn't overbrown;
multitasking isn't wise here.

Make Ahead

Creamy Chicken and Wild Rice Soup

Hands-on: 32 min. Total: 40 min.
*Go ahead and flag this recipe—it's sure to
become a family favorite. For convenience,
we call for precooked wild rice; if you can't
find it, you can substitute 2 cups of your own
cooked wild rice or a package of precooked
brown rice.*

5 bacon slices, chopped
1 cup chopped onion
1 cup thinly sliced carrot
1/2 cup thinly sliced celery
1 tablespoon fresh thyme leaves
1 (8-ounce) package presliced
  cremini mushrooms
4 garlic cloves, minced
4 cups unsalted chicken stock
  (such as Swanson)
1 cup water
4 cups lightly packed chopped curly
  kale
1 teaspoon kosher salt
1/2 teaspoon black pepper
6 ounces shredded skinless, boneless
  rotisserie chicken breast (about
  1 1/2 cups)

1 (8-ounce) package precooked
  wild rice (such as Simply Balanced)
1 cup half-and-half
1 1/2 ounces all-purpose flour (about
  1/3 cup)

1. Heat a Dutch oven over medium-
high. Add bacon to pan; cook
4 minutes or until crisp. Remove
bacon from pan with a slotted spoon,
reserving 1 tablespoon drippings.
Add onion, carrot, and celery to
drippings in pan; sauté 3 minutes.
Add thyme, mushrooms, and garlic;
sauté 5 minutes. Add stock and
1 cup water; bring to a boil. Reduce
heat, and simmer 8 minutes or until
vegetables are tender. Add kale, salt,
and pepper; cook 3 minutes. Stir in
chicken and rice.
2. Combine half-and-half and flour
in a bowl, stirring with a whisk. Stir
into soup; cook 2 minutes or until
thickened. Top with bacon. Serves 6
(serving size: about 1 2/3 cups)

CALORIES 261; FAT 11g (sat 5g, unsat 5g);
PROTEIN 19g; CARB 24g; FIBER 3g; SUGARS 6g
(added sugars 0g); SODIUM 659mg; CALC 9% DV;
POTASSIUM 17% DV

3 WAYS TO USE BRUSSELS

Preshredded or shaved Brussels sprouts (with the prepared produce) is fall's answer to coleslaw mix. Use it to speed up slaws, salads, and sautés.

Fast • Gluten Free
Vegetarian
Caesar Brussels Sprouts Salad with Almonds
Sturdy shaved Brussels sprouts hold the crunchy almonds and a garlicky Parmesan vinaigrette without wilting. Serve with roast chicken or lamb.

1. Heat a large nonstick skillet over medium-high. Add 2 tablespoons sliced almonds, and cook 4 minutes or until toasted and fragrant, stirring occasionally. Combine 2 tablespoons fresh lemon juice, ½ teaspoon black pepper, a dash of kosher salt, and 2 finely chopped garlic cloves in a bowl; let stand 5 minutes.
2. Add 1½ tablespoons olive oil and 2 tablespoons finely grated Parmesan cheese to bowl, stirring with a whisk. Add almonds and 1 (12-ounce) package shaved fresh Brussels sprouts; toss to coat. Serve immediately. Serves 4 (serving size: about 1½ cups)

CALORIES 119; **FAT** 8g (sat 1g, unsat 7g); **PROTEIN** 5g; **CARB** 10g; **FIBER** 4g; **SUGARS** 2g (added sugars 0g); **SODIUM** 97mg; **CALC** 7% DV, **POTASSIUM** 10% DV

Fast • Gluten Free
Vegetarian
Brussels Sprouts Sauté with Pecans and Blue Cheese
Apple cider vinegar helps to quickly braise the Brussels sprouts until tender and adds a gentle tang. If you prefer, you can substitute goat or pecorino Romano cheese for the blue cheese.

1. Heat 1 tablespoon olive oil in a large nonstick skillet over medium-high. Add 1 (12-ounce) package shaved fresh Brussels sprouts; cook 2 to 3 minutes or until slightly wilted, stirring occasionally.
2. Add ¼ cup chopped toasted pecans, 2 tablespoons apple cider vinegar, ¼ teaspoon kosher salt, and ¼ teaspoon black pepper; cook 1 minute or until liquid almost evaporates. Remove pan from heat; stir in 1 teaspoon chopped fresh thyme. Top with 2 tablespoons crumbled blue cheese. Serves 4 (serving size: 1 cup)

CALORIES 133; **FAT** 10g (sat 2g, unsat 7g); **PROTEIN** 5g; **CARB** 9g; **FIBER** 4g; **SUGARS** 2g (added sugars 0g); **SODIUM** 213mg; **CALC** 7% DV; **POTASSIUM** 10% DV

Fast • Gluten Free
Vegetarian
Pomegranate, Avocado, and Citrus Brussels Sprouts Salad
Be sure to toss the salad gently so the pieces of orange and avocado keep their shape. Pair with a fall chili or tacos.

1. Peel and section 2 navel oranges over a medium bowl; reserve sections. Squeeze remaining membranes over bowl; reserve juice. Add ½ cup pomegranate arils, 2 tablespoons olive oil, 2 tablespoons chopped shallot, ¼ teaspoon kosher salt, and ¼ teaspoon black pepper to juice, stirring with a whisk.
2. Add reserved orange sections, 1 (12-ounce) package shaved fresh Brussels sprouts, and 1 cup diced avocado to juice mixture; toss gently to coat. Serves 6 (serving size: about 1 cup)

CALORIES 142; **FAT** 9g (sat 1g, unsat 7g); **PROTEIN** 3g; **CARB** 16g; **FIBER** 6g; **SUGARS** 8g (added sugars 0g); **SODIUM** 97mg; **CALC** 5% DV; **POTASSIUM** 13% DV

4 SAUCES FOR ANY PROTEIN

Fast • Gluten Free
Mushroom–Red Wine Sauce
You don't need to have cooked a beef roast to make this full-bodied sauce. The richness comes instead from sautéed mushrooms and red wine. Spoon the sauce over steak or a baked potato topped with blue cheese.

Melt 1 tablespoon butter with 1 teaspoon olive oil in a medium skillet over medium-high. Add 1 (8-ounce) package presliced cremini mushrooms, 1 teaspoon minced fresh rosemary, ⅛ teaspoon salt, and ⅛ teaspoon pepper; sauté 6 minutes. Add ½ cup red wine, ¾ cup unsalted chicken stock, and 1 teaspoon cornstarch; cook 3 to 4 minutes, stirring occasionally. Sprinkle with ½ teaspoon minced fresh rosemary. Serves 4 (serving size: about ¼ cup)

CALORIES 79; **FAT** 4g (sat 2g, unsat 2g); **PROTEIN** 3g; **CARB** 3g; **FIBER** 1g; **SUGARS** 1g (added sugars 0g); **SODIUM** 111mg; **CALC** 1% DV; **POTASSIUM** 6% DV

Fast • Gluten Free
Make Ahead • Vegetarian
Buttermilk-Dill Sauce
Think of this no-cook sauce as your put-it-on-everything sauce. Spoon over baked fish or chicken. Beyond a main, use it to dress a potato salad or as a veggie dip. We prefer 2% Greek yogurt over nonfat for a milder tang that complements the buttermilk.

Combine ¾ cup plain 2% reduced-fat Greek yogurt, ¼ cup fat-free buttermilk, 1 tablespoon minced fresh dill, 1 teaspoon olive oil, 1 teaspoon fresh lemon juice, ¼ teaspoon kosher salt, and ¼ teaspoon freshly ground black pepper in a bowl, stirring with a whisk. Serves 4 (serving size: about 3 tablespoons)

CALORIES 49; **FAT** 2g (sat 1g, unsat 1g); **PROTEIN** 5g; **CARB** 3g; **FIBER** 0g; **SUGARS** 2g (added sugars 0g); **SODIUM** 151mg; **CALC** 6% DV; **POTASSIUM** 0% DV

Fast • Make Ahead
Vegetarian
Quick Peanut Sauce
The warmth and zing of fresh ginger and garlic put bottled versions of this sauce out of the running. For heat, stir in a generous pinch of crushed red pepper. Drizzle the sauce over grilled chicken or shrimp skewers. You can also use as a dip for spring rolls or toss with a soba noodle salad.

Combine ½ cup creamy peanut butter, ½ cup water, 1 tablespoon reduced-sodium soy sauce, 1 tablespoon grated peeled fresh ginger, 1 teaspoon brown sugar, 1 teaspoon minced fresh garlic, and 1 teaspoon unseasoned rice vinegar in a bowl, stirring with a whisk until smooth. Serves 8 (serving size: about 2 tablespoons)

CALORIES 101; **FAT** 8g (sat 2g, unsat 6g); **PROTEIN** 4g; **CARB** 4g; **FIBER** 1g; **SUGARS** 2g (added sugars 1g); **SODIUM** 141mg; **CALC** 1% DV; **POTASSIUM** 3% DV

Fast • Gluten Free
Make Ahead • Vegetarian
Spinach-Walnut Pesto
An evergreen, everyday pesto will perk up pastas and pizzas when fresh basil is no longer in season. The warmth from the toasted walnuts will help the sauce emulsify; don't skip this step. Try the sauce on seared salmon or chicken.

Place 4 cups fresh spinach, ¼ cup toasted walnuts, 1 ounce grated Parmesan cheese, 1 small chopped garlic clove, 2 teaspoons fresh lemon juice, and ¼ teaspoon crushed red pepper in a food processor; process until finely chopped. With processor on, slowly add 3 tablespoons olive oil through food chute. Add 2 tablespoons warm water; process until blended. Serves 8 (serving size: about 2 tablespoons)

CALORIES 85; **FAT** 8g (sat 1g, unsat 6g); **PROTEIN** 2g; **CARB** 2g; **FIBER** 1g; **SUGARS** 0g (added sugars 0g); **SODIUM** 76mg; **CALC** 5% DV; **POTASSIUM** 3% DV

THE SHORTCUT

Fast • Gluten Free
Make Ahead • Vegetarian
Cauliflower Korma

Hands-on: 15 min. Total: 30 min.
Korma is a creamy, mild curry and a great way to introduce complex and fragrant spices to your cooking to make meatless mains more satisfying. Blend some of the hot cooking liquid with the yogurt first so it won't separate in the finished dish.

1 tablespoon extra-virgin olive oil
⅓ cup prechopped onion
½ cup finely chopped carrot
2 teaspoons curry powder
¾ teaspoon kosher salt
½ teaspoon freshly ground black pepper
½ teaspoon ground ginger
¼ teaspoon garam masala
2 garlic cloves, minced
2 (10-ounce) packages fresh cauliflower florets
2½ cups organic vegetable broth (such as Swanson)
1 (7-ounce) container plain whole-milk Greek yogurt
¾ cup frozen green peas, thawed
2 (8.8-ounce) packages precooked brown rice (such as Uncle Ben's)
½ cup fresh cilantro leaves
½ cup roasted unsalted cashews, chopped

1. Heat oil in a large nonstick skillet over medium. Add onion and carrot; sauté 2 minutes or until onion is translucent. Stir in curry powder and next 5 ingredients (through garlic); cook 1 minute or until fragrant. Add cauliflower; cook 5 minutes or until browned, stirring occasionally. Add broth; bring to a simmer. Cover, and cook 12 minutes or until cauliflower is tender. Remove pan from heat.
2. Combine ½ cup cooking liquid from pan and yogurt in a small bowl, stirring until smooth. Stir yogurt mixture and peas into cauliflower mixture.
3. Heat the rice according to package directions. Place ⅔ cup rice in each of 6 bowls. Top each serving with 1 cup cauliflower mixture, about 1½ tablespoons cilantro, and 1½ tablespoons cashews. Serves 6

CALORIES 270; **FAT** 12g (sat 4g, unsat 8g); **PROTEIN** 9g; **CARB** 33g; **FIBER** 5g; **SUGARS** 4g (added sugars 0g); **SODIUM** 548mg; **CALC** 8% DV; **POTASSIUM** 15% DV

SHORTCUT ITEMS

Look for prechopped onion and cauliflower florets in the prepared produce section. Frozen peas and precooked brown rice are ready in minutes; keep these staples stocked.

Gluten Free • Make Ahead

Slow-Cooked BBQ Pork Roast

(pictured on page 234)

Hands-on: 30 min. Total: 8 hr. 30 min.
The slow cooker makes fall our new favorite season for barbecue. This pork shoulder simmers in a vinegar- and ketchup-laced liquid until tender and juicy. Top with pickled red onions (page 275). Pile the pork onto game-day sandwiches or baked sweet potatoes.

2 tablespoons dark brown sugar
2 teaspoons paprika
1 teaspoon black pepper
1 teaspoon ground cumin
³⁄₄ teaspoon ground red pepper
¹⁄₂ teaspoon ground coriander
1 (4¹⁄₂-pound) bone-in pork shoulder roast (Boston butt), trimmed
1 tablespoon canola oil
1 cup finely chopped white onion
1 tablespoon finely chopped garlic
¹⁄₂ cup unsalted chicken stock (such as Swanson)
¹⁄₂ cup unsalted ketchup
¹⁄₄ cup apple cider vinegar
1 teaspoon kosher salt

1. Combine first 6 ingredients in a bowl. Reserve 2 tablespoons spice mixture. Rub remaining spice mixture evenly over pork, pressing to adhere. Heat oil in a large Dutch oven over medium-high. Add pork to pan; cook 15 minutes, turning to brown on all sides. Place browned pork in a 5- to 6-quart electric slow cooker.
2. Add onion and garlic to Dutch oven; sauté 3 minutes. Add stock to pan, stirring bottom to scrape up browned bits. Remove pan from heat; stir in reserved 2 tablespoons spice mixture, ketchup, and vinegar. Pour stock mixture over pork in slow cooker. Cover, and cook on low 7¹⁄₂ to 8 hours or until tender.

3. Place pork on a cutting board; let stand 20 minutes. Skim fat from cooking liquid; reserve ¹⁄₄ cup liquid. Shred pork into large pieces, discarding bones and fat. Place pork in a bowl; add reserved ¹⁄₄ cup cooking liquid and salt; toss to combine. Serves 10 (serving size: about 3 ounces pork)

CALORIES 193; **FAT** 8g (sat 2g, unsat 5g); **PROTEIN** 20g; **CARB** 10g; **FIBER** 1g; **SUGARS** 7g (added sugars 5g); **SODIUM** 269mg; **CALC** 3% DV; **POTASSIUM** 15% DV

PLAN. SHOP. COOK.

1 LIST
3 DINNERS

Shop this list to feed four for three nights, all for about $30. Read the recipes first to be sure you have the staples on hand.

2 (5-ounce) packages arugula

1 red onion

1 yellow onion

1 bunch flat-leaf parsley

1 (2-pound) butternut squash

1 lemon

Capers

Walnuts

1 (12-inch) prebaked thin whole-grain pizza crust

1 (15-ounce) can unsalted chickpeas

1 (15-ounce) can diced tomatoes

Unsalted tomato paste

2 (8-ounce) packages precooked quinoa (such as Simply Balanced)

1 (32-ounce) container unsalted chicken stock

1¹⁄₂ ounces goat cheese

1 (7-ounce) container plain 2% reduced-fat Greek yogurt

1 (8-ounce) sirloin steak

Fast • Gluten Free

Steak Salad with Salsa Verde Vinaigrette

Hands-on: 15 min. Total: 20 min.
Italian salsa verde, a classic red meat pairing, turns into a quick vinaigrette for this entrée salad. One 8-ounce sirloin steak, thinly sliced, is all you need.

Cooking spray
1 (8-ounce) sirloin steak
¹⁄₂ teaspoon kosher salt, divided
¹⁄₄ teaspoon black pepper
¹⁄₄ cup olive oil
2 tablespoons finely chopped fresh flat-leaf parsley
1¹⁄₂ tablespoons white wine vinegar
1 tablespoon capers, finely chopped
1 teaspoon minced fresh garlic
¹⁄₄ teaspoon crushed red pepper
5 cups arugula (about 5 ounces)
¹⁄₂ cup thinly sliced red onion
1 ounce shaved fresh Parmesan cheese (about ¹⁄₄ cup)

1. Heat a skillet over medium-high. Coat pan with cooking spray. Sprinkle steak with ¹⁄₄ teaspoon salt and black pepper. Add steak to pan; cook 4 to 5 minutes on each side for medium-rare or until desired degree of doneness. Place steak on a cutting board; let stand 5 minutes. Cut across the grain into thin slices.
2. Place the remaining ¹⁄₄ teaspoon salt, oil, parsley, vinegar, capers, garlic, and crushed red pepper in a bowl, stirring with a whisk. Divide arugula evenly among 4 plates. Top evenly with steak, onion, and cheese. Drizzle evenly with oil mixture. Serves 4 (serving size: about 1¹⁄₂ cups)

CALORIES 281; **FAT** 23g (sat 6g, unsat 15g); **PROTEIN** 15g; **CARB** 4g; **FIBER** 1g; **SUGARS** 1g (added sugars 0g); **SODIUM** 458mg; **CALC** 13% DV; **POTASSIUM** 10% DV

Fast • Vegetarian

Arugula Pesto Pizza

Hands-on: 20 min. Total: 25 min.
Wide ribbons of fresh butternut squash become tender while the pizza bakes, a colorful and faintly sweet contrast to the peppery arugula pesto.

1 (12-inch) prebaked thin whole-grain pizza crust (such as Mama Mary's)
Cooking spray
3 cups arugula (about 3 ounces)
½ cup fresh flat-leaf parsley leaves
⅓ cup chopped toasted walnuts
2 tablespoons fresh lemon juice
1 garlic clove, chopped
1 ounce Parmesan cheese, grated (about ¼ cup)
3 tablespoons olive oil, divided
1 tablespoon water
1 cup shaved butternut squash (about 2 ounces)
⅛ teaspoon kosher salt
⅛ teaspoon ground black pepper
1½ ounces goat cheese, crumbled (about ⅓ cup)

1. Preheat oven to 450°F.
2. Place crust on a baking sheet; coat with cooking spray. Bake at 450°F for 5 minutes.
3. Process arugula, parsley, walnuts, juice, garlic, and Parmesan cheese in a mini food processor until finely chopped. With food processor running, slowly add 2½ tablespoons oil. Add 1 tablespoon water; pulse to combine. Spread mixture over crust, leaving a ½-inch border.
4. Combine remaining 1½ teaspoons oil, squash, salt, and pepper in a bowl; arrange over pesto. Sprinkle goat cheese over pizza. Bake at 450°F for 10 minutes. Cut into 8 slices. Serves 4 (serving size: 2 slices)

CALORIES 397; **FAT** 24g (sat 6g, unsat 15g); **PROTEIN** 12g; **CARB** 34g; **FIBER** 1g; **SUGARS** 2g (added sugars 1g); **SODIUM** 572mg; **CALC** 13% DV; **POTASSIUM** 6% DV

Gluten Free

Moroccan Butternut Squash and Chickpea Stew

Hands-on: 18 min. Total: 35 min.

1½ tablespoons olive oil
1½ cups chopped yellow onion
2 garlic cloves, minced
½ teaspoon kosher salt
½ teaspoon ground paprika
½ teaspoon ground cumin
¼ teaspoon ground ginger
¼ teaspoon ground cinnamon
¼ teaspoon ground black pepper
1 tablespoon unsalted tomato paste
3 cups diced peeled butternut squash
1 (15-ounce) can unsalted chickpeas
1 (15-ounce) can diced tomatoes
1½ cups unsalted chicken stock (such as Swanson)
2 (8-ounce) packages precooked quinoa
2 cups arugula (about 2 ounces)
¼ cup plain 2% reduced-fat Greek yogurt

1. Heat oil in a large Dutch oven over medium-high. Add onion and garlic; sauté 5 minutes or until golden. Stir in salt and next 5 ingredients (through pepper); cook 1 minute. Stir in tomato paste; cook 1 minute. Stir in squash and chickpeas; cook 2 minutes. Add tomatoes and stock, scraping pan to loosen browned bits. Bring to a simmer; cook 20 minutes or until squash is tender.
2. Heat quinoa according to package directions. Divide quinoa among 4 shallow bowls. Top evenly with squash mixture, arugula, and yogurt. Serves 4 (serving size: about ½ cup quinoa, about 1¼ cups squash mixture, ½ cup arugula, and 1 tablespoon yogurt)

CALORIES 413; **FAT** 9g (sat 1g, unsat 6g); **PROTEIN** 17g; **CARB** 69g; **FIBER** 12g; **SUGARS** 11g (added sugars 0g); **SODIUM** 578mg; **CALC** 19% DV; **POTASSIUM** 27% DV

A WELL-STOCKED SPICE CABINET IS KEY FOR THIS STEW. EACH SERVING PACKS NEARLY HALF OF YOUR DAILY FIBER, ESSENTIAL FOR BETTER DIGESTION AND WEIGHT CONTROL.

4 GO-WITH-ANYTHING SIDES

Fast • Gluten Free
Vegetarian
Celery, Apple, and Almond Salad
(*pictured on page 234*)
Crunch rules in this fall salad. Cut the celery on a diagonal for long, thin slices that will match the shape of the apple slices. We like a tart-sweet Pink Lady or Fuji apple here.

Combine 2 tablespoons plain 2% reduced-fat Greek yogurt, 1 tablespoon canola mayonnaise, 2 teaspoons apple cider vinegar, 2 teaspoons water, ¼ teaspoon kosher salt, and ¼ teaspoon black pepper in a large bowl. Add 2 cups diagonally sliced celery, 1 cup thinly sliced apple, ¾ cup chopped fresh flat-leaf parsley, and ½ cup chopped roasted unsalted almonds; toss to coat. Serves 4 (serving size: about 1 cup)

CALORIES 145; **FAT** 10g (sat 1g, unsat 9g); **PROTEIN** 5g; **CARB** 10g; **FIBER** 3g; **SUGARS** 5g (added sugars 0g); **SODIUM** 196mg; **CALC** 9% DV; **POTASSIUM** 10% DV

Gluten Free • Vegetarian
Roasted Greek-Style Potatoes
The oven temperature may seem too high, but don't fear: The wedges are thick enough that they will cook through without overbrowning.

Preheat oven to 450°F with a baking sheet in the oven. Combine 3 (8-ounce) baking potatoes, each cut lengthwise into 8 wedges, 1 tablespoon minced fresh oregano, 1½ tablespoons olive oil, 1 teaspoon grated lemon rind, ½ teaspoon kosher salt, and ½ teaspoon black pepper in a bowl. Coat preheated pan with cooking spray. Add potato mixture to pan; bake at 450°F for 30 minutes, stirring after 15 minutes. Sprinkle with 1 teaspoon minced

fresh oregano, 2 teaspoons lemon juice, and 1 ounce crumbled feta. Serves 4 (serving size: 6 wedges)

CALORIES 202; **FAT** 7g (sat 2g, unsat 5g); **PROTEIN** 5g; **CARB** 32g; **FIBER** 2g; **SUGARS** 1g (added sugars 0g); **SODIUM** 314mg; **CALC** 7% DV; **POTASSIUM** 21% DV

Fast • Gluten Free
Vegetarian
Haricots Verts with Warm Shallot Vinaigrette
Applying heat to the dressing allows the shallots to mellow and the mustard and rosemary to steep in the olive oil.

Heat 2 tablespoons extra-virgin olive oil in a small skillet over medium-low. Add ¼ cup minced fresh shallot; sauté 4 minutes. Remove pan from heat; stir in 2 teaspoons sherry vinegar, ½ teaspoon grainy mustard, ½ teaspoon minced fresh rosemary, ¼ teaspoon kosher salt, and ¼ teaspoon black pepper. Cook 1 (8-ounce) package microwave-in-bag haricots verts according to package directions; toss with shallot mixture. Serves 4 (serving size: about ½ cup)

CALORIES 86; **FAT** 7g (sat 1g, unsat 6g); **PROTEIN** 1g; **CARB** 6g; **FIBER** 2g; **SUGARS** 3g (added sugars 0g); **SODIUM** 133mg; **CALC** 3% DV; **POTASSIUM** 21% DV

Fast • Make Ahead
Farro, Mushroom, and Walnut Pilaf
No need to microwave the farro; it will absorb enough liquid and heat through in the pan. Use the green parts of the green onions as well as the white for flecks of color in the finished dish.

Heat 1 tablespoon olive oil in a skillet over medium. Add ½ cup sliced green onions; sauté 2 minutes. Add 2 cups presliced cremini mushrooms and ½ teaspoon chopped fresh thyme; cook 4 minutes. Add ¼ cup unsalted chicken stock and 1 (8-ounce) package precooked farro; cook 1 minute. Stir in ¼ cup chopped toasted walnuts, ½

teaspoon kosher salt, and ¼ teaspoon black pepper. Top with ½ teaspoon chopped fresh thyme. Serves 4 (serving size: about ¾ cup)

CALORIES 167; **FAT** 9g (sat 1g, unsat 7g); **PROTEIN** 5g; **CARB** 20g; **FIBER** 3g; **SUGARS** 1g (added sugars 0g); **SODIUM** 260mg; **CALC** 3% DV; **POTASSIUM** 5% DV

COOKING LIGHT DIET

Fast • Make Ahead
Orange-Almond Chicken-and-Cabbage Bowls

Hands-on: 12 min. Total: 12 min.
Make these low-calorie, no-cook bowls ahead for an easy lunch or dinner when time is tight. Change up the fruit, nut, or protein for whatever you have on hand.

2 navel oranges
1 (12-ounce) package shredded coleslaw mix (about 3 cups)
4 ounces shredded boneless, skinless rotisserie chicken breast (about 1 cup)
3 tablespoons toasted sliced almonds
2 green onions, thinly diagonally sliced
3 tablespoons sesame-ginger salad dressing (such as Newman's Own)

1. Peel and section the oranges over a bowl; reserve sections. Squeeze membranes over bowl; reserve juice for another use. Discard membranes.
2. Divide orange sections, coleslaw mix, chicken, almonds, and green onions between 2 shallow bowls. Drizzle dressing evenly over each serving. Serves 2 (serving size: about 2 cups)

CALORIES 275; **FAT** 11g (sat 1g, unsat 9g); **PROTEIN** 21g; **CARB** 28g; **FIBER** 8g; **SUGARS** 19g (added sugars 3g); **SODIUM** 415mg; **CALC** 8% DV; **POTASSIUM** 13% DV

WHY INGREDIENTS MATTER
LA LISTE

Great French onion soup promises lush texture and exquisite flavor balance. These ingredients deliver.

French Onion Soup

Hands-on: 55 min. Total: 1 hr. 18 min.

¼ cup extra-virgin olive oil
4 pounds large yellow onions, thinly sliced

1 tablespoon chopped fresh thyme, plus more for garnish
½ teaspoon kosher salt
½ teaspoon black pepper
½ cup dry vermouth
4 cups unsalted beef stock
4 cups unsalted chicken stock
1 tablespoon Marmite
8 (½-ounce) slices whole-grain baguette, lightly toasted
4 ounces raclette cheese, grated (about 1 cup)

1. Heat oil in a Dutch oven over medium-high. Add onions; sauté 10 minutes or until tender. Reduce heat to medium-low. Stir in thyme, salt, and pepper; cook 40 minutes or until golden-brown, stirring occasionally.

2. Increase heat to medium-high. Add vermouth, scraping pan to loosen browned bits. Cook until liquid almost evaporates. Stir in stocks; bring to a simmer. Stir in Marmite; cook 5 minutes or until Marmite dissolves.

3. Preheat broiler to high with rack in top position. Place bread on broiler pan; top each slice with 2 tablespoons cheese. Broil 3 minutes or until cheese bubbles and browns in spots. Ladle 1 cup soup into each of 8 bowls; top each with 1 cheese toast, and garnish with thyme. Serves 8

CALORIES 265; **FAT** 12g (sat 4g, unsat 6g); **PROTEIN** 11g; **CARB** 28g; **FIBER** 4g; **SUGARS** 11g (added sugars 0g); **SODIUM** 608mg; **CALC** 16% DV; **POTASSIUM** 12% DV

YELLOW ONION
These grow nicely sweet when caramelized, without becoming cloying the way that sweet onions can.

DRY VERMOUTH
Some recipes use sherry or wine. Dry vermouth, brewed with botanicals and herbs, is like many ingredients in one—it adds complexity.

BEEF AND CHICKEN STOCK
Purists use only beef stock. But the store-bought stuff can taste bitter in large doses. Mellow chicken stock takes the edge off.

MARMITE
This British yeast paste is like an umami explosion, with more meaty flavor per portion than fish sauce, soy sauce, or miso.

WHOLE-GRAIN BAGUETTE
Whole grains are good for you, but the real benefit here is the nutty, hearty flavor they bring to the mix.

RACLETTE CHEESE
This tastes like the Gruyère that most recipes call for, but it's more melty, so your toasts become bubbly in a flash.

MASHED POTATOES, PERFECTED

Whether you like them pillow-fluffy or lush and creamy, four simple tricks deliver top results every time.

Gluten Free • Vegetarian

Silky-Smooth Mashed Potatoes

Hands-on: 14 min. Total: 38 min.

4 pounds russet potatoes, peeled and diced
¹⁄₂ cup whole milk
¹⁄₄ cup unsalted butter
1¹⁄₂ teaspoons kosher salt
¹⁄₂ teaspoon black pepper

1. Place potatoes in a large Dutch oven; cover with cold water by 1 inch. Place pan over medium-high. Bring to a simmer; cook potatoes 17 minutes or until completely tender. Drain well. Return potatoes to pan; place over medium-low. Cook 5 minutes or until all the liquid has evaporated, stirring occasionally (do not brown). Place potatoes in a food mill or large colander with medium-small (¹⁄₈-inch) holes.
2. Combine milk and butter in pan over medium-low; cook until butter melts. Set mill or colander over pan; crank mill, or use the back of a ladle or large spoon to press cooked potato through colander into milk mixture. Add salt and pepper to milled potato in pan; stir well to combine. Serves 8 (serving size: about ¹⁄₂ cup)

CALORIES 255; **FAT** 6g (sat 4g, unsat 2g); **PROTEIN** 4g; **CARB** 46g; **FIBER** 4g; **SUGARS** 3g (added sugars 0g); **SODIUM** 379mg; **CALC** 4% DV; **POTASSIUM** 22% DV

1. PICK THE RIGHT POTATO
Russets rule in mashed potatoes: They're starchy enough to make as fluffy or creamy as you like, without becoming gluey like red potatoes or other waxy varieties. Cook until you can easily slide a fork through a cube without resistance; al dente potatoes won't become silky smooth.

2. STEAM OFF ALL THE WATER
Even after draining the cooked potato, some cooking liquid remains, which waters down flavor and makes the texture leaden. Solve this by heating the cooked cubes in a dry pan for a few minutes until you see all residual water steam out. The dry potatoes are now ready to fully absorb the flavorings.

3. HEAT THE MILK AND BUTTER
Mixing the potatoes in the pan with hot milk and butter is another way to guard against gluey mashers. Hot liquid readily blends with the steaming spuds, so you don't have to over-handle or reheat the potatoes, which makes them release too much sticky starch.

4. PRESS OUT THE LUMPS
Pass the potatoes through a food mill to make them uniformly smooth: Big lumps won't soak up flavorings, creating dead zones in your mashers. No food mill? No problem—just use a potato ricer or a colander with roughly ¹⁄₈-inch holes, and press the potatoes through with the back of a ladle or large spoon.

LIGHTEN UP BEER CHEESE SOUP

With only about 240 calories per serving, this pub-style soup is make-a-double-batch good.

Welcome soup season with a comforting bowl of Beer Cheese Soup. Packed with cheesy flavor and soft undertones of smooth and malty ale, our soup delivers almost a full serving of vegetables in an unexpected way. The classic version is a near 500-calorie indulgence that calls for up to 1 pound of cheese (a whopping 85g sat fat alone), in addition to heavy cream and butter. We use roasted butternut squash to replace the classic butter-and-flour-based roux, lending body and velvety creaminess when pureed. Nutritional yeast amps up the cheesy flavor, letting us dial back on the cheddar. Find it in most health food stores and well-stocked markets. Our stealthy substitutions help shave off 200 calories, 12g sat fat, and 500mg sodium from a traditional recipe, while still delivering the hearty flavor notes of the classic. Plus, what better way to eat your vegetables than in the presence of cheese?

Make Ahead

Beer Cheese Soup

Hands-on: 25 min. Total: 1 hr. 10 min.

1 (2-pound) butternut squash
Cooking spray
1 tablespoon canola oil
1 cup chopped white onion
³/₄ cup chopped carrots
2 garlic cloves, finely chopped

3 tablespoons nutritional yeast
1 teaspoon dry mustard
³/₄ teaspoon kosher salt
¹/₄ teaspoon black pepper
2 teaspoons Dijon mustard
1 (12-ounce) bottle pale ale-style beer
1¹/₂ cups unsalted chicken stock
1¹/₂ cups 2% reduced-fat milk
2 tablespoons cornstarch
2 tablespoons water
4 ounces sharp cheddar cheese, shredded (about 1 cup)
2 tablespoons unsalted pumpkin seeds

1. Preheat oven to 425°F. Slice butternut squash in half lengthwise. Coat each cut side with cooking spray. Place squash halves, cut sides down, on foil-lined baking sheet. Bake at 425°F for 45 minutes. Let stand at room temperature 20 minutes. Scoop out 2½ cups flesh. Set aside.
2. Heat oil in a Dutch oven over medium. Add onion and carrots; cook 5 minutes or until tender. Add garlic, nutritional yeast, dry mustard, salt, pepper, and Dijon mustard; cook, stirring often, 2 minutes or until aromatic. Add beer; bring to a boil, scraping pan to loosen browned bits. Cook 5 minutes or until liquid is reduced by half. Reduce heat to medium, and stir in squash, stock, and milk.
3. Pour mixture into a blender. Remove center piece of blender lid (to allow steam to escape); secure lid on blender. Place a clean towel over opening in lid. Process until smooth. Pour mixture back into Dutch oven.
4. Combine cornstarch and 2 tablespoons water in a small bowl; mix well. Whisk cornstarch mixture into soup; cook 5 minutes, stirring often, until soup begins to thicken. Add cheese, stirring until cheese melts and mixture is smooth. Ladle soup into each of 6 bowls. Top each serving with pumpkin seeds. Serves 6 (serving size: 1½ cups soup and 1 teaspoon pumpkin seeds)

CALORIES 243; FAT 12g (sat 6g, unsat 5g); PROTEIN 10g; CARB 20g; FIBER 3g; SUGARS 6g (added sugars 0g); SODIUM 485mg; CALC 25% DV; POTASSIUM 13% DV

OOEY, GOOEY, HEALTHIER MAC AND CHEESE

By Gina Homolka

Satisfy your family's favorite comfort food craving with this lighter, veggie-packed version.

When the weather gets cooler, my family always craves comfort food classics, especially macaroni and cheese. Creamy and hearty, it's truly one of the most-loved comfort foods of all time. Unfortunately, though, all that cheesy indulgence usually comes with a hefty side of calories and saturated fat, which makes it practically off-limits when I'm sticking to a healthy diet. With my slimmed-down and nutrient-packed version, however, I can have my mac and cheese and indulge my family's craving, too.

So how did I put a healthy spin on a dish that's traditionally so heavy? I created a lighter sauce made with fat-free milk, broth, and a trio of freshly grated cheeses—light cheddar, Havarti, and Parmesan. I also swap out white pasta for whole-grain and roast my favorite seasonal vegetables to fold in at the end. Here, I used a combination of cauliflower, Brussels sprouts, broccoli, and butternut squash, but you can use whatever vegetables your family enjoys. The result is a creamy, delicious comfort food dish packed with healthy goodness.

continued

Make Ahead

Roasted Veggie Mac and Cheese

Hands-on: 55 min. Total: 1 hr. 30 min.

Olive oil cooking spray
10 ounces fresh broccoli florets, cut
   into 1-inch pieces
10 ounces cauliflower florets, cut
   into 1-inch pieces
10 ounces butternut squash, cut
   into ½-inch dice
10 ounces quartered Brussels
   sprouts
1½ teaspoons olive oil
¾ teaspoon kosher salt
12 ounces whole-grain elbow pasta
1½ tablespoons butter
¼ cup minced onion
¼ cup all-purpose flour
2 cups fat-free milk
1 cup reduced-sodium chicken or
   vegetable broth
Freshly ground black pepper
   to taste
5 ounces freshly grated white sharp
   light cheddar cheese (such as
   Cabot) (about 1¼ cups)
4 ounces freshly grated creamy
   Havarti cheese (about 1 cup)
2 tablespoons freshly grated
   Parmesan cheese

1. Preheat oven to 425°F. Line 2 large baking sheets with aluminum foil, and coat with olive oil spray. Toss broccoli, cauliflower, squash, and Brussels sprouts with olive oil, and season with salt. Spread vegetables in an even layer on prepared baking sheets. Bake at 425°F for 25 to 30 minutes, stirring vegetables and rotating pans halfway through cooking time, until vegetables are soft and have begun to brown around edges.
2. While vegetables roast, bring a large pot of water to a boil. Cook pasta according to package directions, omitting fat and salt. Drain, and set aside.

3. Melt butter in a medium saucepan over medium. Add onion, and cook over low about 2 minutes. Add flour, and cook another minute or until the flour mixture is golden and well combined. Add milk and broth; whisk, increasing heat to medium-high until mixture comes to a boil. Cook about 3 to 4 minutes or until it thickens slightly, and then season with pepper.
4. Remove pan from heat; add cheeses, and mix well until cheeses are melted. Add cooked pasta, and mix well; fold in roasted vegetables. Serves 8 (serving size: 1¼ cups)

CALORIES 378; **FAT** 14g (sat 7g, unsat 7g); **PROTEIN** 20g; **CARB** 50g; **FIBER** 8g; **SUGARS** 7g (added sugars 0g); **SODIUM** 568mg; **CALC** 41% DV; **POTASSIUM** 23% DV

THE TEACHER

A CULINARY SKEPTIC TEST-DRIVES THE INSTANT POT

By Andrea Nguyen

More than just a modern-day pressure cooker, this appliance deserves real estate on your counter.

In my kitchen, the stove is my best friend. I stand in front of it for much of the day, watching the transformation of ingredients, recording my observations in recipes. My husband often returns from work and jokes, "There you are, exactly where I left you this morning." So, I was hesitant when *Cooking Light*'s editor-in-chief suggested I try the Instant Pot. I'm a cook who thrives on basic appliances. Counter space is valuable real estate, too; our $30 microwave is in the garage.

But the IP is not just a kitchen appliance. It's a phenomenon. It's a $100 machine that promises to turn kitchen drudgery into culinary joy. Fervent Facebook communities and blog posts discuss its merits and hacks. Dedicated cookbooks have sprung up like mushrooms to capture the mania.

Despite its various functions, the IP is basically a pressure cooker. Never used one, or scared of them? My mom's exploded in the 1970s. Fortunately, modern cookers are safer and easier to operate.

The tight lid and gasket trap in steam, making molecules move faster and hotter to quickly cook and extract flavors. Sure, my simple stovetop pressure cooker, with its steady "shoosh-shoosh" venting, can seem manic, but it has upped my cooking game. I can produce terrific pho, beans, and beets in 65% less time than normal. Curious, I test-drove the Instant Pot 6-quart Duo.

Other than beeps that signal operation, the IP is eerily silent and efficient. There is no venting during cooking, which makes me miss the smell of food being cooked.

An appliance for modern lifestyles, the IP encourages you to tinker and multitask while you use it (it maintains consistent pressure and keeps food warm for hours!). I was emboldened to cook while practicing yoga, meditating, even sleeping.

My near-spills and thrills kept me nimble. Brown jasmine rice cooked on "Multigrain" was borderline mushy; I added water and a frozen chicken carcass and pressed "Porridge" to transform a disaster into dinner. "Beans/Chili" turned heirloom Ayocote Blanco beans into an overcooked mess, to which I added kale, tomato, and herbs to create soup. After seven hours on "Slow Cook," green beans weren't as tender as expected, so I finished the deed with low pressure for three minutes. Complete wins included jiggly soft-boiled eggs cooked via "Steam." The "Rice" function yielded perfect grains after fluffing and resting for 10 minutes. Dreamy homemade yogurt was at my fingertips.

Gathering intel, I reached out to IP superusers. It can ruin delicate seafood, said Coco Morante, author of *The Essential Instant Pot Cookbook*. To safely deal with the pressure release valve, Michelle Tam of nomnompaleo.com uses her left hand to turn its handle and release steam; her hand and arm are out of harm's way.

One weekend, I made eight things in the machine. "You're like Captain Jean-Luc Picard wanting 'tea, Earl Grey, hot,'" my husband said. "I'm an Instant Pot widower." Once averse to programmable cooking gadgets, I am now obsessed with pushing IP buttons and experimenting.

Gluten Free • Make Ahead
Vegetarian

Pressure-Cooked Beets

Hands-on: 16 min. Total: 35 min.
Why pay for precooked beets when the Instant Pot can cook them for you in a flash? These are delicious on their own as a veggie side or to add to salad.

5 medium beets (each about 2 1/2 inches wide, 1 1/4 pounds total), trimmed and unpeeled
2 teaspoons balsamic vinegar
1 teaspoon olive or canola oil
1/8 teaspoon fine sea salt

1. Put 1 to 1½ cups water into the Instant Pot. Set steamer trivet inside, and arrange the beets on top. Lock the lid in place; turn the pressure release valve to seal. Program the IP to cook on Manual, at High Pressure, for 15 minutes.
2. Turn off the IP, and wait 8 to 10 minutes to partially depressurize. Release remaining pressure, remove lid, and then transfer the trivet and beets to a plate. When beets are

cool enough to handle (about 10 minutes), rub off the skins and trim ugly/hard parts. Halve then quarter each beet (or cut each into 6 wedges). Put in a bowl, and toss with vinegar, oil, and salt. Cool completely before eating, or chill for up to 5 days. Return to room temperature to use. Serves 4

CALORIES 73; **FAT** 1g (sat 0g, unsat 1g); **PROTEIN** 2g; **CARB** 14g; **FIBER** 4g; **SUGARS** 10g (added sugars 0g); **SODIUM** 181mg; **CALC** 2% DV; **POTASSIUM** 13% DV

WHY BUY THE INSTANT POT?

The Instant Pot, like most appliances, isn't perfect, but it's well-priced and good for people with little time (set it and forget it). Plus, it's fun—tinker with it and be part of an online tribe (many call themselves "Potheads"). It's a 21st-century cooking experience.

Fast • Gluten Free
Make Ahead • Vegetarian

Beet Yogurt Dip

Hands-on: 26 min. Total: 26 min.
Harness beets' striking color and earthy-sweet flavor in this glorious spread inspired by Jerusalem: A Cookbook by Yotam Ottolenghi and Sami Tamimi. For a little extra heat, use up to 1/4 teaspoon of red pepper. You can try 1 1/2 teaspoons za'atar spice blend as a substitute for fresh thyme, but skip ground thyme because it lends a dirt-like taste. Serve with raw carrot slices, cucumber slices, pita bread, or rice crackers for scooping.

1 garlic clove
8 ounces (1 1/2 cups) cooked beets (or, for raw beets, see recipe at left)
1/2 cup plain 2% reduced-fat Greek yogurt
1 1/2 teaspoons robust-tasting honey, such as amber-colored honey

1 teaspoon minced fresh thyme leaves
1/2 teaspoon fine sea salt
1/8 to 1/4 teaspoon ground red pepper
2 tablespoons olive oil, divided
2 tablespoons crumbled sheep's milk feta cheese
2 tablespoons chopped roasted walnuts or almonds
1 tablespoon chopped fresh mint leaves

1. Make puree in a food processor outfitted with steel blade: Remove the pusher, and with processor running, drop in garlic. Once finely chopped, scrape down sides with a spatula. Add beets. Pulse about 30 times, scraping as needed, until finely chopped.
2. Add yogurt, and then process to a semi-coarse puree. Add honey, thyme, salt, pepper, and 1 tablespoon olive oil. Process to blend well. Let stand 5 minutes to develop flavor. Taste, and adjust flavors if needed. Transfer to a wide, shallow bowl. Drizzle on remaining 1 tablespoon olive oil. Top with cheese, nuts, and mint. Serves 6 (serving size: 1/4 cup)

CALORIES 104; **FAT** 8g (sat 2g, unsat 6g); **PROTEIN** 3g; **CARB** 7g; **FIBER** 1g; **SUGARS** 5g (added sugars 1g); **SODIUM** 269mg; **CALC** 5% DV; **POTASSIUM** 4% DV

FALL HARVEST FAVES

Staff Favorite • Make Ahead
Vegetarian

Cider Doughnuts with Maple-Tahini Glaze

Hands-on: 10 min. Total: 45 min.

¾ cup unfiltered apple cider
7 ounces McIntosh or Cortland apples,
    cored and diced (about 2 cups)
6 ounces whole-wheat pastry flour
    (about 1¾ cups)
1 teaspoon baking powder
½ teaspoon baking soda
½ teaspoon cinnamon
½ teaspoon kosher salt
½ cup sugar
⅓ cup plain whole-milk Greek
    yogurt
3 tablespoons canola oil
1 large egg
Cooking spray
2 tablespoons tahini (sesame seed
    paste)
2 tablespoons dark maple syrup
2 teaspoons water

1. Preheat oven to 350°F.
2. Combine apple cider and apples in a saucepan over medium-high; cover, and cook 10 minutes. Uncover, and cook 2 minutes. Remove from heat; cool 10 minutes. Pour apple mixture into a blender; process until smooth.
3. Weigh or lightly spoon flour into dry measuring cups; level with a knife. Combine flour, baking powder, baking soda, cinnamon, and salt in a medium bowl; stir with a whisk.
4. Combine apple mixture, sugar, yogurt, oil, and egg in a medium bowl; stir with a whisk. Add yogurt mixture to flour mixture, and stir until combined.
5. Coat 2 (6-cavity) doughnut pans with cooking spray. Spoon batter evenly into 12 cavities. Bake at 350°F for 12 minutes or until doughnuts spring back when lightly pressed. Cool in pan 2 minutes. Invert doughnuts onto a wire rack. Cool completely.
6. Combine tahini and maple syrup, stirring with a whisk. Add 2 teaspoons water; whisk until smooth. Spread glaze over tops of doughnuts. Let stand until glaze is set. Serves 12 (serving size: 1 doughnut)

CALORIES 171; **FAT** 6g (sat 1g, unsat 5g); **PROTEIN** 3g; **CARB** 27g; **FIBER** 3g; **SUGARS** 14g (added sugars 10g); **SODIUM** 175mg; **CALC** 5% DV; **POTASSIUM** 3% DV

THE LOWDOWN: APPLE CIDER

FRESH-PRESSED CIDER IS LIKE COLD, CRISP FALL IN A GLASS. HERE'S WHAT TO KNOW.

BUY
Look for unfiltered, fresh cider—deep brown and cloudy, it has a complex, sweet-tart flavor and lush mouthfeel. Find it refrigerated at orchards, farmers' markets, and supermarkets.

SKIP
Avoid shelf-stable, clear "cider"—it's indistinguishable from apple juice, lacks flavor nuance, and doesn't have the naturally thickening pectin that makes fresh cider so great for cooking.

COOK
Adds delightful fall flavor to baked goods. Also shines in sauces or bastes for roasted pork and chicken: Cider's pectin thickens it to a rich, glossy glaze when reduced.

STORE
Refrigerate for up to two weeks. Should be safe if constantly chilled until the "use by" date on the bottle. Raw, unpasteurized cider will have a shorter shelf life.

THANKSGIVING VEGETABLE COOKBOOK

Thanksgiving is truly a celebration of fall's bounty—that's why sides, sauces, and desserts all feature seasonal fruits and vegetables. These are the dishes we love to share, from the annual must-haves to the daringly updated. In the spirit of the season (and our plant-forward mission), this year's cookbook is led by autumn's best produce. You'll find every recipe you need, plus menus, to pull together a complete feast—including two top-rated turkeys—with special attention paid to the sides you love.

GREENS AND GREEN BEANS

Starch is king on Thanksgiving, a great reason to include welcome relief with crisp-tender green beans, vibrant salads, and bumpy, leafy greens like lacinato kale. Quickly make the charred green beans and the citrus and fennel salad at the last minute; the casserole and the braised greens can be made ahead and reheated just before serving.

Staff Favorite • Fast
Gluten Free • Vegetarian

Fennel and Blood Orange Salad

Hands-on: 15 min. Total: 15 min.

2 blood oranges
1/4 cup extra-virgin olive oil
2 tablespoons white wine vinegar
2 teaspoons honey
3/4 teaspoon kosher salt
3/4 teaspoon black pepper
1 (10-ounce) head curly endive, leaves separated
1 (10-ounce) head radicchio, chopped
1 (10-ounce) fennel bulb, cored and thinly sliced
1/3 cup chopped toasted hazelnuts
1/4 cup torn fresh mint
1 small shallot, thinly sliced

1. Peel and section oranges over a bowl; reserve. Squeeze membranes over a bowl to extract juice. Whisk together 2 tablespoons juice, oil, vinegar, honey, salt, and pepper in a bowl.
2. Arrange orange sections, endive, radicchio, and fennel on a large platter. Sprinkle with hazelnuts, mint, and shallot. Drizzle with juice mixture. Serves 8 (serving size: about 1 cup)

CALORIES 142; FAT 10g (sat 1g, unsat 8g); PROTEIN 3g; CARB 12g; FIBER 4g; SUGARS 6g (added sugars 1g); SODIUM 214mg; CALC 7% DV; POTASSIUM 12% DV

Green Bean Casserole with Cauliflower Cream

Hands-on: 20 min. Total: 50 min.

1 cup chopped yellow onion
1/4 cup olive oil, divided
7/8 teaspoon kosher salt, divided
3/4 teaspoon black pepper, divided
1 pound green beans, cut into 2-inch pieces
12 ounces shiitake mushrooms, stemmed and halved
1 (8-ounce) container cremini mushrooms, quartered
3 cups chopped cauliflower (about 9 ounces)
1 1/2 cups 2% reduced-fat milk
1/2 cup water
2 dried bay leaves
2 thyme sprigs
2 garlic cloves, crushed
1 tablespoon dry sherry
1/8 teaspoon ground nutmeg
Cooking spray
3 ounces whole-wheat bread, torn (about 2 1/2 cups)

1. Preheat oven to 425°F.
2. Combine onion, 2 tablespoons oil, 3/8 teaspoon salt, 1/4 teaspoon pepper, green beans, and mushrooms on a foil-lined baking sheet. Bake at 425°F for 15 minutes or until browned.
3. Bring cauliflower and next 5 ingredients (through garlic) to a simmer in a saucepan over medium; cook 25 minutes or until tender. Remove pan from heat. Carefully place cauliflower mixture in a blender; blend until smooth. Return puree to pan; stir in remaining 1/2 teaspoon salt, remaining 1/2 teaspoon pepper, sherry, and nutmeg.

4. Place green bean mixture in an 11- x 7-inch baking dish coated with cooking spray; top with cauliflower mixture. Combine remaining 2 tablespoons oil with bread; sprinkle over dish. Bake at 425°F for 10 minutes. Serves 10 (serving size: about 1/2 cup)

CALORIES 136; FAT 7g (sat 1g, unsat 5g); PROTEIN 5g; CARB 15g; FIBER 4g; SUGARS 6g (added sugars 0g); SODIUM 249mg; CALC 9% DV; POTASSIUM 13% DV

THANKSGIVING MENU ONE

Cider-Glazed Turkey with Roasted Apples (page 314)

Balsamic Cranberry-Onion Jam (page 316)

Triple-Herb Pumpernickel and Sourdough Stuffing (page 308)

Sweet Potato Casserole with Pumpkin Seed–Oat Crumble (page 310)

Garlicky Blistered Green Beans and Tomatoes (page 304)

Garlicky Blistered Green Beans and Tomatoes

Hands-on: 20 min. Total: 20 min.
The broiler does all the work in this easy, impressive side. Pile leftovers on a sandwich or add to a big salad.

2 tablespoons olive oil, divided
1 1/2 tablespoons unsalted butter, melted
1 teaspoon kosher salt
1/2 teaspoon black pepper
1 1/2 pounds haricots verts (French green beans), trimmed
2 garlic cloves, unpeeled
1 pint cherry tomatoes
1 large shallot, sliced crosswise and rings separated
1 tablespoon sherry vinegar

1. Preheat broiler with oven rack in top position.
2. Combine 1 tablespoon oil, butter, salt, pepper, and haricots verts in a bowl; spread in a single layer on a foil-lined rimmed baking sheet. Add garlic cloves to pan. Broil 5 minutes or until beans just begin to char. Add tomatoes and shallots; broil 5 minutes or until tomatoes start to break down.
3. Remove skins from garlic cloves; discard. Place garlic pulp in a bowl; mash. Stir in remaining 1 tablespoon oil and vinegar. Drizzle garlic mixture over green bean mixture; toss. Serves 8 (serving size: about 1/2 cup)

CALORIES 86; FAT 6g (sat 2g, unsat 4g); PROTEIN 2g; CARB 8g; FIBER 3g; SUGARS 4g (added sugars 0g); SODIUM 248mg; CALC 4% DV; POTASSIUM 8% DV

Creamed Greens with Farro

Hands-on: 20 min. Total: 40 min.

1½ tablespoons olive oil, divided
½ cup chopped yellow onion
1 teaspoon minced fresh garlic
12 ounces Swiss chard, stemmed and coarsely chopped (2 bunches)
14 ounces lacinato kale, stemmed and coarsely chopped (2 bunches)
1 cup unsalted chicken stock
½ teaspoon black pepper
¼ teaspoon kosher salt
3 ounces ⅓-less-fat cream cheese, softened
1½ ounces reduced-fat provolone cheese, shredded (⅓ cup)
2 tablespoons grated Parmesan cheese
2 cups cooked unpearled farro
⅓ cup whole-wheat panko (Japanese breadcrumbs)

1. Heat 1 tablespoon oil in an oven-proof skillet over medium-high. Add onion; sauté 4 minutes. Add garlic; cook 30 seconds. Add greens in batches, stirring to wilt. Add stock, pepper, and salt. Reduce heat, and simmer 12 minutes. Stir in cheeses and farro.
2. Preheat broiler with oven rack in top position.
3. Combine remaining 1½ teaspoons oil and panko in a bowl; sprinkle over pan. Broil 4 minutes or until golden. Serves 10 (serving size: about ½ cup)

CALORIES 134; FAT 6g (sat 2g, unsat 2g); PROTEIN 7g; CARB 19g; FIBER 4g; SUGARS 2g (added sugars 0g); SODIUM 236mg; CALC 13% DV; POTASSIUM 9% DV

ONIONS AND MUSHROOMS

Mushrooms and onions often fade into the background in other dishes, but once roasted until rich and browned or slowly sautéed until sweet and meltingly tender, they not only shine brighter but elevate every dish around them.

Make Ahead

Wild Mushroom and Barley Stuffing

Hands-on: 25 min. Total: 1 hr.

3 cups water
1 cup uncooked pearled barley
1 tablespoon unsalted butter
2 teaspoons olive oil
1 cup chopped yellow onion
1 cup chopped celery
½ cup chopped carrots
2 (4-ounce) packages gourmet blend mushrooms
2 teaspoons minced fresh garlic
1 teaspoon chopped fresh rosemary
1 teaspoon chopped fresh thyme
½ cup chopped pecans
½ cup dried cherries, chopped
2 tablespoons chopped fresh flat-leaf parsley
1½ teaspoons kosher salt
½ teaspoon black pepper
1¼ cups unsalted chicken stock
1 large egg, lightly beaten
Cooking spray
3 ounces Gruyère cheese, grated (about ¾ cup)

1. Bring 3 cups water and barley to a boil in a medium saucepan. Reduce heat, and simmer 25 minutes; drain.
2. Preheat oven to 350°F.
3. Heat butter and oil in a large skillet over medium-high. Add onion, celery, carrots, and mushrooms; cook 8 minutes. Add garlic, rosemary, and thyme; cook 1 minute. Combine barley, mushroom mixture, pecans, cherries, parsley, salt, and pepper in a large bowl. Stir in stock and egg. Spoon mixture into a 2-quart baking dish coated with cooking spray.
4. Bake at 350°F for 25 minutes or until liquid is absorbed. Remove dish from oven.
5. Preheat broiler with oven rack in top position.
6. Sprinkle cheese over stuffing. Broil 1 minute or until lightly browned. Let stand 10 minutes before serving. Serves 12 (serving size: ½ cup)

CALORIES 174; FAT 8g (sat 3g, unsat 5g); PROTEIN 6g; CARB 21g; FIBER 4g; SUGARS 6g (added sugars 2g); SODIUM 324mg; CALC 10% DV; POTASSIUM 6% DV

Balsamic-Glazed Pearl Onions

Hands-on: 10 min. Total: 50 min.

1½ tablespoons unsalted butter, divided
2 (14.5-ounce) packages frozen pearl onions, thawed and drained
2 tablespoons sugar
⅓ cup balsamic vinegar
¼ cup water, as needed
¾ teaspoon kosher salt
¼ teaspoon black pepper
2 tablespoons chopped fresh parsley

1. Heat 1 tablespoon butter in a skillet over medium. Add onions; cook 20 minutes, stirring occasionally. Add sugar; cook 2 minutes. Stir in vinegar. Cover, reduce heat, and cook 25 minutes, adding up to ¼ cup water, 1 tablespoon at a time, if pan seems dry. Stir in remaining 1½ teaspoons butter, salt, and pepper. Top with parsley. Serves 6 (serving size: ½ cup)

CALORIES 115; FAT 3g (sat 2g, unsat 1g); PROTEIN 2g; CARB 21g; FIBER 2g; SUGARS 13g (added sugars 4g); SODIUM 249mg; CALC 4% DV; POTASSIUM 7% DV

Garlic-Caper Roasted Mushrooms

Gluten Free • Vegetarian

Hands-on: 10 min. Total: 35 min.
Roasted mushrooms are a revelation—intensely savory yet still tender and juicy. Use cremini or baby bella mushrooms here; white button mushrooms are too mild.

1½ **pounds cremini mushrooms, trimmed and halved (about 4 cups)**
¼ **teaspoon kosher salt**
⅛ **teaspoon freshly ground black pepper**
3 **tablespoons capers, drained and chopped**
1½ **tablespoons unsalted butter**
1 **tablespoon minced fresh garlic**
1 **tablespoon fresh lemon juice**
2 **tablespoons chopped fresh flat-leaf parsley**

1. Preheat oven to 450°F.
2. Place mushrooms on a baking sheet; sprinkle with salt and pepper. Bake at 450°F for 20 minutes or until tender and lightly browned.
3. Combine capers, butter, and garlic in a microwave-safe bowl; microwave at high 1 minute or until butter melts. Drizzle butter mixture over mushrooms; toss. Bake at 450°F for 2 minutes or until browned. Sprinkle lemon juice and parsley over mushroom mixture. Serve warm. Serves 6 (serving size: ½ cup)

CALORIES 55; **FAT** 3g (sat 2g, unsat 1g); **PROTEIN** 3g; **CARB** 6g; **FIBER** 1g; **SUGARS** 2g (added sugars 0g); **SODIUM** 189mg; **CALC** 3% DV; **POTASSIUM** 15% DV

Balsamic Onion and Thyme Tarte Tatin

Make Ahead • Vegetarian

Hands-on: 25 min. Total: 1 hr. 15 min.
Caramelized onion wedges give this tart a lovely stained glass effect once inverted. Use a serrated knife to cut it. The slices won't be precise, but that's part of the charm.

2 **tablespoons olive oil**
½ **teaspoon kosher salt**
½ **teaspoon black pepper**
2 **pounds red onions, halved and cut into wedges (about 2 large)**
2 **tablespoons brown sugar**
2 **tablespoons balsamic vinegar**
1 **teaspoon chopped fresh thyme**
½ **(14.2-ounce) package refrigerated pie dough**
4 **thyme sprigs**

1. Preheat oven to 400°F.
2. Heat oil in a large skillet over medium-low. Add salt, pepper, and onions; sauté 15 minutes or until onions are lightly browned. Add sugar, vinegar, and chopped thyme; cook 5 minutes or until liquid evaporates. Remove pan from heat; cool slightly.
3. Roll pie dough into a 12-inch circle on a lightly floured surface. Place thyme sprigs in bottom of a 9-inch cake pan. Spread onion mixture in bottom of pan in a single layer. Drape dough over pan, folding edges underneath. Prick surface liberally with a fork. Bake at 400°F for 20 minutes. Reduce oven temperature to 350°F (leave pan in oven); bake at 350°F for 15 minutes or until dough is browned and crisp. Remove pan from oven; cool 15 minutes. Carefully invert tart onto a serving plate. Serves 8 (serving size: 1 wedge)

CALORIES 193; **FAT** 10g (sat 3g, unsat 5g); **PROTEIN** 2g; **CARB** 27g; **FIBER** 2g; **SUGARS** 9g (added sugars 3g); **SODIUM** 257mg; **CALC** 3% DV; **POTASSIUM** 5% DV

WINTER SQUASH

We wait all year for these speckled green and gold beauties. Roasted until caramel-sweet, they rival any spud. Try a chile-ginger or molasses-walnut topper, or stuff for a showstopping side. And, save room for pumpkin pie.

Gluten Free • Make Ahead

Acorn Squash with Wild Rice Stuffing
(pictured on page 238)

Hands-on: 45 min. Total: 1 hr.

⅔ **cup uncooked wild rice**
1 **teaspoon olive oil, divided**
4 **(1-pound) acorn squashes, halved lengthwise and seeded**
¾ **teaspoon kosher salt, divided**
2 **(3-ounce) sweet Italian turkey sausage links, casings removed**
1 **cup chopped yellow onion**
½ **cup chopped celery**
3 **ounces fresh shiitake mushrooms, chopped**
1 **tablespoon minced fresh garlic**
1 **teaspoon fresh thyme leaves**
1 **(6-ounce) package fresh spinach**
2 **tablespoons chopped fresh flat-leaf parsley**
1 **tablespoon fresh lemon juice**
½ **teaspoon black pepper**

1. Cook rice according to package directions. Preheat oven to 425°F.
2. Brush ½ teaspoon oil over cut sides of squashes; top with ½ teaspoon salt. Place squashes, cut sides down, on a parchment paper–lined baking sheet. Bake at 425°F for 20 minutes or until almost tender. Remove from oven.
3. Heat remaining ½ teaspoon oil in a skillet over medium. Add sausage; cook 3 minutes, stirring to crumble. Add onion and celery; cook 5 minutes. Add mushrooms; cook 4 minutes. Add garlic and thyme; cook

1 minute. Add spinach, stirring until wilted. Remove from heat; stir in cooked rice, remaining ¼ teaspoon salt, parsley, juice, and pepper.

4. Spoon about ½ cup rice mixture into each squash half. Bake at 425°F for 10 minutes or until squash halves are tender and lightly browned. Serves 8 (serving size: 1 stuffed half)

CALORIES 197; **FAT** 3g (sat 1g, unsat 2g); **PROTEIN** 9g; **CARB** 38g; **FIBER** 6g; **SUGARS** 7g (added sugars 0g); **SODIUM** 297mg; **CALC** 11% DV; **POTASSIUM** 30% DV

Staff Favorite • Make Ahead
Vegetarian

Pumpkin-Praline Pie

Hands-on: 15 min. Total: 2 hr. 55 min.

PIE
½ (14.2-ounce) package refrigerated
   pie dough
Cooking spray
⅔ cup packed light brown sugar
¼ teaspoon kosher salt
2 large egg whites
1 large egg
1 (12-ounce) can fat-free evaporated
   milk
1 (15-ounce) can pumpkin puree
½ teaspoon ground cinnamon
¼ teaspoon ground nutmeg
⅛ teaspoon ground cloves

TOPPING
2.13 ounces all-purpose flour
   (about ½ cup)
¼ cup packed light brown sugar
⅛ teaspoon kosher salt
2 tablespoons unsalted butter, melted
½ cup chopped pecans
2 tablespoons honey

1. Preheat oven to 425°F.
2. To prepare pie, roll dough into an 11-inch circle. Fit dough into a 9-inch pie plate coated with cooking spray; fold edges under, and flute.
3. Combine ⅔ cup brown sugar, ¼ teaspoon salt, egg whites, egg, and

evaporated milk. Whisk in next 4 ingredients. Pour into pie plate; bake at 425°F for 10 minutes. Reduce heat to 350°F (leave pan in oven). Bake at 350°F for 20 minutes (shield piecrust with foil if it gets too brown).
4. To prepare topping, combine flour, ¼ cup brown sugar, and ⅛ teaspoon salt. Stir in melted butter and pecans. Sprinkle over pie. Drizzle with honey. Bake at 350°F for 30 minutes or until center is set. Cool 1 hour Serves 12 (serving size: 1 slice)

CALORIES 262; **FAT** 10g (sat 3g, unsat 6g); **PROTEIN** 5g; **CARB** 39g; **FIBER** 2g; **SUGARS** 24g (added sugars 19g); **SODIUM** 187mg; **CALC** 12% DV; **POTASSIUM** 7% DV

Gluten Free • Make Ahead
Vegetarian

Ginger-Chile Roasted Acorn Squash

Hands-on: 5 min. Total: 35 min.

1 (1½-pound) acorn squash, halved
   lengthwise and seeded
3 tablespoons plus 1 teaspoon olive
   oil, divided
1 tablespoon grated peeled fresh
   ginger
1 tablespoon minced red Fresno
   chile
¾ teaspoon kosher salt
1 tablespoon honey
½ cup pomegranate arils
⅓ cup chopped fresh cilantro

1. Preheat oven to 425°F. Place baking sheet in oven (leave pan in oven as it preheats).
2. Cut squash halves into 1-inch-thick slices. Combine 3 tablespoons oil, ginger, chile, and salt; rub over slices. Arrange in a single layer on preheated pan. Bake at 425°F for 25 minutes; turn over after 15 minutes.
3. Combine remaining 1 teaspoon oil and honey; drizzle over squash.

Top with pomegranate and cilantro. Serves 6 (serving size: about 3 slices)

CALORIES 136; **FAT** 8g (sat 1g, unsat 6g); **PROTEIN** 1g; **CARB** 18g; **FIBER** 2g; **SUGARS** 7g (added sugars 3g); **SODIUM** 245mg; **CALC** 4% DV; **POTASSIUM** 13% DV

Gluten Free • Make Ahead
Vegetarian

Roasted Butternut Squash with Sticky Walnut Topping

Hands-on: 15 min. Total: 55 min.

2 tablespoons chopped fresh sage,
   divided
1 tablespoon olive oil
¾ teaspoon ground cinnamon,
   divided
½ teaspoon kosher salt
¼ teaspoon ground nutmeg
1 (2½-pound) butternut squash,
   halved lengthwise and seeded
2 tablespoons pure maple syrup
1½ tablespoons dark molasses
1 tablespoon apple cider vinegar
⅓ cup coarsely chopped walnuts

1. Preheat oven to 425°F.
2. Combine 1 tablespoon sage, oil, ½ teaspoon cinnamon, salt, and nutmeg; rub over squash. Place squash, cut sides up, on a baking sheet; roast at 425°F for 40 minutes or until tender. Remove pan from oven; let stand 5 minutes. Cut each squash half lengthwise into 4 wedges.
3. Bring remaining 1 tablespoon sage, remaining ¼ teaspoon cinnamon, syrup, molasses, and vinegar to a boil in a small saucepan. Cook 2 to 3 minutes or until syrupy. Remove pan from heat; stir in walnuts. Spoon walnut mixture over squash wedges. Serves 8 (serving size: 1 squash wedge and about 1 tablespoon walnut mixture)

CALORIES 136; **FAT** 5g (sat 1g, unsat 1g); **PROTEIN** 2g; **CARB** 24g; **FIBER** 3g; **SUGARS** 9g (added sugars 6g); **SODIUM** 128mg; **CALC** 9% DV; **POTASSIUM** 17% DV

HERBS

For a burst of bright color in your holiday feast, just add herbs—use a generous mix and your kitchen will also smell amazing. Hard herbs like rosemary, sage, and thyme give dishes a savory backbone, while soft herbs like parsley and chives enliven more muted flavors with freshness. Use all or just two or three, keeping ratios the same for the right balance.

Gluten Free • Make Ahead
Vegetarian

Herb-Roasted Carrots

Hands-on: 10 min. Total: 35 min.
A simple side of roasted carrots is the breather a crowded table needs—a bit of palate relief (and ease for the cook) that still looks elegant.

¼ cup olive oil
2 tablespoons chopped fresh thyme
½ teaspoon kosher salt
½ teaspoon black pepper
3 tablespoons chopped fresh cilantro, divided
3 tablespoons chopped fresh flat-leaf parsley, divided
1½ pounds carrots, peeled and cut diagonally into 2-inch pieces

1. Preheat oven to 400°F.
2. Combine oil, thyme, salt, pepper, 1½ tablespoons cilantro, 1½ tablespoons parsley, and carrots; toss.
3. Arrange carrot mixture on a foil-lined rimmed baking sheet; bake at 400°F for 25 minutes or until lightly browned and tender, stirring once after 15 minutes. Sprinkle with remaining 1½ tablespoons cilantro and remaining 1½ tablespoons parsley. Serves 6 (serving size: ½ cup)

CALORIES 133; **FAT** 10g (sat 1g, unsat 8g); **PROTEIN** 1g; **CARB** 11g; **FIBER** 3g; **SUGARS** 5g (added sugars 0g); **SODIUM** 240mg; **CALC** 4% DV; **POTASSIUM** 11% DV

Triple-Herb Pumpernickel and Sourdough Stuffing

Hands-on: 30 min. Total: 1 hr. 25 min.
This recipe actually boasts five herbs, though hearty sage, rosemary, and thyme are most prominent. Look for packages of poultry herbs at the store; they contain just enough of all three.

1 (1-pound) sourdough bread loaf, cut into ¾-inch cubes (about 9 cups)
4 ounces pumpernickel bread, cubed (about 2 cups)
3 tablespoons unsalted butter, divided
1 tablespoon olive oil
2 cups finely chopped yellow onion
1 cup finely chopped celery
2 tablespoons chopped fresh sage
1 tablespoon chopped fresh thyme
1 tablespoon chopped fresh rosemary
6 garlic cloves, finely chopped
3 cups unsalted chicken stock
2 tablespoons chopped fresh flat-leaf parsley, divided
2 tablespoons chopped fresh chives, divided
½ teaspoon black pepper
2 large eggs, beaten
Cooking spray
⅓ cup celery leaves (optional)

1. Preheat oven to 350°F.
2. Arrange bread cubes in a single layer on a baking sheet; bake at 350°F for 10 minutes or until toasted, stirring once after 5 minutes. Place bread cubes in a large bowl.
3. Heat 1 tablespoon butter and oil in a large nonstick skillet over medium-high. Add onion and celery; sauté 5 minutes. Stir in sage, thyme, rosemary, and garlic; cook 5 minutes. Add herb mixture to bread.
4. Melt remaining 2 tablespoons butter in skillet. Combine butter, stock,

1 tablespoon parsley, 1 tablespoon chives, pepper, and eggs in a bowl. Add to bread mixture; toss gently to combine. Spoon bread mixture into a 2-quart baking dish coated with cooking spray. Bake at 350°F for 40 minutes or until browned. Sprinkle with remaining 1 tablespoon parsley, remaining 1 tablespoon chives, and celery leaves, if using. Serves 12 (serving size: ½ cup)

CALORIES 195; **FAT** 6g (sat 2g, unsat 3g); **PROTEIN** 7g; **CARB** 28g; **FIBER** 2g; **SUGARS** 3g (added sugars 0g); **SODIUM** 337mg; **CALC** 5% DV; **POTASSIUM** 4% DV

Staff Favorite

Herb, Lemon, and Garlic Turkey
(pictured on page 238)

Hands-on: 50 min. Total: 11 hr. 30 min.
Instead of a wet brine, this bird uses an overnight dry salt and sugar cure, which concentrates flavor. If you leave the skin on, it will add 25 calories and 1g of sat fat per serving.

1 (14-pound) whole fresh or frozen turkey, thawed
1 tablespoon kosher salt, divided
1 teaspoon sugar
2 (1-ounce) packages fresh poultry herb blend (or 6 sprigs each fresh rosemary, thyme, and sage), divided
½ cup unsalted butter, melted
1 bunch fresh flat-leaf parsley, divided
2 lemons, halved
1 head garlic, halved horizontally
Cooking spray
1½ cups dry white wine, divided
¼ cup very thinly sliced chives, divided
4 cups unsalted chicken stock, divided (such as Swanson)
1.1 ounces unbleached all-purpose flour (about ¼ cup)
¾ teaspoon freshly ground black pepper

1. Remove giblets and neck from turkey; reserve neck. Trim excess fat. Pat turkey dry. Rub 2 teaspoons salt and sugar over breasts, thighs, and drumsticks. Place turkey in a shallow dish; refrigerate, uncovered, 8 hours or overnight.

2. Let turkey stand at room temperature 1 hour.

3. Preheat oven to 425°F.

4. Chop half of herb blend; combine with butter, and set aside. Chop parsley to equal ¼ cup; reserve.

5. Lift wing tips up and over back; tuck under turkey. Place remaining half of herb blend, remaining parsley, lemons, and garlic in body cavity. Tie legs together with kitchen twine. Place turkey on the rack of a roasting pan coated with cooking spray. Place neck in bottom of pan. Bake at 425°F for 15 minutes.

6. Reduce oven temperature to 350°F (do not remove turkey from oven). Brush reserved butter mixture over turkey. Add 1 cup wine to pan. Bake at 350°F for 1 hour, basting with juices from pan every 20 minutes. Add remaining ½ cup wine to pan. Cover turkey loosely with foil; bake at 350°F for 35 minutes or until a thermometer inserted into the thickest part of the thigh registers 160°F.

7. Remove from oven; place turkey on a cutting board (reserve neck). Let stand, loosely covered with foil, 20 minutes (internal temperature will rise to 165°F). Uncover; sprinkle with 2 tablespoons reserved chopped parsley and 2 tablespoons chives. Remove skin before serving, if desired.

8. Remove all but ¼ cup pan drippings from roasting pan. Heat roasting pan over medium. Add ½ cup stock to ¼ cup drippings in pan; bring to a boil, scraping to loosen browned bits. Pour stock mixture into a medium saucepan. Add reserved neck and 3 cups stock; bring to a boil. Combine remaining ½ cup stock and flour in a bowl. Stir flour mixture into stock mixture; cook 10 minutes or until reduced to about 3 cups, stirring frequently. Stir in remaining 1 teaspoon salt, remaining 2 tablespoons parsley, remaining 2 tablespoons chives, and pepper. Serve gravy with turkey. Serves 16 (serving size: about 6 ounces turkey and 3 tablespoons gravy)

CALORIES 207; FAT 8g (sat 4g, unsat 3g); PROTEIN 27g; CARB 5g; FIBER 1g; SUGARS 1g (added sugars 0g); SODIUM 453mg; CALC 5% DV; POTASSIUM 8% DV

Make Ahead • Vegetarian

Herbed Whole-Grain Yeast Rolls
(pictured on page 238)

Hands-on: 25 min. Total: 3 hr.
Golden whole-grain yeast rolls get a fresh, fragrant hit from a host of seasonal herbs. Make ahead and freeze for up to a month, saving the butter-herb finish for after reheating.

1 package dry yeast (about 2¼ teaspoons)
1½ cups warm whole milk (110°F)
6 tablespoons unsalted butter, melted and divided
1 tablespoon sugar
18 ounces white whole-wheat flour (about 4½ cups)
3 tablespoons chopped fresh flat-leaf parsley, divided
3 tablespoons thinly sliced fresh chives, divided
1 tablespoon kosher salt, divided
1 tablespoon chopped fresh thyme
2 teaspoons chopped fresh sage
1 teaspoon chopped fresh rosemary
Cooking spray

1. Dissolve yeast in warm milk in the bowl of a stand mixer fitted with the paddle attachment; let stand 5 minutes. Add ¼ cup butter and sugar; beat at low speed 1 minute or until combined. Weigh or lightly spoon flour into dry measuring cups, level with a knife. Combine flour, 2 tablespoons parsley, 2 tablespoons chives, 2 teaspoons salt, thyme, sage, and rosemary in a bowl. Add half of flour mixture to milk mixture; beat at low speed until combined, scraping down sides of bowl as needed. Remove paddle attachment; insert dough hook. Add remaining half of flour mixture; beat at low speed 2 minutes or until dough forms a ball. Increase speed to medium-low; beat 7 minutes or until dough is smooth and elastic.

2. Place dough in a large bowl coated with cooking spray, turning to coat. Cover and let rise in a warm place (85°F), free from drafts, 1½ hours or until doubled in size.

3. Turn dough out onto a lightly floured surface; divide into 24 equal portions. Working with 1 portion at a time (cover remaining pieces to avoid drying), gently roll into a smooth ball. Place rolls about 1 inch apart on a rimmed baking sheet coated with cooking spray. Cover and let rise 45 minutes or until doubled in size.

4. Preheat oven to 350°F.

5. Bake rolls at 350°F for 20 to 25 minutes or until browned. Combine remaining 2 tablespoons melted butter with remaining 1 tablespoon parsley and remaining 1 tablespoon chives. Brush butter mixture over hot rolls; sprinkle with remaining 1 teaspoon salt. Cool at room temperature. Serves 24 (serving size: 1 roll)

CALORIES 109; FAT 4g (sat 2g, unsat 1g); PROTEIN 4g; CARB 14g; FIBER 2g; SUGARS 1g (added sugars 1g); SODIUM 247mg; CALC 3% DV; POTASSIUM 19% DV

POTATOES

Everyday spuds become superstars on Thanksgiving, which is why you'll likely need more than one style to please everyone. Go for classic comfort with a bubbly gratin or a streusel-topped sweet potato casserole. Or spruce up a standard with a mash laced with leek and shallot or roasted sweet potatoes doused in smoky-sweet paprika butter.

Gluten Free • Make Ahead
Vegetarian

Roasted Sweet Potatoes with Smoked Paprika-Honey Butter

Hands-on: 5 min. Total: 1 hr. 5 min.

4 (8-ounce) sweet potatoes
1 teaspoon canola oil
3 tablespoons butter
2 tablespoons honey
1 tablespoon smoked paprika
2 tablespoons chopped fresh cilantro
3/4 teaspoon kosher salt

1. Preheat oven to 400°F.
2. Pierce sweet potatoes with a fork; rub with oil. Place potatoes on a jelly-roll pan; bake at 400°F for 1 hour or until tender. Slice potatoes in half.
3. Combine butter, honey, and smoked paprika in a microwave-safe bowl; microwave at HIGH 1 minute, stirring once after 30 seconds. Drizzle butter mixture evenly over potato halves. Sprinkle potato halves with cilantro and salt. Serves 8 (serving size: ½ potato)

CALORIES 159; FAT 5g (sat 3g, unsat 2g); PROTEIN 2g; CARB 28g; FIBER 4g; SUGARS 9g (added sugars 4g); SODIUM 278mg; CALC 4% DV; POTASSIUM 12% DV

Make Ahead • Vegetarian

Sweet Potato Casserole with Pumpkin Seed-Oat Crumble

Hands-on: 10 min. Total: 1 hr. 15 min.

3 pounds sweet potatoes, peeled and cut into 2-inch pieces
5 tablespoons light brown sugar, divided
2 teaspoons grated orange rind
¼ cup fresh orange juice
1 teaspoon ground turmeric, divided
1 teaspoon vanilla extract
½ teaspoon kosher salt
2 large egg whites, lightly beaten
1 (5-ounce) can evaporated milk
Cooking spray
2.1 ounces all-purpose flour (½ cup)
½ cup old-fashioned rolled oats
¼ cup unsalted pumpkin seeds
¼ cup butter, melted
¼ teaspoon ground ginger

1. Preheat oven to 350°F.
2. Bring potatoes to a boil in a large Dutch oven filled with water. Reduce heat; simmer 20 minutes. Drain; return to pan. Add 1 tablespoon brown sugar, rind, juice, ½ teaspoon turmeric, vanilla, salt, egg whites, and milk; mash. Spoon into a 2-quart baking dish coated with cooking spray.
3. Combine flour, remaining ¼ cup brown sugar, oats, pumpkin seeds, and butter in a bowl. Stir in remaining ½ teaspoon turmeric and ginger. Sprinkle oat mixture over potato mixture. Bake at 350°F for 40 minutes. Serves 12 (serving size: about ⅔ cup)

CALORIES 221; FAT 6g (sat 3g, unsat 2g); PROTEIN 5g; CARB 37g; FIBER 4g; SUGARS 12g (added sugars 6g); SODIUM 195mg; CALC 8% DV; POTASSIUM 14% DV

Staff Favorite • Vegetarian

Potato and Parsnip Gratin

Hands-on: 10 min. Total: 1 hr.
Parsnips add an elegant twist to this classic. Parboiling the slices saves baking time and keeps them from absorbing too much sauce.

1 pound russet potatoes, peeled and thinly sliced
1 pound parsnips, peeled and thinly sliced
3 tablespoons canola oil
1.1 ounces all-purpose flour (about ¼ cup)
1 cup half-and-half
1½ teaspoons kosher salt, divided
½ teaspoon black pepper
3 ounces Gruyère cheese, grated (about ¾ cup)
2 tablespoons chopped fresh flat-leaf parsley
Cooking spray
1 ounce Parmigiano-Reggiano cheese, grated (about ¼ cup)

1. Preheat oven to 350°F.
2. Bring potato and parsnip slices to a boil in a large Dutch oven filled with water. Reduce heat, and simmer 6 minutes (slices should be slightly undercooked at the center). Reserve ½ cup cooking liquid; drain. Arrange potato and parsnip slices in a single layer on a baking sheet; cool.
3. Heat oil in a medium saucepan over medium-high; stir in flour. Stir in reserved ½ cup cooking liquid, half-and-half, ½ teaspoon salt, and pepper; bring to a boil. Cook 2 minutes or until slightly thickened. Stir in Gruyère cheese; cook 1 minute. Remove pan from heat. Add potato and parsnip slices, remaining 1 teaspoon salt, and parsley; toss gently to combine. Spoon potato mixture into a 2-quart baking dish coated with cooking spray; sprinkle with Parmigiano-Reggiano cheese. Bake at 350°F for 45 minutes or until

golden brown. Serves 12 (serving size: ½ cup)

CALORIES 157; **FAT** 8g (sat 3g, unsat 4g); **PROTEIN** 4g; **CARB** 17g; **FIBER** 2g; **SUGARS** 2g (added sugars 0g); **SODIUM** 307mg; **CALC** 12% DV; **POTASSIUM** 9% DV

Fast • Gluten Free

Triple-Onion Mashed Potatoes

Hands-on: 15 min. Total: 30 min.

1½ pounds Yukon Gold potatoes, peeled and cubed
½ cup unsalted chicken stock
¼ cup half-and-half
1½ ounces cream cheese, softened and cut into pieces
¾ teaspoon kosher salt
¼ teaspoon black pepper
1½ tablespoons unsalted butter
1 cup chopped leeks
1½ tablespoons canola oil
½ cup sliced shallots
1 tablespoon chopped fresh chives

1. Bring potatoes to a boil in a large Dutch oven filled with water. Reduce heat to medium; simmer 20 minutes or until tender. Drain; return potatoes to pan. Add chicken stock, half-and-half, cream cheese, salt, and pepper; mash to desired consistency.
2. Melt butter in a skillet over medium-high. Add leeks; sauté 5 minutes. Stir leek mixture into potato mixture (do not wipe out skillet).
3. Return skillet to medium-high. Add oil and shallots; cook 3 minutes or until shallots are browned and crisp. Spoon mashed potatoes into a serving dish; top with crispy shallots and chives. Serves 8 (serving size: ½ cup)

CALORIES 146; **FAT** 8g (sat 3g, unsat 4g); **PROTEIN** 3g; **CARB** 18g; **FIBER** 2g; **SUGARS** 3g (added sugars 0g); **SODIUM** 227mg; **CALC** 3% DV; **POTASSIUM** 13% DV

THANKSGIVING MENU TWO

Balsamic Cranberry-Onion Jam (page 316)

Herb, Lemon, and Garlic Turkey (page 308)

Ginger-Chile Roasted Acorn Squash (page 307)

Herb-Roasted Carrots (page 308)

Triple-Onion Mashed Potatoes (page 311)

BRUSSELS SPROUTS AND CAULIFLOWER

Brussels sprouts, the crown jewels of the cabbage world, are a sure sign that fall is here. They're a Thanksgiving favorite, whether sautéed until browned and tender or shredded and served raw. Cauliflower is also at its seasonal peak. Turn it into an impressive side for the table by dredging in Parmesan-flecked breadcrumbs and baking until crisp.

Fast • Vegetarian

Crispy Cauliflower with Italian Salsa Verde

Hands-on: 20 min. Total: 30 min.
How about something completely different? Crispy cauliflower florets and a zingy parsley sauce add texture and vibrancy to the table. These would also be delicious as an appetizer.

6 cups cauliflower florets
Cooking spray
¼ cup fine whole-wheat breadcrumbs
1 tablespoon grated lemon rind
3 ounces Parmesan cheese, grated and divided (about ¾ cup)
¼ cup finely chopped shallots
¼ cup extra-virgin olive oil
3 tablespoons chopped fresh flat-leaf parsley
1½ tablespoons fresh lemon juice
1 tablespoon chopped fresh oregano
¼ teaspoon crushed red pepper

1. Preheat oven to 400°F.
2. Place cauliflower in a bowl; coat cauliflower with cooking spray. Add breadcrumbs, rind, and ½ cup cheese; toss well to coat. Arrange mixture on a foil-lined baking sheet; bake at 400°F for 20 minutes or until cauliflower is golden and tender.
3. Combine shallots and remaining ingredients in a bowl. Arrange cauliflower on a platter; spoon parsley mixture evenly over top. Sprinkle with remaining ¼ cup cheese. Serves 8 (serving size: ⅔ cup cauliflower and about 1 tablespoon sauce)

CALORIES 148; **FAT** 10g (sat 3g, unsat 7g); **PROTEIN** 5g; **CARB** 10g; **FIBER** 2g; **SUGARS** 2g (added sugars 0g); **SODIUM** 217mg; **CALC** 12% DV; **POTASSIUM** 8% DV

Maple-Caraway Brussels Sprouts

(pictured on page 238)

Hands-on: 20 min. Total: 25 min.
Caraway seeds toast and infuse the butter as it browns, giving the Brussels sprouts a beautifully bronzing and nutty depth.

1½ tablespoons unsalted butter, divided
1½ teaspoons olive oil
1 tablespoon chopped fresh thyme
2 teaspoons caraway seeds
1 pound Brussels sprouts, trimmed and halved
2 cups thinly vertically sliced onion (about 1 large onion)
6 garlic cloves, thinly sliced
¼ cup pure maple syrup
3 tablespoons sherry vinegar
1 teaspoon Dijon mustard
½ teaspoon kosher salt
½ teaspoon black pepper

1. Heat 1½ teaspoons butter, oil, thyme, and caraway in a large non-stick skillet over medium-low, swirling until butter melts. Cook 2 to 3 minutes or until butter starts to foam.
2. Increase heat to medium-high. Add Brussels sprouts to pan; cook 6 to 7 minutes or until browned and crisp-tender. Remove from pan. Add onion and garlic to pan; sauté 6 minutes. Return Brussels sprouts to pan. Stir in syrup, vinegar, mustard, and salt; cook 2 minutes. Remove pan from heat; stir in remaining 1 tablespoon butter and pepper. Serves 6 (serving size: ½ cup)

CALORIES 129; **FAT** 4g (sat 2g, unsat 2g); **PROTEIN** 3g; **CARB** 21g; **FIBER** 4g; **SUGARS** 11g (added sugars 8g); **SODIUM** 203mg; **CALC** 7% DV; **POTASSIUM** 12% DV

Bacon and Brussels Sprout Slaw

Hands-on: 10 min. Total: 20 min.
Crunchy, creamy, tangy slaws aren't just for summer; they add a welcome contrast to the heartier dishes of fall—and free up much-needed oven space on Turkey Day.

1 cup thinly diagonally sliced carrots
⅓ cup thinly sliced green onions
¼ cup canola mayonnaise
3 tablespoons apple cider vinegar
1 teaspoon sugar
½ teaspoon black pepper
2 bacon slices, cooked and crumbled
12 ounces Brussels sprouts, shredded (about 5 cups)
2 tablespoons toasted sliced almonds

1. Combine first 8 ingredients in a large bowl, stirring to coat. Let stand at room temperature 10 minutes. Sprinkle with almonds. Serves 6 (serving size: about 1 cup)

CALORIES 90; **FAT** 5g (sat 0g, unsat 4g); **PROTEIN** 4g; **CARB** 9g; **FIBER** 3g; **SUGARS** 3g (added sugars 1g); **SODIUM** 146mg; **CALC** 4% DV; **POTASSIUM** 9% DV

ROOTS

Beneath their skins, these humble roots hide deep, earthy-sweet flavors that enrich everything else on the table. Celery root becomes a velvety puree once peeled and slowly simmered. Turnips turn tender and sweet when roasted. Others boast wild hues: Multicolored beets and carrots go full peacock once combined in a stunning salad.

Cranberry-Beet Chutney

Hands-on: 40 min. Total: 1 hr. 30 min.

4 (4-ounce) red beets, trimmed and halved
1 tablespoon whole coriander seeds
2 teaspoons whole brown mustard seeds
1 tablespoon olive oil
1 cup chopped red onion
¼ cup dried cranberries
¼ cup golden raisins
¼ cup pomegranate juice
¼ cup sherry vinegar
2 tablespoons sugar
¼ teaspoon kosher salt

1. Fill a large saucepan with water to a depth of 1 inch. Place a steamer basket in saucepan; place beets in basket. Cover, bring to a boil, and steam 12 to 15 minutes or until tender. Drain. Once cool, peel and cut into cubes.
2. Heat a small skillet over medium-high. Add coriander and mustard seeds; cook 5 minutes or until toasted. Crush toasted seeds with a small heavy skillet until coarsely ground.
3. Heat olive oil in a large skillet over medium-high. Add beets, crushed seeds, and onion; cook 6 minutes. Reduce heat to medium-low. Add cranberries and next 4 ingredients (through sugar) to pan; cook 20 minutes or until thickened. Stir in salt; cool. Refrigerate in an airtight container up to 1 week. Serves 16 (serving size: about 3½ tablespoons)

CALORIES 51; **FAT** 1g (sat 0g, unsat 1g); **PROTEIN** 1g; **CARB** 10g; **FIBER** 1g; **SUGARS** 8g (added sugars 3g); **SODIUM** 54mg; **CALC** 1% DV; **POTASSIUM** 4% DV

Gluten Free • Make Ahead
Vegetarian

Celery Root Puree with Almond-Mint Gremolata

Hands-on: 30 min. Total: 40 min.
If you have celery stalks on hand, save the fresh leaves for a pretty garnish that hints at the main ingredient.

1½ cups chopped yellow onion
2½ pounds celery root, peeled and cut into ½-inch pieces (about 4 medium or 8 cups)
1 (15-ounce) can unsalted cannellini beans, rinsed and drained
¼ cup 2% reduced-fat milk, divided
6 tablespoons reduced-fat sour cream
3 tablespoons butter
1¼ teaspoons kosher salt
1½ tablespoons fresh lemon juice, divided
2 ounces Parmigiano-Reggiano cheese, grated (about ½ cup)
1 teaspoon grated lemon rind
¼ cup toasted sliced almonds, coarsely chopped
2 tablespoons chopped fresh mint
½ cup fresh celery leaves, coarsely chopped (optional)

1. Bring onion and celery root to a boil in a large Dutch oven filled with water. Reduce heat, and simmer 15 minutes or until tender. Add beans; cook 2 minutes. Drain. Place half of celery root mixture and 2 table-spoons milk in a blender; blend until smooth. Return puree to pan. Repeat procedure with remaining half of celery root mixture and remaining 2 tablespoons milk. Stir in sour cream, butter, salt, 1½ teaspoons juice, and cheese.

2. Combine rind, remaining 1 tablespoon juice, almonds, and mint in a bowl. Spoon puree into a serving dish; sprinkle with almond mixture and celery leaves, if desired. Serves 12 (serving size: about ¾ cup)

CALORIES 131; **FAT** 6g (sat 3g, unsat 2g);
PROTEIN 5g; **CARB** 17g; **FIBER** 4g; **SUGARS** 4g
(added sugars 0g); **SODIUM** 343mg; **CALC** 10% DV;
POTASSIUM 13% DV

THANKSGIVING MENU THREE

Cranberry-Beet Chutney
(page 312)

Cider-Glazed Turkey with Roasted Apples
(page 314)

Herb- Roasted Carrots
(page 308)

Pear, Sage, and Golden Raisin Stuffing (page 315)

Maple-Caraway Brussels Sprouts (page 312)

Celery Root Puree with Almond-Mint Gremolata
(page 313)

Staff Favorite • Fast
Gluten Free • Make Ahead
Vegetarian

Tricolor Beet-and-Carrot Salad

(pictured on page 239)

Hands-on: 30 min. Total: 1 hr. 30 min.

4 (4-ounce) red beets, trimmed
4 (4-ounce) golden beets, trimmed
4 (4-ounce) Chioggia beets, trimmed
3 medium-sized orange carrots, peeled
3 medium-sized purple carrots, peeled
3 medium-sized yellow carrots, peeled
1 cup packed baby arugula leaves
½ cup thinly sliced shallots
6 tablespoons extra-virgin olive oil
¼ cup red wine vinegar
1 tablespoon honey
¾ teaspoon kosher salt
½ teaspoon black pepper
2 ounces goat cheese, crumbled (about ½ cup)
¼ cup unsalted roasted pistachios, chopped

1. Preheat oven to 400°F.
2. Wrap red beets, golden beets, and Chioggia beets separately in foil. Bake at 400°F for 1 hour or until tender. Peel and cut into ½-inch wedges.
3. Shave carrots into wide ribbons using a vegetable peeler. Combine carrot ribbons, arugula, and shallots in a bowl; arrange on a platter. Top carrot mixture with beets. Combine oil, vinegar, honey, salt, and pepper in a bowl; drizzle over salad. Sprinkle with goat cheese and pistachios. Serves 12 (serving size: about 1 cup)

CALORIES 155; **FAT** 9g (sat 2g, unsat 7g);
PROTEIN 3g; **CARB** 16g; **FIBER** 4g; **SUGARS** 10g
(added sugars 1g); **SODIUM** 242mg; **CALC** 5% DV;
POTASSIUM 14% DV

Roasted Turnips with Sage Browned Butter

Hands-on: 15 min. Total: 1 hr. 10 min.
Sage and browned butter is a classic pairing that enhances roasted turnips (which look like white, oversized radishes). Toss with the butter mixture as soon as the turnips are done.

3 pounds turnips, peeled and cut into
**   ¹/₂-inch wedges**
Cooking spray
1¹/₂ teaspoons kosher salt
¹/₂ teaspoon black pepper
¹/₄ cup unsalted butter
12 small fresh sage leaves, divided
2 teaspoons grated lemon rind,
**   divided**
1 tablespoon fresh lemon juice

1. Preheat oven to 400°F.
2. Place turnips on a baking sheet coated with cooking spray; sprinkle with salt and pepper. Bake at 400°F for 50 minutes or until tender and lightly browned, stirring once after 30 minutes.
3. Combine butter and 6 sage leaves in a small saucepan over medium; cook 3 minutes or until butter is lightly browned and fragrant. Remove pan from heat; stir in 1 teaspoon rind and juice. Combine turnips and butter mixture in a bowl; toss to coat. Arrange turnip mixture on a platter; sprinkle with remaining 6 sage leaves and remaining 1 teaspoon rind. Serves 12 (serving size: ½ cup)

CALORIES 67; **FAT** 4g (sat 2g, unsat 1g); **PROTEIN** 1g; **CARB** 8g; **FIBER** 2g; **SUGARS** 4g (added sugars 0g); **SODIUM** 317mg; **CALC** 4% DV; **POTASSIUM** 6% DV

APPLES, PEARS, AND CRANBERRIES

Tart, jammy sauces and mile-high pies are reason enough to love cranberries, apples, and pears. These fruits also have a savory side worth exploring, from cider-infused turkey to a tangy cranberry and onion jam (amazing on post-Thanksgiving Day sandwiches). Use extra fresh fruits to decorate the table.

Gluten Free

Cider-Glazed Turkey with Roasted Apples

Hands-on: 30 min. Total: 16 hr. 30 min.
An overnight brine infuses and plumps up the meat so it stays moist. Line a roasting pan with the brining bag before adding the liquid and the turkey so everything stays in place.

BRINE
6 cups apple cider, divided
³/₄ cup sugar
¹/₂ cup kosher salt
2 tablespoons black peppercorns
8 garlic cloves, smashed
4 fresh bay leaves
2 small yellow onions, quartered
6 cups water

TURKEY
1 (12-pound) whole fresh or frozen
**   turkey, thawed**
6 tablespoons unsalted butter,
**   softened and divided**
1 tablespoon chopped fresh thyme
1 teaspoon black pepper
¹/₂ teaspoon kosher salt
4 small yellow onions, quartered
**   and divided**
4 small apples, quartered and
**   divided**
4 small carrots, halved and divided

4 fresh thyme sprigs, divided
Cooking spray
2 cups cider
¹/₄ cup apple jelly

1. To prepare brine, bring 2 cups cider, sugar, ½ cup salt, and peppercorns to a simmer in a large saucepan over medium-high. Cook 5 minutes or until salt and sugar dissolve. Remove pan from heat. Stir in remaining 4 cups cider, garlic, bay leaves, and 2 onions. Cool completely. Combine brine with 6 cups water in a brining bag.
2. To prepare the turkey, remove giblets and neck; discard. Add turkey to brine. Add water to bag, ½ cup at a time, as needed to cover turkey. Refrigerate 12 to 24 hours.
3. Preheat oven to 350°F.
4. Remove turkey from brine; discard brine. Pat turkey dry. Combine ¼ cup butter, chopped thyme, pepper, and ½ teaspoon salt in a small bowl. Starting at neck cavity, loosen skin from breast and drumsticks by inserting fingers and gently pushing between skin and meat. Rub butter mixture under loosened skin. Lift wing tips up and over back; tuck under turkey. Place 1 onion, 1 apple, 1 carrot, and 2 thyme sprigs in body cavity. Tie legs with kitchen twine.
5. Place turkey on the rack of a roasting pan coated with cooking spray. Place remaining onions, apples, carrots, and thyme sprigs in bottom of pan; place rack with turkey in pan. Add 2 cups cider to pan. Bake at 350°F for 1½ hours.
6. Combine remaining 2 tablespoons butter and jelly in a small saucepan over medium-high; cook 2 minutes. Brush half of jelly mixture over turkey. Bake at 350°F for 30 minutes. Brush turkey with remaining half of jelly mixture; bake at 350°F for 30 minutes or until a thermometer inserted into the thickest part of the thigh registers 160°F.
7. Place turkey on a cutting board. Let stand, loosely covered with foil, 20 minutes (internal temperature will

rise to 165°F). Remove skin before serving. Reserve pan drippings for gravy, if using. Serve with roasted apples and vegetables from pan. Serves 12 (serving size: 6 ounces turkey and ¼ cup vegetable mixture)

CALORIES 252; **FAT** 8g (sat 4g, unsat 3g); **PROTEIN** 26g; **CARB** 18g; **FIBER** 2g; **SUGARS** 14g (added sugars 4g); **SODIUM** 539mg; **CALC** 4% DV; **POTASSIUM** 11% DV

Staff Favorite • Make Ahead Vegetarian

Salted Caramel Apple Pie

(pictured on page 240)

Hands-on: 40 min. Total: 2 hr. 40 min.
Grated apple is the secret to a syrupy pie filling—it releases more pectin (a natural thickener) than the sliced apples alone.

CRUST
6.4 ounces all-purpose flour (about 1½ cups)
3.5 ounces whole-wheat pastry flour (about 1 cup)
1 tablespoon sugar
¼ teaspoon kosher salt
6 tablespoons chilled unsalted butter, cut into ½-inch pieces (3 ounces)
¼ cup canola oil
¼ cup ice water

FILLING
½ cup packed dark brown sugar
2 tablespoons unsalted butter
2 tablespoons water, divided
⅜ teaspoon kosher salt
2 tablespoons whole milk
1 teaspoon vanilla extract
Cooking spray
3 pounds Fuji apples, peeled, cored, and quartered (about 5 medium)
1.1 ounces all-purpose flour (about ¼ cup), divided
1 large egg white, lightly beaten

1. To prepare crust, weigh or lightly spoon flours into dry measuring cups; level with a knife. Place 1½ cups all-purpose flour, pastry flour, 1 tablespoon sugar, and ¼ teaspoon salt in a food processor; pulse 3 to 4 times to combine. Add 6 tablespoons butter and canola oil; pulse 8 to 10 times or until mixture resembles coarse meal. Add ¼ cup ice water; pulse until dough begins to form a ball. Turn dough out onto a work surface; divide and shape into 2 (8-inch) disks. Wrap in plastic wrap, and refrigerate 1 hour or overnight.
2. To prepare filling, combine brown sugar, 2 tablespoons butter, 1 tablespoon water, and ⅜ teaspoon salt in a small saucepan over medium-high. Cook 7 minutes or until mixture begins to bubble and thicken, stirring frequently. Remove pan from heat; stir in milk and vanilla. Return pan to medium-high; bring to a boil. Cook 1 minute, stirring constantly. Remove pan from heat; cool slightly.
3. Preheat oven to 425°F.
4. Unwrap 1 dough disk and place between 2 large sheets of parchment paper. Roll to an 11-inch circle. Place into a 9-inch pie plate coated with cooking spray. Refrigerate until ready to use.
5. Grate enough apple quarters to equal 1 cup. Combine grated apple and 1 tablespoon all-purpose flour in a bowl. Cut remaining apple quarters into ½-inch-thick slices; combine with remaining 3 tablespoons flour. Add grated apple mixture to sliced apple mixture. Pour cooked brown sugar mixture over top; stir to coat. Spoon filling into prepared pie shell.
6. Unwrap remaining dough disk; roll to an 11-inch circle. Cut circle into 10 (½-inch) strips. Arrange in a lattice pattern over apple mixture, sealing dough strips to edge of crust. Combine remaining 1 tablespoon water and egg white in a bowl; brush lattice and dough edges. Bake at 425°F for 45 minutes. Cover loosely with foil, and bake at 425°F for 15 more minutes or until filling is bubbly and crust is golden brown. Cool

at least 20 minutes before serving. Serves 12 (serving size: 1 slice)

CALORIES 299; **FAT** 13g (sat 5g, unsat 7g); **PROTEIN** 3g; **CARB** 44g; **FIBER** 3g; **SUGARS** 22g (added sugars 10g); **SODIUM** 110mg; **CALC** 2% DV; **POTASSIUM** 4% DV

Pear, Sage, and Golden Raisin Stuffing

Hands-on: 45 min. Total: 1 hr. 5 min.

12 ounces whole-wheat sourdough bread, cut into ¾-inch cubes
¼ cup golden raisins
¼ cup hot water
2 thick-cut bacon slices (about 2½ ounces)
2 cups chopped yellow onion
1 cup chopped carrots
1 cup chopped celery
5 teaspoons chopped fresh sage, divided
1 tablespoon minced fresh garlic
2¼ cups unsalted chicken stock
3 tablespoons unsalted butter, melted
½ teaspoon black pepper
2 large eggs
1½ cups chopped ripe Bosc pear
Cooking spray

1. Preheat oven to 400°F.
2. Arrange bread cubes in a single layer on a rimmed baking sheet. Bake at 400°F for 20 minutes or until golden, stirring after 10 minutes. Place bread cubes in a large bowl.
3. Reduce oven temperature to 350°F.
4. Place raisins in a small bowl; cover with ¼ cup hot water. Let stand 10 minutes; drain.
5. Cook bacon slices in a skillet over medium 10 minutes or until crisp. Remove to a paper towel–lined plate with a slotted spoon; crumble. Add onion, carrot, and celery to bacon

continued

drippings in pan; sauté 6 minutes. Add 1 tablespoon sage and garlic; cook 1 minute. Remove from heat. **6.** Combine stock, butter, pepper, and eggs in a large bowl. Add stock mixture, drained raisins, bacon, pear, and vegetable mixture to bread; toss to combine. Spoon into a 2-quart baking dish coated with cooking spray. Bake at 350°F for 25 minutes. Top with remaining 2 teaspoons sage. Serves 10 (serving size: ⅔ cup)

CALORIES 217; **FAT** 8g (sat 3g, unsat 3g); **PROTEIN** 9g; **CARB** 27g; **FIBER** 4g; **SUGARS** 9g (added sugars 1g); **SODIUM** 331mg; **CALC** 5% DV; **POTASSIUM** 5% DV

Gluten Free • Make Ahead Vegetarian

Balsamic Cranberry-Onion Jam

Hands-on: 15 min. Total: 1 hr. 15 min.

⅓ **cup extra-virgin olive oil**
4 cups chopped sweet onions
1 teaspoon kosher salt
¼ **cup honey**
¼ **teaspoon black pepper**
2 fresh thyme sprigs
1 (12-ounce) package fresh or frozen cranberries, thawed
1 tablespoon balsamic vinegar

1. Heat oil in a large heavy saucepan over medium. Add onions and salt; cover and cook 30 minutes or until caramelized. Add honey, pepper, thyme, and cranberries; cook, uncovered, 30 minutes or until cranberries break down and mixture is syrupy. **2.** Remove pan from heat; discard thyme sprigs. Stir in vinegar. Serves 16 (serving size: about 2 tablespoons)

CALORIES 78; **FAT** 5g (sat 1g, unsat 4g); **PROTEIN** 0g; **CARB** 10g; **FIBER** 1g; **SUGARS** 7g (added sugars 4g); **SODIUM** 124mg; **CALC** 1% DV; **POTASSIUM** 2% DV

30 WAYS TO BE A HEALTHIER COOK

After three decades of creating delicious, nutritious recipes, we've mastered the art of healthy cooking. Use these insights to boost your own skills in the kitchen.

Since *Cooking Light* launched in 1987, nutrition science and our food culture have certainly evolved—and so have we. Not that we're fickle, mind you. We've never been about chasing after fleeting trends; instead, our goal—always—has been to distill the rather nuanced and complicated world of nutrition science into recipes, advice, tips, and techniques that make sense for home cooks. After all, the journey to healthy starts in the kitchen. We've taken a look back over our history to share our most game-changing healthy cooking lessons. Use them to become a smarter, more intuitive cook.

1. COOK MORE OFTEN. ▼
It's the healthiest thing you can do for yourself and your family. You will automatically make better choices that have you eating less saturated fat, sodium, added sugar, and processed foods.

Fast • Gluten Free

Mussels with Buttery Turmeric Broth

(pictured on page 237)

Hands-on: 20 min. Total: 20 min.
Mussels are surprisingly affordable and easy to cook.

2½ **tablespoons unsalted butter**
1½ **tablespoons olive oil**
⅔ **cup thinly sliced shallot**
6 garlic cloves, thinly sliced
2 teaspoons grated peeled fresh turmeric or ½ **teaspoon dried ground turmeric**

¾ **cup dry white wine**
½ **teaspoon black pepper**
⅛ **teaspoon kosher salt**
2 pounds mussels, scrubbed and debearded
⅓ **cup coarsely chopped fresh flat-leaf parsley**

1. Heat butter and oil in a large Dutch oven over medium-high. Add shallot and garlic; cook, stirring often, until starting to soften, about 3 minutes. Add turmeric; cook, stirring constantly, 30 seconds. Stir in wine, pepper, and salt. Bring to a boil; cook 1 minute. Add mussels; cover, and cook until shells open, about 3 minutes, shaking Dutch oven once or twice during cooking time. Remove and discard any unopened mussels. Divide mussels and broth evenly among 4 bowls; sprinkle with parsley. Serves 4 (serving size: about 12 mussels and ¼ cup broth)

CALORIES 338; **FAT** 17g (sat 6g, unsat 9g); **PROTEIN** 24g; **CARB** 14g; **FIBER** 1g; **SUGARS** 2g (added sugars 0g); **SODIUM** 617mg; **CALC** 8% DV; **POTASSIUM** 22% DV

2. TOAST FOR FLAVOR.
Nuts taste nuttier when toasted, and butter takes on a caramel richness when you brown it—making a small amount taste bigger. Toasting also enhances the flavor of everything from tomato paste to spices.

3. USE FAT WHERE IT WILL HAVE THE BIGGEST IMPACT. ▼
If you're cutting back on saturated fat, use it where it counts. If you're making a potpie or these dessert bars, for example, put the butter in the crust; the filling can do without.

4. BE GENTLE WITH LOWER-FAT DOUGH.
It can toughen easily if overworked, so use a gentle hand: Pat out biscuit dough, lightly tamp crumb crusts into place, and softly glide a rolling pin over cookie dough.

5. USE SALT WISELY. ▶
Think about where the salt goes. Flaked salt, for example, will hit the palate first when sprinkled onto a plated salad—so you use less and still have a big impact. Cut back on the salt in a marinade or breading (half of which will get tossed), and reserve some to add at the end.

Staff Favorite • Make Ahead
Vegetarian

Grapefruit-Campari Bars with Shortbread Crust

Hands-on: 40 min. Total: 5 hr.

This grown-up treat embraces the bitterness in both grapefruit and Campari, balancing the flavor with a rich, buttery crust.

CRUST
4 ounces whole-wheat pastry flour (about 1 cup)
¼ cup powdered sugar
2 tablespoons cornstarch
½ teaspoon kosher salt
6 tablespoons cold unsalted butter, cut into small pieces
2 tablespoons canola oil
Cooking spray

TOPPING
¾ cup granulated sugar
¾ cup fresh red grapefruit juice
3 tablespoons cornstarch
¼ teaspoon kosher salt
2 large egg yolks, lightly beaten
1½ tablespoons Campari

1. To prepare the crust, preheat oven to 350°F. Weigh or spoon flour into a dry measuring cup; level with a knife. Pulse flour, powdered sugar, 2 tablespoons cornstarch, and ½ teaspoon salt in a food processor until combined. Top with butter pieces; pulse until mixture resembles coarse meal, 4 to 5 times. Drizzle evenly with oil; pulse just until moistened, about 2 times. (Mixture will be crumbly.) Transfer mixture to an 8-inch square glass baking dish coated with cooking spray. Pat into an even layer, being careful not to compact it. (Pressing too firmly will create a dense, tough crust.) Bake at 350°F until lightly browned all over, 25 to 30 minutes. Cool to room temperature.
2. To prepare the topping, combine granulated sugar, grapefruit juice, 3 tablespoons cornstarch, and ¼ teaspoon salt in a heavy saucepan. Bring to a boil over medium, stirring constantly. Cook, stirring often, until thickened, about 2 minutes.
3. Place egg yolks in a medium bowl. Gradually whisk in half of grapefruit mixture. Add egg mixture to remaining grapefruit mixture in pan. Bring to a boil over medium, whisking constantly. Remove from heat; whisk in Campari. Pour through a fine-mesh strainer into a bowl; discard solids.
4. Spread grapefruit mixture onto crust. Cover and chill until set, 3 to 4 hours. Cut into 16 squares. Serves 16 (serving size: 1 bar)

CALORIES 148; **FAT** 7g (sat 3g, unsat 3g); **PROTEIN** 1g; **CARB** 21g; **FIBER** 1g; **SUGARS** 12g (added sugars 11g); **SODIUM** 92mg; **CALC** 1% DV; **POTASSIUM** 1% DV

Gluten Free

Garlicky New York Strip Steak

Hands-on: 15 min. Total: 1 hr.
To make your next steak night a success, watch over the temperature of the meat with a thermometer. This works best on steaks of 1-inch (or more) thickness; it's hard to get a good reading on anything thinner.

4 large garlic cloves, grated
2 (8-ounce) New York strip steaks (1-inch thick), trimmed
2 tablespoons fresh lemon juice
3 tablespoons olive oil, divided
½ teaspoon black pepper
¼ teaspoon kosher salt
1 tablespoon fresh rosemary leaves
¾ teaspoon flaked sea salt

1. Rub garlic over steaks. Place juice and 2 tablespoons oil in a shallow dish. Add steaks; turn to coat. Let stand at room temperature 30 minutes.
2. Remove steaks from marinade; discard marinade. Pat steaks dry with paper towels, leaving any bits of garlic that stick. Sprinkle tops of steaks with pepper and kosher salt.
3. Heat remaining 1 tablespoon oil in a large cast-iron skillet over high. Add steaks; cook until a meat thermometer inserted in thickest portion registers 127°F to 130°F for medium-rare or to desired degree of doneness, 2 to 2½ minutes per side.
4. Place steaks on a cutting board; reserve pan drippings. Tent steaks loosely with foil. Let stand 5 minutes. Discard foil. Cut steaks across the grain into slices. Arrange slices on a platter; drizzle with pan drippings. Sprinkle with rosemary and sea salt. Serves 4 (serving size: 3 ounces steak)

CALORIES 213; **FAT** 13g (sat 3g, unsat 8g); **PROTEIN** 22g; **CARB** 1g; **FIBER** 0g; **SUGARS** 0g; **SODIUM** 493mg; **CALC** 2% DV; **POTASSIUM** 8% DV

6. WEIGH MEAT, PASTA & CHEESE.
At least until you've done it enough times to accurately eyeball it. You might be surprised at how much you underestimate when winging it: What looks to you like a 6-ounce chicken breast might be 11 ounces—which means almost double the calories.

7. PAIR BOLD FLAVORS WITH WHOLE-GRAIN PASTAS.
Depending on the product, whole-grain pastas can taste mildly nutty or profoundly earthy. Match the robust taste with equally hearty ingredients. Think garlic, red pepper, anchovies, tangy tomato sauces, and strong cheeses.

8. COOK SEASONALLY. ▼
In-season produce—kale in fall, tomatoes in summer—tastes far superior to out-of-season produce and has likely traveled a much shorter distance to reach your market. There are nutrition bonuses, too, including more vitamins and antioxidants.

9. EAT MORE WHOLE FOODS. ▶
Opt for whole grains, use fresh and frozen produce, and buy fresh fish, meat, and poultry instead of preseasoned. You'll get more vitamins and antioxidants and less sodium. This applies to dessert as well as dinner—go whole-grain for sweet treats.

10. EAT MINDFULLY.
Mindless eating—scarfing down food with little thought to what it is—is not a healthy practice. But mindful eating—appreciating each bite with an awareness of what you're putting into your body—isn't just a healthier approach; it's a deeply joyful way of eating.

11. GET A STURDY DUTCH OVEN.
Like a cast-iron skillet, this durable pot has limitless uses: boiling pasta, braising pot roast, simmering soup, baking bread, and more. Go for an enamel-coated cast-iron one, like Le Creuset's 5½ Qt. Round Dutch Oven, $330, lecreuset.com; or Lodge's 4.6 Qt. Dutch Oven, $100, lodgemfg.com.

Fast

Pasta with Browned Butter, Anchovy, and Kale

Hands-on: 20 min. Total: 20 min.
Match the hearty taste of whole-grain noodles with anchovy, red pepper, and pecorino Romano cheese. Lest those flavors get too heavy, brighten with a squeeze of lemon juice.

8 ounces uncooked whole-grain fettuccine or linguine
2 tablespoons unsalted butter
2 tablespoons olive oil
6 garlic cloves, thinly sliced
5 anchovy fillets, finely chopped
1 tablespoon fresh thyme leaves
½ teaspoon crushed red pepper
6 cups lightly packed thinly sliced lacinato kale (6 ounces)
½ teaspoon kosher salt
1 ounce pecorino Romano cheese, grated (about ¼ cup)
4 lemon wedges

1. Cook pasta according to directions. Reserve 1 cup cooking liquid; drain.
2. While pasta cooks, melt butter in a large skillet over medium. Cook until butter is browned and very fragrant, 2 to 3 minutes. Add oil, garlic, anchovies, thyme, and pepper. Cook, stirring constantly, until anchovies dissolve and garlic begins to brown, about 1 minute. Add kale; cook, stirring often, just until wilted, 1 to 2 minutes. Add pasta, salt, and ⅔ cup reserved cooking liquid; toss to coat. If pasta seems dry, add additional cooking liquid, a splash at a time.
3. Divide pasta mixture among 4 shallow bowls. Top evenly with cheese, and serve with lemon wedges. Serves 4 (serving size: about 1¼ cups pasta mixture, 1 tablespoon cheese, and 1 lemon wedge)

CALORIES 382; **FAT** 17g (sat 6g, unsat 8g); **PROTEIN** 15g; **CARB** 51g; **FIBER** 8g; **SUGARS** 2g (added sugars 0g); **SODIUM** 570mg; **CALC** 26% DV; **POTASSIUM** 16% DV

Make Ahead • Vegetarian

Apple Spice Bundt Cake with Cider Glaze

(pictured on page 236)

Hands-on: 35 min. Total: 3 hr. 20 min.
Don't be afraid to go 100% whole-grain with desserts; we use all spelt flour here with amazing results. The nutty flour boosts the taste of the butter, spices, and vanilla, unlike all-purpose flour, whose bland nature would dilute those flavors. Be sure to weigh the flour for accuracy; using too much will make the cake dry.

½ cup canola oil
1 vanilla bean pod
¼ cup unsalted butter, softened
1 cup packed light brown sugar
2 large eggs
2 cups shredded peeled Honeycrisp or Gala apples (about 3 medium apples)
13.5 ounces spelt or whole-wheat flour (about 3 cups)
1 tablespoon baking powder
2 teaspoons ground cinnamon
¼ teaspoon ground nutmeg
¼ teaspoon ground cloves
1⅛ teaspoons kosher salt, divided
¾ cup evaporated whole milk
Baking spray with flour
1 cup powdered sugar (4 ounces)
1 tablespoon unsalted butter, melted
1½ to 2 tablespoons apple cider

1. Pour oil into a small skillet or saucepan. Split vanilla pod lengthwise; scrape out seeds. Add seeds and pod to oil. Heat over medium just until pod begins to sizzle, about 3 minutes. Reduce heat to low; cook 5 minutes. Remove from heat. Cool to room temperature. Discard bean pod.
2. Preheat oven to 350°F. Place softened butter in a large bowl; beat with a mixer on medium speed until light and fluffy, about 2 minutes. With

mixer on low speed, add oil mixture. Increase speed to medium, and beat until combined (mixture will not be smooth); scrape down sides of bowl as necessary. Add brown sugar; beat on medium speed until softened and well combined, about 2 minutes. Add eggs; beat until well combined, about 1 minute. Add apples; beat on low speed just until combined.

3. Weigh or lightly spoon flour into dry measuring cups; level with a knife. Whisk together flour, baking powder, cinnamon, nutmeg, cloves, and 1 teaspoon salt. Add flour mixture and evaporated milk alternately to butter mixture, beginning and ending with flour mixture, and beating on low speed after each addition just until combined. Pour batter into a 10-cup Bundt pan coated with baking spray. Bake at 350°F until a wooden pick inserted in center comes out clean, 45 to 50 minutes.

4. Cool cake in pan on a wire rack 10 minutes. Carefully invert cake onto rack; cool completely.

5. Stir together powdered sugar, melted butter, and remaining ⅛ teaspoon salt in a medium bowl. Stir in 1½ tablespoons cider until mixture is smooth. If mixture is too thick, stir in ½ tablespoon cider. Drizzle over cake. Serves 16 (serving size: 1 slice)

CALORIES 290; **FAT** 13g (sat 4g, unsat 8g); **PROTEIN** 5g; **CARB** 42g; **FIBER** 2g; **SUGARS** 24g (added sugars 21g); **SODIUM** 253mg; **CALC** 10% DV; **POTASSIUM** 5% DV

12. STOCK UP ON HEALTHY CONVENIENCE ITEMS.
Unsalted canned beans and tomatoes, precooked unseasoned brown rice, and unsalted chicken stock are the hardworking convenience heroes of a healthy kitchen because—let's get real—they allow a healthy meal to happen when you have almost no time to cook. Use fresh ingredients to perk them up: a little citrus, perhaps, or some herbs.

13. BE PATIENT.
Fully preheat your oven or skillet; otherwise, you won't get the proper rise or sear. Thoroughly mix ingredients until they're emulsified, creamed, or pureed. Use restraint when you're tempted to futz with the steak you're trying to sear. And let food stand after it's cooked if necessary: Rest meat to allow juices to settle, or cool a cake to prevent the glaze from sliding off.

14. DEPLOY HERBS AND CITRUS.
If you think of fresh herbs as a garnish, you're missing out. A handful can turn ho-hum pasta into a fragrant delight. Or if a dish tastes flat, a spritz of lemon or lime juice—or a sprinkling of zest—will bring it to life. Oh, and with basically no calories, sodium, or fat.

15. ADD, DON'T SUBTRACT.
It used to be that healthy eating was about what you shouldn't eat. Now, our focus is on all the fresh, delicious, interesting foods you should be eating—from avocados to beets, mussels to fried eggs, kimchi to artisan salumi. Healthy eating is a celebration of color, variety, balance, and the intrinsic pleasures of food that makes you feel good. And if you eat this way, you'll be a much healthier, happier cook.

16. GO SAVORY AT BREAKFAST.
Many sweet breakfast options (pancakes, doughnuts, pastries) are full of refined carbs and added sugars. Even wholesome foods like steel-cut oats and whole-grain toast can go awry if you pile on jam, syrup, or honey. The USDA recommends limiting added sugars to 10% of daily calories—that's 12.5 teaspoons for a 2,000-calorie diet. We aim to consume as little added sugar as possible. Start your day savory with a veggie omelet or a hearty breakfast salad, and you're much more likely to stick to that goal.

17. BE GOOD TO YOUR GUT.
Science is uncovering more and more potential benefits to having a thriving gut microbiome (the bacterial community in your GI tract): lower risk of obesity, type 2 diabetes, heart disease, dementia, depression, and more. Put more of the good bugs into your gut by eating probiotic-rich foods, such as yogurt and kefir, and fermented foods like sauerkraut, kombucha, and kimchi. And be sure to fuel your bacterial team with plenty of prebiotics (food for probiotics), including whole wheat, garlic, onions, asparagus, and leeks. So what's not good for your gut? It's not surprising, but try to avoid artificial sweeteners and highly processed foods, and cut back on sugar. You'll hear a lot more from us on gut health in the near future, so stay tuned.

18. DON'T STRESS TOO MUCH ABOUT DIETARY CHOLESTEROL.
We've recently removed it from the numbers we report with our recipes. The link between the cholesterol you consume and the cholesterol that ends up in your blood is not as direct as once thought. The USDA's 2015 Dietary Guidelines removed the daily cholesterol cap in favor of advising that you "eat as little dietary cholesterol as possible." Bottom line: If you eat an overall healthy diet that goes easy on foods high in saturated fat, you shouldn't have to worry.

19. BAKE WITH PRECISION.
Making a cake successfully depends on exact measurements. Lighter baking requires even more precision; there's a smaller margin of error when you're using less fat and sugar. So weigh your flour: It's the most accurate way to measure. Use a spouted liquid measuring cup for milk, oil, and other liquids, and check the amount at eye level. Your cakes (and your family) will thank you.

20. MAKE SNACKS COUNT.
First, make sure they offer some fat, protein, and fiber, not just carbs, so they'll satisfy your hunger. Try Greek yogurt and berries, an apple with almond butter, grape tomatoes with a stick of string cheese, or carrots dipped in hummus. And think of your snacks as opportunities to fill your daily fruit and veggie quota. If dinner ends up being pizza delivery, well, at least you will have had all those carrots earlier in the day.

Charred Broccolini and Onion Chickpea Bowls

Hands-on: 30 min. Total: 30 min.

5 tablespoons olive oil, divided
1 small red onion (8 ounces), root end intact, cut into 12 wedges
1 teaspoon kosher salt, divided
1 pound Broccolini, trimmed
3/4 teaspoon smoked paprika
2 (15-ounce) cans unsalted chickpeas, rinsed and drained
1 large garlic clove, grated
2 teaspoons grated lemon rind
2 tablespoons fresh lemon juice
1 teaspoon Dijon mustard
1/2 teaspoon black pepper
1/4 cup chopped fresh parsley
8 lemon wedges

1. Heat 1 tablespoon oil in a large cast-iron skillet over medium-high. Add onion wedges; cook until charred, about 2 minutes per side. Transfer to a plate; sprinkle with 1/4 teaspoon salt.
2. Heat 1 tablespoon oil in skillet. Add Broccolini in a single layer; cook, turning occasionally, until charred, 8 to 10 minutes. Transfer to a plate; sprinkle with 1/4 teaspoon salt.
3. Add 1 tablespoon oil, paprika, chickpeas, and garlic to skillet. Cook, stirring occasionally, until starting to brown, 3 minutes. Remove from heat.
4. Combine rind, juice, mustard, pepper, remaining 2 tablespoons oil, and remaining 1/2 teaspoon salt in a medium bowl. Add chickpea mixture and parsley; toss to combine. Spoon chickpea mixture into each of 4 bowls. Top with Broccolini and onion; serve with lemon wedges. Serves 4 (serving size: 3/4 cup chickpea mixture, 4 ounces Broccolini, 3 onion wedges, and 2 lemon wedges)

CALORIES 423; FAT 19g (sat 2g, unsat 14g); PROTEIN 16g; CARB 49g; FIBER 10g; SUGARS 5g (added sugars 0g); SODIUM 596mg; CALC 18% DV; POTASSIUM 24% DV

---

21. MASTER THE TECHNIQUE OF CHARRING. ▲
Those deliberately overbrowned edges make an enormous flavor impact with zero added calories, sodium, or fat. Charred vegetables—onions, cabbage, Broccolini, Brussels sprouts—are particularly delicious.

22. LEARN HOW TO BALANCE TEXTURES AND FLAVORS.
Sometimes, a one-note dish is a good thing. A sloppy joe, for example, is a delightful monotextured combo of squishy filling inside smushy bun. More often, though, dishes need balance. A creamy pureed soup might be A-OK as is, but it turns into a phenomenal experience when topped with crunchy croutons. And consider salted caramel, arguably the superior caramel. It's delicious precisely because the sweetness is balanced by the contrasting taste and crunch of the salt; without it, the flavor might simply be cloying. Sautéed greens too bitter? Balance with a splash of acid from vinegar or lemon juice. Embrace the idea of culinary yin and yang.

23. USE A TIMER.
How many times have you trusted yourself to take the nuts out of the oven after 10 or so minutes, but then you forget and burn them? Life has a way of constantly distracting us—we need the "ding."

24. USE QUALITY INGREDIENTS.
When you're cooking in a healthier way, it's crucial to start with the best ingredients you can afford. Without a ton of butter, sugar, or salt, you can't make up for poor quality.

25. EMBRACE AFFORDABLE AQUACULTURE.
You (yes, you!) can make a difference in the health of the planet's fish stocks by purchasing sustainable seafood, such as farmed mussels or salmon, and laying off species that are overfished, such as Atlantic cod. One of the most affordable ways to do so is to look to aquaculture—farmed fish and shellfish raised in a responsible way. Download the Seafood Watch app from Monterey Bay Aquarium for guidance, or ask at the seafood counter.

26. EAT MORE FLORA, LESS FAUNA.
Doing so is better for your health and the health of the planet. We're not saying you need to go vegetarian, but do try to eat a more plant-based diet. Maybe that means Meatless Monday and Wednesday or using meat as an accent rather than the center of the plate. When you do eat meat as an entrée, use the 50/25/25 rule to keep portions in check: half the plate devoted to vegetables and fruit and a quarter each to starch and protein.

27. BUY AN INSTANT-READ THERMOMETER.
Ever look forward to a juicy steak, only to find it more gray than pink inside? Leaner meats can be easy to overcook. Don't risk it; use a meat thermometer. See page 356 for more info.

28. DRINK UP!
If you drink alcohol, enjoy a guilt-free glug. All types offer heart-health benefits when enjoyed in moderation: one serving (5 ounces wine, 1.5 ounces spirits, a 12-ounce beer) per day for women and two for men.

29. GET A CAST-IRON SKILLET.
Once seasoned, it will be one of the most versatile pans you own, with a nonstick surface for gently scrambling eggs or heating screaming-hot for seared scallops. One we love: Lodge 10.25-inch, $27, lodgemfg.com.

30. WIELD FLAVOR BOMBS FROM A GLOBAL PANTRY.
Some of our favorite flavor boosters are miso, fish sauce, harissa, sambal oelek, and chipotle chiles. Don't think you only have to use them in "ethnic" recipes; any of those ingredients would make for a killer take on mac and cheese or to amp up your everyday sandwiches and soups.

Fast

Turkey Sandwiches with Kimchi Slaw and Miso Sauce

Hands-on: 15 min. Total: 20 min.
Give your day-after-Thanksgiving sandwich a modern update with global ingredients. The robust flavors of nutty sesame oil, tangy-garlicky-pungent kimchi, and salty-sweet white miso give your palate a welcome change of pace. The sandwich also feeds your gut healthy probiotics (kimchi, yogurt, and miso) plus prebiotics (whole-wheat bread) to keep the good bacteria well fed.

1½ cups very thinly sliced red cabbage
1 tablespoon rice vinegar
2 teaspoons toasted sesame oil
⅓ cup very thinly sliced kimchi
⅓ cup plain 2% reduced-fat Greek yogurt
2 tablespoons extra-virgin olive oil
1½ tablespoons white miso
8 (1-ounce) 100% whole-wheat bread slices, toasted
12 ounces sliced skinless roasted turkey breast

1. Combine cabbage, vinegar, and sesame oil in a medium bowl; toss well to coat. Add kimchi; toss well to combine. Let stand 10 minutes.
2. Meanwhile, whisk together yogurt, olive oil, and miso until smooth.
3. Spread about 2 tablespoons yogurt mixture on each of 4 bread slices. Top each with 3 ounces turkey and about ⅓ cup kimchi slaw. Cover with remaining 4 bread slices. Serves 4 (serving size: 1 sandwich)

CALORIES 388; **FAT** 13g (sat 2g, unsat 10g); **PROTEIN** 35g; **CARB** 32g; **FIBER** 6g; **SUGARS** 8g (added sugars 2g); **SODIUM** 608mg; **CALC** 8% DV; **POTASSIUM** 11% DV

THOROUGHLY MODERN MEDITERRANEAN

The saying "what's old is new again" rings true when it comes to the Mediterranean diet. This delicious, intrinsically healthy way of eating is the OG diet—and the heart of what healthy means now.

You've heard it, you know it: The Mediterranean diet is crazy healthy. In fact, if the typical American ate a traditional Mediterranean diet, this could lower heart disease and stroke risk by about 30 to 40%, says Walter Willett, MD, DrPH, of the Harvard T.H. Chan School of Public Health. But guess what else it is? It's hands-down one of the easiest and most delicious diets in the world. It's rooted in diversity and flavor. And it's millennia old. People eating the Mediterranean way in Italy, Spain, or Greece are not sneaking greens into their smoothies. They're not Pinning complicated recipes that require multiple cooking methods. Instead, they're leisurely dining on an abundance of produce, fish, whole grains, olive oil, and what we now dub "artisanal" cheeses. They're embracing fresh, local ingredients. In essence, old-school Mediterranean dining is the ultimate in modern eating. It's minimalist without the hoity-toityness of it all. It's healthy without the blinding halo. It's a celebration of real food made with whole ingredients. Here's everything you need to know about the most modern of ancient diets, starting with the big-hitter tentpoles that hold it all together.

YOUR GUIDE TO GOING MEDITERRANEAN

This is where you'd expect to see the down and dirty details for how many fruits and veggies to eat daily and the exact whole-grain serving size to heap onto your plate. But that's not how the Mediterranean diet works. Rather, it suggests examples of what to eat over time—not just at one meal. The keys are variety, frequency, and relative proportions to other items on your plate. Fruits, veggies, whole grains, olive oil, legumes, herbs, and nuts should be the core of most meals, enjoyed multiple times a day. Fish and poultry are at least a twice-a-week thing. Dairy and eggs are a few times weekly (or daily), but in small amounts. Red meat is a few times a month. Wine is enjoyed in moderation with dinner, and when it isn't poured, the beverage is water. "Don't get caught up in too many do's and don'ts," says Connie Diekman, RD, author of *The Everything Mediterranean Diet Book*. "A good first step is to add more veggies to what you're already eating."

Staff Favorite • Gluten Free
Vegetarian

Fall Vegetable and Lentil Salad

Hands-on: 30 min. Total: 40 min.
We love firm French green lentils, but you can also use standard brown lentils. You're not likely to find a whole butternut squash that's only 1 pound; just buy the smallest one you can find, and use 1 pound of it.

²/₃ cup uncooked French green lentils
2 bay leaves
1 pound butternut squash, peeled
1 pound large carrots
1 small red onion (about 8 ounces)
¼ cup extra-virgin olive oil, divided
1 teaspoon ground cumin
³/₈ teaspoon ground red pepper
¼ teaspoon ground cinnamon
1½ teaspoons kosher salt, divided
2 cups plain 2% reduced-fat Greek yogurt
2 teaspoons grated lemon rind
1 garlic clove, grated
1 tablespoon fresh lemon juice
³/₄ cup pomegranate arils
½ cup roughly chopped fresh flat-leaf parsley

1. Preheat oven to 425°F.
2. Place lentils and bay leaves in a small saucepan; cover with water to 2 inches above lentils. Bring to a boil over high; reduce heat to medium-low, and simmer until tender, 25 to 30 minutes.
3. Meanwhile, cut squash in half lengthwise; discard seeds and membranes. Cut squash halves crosswise into ¼-inch-thick slices; cut any wide slices in half lengthwise. Cut carrots into ¼-inch-thick slices on an extreme diagonal to create similar-sized pieces. Cut onion into 12 thin wedges. Place vegetables in an even layer on a rimmed baking sheet lined with parchment paper. Place 2 tablespoons oil in a small bowl. Whisk in cumin, red pepper, cinnamon, and ¾ teaspoon salt; drizzle over vegetables, and toss gently to coat. Bake vegetables at 425°F until tender and lightly browned, 25 to 30 minutes.
4. Whisk together yogurt and 1 tablespoon oil in a small bowl; whisk in lemon rind, garlic, and ¼ teaspoon salt. Set aside.
5. Drain lentils, and place in a large bowl. Discard bay leaves. Stir lemon juice, remaining 1 tablespoon oil, and remaining ½ teaspoon salt into lentils.
6. To serve, spread ⅓ cup yogurt mixture on each of 6 plates; top with about 1 cup vegetables, about ⅓ cup lentils, 2 tablespoons pomegranate arils, and 4 teaspoons parsley.
Serves 6

CALORIES 250; FAT 10g (sat 1g, unsat 8g); PROTEIN 7g; CARB 37g; FIBER 9g; SUGARS 10g (added sugars 0g); SODIUM 543mg; CALC 9% DV; POTASSIUM 23% DV

THE MODERN MEDITERRANEAN STAPLES

Keep these items on hand to incorporate the Mediterranean diet into your everyday eating—in addition, of course, to fresh fruits, veggies, and fish.

EXTRA-VIRGIN OLIVE OIL

CANNED FISH
Sustainable tuna, salmon, anchovies, clams, and sardines

DRIED FRUIT
Apricots, blueberries, cherries, cranberries, figs, raisins, and prunes

RAW OR ROASTED NUTS AND SEEDS
Walnuts, almonds, pistachios, pine nuts, and tahini (sesame seed paste)

WHOLE-GRAIN STAPLES
Pasta, bulgur wheat (the base of tabbouleh), farro, millet, whole-grain cornmeal or corn grits

TOMATOES
Canned, paste, sauce, and sun-dried

OLIVES

WHOLE-GRAIN CRACKERS

CANNED BEANS
Chickpeas, cannellini, fava, kidney beans, and lentils

HERBS AND SPICES
Oregano, cumin, basil, bay leaves, black pepper, crushed red pepper, curry powder, dill, garlic powder, ginger, paprika, rosemary, saffron, sage, thyme, and turmeric; also stock blends like Italian seasoning or za'atar, which often contains sumac, sesame seeds, thyme, and other herbs

ONIONS AND GARLIC

PLAIN GREEK YOGURT

ARTISANAL CHEESES
Feta, Parmesan, etc.

LEGUMES

While beans are the most famous of the legume family, peas, lentils, chickpeas, and even peanuts are also part of the clan. "Legumes became a huge part of the Mediterranean diet because they were affordable sources of protein when meat wasn't," says Toups—and because they're high in fiber and antioxidants, which protect against cancer and heart disease. Legumes are diverse, too: They're a perfect addition to ragouts or whole-grain dishes, and they can be mashed and blended with herbs and spices to make amazing dips and spreads.

RED WINE

Who doesn't love a diet that features a daily 5-ounce glass of red? Wine, says Toups, is sipped slowly and enhances food's enjoyment. For women, one glass is on the menu; for men, it's up to two. For the most heart-healthy antioxidants, toast with a Cannonau, Pinot Noir, Syrah, Shiraz, Zinfandel, Cabernet Sauvignon, or Merlot. Moderate drinking lowers your heart disease risk better than abstaining, notes a 2017 study. But no matter what's in your cup, it's just as important to clink glasses with friends, so teetotalers, don't sweat.

Fast • Vegetarian

Chickpea "Meatballs" with Crunchy Romaine Salad

Hands-on: 30 min. Total: 30 min.
The expected chickpea dish might be falafel, but the flavor here is more akin to hummus. The chickpea mixture will be soft at first; it firms up as it cooks.

3 cups torn romaine lettuce (about 3 ounces)
1 cup loosely packed fresh flat-leaf parsley leaves
1 cup chopped English cucumber
1 cup quartered grape tomatoes (about 5 ounces)
⅓ cup slivered red onion
3 garlic cloves, divided
3 tablespoons fresh lemon juice
1½ tablespoons water
¼ teaspoon black pepper
5 tablespoons tahini (sesame seed paste), divided
¼ cup extra-virgin olive oil, divided
1⅛ teaspoons kosher salt, divided
1 (15-ounce) can unsalted chickpeas, drained
½ cup whole-wheat panko (Japanese breadcrumbs)
1 teaspoon ground cumin
½ teaspoon smoked paprika
1 large egg

1. Combine lettuce, parsley, cucumber, tomatoes, and onion; set aside.
2. Grate 1 garlic clove. Whisk together lemon juice, 1½ tablespoons water, pepper, grated garlic, 3 tablespoons tahini, 1 tablespoon olive oil, and ⅜ teaspoon salt; set dressing aside.
3. Chop remaining 2 garlic cloves. Process chickpeas in a food processor until almost ground, about 15 seconds. Add panko, cumin, paprika, chopped garlic, remaining 2 tablespoons tahini, and remaining ¾ teaspoon salt; process until almost smooth, about 15 seconds, stopping to scrape down sides as needed. Add egg; pulse just until combined, 5 to 6 times. Shape mixture into 20 balls (about 1 slightly heaping tablespoon each).
4. Heat a large nonstick skillet over medium-high. Add remaining 3 tablespoons oil; swirl to coat. Add chickpea balls to skillet. Cook, turning occasionally, until browned all over and crisp on the outside, 8 to 10 minutes. Serve chickpea balls with salad; drizzle with tahini dressing. Serve immediately. Serves 4 (serving size: 5 chickpea balls, 2 cups salad, and about 2 tablespoons dressing)

CALORIES 424; **FAT** 26g (sat 4g, unsat 20g); **PROTEIN** 14g; **CARB** 36g; **FIBER** 8g; **SUGARS** 4g (added sugars 0g); **SODIUM** 616mg; **CALC** 14% DV; **POTASSIUM** 18% DV

GO MED, GET HEALTHIER

It's not an overstatement to say that the Mediterranean diet saves—and extends—lives. Here's how:

IMPROVES HEART HEALTH

That's in large part a result of the heart-helping benefits from the monounsaturated fatty acids that abound in olive oil and nuts, which take a leading role in the Med diet, pushing artery-clogging saturated and trans fats to the side. Plus, extra-virgin olive oil spurs a decrease in bad cholesterol and an uptick in HDL cholesterol (aka the good stuff). HDL works to eliminate excess cholesterol from your arteries and keep your blood vessels open and blood flowing, notes new research in *Circulation*.

FIGHTS OTHER CHRONIC CONDITIONS

Olive oil's phytochemicals are also believed to quell inflammation and insulin resistance, the root of many diseases like breast cancer and diabetes, according to Diekman. To wit: A Mediterranean diet has been shown to reduce one's risk of breast cancer by 57% and diabetes by 30%, according to a 2016 study in the *Annals of Internal Medicine*. That inflammation reduction? It decreases pain, too, and it helps the brain, notes a 2017 study at The Ohio State University.

BOLSTERS BRAIN POWER

The Mediterranean diet's ability to tamp down inflammatory responses is part of the reason it's been shown to slow rates of cognitive decline and boost brain function. Further brain-fortifying news came earlier this year when Australian researchers found that one-third of clinically depressed individuals who ate a Mediterranean diet for three months reported a significant improvement in their mood and depressive symptoms.

Fast • Gluten Free
Make Ahead

Pan-Grilled Mackerel with Creamy Millet Puree

Hands-on: 30 min. Total: 35 min.
While fresh sardines and anchovies are plentiful in the Mediterranean, those species can be hard to find in the U.S. We look instead to rich mackerel, a sustainable option with a similar fat profile.

⅓ cup uncooked millet

2 garlic cloves, smashed

1½ cups water

3 cups small cauliflower florets (about 9 ounces)

3 tablespoons extra-virgin olive oil, divided

⅓ cup thinly sliced shallots

⅓ cup red wine vinegar

¼ cup golden raisins

1 tablespoon light brown sugar

1½ tablespoons drained capers

2 tablespoons toasted pine nuts

⅝ teaspoon kosher salt, divided

½ teaspoon black pepper, divided

4 (6-ounce) sustainable skin-on mackerel fillets

Cooking spray

¼ cup roughly chopped fresh flat-leaf parsley

4 teaspoons chopped fresh dill

1. Heat a medium saucepan over medium-high. Add millet and garlic to dry pan; cook, stirring occasionally, until millet is lightly toasted, about 5 minutes. Add 1½ cups water; bring to a boil. Cover, reduce heat to medium-low, and simmer 10 minutes. Add cauliflower; cover and simmer until cauliflower is tender and liquid is absorbed, about 15 minutes. Set aside.
2. Meanwhile, heat a small skillet over medium. Add 1 tablespoon oil; swirl to coat. Add shallots; cook, stirring often, until softened, about 2 minutes. Stir in vinegar, raisins, sugar, and capers. Reduce heat to medium-low; cook, stirring occasionally, until slightly syrupy, 8 to 10 minutes. Remove from heat; stir in pine nuts.
3. Transfer millet mixture to a food processor. Add 1 tablespoon oil, ½ teaspoon salt, and ¼ teaspoon pepper; process until smooth, about 20 seconds. (If mixture is too thick, add water, 1 tablespoon at a time, and process until desired consistency is reached.)
4. Heat a large grill pan over high. Brush flesh side of fish evenly with remaining 1 tablespoon oil; sprinkle evenly with remaining ⅛ teaspoon salt and remaining ¼ teaspoon pepper. Coat pan with cooking spray. Add fish to pan, skin side down; cook until crisp, about 3 minutes. Turn fish over; cook until flesh flakes easily when tested with a fork, about 3 minutes. Spread about ½ cup millet puree on each of 4 plates. Top each serving with 1 fillet, skin side up, and about 2 tablespoons relish. Sprinkle servings evenly with parsley and dill. Serves 4

CALORIES 456; **FAT** 18g (sat 3g, unsat 14g); **PROTEIN** 43g; **CARB** 31g; **FIBER** 4g; **SUGARS** 12g (added sugars 3g); **SODIUM** 706mg; **CALC** 10% DV; **POTASSIUM** 36% DV

Chunky Muhammara

Hands-on: 10 min. Total: 25 min.
Build a healthy "snack dinner" platter with this flavor-packed dip at the center—surround it with crunchy vegetables and whole-wheat flatbread for dipping, and add a tin of oil-packed sardines, olives, nuts, feta cheese, marinated artichokes, and some dried and fresh fruit for a colorful, well-rounded meal.

2 large red bell peppers (about 1¼ pounds), halved and seeded
1½ ounces whole-wheat pita or lavash
1½ tablespoons extra-virgin olive oil
1 tablespoon pomegranate molasses
2 teaspoons Aleppo pepper
1 teaspoon ground cumin
¾ teaspoon kosher salt
1 large garlic clove, chopped
⅔ cup chopped toasted walnuts

1. Preheat broiler with oven rack in top position. Place bell pepper halves on a foil-lined baking sheet, skin sides up; flatten slightly by pressing with heel of hand. Broil until blackened, 8 to 10 minutes. Remove from oven, and wrap in foil used to line pan. Let stand 10 minutes. Rub off and discard skins.
2. Place pita in a food processor; process until coarsely ground, about 30 seconds. Add bell peppers, oil, pomegranate molasses, Aleppo pepper, cumin, salt, and garlic; process until smooth, stopping to scrape sides as needed. Add walnuts; pulse until almost smooth but with some small chunks, 4 to 5 times. Serves 8 (serving size: ¼ cup)

CALORIES 121; **FAT** 9g (sat 1g, unsat 8g);
PROTEIN 3g; **CARB** 8g; **FIBER** 2g; **SUGARS** 3g
(added sugars 0g); **SODIUM** 206mg; **CALC** 2% DV;
POTASSIUM 4% DV

QUALITY DAIRY
It's hard to imagine a Mediterranean meal sans cheeses or yogurt. They do love their dairy, but quality beats quantity. Often, instead of dairy serving as a main component, Toups says, "dairy is integrated as a flavor into the meal." Think: a dollop of tangy yogurt atop veggies or a kebab accented with ever-so-slightly grilled chunks of cheese. (Folks are not short on calcium. The Med diet leans heavily on nondairy calcium-rich foods, such as leafy greens, beans, and bony fish like sardines and anchovies.)

Gluten Free

Harissa-Roasted Eggplant with Minced Chicken

Hands-on: 30 min. Total: 55 min.
Here we play with the concept of meat as condiment, using a small amount of rich chicken thighs as a sort of relish on spicy roasted eggplant. Creamy Greek yogurt offers cooling balance to the heat of harissa.

2 (1-pound) eggplants, halved lengthwise
¼ cup extra-virgin olive oil, divided
¼ cup harissa sauce or paste
1 teaspoon kosher salt, divided
¾ teaspoon black pepper, divided
8 ounces boneless, skinless chicken thighs
2 garlic cloves, minced
½ teaspoon dried oregano
½ teaspoon ground coriander
¼ teaspoon ground turmeric
1 tablespoon fresh lemon juice
¾ cup plain 2% reduced-fat Greek yogurt
¼ cup roughly chopped fresh cilantro
1 red Fresno chile, thinly sliced

1. Preheat oven to 400°F.
2. Score flesh side of each eggplant half in a cross-hatch pattern, being careful not to cut through the skin. Place eggplant halves on a foil-lined rimmed baking sheet. Brush 2 tablespoons oil evenly over flesh side of eggplant halves; brush evenly with harissa. Bake at 400°F until tender, 40 to 45 minutes. Sprinkle evenly with ½ teaspoon salt and ¼ teaspoon pepper.
3. Meanwhile, heat a small skillet over medium-high. Add 1 tablespoon oil; swirl to coat. Add chicken; cook until golden on both sides and cooked through, about 4 minutes per side. Transfer chicken to a cutting board. (Do not wipe skillet clean.) Cool chicken about 10 minutes. Finely chop chicken.
4. Heat skillet over medium-high. Add remaining 1 tablespoon oil; stir in garlic. Cook, stirring constantly, until garlic is lightly golden, about 30 seconds. Add oregano, coriander, turmeric, ¼ teaspoon salt, and ¼ teaspoon pepper; cook, stirring constantly, until fragrant, about 30 seconds. Add chicken and lemon juice; cook until chicken is crisped, about 4 to 5 minutes.
5. Stir remaining ¼ teaspoon salt and remaining ¼ teaspoon pepper into yogurt. Spoon 3 tablespoons yogurt mixture over each eggplant half; top each with about ¼ cup chicken mixture. Sprinkle evenly with cilantro and chile slices. Serves 4 (serving size: 1 topped eggplant half)

CALORIES 265; **FAT** 17g (sat 3g, unsat 13g);
PROTEIN 14g; **CARB** 17g; **FIBER** 7g; **SUGARS** 8g
(added sugars 0g); **SODIUM** 601mg; **CALC** 4% DV;
POTASSIUM 21% DV

Fast • Gluten Free

Seared Sea Bass with Lemon-Olive White Beans

Hands-on: 20 min. Total: 20 min.
Meaty, buttery Castelvetrano olives are lower in sodium than many other olive types. They pair particularly well with rich sea bass and creamy white beans, but if you can't find them, you can use any olive you like.

4 (6-ounce) sustainable skinless sea bass fillets
³/₄ teaspoon kosher salt, divided
½ teaspoon black pepper, divided
3 tablespoons extra-virgin olive oil, divided
5 garlic cloves, sliced
2 teaspoons fresh thyme leaves
8 cherry tomatoes, quartered
²/₃ cup unsalted chicken stock
1 (15-ounce) can unsalted cannellini beans, rinsed and drained
5 ounces fresh baby spinach
2 tablespoons fresh lemon juice
1 ounce pitted Castelvetrano olives, quartered (about ¹/₃ cup)

1. Heat a large nonstick skillet over medium-high. Sprinkle fish with ¼ teaspoon salt and ¼ teaspoon pepper. Add 1 tablespoon oil to skillet; swirl to coat. Add fish; cook to desired degree of doneness, about 3 minutes on each side for medium. Remove fish from pan; discard drippings.

(Do not wipe skillet clean.) Lightly tent fish with foil to keep warm.
2. Heat remaining 2 tablespoons oil in skillet over medium-high. Add garlic; cook, stirring often, until light golden brown, about 1 minute. Stir in thyme and tomatoes; cook, stirring often, until heated through, about 1 minute. Add stock and beans; bring to a simmer. Add spinach in batches, and cook, tossing gently, until spinach is wilted after each addition. Stir in lemon juice, olives, remaining ½ teaspoon salt, and remaining ¼ teaspoon pepper. Divide bean mixture among 4 shallow bowls; nestle 1 fillet into each bowl. Serves 4 (serving size: about ¾ cup bean mixture and 1 fillet)

CALORIES 382; FAT 16g (sat 3g, unsat 12g); PROTEIN 40g; CARB 19g; FIBER 6g; SUGARS 2g (added sugars 0g); SODIUM 708mg; CALC 10% DV; POTASSIUM 28% DV

Fast • Vegetarian

Stewed Chickpeas and Chard over Garlic Toast

Hands-on: 20 min. Total: 20 min.
This is one of those go-to dishes for busy weeknights—it's fast, easy, and filling. Though we're calling this dinner, it would be splendid for breakfast, too.

1 (14.5-ounce) can unsalted diced tomatoes
8 ounces rainbow chard
6 garlic cloves, divided
3 tablespoons extra-virgin olive oil, divided
1 cup chopped yellow onion
1 teaspoon ground cumin
³/₄ teaspoon smoked paprika
½ teaspoon kosher salt
¼ teaspoon crushed red pepper
1 (15-ounce) can unsalted chickpeas, drained
4 (1¹/₂-ounce) slices whole-wheat boule or country bread

1. Preheat broiler with oven rack in top position.
2. Place tomatoes in a mini food processor; pulse until pureed but not completely smooth, 4 to 5 times.
3. Strip chard leaves from stems; coarsely chop leaves. Cut stems into ½-inch pieces.
4. Mince 5 garlic cloves. Heat a large skillet over medium. Add 2 tablespoons oil; swirl to coat. Add onion and minced garlic; cook, stirring occasionally, 3 minutes. Add chard stem pieces; cook, stirring occasionally, until onion is tender, about 3 minutes. Add cumin, paprika, salt, and pepper; cook, stirring constantly, until heated through, about 30 seconds. Stir in chickpeas and pureed tomatoes; bring to a simmer. Add chard leaves. Reduce heat to medium-low, cover, and simmer until leaves wilt, about 5 minutes.
5. Cut remaining garlic clove in half. Place bread in a single layer on a baking sheet. Broil until toasted, about 1 minute. Turn bread over; brush with remaining 1 tablespoon oil. Broil until toasted, about 1 minute. Rub cut sides of halved garlic clove over oiled side of toasted bread. Place 1 toast slice on each of 4 plates; top each with about 1 cup chickpea mixture. Serves 4 (serving size: 1 topped toast)

CALORIES 352; FAT 13g (sat 2g, unsat 10g); PROTEIN 13g; CARB 48g; FIBER 9g; SUGARS 7g (added sugars 0g); SODIUM 586mg; CALC 18% DV; POTASSIUM 21% DV

SIMPLE SOUPS

The hustle and bustle of the holidays can leave you feeling drained. Nourish yourself with these supereasy soups and stews.

Gluten Free • Make Ahead

Turmeric Chicken-and-Chickpea Soup

Hands-on: 15 min. Total: 50 min.
In place of noodles, which tend to swell in soups, we look to canned chickpeas, which add texture and boost fiber.

1 tablespoon olive oil
1 pound boneless, skinless chicken thighs
1 teaspoon kosher salt, divided
½ teaspoon black pepper, divided
1 cup chopped red bell pepper
1 cup chopped onion
2 teaspoons ground turmeric
1 teaspoon freshly grated ginger
2 garlic cloves, minced
4 cups unsalted chicken stock (such as Swanson)
2 (15-ounce) cans unsalted chickpeas, rinsed and drained
1 cup canned light coconut milk
½ cup torn fresh basil
2 tablespoons fresh lime juice

1. Heat olive oil in a Dutch oven over medium-high. Season chicken with ½ teaspoon salt and ¼ teaspoon pepper. Add chicken to pan; cook 3 minutes on each side or until browned. Transfer to a plate.
2. Reduce heat to medium. Add bell pepper and onion; cook, stirring occasionally, until softened, about 5 minutes. Add turmeric, ginger, garlic, remaining ½ teaspoon salt, and remaining ¼ teaspoon pepper; cook 1 minute. Add stock and chickpeas. Return chicken to pot; increase heat to high. Bring mixture to a boil. Reduce heat to medium; simmer 15 minutes or until chicken is cooked through.
3. Place chicken on a cutting board, and use two forks to shred; return to pot. Stir in coconut milk, basil, and lime juice; cook 5 minutes. Serves 6 (serving size: about 1⅓ cups)

CALORIES 314; **FAT** 9g (sat 3g, unsat 4g); **PROTEIN** 27g; **CARB** 31g; **FIBER** 7g; **SUGARS** 4g (added sugars 0g); **SODIUM** 518mg; **CALC** 10% DV; **POTASSIUM** 11% DV

Gluten Free • Make Ahead Vegetarian

Creamy Carrot and Lemongrass Soup

Hands-on: 15 min. Total: 40 min.
Look for lemongrass paste in the refrigerated produce section, near the packages of fresh herbs. Bonus: One serving of this soup delivers 100% of your daily dose of vitamin A.

1 tablespoon olive oil
2½ cups chopped carrots
1 (12-ounce) bag prechopped fresh butternut squash
1 cup chopped onion
¼ teaspoon kosher salt
3½ cups unsalted vegetable or chicken stock
2 teaspoons lemongrass paste
1 teaspoon Thai red curry paste
½ teaspoon ground ginger
1 cup plain 2% reduced-fat Greek yogurt, divided
1 tablespoon fresh lime juice (from 1 lime)
4 teaspoons toasted pumpkin seeds

1. Heat oil in a Dutch oven over medium. Add carrots, squash, onion, and salt; cook, stirring occasionally, until softened, about 8 minutes. Add stock, pastes, and ginger; increase heat to high. Bring mixture to a boil. Reduce heat to medium, and cook, covered, until vegetables are very tender, about 15 minutes.
2. Pour carrot mixture into a blender; add ¾ cup yogurt. Remove center piece of blender lid (to allow steam to escape); secure lid on blender. Place a clean towel over opening in lid. Process until smooth. Add lime juice; process until combined. Ladle soup into 4 bowls; top evenly with remaining ¼ cup yogurt and pumpkin seeds. Serves 4 (serving size: about 1⅔ cups soup, 1 tablespoon yogurt, and 1 teaspoon pumpkin seeds)

CALORIES 200; **FAT** 7g (sat 2g, unsat 4g); **PROTEIN** 10g; **CARB** 29g; **FIBER** 5g; **SUGARS** 11g (added sugars 0g); **SODIUM** 517mg; **CALC** 14% DV; **POTASSIUM** 18% DV

Gluten Free • Make Ahead • Vegetarian

Smoky Lentil Stew

Hands-on: 15 min. Total: 50 min.
Be prepared: You will want crusty bread to dip into the runny egg and sop up the remains.

1 tablespoon olive oil
1 cup chopped onion
1 cup chopped carrots
3 garlic cloves, minced
3 tablespoons tomato paste
1½ teaspoons smoked paprika
1 teaspoon ground cumin
¾ teaspoon kosher salt
½ teaspoon freshly ground black pepper
¼ teaspoon crushed red pepper
1 bunch lacinato kale, stemmed and chopped (about 5 cups)
1½ cups dried brown lentils
4 cups unsalted vegetable stock
2½ cups water
5 large eggs

1. Heat oil in a Dutch oven over medium. Add onion and carrots; cook, stirring occasionally, until tender, about 5 minutes. Add garlic, tomato paste, smoked paprika, cumin, salt, black pepper, and red pepper; cook 1 minute. Add kale and lentils; cook, stirring often, until kale begins to soften, about 2 minutes. Add stock and 2½ cups water; increase heat to high. Bring to a boil. Reduce heat to medium, and simmer until lentils are tender, about 30 minutes.
2. Form 5 indentations in soup. Crack eggs, 1 at a time, into a small custard cup. Gently slip 1 egg into each indentation. Cover and cook over medium-low until egg whites are set, about 6 to 8 minutes. Serves 5 (serving size: about 1¾ cups soup and 1 egg)

CALORIES 382; **FAT** 8g (sat 2g, unsat 6g); **PROTEIN** 25g; **CARB** 55g; **FIBER** 10g; **SUGARS** 5g (added sugars 0g); **SODIUM** 635mg; **CALC** 18% DV; **POTASSIUM** 20% DV

Gluten Free • Make Ahead • Vegetarian

Three-Bean Miso Chili

Hands-on: 10 min. Total: 40 min.
Find white miso in the refrigerated section near the produce.

1 tablespoon olive oil
1 cup chopped onion
2 tablespoons seeded and chopped poblano chile
¼ teaspoon kosher salt
¼ teaspoon black pepper
2 garlic cloves, minced
2 tablespoons natural creamy peanut butter
1½ tablespoons white miso paste
2 teaspoons cumin
2 teaspoons chili powder
1 (15-ounce) can unsalted Great Northern beans, rinsed and drained
1 (15-ounce) can unsalted chickpeas, rinsed and drained
1 (15-ounce) can unsalted kidney beans, rinsed and drained
4 cups unsalted vegetable stock
5 tablespoons plain 2% reduced-fat Greek yogurt
1 ripe avocado, sliced

1. Heat oil in a Dutch oven over medium. Add onion, poblano chile, salt, and black pepper; cook, stirring often, until softened, about 5 minutes. Add garlic, peanut butter, miso, cumin, and chili powder; cook 1 minute, stirring constantly.
2. Add beans and vegetable stock; increase heat to high. Bring to a boil. Reduce heat to medium, and simmer, uncovered, until thickened, about 30 minutes. Ladle into 5 bowls; top evenly with yogurt and avocado slices. Serves 5 (serving size: 1¼ cups chili, 1 tablespoon yogurt, and ⅓ avocado)

CALORIES 401; **FAT** 14g (sat 2g, unsat 10g); **PROTEIN** 19g; **CARB** 50g; **FIBER** 14g; **SUGARS** 5g (added sugars 0g); **SODIUM** 586mg; **CALC** 13% DV; **POTASSIUM** 21% DV

Gluten Free • Make Ahead

Beans-and-Greens Soup

Hands-on: 15 min. Total: 1 hr. 15 min.
Escarole is transformed by heat, changing from a bitter green into something soft, mellow, and sultry. If you crave extra crunch, use fresh green beans instead of canned. As with most soups, the longer it sits, the better it gets, making this a great make-ahead option.

2 tablespoons extra-virgin olive oil
2 ounces diced pancetta
5 garlic cloves, minced
½ teaspoon freshly ground black pepper
¼ teaspoon crushed red pepper
2 large heads escarole, cored and roughly chopped (about 2½ pounds)
1 (14.5-ounce) can cut Italian green beans, rinsed and drained
2 (15-ounce) cans unsalted cannellini beans, rinsed and drained
3 cups unsalted chicken stock (such as Swanson)
2 tablespoons chopped fresh basil
1 teaspoon red wine vinegar
1½ ounces Parmesan cheese, grated (about ⅓ cup)

1. Heat oil in a Dutch oven over medium. Add pancetta and garlic; cook, stirring often, until pancetta is crisp and garlic is aromatic, about 5 minutes. Add black pepper, red pepper, and escarole; cook, stirring often, until escarole begins to wilt, about 5 minutes. Add green beans, cannellini beans, stock, and basil; increase heat to high. Bring to a boil. Cover and reduce heat to medium-low; simmer 1 hour. Stir in vinegar and Parmesan cheese. Serves 5 (serving size: 1½ cups)

CALORIES 338; **FAT** 13g (sat 4g, unsat 8g); **PROTEIN** 18g; **CARB** 37g; **FIBER** 15g; **SUGARS** 4g (added sugars 0g); **SODIUM** 644mg; **CALC** 27% DV; **POTASSIUM** 29% DV

Easy Pork Posole

Hands-on: 10 min. Total: 35 min.
Hominy is a hallmark of posole; find it canned in the Latin and Mexican foods section. This low-stress soup is great for serving a crowd and even better for leftovers the next day.

1 tablespoon olive oil
1 pound ground pork
1 cup chopped onion
3 garlic cloves, minced
2 teaspoons dried oregano
1 teaspoon ancho chile powder
½ teaspoon kosher salt
½ teaspoon black pepper
1 bay leaf
1 (14.5-ounce) can unsalted diced
  tomatoes
1 (25-ounce) can white hominy,
  rinsed and drained
5 cups unsalted chicken stock
  (such as Swanson)
½ cup uncooked tricolor quinoa
6 tablespoons queso fresco, crumbled
⅓ cup shaved radishes
½ cup loosely packed cilantro leaves

1. Heat oil in a Dutch oven over medium. Add pork; cook 5 minutes or until browned, stirring to crumble. Add onion, garlic, oregano, ancho chile powder, salt, and pepper; cook, stirring often, until softened, about 4 minutes. Add bay leaf, tomatoes, hominy, stock, and quinoa; increase heat to high. Bring mixture to a boil. Reduce heat to medium, and simmer, covered, until quinoa is cooked, about 20 to 25 minutes.
2. Discard bay leaf. Ladle soup into each of 6 bowls; top evenly with queso fresco, radishes, and cilantro. Serves 6 (serving size: about 1½ cups soup, 1 tablespoon queso fresco, about 1 tablespoon radish, and 1½ tablespoons cilantro)

CALORIES 341; FAT 12g (sat 4g, unsat 8g), PROTEIN 24g; CARB 33g; FIBER 5g; SUGARS 6g (added sugars 0g); SODIUM 596mg; CALC 9% DV; POTASSIUM 8% DV

THE RECIPE MAKEOVER

LIGHTEN UP CLASSIC PECAN PIE

Whole grains and naturally sweet dates give this traditional holiday dessert a more virtuous profile.

Our rendition of pecan pie features everything you love about the Southern classic: the deep flavor of roasted pecans, a gooey filling, and just enough sticky sweetness enveloped in a buttery, flaky crust. Of all tree nuts, pecans are the top source of antioxidants and contain the largest variety of vitamins and minerals, including vitamins A and E, B vitamins, magnesium, and potassium. A slice of traditional pecan pie may deliver as much as 10g sat fat (half the daily recommended limit) and 40g added sugar (10 teaspoons and 80% of the USDA's recommended daily limit for a 2,000-calorie diet). Our healthier version dials back on the heft while keeping all the flavor and soul of the original.

Gluten Free • Make Ahead
Vegetarian

Pecan-Date Pie

Hands-on: 30 min. Total: 3 hr. 45 min.

CRUST
5 ounces oat flour (about 1¼ cups),
  divided
1 tablespoon sugar
1 tablespoon nonfat dry milk powder
½ teaspoon kosher salt
¼ teaspoon baking powder
¼ cup vegetable shortening
  (such as Spectrum), chilled
2 tablespoons cold unsalted butter,
  cut into small pieces
3 to 4 tablespoons ice-cold water

FILLING
1 cup pecan halves
1 cup whole pitted Medjool dates
2 tablespoons unsalted butter
¾ cup dark-colored corn syrup
1 teaspoon vanilla extract
¼ teaspoon kosher salt
3 large eggs

1. To prepare the crust: Place two-thirds of the flour with the sugar, milk powder, salt, and baking powder in a food processor. Pulse twice to mix. Add shortening and cold butter; pulse until dough begins to clump, about 20 pulses. Add remaining flour; pulse 5 times. Place in a bowl. Add up to 4 tablespoons ice-cold water, 1 tablespoon at a time, mixing with a rubber spatula until combined. Turn out on a floured surface; shape into a flattened disk; wrap in plastic wrap. Chill 2 hours.
2. Unwrap dough; transfer to a floured surface. Let stand 10 minutes. Roll to a 10- to 11-inch circle; fit into a 9-inch glass or ceramic pie plate. Fold edges under, and crimp. Chill until ready to fill.
3. Preheat oven to 350°F.
4. To prepare the filling: Spread pecans on a baking sheet; toast at 350°F until fragrant, 8 to 10 minutes. Pulse dates in a food processor until finely chopped. Set aside.
5. Melt butter in a small skillet over medium; cook 90 seconds or until browned and fragrant, swirling pan frequently.
6. Combine corn syrup, vanilla, and salt in a bowl. Whisk in eggs, and gradually whisk in browned butter until smooth.
7. Spread dates in crust; sprinkle pecans over top. Pour in egg mixture. Bake at 350°F for 40 minutes or until filling is set around the edges. Loosely cover with foil; bake 10 minutes. Cool 30 minutes. Serves 12

CALORIES 298; FAT 17g (sat 5g, unsat 10g); PROTEIN 5g; CARB 35g; FIBER 3g; SUGARS 25g (added sugars 16g); SODIUM 207mg; CALC 4% DV; POTASSIUM 4% DV

THE COOKING LIGHT 3-DAY PRETOX

Follow this meal plan to make room in your diet for your favorite holiday indulgences.

As we head into the feasting season, use this pretox as your reset button either before or in between Thanksgiving and Christmas—a way to dial back before and after so you can indulge in that extra cookie or decadent slice of pie. "Detox" can be an illusive term, often associated with fad diets, supplements, or calorically replete cleanses. But detoxification is a natural human body process carried out by your organs and immune system, and it is best supported by a nutritious diet along with plenty of fluids. Our pretox is a whole-foods prescription—one that front-loads your system with good-for-you nutrients and ingredients and is devoid of added sugars, to help you feel energized and balanced as you enter the holiday season. Each day of the pretox clocks in at under 1,500 calories (an amount that most people will lose weight on) with delicious, fresh recipes that won't leave you feeling deprived. Ready to get started?

SHOPPING LIST

We zeroed in on price, convenience, and reduced food waste to bring you a streamlined shopping list—all for under $54.

STAPLES YOU HAVE ON HAND
Cooking spray
Cumin
Dijon mustard
Garlic powder
Ground turmeric
Large eggs
Olive oil
Paprika
Red wine vinegar
Kosher salt and black pepper
White vinegar

DAIRY
Crumbled feta cheese (4 ounces)
Plain 2% reduced-fat Greek yogurt (1 [17.6-ounce] container)
Unsweetened almond milk (1 [32-ounce] carton)

PRODUCE
Apples (2)
Arugula (1 [5-ounce] bag)
Bananas (2)
Brussels sprouts (8 ounces)
Butternut squash (1 [2-pound])
Cucumber (1)
Garlic (1 head)
Ginger (1 [2-inch] piece)
Lacinato kale (1 bunch)
Lemons (2)
Parsley (1 bunch)
Plain hummus (1 [7-ounce] container)
Red bell peppers (2)

Ripe avocado (1 medium)
Steamed and peeled beets (1 [8-ounce] package)

MEAT AND SEAFOOD
Boneless, skinless chicken breast (2 [4-ounce] pieces)
Wild salmon fillet (6-ounce)

FROZEN
Frozen mixed berries (12 ounces)

DRY GOODS
Chia seeds (1 tablespoon)
Dried green lentils (½ cup)
Low-sodium white tuna in water (1 [2.6-ounce] pouch)
Old-fashioned oats (1 cup)
Tahini (sesame seed paste) (1 [12-ounce] jar)
Uncooked farro (½ cup)
Uncooked quinoa (½ cup)
Unsalted walnut halves (⅔ cup)

START HERE

Get ahead by preparing the tahini dressing and overnight oats the night before starting the pretox.

Fast • Gluten Free
Make Ahead • Vegetarian

All-Purpose Tahini Dressing

Hands-on: 5 min. Total: 5 min.
Tahini is made from ground hulled sesame seeds, which are rich in cholesterol-lowering phytosterols. We look to this rich and nutty pantry staple to add savory depth and sumptuous creaminess to salads and grains. If the dressing thickens up too much after being refrigerated, whisk in an extra teaspoon of water.

3 tablespoons tahini (sesame seed paste), well stirred
1 tablespoon fresh lemon juice
¼ teaspoon garlic powder
⅛ teaspoon kosher salt
⅛ teaspoon black pepper
3 tablespoons warm water

1. Combine tahini, lemon juice, garlic powder, salt, and pepper in a small bowl; mix well. Whisk in water, 1 tablespoon at a time, until dressing reaches desired consistency. Refrigerate in an airtight container. Serves 3 (serving size: 2 tablespoons)

CALORIES 91; **FAT** 8g (sat 1g, unsat 6g); **PROTEIN** 3g; **CARB** 4g; **FIBER** 1g; **SUGARS** 0g (added sugars 0g); **SODIUM** 102mg; **CALC** 2% DV; **POTASSIUM** 2% DV

DAY 1

Total: 1,442 calories

Breakfast

Gluten Free • Make Ahead Vegetarian

Berry-Banana Overnight Oats

Hands-on: 5 min. Total: 6 hr. 5 min.
Speed up your morning routine with a low-maintenance breakfast made the night before. Studies show frozen blueberries have considerably greater polyphenol concentrations than fresh, while most other nutrient levels are comparable between the two. Walnuts deliver a one-two punch of crunch and nutrition: They are a top nut for brain health thanks to the powerful combination of omega-3 fats, vitamin E, and antioxidants.

½ **medium-sized ripe banana**
¼ **cup plain 2% reduced-fat Greek yogurt**
½ **cup old-fashioned rolled oats**
1 **teaspoon chia seeds**
⅛ **teaspoon kosher salt**
⅔ **cup unsweetened almond milk**
¼ **cup frozen thawed mixed berries**
1 **tablespoon chopped walnuts**

1. Place banana in a small bowl, and use a fork to thoroughly mash. Add yogurt; mix to combine.

2. Add oats, chia seeds, salt, and almond milk; mix well. Cover and refrigerate overnight or at least 6 hours.
3. Top with mixed berries and walnuts. Serves 1 (serving size: about 1 cup)

CALORIES 359; **FAT** 13g (sat 2g, unsat 9g); **PROTEIN** 14g; **CARB** 52g; **FIBER** 10g; **SUGARS** 14g (added sugars 0g); **SODIUM** 397mg; **CALC** 26% DV; **POTASSIUM** 16% DV

SNACKS

MORNING: 1 large hard-boiled egg with 1 cup red bell pepper slices and 3 tablespoons hummus (175 calories)

AFTERNOON: 1 medium apple with 5 walnut halves (160 calories)

Lunch

Gluten Free • Make Ahead Vegetarian

Autumn Glow Salad

Hands-on: 10 min. Total: 40 min.
This plant-powered salad delivers over 50% of your daily fiber and one-third of your daily potassium goal. Butternut squash is an excellent source of eye-healthy vitamin A and a good source of immune-boosting vitamin C and blood pressure–supporting potassium.

1 **(2-pound) butternut squash, peeled and cut into ½-inch cubes**
1 **tablespoon olive oil**
½ **teaspoon kosher salt, divided**
¼ **teaspoon freshly ground black pepper**
½ **cup dried green lentils**
½ **teaspoon cumin**
½ **teaspoon red wine vinegar**
2 **cups arugula**
1 **tablespoon crumbled feta cheese**
2 **tablespoons All-Purpose Tahini Dressing (page 330)**

1. Preheat oven to 400°F.
2. Place squash, oil, ¼ teaspoon salt, and pepper in a bowl; toss to combine. Spread mixture in a single layer on a foil-lined baking sheet. Bake at 400°F for 28 to 30 minutes, tossing once halfway through.
3. While squash bakes, place lentils in a medium saucepan. Cover with water to 3 inches above lentils; bring to a boil. Reduce heat, and simmer 20 minutes or until lentils are tender. Drain. Stir in remaining ¼ teaspoon salt, cumin, and red wine vinegar. Let stand 10 minutes.
4. Arrange arugula on a plate. Top with 1 cup butternut squash (reserve remaining for Day 2 Breakfast), ½ cup cooked lentils (reserve remaining for Day 3 Dinner), and cheese. Drizzle All-Purpose Tahini Dressing over top. Serves 1 (serving size: about 3 cups)

CALORIES 366; **FAT** 15g (sat 3g, unsat 11g); **PROTEIN** 16g; **CARB** 48g; **FIBER** 16g; **SUGARS** 8g (added sugars 0g); **SODIUM** 503mg; **CALC** 27% DV; **POTASSIUM** 35% DV

PRO TIP:
HIT UP THE BULK BIN SECTION OF YOUR GROCERY STORE FOR WHOLE GRAINS, NUTS, SEEDS, AND PULSES TO SAVE MONEY AND REDUCE PACKAGING WASTE.

THE 5 PILLARS OF THE *COOKING LIGHT* PRETOX

REGARDLESS OF THE TIME OF YEAR, IF YOU VEER OFF YOUR USUAL COURSE OF HEALTHY EATING, USE THESE GUIDING PRINCIPLES TO HELP GET YOU BACK ON TRACK.

1. SLASH ADDED SUGARS.
The average American consumes around 17 teaspoons of added sugars (sugars or syrups added to foods or beverages during preparation or processing) every day—that's 270 calories and more than double the amount recommended by the American Heart Association. Eating too much added sugar will not only leave you feeling sluggish; it has been linked to obesity and a higher risk of cardiovascular disease.

2. LET PRODUCE TAKE PRECEDENCE.
Move plants to the center of the plate and allow meat, nuts, and whole grains to take supporting roles. Each day of our pretox delivers between 3 and 5 cups of vegetables and 1½ to 3 cups of fruit (experts recommend 2 to 3 cups of vegetables and 1½ to 2 cups of fruit daily). The extra volume and fiber will help keep you full and satisfied.

3. CHOOSE WHOLE OVER REFINED GRAINS.
Half of the grains we eat should be whole, says the USDA, but we say go all in. More and more research says that regularly eating whole grains could help protect against cardiovascular disease, metabolic syndrome, type 2 diabetes, and certain cancers, including colon cancer. Diversify your grain selection and reap the benefits of fiber, disease-fighting phytosterols, and a slew of vitamins and minerals, including B vitamins, vitamin E, and magnesium.

4. FOCUS ON FUNCTIONAL FOODS.
A functional food is one that delivers benefits beyond basic nutrition and may lower your risk of chronic disease. For example, cold-water fish such as salmon has high amounts of omega-3 fatty acids, which can lower risk of heart disease and improve brain function. Find salmon along with berries, probiotic-rich yogurt, nuts, and turmeric throughout the pretox, all of which are functional foods.

5. DITCH THE BOOZE.
One of the easiest ways to cut calories is to lay off the alcohol; plus, it helps you stay hydrated and keep your head clear. If you're used to a night-cap, try getting a fizzy fix from kombucha instead. Although this fermented tea beverage contains trace amounts of alcohol (typically less than 0.5% per serving), it's rich in gut-healthy probiotics and typically low in sugar.

Dinner

Make Ahead

Turmeric-Roasted Chicken with Farro

Hands-on: 10 min. Total: 35 min.

½ cup uncooked farro
1 cup water
2 tablespoons plain 2% reduced-fat Greek yogurt
1 garlic clove, minced
½ teaspoon ground turmeric
½ teaspoon paprika
⅜ teaspoon kosher salt, divided
¼ teaspoon black pepper, divided
2 (4-ounce) boneless, skinless chicken breasts
Cooking spray
4 ounces Brussels sprouts, trimmed and halved (about 1 cup)
2 teaspoons olive oil
⅛ teaspoon garlic powder

1. Preheat oven to 425°F. Combine farro and 1 cup water in a saucepan over medium-low; cover, and cook 25 minutes or until tender. Drain.
2. Mix yogurt, garlic, turmeric, paprika, ¼ teaspoon salt, and ⅛ teaspoon pepper. Add chicken; thoroughly coat with yogurt mixture.
3. Place chicken on 1 half of a foil-lined baking sheet coated with cooking spray. Arrange Brussels sprouts on other half. Toss sprouts with oil, remaining ⅛ teaspoon salt, remaining ⅛ teaspoon pepper, and garlic powder. Bake at 425°F for 18 to 20 minutes, tossing once halfway through.
4. Place ½ cup farro on a plate. Top with 1 chicken breast; serve with sprouts. Reserve remaining chicken breast and farro for Day 2 Lunch. Serves 1 (serving size: ½ cup farro, 4 ounces chicken, and 4 ounces Brussels sprouts)

CALORIES 382; **FAT** 14g (sat 2g, unsat 9g); **PROTEIN** 35g; **CARB** 38g; **FIBER** 8g; **SUGARS** 3g (added sugars 0g); **SODIUM** 566mg; **CALC** 7% DV; **POTASSIUM** 24% DV

DAY 2

Total: 1,465 calories

Breakfast

Fast • Gluten Free
Vegetarian

Butternut-Kale Frittata

Hands-on: 10 min. Total: 10 min.
Frittatas are some of the most efficient vehicles for leftover vegetables. Here, we combine roasted butternut squash with quick-cooking kale for a fiber-rich breakfast duo. A touch of dairy lends custardlike creaminess to the egg mixture.

Cooking spray
1 cup chopped lacinato kale
1 cup roasted butternut squash (from Day 1 Lunch, page 331)
2 large eggs
2 teaspoons plain 2% reduced-fat Greek yogurt
⅛ teaspoon kosher salt
⅛ teaspoon freshly ground black pepper
¼ ripe avocado, sliced

1. Preheat broiler to high with oven rack in upper middle position.
2. Heat an 8-inch ovenproof skillet over medium. Coat pan with cooking spray. Add kale and roasted butternut squash; cook 2 to 3 minutes.
3. Whisk together eggs, yogurt, salt, and pepper. Add eggs to pan, and cook 2 minutes, stirring slowly and tilting the skillet a few times so runny parts hit the pan.
4. Place pan under broiler; broil 1 minute or until eggs are almost set. Top frittata with avocado. Serves 1 (serving size: 1 frittata)

CALORIES 332; **FAT** 19g (sat 4g, unsat 13g); **PROTEIN** 17g; **CARB** 29g; **FIBER** 11g; **SUGARS** 6g (added sugars 0g); **SODIUM** 403mg; **CALC** 18% DV; **POTASSIUM** 30% DV

Lunch

Make Ahead

Turmeric Chicken-Stuffed Peppers

Hands-on: 10 min. Total: 40 min.

1 red bell pepper
Cooking spray
4 ounces Turmeric-Roasted Chicken (from Day 1 Dinner, page 332)
½ cup cooked farro (from Day 1 Dinner, page 332)
2 teaspoons olive oil
2 tablespoons crumbled feta cheese
1 tablespoon chopped fresh parsley
1 tablespoon fresh lemon juice

1. Preheat oven to 350°F.
2. Cut pepper in half lengthwise; discard seeds and membranes, leaving stem intact. Place pepper halves, cut sides up, in a small baking dish. Coat with cooking spray, and cover with foil. Bake at 350°F for 25 minutes.
3. Chop chicken, and place in a bowl. Stir in farro and olive oil. Divide mixture evenly into both bell pepper halves. Bake at 350°F, uncovered, for 6 to 7 minutes, until chicken mixture is heated through.
4. Sprinkle feta cheese, parsley, and lemon juice evenly over top. Serves 1 (serving size: 2 stuffed bell pepper halves)

CALORIES 426; **FAT** 18g (sat 5g, unsat 10g); **PROTEIN** 35g; **CARB** 37g; **FIBER** 6g; **SUGARS** 7g (added sugars 0g); **SODIUM** 476mg; **CALC** 13% DV; **POTASSIUM** 20% DV

SNACKS

MORNING: ½ cup plain 2% reduced-fat Greek yogurt with ½ cup frozen thawed berries (117 calories)

AFTERNOON: 8 walnut halves (105 calories)

Dinner

Gluten Free • Make Ahead

Supercharged Salmon Salad

Hands-on: 15 min. Total: 35 min.
Aim to eat salmon (or other fatty fish) twice a week to maximize your heart-protective and brain-boosting benefits.

1 cup water
½ cup uncooked quinoa, rinsed and drained
¼ teaspoon kosher salt, divided
1 (6-ounce) wild salmon fillet
Cooking spray
½ teaspoon olive oil
⅛ teaspoon black pepper
2 cups roughly chopped lacinato kale
3 ounces shredded Brussels sprouts (about 1 cup)
2 tablespoons All-Purpose Tahini Dressing (page 330)
⅓ cup steamed and peeled beets

1. Bring 1 cup water and quinoa to a boil in a small saucepan. Reduce heat, cover, and simmer 15 minutes or until liquid is absorbed. Remove pan from heat; let stand 5 minutes. Stir in ⅛ teaspoon salt.
2. Preheat broiler to high with oven rack in upper middle position.
3. Place salmon on a foil-lined baking sheet coated with cooking spray. Rub salmon with oil, remaining ⅛ teaspoon salt, and pepper. Broil for 6 minutes.
4. Place kale, Brussels sprouts, and All-Purpose Tahini Dressing in a bowl. Use your hands to massage dressing into kale and Brussels sprouts. Mix in ¼ cup cooked quinoa (reserve remaining for Day 3 Dinner) and beets. Top with salmon. Serves 1 (serving size: about 3½ cups)

CALORIES 485; **FAT** 23g (sat 3g, unsat 17g); **PROTEIN** 44g; **CARB** 30g; **FIBER** 8g; **SUGARS** 8g (added sugars 0g); **SODIUM** 515mg; **CALC** 14% DV; **POTASSIUM** 47% DV

DAY 3

Total: 1,455 calories

Breakfast

Fast • Gluten Free
Vegetarian

Kale-Ginger Smoothie

Hands-on: 5 min. Total: 5 min
Smoothies are a great way to front-load your day with produce and nutrition. Just one serving of this power breakfast offers about two-thirds of the day's calcium and nearly a quarter of potassium in a low-calorie package. Chia seeds amp up fiber and protein, plus they're one of the richest plant sources of heart-healthy alpha-linoleic acid (an omega-3 fatty acid).

1 cup roughly torn lacinato kale
1 medium-sized frozen banana
1 cup unsweetened almond milk
½ cup plain 2% reduced-fat Greek yogurt
1 teaspoon chia seeds
¼ ripe avocado
½ teaspoon sliced peeled fresh ginger

1. Place all ingredients in a blender; process until smooth. Serves 1 (serving size: about 1¾ cups)

CALORIES 331; **FAT** 14g (sat 3g, unsat 8g); **PROTEIN** 16g; **CARB** 40g; **FIBER** 9g; **SUGARS** 20g (added sugars 0g); **SODIUM** 224mg; **CALC** 63% DV; **POTASSIUM** 22% DV

SNACKS

MORNING: 1 medium apple with 5 walnut halves (160 calories)

AFTERNOON: 3 tablespoons hummus with 1 cup sliced cucumber (90 calories)

Lunch

Fast • Gluten Free
Make Ahead

Crispy Tuna Cakes

Hands-on: 10 min. Total: 15 min.

½ cup old-fashioned rolled oats
1 large egg, lightly beaten
1 (2.6-ounce) pouch solid white tuna in water
1 teaspoon Dijon mustard
2 teaspoons chopped fresh parsley, plus more for garnish
½ teaspoon grated lemon rind
⅛ teaspoon kosher salt
⅛ teaspoon black pepper
¼ teaspoon garlic powder
2 teaspoons olive oil
2 cups arugula
2 tablespoons fresh lemon juice, divided
1 tablespoon hummus

1. Place oats in a food processor. Pulse until ground, about 10 seconds. Transfer to a bowl. Add egg, tuna, mustard, 2 teaspoons parsley, lemon rind, salt, pepper, and garlic powder. Mix to combine.
2. Fill a ⅓-cup dry measuring cup with tuna mixture. Invert onto work surface; pat into a ¾-inch-thick patty. Repeat with remaining tuna mixture.
3. Heat oil in a large skillet over medium. Add tuna cakes to pan; cook 3 to 4 minutes on each side, until bottoms are golden.
4. Arrange arugula on a plate. Toss with 1 tablespoon lemon juice. Place tuna cakes over arugula. Add hummus and remaining 1 tablespoon lemon juice. Garnish with chopped fresh parsley, if desired. Serves 1 (serving size: 2 tuna cakes, 2 cups arugula, and 1 tablespoon hummus)

CALORIES 423; **FAT** 20g (sat 4g, unsat 15g); **PROTEIN** 30g; **CARB** 33g; **FIBER** 6g; **SUGARS** 2g (added sugars 0g); **SODIUM** 614mg; **CALC** 9% DV; **POTASSIUM** 11% DV

Dinner

Fast • Gluten Free
Vegetarian

Poached Egg Power Bowls

Hands-on: 10 min. Total: 10 min.
This 10-minute dinner features the power trio of protein-packed legumes, seeds, and crisp greens. The runny, nutrient-rich egg yolk doubles as a silky dressing in this vegetarian main.

2 quarts water
1 teaspoon ground turmeric
1 tablespoon white vinegar
1 large egg
1 cup arugula
1 teaspoon olive oil
½ cup cooked lentils (from Day 1 Lunch, page 331)
½ cup cooked quinoa (from Day 2 Dinner, page 333)
⅓ ripe avocado, peeled and sliced
¼ teaspoon kosher salt
¼ teaspoon freshly ground black pepper

1. Bring 2 quarts water, turmeric, and vinegar to a gentle simmer in a medium saucepan over medium. Adjust heat as necessary to maintain a gentle simmer.
2. Using a whisk, swirl water in a circular motion until a whirlpool forms. Gently crack egg into center of whirlpool. Cook until white is set, about 3 minutes. Using a slotted spoon, remove egg from pan; place on a plate lined with paper towels.
3. Toss arugula with olive oil in a medium bowl. Arrange lentils, quinoa, and avocado in bowl. Sprinkle salt and pepper over top. Place egg in center of bowl. Serves 1 (serving size: 1 bowl)

CALORIES 451; **FAT** 21g (sat 4g, unsat 16g); **PROTEIN** 21g; **CARB** 47g; **FIBER** 15g; **SUGARS** 4g (added sugars 0g); **SODIUM** 570mg; **CALC** 10% DV; **POTASSIUM** 28% DV

HOW TO MAKE FAUX-FRIED CHICKEN

By Gina Homolka

Save yourself the calories and still bring the family together for crunchy, irresistible "fried" chicken.

When I was a kid, I loved the nights that my mom made good old-fashioned fried chicken—it's crunchy, it's juicy, and it's still one of my favorites. What I don't love, however, are the fat and the calories (not to mention the mess!) that come with frying. My light and easy solution is to bake (aka "faux fry") skinless chicken drumsticks instead. My kids love them—they come out moist and delicious on the inside, and the seasoned panko and Parmesan crust cooks up to a crispy golden coating on the outside. And trust me, no one will miss the skin.

One-dish dinners (often on a sheet pan) are by far my favorite way to cook on busy weeknights. Technically this dish uses two sheet pans, but lining the pans with foil makes cleanup a snap, so this is still a great weeknight meal. The key for making this work is timing. I start the chicken, which takes more time to bake, then I add the sweet potatoes (a healthier alternative to French fries), and when they're just about done, I add the broccoli. And then (voilà!) everything comes out at the same time. This entire veggie-packed meal is ready in an hour.

Sheet Pan Parmesan "Fried" Chicken with Broccoli and Sweet Potato Wedges

Hands-on: 30 min. Total: 1 hr.

8 (3½-ounce) chicken drumsticks, skinned
1 tablespoon fresh lemon juice
1⅛ teaspoons kosher salt, divided
½ teaspoon poultry seasoning
1 teaspoon garlic powder, divided
⅛ teaspoon freshly ground black pepper
2 large eggs, lightly beaten
1 cup panko (Japanese breadcrumbs)
1½ ounces Parmesan cheese, grated (about ⅓ cup)
1 teaspoon dried oregano
1 teaspoon dried parsley flakes (optional)
Cooking spray
2 (7-ounce) sweet potatoes, each cut into 8 wedges
2 tablespoons olive oil, divided
½ teaspoon paprika
½ teaspoon chili powder
7 cups broccoli florets (about 12 ounces)
1 garlic clove, crushed or grated
5 lemon wedges

1. Preheat oven to 425°F.
2. Place chicken in a large bowl. Drizzle with lemon juice, and sprinkle with ⅜ teaspoon salt, poultry seasoning, ½ teaspoon garlic powder, and black pepper; toss to combine.
3. Place eggs in a shallow dish. Combine panko, Parmesan, oregano, and parsley, if using, in another shallow dish. Dip each drumstick in eggs then dredge in panko mixture. Place drumsticks on a rimmed baking sheet coated with cooking spray, and discard remaining egg and panko mixture. Coat tops of drumsticks with cooking spray. Bake at 425°F for 15 minutes.
4. Combine potatoes, 1 tablespoon oil, remaining ½ teaspoon garlic powder, paprika, chili powder, and ⅜ teaspoon salt; toss to coat. Arrange potatoes on one half of another rimmed baking sheet coated with cooking spray. Place in oven with chicken, and bake at 425°F for 10 minutes.
5. Combine broccoli, remaining 1 tablespoon oil, garlic clove, and remaining ⅜ teaspoon salt. Remove baking sheet with potatoes from oven; turn potatoes over, and add broccoli to other half of pan. Place in oven with chicken, and bake at 425°F for 20 minutes or until chicken and potatoes are done. Squeeze 1 lemon wedge over broccoli. Serve remaining lemon wedges with the meal. Serves 4 (serving size: 2 drumsticks, 4 potato wedges, and about 1 cup broccoli)

CALORIES 425; FAT 17g (sat 4g, unsat 12g); PROTEIN 34g; CARB 35g; FIBER 7g; SUGARS 7g (added sugars 0g); SODIUM 902mg; CALC 19% DV; POTASSIUM 31% DV

A CRUCIFER WITH CHARACTER

Think cabbage is a little too ordinary? Chef Jenn Louis, the queen of greens, is here to convince you that with the right techniques and accompaniments, the humble cabbage is nothing short of magnificent.

Chef Jenn Louis grew up in the 1970s with limp, overboiled cabbage and Brussels sprouts. "People's education on ingredients and how to cook wasn't as developed then," she says. "We learned later that roasting, frying, searing, sautéing, and eating cabbage raw is really delicious."

Cabbage was one of the first subjects Louis tackled for her latest cookbook, *The Book of Greens*, "because it's easy, inexpensive, and so versatile." She always keeps a head or two in her fridge (wrapped in plastic, they stay fresh for up to two weeks). Cabbage is also incredibly healthy—brimming with vitamin C; fiber; and isothiocyanates, compounds that research has linked with a lower risk of cancer.

Once considered bland and boring, cabbage is now undeniably cool—a key player in the fermentation trend (kraut and kimchi) and the center-of-the-plate, knife-and-fork vegetable movement (cabbage "steaks" and wedges). The potential is endless and so delicious, Louis says.

Make Ahead

Pork and Broken Rice Cabbage Rolls

Hands-on: 15 min. Total: 1 hr. 15 min.
Though typically thought of as an Eastern European dish, cabbage rolls can actually be found in several cuisines, Louis says. She adopts a Far East approach here, using soy sauce, ginger, sesame, and broken jasmine rice. Broken rice is exactly what it sounds like—fragments of rice grains. Look for it in Asian markets, or use standard jasmine rice.

DRESSING
1/4 cup reduced-sodium soy sauce
1/4 cup water
2 teaspoons Sriracha chili sauce
1 teaspoon rice wine vinegar
1 teaspoon minced fresh ginger
1/2 teaspoon toasted sesame seeds
1/4 teaspoon toasted sesame oil
1/4 teaspoon sugar
2 garlic cloves, thinly sliced
2 green onions, thinly sliced

CABBAGE ROLLS
8 cups water
1 teaspoon kosher salt, divided
12 large inner savoy cabbage leaves
3/4 teaspoon toasted sesame oil
1 cup uncooked broken or regular jasmine rice
3/4 cup finely chopped yellow onion
1/4 cup chopped fresh cilantro leaves and stems
1 tablespoon minced peeled fresh ginger
1/2 teaspoon crushed red pepper
1 pound ground pork
1 cup unsalted chicken stock
1/2 teaspoon fish sauce

1. To prepare the dressing, combine first 10 ingredients in a bowl, stirring with a whisk. Let stand at room temperature 1 hour.
2. Preheat oven to 375°F.
3. To prepare cabbage rolls, bring 8 cups water and 3/4 teaspoon salt to a boil in a large stockpot. Add cabbage leaves; cook 3 minutes or until leaves are very tender. Drain; plunge leaves into a bowl filled with ice water. Let stand 2 minutes; drain and pat dry. Remove center rib of each leaf with a knife.
4. Combine remaining 1/4 teaspoon salt, 1/4 teaspoon of the oil, rice, and next 5 ingredients. Divide and shape pork mixture into 12 oval-shaped meatballs, each about the width of a cabbage leaf. Place 1 cabbage leaf on a work surface with the stem end facing toward you. Place 1 meatball in center of leaf. Fold sides of leaf over filling; roll up. Place, seam side down, in an 11- x 7-inch glass or ceramic baking dish. Repeat procedure with remaining cabbage and meatballs.
5. Combine remaining 1/2 teaspoon oil, stock, and fish sauce in a glass measure; pour over cabbage rolls in dish. Cover with foil; bake at 375°F for 45 minutes. Remove foil; bake at 375°F for 15 minutes, basting cabbage rolls with pan juices every 5 minutes. Arrange cabbage rolls on a platter; spoon remaining pan juices over top. Serve with dressing. Serves 6 (serving size: 2 cabbage rolls and about 1 tablespoon dressing)

CALORIES 355; **FAT** 17g (sat 6g, unsat 9g); **PROTEIN** 18g; **CARB** 32g; **FIBER** 2g; **SUGARS** 4g (added sugars 0g); **SODIUM** 644mg; **CALC** 6% DV; **POTASSIUM** 13% DV

Cabbage Salad with Miso Vinaigrette

Hands-on: 10 min. Total: 10 min.
Fresh cabbage is all about crunch; the more texture, the better. Napa cabbage can absorb bold vinaigrettes without losing its crisp bite. Carrots, red onion, and daikon radish add even more crunch to the salad.

3 tablespoons unseasoned rice vinegar
2 tablespoons red miso paste
1 tablespoon canola oil
1 tablespoon toasted sesame oil
2 teaspoons reduced-sodium soy sauce
2 teaspoons honey
1 garlic clove, thinly sliced
1 cup julienne-cut carrot (about 2 medium)
3/4 cup thinly vertically sliced red onion
1 (1-pound) head napa cabbage, coarsely chopped (about 5 cups)
1 medium daikon radish, peeled, halved lengthwise, and thinly sliced (about 8 ounces)
1/4 teaspoon kosher salt
1/4 teaspoon freshly ground black pepper
1/2 cup roasted unsalted cashews
1/4 cup fresh cilantro leaves
2 tablespoons toasted sesame seeds

1. Combine first 7 ingredients in a small bowl, stirring with a whisk. Combine carrot, onion, cabbage, and radish in a large bowl. Add vinegar mixture, salt, and pepper to cabbage mixture; toss well to coat. Sprinkle cashews, cilantro, and sesame seeds over salad. Serves 8 (serving size: about 2/3 cup)

CALORIES 172; **FAT** 12g (sat 2g, unsat 9g);
PROTEIN 4g; **CARB** 14g; **FIBER** 3g; **SUGARS** 6g
(added sugars 2g); **SODIUM** 249mg; **CALC** 10% DV;
POTASSIUM 8% DV

Brussels Sprouts Giardiniera

Hands-on: 15 min. Total: 4 days
Now that we know to roast or shred fresh Brussels sprouts rather than boil them, the possibilities are endless. The next frontier, according to Louis, is to pickle for giardiniera. Try this condiment on sandwiches, baked fish, or a charcuterie or cheese board.

4 cups sliced fresh Brussels sprouts (about 1 pound)
2 cups thinly sliced carrots
2 cups diced fennel bulb
1 cup thinly sliced celery
1/2 cup thinly sliced shallots
1/4 cup kosher salt
1 large jalapeño, thinly sliced
1 cup Champagne vinegar
1 cup canola oil
2 tablespoons fresh oregano leaves
1 1/2 teaspoons crushed red pepper
1/2 teaspoon celery seeds
2 garlic cloves, thinly sliced
1/2 cup water (optional)

1. Place first 7 ingredients in a large bowl, tossing to combine. Cover with plastic wrap; chill 8 hours or overnight. Drain; rinse well. Drain.
2. Combine vinegar, oil, oregano, red pepper, celery seeds, and garlic in a bowl, stirring with a whisk until blended. Pack vegetable mixture into 1 (2-quart) jar; pour vinegar mixture over vegetable mixture. Add up to 1/2 cup water as needed to cover vegetables. Cover; refrigerate 3 days. Drain before serving. Serves 16 (serving size: 1/2 cup)

CALORIES 60; **FAT** 4g (sat 0g, unsat 3g);
PROTEIN 1g; **CARB** 7g; **FIBER** 2g; **SUGARS** 2g
(added sugars 0g); **SODIUM** 210mg; **CALC** 3% DV;
POTASSIUM 7% DV

Red Cabbage Agrodolce with Dried Cherries

Hands-on: 20 min. Total: 20 min.
This sweet-and-sour cabbage side will perk up any pot roast or pork loin. Plump dried cherries are the tart, hidden gems in the dish. A little butter rounds out the acidity and helps bind everything together.

1/4 cup unsweetened dried tart cherries
1/4 cup olive oil
1 1/2 cups (1/4-inch) diced fennel bulb
1/2 cup (1/4-inch) diced yellow onion
2 small garlic cloves, thinly sliced
1 fresh rosemary sprig
1 (1 3/4-pound) head red cabbage, shredded (about 8 cups)
1/2 teaspoon kosher salt
1 tablespoon sugar
1 tablespoon red wine vinegar
1 tablespoon unsalted butter

1. Place cherries in a small bowl; cover with boiling water. Let stand 10 minutes; drain.
2. Heat oil in a medium saucepan over medium. Add fennel and onion; sauté 3 to 5 minutes or until translucent. Add garlic and rosemary; cook 1 minute, stirring constantly (do not let garlic brown). Add cabbage and salt; cook 5 minutes or until wilted, stirring occasionally. Stir in cherries, sugar, vinegar, and butter. Remove pan from heat; discard rosemary. Serves 6 (serving size: 3/4 cup)

CALORIES 176; **FAT** 11g (sat 2g, unsat 8g);
PROTEIN 3g; **CARB** 19g; **FIBER** 4g; **SUGARS** 11g
(added sugars 2g); **SODIUM** 208mg; **CALC** 8% DV;
POTASSIUM 12% DV

Fast

Cabbage Okonomiyaki (Pancakes)

Hands-on: 15 min. Total: 30 min.
Find togarashi (also called Japanese seven spice) at Asian markets.

1 pound green cabbage, finely shredded (about 5 cups)
4 teaspoons shichimi togarashi (Japanese spice blend), divided
1¹/₂ teaspoons sugar
¹/₂ teaspoon kosher salt
¹/₃ cup thinly sliced green onions, divided
5 large eggs, lightly beaten
4 center-cut bacon slices, cooked and crumbled
2.9 ounces all-purpose flour (about ²/₃ cup)
2 tablespoons canola oil, divided
¹/₄ cup canola mayonnaise
1 tablespoon unseasoned rice vinegar
1 tablespoon water

1. Preheat oven to 200°F.
2. Combine cabbage, 1 tablespoon togarashi, sugar, and salt in a bowl; let stand 15 minutes, stirring occasionally. Stir in 3 tablespoons green onions, eggs, and bacon. Fold in flour.
3. Heat 1½ teaspoons oil in an 8-inch nonstick skillet over medium-high. Add 1 cup cabbage mixture; flatten with a spatula. Cook 2 to 3 minutes on each side or until golden brown. Place pancake on a baking sheet; keep warm in 200°F oven. Repeat procedure 3 times with remaining 1½ tablespoons oil and cabbage mixture.
4. Combine remaining 1 teaspoon togarashi, mayonnaise, vinegar, and 1 tablespoon water in a bowl; drizzle over each pancake. Top with remaining green onions. Serves 4 (serving size: 1 pancake and about 1 tablespoon mayonnaise mixture)

CALORIES 346; FAT 20g (sat 4g, unsat 16g); PROTEIN 15g; CARB 26g; FIBER 4g; SUGARS 6g (added sugars 2g); SODIUM 602mg; CALC 10% DV; POTASSIUM 11% DV

Gluten Free • Vegetarian

Roasted Cabbage Wedges with Orange and Caraway

Hands-on: 15 min. Total: 1 hr.
These slow-roasted wedges will make a cabbage convert out of anyone and are a beautiful first course sub for the usual appetizer salad. Leave the core intact so the wedges hold their shape.

1 teaspoon caraway seeds, crushed
1 teaspoon grated orange rind
¹/₂ teaspoon crushed red pepper
³/₈ teaspoon kosher salt, divided
¹/₄ teaspoon ground turmeric
3 tablespoons unsalted butter, softened
1 (3-pound) head green cabbage
1 tablespoon olive oil
Cooking spray
2 tablespoons chopped fresh dill

1. Preheat oven to 350°F.
2. Combine caraway, rind, pepper, ⅛ teaspoon salt, turmeric, and butter in a small bowl. Chill 5 minutes or until slightly firm.
3. Remove outer leaves of cabbage; discard. Cut cabbage vertically into quarters; cut each quarter in half to equal 8 wedges (leave core intact). Brush cabbage wedges evenly with oil. Heat a large skillet over medium. Coat pan with cooking spray. Add cabbage wedges to pan; cook 3 minutes on each side or until browned.
4. Arrange cabbage wedges, cut sides up, on a baking sheet. Spread half of butter mixture evenly over cut sides of cabbage. Bake at 350°F for 25 minutes. Remove pan from oven; spread remaining half of butter mixture over wedges. Bake at 350°F for 20 minutes or until tender. Sprinkle with remaining ¼ teaspoon salt and dill. Serve immediately. Serves 8 (serving size: 1 cabbage wedge)

CALORIES 106; FAT 6g (sat 3g, unsat 3g); PROTEIN 2g; CARB 10g; FIBER 4g; SUGARS 6g (added sugars 0g); SODIUM 131mg; CALC 9% DV; POTASSIUM 11% DV

GIRLS NIGHT IN

Throw a casual dinner party that wows guests and keeps your effort to a minimum. Cookbook author and entertaining maven Alison Roman shares dishes from her new book, *Dining In*, along with expert tips for a memorable Middle Eastern–accented spread.

Gluten Free • Vegetarian

Raw and Roasted Carrots and Fennel

Hands-on: 10 min. Total: 35 min.
This salad demonstrates the magic that happens when you showcase both the raw and cooked sides of ingredients.

1 large fennel bulb, halved lengthwise and divided
1 bunch small carrots with tops, divided
1 bunch scallions, halved crosswise and divided
5 tablespoons olive oil, divided
½ teaspoon kosher salt, divided
½ teaspoon black pepper, divided
3 tablespoons fresh lemon juice
1 cup chopped fresh cilantro (tender leaves and stems, from 1 bunch)
3 ounces feta cheese, crumbled (about ¾ cup)
¼ cup toasted unsalted pistachios, chopped

1. Preheat oven to 425°F.
2. Cut one of the fennel bulb halves into ½-inch-thick wedges, and place on a parchment paper–lined baking sheet. Trim tops from carrots, and chop tops to equal 1 cup; set aside. Scrub carrots (do not peel), and add half of carrots to fennel wedges. Add half of scallions and 3 tablespoons olive oil. Sprinkle with ¼ teaspoon each salt and pepper; toss to coat. Roast at 425°F for 18 minutes or until carrots and fennel are completely tender and scallions begin to char, tossing occasionally. Remove from oven; cool to room temperature.
3. Thinly slice remaining carrots, fennel, and scallions diagonally into 3-inch-long pieces; place in a large bowl.
4. Add cooled roasted vegetables to raw vegetables in bowl. Add juice, cilantro, and carrot tops; toss. Sprinkle with remaining ¼ teaspoon each salt and pepper; drizzle with remaining 2 tablespoons olive oil, and top with feta and pistachios. Serve immediately, or let stand at room temperature 1 hour. Serves 8 (serving size: ¾ cup)

CALORIES 168; **FAT** 13g (sat 3g, unsat 9g); **PROTEIN** 4g; **CARB** 11g; **FIBER** 3g; **SUGARS** 5g (added sugars 0g); **SODIUM** 276mg; **CALC** 10% DV; **POTASSIUM** 12% DV

Gluten Free

Paprika-Rubbed Sheet-Tray Chicken

Hands-on: 5 min. Total: 1 hr. 15 min.
Roman also uses this paprika rub to smear on pork roasts or to marinate chicken.

1 (3½- to 4-pound) chicken, spatchcocked
1 tablespoon fennel seeds
2 teaspoons hot paprika
1 teaspoon kosher salt
1 teaspoon smoked paprika
1 teaspoon black pepper
2 garlic cloves, finely grated
¼ cup olive oil
2 lemons, quartered

1. Preheat oven to 325°F.
2. Pat chicken dry with paper towels. Grind fennel seeds in a spice mill or with a mortar and pestle. Combine fennel, hot paprika, salt, smoked paprika, black pepper, garlic, and olive oil in a medium bowl; rub spice mixture all over chicken. Rub any leftover spice mixture onto lemon quarters.
3. Place chicken, breast side up, on a rimmed baking sheet or in a 12-inch ovenproof skillet; scatter lemons around chicken. Roast at 325°F for 1 hour or until chicken is tender, lemons are soft and jammy, and a meat thermometer inserted into thickest portion of breast registers 160°F, basting chicken with drippings every 30 minutes. Remove from oven; rest 15 minutes. Squeeze lemons over chicken, or serve lemons with warm chicken. Serves 6 (serving size: about 3 ounces chicken)

CALORIES 261; **FAT** 14g (sat 2g, unsat 11g); **PROTEIN** 32g; **CARB** 1g; **FIBER** 1g; **SUGARS** 0g; **SODIUM** 437mg; **CALC** 3% DV; **POTASSIUM** 11% DV

Make Ahead • Vegetarian

Brown Butter Cake with Cocoa

Hands-on: 15 min. Total: 1 hr. 50 min.
A good bit of salt enhances all the flavors here.

Cooking spray
6 tablespoons unsalted butter (3 ounces)
7¹/₂ ounces all-purpose flour (about 1³/₄ cups)
¹/₂ cup unsweetened cocoa
¹/₂ cup packed light or dark brown sugar
1³/₄ teaspoons baking powder
¹/₂ teaspoon baking soda
1 teaspoon kosher salt
¹/₂ cup plus 1 tablespoon granulated sugar, divided
1¹/₄ cups whole buttermilk
2 large eggs
1 teaspoon vanilla extract
2 tablespoons coconut oil
¹/₂ cup unsweetened coconut flakes

1. Preheat oven to 350°F.
2. Spray a 9-inch round cake pan with 2-inch sides or a 9-inch springform pan with cooking spray. Line pan with parchment paper; spray with cooking spray.
3. Melt butter in a small saucepan over medium-low, swirling pan occasionally, until butter is foamy and starting to brown on the bottom, about 5 minutes. (It should smell like hazelnuts.) Scrape browned bits from bottom; remove from heat, and cool 5 minutes.
4. Whisk together flour, cocoa, brown sugar, baking powder, baking soda, salt, and ½ cup granulated sugar in a large bowl until no lumps of brown sugar remain. (Break up lumps with hands, if necessary.)
5. Whisk together buttermilk, eggs, and vanilla in a medium bowl until no visible bits of egg remain. Add buttermilk mixture to flour mixture,

whisking just until blended (a few streaks of flour are fine). Add brown butter and coconut oil, and whisk just until blended.
6. Pour batter into prepared pan; sprinkle with coconut flakes and remaining 1 tablespoon granulated sugar. Bake at 350°F for 35 minutes or until coconut is golden brown, cake pulls away from the sides of the pan, and a wooden pick inserted into center of cake comes out clean. Cool cake in pan 10 minutes. Remove cake from pan to a wire rack; cool to room temperature. Serves 12 (serving size: 1 slice)

CALORIES 258; **FAT** 13g (sat 7g, unsat 5g); **PROTEIN** 5g; **CARB** 34g; **FIBER** 2g; **SUGARS** 17g (added sugars 14g); **SODIUM** 330mg; **CALC** 6% DV; **POTASSIUM** 3% DV

Fast • Gluten Free
Vegetarian

Crunchy Greens with Radish

Hands-on: 10 min. Total: 15 min.
Letting the raw shallot stand with the salt and vinegar pickles it slightly and mellows the harshness. Long spears of romaine make for a dramatic presentation. Once it's brought to the table, you can coarsely chop the lettuce for easier serving.

1 shallot, thinly sliced into rings
2 tablespoons white or red wine vinegar
¹/₂ teaspoon kosher salt, divided
¹/₂ teaspoon black pepper, divided
¹/₃ cup fresh pomegranate arils (from about ¹/₂ pomegranate)
2 tablespoons olive oil
1 tablespoon pomegranate molasses or honey
1 small head romaine or other long-leaf lettuce (such as green leaf)
1 watermelon radish or black radish (or 3 red radishes), thinly sliced into rounds
¹/₂ cup chopped fresh flat-leaf parsley (tender stems and leaves)

1. Combine shallot and vinegar in a small bowl. Stir in ¼ teaspoon each salt and pepper, and let stand 5 minutes.
2. Stir together pomegranate arils, olive oil, and pomegranate molasses in a small bowl. Stir in remaining ¼ teaspoon each salt and pepper; set aside.
3. Remove and discard any limp, larger leaves on the outside of lettuce head, and trim end of lettuce. Quarter lettuce lengthwise.
4. Arrange lettuce on a large platter or divide between 2 plates. Scatter radish slices and parsley over lettuce. Spoon shallots and any liquid over salad, and top with pomegranate mixture. Serves 6 (serving size: ¾ cup)

CALORIES 85; **FAT** 5g (sat 1g, unsat 4g); **PROTEIN** 2g; **CARB** 10g; **FIBER** 2g; **SUGARS** 4g (added sugars 2g); **SODIUM** 175mg; **CALC** 4% DV; **POTASSIUM** 8% DV

Staff Favorite • Gluten Free
Make Ahead • Vegetarian

Maple-Sumac Roasted Walnuts

Hands-on: 5 min. Total: 35 min.
Here's a perfectly simple and delicious snack. A little sumac adds a bright piney-citrusy note. Look for it at specialty spice stores. A tablespoon of lemon rind can sub for sumac, if you prefer.

4 cups raw walnuts (about 12 ounces)
¹/₃ cup pure maple syrup
¹/₄ cup raw white sesame seeds
2 tablespoons olive oil
¹/₂ teaspoon ground red pepper (optional)
¹/₂ teaspoon black pepper
1¹/₂ teaspoons kosher salt, divided
1 tablespoon ground sumac

1. Preheat oven to 325°F.
2. Place walnuts on a rimmed baking sheet or in a large ovenproof skillet, and break up walnuts slightly into smaller pieces with your hands. Add maple syrup, sesame seeds, olive oil,

and, if desired, red pepper. Sprinkle with black pepper and 1 teaspoon salt, and toss until evenly coated. **3.** Place in oven, and roast at 325°F, stirring occasionally, until walnuts are golden brown and maple syrup is caramelized, 15 to 20 minutes. Remove from heat, and immediately sprinkle with sumac and remaining ½ teaspoon salt, tossing to coat. Let cool completely before serving, about 10 minutes. Serves 18 (serving size: ½ cup)

CALORIES 329; FAT 17g (sat 2g, unsat 14g); PROTEIN 4g; CARB 7g; FIBER 2g; SUGARS 5g (added sugars 5g); SODIUM 165mg; CALC 3% DV; POTASSIUM 3% DV

Fast • Gluten Free
Make Ahead • Vegetarian

Preserved Lemon Labneh

Hands-on: 5 min. Total: 5 min.
This is the ideal condiment: tangy, rich, salty, and lemony, all without trying too hard. It works well with Greek yogurt or sour cream if you can't find labneh (strained yogurt).

1 cup labneh, Greek yogurt, or sour cream
½ preserved lemon, finely chopped and seeds removed
1 teaspoon black pepper
1 tablespoon extra-virgin olive oil
Pinch of ground turmeric (optional)

1. Combine labneh and preserved lemon in a medium bowl; season with black pepper. Place mixture in a serving bowl. Drizzle with olive oil; sprinkle with ground turmeric, if desired. Serve with flatbreads and vegetables. Serves 8 (serving size: 2 tablespoons labneh)

CALORIES 47; FAT 3g (sat 1g, unsat 2g); PROTEIN 3g; CARB 1g; FIBER 0g; SUGARS 1g (added sugars 0g); SODIUM 308mg; CALC 3% DV; POTASSIUM 0% DV

A COOKING CLUB WE LOVE

Going strong since 2002, this Nebraska group meets monthly to share great stories, delicious food, and powerful bonds.

Fifteen years ago, Jennifer Allen found herself in a new city (Omaha, Nebraska), with a love of healthy cooking but no one to cook with. She was a fan of *Cooking Light* and had been a subscriber for years, so she knew about the rising trend of *Cooking Light* Supper Clubs—groups of like-minded people who found each other through the budding technology of the time, the bulletin boards on cookinglight.com. Allen says she searched the boards for the Midwest and "stumbled upon another gal [Pam Campbell] who also wanted to meet other healthy-cooking ladies." In 2002, she and Campbell gathered some of their friends and got together for their first meeting, bonding through a shared love of food.

Although the online bulletin boards no longer exist, from 1999 to the early 2000s they served as a sort of first wave of social media, allowing people to connect with each other in a virtual realm. Reader Amy Fong Lai is credited with starting the first *Cooking Light* Supper Club in the San Francisco Bay Area in 1999, and quickly more readers in other cities founded their own clubs. The appeal was simple: Meet new people, try new healthy food, and learn new skills.

Allen's supper club has held steady at six members who gather monthly, with herself and Campbell at the core. Occasionally, when a member would move away, the group would absorb a new one to take her place. And though they now share news through email, the way they approach the menu each month hasn't changed much; they take their cues from the recipes in this magazine. They do this even for their December food gift exchange, "be it cranberry liqueur, homemade granolas, delicious caramel sauces and fudge sauces," Allen says. Or even a decadent cake with a secret (vegetable) ingredient, which we've given a makeover here.

Despite busy schedules and competing responsibilities, these women make it a priority to stay connected. "Our group has been through many things—moves, a divorce, marriage, births of children, births of grandchildren, new houses, surgeries, and breakups and get-back-togethers," Allen explains. But they still manage to find time for each other. This fellowship at the table has created cherished memories and lasting friendships that have spanned 15 years. "Our group loves to get together," says Allen, "and has no plans of slowing down."

Parsnip Spice Cake with Caramel Icing

Make Ahead • Vegetarian

Hands-on: 30 min. Total: 1 hr. 45 min.
One of the Omaha supper club's favorite recipes is a parsnip layer cake we published in 2003. We took a look at the recipe and decided to update it with less sugar and more whole grains. A few tweaks later, we had a moist, tender, tastier spice cake capped with an indulgent caramel-flavored cream cheese icing.

CAKE

1 pound parsnips, peeled
½ cup canola oil, divided
¼ cup water
9 ounces whole-wheat pastry flour (about 2½ cups)
1½ teaspoons baking soda
1 teaspoon ground cinnamon
½ teaspoon kosher salt
⅜ teaspoon dried ground ginger
¼ teaspoon ground nutmeg
¾ cup dark brown sugar
1 teaspoon vanilla extract
2 large eggs
¾ cup fat-free buttermilk
Cooking spray

ICING

¼ cup unsalted butter, softened
8 ounces ⅓-less-fat cream cheese, softened
¾ cup powdered sugar
⅓ cup dark brown sugar
½ teaspoon vanilla extract
¼ teaspoon kosher salt
¼ cup chopped pecans, toasted

1. Preheat oven to 350°F.
2. To prepare cake, cut thin ends of parsnips into ¾-inch pieces. Cut wide ends of parsnips lengthwise into quarters. Cut out and discard core from each piece; cut pieces into ¾-inch pieces. Place parsnips on a foil-lined baking sheet. Drizzle with 1 tablespoon oil; toss to coat. Bake at 350°F for 25 minutes or until tender. (Leave oven on.) Place parsnips in a mini food processor with ¼ cup water; process until smooth. Cool slightly.
3. Weigh or lightly spoon flour into dry measuring cups; level with a knife. Whisk together flour and next 5 ingredients (through nutmeg). Place remaining 7 tablespoons oil, ¾ cup brown sugar, 1 teaspoon vanilla, and eggs in a large bowl; beat with a mixer at medium speed until well combined (about 2 minutes). With mixer on low speed, gradually add flour mixture and buttermilk alternately to oil mixture, beginning and ending with flour mixture. Add parsnips; beat just until combined. Spread batter into a 13- x 9-inch light-colored metal baking pan coated with cooking spray. Bake at 350°F for 25 minutes or until a wooden pick inserted in center comes out clean. Cool completely in pan.
4. To prepare icing, place butter and cream cheese in a large bowl; beat with a mixer at medium speed until smooth. Add powdered sugar, ⅓ cup brown sugar, ½ teaspoon vanilla, and ¼ teaspoon salt; beat just until combined. Spread icing over cake; sprinkle with pecans. Serves 15 (serving size: 1 piece)

CALORIES 307; **FAT** 16g (sat 5g, unsat 10g); **PROTEIN** 4g; **CARB** 39g; **FIBER** 3g; **SUGARS** 22g (added sugars 20g); **SODIUM** 314mg; **CALC** 5% DV; **POTASSIUM** 4% DV

THE TEACHER

COOKIES ON DEMAND
By Andrea Nguyen

This make-ahead freezer method will be your new go-to for sweet treats, precisely when you want them.

When it comes to cookies, occasional indulgence is not the same as gluttony. I adopted that philosophical approach years ago from my landlord's fiancée, Diane, a middle-aged woman who was formerly married to the owner of a fast-food franchise. In her new life, she decided to pursue her longtime goal of becoming a nurse. During her first semester at community college, she announced that she'd started "eating healthy."

Diane had a large garden installed on the property. We grew closer through seeding and weeding, discussing nutrition and diet, and sharing recipes and meals. Despite her lifestyle changes, Diane didn't relinquish her love of baking: Every November, for example, her kitchen was filled with homemade sweets for family and friends.

One day, after biting into a warm snickerdoodle, she blissfully proclaimed that the best cookies were ones just a few minutes out of the oven. The fragrant, tender-crisp cookie was delicious, and I wanted more. My husband intervened by asking, "What about eating healthy?"

"It's not what you do one day but what you do every day that matters," Diane quipped.

She was right. When it comes to healthy eating, you shouldn't consistently deprive yourself. Sometimes you want—and need—a little treat.

Cue cookies. Many don't age well. They're most brilliant in their fleeting prime-time state. Unless you're feeding a crowd, making and baking an entire batch isn't necessary. Small-batching cookies is smart cooking and living. That's why I maintain a stash of frozen cookie dough and make small batches of cookies on demand. Store-bought dough pales by comparison, plus I can't get ones I really enjoy. Good candidates for frozen cookie dough are unfussy. My choices include old-fashioned drop cookies such as oatmeal raisin and chocolate chip, elegant hand-molded Chinese almond cookies, and slice-and-bake ginger coins. I've been baking and tweaking the recipe below since the mid-1990s; it comes from Barbara Tropp's *China Moon Cookbook*. She, too, was a proponent of freezing cookie dough, so I knew the recipe was a keeper. Three kinds of ginger define the zippy cookie recipe (though if you don't have the crystallized ginger at baking time, they'll still be tasty).

Quick cookie fixes shouldn't involve fancy cutouts, pastry bags, presses, or irons. They also shouldn't be overly healthy. Enjoy that butter, sugar, or salt. Make them fabulous.

It typically goes like this: I thaw and finish readying the dough as part of dinner prep, bake the cookies while we're eating, and cool them as we're cleaning up. The timing usually works out for us to savor the cookies at peak perfection. The house smells wonderful, and eating a couple of perfect cookies is a remarkably sati-ating, over-the-top experience that always makes me happy. Life is too short to curtail cookie love.

Make Ahead • Vegetarian

Ginger Coins

Hands-on: 15 min. Total: 50 min.

½ cup room-temperature unsalted butter, cut into 4 to 6 nuggets (4 ounces)
½ cup packed light or dark brown sugar (3.5 ounces)

2 rounded teaspoons grated peeled fresh ginger [I used a rasper, also known as a Microplane]
1 tablespoon ground ginger
½ teaspoon vanilla extract
¼ teaspoon baking soda
Generous pinch fine sea salt
4.5 ounces all-purpose flour (1 cup plus 2 tablespoons), plus more as needed
3 tablespoons finely diced crystallized ginger

1. Use an electric hand mixer on medium speed (or a stand mixer outfitted with the paddle attach-ment) to mix the butter for about 10 seconds. Pause to add the sugar. Beat for 3 to 4 minutes until pale colored and aerated. Remove the beaters (or paddle).
2. Add the fresh ginger, ground ginger, vanilla, baking soda, salt, and flour. Use a spatula to combine. If it's dry, crumbly, and doesn't come together, add 1 teaspoon water. Transfer onto a lightly floured work surface, and then gather and gently knead dough into a ball.
3. Divide into 4 portions, rolling each into a generous 1-inch-thick log. Wrap each in parchment paper and then plastic wrap. Label with masking tape, and freeze for up to 3 months. If the cookies are to be baked immediately, cover, and then chill the dough for 20 minutes, which will make it easy to slice.
4. To bake, heat the oven to 350°F with a rack in the middle position. Line a baking sheet with parchment paper.
5. Partially or fully thaw the dough log before using. Cut it into ¼-inch-thick slices (about 16 total). Place the flat rounds 1½ inches apart on the prepared baking sheet. Press a crystallized ginger piece in the cen-ter of each. Bake at 350°F for 10 to 12 minutes, until spread out, lightly puffed up, and lightly golden at the edges. Cool cookies on the baking sheet on a wire rack for 8 to 10 min-

utes before eating. Serves 64 (serving size: 1 cookie)

CALORIES 28; FAT 1g (sat 1g, unsat 0g); PROTEIN 0g; CARB 4g; FIBER 0g; SUGARS 2g (added sugars 2g); SODIUM 8mg; CALC 0% DV; POTASSIUM 0% DV

HOW TO PREPARE AND FREEZE DOUGH

Set aside time to make one or two batches of your favorite dough (this method works for any kind), and then follow these steps to load up your freezer with cookie gold.

STEP 1 Divide each batch into three or four portions. Wrap each dough portion in parchment paper, and then plastic wrap. When it's time to bake, you can recycle the parchment.

STEP 2 Use masking tape to label the dough with the cookie name, oven temperature, and yield to avoid scrambling for recipe instructions. If the dough is soft, freeze it on a tray to a rock-hard state.

STEP 3 Transfer wrapped dough to an airtight container or ziplock bag to freeze for up to three months. When it's time to bake, see step 5 in the recipe for freezer-to-oven instructions.

TOP RATED!

Best Chili Recipe

**Gluten Free • Make Ahead
Vegetarian**

Quinoa and Roasted Pepper Chili

Hands-on: 25 min. Total: 45 min.
This hearty vegetarian chili from December 2011 uses quinoa, which adds body, texture, and protein.

2 red bell peppers, halved
2 poblano chiles, halved
4 teaspoons olive oil
3 cups chopped zucchini
1½ cups chopped onion
4 garlic cloves, minced
1 tablespoon chili powder
1 teaspoon ground cumin
½ teaspoon smoked paprika
1 cup low-sodium vegetable juice
½ cup water
⅓ cup uncooked quinoa, rinsed and drained
1 tablespoon minced chipotle chiles in adobo sauce
½ teaspoon kosher salt
1 (15-ounce) can unsalted pinto beans, rinsed and drained
1 (14.5-ounce) can unsalted fire-roasted diced tomatoes, undrained

1. Preheat broiler.
2. Discard seeds and membranes from bell peppers and chiles. Place halves, skin sides up, on a foil-lined baking sheet; flatten. Broil 10 minutes or until blackened. Wrap in foil from pan; let stand 10 minutes. Peel and chop.
3. Heat oil in a large Dutch oven over medium-high. Add zucchini, onion, and garlic; sauté 4 minutes. Stir in chili powder, cumin, and paprika; sauté 30 seconds. Add bell peppers, chiles, juice, and remaining ingredients; bring to a boil. Reduce heat to medium-low, cover, and simmer 20 minutes. Serves 4 (serving size: 1½ cups)

CALORIES 292; FAT 6g (sat 1g, unsat 5g); PROTEIN 12g; CARB 48g; FIBER 12g; SUGARS 13g (added sugars 0g); SODIUM 414mg; CALC 11% DV; POTASSIUM 31% DV

Best Cheesy Recipe

Make Ahead

Creamy, Light Macaroni and Cheese

Hands-on: 1 hr. Total: 1 hr. 25 min.
A trio of bold, nutty cheeses and a velvety butternut squash puree helped create our cheesiest mac and cheese in September 2011. The squash trick lets us cut back on cheese overall for an impressive makeover, shaving 500 calories and 30g sat fat.

3 cups cubed peeled butternut squash (about 1 pound)
1½ cups 1% low-fat milk
1¼ cups unsalted chicken stock
2 garlic cloves, peeled
2 tablespoons plain fat-free Greek yogurt
¾ teaspoon kosher salt
½ teaspoon freshly ground black pepper
4 ounces Gruyère cheese, shredded (about 1 cup)
4 ounces pecorino Romano cheese, grated (about 1 cup)
1 ounce Parmigiano-Reggiano cheese, finely grated and divided (about ¼ cup)
1 pound uncooked cavatappi pasta
Cooking spray
1 teaspoon olive oil
½ cup whole-wheat panko (Japanese breadcrumbs)
2 tablespoons chopped fresh flat-leaf parsley

1. Preheat oven to 375°F.
2. Bring first 4 ingredients to a boil in a medium saucepan over medium-high; reduce heat to medium, and simmer 25 minutes or until squash is tender.
3. Carefully place squash mixture in a blender with yogurt, salt, and pepper. Remove center piece of blender lid (to allow steam to escape); secure blender lid on blender. Place a clean towel over opening in lid (to avoid splatters). Blend until smooth. Place squash puree in a bowl; stir in Gruyère, pecorino Romano, and 2 tablespoons Parmigiano-Reggiano cheese.
4. Cook pasta according to package directions, omitting salt and fat; drain well. Add pasta to squash mixture, stirring to combine. Spoon pasta mixture into a 13- x 9-inch glass or ceramic baking dish coated with cooking spray.
5. Heat oil in a medium skillet over medium. Add panko; cook 2 minutes or until toasted. Remove pan from heat; stir in remaining 2 tablespoons Parmigiano-Reggiano cheese. Sprinkle panko mixture evenly over pasta; lightly coat with cooking spray. Bake at 375°F for 25 minutes or until bubbly. Sprinkle evenly with chopped parsley. Serves 8 (serving size: about 1⅓ cups)

CALORIES 418; FAT 13g (sat 7g, unsat 3g); PROTEIN 20g; CARB 56g; FIBER 4g; SUGARS 2g (added sugars 0g); SODIUM 681mg; CALC 40% DV; POTASSIUM 8% DV

Chicken Piccata

Hands-on: 31 min. Total: 31 min.
Easy and quick (and starring our favorite dinner bird), this January 2012 classic continues to be a weeknight rock star. Serve the chicken with polenta or whole-wheat angel hair pasta to catch all the lemony, garlicky pan sauce.

4 (6-ounce) skinless, boneless chicken breast halves
½ teaspoon kosher salt
¼ teaspoon freshly ground black pepper
³/₄ cup unsalted chicken stock, divided
2 ounces all-purpose flour, divided (about ½ cup)
2 tablespoons butter, divided
2 tablespoons olive oil, divided
¼ cup finely chopped shallots
Lemon slices (optional)
4 medium garlic cloves, thinly sliced
½ cup dry white wine
2 tablespoons fresh lemon juice
1½ tablespoons drained capers
3 tablespoons fresh flat-leaf parsley leaves

1. Place each chicken breast half between 2 sheets of heavy-duty plastic wrap; pound to ½-inch thickness using a meat mallet or small heavy skillet. Sprinkle both sides of chicken evenly with salt and pepper. Combine ¼ cup stock and 1 teaspoon flour in a bowl; set aside. Place remaining flour in a shallow dish. Dredge chicken in remaining flour, shaking off excess.
2. Heat 1 tablespoon butter and 1 tablespoon oil in a large skillet over medium-high; swirl until butter melts. Add chicken to pan; cook 4 minutes on each side or until done. Remove chicken from pan; keep warm.
3. Add remaining 1 tablespoon oil to pan. Add shallots and lemon slices, if using; sauté 3 minutes. Add garlic; sauté 1 minute. Add wine; cook 2 minutes or until liquid almost evaporates, scraping pan to loosen browned bits. Add remaining ½ cup stock; bring to a boil. Cook 5 minutes or until liquid is reduced by half.
4. Stir in reserved stock and flour mixture; cook 1 minute. Remove pan from heat; stir in remaining 1 tablespoon butter, juice, and capers. Place 1 chicken breast half on each of 4 plates; top each serving with 2 tablespoons sauce and about 2 teaspoons parsley leaves. Serves 4

CALORIES 398; **FAT** 17g (sat 6g, unsat 9g); **PROTEIN** 41g; **CARB** 15g; **FIBER** 1g; **SUGARS** 1g (added sugars 0g); **SODIUM** 466mg; **CALC** 3% DV; **POTASSIUM** 19% DV

Fast • Gluten Free
Make Ahead • Vegetarian

Fall Vegetable Curry

Hands-on: 13 min. Total: 25 min.
You'll use this staff fave from October 2010 in heavy rotation as the days turn cooler. Madras curry powder is a blend of several fragrant spices and has more depth than regular curry powder; it's the only spice you need here (look for it in specialty stores or online).

1 tablespoon olive oil
1 cup diced peeled sweet potato
1 cup small cauliflower florets
¼ cup thinly sliced yellow onion
2 teaspoons Madras curry powder
½ cup organic vegetable broth (such as Swanson)
½ teaspoon salt, divided
1 (15-ounce) can unsalted chickpeas, rinsed and drained
1 (14.5-ounce) can unsalted diced tomatoes, undrained
2 (8.8-ounce) packages precooked brown rice (such as Uncle Ben's)
½ cup plain 2% reduced-fat Greek yogurt
¼ cup unsalted cashews
2 tablespoons chopped fresh cilantro

1. Heat olive oil in a large nonstick skillet over medium-high. Add sweet potato; sauté 3 minutes. Reduce heat to medium. Add cauliflower, onion, and curry powder; cook 1 minute, stirring constantly. Add broth, ¼ teaspoon salt, chickpeas, and tomatoes; bring to a boil. Cover, reduce heat, and simmer 10 minutes or until vegetables are tender, stirring occasionally.
2. Heat rice according to package directions. Place rice in a bowl; stir in remaining ¼ teaspoon salt. Divide rice among 4 bowls; top evenly with vegetable mixture, yogurt, cashews, and chopped cilantro. Serves 4 (serving size: ½ cup rice, about 1 cup curry, and 2 tablespoons yogurt)

CALORIES 428; **FAT** 13g (sat 2g, unsat 8g); **PROTEIN** 15g; **CARB** 67g; **FIBER** 11g; **SUGARS** 7g (added sugars 0g); **SODIUM** 522mg; **CALC** 10% DV; **POTASSIUM** 12% DV

CHANGE IT UP

Keep the broth, curry, and tomato base, but switch up the vegetables. Try butternut squash and red bell pepper, spinach and eggplant, or lacinato kale and potato.

Fast

Shrimp and Broccoli Rotini

Hands-on: 20 min. Total: 20 min.
Keep pasta in the pantry and shrimp in the freezer, and you've got an easy last-minute meal—which is why this recipe from September 2015 remains a regular go-to for busy weeknights.

6 cups water
8 ounces uncooked rotini pasta
3 cups packaged fresh broccoli florets
2 tablespoons olive oil
1 pound large shrimp, peeled and deveined
2 teaspoons grated lemon rind
2½ tablespoons unsalted butter
2 tablespoons fresh lemon juice
⁵/₈ teaspoon kosher salt
½ teaspoon freshly ground black pepper

1. Bring 6 cups water to a boil in a large saucepan. Add pasta; cook according to package directions, omitting salt and fat. Add broccoli during last 3 minutes of cooking; drain.
2. Heat oil in a large skillet over high. Add shrimp to pan; sauté 2 minutes. Stir in rind; cook 1 minute. Add pasta mixture, butter, lemon juice, and salt to pan; toss to coat. Sprinkle with pepper. Serve immediately. Serves 4 (serving size: about 1½ cups)

CALORIES 428; **FAT** 16g (sat 6g, unsat 8g); **PROTEIN** 25g; **CARB** 47g; **FIBER** 4g; **SUGARS** 3g (added sugars 0g); **SODIUM** 486mg; **CALC** 10% DV; **POTASSIUM** 11% DV

Gluten Free

Sumac Chicken with Cauliflower and Carrots

Hands-on: 10 min. Total: 55 min.
This sheet pan dinner made chicken a winner in January 2017, with a ground sumac and brown sugar rub. You can also use sumac on roasted vegetables or stir it into vinaigrette.

6 tablespoons olive oil, divided
1 tablespoon sumac
1¼ teaspoons kosher salt, divided
1 teaspoon light brown sugar
1 teaspoon paprika
¼ teaspoon ground red pepper
1 pound cauliflower florets
2 (6-ounce) packages small rainbow carrots, halved lengthwise
1 pound bone-in chicken thighs, skinned
1 pound chicken drumsticks, skinned
1 small lemon, halved lengthwise and thinly sliced
1 small red onion, cut into ³/₄-inch wedges
½ cup finely chopped fresh flat-leaf parsley
½ cup chopped fresh cilantro
1 tablespoon fresh lemon juice
1 small garlic clove, minced

1. Preheat oven to 425°F.
2. Combine 3 tablespoons oil with sumac, 1 teaspoon salt, brown sugar, paprika, and red pepper in a medium bowl. Place cauliflower and carrots on a foil-lined baking sheet. Add half of oil mixture; toss to coat. Add chicken thighs, drumsticks, and lemon slices to pan. Rub remaining oil mixture over chicken. Bake at 425°F for 20 minutes. Stir vegetables. Sprinkle onion wedges over pan. Bake at 425°F for 20 more minutes or until chicken is done.
3. Combine remaining 3 tablespoons oil, remaining ¼ teaspoon salt, parsley, and remaining ingredients in a small bowl. Spoon parsley mixture evenly over chicken and vegetables. Serves 6 (serving size: about 5 ounces chicken and 1 cup vegetables)

CALORIES 313; **FAT** 20g (sat 4g, unsat 15g); **PROTEIN** 22g; **CARB** 13g; **FIBER** 4g; **SUGARS** 6g (added sugars 1g); **SODIUM** 562mg; **CALC** 6% DV; **POTASSIUM** 20% DV

USE THE BEST

Few ingredients and a simple preparation mean there's less to hide behind. Start with the freshest produce, high-quality pork, and an olive oil you love.

Fast • Gluten Free

Pork Medallions with Scallions and Magic Green Sauce

Hands-on: 20 min. Total: 20 min.
This August 2015 dish is way more than the sum of its parts. Green onions do triple duty: in the sauce, with the pork in the pan, and as a curly garnish. Caper brine thins and brightens the sauce, a brilliant second use for the jar.

1 cup packed chopped fresh cilantro (about 1 bunch)
¼ cup extra-virgin olive oil, divided
2 tablespoons capers, drained
1 tablespoon caper brine
1 tablespoon water
2 bunches scallions, divided

4 (4-ounce) boneless center-cut loin
   pork chops
$^3/_8$ teaspoon salt, divided
$^1/_4$ teaspoon freshly ground black
   pepper
16 red and yellow heirloom cherry
   tomatoes, halved

1. Place cilantro, 3 tablespoons oil, capers, caper brine, and 1 tablespoon water in a mini food processor. Chop scallions to measure 3 tablespoons. Add chopped scallions to cilantro mixture; process until smooth.
2. Cut remaining scallions diagonally into 2-inch pieces. Cut 8 of those pieces lengthwise into slivers; set aside.
3. Heat remaining 1 tablespoon oil in a large skillet over medium-high. Sprinkle pork chops with $^1/_4$ teaspoon salt and pepper. Add pork and 2-inch scallion pieces to pan; cover, and cook 4 minutes. Turn pork over. Add tomatoes and remaining $^1/_8$ teaspoon salt to pan; cook 2 minutes. Arrange pork mixture on a platter; top with cilantro mixture and reserved slivered onions. Serves 4 (serving size: 1 chop, about $^1/_2$ cup tomato mixture, and 2 tablespoons sauce)

CALORIES 303; FAT 21g (sat 5g, unsat 15g); PROTEIN 23g; CARB 6g; FIBER 2g; SUGARS 1g (added sugars 0g); SODIUM 406mg; CALC 6% DV; POTASSIUM 19% DV

Best Makeover Recipe

Make Ahead • Vegetarian

Eggplant Parmesan

Hands-on: 35 min. Total: 1 hr. 45 min.
Traditional versions of this dish can tip the scales at nearly 1,000 calories and 30g sat fat per serving. Our September 2010 makeover cuts that by more than two-thirds and still has plenty of marinara, melty cheese, and crispy baked eggplant.

3 large eggs, divided
1 tablespoon water
2 cups whole-wheat panko (Japanese
   breadcrumbs)
2 ounces Parmigiano-Reggiano
   cheese, grated and divided
   (about $^1/_2$ cup)
2 (1-pound) eggplants, peeled and
   cut crosswise into $^1/_2$-inch-thick
   slices
Cooking spray
$^1/_2$ cup torn fresh basil
$^1/_2$ teaspoon crushed red pepper
$1^1/_2$ teaspoons minced fresh garlic
$^3/_8$ teaspoon kosher salt, divided
1 (16-ounce) container part-skim
   ricotta cheese
3 cups lower-sodium marinara sauce
   (such as Dell'Amore)
6 ounces thinly sliced mozzarella
   cheese
2 ounces fontina cheese, finely grated
   (about $^1/_2$ cup)

1. Preheat oven to 375°F.
2. Combine 2 eggs and 1 tablespoon water in a shallow dish, stirring with a whisk. Combine panko and $^1/_4$ cup Parmigiano-Reggiano in a shallow dish. Dip eggplant in egg mixture; dredge in panko mixture, pressing gently to adhere. Place eggplant slices 1 inch apart on 2 baking sheets coated with cooking spray. Bake at 375°F for 30 minutes or until golden, flipping eggplant and rotating pans from front to back after 15 minutes.
3. Combine remaining egg, basil, pepper, garlic, $^1/_4$ teaspoon salt, and ricotta in a bowl. Spoon $^1/_2$ cup marinara sauce in bottom of a 13- x 9-inch glass baking dish coated with cooking spray. Layer half of eggplant slices over sauce. Top with about $^3/_4$ cup sauce, half of ricotta mixture, one-third of mozzarella cheese, and $^1/_4$ cup fontina cheese. Repeat layers once. Top with remaining $^1/_2$ cup marinara sauce and remaining $^1/_8$ teaspoon salt. Cover tightly with foil coated with cooking spray. Bake at 375°F for 35 minutes. Remove foil; top dish with remaining one-third of mozzarella cheese and remaining $^1/_4$ cup Parmigiano-Reggiano cheese. Bake at 375°F for 10 minutes or until sauce is bubbly and cheese melts. Cool 10 minutes. Serves 10

CALORIES 305; FAT 15g (sat 7g, unsat 4g); PROTEIN 19g; CARB 26g; FIBER 5g; SUGARS 7g (added sugars 0g); SODIUM 572mg; CALC 36% DV; POTASSIUM 8% DV

Best Mash-Up Recipe

Fast

Chicken Potpie Skillet Pizza

(pictured on page 234)

Hands-on: 20 min. Total: 20 min.
The genius of this November 2016 recipe is the skillet-seared crust, which gives you a pizzeria-quality pie in less than half the bake time. The potpie-style topper is a fun twist on a white pizza and a great way to pack extra veggies onto each slice.

4 teaspoons olive oil, divided
¼ cup prechopped onion
¼ cup matchstick-cut carrot
¼ cup prechopped celery
¼ cup frozen green peas
1½ tablespoons all-purpose flour
1 cup unsalted chicken stock
10 ounces refrigerated fresh whole-wheat pizza dough
3 ounces skinless, boneless rotisserie chicken breast, shredded (about ¾ cup)
3 ounces preshredded part-skim mozzarella cheese (about ¾ cup)
1 teaspoon fresh thyme leaves
¼ teaspoon black pepper
⅛ teaspoon kosher salt

1. Preheat oven to 500°F. Place a 12-inch cast-iron skillet in oven (leave pan in oven as it preheats). **2.** Heat 1 teaspoon oil in a large nonstick skillet over medium-high. Add onion; sauté 2 minutes. Add carrot, celery, and peas; sauté 1 minute. Remove vegetable mixture from nonstick skillet; set aside.

3. Add flour and remaining 1 tablespoon oil to nonstick skillet. Cook 30 seconds, stirring constantly. Slowly add stock, stirring constantly. Bring to a boil; reduce heat, and simmer 3 minutes or until thickened, stirring frequently. Remove from heat. **4.** Place dough on a lightly floured surface; roll into a 12-inch circle. Carefully place dough in preheated cast-iron skillet; flatten to cover bottom of pan. Bake at 500°F for 5 minutes or until crust is lightly browned. Remove from oven. **5.** Preheat broiler to high. **6.** Top pizza crust with ½ cup stock mixture, vegetable mixture, chicken, and cheese. Broil 2 minutes or until cheese is melted. Drizzle with remaining stock mixture. Sprinkle with thyme, pepper, and salt. Cut into 8 slices. Serves 4 (serving size: 2 slices)

CALORIES 311; **FAT** 12g (sat 3g, unsat 8g); **PROTEIN** 18g; **CARB** 36g; **FIBER** 6g; **SUGARS** 2g (added sugars 0g); **SODIUM** 630mg; **CALC** 19% DV; **POTASSIUM** 4% DV

Best Fast Fish Recipe

Fast

Dijon-Herb Crusted Salmon with Creamy Dill Sauce

Hands-on: 10 min. Total: 20 min.
Simple and kid friendly, this April 2017 main is an easy way to work more fish into your diet. Look for thicker center-cut fillets, which will stay more moist.

4 (6-ounce) salmon fillets, skinned (about 1½ inches thick)
½ teaspoon kosher salt
½ teaspoon freshly ground black pepper

½ cup whole-wheat panko (Japanese breadcrumbs)
2 tablespoons finely chopped fresh flat-leaf parsley
2 tablespoons canola oil
2 teaspoons chopped fresh thyme
2 teaspoons Dijon mustard
¼ cup plain 2% reduced-fat Greek yogurt
4 teaspoons chopped fresh dill
1 tablespoon 2% reduced-fat milk
2 teaspoons red wine vinegar

1. Preheat oven to 450°F. **2.** Arrange fish fillets on a parchment paper–lined baking sheet. Sprinkle with salt and pepper. Bake at 450°F for 10 minutes or until desired degree of doneness. Remove pan from oven. Turn on broiler. **3.** Combine panko, parsley, oil, thyme, and Dijon in a small bowl. Spoon panko mixture evenly over fish, pressing to adhere. Place pan in oven; broil 1 to 2 minutes or until the topping is browned and crisp. **4.** Combine yogurt, dill, milk, and vinegar in a small bowl, stirring with a whisk. Serve with fish. Serves 4 (serving size: 1 fillet and about 1½ tablespoons sauce)

CALORIES 356; **FAT** 17g (sat 3g, unsat 13g); **PROTEIN** 39g; **CARB** 8g; **FIBER** 1g; **SUGARS** 1g (added sugars 0g); **SODIUM** 400mg; **CALC** 4% DV; **POTASSIUM** 17% DV

Best Quick Chinese Recipe

Fast

Szechuan Chicken Stir-Fry

Hands-on: 25 min. Total: 25 min.
Ginger and sambal oelek, a chile-garlic paste that's now in most supermarkets' international aisles, made this January 2012 recipe a favorite by providing bold flavor in no time. Have all the ingredients ready so they can go in at just the right moment.

1 tablespoon toasted sesame oil, divided
1/2 cup unsalted chicken stock
2 tablespoons reduced-sodium soy sauce
1 tablespoon rice vinegar
2 teaspoons sambal oelek (ground fresh chile paste)
2 teaspoons cornstarch
1/4 teaspoon salt
2 tablespoons canola oil, divided
1 pound skinless, boneless chicken breast halves, cut into bite-sized pieces
1 yellow bell pepper, cut into strips
1 red bell pepper, cut into strips
1 cup diagonally cut snow peas
1/2 cup vertically sliced onion
1 tablespoon grated peeled fresh ginger
1 tablespoon minced fresh garlic
2 cups hot cooked brown rice
1/4 cup (1-inch) green onion slices
1/4 cup unsalted roasted peanuts, chopped

1. Combine 2 teaspoons sesame oil and next 6 ingredients (through salt) in a small bowl. Heat remaining 1 teaspoon sesame oil and 1 tablespoon canola oil in a wok or large skillet over medium-high. Add chicken; stir-fry 2 minutes. Remove chicken from pan.
2. Add remaining 1 tablespoon canola oil to pan. Add bell peppers and next 4 ingredients (through garlic); stir-fry 1 minute. Add stock mixture; cook 30 seconds or until thickened. Add chicken to pan; cook 4 minutes or until chicken is done. Spoon ½ cup rice onto each of 4 plates; top each serving with 1 cup chicken mixture, 1 tablespoon green onions, and 1 tablespoon peanuts. Serves 4

CALORIES 457; FAT 19g (sat 3g, unsat 14g); PROTEIN 33g; CARB 38g; FIBER 5g; SUGARS 5g (added sugars 0g); SODIUM 567mg; CALC 4% DV; POTASSIUM 20% DV

Best One-Pan Recipe

Fast

One-Pot Pasta with Spinach and Tomatoes

Hands-on: 29 min. Total: 29 min.
In March 2015 we made pasta night easier by cooking the noodles in the sauce. This not only saves on cleanup; the stock also infuses the pasta with flavor as it cooks, and the starch helps to thicken the sauce so it clings.

1 tablespoon olive oil
1 cup chopped onion
6 garlic cloves, finely chopped
1 (14.5-ounce) can unsalted petite diced tomatoes, undrained
1 1/2 cups unsalted chicken stock
1/2 teaspoon dried oregano
8 ounces uncooked whole-grain spaghetti or linguine (such as Barilla)
1/2 teaspoon salt
10 ounces fresh spinach
1 ounce Parmesan cheese, grated (about 1/4 cup)

1. Heat oil in a Dutch oven or large saucepan over medium-high. Add onion and garlic; sauté 3 minutes or until onion starts to brown. Add tomatoes, stock, oregano, and pasta, in that order, pressing with a spoon to submerge the pasta in liquid. Bring to a boil. Cover, reduce heat to medium-low, and cook 7 minutes or until pasta is almost done.
2. Uncover pan; stir in salt. Add spinach in batches, stirring until the spinach wilts before adding more. Remove pan from heat; let stand 5 minutes. Divide pasta mixture among 4 plates; sprinkle evenly with cheese. Serves 4 (serving size: about 2 cups pasta mixture and 1 tablespoon cheese)

CALORIES 331; FAT 7g (sat 2g, unsat 4g); PROTEIN 15g; CARB 55g; FIBER 9g; SUGARS 6g (added sugars 0g); SODIUM 522mg; CALC 19% DV; POTASSIUM 14% DV

Best Steak Recipe

Gluten Free

Pan-Seared Strip Steak

Hands-on: 11 min. Total: 51 min.
Master techniques stand the test of time, which is why our April 2011 method for grass-fed strip steak (a lean, flavorful cut) remains one of our favorites.

2 (12-ounce) lean, grass-fed New York strip steaks
1 teaspoon kosher salt
3/4 teaspoon black pepper
1 teaspoon olive oil
2 tablespoons butter
2 fresh thyme sprigs
2 garlic cloves, crushed

1. Let steaks stand 30 minutes at room temperature.
2. Sprinkle salt and pepper evenly over steaks. Heat oil in a large cast-iron skillet over high. Add steaks to pan; cook 3 minutes on each side or until browned. Reduce heat to medium-low; add butter, thyme, and garlic to pan. Carefully grasp pan handle using an oven mitt or folded dish towel. Tilt pan toward you so butter pools on one side; cook 1½ minutes, basting steaks with butter mixture constantly. Remove steaks from pan; reserve butter mixture. Cover steaks loosely with foil. Let stand 10 minutes.
3. To serve, cut steaks across grain into thin slices. Discard thyme and garlic; spoon reserved butter mixture over steaks. Serves 6 (serving size: 3 ounces beef and about ¾ teaspoon butter mixture)

CALORIES 176; FAT 8g (sat 4g, unsat 3g); PROTEIN 26g; CARB 1g; FIBER 0g; SUGARS 0g; SODIUM 413mg; CALC 2% DV; POTASSIUM 11% DV

Best Meatless Recipe

Make Ahead • Vegetarian

Vegetable "Meat" Loaf

Hands-on: 1 hr. Total: 1 hr. 47 min.
This umami-rich recipe received our Test Kitchen's highest rating in March 2012 and continues to get raves from both vegetarians and meat lovers. Be sure to tightly pack the mushroom mixture into the pan so the slices hold their shape after baking.

MEAT LOAF
1 large red bell pepper, halved
1 large green bell pepper, halved
2 pounds cremini mushrooms, coarsely chopped
1 tablespoon olive oil
1 cup ½-inch asparagus pieces
½ cup chopped red onion
1 cup panko (Japanese breadcrumbs), toasted
1 cup chopped walnuts, toasted
2 tablespoons chopped fresh basil
1 tablespoon ketchup
1 teaspoon Dijon mustard
½ teaspoon kosher salt
½ teaspoon freshly ground black pepper
4 ounces Parmigiano-Reggiano cheese, grated (about 1 cup)
2 large eggs, lightly beaten
Cooking spray

TOPPING
2 tablespoons ketchup
1 tablespoon organic vegetable broth
¼ teaspoon Dijon mustard

1. Preheat broiler to high.
2. To prepare meat loaf, place bell pepper halves, skin sides up, on a foil-lined baking sheet; flatten. Broil 10 minutes or until blackened. Wrap in foil from pan; let stand 10 minutes. Peel, seed, and finely chop. Place bell peppers in a bowl.
3. Reduce oven temperature to 350°F.
4. Place about one-fourth of mushrooms in a food processor; pulse 10 times or until finely chopped. Place chopped mushrooms in a bowl. Repeat procedure 3 times with remaining mushrooms.
5. Heat oil in a large nonstick skillet over medium-high. Add mushrooms; sauté 15 minutes or until liquid evaporates. Add mushrooms to bell peppers. Wipe out pan with paper towels.
6. Return pan to medium-high. Add asparagus and onion; sauté 6 minutes. Add onion mixture to mushroom mixture. Add panko and next 8 ingredients (through eggs), stirring well.
7. Spoon mixture into a 9- x 5-inch loaf pan coated with cooking spray, pressing gently to pack into pan. Bake at 350°F for 45 minutes or until a thermometer registers 155°F.
8. To prepare the topping, combine 2 tablespoons ketchup and remaining ingredients in a bowl; brush over loaf. Bake at 350°F for an additional 10 minutes. Let stand 10 minutes; cut into 6 slices. Serves 6 (serving size: 1 slice)

CALORIES 351; **FAT** 22g (sat 5g, unsat 14g); **PROTEIN** 19g; **CARB** 22g; **FIBER** 5g; **SUGARS** 8g (added sugars 1g); **SODIUM** 506mg; **CALC** 29% DV; **POTASSIUM** 22% DV

Best Get-Together Recipe

Gluten Free • Make Ahead
Classic Beef Pot Roast

Hands-on: 22 min. Total: 2 hr. 35 min.
This dish is our most popular recipe ever. It has kept that distinction since it was first published in October 2006, probably because it's such a crowd-pleaser. To serve, carve the roast into large pieces, ladle the rich broth over the top, and sprinkle with fresh flat-leaf parsley.

1 teaspoon olive oil
1 (3-pound) boneless chuck roast, trimmed
1 teaspoon kosher salt
¼ teaspoon freshly ground black pepper
2 cups coarsely chopped onion
1¾ cups unsalted beef stock
1 cup dry red wine
4 thyme sprigs
3 garlic cloves, chopped
1 bay leaf
4 large carrots, peeled and cut diagonally into 1-inch pieces
2 pounds Yukon Gold potatoes, peeled and cut into 2-inch pieces

1. Preheat oven to 350°F.
2. Heat oil in a large Dutch oven over medium-high. Sprinkle beef with salt and pepper. Add to pan; cook 5 minutes, turning to brown on all sides. Remove beef from pan. Add onion to pan; sauté 8 minutes or until tender.
3. Return beef to pan, and add stock, wine, thyme sprigs, garlic, and bay leaf; bring to a simmer. Cover, place pan in oven, and bake at 350°F for 1½ hours or until beef is almost tender.
4. Add carrots and potatoes to pan. Cover, and bake at 350°F for an additional 1 hour or until vegetables are tender. Remove thyme sprigs and bay leaf from pan; discard.

Place beef on a cutting board; carve into large pieces. Remove vegetables to a platter with a slotted spoon. Strain cooking liquid over a bowl; discard solids. Serve beef with vegetables and cooking liquid. Serves 10 (serving size: 3 ounces beef and about ¾ cup vegetables)

CALORIES 299; **FAT** 7g (sat 3g, unsat 3g); **PROTEIN** 29g; **CARB** 24g; **FIBER** 3g; **SUGARS** 4g (added sugars 0g); **SODIUM** 288mg; **CALC** 4% DV; **POTASSIUM** 19% DV

Best Slow Cooker Recipe

Make Ahead

Slow Cooker Pork with Peach Barbecue Sauce

Hands-on: 30 min. Total: 7 hr.
A generous spice rub and a good sear gave this July 2014 roast the crust and smoke of great barbecue with the hands-off ease of the slow cooker. The sauce alone—thick, smoky, sweet, and tangy—is reason enough to make this dish year-round.

Cooking spray
2 teaspoons smoked paprika
1¼ teaspoons kosher salt, divided
1 teaspoon freshly ground black pepper
1 (3½-pound) bone-in pork shoulder roast (Boston butt), trimmed
½ cup unsalted chicken stock (such as Swanson)
⅓ cup balsamic vinegar
⅓ cup molasses
2 teaspoons reduced-sodium soy sauce
1 teaspoon crushed red pepper
½ cup peach preserves
2 cups vertically sliced onion
5 garlic cloves, thinly sliced
¼ cup bourbon
2 tablespoons cold water
2 teaspoons cornstarch

1. Heat a large skillet over medium-high. Coat pan with cooking spray. Combine paprika, ½ teaspoon salt, and black pepper in a bowl; rub evenly over pork. Add pork to pan; cook 10 minutes, turning to brown on all sides. Place pork in a 6-quart electric slow cooker.
2. Add stock and next 4 ingredients (through crushed red pepper) to skillet; bring to a boil, scraping pan to loosen browned bits. Add preserves, stirring with a whisk. Pour stock mixture over pork; top with onion and garlic. Cover, and cook on low 6 ½ hours or until pork is very tender. Place pork on a cutting board; reserve cooking liquid. When cool enough to handle, shred pork into large pieces, and place on a platter. Remove onion from slow cooker with a slotted spoon; add to pork.
3. Place a large ziplock bag inside a 4-cup glass measuring cup. Carefully add cooking liquid; let stand 10 minutes (fat will rise to the top). Seal bag; carefully snip off a bottom corner. Drain drippings into the skillet, stopping before fat layer reaches opening; discard fat. Stir bourbon into drippings; bring to a boil. Cook 10 minutes or until reduced to about 1½ cups.
4. Combine 2 tablespoons cold water and cornstarch in a small bowl. Stir cornstarch mixture and remaining ¾ teaspoon salt into cooking liquid mixture; cook 1 to 2 minutes or until thickened. Drizzle sauce over pork and onion; toss gently to coat. Serves 12 (serving size: about 3 ounces pork and 2 tablespoons sauce)

CALORIES 212; **FAT** 6g (sat 2g, unsat 3g); **PROTEIN** 17g; **CARB** 20g; **FIBER** 1g; **SUGARS** 16g (added sugars 14g); **SODIUM** 369mg; **CALC** 41% DV; **POTASSIUM** 13% DV

Best Family-Friendly Recipe

Fast • Make Ahead

Hamburger Steak with Onion Gravy

Hands-on: 20 min. Total: 20 min.
These smothered burger patties from April 2013 are a unanimous family favorite—easy, filling, and fun. Serve with speedy sides like frozen mashed potatoes and microwave-in-bag haricots verts (slender green beans).

1 pound 90% lean ground sirloin
½ teaspoon salt, divided
½ teaspoon freshly ground black pepper, divided
1 tablespoon canola oil, divided
1½ cups vertically sliced onion
4 ounces cremini mushrooms, quartered
2 teaspoons all-purpose flour
1 cup unsalted beef stock

1. Divide and shape ground beef into 4 (½-inch-thick) patties; sprinkle evenly with ¼ teaspoon salt and ¼ teaspoon pepper. Heat 2 teaspoons oil in a large skillet over medium-high. Add patties to pan; cook 3 minutes on each side or until browned (patties will not be cooked through); remove from pan.
2. Add remaining 1 teaspoon oil to pan. Add vertically sliced onion; sauté 3 minutes or until lightly browned and tender. Add mushrooms; cook 3 minutes. Sprinkle flour over pan; cook 30 seconds. Add stock, remaining ¼ teaspoon salt, and remaining ¼ teaspoon pepper; bring to a boil. Return patties to pan; reduce heat to medium, partially cover, and cook 5 minutes or until gravy is slightly thickened. Serves 4 (serving size: 1 patty and about ¼ cup gravy)

CALORIES 263; **FAT** 15g (sat 5g, unsat 8g); **PROTEIN** 25g; **CARB** 6g; **FIBER** 1g; **SUGARS** 3g (added sugars 0g); **SODIUM** 411mg; **CALC** 3% DV; **POTASSIUM** 15% DV

Gluten Free • Make Ahead

Spaghetti Squash Lasagna with Spinach

Hands-on: 40 min. Total: 1 hr. 50 min.
This reader favorite from December 2015 has half the carbs of classic lasagna. If you bake the squash ahead, store the squeeze-dried strands in a ziplock bag, and stack the empty squash "boats" between damp paper towels before refrigerating.

2 small spaghetti squash (about 1½ pounds each)
2 teaspoons olive oil
4 garlic cloves, thinly sliced
1 (8-ounce) package fresh baby spinach
½ cup part-skim ricotta cheese
⅛ teaspoon kosher salt
2 ounces part-skim mozzarella cheese, shredded and divided (about ½ cup)
8 ounces 93% lean ground turkey
1½ cups lower-sodium marinara sauce (such as Dell'Amore)
1 ounce Parmesan cheese, grated (about ¼ cup)

1. Preheat oven to 350°F.
2. Cut each squash in half lengthwise; remove seeds. Place squash halves, cut sides up, on a baking sheet. Bake at 350°F for 50 minutes. Let stand 10 minutes. Scrape inside of squash with a fork to remove spaghetti-like strands. Place strands on a clean dish towel; squeeze until barely moist. Reserve squash halves.
3. Increase oven temperature to 425°F.
4. Heat oil in a large skillet over medium-high. Add garlic; sauté 30 seconds. Add spinach, stirring to wilt. Remove from heat. Combine spinach mixture, squash strands, ricotta cheese, salt, and ¼ cup mozzarella cheese in a medium bowl.

5. Return skillet to medium-high. Add turkey to pan; cook 4 minutes or until browned, stirring to crumble. Add marinara sauce; cover, reduce heat to medium, and simmer 4 minutes.
6. Arrange reserved squash halves on baking sheet. Spoon sauce evenly into the bottom of each squash half. Top with squash mixture. Sprinkle evenly with remaining ¼ cup mozzarella cheese and Parmesan cheese. Bake at 425°F for 20 minutes.
7. Preheat broiler to high (keep pan in oven). Broil 1 to 2 minutes or until cheese is golden brown and bubbly. Remove from oven; let stand 10 minutes. Serves 4 (serving size: 1 squash half)

CALORIES 373; **FAT** 19g (sat 6g, unsat 8g); **PROTEIN** 25g; **CARB** 31g; **FIBER** 6g; **SUGARS** 12g (added sugars 0g); **SODIUM** 628mg; **CALC** 39% DV; **POTASSIUM** 22% DV

Fast

Crab Cakes with Spicy Rémoulade

Hands-on: 20 min. Total: 20 min.
These light, tender crab cakes from April 2012 are ready in just 20 minutes, making them an easy, elegant main. Look for fresh lump crabmeat at the fish counter for a sweet, clean flavor. Serve with a salad of mixed greens and fennel.

CRAB CAKES
1 pound fresh jumbo lump crabmeat, picked and drained
2 tablespoons finely chopped green bell pepper
1½ tablespoons canola mayonnaise
¼ teaspoon black pepper
2 green onions, finely chopped
1 large egg, lightly beaten
1 cup panko (Japanese breadcrumbs), divided
2 tablespoons canola oil, divided

RÉMOULADE
¼ cup canola mayonnaise
2 teaspoons minced shallots
1 teaspoon chopped fresh tarragon
1 teaspoon chopped fresh parsley
1½ teaspoons Dijon mustard
¾ teaspoon capers, chopped
¾ teaspoon white wine vinegar
¼ teaspoon ground red pepper

1. To prepare crab cakes, pat crabmeat dry with paper towels. Place crabmeat, bell pepper, and next 4 ingredients in a bowl; stir gently to combine. Stir in ¼ cup panko. Place remaining ¾ cup panko in a shallow dish. Shape crab mixture into 8 (¾-inch-thick) patties; dredge in panko.
2. Heat 1 tablespoon oil in a large nonstick skillet over medium-high. Add 4 patties to pan; cook 3 minutes on each side or until golden. Remove from pan. Repeat procedure with remaining 1 tablespoon oil and remaining patties.
3. To prepare the rémoulade, combine ¼ cup mayonnaise and remaining ingredients in a bowl. Serve with crab cakes. Serves 4 (serving size: 2 crab cakes and about 2 tablespoons sauce)

CALORIES 310; **FAT** 16g (sat 1g, unsat 13g); **PROTEIN** 27g; **CARB** 12g; **FIBER** 1g; **SUGARS** 1g (added sugars 0g); **SODIUM** 583mg; **CALC** 2% DV; **POTASSIUM** 12% DV

Fast • Make Ahead

20-Minute Chicken Enchiladas

Hands-on: 20 min. Total: 20 min.
We hacked this Mexican favorite in July 2013 to get it to the table fast. One richly spiced sauce doubles as the filling and the topper. And since every element is already cooked, it needs just 3 minutes under the broiler to melt the cheese.

1 cup prechopped onion
1 cup unsalted chicken stock
1 tablespoon all-purpose flour
1½ tablespoons chili powder
2 teaspoons ground cumin
¾ teaspoon garlic powder
½ teaspoon crushed red pepper
¼ teaspoon salt
1 (15-ounce) can unsalted tomato
    sauce
12 ounces skinless, boneless rotisserie
    chicken breast, shredded (about
    3 cups)
1 (15-ounce) can unsalted black
    beans, rinsed and drained
12 (6-inch) corn tortillas
Cooking spray
3 ounces preshredded 4-cheese
    Mexican-blend cheese (about
    ¾ cup)
1 cup chopped tomato
¼ cup chopped fresh cilantro
6 tablespoons sour cream

1. Preheat broiler to high.
2. Combine first 9 ingredients in a
medium saucepan. Bring to a boil
over high; cook 2 minutes or until
thickened. Place 1½ cups tomato
mixture in a bowl; reserve. Add
chicken and beans to remaining
sauce mixture in pan; cook 2 minutes.
3. Stack tortillas; wrap stack in
damp paper towels, and microwave
at high for 25 seconds. Spoon about
⅓ cup chicken mixture in center of
each tortilla; roll up. Arrange filled
tortillas, seam sides down, in bottom
of a 13- x 9-inch glass or ceramic
baking dish coated with cooking
spray. Top with reserved 1½ cups
sauce and cheese. Broil 3 minutes or
until cheese is lightly browned and
sauce is bubbly. Top with tomato
and cilantro. Serve with sour cream.
Serves 6 (serving size: 2 enchiladas
and 1 tablespoon sour cream)

CALORIES 398; FAT 11g (sat 5g, unsat 5g);
PROTEIN 29g; CARB 50g; FIBER 9g; SUGARS 7g
(added sugars 0g); SODIUM 485mg; CALC 21% DV;
POTASSIUM 19% DV

CHEERS TO YOUR HEALTH

Fast • Gluten Free
Vegetarian

Pomegranate Paloma

Hands-on: 5 min. Total: 5 min.
Classic palomas call for grapefruit soda.
Here, we use fresh grapefruit juice for a
fruit-forward beverage with less sugar and
more vitamin C. Pomegranate juice boosts
fruity flavor and packs a punch of heart-
healthy polyphenols.

Muddle 2 tablespoons pomegranate
arils, 2 teaspoons thinly sliced
ginger, and 1 (1-inch) lime wedge
in a cocktail shaker. Add ⅓ cup
pomegranate juice, ⅔ cup fresh red
grapefruit juice, 2 ounces silver
tequila, and 3 ice cubes; cover, and
shake well for 15 seconds. Strain
evenly into 2 highball glasses filled
with ice. Top each glass with 2
ounces club soda. Garnish with a
grapefruit wedge, if desired. Serves 2
(serving size: about 1 cup)

CALORIES 127; FAT 0g; PROTEIN 1g; CARB 15g;
FIBER 0g; SUGARS 14g (added sugars 0g);
SODIUM 19mg; CALC 2% DV; POTASSIUM 4% DV

┌─────────────────────────────────┐

MAKE IT A MOCKTAIL

Omit the tequila and top each drink with
2 ounces tonic water for a refreshing,
booze-free spin.

└─────────────────────────────────┘

YOUR GUIDE TO GRACIOUSNESS

Staff Favorite • Fast
Gluten Free • Make Ahead
Vegetarian

Beet Chips with Turmeric-Yogurt Dip

Hands-on: 22 min. Total: 22 min.
Here's a lighter, more colorful take on the
usual chips and dip. Beet chips crisp up in a
flash in the microwave. Keep close watch on
them to make sure they don't scorch.

3 medium beets, peeled and sliced to
    1/16-inch thickness on a mandoline
1 cup plain whole-milk Greek yogurt
2 tablespoons chopped fresh chives
1 tablespoon extra-virgin olive oil
2 teaspoons fresh lemon juice
1 teaspoon ground turmeric
1 teaspoon onion powder
¾ teaspoon kosher salt
⅛ teaspoon ground red pepper

1. Line a large microwave-safe
plate with paper towels. Working
in batches, spread beet slices on
towel-lined plate; microwave at
HIGH for 3 minutes or until crisp.
2. Combine yogurt and remaining
ingredients; stir well. Serve dip with
beet chips. Serves 8 (serving size:
about ¼ cup chips and 2 tablespoons
dip)

CALORIES 64; FAT 3g (sat 1g, unsat 2g);
PROTEIN 3g; CARB 7g; FIBER 2g; SUGARS 5g
(added sugars 0g); SODIUM 230mg; CALC 4% DV;
POTASSIUM 6% DV

WHY PRECISE TEMPERATURE MATTERS

Regardless of your skill level, you cook and think like a chef more than you know. Consider how game-changing ideas and innovative equipment constantly trickle down from professional restaurants to home kitchens. Your Thanksgiving gravy and homemade marinara owe debts to Escoffier's mother sauces. The art and craft of healthy cooking is based in part on principles French chef Michel Guérard laid out more than 40 years ago with his cuisine minceur. The chef's cherished Robot-Coupe spawned the food processor, an essential appliance in today's home kitchen. Most recently, modernist cuisine, aka molecular gastronomy—the prevailing haute cuisine mode for much of the new century—has given home cooks the gift of precision. Specifically, the lesson that cooking food to exact temperatures—rather than using the broad, vague sensory cues that guided us for generations—is a foolproof way to achieve deliciousness.

Of course, we all have our own ideas of what "coating the back of a spoon" and "fork-tender" look like, but that's the point: Those cues are subjective, while the readout on a digital thermometer is not. If the hallmark of a great cook is consistently turning out delicious food, cooking to exact temperatures is the surest way to nail those dishes every time. Chefs rely heavily on temps for sous vide cooking (see page 355 for home sous vide gear), where food in vacuum-sealed bags poaches for hours in water heated to a specific temperature so the ingredients are guaranteed to be perfectly cooked. The same principle applies at home. Here, we share temperatures that bring us brilliant results for slow-roasted meat, creamy custard, fresh-baked bread, crispy tempura green beans, poached fish, and more. So grab your digital thermometer (see our recommendations on page 356) and learn how it can take your cooking to the next level.

POACHING LIQUID
Old Cue Simmering water
New Cue 160°F (meat and fish)/ 180°F (eggs)

Cooks often think of a simmer as just barely below a boil (which is not technically wrong, though "simmer" has a broad temperature range). But when you poach fish or chicken in liquid in the 180°F to 200°F range, they end up tough and dry, because the high temps scald the meat and squeeze the life out of them. Instead, heat the water only to 160°F, which is closer to the end temperature you want the food to be (chicken breasts are ready at 160°F; white fish at 145°F; medium-cooked salmon at 125°F). When you gently submerge your food, the water temperature will drop immediately, so adjust the burner heat until the water comes back to 160°F. This approach yields incredibly supple and juicy proteins. Quick-cooking eggs need a higher temp and some bubbles, so 180°F works best for poaching them.

DEEP-FRYING OIL

Old Cue Toss in a spoonful of batter and see if it bubbles rapidly
New Cue 375°F/340°F

Frying oil temps can range from 325°F to 400°F or so. For healthy frying, the oil needs to be hot enough to turn the food's water content to steam, which prevents the food from absorbing oil. Oil that's too cool will seep into the food, making a soggy grease bomb instead of crunchy, golden perfection. We find 375°F ideal for quick-frying veggies and dumplings, while 340°F is great for dense items like chicken and fish.

SLOW-COOKED MEATS

Old Cue Until fork-tender
New Cue 195°F

You've probably had overcooked pot roast. And strange as it seems, you can dry out stewed and braised meat, too, even though they cook in liquid. Cooked too long, the meat surrenders its juices and turns stringy. The sweet spot is said to be when you can insert a fork and easily pry the meat into shreds. But this leaves plenty of room for error. Tough connective tissue that binds cuts like pork shoulder, beef chuck roast, and lamb shanks is made up mostly of collagen, which starts to melt at around 140°F. When the meat reaches 195°F, the collagen has all turned to creamy gelatin that coats the meat and gives it seductively rich mouthfeel. The meat stays superjuicy at this temp, too. Recipes that call for shreds of meat

(like pulled pork) can go to 200°F for a little extra fall-off-the-bone tenderness without drying out.

MAC AND CHEESE

Old Cue Until browned and bubbly
New Cue 155°F

Face it: The macaroni is just a vehicle for the rich, velvety cheese sauce. But lighter versions with reduced-fat dairy can curdle easily, and broken sauce kills this comfort food. Even whole milk and half-and-half curdle if cooked too hot or too long. The trick is to heat the sauce no higher than 155°F, just enough to melt the cheese into the milk mixture. No need for the sauced mac to bake long in the oven—a few minutes under the broiler will brown any added topping nicely.

CUSTARD

Old Cues Mixture "thickens slightly" or "coats the back of a spoon"
New Cue 165°F (sauce)/179°F (ice cream base)

The terror of making any egg emulsion (hollandaise sauce, carbonara pasta, mayo) is that the egg will overcook and curdle into a sad, coagulated mess. A custard like crème anglaise, the sweet base for crème brûlée and ice creams, is just as delicate. And even experienced chefs can differ on exactly what a slightly thickened custard looks like or how it should coat the back of a spoon. It's important to heat the mixture gradually, so it cooks evenly and doesn't scald. But for a sauce base, the only visual cue you need to guarantee perfect consistency is a readout of 165°F on your digital thermometer. Then chill it down, and you're golden. Because a custard that will be an ice cream base needs to be a little thicker, we carefully take it to 179°F.

TEMPERING CHOCOLATE

Old Cues Temp range, touch test
New Cues 115°F/81°F/89°F

To temper chocolate, you melt it down, then cool it back into solid form, giving it shiny gloss and snappy texture. Chocolate can be finicky, so precision is critical. Look to hit three marks during the process: first, 115°F when you melt the chocolate in a double boiler or the microwave; next, 81°F when you add whole chunks to cool the mixture; and last, 89°F when you reheat the whole mixture. This temp combo leads to Wonka-level magic every time.

OUR FAVORITE DIGITAL THERMOMETERS

THERMOPRO WIRELESS REMOTE THERMOMETER
For slow roasts that take hours to hit the right temp, we like remote probe thermometers. The ThermoPro's unit lets you conveniently monitor your food from 300 feet away, so you don't need to be glued to the oven, grill, or smoker when you have guests. And while the probe wires of some other brands suffer damage at oven temps over 400°F, this cable can handle up to 716°F, making it safe for most cooking, even on turbocharged kamado-style grills. (homedepot.com, $22)

OXO'S NEW CHEF'S PRECISION THERMOCOUPLE THERMOMETER
The Chef's Precision Thermocouple Thermometer from OXO delivers a temperature readout within about two seconds, accurate to +/- 0.9°F. Its range from -58°F to 572°F covers everything you could possibly want to temp and then some; its folding style makes it easy to store. (oxo.com, $100)

BREAD LOAF

Old Cue Tap on the bottom of the loaf and listen for a hollow sound
New Cue 200°F/185°F

Unless you're practiced in the art of bread loaf tapping, underbaked bread can make a very similar "hollow" sound to a fully baked loaf. It's like thumping a watermelon to check for ripeness: Do you *really* know what you're listening for? The thump test for bread works just fine for seasoned bakers, but the rest of us need a more exact guideline.

Our in-house baking experts find that at 200°F, yeast bread like baguettes, sourdough boules, and whole-grain loaves are ready to pull from the oven and cool. Sweet and egg-enriched breads like challah and brioche that are softer than "lean-dough" breads will be done sooner: Our bakers aim for 185°F. And to keep the loaf looking pristine, insert the thermometer into the bottom, if possible.

PROOFING YEAST

Old Cues "Lukewarm" water, touch test, temp range
New Cue 110°F

Active dry yeast is alive, made up of good-guy microbes that give rise (in every sense) to fresh-baked bread. The first step in bread making is to combine the yeast with water to proof, or "bloom," the yeast, bringing the microbes back to life. Old-school bakers will tell you to test the temp with your finger: Water that's about 98°F won't feel like anything at all, since it's approximately the same as your body temperature. They say the right temp of water will feel slightly warm to the touch, but this is pretty imprecise. Many recipes offer a range as wide as 105°F to 115°F. We aim for dead center—110°F, warm enough to activate the yeast but not too hot to kill it and allowing for 5 degrees leeway either way.

A FEAST FOR FRIENDS

During the busy rush of the season, making time for dear friends nurtures your soul. Invite them over, keep the menu simple and the hospitality warm, and renew your ties. Cookbook author Sarah Copeland shares just how easy it can be.

I n our small corner of the world, 90 miles north of New York City, we're blessed with an amazing community—almost all city expats looking for a simpler, slower life for their families. We have our tree-trimming tradition to thank for it.

When we lived in New York City, I always dreamed of an evening with many hands filling our tree with our hodgepodge of ornaments, Bing Crosby's Christmas songs crooning from a record player in the background. One year, as my husband, András, our two young children, Greta and Mátyás, and I were making our own transition from city life, we decided to invite a few new acquaintances over to our home in Hurley, in the Hudson Valley, to join us for a feast, some carols, and treats—hoping everyone would get along. András had just launched a new furniture business (Hudson Workshop), and as an inaugural project, built us a beautiful dining room table with room for eight, plus a half-dozen small kids squeezed in between. It felt like a sign. And with that one simple meal, we opened our home, our table, and our circle of friends a little wider.

It was magic: babies playing in the shadow of our freshly cut fir, little girls sneaking chocolate-stained hands into towers of treats stacked high on cake stands (my signature, no-fuss dessert for a crowd), and the guys, huddled in a corner by the coffee and beer, exchanging notes about house renovations, barn projects, and new businesses in the works.

Three years later, the same crew are our very dear friends, the ones we spend many holidays with all around the year. The easy meal I serve for this now-annual gathering is roughly the same, with some tweaks as each member contributes something from their own artistic arsenal.

After dinner, our kids circled us playing the piano and tiny guitars, begging for more chocolate while we discussed life, politics, business strategy, and local schools—enriching our families, each, while urging each other forward.

Somehow, the magic never fades.

At the holidays, but really any day, nothing feels quite like belonging—like feeling a part of something bigger than you. This crew, this meal, and the way it feeds our lives, all year long—they're one mighty gift.

Fast • Gluten Free
Vegetarian

Winter Radish Salad with Parsley and Olives

Hands-on: 20 min. Total: 30 min.
Watermelon radishes tend to be sweeter and can be cut a little thicker for heartier crunch. If you can't find them, use classic red radishes.

- ⅓ cup kalamata olives, finely chopped
- ¼ cup extra-virgin olive oil
- 2 tablespoons fresh lime juice
- 2 tablespoons kalamata olive brine (from jar)
- 2 medium watermelon radishes (about 4 ounces), thinly sliced
- 2 black radishes (about 4 ounces), sliced paper-thin
- 1 bunch watercress (about 4 ounces), trimmed
- 1 cup packed fresh flat-leaf parsley leaves
- 2 ounces feta-style goat's milk cheese or feta cheese, crumbled (about ½ cup)
- ¼ teaspoon flaky sea salt

1. Place olives, oil, juice, and brine in a large bowl; whisk to combine. Add radishes to olive mixture; toss to combine. Let stand at room temperature 20 minutes, or chill up to 1 hour.

2. Just before serving, add watercress and parsley to bowl, and toss to combine. Transfer to a platter, and sprinkle with cheese and salt. Serves 8 (serving size: about ½ cup)

CALORIES 101; FAT 10g (sat 2g, unsat 6g); PROTEIN 2g; CARB 2g; FIBER 0g; SUGARS 0g; SODIUM 261mg; CALC 6% DV; POTASSIUM 3% DV

Smoked Beer-Braised Pork Shoulder Tacos

Hands-on: 25 min. Total: 4 hr. 20 min.
Copeland uses Arrowood smoked lager (it's local for her). You can use any smoked beer—or if you can't find one, try a nut ale, a porter, or 1½ cups chicken stock. This recipe makes enough for leftovers (or hungrier guests).

1 tablespoon light brown sugar
1 tablespoon smoked paprika
2 teaspoons coarse sea salt
1 teaspoon black pepper
1 teaspoon ground red pepper
1 teaspoon fennel seeds
1 (4-pound) bone-in pork shoulder
   (Boston butt), fat trimmed to
   ¼ inch
1 (12-ounce) bottle smoked beer
24 (6-inch) corn tortillas, warmed
3 ripe avocados, quartered
4 limes, cut into wedges

1. Stir together first 6 ingredients; rub over all sides of pork shoulder. Wrap tightly in aluminum foil, and chill 1 hour or up to overnight.
2. Preheat oven to 450°F. Unwrap pork; discard foil. Place pork shoulder, fat side up, in a large ovenproof Dutch oven, and cook at 450°F, uncovered, until lightly browned, about 45 minutes. Pour beer over pork shoulder; reduce temperature to 300°F, and cover with lid. Cook pork at 300°F, basting occasionally, until a thermometer inserted just next to (but not touching) bone registers 196°F and meat pulls easily from bone, about 2 hours.
3. Remove pork from oven, and transfer to a plate. Remove and discard bone. Transfer cooking liquid to a 2-cup glass measuring cup. Let stand 10 minutes.

4. Meanwhile, shred pork, using 2 forks. Skim fat from cooking liquid. Return pork and cooking liquid to Dutch oven, and stir to combine. Serve with tortillas, avocados, and limes, or cover with lid to keep warm up to 1 hour. Serves 12 (serving size: about 3¼ ounce pork, 2 tortillas, and 1 avocado quarter)

CALORIES 360; FAT 14g (sat 3g, unsat 9g); PROTEIN 26g; CARB 37g; FIBER 6g; SUGARS 3g (added sugars 1g); SODIUM 489mg; CALC 6% DV; POTASSIUM 15% DV

> "THIS YEAR, I SLOW-ROASTED THE PORK IN ARROWOOD FARMS BREWERY'S SMOKED BEER, BREWED BY OUR FRIEND TAIT. DEAR BUDDY AND CHEF CHRIS LANIER (OF RAVENWOOD FARM) AND I COOKED THE PLANTAINS AND BEANS SIDE BY SIDE AT THE STOVE."
>
> —Sarah Copeland

Easy Smoky Black Beans

Hands-on: 10 min. Total: 10 min.
Since everything else in this menu requires a bit more of your attention, it's good to have one dish that's simpler to prepare. Gussied-up canned beans are easy and delicious.

2 tablespoons olive oil
1 tablespoon minced fresh garlic
½ teaspoon smoked paprika
½ teaspoon ground cumin
2 (15.5-ounce) cans reduced-sodium
   black beans, rinsed and drained
¼ cup water
½ teaspoon kosher salt
3 tablespoons fresh lime juice
¼ cup chopped fresh cilantro

1. Heat oil in a medium saucepan over medium-low. Add garlic, paprika, and cumin; cook, stirring often, until fragrant, about 1 minute. Add beans, ¼ cup water, and salt; cook until warmed through, 3 to 4 minutes. Remove from heat; cover to keep warm. Just before serving, stir in juice and cilantro. Serves 8 (serving size: ½ cup)

CALORIES 134; FAT 4g (sat 1g, unsat 3g); PROTEIN 7g; CARB 19g; FIBER 8g; SUGARS 0g; SODIUM 297mg; CALC 4% DV; POTASSIUM 10% DV

Baked Coconut Plantains

Hands-on: 10 min. Total: 40 min.
With their crisp exterior, tender and creamy interior, and hint of coconut flavor, these plantains are irresistible.

4 very ripe plantains, diagonally sliced
¼ cup coconut oil, melted
½ teaspoon kosher salt
½ teaspoon flaky sea salt

1. Preheat oven to 400°F with rack 6 inches from heat.
2. Toss together plantain slices, oil, and kosher salt; spread in a single layer on a baking sheet. Roast at 400°F until plantains are lightly golden on bottom, about 15 minutes. Turn slices over, and continue roasting until evenly cooked and soft, about 15 minutes. Increase oven temperature to broil, and broil until deeply golden, 1 to 2 minutes. Sprinkle with flaked salt; serve warm. Serves 8 (serving size: ½ cup)

CALORIES 170; **FAT** 7g (sat 6g, unsat 1g); **PROTEIN** 1g; **CARB** 29g; **FIBER** 2g; **SUGARS** 13g (added sugars 0g); **SODIUM** 258mg; **CALC** 0% DV; **POTASSIUM** 13% DV

Fast • Gluten Free
Make Ahead • Vegetarian

Spicy Tomatillo-Lime Sauce

Hands-on: 15 min. Total: 30 min.

10 tomatillos (about 1¾ pounds), husks removed
2 serrano chiles
1 medium-sized yellow onion, peeled and quartered
1 bunch cilantro leaves and stems
½ cup water
2 tablespoons extra-virgin olive oil
1 tablespoon fresh lime juice
1 tablespoon honey
1½ teaspoons kosher salt

1. Preheat broiler with oven rack 6 inches from heat. Arrange tomatillos, chiles, and onion in a single layer on a rimmed baking sheet. Broil until tomatillos are soft and browned, 15 to 20 minutes, turning after 8 minutes. Cool 10 minutes.
2. Transfer vegetables and any liquid in pan to a blender. Add cilantro, ½ cup water, oil, juice, honey, and salt; process until almost smooth. Keep

at room temperature until ready to serve (up to 2 hours), or store, covered, in refrigerator up to 1 week. Makes 4 cups (serving size: ¼ cup)

CALORIES 39; **FAT** 2g (sat 0g, unsat 2g); **PROTEIN** 1g; **CARB** 5g; **FIBER** 1g; **SUGARS** 3g (added sugars 1g); **SODIUM** 220mg; **CALC** 1% DV; **POTASSIUM** 5% DV

Fast • Gluten Free
Make Ahead • Vegetarian

Pickled Farm Vegetables

Hands-on: 10 min. Total: 30 min.

CARROTS
3 large multicolored carrots (about 10 ounces), thinly sliced
½ cup apple cider vinegar
½ cup water
1 tablespoon granulated sugar
1 teaspoon kosher salt
1 garlic clove, halved

ONIONS
1 large red onion, thinly sliced
½ cup apple cider vinegar
½ cup water
1 tablespoon granulated sugar
1 teaspoon kosher salt
1 garlic clove, halved

1. To prepare carrots, combine first 6 ingredients in a 1-pint jar. Cover with lid, and shake well. Let stand at room temperature 20 minutes. Chill until ready to use (up to 2 weeks).
2. To prepare onions, combine onion slices and remaining ingredients in a 1-pint jar. Cover with lid; shake well. Let stand at room temperature 20 minutes. Chill until ready to use (up to 2 weeks). Serves 8 (serving size: about ¼ cup drained pickles)

CALORIES 25; **FAT** 0g; **PROTEIN** 1g; **CARB** 6g; **FIBER** 1g; **SUGARS** 3g (added sugars 1g); **SODIUM** 168mg; **CALC** 2% DV; **POTASSIUM** 4% DV

RECIPES WITH ROOTS

Five of our favorite writers share their fondest holiday traditions, with stories in recipe format crafted to make you laugh, think, and savor.

SHANE MITCHELL

When my sister Kaki laughed, a few age lines appeared around her mouth and eyes. We were rolling out cookie dough in my kitchen on that last Christmas spent together, and because she was a dead ringer for our grandmother, a prescient thought occurred to me. "I know what she's going to look like when she's old." Didn't say it aloud. If I had, maybe life would be different, but that's magical thinking for you.

The first gingerbread man is credited to the court of Queen Elizabeth I, who favored important guests with a likeness baked as a cookie. Four centuries later, my sister, an artist and graphic designer, turned her own crisply browned wafers into an X-rated gender statement; her sense of humor always a little darker and definitely a lot dirtier than mine. The androgynous cookies swiftly developed body parts, with cinnamon red hots and sprinkles explicitly applied.[1] She even smashed dough through a garlic press to create a hirsute effect. Santa undoubtedly laugh-snorted his milk when he saw our offering next to the chimney later that night.

Full-frontal cookies are Kaki's holiday legacy to our family.[2] Recently, I mailed vintage tin cutters and the recipe to a niece named in her honor after Kaki left us too soon, never destined to be old, though her naughty spirit lingers when I slide a batch of her mature audience gingerbread into the oven this time of year.

Some kids don't get Christmas cookies. Please be Santa's helper and donate to No Kid Hungry (nokidhungry.org): It's a cause close to my heart.

Make Ahead • Vegetarian

Gingerfolk Cookies

Hands-on 20 min. Total 4 hr. 40 min.

- **1¹⁄₂ cups (about 6³⁄₈ ounces) all-purpose flour**
- **2 teaspoons ground ginger**
- **¹⁄₄ teaspoon ground cinnamon**
- **¹⁄₄ teaspoon ground cloves**
- **¹⁄₄ teaspoon ground nutmeg**
- **¹⁄₂ teaspoon baking soda**
- **¹⁄₂ cup (4 ounces) unsalted butter, softened**
- **¹⁄₂ cup packed light brown sugar**
- **¹⁄₄ cup unsulfured molasses[3]**
- **1 large egg yolk**
- **1 teaspoon grated orange zest**
- **¹⁄₂ teaspoon finely grated peeled fresh ginger[4]**
- **¹⁄₂ teaspoon vanilla extract**
- **1 cup assorted sprinkles**

1. Weigh or lightly spoon flour into dry measuring cups; level with a knife. Sift flour, spices, and baking soda into a medium bowl. With a hand or standing mixer on medium speed, cream butter in a separate bowl until whipped, about 1 minute. Then add brown sugar, beating until fluffy, about 2 more minutes. Beat in molasses, egg yolk, orange zest, fresh ginger, and vanilla on medium-low speed. Add flour mixture, and beat until just blended. Gather dough into a ball; divide and flatten into 2 disks. Wrap each in plastic wrap, and chill until firm, about 4 hours.
2. Preheat oven to 350°F.
3. Line 2 baking sheets with parchment paper. Working with 1 dough disk at a time, unwrap and place on a lightly floured surface. Roll out dough disk to ¼-inch thickness. Using a 2-inch cookie cutter[5], cut each dough disk into 12 cookies. Transfer to prepared sheets, placing about 1 inch apart. Bake at 350°F until puffed and slightly dark around edges, about 10 minutes. Cool on sheets 2 minutes; remove with a spatula to a wire rack. Cool 10 minutes. Decorate provocatively with sprinkles. Serves 24 (serving size: 1 cookie)

CALORIES 126; **FAT** 6g (sat 2g, unsat 1g); **PROTEIN** 1g; **CARB** 17g; **FIBER** 0g; **SUGARS** 9g (added sugars 9g); **SODIUM** 30mg; **CALC** 2% DV; **POTASSIUM** 2% DV

---

[1] For my family, Christmas has always been a time to be creative. Even cookies are a palette for self-expression.
[2] But not the only one: Kaki once designed felt Santa hats for pets, so now every Christmas my dog Dharma dons hers.
[3] Unsulfured molasses is made from mature sugarcane ripened naturally. Blackstrap is rich in flavor and antioxidants.
[4] A few years ago I started adding grated fresh ginger to our family recipe. It gives these cookies extra kick.
[5] On my wish list? Williams Sonoma's classic welded copper gingerbread man cookie cutter set. ($15, williams-sonoma.com)

TAMAR ADLER

There is a version of my parents' story that is best told in numbers, making it particularly well-suited to a recipe—a narrative in measurements. Twenty was my mother's age when she married my father, who was 30. She was 39 when he died. Just over zero is about the amount we know about his life in Israel, where he lived until marrying my mother[1]. We have fractions: a tan photograph of him as a smiling 4-year-old in Jerusalem; a story about his surviving the siege of Jerusalem alone, on potatoes[2]. All that we have that is whole was his food. In the place of ketchup and mayonnaise, our table in suburban New York featured hummus, tehinah, pickled hot peppers, Israeli salad. And on Shabbat and Hannukah, my mother made mujadara—a festive but simple one-pot meal of fried onion, lentils, and rice[3]. She has made variations on the basic dish, trying duck fat[4], Urfa pepper, lentils de puy. But this is where she has landed—very much, she says, like where she began.

Adding thyme and bay leaf might be heresy. I haven't seen either in mujadara recipes I've read, and my mother doesn't include them. But I never cook rice or lentils without them.

We always ate this with white rice. I like brown better. If you use white, the benefit is not having to parboil it. But the benefits of brown far outweigh that small step: It tastes like something, it is healthier, it retains a bit of structure and body and reminds you that you're eating.

Staff Favorite • Gluten Free
Vegetarian

Mujadara

Hands-on: 30 min. Total: 1 hr. 30 min.

7 cups water, divided
1 cup uncooked long-grain brown rice
1½ teaspoons kosher salt, divided
3 large yellow onions
¼ cup good-quality extra-virgin olive oil (such as Lucini), divided
6 thyme sprigs
1 tablespoon ground cumin
1 bay leaf
1 cup uncooked brown or green lentils, rinsed
¼ cup toasted pine nuts
Plain whole-milk yogurt

1. Bring 4 cups of the water to a boil in a small pot over high. Add rice and ½ teaspoon of the salt, and boil for 10 minutes. Drain. While the rice par-cooks, halve and thinly slice the onions horizontally.
2. Heat a medium pot or baking dish with a lid over medium-high, and then add 3 tablespoons of the olive oil. Add sliced onions, thyme, and remaining 1 teaspoon kosher salt. Reduce heat to medium, and cook, stirring often, until onions are softened and quite browned, about 20 to 25 minutes. Add a sprinkle of water if needed to keep from burning. Remove half the onions (about 1 cup), and set aside. Add par-cooked rice, cumin, bay leaf, and remaining 1 tablespoon olive oil to pot. Cook, stirring often, until toasted and fragrant, 1 to 2 minutes. Add lentils and remaining 3 cups water. Increase heat to medium-high, and bring to a boil. Then reduce heat to a very low simmer. Cover and cook until rice and lentils are tender and water is absorbed, about 40 minutes.
3. While mujadara cooks, put reserved half of onions in a small pan, and cook over medium-high, stirring often, until fried and crisp, even blackened in places, about 5 minutes. Set aside.
4. To serve, stir toasted pine nuts into mujadara, and sprinkle with fried onions. If you like, drizzle with additional olive oil and a dollop of yogurt[5]. Serves 8 (serving size: about ¾ cup)

CALORIES 276; FAT 11g (sat 1g, unsat 8g); PROTEIN 8g; CARB 37g; FIBER 6g; SUGARS 3g (added sugars 0g); SODIUM 367mg; CALC 3% DV; POTASSIUM 10% DV

[1]He was the only Israeli generation, perhaps part of why I cling to his food so vehemently.
[2]My father's mother died when he was 12, and his father died when he was 18. If zero is what we knew about him, the amount I know of his parents is some deep negative number.
[3]An almost-child bride, my mother was taught Israeli cuisine by the wives of my father's émigré friends. She has become a formidable cook, outpacing her teachers.
[4]I recently tried making this with ghee because it sounded good. It was too buttery, and I've reverted to olive oil, which is perfect, and usually the best fat in my book, anyway.
[5]This can be a side dish, but I serve it as a main dish, with yogurt with pounded-up garlic and sometimes mint mixed in, some boiled egg wedges, and an herb salad.

ROBB WALSH

I dimly remember a Christmas Eve dinner at Nana's house that started with raw garlic and a bowl of dark brown mushroom soup. There were carolers at the front door singing Christmas songs in Ruthenian[1,2]. We left Pittsburgh when I was 7 and quit the tradition[3]. When I had kids of my own, I felt a need to reconnect with my heritage. I was invited to the Ukrainian Cultural Center in Chicago one October—they made a full-scale Christmas Eve dinner for my visit[4]. The food brought back memories, but when a group of carolers appeared singing the old Christmas songs, tears rolled down my cheeks. My family has prepared the Ruthenian feast every year since. The raw garlic freaks out kids, but everybody loves the mushroom soup.

This recipe calls for a mix of dried mushrooms and fresh button mushrooms, but the soup was originally prepared with freshly foraged wild mushrooms—feel free to use what you like.

If you forget the first step, don't panic. The shortcut: combine dried mushrooms and 4 cups of water in a saucepan over low, simmer for 30 minutes. Save the liquid.

Make Ahead • Vegetarian

Ruthenian Mushroom Soup

Hands-on: 45 min. Total: 10 hr.

2 ounces dried porcini mushrooms
3 tablespoons canola oil
1 pound sliced fresh button mushrooms
1 medium-sized yellow onion, finely chopped (about 1½ cups)
1 cup finely chopped celery
3 garlic cloves, minced
½ teaspoon dried powdered thyme
½ teaspoon dried dill
½ teaspoon ground white pepper
Pinch of cayenne pepper
2 tablespoons all-purpose flour
1 bay leaf
1 pound russet potatoes, peeled and cut into quarter-inch dice
3 tablespoons sherry vinegar[5]
1½ teaspoons kosher salt
Hot pepper sauce (such as Tabasco)
Fresh dill leaves

1. Ideally, you should soak the dried mushrooms in a quart of warm water overnight to rehydrate them. If you forget this first step, don't panic. The shortcut: Combine dried mushrooms and 4 cups of water in a saucepan over low; simmer for 30 minutes. Save the liquid. The soaking liquid is the soup stock, so be careful not to throw it away.
2. When the mushrooms are soft, remove from water, squeezing most of the liquid back into the bowl. Trim away hard woody parts of the mushroom stems. Coarsely chop mushrooms, and set aside. Pour liquid through a cheesecloth-lined sieve over a bowl—stop when a tablespoon or so of the liquid remains and discard it along with the grit. Combine the strained liquid with water until you have 10 cups.
3. Heat the oil in a large soup pot over medium-high. Add the fresh mushrooms, onion, celery, and garlic, and cook, stirring now and then, until the mushrooms give up their water, about 10 minutes. Add thyme, dill, white pepper, and cayenne, and keep stirring. Sprinkle the flour over the mushroom mixture, and stir constantly for a few minutes until flour begins to stick to the pot. Add porcini mushrooms, the 10 cups of mushroom liquid, and bay leaf. Stir while scraping to deglaze the bottom of the pot. Cook 15 minutes, stirring as it thickens.
4. Reduce heat to a simmer, stir in potatoes, and cook until meltingly tender, another 45 minutes. Season with vinegar, salt, and hot pepper sauce to taste. Simmer for a few more minutes. Remove bay leaf. Serve family style in a tureen; garnish each bowl with fresh dill. Serves 12 (serving size: about 1 cup)

CALORIES 100; **FAT** 4g (sat 0g, unsat 3g); **PROTEIN** 4g; **CARB** 13g; **FIBER** 3g; **SUGARS** 2g (added sugars 0g); **SODIUM** 251mg; **CALC** 2% DV; **POTASSIUM** 9% DV

---

[1] Ruthenian-Americans are citizens with ancestors from areas of the Carpathian mountains of Central Europe, including parts of Slovakia, Poland, and Ukraine.
[2] Ruthenian vegetarian Christmas Eve dinner originated from a pre-Christian winter feast that honored farm animals.
[3] Pittsburgh has the Byzantine Catholic Archeparchy and a large Ruthenian population. Andy Warhol, the most famous Ruthenian-American, was a Pittsburgh native.
[4] The menu consisted of 12 vegetarian dishes, each representing part of nature: wheat from the fields, vegetables from the garden, mushrooms from the forest, etc.
[5] In earlier times, the sour flavor often came from kvass, a fermented bread beverage. As kvass became less common, vinegar and lemon juice were adopted as modern alternatives.

PETER MEEHAN

Christmastime travel is garbage unless you drive a flying sleigh. One year I decided I was done with it. I'd stay in New York instead of swimming upstream to my parents' house and would gather the other misfits on the island of misfit toys to celebrate it. My plan was to make an Italianate Feast of the Seven Fishes[1] on Christmas Eve, a rewrite of my family's fish-free Midwestern traditions. But as the RSVP tally climbed[2], I had to accept that I definitely didn't own enough plates to do it for 30. (Where would I even get all the eels?)

My wife and I racked our brains for a menu solution. We needed seafood for a crowd, without being at the stove all night. We landed on lobster rolls: They were highly desirable, but also hand-food, and easier to make than anything, like tuna salad in white tie and tails[3]. So we stacked them high, in near-criminal *abbondanza*, and started a tradition that's been running for a decade-plus. Now "home" is where we and the misfits gather on Christmas Eve and where there's no end to the lobster rolls—at least until it's time to put the cookies and milk out and try to get the kids into bed.

Make Ahead

Lobster Rolls

Hands-on: 40 min. Total: 1 hr. 10 min.

**2 pounds fully cooked lobster meat[4]
(from about 10 pounds of live
lobsters)**
2 cups finely diced English cucumber
3/4 cup mayonnaise
2 teaspoons minced fresh tarragon
6 small scallions, very thinly sliced
1 teaspoon kosher salt
1/2 teaspoon black pepper
**12 Martin's Long Potato Rolls (aka
hot dog buns)**
1/4 cup unsalted butter, softened

1. If using live lobsters, steam or boil them. Let cool at room temperature. Use a cleaver to crack and remove the meat from the claws, knuckles, and tails. Remove and discard the cartilage from the claws and the intestines from the tails of the cooked meat. Cut the meat into ½-inch pieces.
2. Place diced cucumber in a colander for at least 5 minutes to drain the excess liquid. Combine the lobster, cucumber, mayonnaise, and tarragon (or chervil). If the salad is to be served within the hour, add the scallions (or chives). If not, add them 30 minutes before serving. Season with salt, if needed, and pepper. Cover with plastic wrap and chill for at least 30 minutes before serving, or as far ahead as the night before.
3. When you're ready to party: preheat a griddle over medium-low. Taste the lobster salad—does it need more salt? Does it want more mayonnaise? Now's the time to fix it.
4. Lightly butter the insides of the buns. (The split-top buns common to New England lobster roll joints are rare in New York, but Martin's Potato Rolls—from Central Pennsylvania, famous for being Shake Shack's buns—are easy to score. If Martin's aren't available, other potato roll brands will work just fine.) Griddle them for about 2 minutes, until golden brown[5]. Stuff the rolls with the chilled lobster salad. Stack 'em high and serve 'em hot. Serves 12 (serving size: 1 lobster roll)

CALORIES 358; **FAT** 20g (sat 5g, unsat 12g); **PROTEIN** 20g; **CARB** 25g; **FIBER** 1g; **SUGARS** 4g (added sugars 0g); **SODIUM** 757mg; **CALC** 13% DV; **POTASSIUM** 10% DV

---

[1] The feast is an Italian Catholic Christmas Eve tradition of meat-free feasting that often includes salt cod, mussels, eels, and other sea beasts common to the Southern Italian table.
[2] Truth is, I would have fudged up seven courses for just seven people.
[3] This was when lobster rolls ran you 20 bucks and required a wait in line in Manhattan at places like Mary's Fish Camp or Pearl Oyster Bar.
[4] This time of year, lobsters tend to be hard-shell, which have more meat per pound than the soft-shell lobsters of summer.
[5] You could toast the buns a little further in a broiler or oven, but that butter-crisped, just-warm interior is the necessary magic.

CARLA HALL

Green beans were often a staple of our regular Sunday suppers at Granny's house, but the simple addition of the little potatoes with the skin peeled off in the middle was saved for holidays and special occasions. The green beans and potatoes[1] were cooked in flavored chicken stock, and the potatoes would fall apart just enough to coat the beans with starchy goodness.

The best part of this memory was stringing the green beans, because it was one of the few tasks that I was allowed to do when it came to preparing dinner for the holidays when I was a kid—probably because it was tedious and rarely actually done in the kitchen[2]. Today our family holiday tradition includes everyone in the family taking charge of a recipe, and I tend to move around between them helping out here and there as needed. The green beans and potatoes still live on in our yearly menu, only now it's my nieces and nephews who cook it. The dish is just as simple and delicious as it was when I had it at Granny's table, and it's still the one thing that officially tells my taste buds that it's a special occasion.

---

[1] We peel the strip for a couple of reasons: It looks nice, and it helps the potatoes release more starch.
[2] Pulling strings off the green beans is a great kitchen job for kids—or anyone else who wants to help. It's simple enough that you can chat while stringing.
[3] To avoid an over-salted dish, be sure to use low- or no-sodium chicken stock. Vegetable stock works great, too, if you want to make the dish vegetarian.
[4] I also like to cut a few of the potatoes into quarters—that way they'll help thicken the stock even more.
[5] The reduced stewing liquid is a built-in sauce for the vegetables. Make sure to spoon it all on there—it's like veggie gravy!

continued

Gluten Free

Southern Green Beans and Potatoes

Hands-on: 15 min. Total: 37 min.

2 teaspoons olive oil
1 medium onion, halved and very
   thinly sliced
2 garlic cloves, sliced
¼ teaspoon crushed red chile flakes
3 cups unsalted chicken stock[3]
¾ teaspoon kosher salt
1½ pounds small red and gold
   potatoes, a strip peeled from the
   center of each[4]
1 pound green beans, trimmed

1. Heat the oil in a 5-quart saucepan over medium-high heat. Add the onion. Cook, stirring occasionally, until just tender, about 2 minutes. Add the garlic and chile flakes and cook, stirring frequently, until the onions are tender, about 3 minutes.
2. Add the stock, salt, and potatoes. Bring to a boil, and then reduce to a steady simmer. Simmer 10 minutes or until the potatoes are just tender enough to be pierced with a fork, but still firm.
3. Add the green beans, cover, and simmer until very tender, about 6 minutes. (The secret to these beans is that they should be tender, not crisp, just as my granny made them. For me, they are true comfort food.) Use a slotted spoon to transfer the potatoes and green beans to a serving dish. Bring the liquid to a boil and boil until reduced to 1 cup, about 6 minutes. Spoon[5] over the vegetables and gently fold to mix. Serve hot. Serves 4 (serving size: about 1 cup)

CALORIES 198; FAT 3g (sat 0g, unsat 2g);
PROTEIN 8g; CARB 39g; FIBER 8g; SUGARS 8g
(added sugars 0g); SODIUM 346mg; CALC 5% DV;
POTASSIUM 8% DV

SUPERPOWER SIPPERS

Start and end your day with delicious drinks that give you a nutritional boost. From spicy morning elixirs to soothing nightcaps, these better-for-you beverages keep your immune system humming and your gut health optimized, and fill in the nutrient voids you may be experiencing this holiday season.

Fast • Gluten Free
Vegetarian

Restorative Turmeric Elixir

Hands-on: 5 min. Total: 5 min.
When the hustle of the holidays leaves you feeling overtaxed, your immune function can suffer. This invigorating morning beverage delivers a quarter of your daily goal for immune-boosting vitamin C, along with turmeric and ginger, which help quell inflammation. New research shows ginger also helps promote the growth of gut-healthy bacteria.

1 tablespoon thinly sliced fresh
   turmeric
1 tablespoon fresh mint leaves
1 teaspoon thinly sliced peeled fresh
   ginger
½ teaspoon sugar
¼ teaspoon grated lime zest
Dash of salt
Pinch of crushed red pepper
   (optional)
½ cup fresh pineapple juice
1½ tablespoons fresh lime juice
5 ice cubes
⅓ cup seltzer water
1 lime wedge (optional)

1. Muddle turmeric, mint, ginger, sugar, lime zest, salt, and red pepper, if using, in a cocktail shaker. Add pineapple juice, lime juice, and 5 ice cubes; cover and shake for 15 seconds.
2. Strain into a highball glass filled with ice. Add seltzer; stir. Garnish with lime wedge, if desired. Serves 1 (serving size: about 1 cup)

CALORIES 90; FAT 0g; PROTEIN 1g; CARB 22g;
FIBER 1g; SUGARS 15g (added sugars 2g);
SODIUM 124mg; CALC 3% DV; POTASSIUM 8% DV

Rejuvenating Rosé Spritzer

Hands-on: 5 min. Total: 5 min.
Stress runs high during the holidays, which could compromise digestion. Kombucha is packed with gut-friendly probiotics to help maintain healthy gut flora, in addition to compounds that fight harmful free radicals. Light and bright, rosé is a great match for effervescent grapefruit, both of which contain rich amounts of flavonoids— powerful plant antioxidants shown to help reduce blood pressure, fight inflammation, and improve vascular function.

⅓ cup fresh grapefruit juice
½ ounce St-Germain (elderflower liqueur)
½ cup ice
3 ounces original (unflavored) kombucha
2 ounces sparkling rosé
1 lemon slice

1. Place grapefruit juice and St-Germain in a lowball glass. Add ½ cup ice; top with kombucha and rosé. Garnish with lemon slice. Serves 1 (serving size: about 1 cup)

CALORIES 146; **FAT** 0g; **PROTEIN** 1g; **CARB** 17g; **FIBER** 0g; **SUGARS** 14g (added sugars 6g); **SODIUM** 7mg; **CALC** 1% DV; **POTASSIUM** 4% DV

Soothing Cardamom Sipper

Hands-on: 10 min. Total: 15 min.
Wind down at the end of the day with the adult version of a glass of warm milk. Research shows cardamom may help ward off stomach ulcers. It and sesame seeds (the essential ingredient in tahini) also have heart-healthy and anti-inflammatory benefits. Be sure to use refrigerated coconut milk (found with nut milks in the dairy case) and not canned coconut milk.

1 cup refrigerated unsweetened coconut milk (such as Silk)
3 green cardamom pods, crushed
1 cinnamon stick
1 tablespoon maple syrup
1 teaspoon tahini (sesame seed paste)
¾ ounce bourbon

1. Bring milk, cardamom, cinnamon, and maple syrup to a simmer in a small saucepan over medium, stirring occasionally. Remove from heat; stir in tahini, cover, and let stand 5 minutes. Strain into a glass; discard cardamom pods, and reserve cinnamon stick. Add bourbon; stir. Garnish with reserved cinnamon stick. Serves 1 (serving size: about 1 cup)

CALORIES 174; **FAT** 7g (sat 4g, unsat 0g); **PROTEIN** 1g; **CARB** 16g; **FIBER** 1g; **SUGARS** 12g (added sugars 12g); **SODIUM** 43mg; **CALC** 52% DV; **POTASSIUM** 1% DV

Supercharged Kale-Avocado Smoothie

Hands-on: 5 min. Total: 5 min.
This hydrating smoothie is jam-packed with nutrients, delivering one-third of your daily goal of vitamin A and 100% of vitamin K— two important nutrients many of us don't get enough of. Matcha green tea powder delivers a jolt of caffeine without the jittery side effects, helping you power through your holiday to-do list with sustained energy and alertness.

1 cup coconut water
1 tablespoon fresh lemon juice
1 teaspoon matcha powder
1 cup fresh kale, stemmed
1 cup fresh spinach
¼ ripe avocado
2 pitted Medjool dates
1 cup ice

1. Place coconut water, lemon juice, and matcha in a blender; top with kale, spinach, avocado, dates, and ice. Start blender at lowest setting and gradually increase to half-power; process for 1 minute or until very smooth. Serves 1 (serving size: about 1½ cups)

CALORIES 200; **FAT** 8g (sat 1g, unsat 6g); **PROTEIN** 3g; **CARB** 32g; **FIBER** 7g; **SUGARS** 21g (added sugars 0g); **SODIUM** 70mg; **CALC** 14% DV; **POTASSIUM** 26% DV

SHARP KNIFE ADVICE

By Andrea Nguyen

This culinary guru tells you why when it comes to knives, quality trumps quantity.

My mother taught me many things about cooking, but knife skills were not among them. I learned to chop, dice, and slice by watching Jacques Pépin and Martin Yan on 1980s public television. Pépin chattered effortlessly while rendering an onion into perfect squares. Within seconds, Yan smacked and smeared garlic into a minced state.

I wanted to be like them and practiced whenever I could. A dull knife accident that led to stitches didn't deter me. It only underscored the need for sharp blades.

In college, my brother indulged me with a set of Cutco knives. For my first restaurant job, I bought a Chicago Cutlery chef's knife. Our wedding registry included J.A. Henckels. I sharpened the blades often, but they never held their edges long. I wasn't yet chopping at Pépin and Yan levels.

One day at a Japanese hardware store in Los Angeles, I bought a Mac knife for my sister as a housewarming gift. She wasn't a great cook, and the light, thin blade gave her confidence. I added inexpensive Japanese knives to my collection, too. We marveled at how the Asian knives were easier to work with than their European cousins. I was chopping more like my PBS heroes.

My local knife-sharpening guru taught me how to gently draw a blade along a steel to maintain its edge between his intense sharpenings. He has sharpened more than 60,000 knives in 13 years, but "no one makes knives like the Japanese," he told me. Their craft developed from making samurai swords centuries ago, and their knife designs are formulated for efficiency.

The hardware-store Japanese knives were fine tools, but over time my cutting hand and forearm began to tingle and hurt. A tendinitis brace helped, but the pain lingered. Would pricier blades relieve my pain?

I spent hours researching blade steels and knife designs (going down the Japanese cutlery rabbit hole is an adventure characterized by metallurgy and artisanal makers). I eventually settled on a guyto (aka gyutou) chef's knife and a nakiri vegetable knife featuring HAP40 semi-stainless blades, a high-tech combo of metals that enables blades to stay sharp longer. (See buying tips on the next page.)

You must wipe these knives dry after prep sessions to prevent them from rusting. (Any careless rust spots got removed with Flitz metal polish.) But the slight inconvenience was worth it. As I chopped, diced, and minced like a crazy fool, the edges barely dulled. My quarterly knife tune-ups are now needed just once a year.

Tackling a dish involving lots of knife work became less of a chore. Paper-thin sliced onion, matchstick-cut jicama, and finely chopped ginger? No problem with the guyto. A mandoline for potatoes au gratin? Nah. The nakiri glides through the potato like butter. My arm pain disappeared.

I had developed pretty good knife skills during decades of cooking, but using the new Japanese knives upped my game—and it may do the same for you, too.

Gluten Free

Shrimp-and-Orange Salad

Hands-on: 30 min. Total: 35 min.
Practice and show off your knife skills by making this main course salad. To give precooked shrimp a refresh, toss them in a good 1/2 teaspoon salt, and then rinse and pat dry. Cutting the shrimp in half symmetrically makes them easier to eat.

3 tablespoons canola oil
2 tablespoons strained fresh lemon juice (from 1 lemon)
2 tablespoons unseasoned Japanese rice vinegar
1 tablespoon honey
1 1/2 teaspoons grated orange rind
1 teaspoon fish sauce (such as Red Boat or Three Crabs)
1/2 teaspoon fine sea salt
1/2 teaspoon black pepper, freshly ground is best
3/4 cup thinly sliced red onion, quickly rinsed to reduce harshness and drained well [the onion may be a little harsh for date night if it's not rinsed]
5 cups thinly sliced savoy cabbage (about 10 ounces)
1 1/2 cups peeled, matchstick-cut jicama
1/2 cup coarsely chopped fresh mint leaves [a coarse chop allows the mint to pop in flavor and color]
16 large cooked shrimp, peeled, deveined and halved symmetrically into 32 pieces (about 9 ounces)
3 large navel oranges, peeled and cut into segments

1. For the dressing: whisk together canola oil, lemon juice, vinegar, honey, orange rind, fish sauce, sea salt, and pepper in a small bowl.

Add the onion, and set aside for a few minutes to soften and slightly pickle the onion.

2. Combine the cabbage, jicama, mint, shrimp, and orange segments in a large bowl. Pour on the dressing and onion, and then toss well. If you want to soften the cabbage and develop flavor, let the salad sit for about 5 minutes. Divide among 4 plates to serve. Serves 4 (serving size: 2 cups)

CALORIES 250; **FAT** 11g (sat 1g, unsat 10g); **PROTEIN** 12g; **CARB** 28g; **FIBER** 7g; **SUGARS** 17g (added sugars 4g); **SODIUM** 516mg; **CALC** 12% DV; **POTASSIUM** 15% DV

JAPANESE KNIFE BUYING TIPS

When you're shopping for a Japanese knife, shop by knife type. Mac, Miyabi, Tojiro, and Shun are all well-regarded, well-distributed brands. Or geek out on artisanal makers at chefknivestogo.com or knifewear.com. Prices vary a lot: $50 to $100 for a good petty; $150 to $225 for quality representatives of other kinds of knives.

SANTOKU
Santokus are good all-purpose knives. A 7-inch santoku can handle many tasks with ease. Dimples on the blade help food release, but they're not a must.

GYUTO
This Western-style chef's knife is crafted with Japanese sensibilities. An 8-inch blade is good, but one that's longer offers greater leverage for chopping.

PETTY KNIFE
A petty knife (aka a utility knife) is versatile, like a petite chef's knife crossed with a paring knife, and it's terrific for small tasks, such as chopping apples.

NAKIRI
For veggie prep, buy a rectangular nakiri. Its straight cutting edge means you can't rock and chop with it, but you'll produce precise, uniform cuts.

THE PICKY EATER GURU

EAT MORE VEGGIES WITH THIS FAMILY FAVORITE

By Gina Homolka

This mom shares her secret to getting kids to eat their vegetables, no bickering included. Better yet? Adults will be happy to have a healthier version of this old-school fave, too.

I've combined two kid-friendly classics—cheeseburgers and sloppy joes—to make a meal no picky kid could resist. The best part? There are veggies hiding in the meat! But not to worry—the kids won't even notice.

I've talked to so many parents about the challenges of getting their picky children to eat their veggies. It's actually one of the most common problems parents face at the dinner table. The good news is that most children eventually outgrow their picky palates. In fact, as a kid I was a pretty picky eater myself. I remember many nights sitting at the dinner table pushing my peas and carrots around on my plate waiting to be excused from the table. But rather than fighting with my kids and coaxing them to eat something they don't like, my solution is to hide the good stuff in some of their favorite meals. In this dish I created a nutrient-packed sauce by pureeing the veggies in with the tomato sauce. I used onions, carrots, and red bell pepper, and avoided anything green since (as I am sure you know) most picky kids won't touch the green stuff.

This is perfect served over whole-wheat burger buns with the same toppings you like on your burger. One of my favorite—and less messy—ways to eat this is served over a baked potato.

Turkey Cheeseburger Sloppy Joe

Hands-on: 20 min. Total: 52 min.

1 pound 93% lean ground turkey
½ teaspoon kosher salt
1 (8-ounce) can tomato sauce
1 cup water
¼ cup ketchup
½ small yellow onion, roughly chopped (about 4 ounces)
¼ red bell pepper, roughly chopped (about 2½ ounces)
1 carrot, roughly chopped (about 4 ounces)
2 garlic cloves
1 teaspoon yellow mustard
1 teaspoon Worcestershire sauce
¾ cup preshredded part-skim cheddar cheese
6 whole-wheat hamburger buns

1. Brown the turkey in a large skillet over high, breaking it up as it cooks, about 1 to 2 minutes. Season with salt; drain liquid.
2. While turkey browns, place tomato sauce, 1 cup water, ketchup, onion, bell pepper, carrot, garlic, mustard, and Worcestershire sauce in a blender, and blend until smooth, about 30 seconds. Pour over browned meat, and stir well. Bring to a boil over high; reduce heat to low. Cover and simmer 30 minutes. Uncover, increase heat to high, and cook, stirring, until thickened, about 1 to 2 minutes. Remove from heat, and stir in cheese. To serve, spoon ½ cup meat mixture over bottom halves of buns, and top with your favorite toppings and top halves of buns. Serves 6 (serving size: 1 sandwich)

CALORIES 318; **FAT** 10g (sat 4g, unsat 6g); **PROTEIN** 20g; **CARB** 31g; **FIBER** 4g; **SUGARS** 8g (added sugars 1g); **SODIUM** 648mg; **CALC** 27% DV; **POTASSIUM** 7% DV

WEEKNIGHT MAINS

Fast • Gluten Free

Curried Butternut Squash and Apple Soup

Hands-on: 20 min. Total: 25 min.
Winter squash is high in vitamin A, important for vision and bone health. Frozen, precooked squash saves time here. You can also roast a 2-pound peeled, diced butternut squash instead—do this a day ahead so the soup is quick to prepare the next night.

1 tablespoon unsalted butter
1 tablespoon olive oil
1 medium leek, chopped (about 1 cup)
1 cup peeled, chopped Golden
   Delicious apple
1 tablespoon Madras curry powder
1/2 cup dry white wine
3 (10-ounce) packages frozen cooked
   butternut squash, thawed
4 cups unsalted chicken stock
2 tablespoons pure maple syrup
1 1/2 tablespoons apple cider vinegar
3/4 teaspoon kosher salt
1/2 teaspoon black pepper
3/4 cup plain 2% reduced-fat Greek
   yogurt
2 tablespoons water
1/2 cup julienne-cut Golden Delicious
   apple

1. Heat butter and oil in a large Dutch oven over medium until butter melts. Add leek and chopped apple; cook 6 minutes, stirring occasionally. Stir in curry powder; cook 1 minute. Increase heat to medium-high. Add wine; cook 2 minutes or until liquid is reduced and slightly syrupy, stirring to scrape up browned bits. Add squash and stock to pan; bring to a boil. Reduce heat to medium-low; cover and simmer 8 minutes or until apple and squash are very tender.
2. Place half of squash mixture in a blender. Remove center piece of blender lid (to allow steam to escape); secure blender lid on blender. Cover opening in lid with a kitchen towel (to avoid splatters); blend until smooth. Repeat procedure with remaining half of squash mixture. Return soup to pan; stir in maple syrup, vinegar, salt, and pepper. Combine yogurt and 2 tablespoons water in a bowl. Divide soup among 4 bowls; top with yogurt mixture and julienne-cut apple. Serves 4 (serving size: 2 cups soup, 3 tablespoons yogurt, and 2 tablespoons apple)

CALORIES 322; FAT 8g (sat 3g, unsat 4g); PROTEIN 13g; CARB 51g; FIBER 5g; SUGARS 20g (added sugars 6g); SODIUM 519mg; CALC 14% DV; POTASSIUM 17% DV

MADRAS CURRY

Earthy Madras curry powder has a bit more heat than regular curry powder, though either can be used here. For extra kick, add a dash of ground red pepper to the soup.

Gluten Free

Miso-Ginger Noodle Bowls

Hands-on: 40 min. Total: 40 min.
Use miso to enrich broths, marinades, or salad dressings, keeping in mind that a little goes a long way. Look for it in the refrigerated section with the soy products.

3 center-cut bacon slices, chopped
8 cups stemmed, sliced collard
   greens or kale
3 garlic cloves, sliced
1 tablespoon canola oil
1 (6-ounce) package shiitake
   mushroom caps, sliced
2 tablespoons white miso paste
2 teaspoons grated peeled fresh
   ginger
4 cups unsalted chicken stock
4 large eggs (in shells), rinsed
4 ounces dried flat brown rice
   noodles (such as Annie Chun's Pad
   Thai noodles)
1 cup matchstick-cut carrot

1. Heat bacon in a large saucepan over medium-high; cook 5 minutes or until crisp. Add greens and garlic; sauté 6 minutes. Place greens in a bowl; keep warm.
2. Heat oil in pan over medium-high. Add mushrooms; cook 3 minutes or until softened. Stir in miso and ginger; cook 30 seconds, stirring constantly. Add stock; bring to a boil.
3. Reduce heat to medium. Add eggs in shells; cover and cook 7 minutes. Remove eggs with a slotted spoon; plunge into ice water. Let stand 3 minutes; drain. Peel and halve eggs.
4. Bring soup to a boil. Add noodles; cook 2 minutes or until tender. Divide stock mixture among 4 bowls; top evenly with greens, eggs, and carrots. Serves 4 (serving size: 1 cup soup, 1/2 cup greens, 1 egg, and 1/4 cup carrots)

CALORIES 304; FAT 11g (sat 3g, unsat 6g); PROTEIN 18g; CARB 36g; FIBER 6g; SUGARS 6g (added sugars 0g); SODIUM 542mg; CALC 21% DV; POTASSIUM 13% DV

Staff Favorite • Fast Vegetarian

Creamy Kale Caesar Salad with Soft-Boiled Eggs

Hands-on: 25 min. Total: 25 min.
A quick massage tenderizes hearty lacinato kale leaves so that they absorb more of the creamy dressing. Start with cold eggs so the yolks cook to a deliciously jammy texture.

4 large eggs (in shells), refrigerator cold

1 pound lacinato kale, stemmed and chopped

2 tablespoons fresh lemon juice, divided

1 tablespoon olive oil

1/4 cup canola mayonnaise

2 tablespoons water

1/4 teaspoon kosher salt

1/2 teaspoon black pepper

2 garlic cloves, grated

1 ounce Parmesan cheese, grated and divided (about 1/4 cup)

Cooking spray

1/2 large red onion, cut into 4 wedges

1 1/2 ounces whole-wheat French bread baguette, cut into 8 thin slices

1. Bring a large saucepan filled with water to a boil. Carefully add eggs; cook 7 minutes. Plunge eggs into a bowl filled with ice water; let stand 3 minutes. Peel and halve.
2. Combine kale, 1 tablespoon juice, and oil in a large bowl; massage by squeezing and tossing the kale mixture 1 minute or until slightly wilted.
3. Combine remaining 1 tablespoon juice, mayonnaise, 2 tablespoons water, salt, pepper, and garlic in a bowl. Stir in half of cheese. Add mayonnaise mixture to kale mixture; toss.
4. Heat a grill pan over medium-high. Coat pan with cooking spray. Add onion and bread slices; cook onion 4 minutes on each side and bread for 2 minutes on each side. Separate onion wedges into pieces, if desired.
5. Divide kale mixture among 4 plates. Top with egg halves, red onion, bread, and remaining cheese. Serves 4 (serving size: 3 cups kale mixture, 1 egg, and 2 bread slices)

CALORIES 316; FAT 22g (sat 4g, unsat 17g); PROTEIN 13g; CARB 20g; FIBER 3g; SUGARS 1g (added sugars 0g); SODIUM 503mg; CALC 28% DV; POTASSIUM 3% DV

3 WAYS TO
SPEED UP A KALE SALAD

1. While the water comes to a boil, prep all the other elements for the dish: Stem and chop kale, grate the cheese and garlic, and slice the bread.

2. Squeeze the kale for just a minute to soften the leaves far faster than marinating would. The slightly wilted greens will be easier to eat.

3. Reach for a grill pan to cook the onion and toast the bread; the stovetop pan heats up more quickly than the oven or broiler does.

Make Ahead

Chicken-and-Kale Alfredo Bake

Hands-on: 40 min. Total: 40 min.
Whole-grain pasta holds up nicely throughout boiling and baking and gives you twice as much fiber per serving as white pasta; opt for a ridged pasta like penne.

6 ounces uncooked whole-wheat penne

2 cups stemmed chopped kale (about 2 ounces)

1 1/2 tablespoons olive oil

2 (6-ounce) skinless, boneless chicken breasts, cut into bite-sized pieces

1/2 teaspoon black pepper

1/4 teaspoon kosher salt

2 cups fat-free milk

2 tablespoons all-purpose flour

2 ounces Parmesan cheese, grated and divided (about 1/2 cup)

1/2 cup chopped shallots

1 teaspoon grated lemon rind

1 tablespoon fresh lemon juice

Cooking spray

2 ounces preshredded part-skim mozzarella cheese (about 3/4 cup)

1 1/2 tablespoons whole-wheat panko (Japanese breadcrumbs)

1. Preheat oven to 400°F.
2. Bring a large saucepan filled with water to a boil. Add pasta; cook 6 minutes. Add kale; cook 2 minutes or until pasta is al dente. Drain. Place pasta mixture in a large bowl.
3. Heat oil in a large nonstick skillet over medium-high. Sprinkle chicken with pepper and salt. Add chicken to pan; cook 8 minutes or until done. Add chicken to pasta (do not wipe out pan).
4. Combine milk, flour, and 1/4 cup Parmesan cheese in a bowl. Heat pan over medium. Add shallot to drippings in pan; cook 2 minutes. Stir in rind and juice; cook 1 minute. Add milk mixture; bring to a boil. Cook 2 minutes or until thickened. Add milk mixture to pasta mixture; toss to coat.
5. Spoon pasta mixture into a 2-quart glass or ceramic baking dish coated with cooking spray. Sprinkle with remaining 1/4 cup Parmesan, mozzarella cheese, and panko. Bake at 400°F for 10 minutes or until browned. Serves 4 (serving size: about 2 cups)

CALORIES 463; FAT 15g (sat 5g, unsat 8g); PROTEIN 38g; CARB 49g; FIBER 6g; SUGARS 8g (added sugars 0g); SODIUM 561mg; CALC 42% DV; POTASSIUM 18% DV

3 WAYS TO
SPEED UP A PASTA BAKE

1. To quickly remove the stems from the kale, pinch each leaf at the bottom (the wide part of the stem) and slide upward.

2. Cook all the elements separately (boil the pasta, wilt the kale, and cook the chicken). Then the oven's only job is to meld the flavors and melt the cheese.

3. Adding flour to the sauce will help it thicken in just 2 minutes, no need to reduce, reduce, reduce. Stir often so the sauce doesn't scorch.

Lentil Cakes with Mint Yogurt

Hands-on: 30 min. Total: 30 min.
A food processor brings these cakes together in minutes.

2½ tablespoons olive oil, divided
½ cup chopped yellow onion
1 tablespoon minced fresh garlic
¾ cup old-fashioned rolled oats
2 tablespoons red wine vinegar, divided
1 teaspoon kosher salt, divided
½ teaspoon black pepper
2 large eggs
1 (17.6-ounce) package steamed brown lentils (such as Melissa's)
2 cups packed baby arugula
2 cups packed baby spinach
¾ cup plain whole-milk Greek yogurt
2 tablespoons fresh lemon juice
2 tablespoons chopped fresh mint
3 tablespoons unsalted pistachios

1. Heat 1½ teaspoons oil in a large nonstick skillet over medium. Add onion and garlic; sauté 3 minutes. Place onion mixture, oats, 1 tablespoon vinegar, ¾ teaspoon salt, pepper, eggs, and lentils in a food processor; pulse 3 to 4 times. Divide and shape mixture into 12 patties (about ¼ cup each).
2. Heat 1½ teaspoons oil in pan over medium-high. Add 6 patties to pan; cook 2 minutes on each side. Remove from pan. Repeat with 1½ teaspoons oil and remaining 6 patties.
3. Combine remaining 1 tablespoon vinegar and remaining 1 tablespoon oil in a large bowl, stirring with a whisk. Add arugula and spinach; toss.
4. Combine remaining ¼ teaspoon salt, yogurt, juice, and mint in a bowl. Divide arugula mixture evenly among 4 plates; top each serving with 3 patties and 2 tablespoons yogurt mixture. Sprinkle evenly with pistachios. Serves 4

CALORIES 413; FAT 18g (sat 4g, unsat 13g); PROTEIN 23g; CARB 43g; FIBER 13g; SUGARS 6g (added sugars 0g); SODIUM 552mg; CALC 15% DV; POTASSIUM 25% DV

Roasted Salmon with Oranges, Beets, and Carrots

Hands-on: 8 min. Total: 18 min.
For individual fillets, bake at 400°F for 10 minutes and roast the veggies separately for 15 minutes.

1 (1½-pound) salmon fillet
2 blood oranges, cut into 8 wedges
1 navel orange, cut into 8 wedges
1 small red onion, cut into thin wedges
1 medium-sized golden beet, cut into ⅛-inch-thick slices
1 small Chioggia beet, cut into ⅛-inch-thick slices
1 large carrot, cut into ⅛-inch-thick slices
2 tablespoons olive oil
1 teaspoon fennel seeds, crushed
1 teaspoon kosher salt
½ teaspoon black pepper
2 tablespoons fresh lemon juice
2 teaspoons chopped fresh tarragon

1. Preheat oven to 450°F.
2. Pat fish dry with paper towels. Place fish in the center of a rimmed baking sheet lined with parchment paper. Arrange oranges, onion, beets, and carrot around fish. Combine oil, fennel seeds, salt, and pepper in a bowl; drizzle oil mixture over fish and vegetable mixture.
3. Bake at 450°F for 10 to 12 minutes or until fish flakes easily when tested with a fork. Sprinkle juice and tarragon over fish and vegetable mixture. Serves 4 (serving size: 4½ ounces fish and about 1 cup vegetable mixture)

CALORIES 390; FAT 17g (sat 3g, unsat 12g); PROTEIN 38g; CARB 21g; FIBER 5g; SUGARS 14g (added sugars 0g); SODIUM 606mg; CALC 9% DV; POTASSIUM 25% DV

20-MINUTE MAINS

Orange, Tofu, and Bell Pepper Stir-Fry

Hands-on: 20 min. Total: 20 min.
Cornstarch helps the tofu crisp without needing lots of oil. Have every element at the ready before you cook, as the stir-fry comes together quickly.

¼ cup canola oil, divided
5 tablespoons cornstarch, divided
1 (14-ounce) package extra-firm water-packed tofu, drained and cut into ¾-inch cubes
½ cup fresh orange juice
1 cup thinly sliced yellow onion
1 cup sliced green bell pepper
1 cup sliced red bell pepper
1 tablespoon thinly sliced garlic
½ teaspoon grated orange rind
½ teaspoon crushed red pepper
3 tablespoons lower-sodium soy sauce
1 tablespoon unseasoned rice vinegar
1 teaspoon light brown sugar
½ teaspoon kosher salt
2 (8.8-ounce) packages precooked brown rice (such as Uncle Ben's)
2 tablespoons chopped fresh cilantro

1. Heat 3 tablespoons oil in a large nonstick skillet over medium-high. Combine 4 tablespoons cornstarch and tofu in a bowl; toss. Add tofu to pan; cook 8 minutes or until golden brown. Remove from pan.
2. Combine remaining 1 tablespoon cornstarch and orange juice in a small bowl. Heat remaining 1 tablespoon oil in pan over medium-high. Add onion and bell peppers; cook 5 minutes. Add garlic, orange rind, and crushed red pepper; cook 1 minute. Add juice mixture, soy sauce, vinegar, sugar, and salt; bring to a boil. Stir in tofu. Place ½ cup rice on each of 4 plates; top each serving with ¾ cup tofu mixture. Sprinkle evenly with cilantro. Serves 4

CALORIES 488; FAT 22g (sat 2g, unsat 20g); PROTEIN 17g; CARB 59g; FIBER 6g; SUGARS 8g (added sugars 1g); SODIUM 695mg; CALC 10% DV; POTASSIUM 1% DV

Fast • Gluten Free

Coriander-Crusted Pork Tenderloin with Roasted Potatoes

Hands-on: 20 min. Total: 20 min.
Coarsely ground spices make a lovely crust on pork tenderloin. Coat and sear the pork while the oven preheats, and make the yogurt sauce while it roasts.

1 tablespoon black peppercorns
1 tablespoon coriander seeds
1 teaspoon kosher salt, divided
1 tablespoon Dijon mustard
1 (1-pound) pork tenderloin, trimmed
3 tablespoons olive oil, divided
1 pound refrigerated potato wedges (such as Simply Potatoes) (about 3 cups)
½ cup plain whole-milk yogurt
2 tablespoons chopped fresh cilantro
½ teaspoon grated lime rind
1 teaspoon fresh lime juice

1. Preheat oven to 475°F.
2. Crush peppercorns and coriander seeds with a mortar and pestle or small heavy skillet until coarsely ground. Combine with ¾ teaspoon salt in a small bowl. Spread mustard evenly over pork; coat with spice mixture.
3. Heat 2 tablespoons oil in a large nonstick skillet over medium-high. Add pork; cook 5 minutes, turning to brown on all sides. Place pork and potatoes on a parchment paper-lined baking sheet; drizzle with drippings from skillet. Bake at 475°F for 10 to 12 minutes or until a meat thermometer inserted into the center of the pork registers 145°F. Let pork stand 5 minutes. Cut across the grain into slices.
4. Combine remaining ¼ teaspoon salt, remaining 1 tablespoon oil, yogurt, cilantro, rind, and juice in a bowl; serve with pork and potatoes. Serves 4 (serving size: 3 ounces pork, ¾ cup potatoes, and 2 tablespoons sauce)

CALORIES 342; FAT 15g (sat 3g, unsat 10g); PROTEIN 26g; CARB 22g; FIBER 3g; SUGARS 3g (added sugars 0g); SODIUM 683mg; CALC 8% DV; POTASSIUM 24% DV

Fast • Gluten Free

Apricot-Sage Chicken with Carrots

Hands-on: 20 min. Total: 20 min.
Much more than a spread for toast, tart-sweet apricot preserves balance the pungent mustard in the sauce and give everything a glossy coat.

1 tablespoon olive oil
4 (4-ounce) skinless, boneless chicken thighs
¾ teaspoon kosher salt, divided
¼ teaspoon black pepper, divided
½ cup unsalted chicken stock
¼ cup apricot preserves
1 tablespoon Dijon mustard
2 cups thinly diagonally sliced carrots
4 teaspoons finely chopped fresh sage, divided
1 tablespoon thinly sliced garlic
2 tablespoons unsalted butter

1. Heat olive oil in a large skillet over medium-high. Sprinkle chicken with ½ teaspoon salt and ½ teaspoon pepper. Add chicken to pan; cook 3 minutes per side or until browned (chicken will not be cooked through). Remove chicken from pan (do not wipe out pan).
2. Combine stock, apricot preserves, and mustard in a bowl, stirring with a whisk. Add carrots, 1 tablespoon sage, and garlic to pan; sauté 4 minutes. Add apricot mixture and chicken to pan. Reduce heat to medium; cover and cook 8 minutes or until chicken is done. Remove pan from heat. Place chicken and carrots on a platter. Add remaining ¼ teaspoon salt, remaining ¼ teaspoon pepper, and butter to pan, swirling until butter melts. Spoon pan sauce over chicken; sprinkle with remaining 1 teaspoon sage. Serves 4 (serving size: 1 chicken thigh, ½ cup carrots, and 3 tablespoons sauce)

CALORIES 313; FAT 14g (sat 5g, unsat 8g); PROTEIN 24g; CARB 22g; FIBER 3g; SUGARS 13g (added sugars 5g); SODIUM 642mg; CALC 6% DV; POTASSIUM 17% DV

4 GO-WITH-ANYTHING SIDES

Fast • Gluten Free
Make Ahead
Bacon and Apple Braised Cabbage
We add sweet (brown sugar) and tangy (sherry vinegar) flavors toward the end of braising so they stand out in the finished dish. Serve with roast pork or braised beef.

Cook 2 chopped bacon slices in a saucepan over medium 5 minutes. Add 1 teaspoon fennel seeds; cook 30 seconds. Add 6 cups chopped red cabbage and ½ cup water; bring to a boil. Cover; reduce heat, and simmer 20 minutes. Stir in 2 cups chopped peeled Fuji apple, 3 tablespoons sherry vinegar, 2 teaspoons light brown sugar, ¾ teaspoon black pepper, and ⅛ teaspoon kosher salt. Cover and simmer 5 minutes. Stir in 1½ teaspoons unsalted butter. Serves 4 (serving size: ¾ cup)

CALORIES 108; FAT 3g (sat 1g, unsat 1g); PROTEIN 3g; CARB 19g; FIBER 4g; SUGARS 13g (added sugars 2g); SODIUM 139mg; CALC 6% DV; POTASSIUM 9% DV

Fast • Gluten Free
Make Ahead • Vegetarian
Maple-Butternut Puree
A food processor will get the mixture silky smooth. Pair with any seared or roasted protein.

Bring a large saucepan filled with water to a boil. Add 4 cups cubed peeled butternut squash; cook 10 minutes or until tender. Drain. Place squash in a food processor with 2 tablespoons pure maple syrup, 1 tablespoon unsalted butter, 1 teaspoon grated peeled fresh ginger, ⅝ teaspoon kosher salt, ½ teaspoon black pepper, and

1 grated garlic clove; process until smooth. Top with 4 teaspoons roasted unsalted pumpkinseed kernels. Serves 4 (serving size: ⅔ cup)

CALORIES 130; FAT 4g (sat 2g, unsat 1g); PROTEIN 2g; CARB 24g; FIBER 3g; SUGARS 9g (added sugars 6g); SODIUM 323mg; CALC 8% DV; POTASSIUM 15% DV

Fast • Gluten Free
Make Ahead
Warm Potato and Pancetta Salad
Buttery, thin-skinned fingerlings cook quickly and pre-diced pancetta (such as Boar's Head) saves prep time. Serve with a greens-stuffed omelet or seared fish fillets.

Preheat oven to 450°F. Combine 1 tablespoon olive oil, ¼ teaspoon kosher salt, ¼ teaspoon black pepper, and 1 pound halved fingerling potatoes on a baking sheet. Bake at 450°F for 20 minutes. Cook ⅓ cup diced pancetta in a skillet over medium 5 minutes. Add ⅔ cup sliced red onion; cook 2 minutes. Stir in 2 tablespoons red wine vinegar, 1 tablespoon olive oil, and 2 teaspoons grainy Dijon mustard. Add pancetta mixture, 2 tablespoons chopped fresh chives, and 1 tablespoon chopped fresh tarragon to potatoes. Serves 4 (serving size: 1 cup)

CALORIES 210; FAT 11g (sat 3g, unsat 6g); PROTEIN 4g; CARB 22g; FIBER 3g; SUGARS 2g (added sugars 0g); SODIUM 335mg; CALC 2% DV; POTASSIUM 1% DV

Fast • Make Ahead
Vegetarian
Kale, Farro, and Feta Salad
This satisfying winter salad is full of texture and color. Pair with roasted chicken thighs or serve as a side for pureed veggie soup. Top leftovers with cooked chicken and diced apple for tomorrow's lunch.

Combine 2 tablespoons extra-virgin olive oil, 1½ tablespoons apple cider vinegar, 1 tablespoon honey, ⅜ teaspoon kosher salt, and ½ teaspoon

black pepper in a large bowl. Add 2 cups stemmed, thinly sliced lacinto kale, ¼ cup sliced shallots, and 1 (8.5-ounce) package precooked farro, heated according to microwave directions, to oil mixture; toss. Top with 1 teaspoon chopped fresh mint and 2 ounces crumbled feta cheese. Serves 4 (serving size: 1¼ cups)

CALORIES 183; FAT 11g (sat 3g, unsat 7g); PROTEIN 5g; CARB 21g; FIBER 3g; SUGARS 6g (added sugars 4g); SODIUM 315mg; CALC 9% DV; POTASSIUM 3% DV

4 SAUCES FOR ANY PROTEIN

Fast • Gluten Free
Make Ahead • Vegetarian
Horseradish-Dill Sour Cream Sauce
While too pungent to eat alone, prepared horseradish sings in a rich sour cream sauce. It's also tasty stirred into a little cheese sauce or creamy coleslaw. Dollop the sauce over seared steak or salmon, or serve with roasted potato wedges.

Combine ½ cup light sour cream, 2 tablespoons minced fresh dill, 1 tablespoon prepared horseradish, 2 teaspoons fresh lemon juice, ¼ teaspoon kosher salt, and ¼ teaspoon black pepper in a small bowl, stirring with a whisk until smooth. Serves 4 (serving size: about 2 tablespoons)

CALORIES 45; FAT 3g (sat 2g, unsat 1g); PROTEIN 1g; CARB 3g; FIBER 0g; SUGARS 0g; SODIUM 162mg; CALC 5% DV; POTASSIUM 2% DV

Fast • Gluten Free
Maple-Bacon-Tarragon Dressing
Spoon this sauce over simply baked chicken breasts for an impressive main. Remove the pan from the heat first and carefully add the liquid to avoid splatters. You can sub fresh rosemary or thyme for the tarragon.

Cook 2 bacon slices in a medium skillet over medium-high until crisp. Remove bacon from pan; finely chop. Remove pan from heat. Add ⅓ cup water, 1 tablespoon minced shallots, 1 tablespoon sherry vinegar, 2 teaspoons Dijon mustard, 2 teaspoons pure maple syrup, and 1 teaspoon minced fresh tarragon to pan, stirring to scrape up browned bits. Stir in bacon, ¼ teaspoon black pepper, and ⅛ teaspoon kosher salt. Serves 4 (serving size: about 1 tablespoon)

CALORIES 73; FAT 6g (sat 2g, unsat 3g); PROTEIN 2g; CARB 3g; FIBER 0g; SUGARS 2g (added sugars 2g); SODIUM 213mg; CALC 1% DV; POTASSIUM 1% DV

Fast • Make Ahead
Peppered Gravy
This quick, easy gravy delivers rich flavor without any need for pan drippings. Cooking the flour (before adding the stock) adds a slight toasty note. Serve the sauce over roast chicken or pork, or use to perk up leftover turkey or a store-bought rotisserie chicken.

Heat 2½ tablespoons olive oil in a medium skillet over medium-high. Add ⅓ cup chopped shallots and 2 teaspoons chopped fresh thyme; sauté 3 minutes. Stir in 2 tablespoons all-purpose flour; cook 1 minute. Gradually stir in 1¾ cups unsalted chicken stock, 1 teaspoon black pepper, and ½ teaspoon kosher salt; cook 4 minutes or until thickened, whisking often. Remove

from heat; add 1½ tablespoons unsalted butter, whisking until butter melts. Serves 8 (serving size: about 3½ tablespoons)

CALORIES 74; FAT 6g (sat 2g, unsat 4g); PROTEIN 1g; CARB 3g; FIBER 0g; SUGARS 1g (added sugars 0g); SODIUM 167mg; CALC 1% DV; POTASSIUM 1% DV

Fast • Gluten Free
Make Ahead • Vegetarian
Citrus-Cilantro Salsa
Serve the salsa over seared salmon, halibut, or shrimp, or tuck into fish or shrimp tacos for a next-level dinner.

Peel and section 2 navel oranges and 1 red grapefruit; coarsely chop sections. Peel and section 1 lime; finely chop sections. Place citrus in a medium bowl. Add ⅓ cup pomegranate arils, ¼ cup finely chopped red onion, 2 tablespoons chopped fresh cilantro, ¼ teaspoon kosher salt, and 1 finely chopped seeded jalapeño pepper; toss gently to combine. Serves 4 (serving size: about ½ cup)

CALORIES 79; FAT 0g; PROTEIN 1g; CARB 20g; FIBER 4g; SUGARS 9g (added sugars 0g); SODIUM 122mg; CALC 4% DV; POTASSIUM 8% DV

> ## WE SECTION ALL THE CITRUS, INCLUDING A LIME, AND CHOP THE FLESH FOR JUICY BITS THAT BURST WITH FRESHNESS.

SHARE THIS

Gluten Free • Make Ahead
Vegetarian
Marinated Olives

Hands-on: 15 min. Total: 2 hr. 35 min.
This recipe from Elizabeth Heiskell's What Can I Bring? *is easy to tote to holiday cocktail or dinner parties.*

1 orange
1 lemon
¼ cup extra-virgin olive oil
2 teaspoons red wine vinegar
5 bay leaves
4 garlic cloves
2 thyme sprigs
1 rosemary sprig
4 cups mixed black and green olives, pitted

1. Cut 3 (¼-inch-thick) slices from the orange; set aside. Squeeze the juice from the remaining orange to equal 3 tablespoons. Cut 3 (¼-inch-thick) slices from the lemon; set aside. Squeeze the juice from the remaining lemon to equal 1½ tablespoons.
2. Stir together the olive oil, vinegar, bay leaves, garlic, lemon juice, and orange juice in a small saucepan; cook over medium-low until just warmed, about 10 minutes. Remove from heat. Add the reserved lemon and orange slices, thyme, and rosemary. Let stand 20 minutes.
3. Place the olives in a wide-mouthed 1-quart jar with a tight-fitting lid. Pour the citrus-herb mixture over the olives. Cover with the lid, and chill 2 hours. Shake the jar to redistribute seasonings before serving. Store in the refrigerator up to 2 weeks. Serves 32 (serving size: 2 tablespoons)

CALORIES 36; FAT 4g (sat 1g, unsat 3g); PROTEIN 0g; CARB 1g; FIBER 1g; SUGARS 0g; SODIUM 124mg; CALC 2% DV; POTASSIUM 0% DV

WHY INGREDIENTS MATTER

ALL DRESSED UP

A crunchy, bright-flavored winter salad is a delicious counter to cold-weather comfort food.

Fast • Gluten Free
Vegetarian

Winter Greens Salad with Citrus and Blue Cheese

Hands-on: 13 min. Total: 23 min.
A great salad is all about balancing flavors and textures. This one gives you all the taste elements in each bite—salty, sour, bitter, sweet, and umami—while rich, creamy cheese complements the crunchy components.

1 tablespoon thinly sliced shallots
2 tablespoons red wine vinegar
2 teaspoons honey
¾ teaspoon kosher salt
½ teaspoon freshly ground black pepper
6 cups baby kale
3 cups chopped radicchio
2 tablespoons extra-virgin olive oil
1 cup navel or blood orange segments
½ cup pecan halves, toasted
1½ tablespoons pomegranate arils
1½ ounces blue cheese, crumbled (about ⅓ cup)

1. Combine first 5 ingredients (through pepper) in a small bowl. Let stand 10 minutes.
2. Combine kale and radicchio in a large serving bowl. Add oil to shallot mixture, stirring well to combine. Drizzle dressing over greens; toss well to coat.
3. Top salad evenly with citrus segments, nuts, pomegranate arils, and cheese. Serves 8 (serving size: 1 cup)

CALORIES 129; **FAT** 10g (sat 2g, unsat 8g); **PROTEIN** 3g; **CARB** 8g; **FIBER** 2g; **SUGARS** 4g (added sugars 2g); **SODIUM** 277mg; **CALC** 10% DV; **POTASSIUM** 4% DV

 +  +

WINTER GREENS
Hearty kale and radicchio deliver bold flavor, unlike mild spring greens such as butter lettuce and mâche.

RED WINE VINEGAR
This salad can handle a strong vinegar that stands up to the greens' peppery mineral flavors.

WINTER FRUIT
Sweet-tart orange segments and pomegranate arils play well together and add a dazzling pop of color.

 +  +

HONEY
It gives the dressing a little body, offsets bitterness, and pairs perfectly with blue cheese.

BLUE CHEESE
The up-front flavors here cry out for cheese with plenty of oomph. Blue also adds luxe creaminess to each bite.

NUTS
For extra crunch and a touch of umami, nuts are a must. Pecans are better here than slightly bitter walnuts.

Fast • Gluten Free
Vegetarian

Roasted Vegetable Plate with Herbed Dressing

Hands-on: 20 min. Total: 30 min.
This filling plate of seasonal veggies will help you stick to your calorie goal in winter months when holiday braises, hearty stews, and centerpiece roasts tend to take over. You can easily change up the vegetables depending on what's available.

1 cup chopped peeled sweet potato (about 1 small)
¼ cup olive oil, divided
1 teaspoon grated lemon rind
⅝ teaspoon kosher salt, divided
½ teaspoon freshly ground black pepper
8 ounces Brussels sprouts, trimmed and halved
1 ounce Parmesan cheese, grated (about ¼ cup), divided
2 large shallots, quartered lengthwise
1 (10-ounce) package cauliflower florets
2 tablespoons chopped fresh tarragon
2 tablespoons white wine vinegar
1 (5-ounce) package baby arugula
3 tablespoons chopped almonds, toasted

1. Preheat oven to 500°F. Place a rimmed baking sheet in oven (leave pan in oven while it preheats).
2. Combine sweet potato, 2 tablespoons oil, rind, ⅜ teaspoon salt, pepper, Brussels sprouts, 2 tablespoons Parmesan cheese, shallots, and cauliflower in a bowl. Spread potato mixture on preheated pan; bake at 500°F for 15 minutes or until golden-brown.
3. Combine remaining 2 tablespoons oil, remaining ¼ teaspoon salt, tarragon, and vinegar in a large bowl. Add arugula; toss to coat. Divide arugula mixture evenly among 4 plates. Top evenly with vegetable mixture, remaining 2 tablespoons Parmesan cheese, and almonds. Serves 4 (serving size: about 1½ cups)

CALORIES 290; **FAT** 19g (sat 3g, unsat 15g); **PROTEIN** 9g; **CARB** 24g; **FIBER** 6g; **SUGARS** 5g (added sugars 0g); **SODIUM** 482mg; **CALC** 20% DV; **POTASSIUM** 18% DV

SLOW COOKER

Staff Favorite • Make Ahead

Korean-Style Short Ribs with Chile-Scallion Rice

Hands-on: 20 min. Total: 8 hr. 20 min.
Beef short ribs become tender in the slow cooker as the cooking liquid reduces to a sauce. Kimchi (Korean fermented cabbage) adds heat and a hint of tang to the dish. Find more ways to use it on page 380.

1½ tablespoons extra-virgin olive oil, divided
3 pounds bone-in beef short ribs
1 cup chopped yellow onion
½ cup sake
½ cup unsalted beef stock
⅓ cup jarred kimchi (Korean fermented cabbage), chopped
¼ cup lower-sodium soy sauce
¼ cup packed light brown sugar
2 tablespoons mirin
2 teaspoons minced peeled fresh ginger
3 garlic cloves, crushed
2 red Fresno chiles, seeded, minced, and divided
½ cup sliced scallions, divided
3 cups hot cooked brown rice
2 tablespoons chopped fresh cilantro

1. Heat 1 tablespoon oil in a large skillet over high. Add 1½ pounds short ribs; cook 6 to 8 minutes, turning to brown on all sides. Remove browned short ribs from pan. Repeat procedure with remaining 1½ pounds short ribs. Place browned short ribs and next 9 ingredients (through garlic) in a 6-quart electric slow cooker. Stir in 1 minced fresno chile. Cover and cook on low 8 hours or until meat is very tender.
2. Remove short ribs from slow cooker. Skim fat from cooking liquid; discard. Reserve cooking liquid.
3. Stir remaining 1½ teaspoons oil, remaining minced fresno chile, and ¼ cup chopped green onions into rice. Divide short ribs and rice mixture among 8 shallow bowls; spoon about ¼ cup cooking liquid over each serving. Sprinkle evenly with remaining ¼ cup green onions and cilantro. Serves 8 (serving size: 1 short rib and about ⅓ cup rice mixture)

CALORIES 317; **FAT** 11g (sat 4g, unsat 6g); **PROTEIN** 17g; **CARB** 33g; **FIBER** 2g; **SUGARS** 10g (added sugars 7g); **SODIUM** 408mg; **CALC** 3% DV; **POTASSIUM** 12% DV

**Staff Favorite • Fast
Gluten Free**

Cheesy Polenta Skillet

Hands-on: 15 min. Total: 20 min.
We keep the polenta slices on the thick side so they have a creamy texture when heated through. A little ground turkey goes a long way in this dish; stir the rest into chili, make burger patties, or use as a filling for lettuce cups. Add any vegetables you have on hand, like spinach or chopped broccoli, to the sautéed mushroom mixture.

4 teaspoons olive oil, divided
**1 (8-ounce) tube prepared polenta,
  cut into 4 (³/₄-inch-thick) slices**
6 ounces ground turkey
**2 cups sliced fresh cremini
  mushrooms (about 6 ounces)**
1 cup finely chopped red onion
5 garlic cloves, thinly sliced
**1¹/₂ cups lower-sodium marinara
  sauce (such as Dell 'Amore)**
2 tablespoons chopped fresh oregano
1 tablespoon red wine vinegar
**2 ounces preshredded part-skim
  mozzarella cheese (about ¹/₂ cup)**
**1 ounce Parmesan cheese, grated
  (about ¹/₄ cup)**

1. Preheat broiler with oven rack in top position.
2. Heat 2 teaspoons oil in a 10-inch ovenproof skillet over medium-high. Add polenta slices; cook 4 minutes on each side or until golden brown. Remove pan from heat.
3. Heat remaining 2 teaspoons oil in a medium saucepan over medium-high. Add turkey; cook 7 minutes or until browned, stirring to crumble. Add mushrooms, onion, and garlic; cook 6 minutes. Stir in marinara sauce, oregano, and vinegar; cook 5 minutes. Pour turkey mixture over polenta in skillet. Sprinkle mozza-rella and Parmesan cheeses over pan. Place pan in oven; broil 2 minutes or until cheese is melted and browned. Serves 4 (serving size: 1 polenta slice and about 1 cup sauce)

CALORIES 292; **FAT** 15g (sat 4g, unsat 10g); **PROTEIN** 18g; **CARB** 23g; **FIBER** 4g; **SUGARS** 7g (added sugars 0g); **SODIUM** 494mg; **CALC** 20% DV; **POTASSIUM** 9% DV

SHORTCUT ITEMS

Find tube polenta in the grain aisle. Slice and toast, sear, or layer and bake. Keep a great marinara in the pantry for last-minute mains. Preshredded cheese also saves time.

1 INGREDIENT, 3 SIDES

3 WAYS TO USE COUSCOUS

Israeli (pearl) couscous is a fun alternative to rice. Try it in salads, stir into soups, or toast the pasta pebbles in a little oil and simmer for a pilaf-style side.

**Fast • Make Ahead
Vegetarian**
**Golden Raisin and Charred
Radicchio Couscous**
Searing the radicchio until lightly charred helps to mellow its bitter edge and adds smokiness to the couscous.

1. Bring 1¹/₂ cups water to a boil in a small saucepan; stir in ³/₄ cup un-cooked whole-wheat Israeli couscous and ¹/₄ cup golden raisins. Cover, reduce heat, and simmer 12 minutes or until liquid is absorbed. Place couscous mixture in a bowl.
2. Heat 1 tablespoon extra-virgin olive oil in a cast-iron skillet over medium-high. Add 1 head radicchio, cut lengthwise into quarters, to pan; cook 5 minutes, turning to brown on all sides. Remove from pan; finely chop. Add radicchio, 2 tablespoons finely grated Parmesan cheese, 1 tablespoon extra-virgin olive oil, 1 tablespoon apple cider vinegar, ¹/₂ teaspoon kosher salt, and ¹/₄ teaspoon black pepper to couscous mixture; toss. Serves 4 (serving size: 1 cup)

CALORIES 226; **FAT** 8g (sat 1g, unsat 6g); **PROTEIN** 6g; **CARB** 34g; **FIBER** 3g; **SUGARS** 6g (added sugars 0g); **SODIUM** 298mg; **CALC** 5% DV; **POTASSIUM** 8% DV

**Fast • Make Ahead
Vegetarian**
Cherry-and-Leek Couscous
Add the dried cherries to the cooking liquid with the couscous so they can plump, soften, and flavor the grains.

1. Bring 1¹/₄ cups water to a boil in a small saucepan; stir in ³/₄ cup un-cooked whole-wheat Israeli couscous and 3 tablespoons chopped dried cherries. Cover; reduce heat, and simmer 12 minutes or until liquid is absorbed.
2. Place couscous mixture in a bowl. Heat 1¹/₂ teaspoons extra-virgin olive oil in a medium skillet over medi-um-high. Add 1 cup thinly sliced leek; sauté 5 minutes. Add leek mixture, 2 tablespoons white wine vinegar, 1 tablespoon extra-virgin olive oil, ⁵/₈ teaspoon kosher salt, and ¹/₄ teaspoon black pepper to couscous; toss. Sprinkle with 3 tablespoons chopped toasted walnuts. Serves 4 (serving size: about 1 cup)

CALORIES 232; **FAT** 9g (sat 1g, unsat 8g); **PROTEIN** 5g; **CARB** 34g; **FIBER** 3g; **SUGARS** 6g (added sugars 3g); **SODIUM** 306mg; **CALC** 2% DV; **POTASSIUM** 3% DV

**Fast • Make Ahead
Vegetarian**
Pear-and-Pesto Couscous
This vibrant side is a fun play on the classic arugula, pear, and walnut salad. Use a red pear for a pop of color.

1. Bring 2 cups water to a boil in a small saucepan; stir in ³/₄ cup uncooked whole-wheat Israeli couscous. Cover, reduce heat, and simmer 12 minutes or until liquid is absorbed. **2.** Place the couscous in a bowl. Place 2 packed cups baby arugula, 2 tablespoons olive oil, 2 tablespoons fresh lemon juice, ⅝ teaspoon kosher salt, ½ teaspoon sugar, ¼ teaspoon black pepper, and 1 smashed garlic clove in a food processor; process until smooth. Add pesto, 2 tablespoons chopped toasted walnuts, and 1 chopped ripe Anjou pear to couscous; toss. Sprinkle with 2 tablespoons chopped toasted walnuts. Serves 4 (serving size: about 1 cup)

CALORIES 255; **FAT** 12g (sat 1g, unsat 10g); **PROTEIN** 5g; **CARB** 34g; **FIBER** 4g; **SUGARS** 6g (added sugars 1g); **SODIUM** 305mg; **CALC** 4% DV; **POTASSIUM** 4% DV

THE RECIPE MAKEOVER

MAKE AHEAD BREAKFAST

Slimmed down and simplified, our 330 calorie casserole is a great offering for hungry houseguests.

When you're looking for a breakfast that is both elegant and easy this holiday season, our crowd-pleasing casserole is just the ticket. This multilayered marvel is loaded with crispy potatoes, hot-smoked salmon, and a smattering of fresh herbs. Cottage cheese naturally melds into the eggs, creating pillowy lightness throughout the mixture, while goat cheese creates dense pockets of creaminess. Hot-smoked salmon, unlike cured, is fully cooked—look for it in the fish case or packaged in the meat aisle of your grocery store. Our recipe hits all the marks for a hearty one-dish meal, with 25% fewer calories, 7g less saturated fat, and over 600mg less sodium than traditional meat-and-cheese breakfast casseroles. Use a well-seasoned cast-iron skillet for best results.

Staff Favorite • Gluten Free
Make Ahead

Smoked Salmon Breakfast Casserole

Hands-on: 15 min. Total: 45 min.
If making ahead, prepare the potato and salmon mixture the night before and refrigerate, covered, overnight. The next morning, whip up the egg mixture and proceed with the final steps. To reheat leftovers, place the whole skillet back in the oven or microwave individual portions on a microwave-safe plate.

6 large eggs
3 large egg whites
¾ cup 2% reduced-fat milk
½ cup plain whole-milk cottage cheese
2 tablespoons minced fresh chives
1 teaspoon Dijon mustard
¼ teaspoon freshly ground black pepper
1 tablespoon canola oil
1 pound russet potatoes, peeled and cut into ½-inch cubes (about 3½ cups)
½ cup thinly sliced leeks
¼ cup minced shallots
8 ounces hot-smoked salmon, flaked
2 ounces goat cheese, crumbled (about ½ cup)
2 tablespoons chopped fresh dill

1. Preheat oven to 350°F.
2. Place eggs, egg whites, milk, cottage cheese, chives, mustard, and black pepper in a large bowl; whisk to combine. Set aside.
3. Heat oil in a 10-inch ovenproof skillet over medium. Add potatoes; stir to coat, and arrange in a single layer. Cover and cook until potatoes are almost tender, about 8 minutes, stirring occasionally. Uncover; add leeks and shallots; cook 5 minutes, stirring occasionally, until soft.

4. Scatter salmon evenly over potatoes in pan. Pour egg mixture over salmon and potatoes. Sprinkle cheese evenly over top. Bake at 350°F for 25 minutes or until egg mixture is set. Garnish with dill. Serves 6 (serving size: 1½ cups)

CALORIES 330; **FAT** 15g (sat 5g, unsat 8g); **PROTEIN** 26g; **CARB** 22g; **FIBER** 2g; **SUGARS** 5g (added sugars 0g); **SODIUM** 592mg; **CALC** 15% DV; **POTASSIUM** 19% DV

HEALTHY TIPS AND SOLUTIONS

OUR FRESH SPIN ON A BREAKFAST CLASSIC DIALS DOWN ON CALORIES WHILE STILL DELIVERING HEARTY HOLIDAY FARE TO THE TABLE THIS SEASON.

Adding cottage cheese to the egg mixture offers some insurance against overcooking.

Precooking the potatoes in the same pan as the casserole lightens your dish load.

For a fiber and flavor boost, leave the skins on half the potatoes.

COTTAGE CHEESE
The extra dairy fat in whole-milk cottage cheese enriches the egg mixture with custard-like creaminess, coupled with an extra hit of protein.

SALMON
Bearing all the smoky, saltiness of classic breakfast meat with a fraction of the sat fat, hot-smoked salmon lends meatiness and heart-healthy fats.

POTATOES
Rich in vitamin C and potassium, russet potatoes add more nutritious heft than bread or biscuits and save up to 3g sat fat per serving.

1 LIST
3 DINNERS

Shop this list to feed four for three nights, all for about $30. Read the recipes to be sure you have the staples.

2 bunches curly kale

10 ounces shiitake mushroom caps

1 (6-ounce) bunch Broccolini

1 yellow onion

2 medium carrots

1 whole-wheat baguette

Golden raisins

Whole-wheat panko (Japanese breadcrumbs)

1 (32-ounce) container unsalted chicken stock

Sriracha chili sauce

2 (8.8-ounce) packages precooked brown rice

2 (15-ounce) cans unsalted cannellini beans

Whole milk

Eggs

2 (1-pound) pork tenderloins

Staff Favorite

Mushroom and Pork Meatballs with Broccolini Rice

Hands-on: 35 min. Total: 35 min.
A quick spin in the food processor turns pork tenderloin into lean ground pork—perfect for rich, tender meatballs. Broccolini, a cousin of broccoli, have long stalks and small florets; they'll add plenty of texture to the rice once chopped and sautéed.

1½ cups shiitake mushroom caps (about 4 ounces)
10 ounces pork tenderloin, cut into ½-inch pieces
6 tablespoons whole-wheat panko (Japanese breadcrumbs)
½ teaspoon kosher salt, divided
½ teaspoon black pepper, divided
1 large egg, lightly beaten
2 tablespoons canola oil, divided
1 (6-ounce) bunch Broccolini, finely chopped
1 cup unsalted chicken stock (such as Swanson), divided
2 tablespoons rice or apple cider vinegar, divided
1 tablespoon light brown sugar
1 tablespoon lower-sodium soy sauce
1 tablespoon Sriracha
2 teaspoons cornstarch
2 (8.8-ounce) packages precooked brown rice (such as Uncle Ben's)

1. Place mushrooms and pork in a food processor; pulse 15 to 20 times or until finely chopped. Place pork mixture in a bowl with panko, ¼ teaspoon salt, ¼ teaspoon pepper, and egg; stir to combine. Divide and shape pork mixture into 24 meatballs (about 1 tablespoon each).

2. Heat 1½ teaspoons oil in a large skillet over medium-high. Add Broccolini; cook 2 minutes. Place Broccolini mixture in a bowl; set aside.
3. Add remaining 1½ tablespoons oil to pan. Add meatballs; cook 5 minutes, turning to brown on all sides.
4. Combine ¾ cup chicken stock, 1 tablespoon rice vinegar, brown sugar, soy sauce, and Sriracha in a bowl; add to pan. Cover, reduce heat, and simmer 3 minutes or until meatballs are done. Combine remaining ¼ cup stock and cornstarch in a bowl; stir into meatball mixture. Cook 1 minute or until sauce is thickened.
5. Heat rice according to package directions. Stir rice, remaining ¼ teaspoon salt, remaining ¼ teaspoon pepper, and remaining 1 tablespoon vinegar into Broccolini. Serve with meatball mixture. Serves 4 (serving size: 6 meatballs, ¼ cup sauce, and 1 cup broccolini mixture)

CALORIES 419; FAT 13g (sat 2g, unsat 10g); PROTEIN 26g; CARB 53g; FIBER 5g; SUGARS 8g (added sugars 3g); SODIUM 705mg; CALC 5% DV; POTASSIUM 16% DV

Make Ahead

White Bean Soup with Garlicky Croutons

Hands-on: 25 min. Total: 40 min.
A little whole milk enriches this simple soup without making it as heavy as a classic chowder. The golden color of the broth comes from the sautéed onion and carrot; keep an eye on the mixture as it cooks to make sure it doesn't overbrown.

5 teaspoons olive oil, divided
1 cup peeled, chopped carrots
½ cup chopped yellow onion
2 teaspoons minced fresh garlic, divided
2 cups unsalted chicken stock (such as Swanson)
1 cup water
½ teaspoon freshly ground black pepper
³/₈ teaspoon kosher salt
2 (15-ounce) cans unsalted cannellini beans, rinsed and drained
4 cups stemmed chopped curly kale (about 1 bunch)
½ cup whole milk
1 ounce Parmesan cheese, finely grated (about ¼ cup)
3 ounces whole-wheat baguette, cut into 1-inch pieces (about 1 cup)

1. Heat 2 teaspoons oil in a Dutch oven over medium-high. Add carrots and onion; sauté 7 minutes. Add 1 teaspoon garlic; cook 30 seconds. Stir in stock, 1 cup water, pepper, salt, and beans; bring to a boil. Reduce heat and simmer 20 minutes. Stir in kale, milk, and Parmesan cheese; let stand 5 minutes.

2. Preheat broiler with oven rack in top position.
3. Place the bread pieces on a foil-lined baking sheet. Combine the remaining 1 tablespoon oil and remaining 1 teaspoon garlic in a bowl; drizzle over bread. Broil 2 minutes or until golden, stirring once after 1 minute. Place 1½ cups soup in each of 4 bowls; top evenly with bread pieces. Serves 4

CALORIES 349; **FAT** 11g (sat 2g, unsat 7g); **PROTEIN** 18g; **CARB** 47g; **FIBER** 11g; **SUGARS** 6g (added sugars 0g); **SODIUM** 571mg; **CALC** 21% DV; **POTASSIUM** 20% DV

Pork Milanese with Kale Salad

Hands-on: 40 min. Total: 40 min.
Milanese is an Italian way of preparing meat by breading and sautéing until golden—an easy, fast way to dress up pork tenderloin. Golden raisins seem to elevate everything they touch; here they brighten up earthy kale. Try sprinkling them over rice pilaf or roasted vegetables, too.

4 cups stemmed chopped curly kale (about 1 bunch)
3 tablespoons olive oil, divided
3 tablespoons golden raisins
1 tablespoon red wine vinegar
1 teaspoon kosher salt, divided
1 teaspoon black pepper, divided
1 cup whole-wheat panko (Japanese breadcrumbs)
1 large egg, lightly beaten
1 tablespoon water
1 (1-pound) pork tenderloin, cut crosswise into 12 slices
6 ounces shiitake mushroom caps, sliced
1 tablespoon all-purpose flour
1 cup whole milk

1. Combine kale, 1 tablespoon oil, raisins, vinegar, ¼ teaspoon salt, and ¼ teaspoon pepper in a large bowl. Let stand 10 minutes.
2. Combine ¼ teaspoon salt, ½ teaspoon pepper, and panko in a shallow dish. Combine egg and 1 tablespoon water in a shallow dish. Dip pork slices in egg mixture; dredge in panko mixture.
3. Heat 1½ teaspoons oil in a large nonstick skillet over medium-high. Add half of pork slices to pan; cook 3 minutes on each side. Place cooked slices on a plate. Repeat procedure with 1½ teaspoons oil and remaining half of pork slices.
4. Heat remaining 1 tablespoon oil in pan. Add mushrooms; sauté 4 minutes. Sprinkle flour over pan; cook 1 minute, stirring constantly. Add remaining ½ teaspoon salt, remaining ¼ teaspoon pepper, and milk; cook 2 minutes or until slightly thickened, stirring occasionally. Top pork with mushroom sauce. Serve with salad. Serves 4 (serving size: 3 pork slices, about ¼ cup sauce, and 1 cup salad)

CALORIES 391; **FAT** 17g (sat 4g, unsat 11g); **PROTEIN** 32g; **CARB** 29g; **FIBER** 4g; **SUGARS** 9g (added sugars 0g); **SODIUM** 618mg; **CALC** 11% DV; **POTASSIUM** 23% DV

3 WAYS TO USE KIMCHI

This spicy, pungent, fermented cabbage peps up the short ribs on page 375 and adds kick to everyday dishes like dips and sandwiches. Find this Korean staple near the tofu in large supermarkets or at Asian markets.

Fast
Kimchi Grilled Cheese
Mild mozzarella and creamy Monterey Jack melt nicely. Kimchi brightens the sandwich and adds crunch.

1. Brush 2 tablespoons canola oil evenly over 1 side of 8 (1-ounce) whole-wheat bread slices. Arrange 4 bread slices, oiled side down, on a work surface. Divide 3 ounces thinly sliced fresh mozzarella cheese and 1½ ounces (⅓ cup) shredded Monterey Jack cheese evenly among bread slices; top each with 2 tablespoons chopped kimchi and 1 bread slice, oiled side up.
2. Cook sandwiches in a large nonstick skillet over medium-high until toasted and cheese is melted, about 3 minutes on each side. Serves 4 (serving size: 1 sandwich)

CALORIES 308; **FAT** 17g (sat 6g, unsat 10g); **PROTEIN** 14g; **CARB** 25g; **FIBER** 4g; **SUGARS** 3g (added sugars 1g); **SODIUM** 476mg; **CALC** 29% DV; **POTASSIUM** 5% DV

Fast • Make Ahead
Kimchi Fried Rice
Chopped kimchi and kimchi juice add lots of tangy-spicy goodness to this quick meatless main. Though there's no meat, do be aware that most traditional kimchi isn't vegetarian (it includes fish).

1. Heat 1½ teaspoons toasted sesame oil in a large nonstick skillet over medium-high. Add 2 lightly beaten large eggs; cook 30 seconds or until scrambled, stirring constantly. Remove from pan. Heat 1½ tablespoons toasted sesame oil in pan. Add 1 cup chopped green onions and 4 minced garlic cloves; sauté 1 minute.
2. Add ¾ cup chopped kimchi and 2 (8.8-ounce) pouches precooked brown rice (such as Uncle Ben's); sauté 4 minutes. Gradually add 8 ounces fresh spinach, stirring until spinach wilts. Stir in ½ cup thawed frozen green peas, ¼ cup kimchi juice, 2 tablespoons reduced-sodium soy sauce, and eggs. Serves 4 (serving size: 1½ cups)

CALORIES 316; **FAT** 13g (sat 2g, unsat 10g); **PROTEIN** 11g; **CARB** 44g; **FIBER** 6g; **SUGARS** 3g (added sugars 0g); **SODIUM** 597mg; **CALC** 11% DV; **POTASSIUM** 16% DV

Fast • Gluten Free
Make Ahead
Kimchi-Sesame Hummus
Here's a fun Korean spin on a classic Mediterranean appetizer. Toasted sesame oil enhances the nuttiness of tahini (sesame seed paste) in this easy make-ahead dip.

1. Drain 1 (15-ounce) can unsalted chickpeas. Place drained chickpeas, ½ cup kimchi, ¼ cup tahini (sesame seed paste), 3 tablespoons water, 2 tablespoons toasted sesame oil, 1 tablespoon rice vinegar, ½ teaspoon kosher salt, and 1 chopped garlic clove in a mini food processor; process until well blended (about 2 minutes).
2. Spoon hummus into a bowl; top with 2 tablespoons chopped kimchi and 1½ tablespoons thinly sliced green onions. Serves 8 (serving size: about ¼ cup)

CALORIES 126; **FAT** 8g (sat 1g, unsat 6g); **PROTEIN** 4g; **CARB** 10g; **FIBER** 2g; **SUGARS** 1g (added sugars 0g); **SODIUM** 193mg; **CALC** 4% DV; **POTASSIUM** 4% DV

QUITTIN' TIME

Staff Favorite • Fast Gluten Free • Make Ahead Vegetarian

Holiday Coconut Cooler

Hands-on: 5 min. Total: 5 min.
Wow your guests this holiday season with a whimsical white cocktail. A mix of coconut milk and coconut rum adds Caribbean flair, making even the coldest winter days feel bright and blissful. Entertain a crowd with ease by making a double or triple batch ahead of time—just give it a stir right before garnishing.

Muddle ½ cup fresh mint leaves, 1 (1-inch) lime wedge, 2 tablespoons sugar, and ¼ teaspoon kosher salt in a cocktail shaker. Add 3 ounces white rum, ½ cup coconut water, and 5 ice cubes; shake for 15 seconds. Strain into a serving pitcher. Add 3 ounces coconut rum, 1 tablespoon fresh lime juice, and 2 cups refrigerated unsweetened coconut milk (such as Silk). Stir to combine. Pour into 4 lowball glasses filled with ice. Garnish with fresh mint leaves and pomegranate arils. Serves 4 (serving size: about ¾ cup)

CALORIES 141; **FAT** 2g (sat 2g, unsat 0g); **PROTEIN** 0g; **CARB** 12g; **FIBER** 0g; **SUGARS** 7g (added sugars 6g); **SODIUM** 142mg; **CALC** 23% DV; **POTASSIUM** 2% DV

MAKE IT A MOCKTAIL

Omit both rums. Add an extra ½ cup coconut water, 1 tablespoon fresh lime juice, and ½ teaspoon coconut extract.

PORK LOIN, DRESSED TO IMPRESS

Stuffed pork loin gets oohs and aahs at the table. Our expert tips for better butterflying and genius twine-tying make it easy, too. The dazzling result of a basic technique you need to know.

Roasted Pork Loin Stuffed with Prosciutto and Broccoli Rabe

Hands-on: 30 min. Total: 1 hr. 40 min.
Make this centerpiece roast more festive by sprinkling with pomegranate arils. The sauce gets a deeply savory flavor boost from a bit of Marmite (British yeast paste); look for it on the international foods aisle.

1 bunch broccoli rabe, trimmed
3 tablespoons olive oil, divided
1 teaspoon kosher salt, divided
⅛ teaspoon crushed red pepper
3 garlic cloves, minced
1 (2-pound) pork loin, trimmed
4 ounces very thinly sliced prosciutto
2 cups unsalted chicken stock (such as Swanson)
¼ cup dry white wine
1½ teaspoons Marmite
2 tablespoons salted butter

1. Cook broccoli rabe in boiling water 3 minutes; plunge into an ice bath for 1 minute. Drain well. Wrap rabe in paper towels; squeeze dry. Chop rabe into 1½-inch pieces. Place in a bowl with 1 tablespoon oil, ¼ teaspoon salt, pepper, and garlic; stir well.
2. Preheat oven to 325°F.
3. Cut into pork loin lengthwise from right to left, ¾ inch from bottom, keeping knife parallel with cutting board; do not cut through the other side. Continue slicing lengthwise from right to left, unrolling loin as you slice, to form a ¾-inch-thick rectangle. Season with remaining ¾ teaspoon salt.
4. Arrange prosciutto in layers to cover inside of loin. Spread rabe mixture on top, leaving a 1-inch border. Roll pork up, left to right. Tie with twine in surgeon's knots at 2-inch intervals.
5. Combine stock, wine, and Marmite in a roasting pan. Place pan over medium heat; cook until Marmite dissolves, stirring. Set a roasting rack in pan.
6. Heat a large skillet over medium-high. Add remaining 2 tablespoons oil. Place loin in pan; cook 12 minutes or until browned. Place loin on rack; cover loosely with foil. Roast at 325°F for 50 minutes or until meat registers 150°F. Remove pork from pan; let pork stand 20 minutes. Swirl butter into pan juices until butter melts. Cut pork into ¾-inch slices; serve with jus. Serves 8 (serving size: about 3 ounces pork and 2 tablespoons jus)

CALORIES 264; **FAT** 15g (sat 5g, unsat 9g); **PROTEIN** 29g; **CARB** 2g; **FIBER** 1g; **SUGARS** 0g; **SODIUM** 631mg; **CALC** 4% DV; **POTASSIUM** 12% DV

1. BUTTERFLY
Slice along long side of loin, ¾ inch from board. With knife parallel to board, continue slicing lengthwise; roll pork out right to left (if you're right-handed).

2. SPREAD SMART
The first layer is prosciutto, which seasons the loin from the inside as it roasts, while moisture from the broccoli rabe retains the proscuitto's supple, buttery texture.

3. KNOT SECURELY
For a snug tie, use a surgeon's knot: Loop the ends of the twine together, then loop a second time before tying the knot—the extra friction holds the twine fast.

4. STEAM-ROAST
Lean pork loin dries out easily. Wine and stock in the roasting pan, plus covering loosely with foil, creates a sauna for the pork, which in turn flavors the meaty jus.

DELICIOUS GIFTS FOR ALL ON YOUR LIST

These edible offerings will fill your friends and family with comfort and joy.

Staff Favorite • Make Ahead
Vegetarian

Molasses Crinkle Cookies

Hands-on: 20 min. Total: 2 hr. 30 min.

8.5 ounces all-purpose flour (about 2 cups)
4 ounces whole-wheat flour (about 1 cup)
3/4 cup packed brown sugar
4 teaspoons ground ginger
1 tablespoon ground cinnamon
3/4 teaspoon baking soda
1/2 teaspoon kosher salt
3/4 cup unsalted butter, softened
3/4 cup molasses
1 tablespoon whole milk
1/4 cup granulated sugar
1/4 cup powdered sugar

1. Weigh or lightly spoon flours into measuring cups; level with a knife. Place flours and next 5 ingredients in the bowl of a stand mixer fitted with a whisk attachment; beat at medium speed until combined. Add butter; beat 2 minutes, scraping sides of bowl as needed. Add molasses and milk; beat just until combined. Divide dough into 2 portions; wrap each portion in plastic wrap. Chill 2 hours or until firm.

2. Preheat oven to 350°F.
3. Line 3 baking sheets with parchment paper. Shape dough into 36 balls (1 tablespoon each). Place granulated sugar in a small dish. Place powdered sugar in a small dish. Roll each ball in granulated sugar, and then powdered sugar. Place 2 inches apart on baking sheets. Bake at 350°F for 12 minutes or until set but slightly soft in the center. Cool 5 minutes on wire racks before serving, or cool completely before packaging. Serves 36 (serving size: 1 cookie)

CALORIES 113; **FAT** 4g (sat 2g, unsat 1g); **PROTEIN** 1g; **CARB** 19g; **FIBER** 1g; **SUGARS** 11g (added sugars 11g); **SODIUM** 56mg; **CALC** 2% DV; **POTASSIUM** 3% DV

HOW TO PACKAGE

Stack the Molasses Crinkle Cookies in tall, slender cellophane bags or small boxes; less room means less crumbling.

Gluten Free • Make Ahead
Vegetarian

Pumpkin Spice Fudge

Hands-on: 20 min. Total: 2 hr. 20 min. Fudge is easier to make than other made-from-scratch candies because it doesn't require tempering, rolling, or shaping.

Cooking spray
13/4 cups sugar
3/4 cup canned pumpkin puree
2/3 cup fat-free sweetened condensed milk
1/2 cup pure maple syrup
2 tablespoons unsalted butter
1 teaspoon kosher salt
1 teaspoon pumpkin pie spice
4 ounces 1/3-less-fat cream cheese
1 (12-ounce) package white chocolate chips

1. Line an 11- x 7-inch glass or ceramic baking dish with foil; coat with cooking spray.
2. Combine sugar, pumpkin, milk, and syrup in a large saucepan over medium; cook 30 minutes or until a candy thermometer registers 237°F, stirring frequently. Stir in butter, salt, spice, cream cheese, and chocolate until melted (mixture will be very thick).
3. Coat a spatula with cooking spray; spoon mixture into prepared dish, smoothing into an even layer. Cool completely at room temperature, 1½ to 2 hours. Cut into 32 squares. Serves 32 (serving size: 1 square)

CALORIES 149; **FAT** 5g (sat 3g, unsat 1g); **PROTEIN** 1g; **CARB** 25g; **FIBER** 0g; **SUGARS** 25g (added sugars 23g); **SODIUM** 91mg; **CALC** 5% DV; **POTASSIUM** 1% DV

HOW TO PACKAGE

For the Pumpkin Spice Fudge, separate the pieces among mini cupcake liners or squares of parchment paper so they don't stick. Tie packages of treats with ribbon or baker's twine.

Make Ahead • Vegetarian

Eggnog Banana Bread

Hands-on: 15 min. Total: 1 hr.

8 ounces white whole-wheat flour
(about 2 cups)
1 teaspoon kosher salt
3/4 teaspoon baking soda
3/4 teaspoon ground nutmeg
1 cup packed brown sugar
1/4 cup unsalted butter, softened
2 large eggs
1 1/2 cups mashed ripe banana
(about 3 medium)
1/3 cup plain whole-milk yogurt
(not Greek-style)
2 teaspoons vanilla extract
Cooking spray
3/4 cup powdered sugar
1 1/2 tablespoons bourbon or rum
1 tablespoon heavy cream
Dash of ground cinnamon

1. Preheat oven to 350°F.
2. Combine first 4 ingredients. Combine brown sugar and butter in the bowl of a stand mixer; beat at medium speed 1 minute. Add eggs; beat just until combined. Add banana, yogurt, and vanilla; beat to combine. Reduce speed to medium-low; add flour mixture, beating just until combined.
3. Divide batter among 6 (5- x 3-inch) mini loaf pans or 12 muffin cups coated with cooking spray. Bake at 350°F for 25 to 30 minutes or until a toothpick inserted in center comes out with a few moist crumbs clinging. Cool in pans on wire racks 10 minutes. Remove bread to wire racks; cool completely.
4. Combine powdered sugar, bourbon, and cream; drizzle over bread. Top with cinnamon. Serves 12 (serving size: 1/2 mini loaf or 1 muffin)

CALORIES 256; **FAT** 6g (sat 3g, unsat 2g);
PROTEIN 4g; **CARB** 46g; **FIBER** 3g; **SUGARS** 31g
(added sugars 26g); **SODIUM** 262mg; **CALC** 5% DV;
POTASSIUM 4% DV

HOW TO PACKAGE

Wrap completely cooled, unsliced Eggnog Banana Bread or Savory Fig, Olive, and Pistachio Fruitcake loaves in plastic wrap. Cut a collar of parchment or butcher paper to fit around the center of each loaf, and label with the name of the recipe. Tape the collar around each loaf, and then tie decorative ribbon or butcher's twine over the collar. You can also package individual slices in food-safe wax paper envelopes (make your own or find them at craft stores), and seal with a holiday sticker.

Make Ahead • Vegetarian

Savory Fig, Olive, and Pistachio Fruitcake

Hands-on: 20 min. Total: 1 hr. 20 min.

2 teaspoons grated orange rind
7 ounces dried mission figs, stemmed
and quartered (about 1 1/4 cups)
1 cup golden raisins (4 ounces)
1/2 cup cream sherry
3.25 ounces all-purpose flour
(about 3/4 cup)
2.6 ounces whole-wheat pastry flour
(about 3/4 cup)
1 1/2 teaspoons kosher salt
3/4 teaspoon ground cardamom
3/4 teaspoon baking powder
1/4 teaspoon ground cloves
1/4 teaspoon baking soda
4 large eggs
1/4 cup extra-virgin olive oil
1/4 cup fat-free buttermilk
1 1/2 tablespoons honey
2 teaspoons vanilla extract
1 cup roasted unsalted pistachios
3 ounces pitted Castelvetrano olives,
drained and coarsely chopped
(3/4 cup)
Baking spray with flour

1. Preheat oven to 375°F.
2. Combine rind, figs, and raisins in a bowl. Bring sherry to a boil in a saucepan; pour over fig mixture. Let stand 15 minutes.
3. Weigh or lightly spoon flours into dry measuring cups; level with a knife. Combine flours, salt, and next 4 ingredients (through baking soda) in a bowl. Place eggs in the bowl of a stand mixer fitted with a whisk attachment; beat 2 minutes. Add oil, buttermilk, honey, and vanilla; beat until combined. Reduce speed to low. Add flour mixture; beat just until combined. Use a spatula to stir in fig mixture (including liquid), pistachios, and olives.
4. Spoon mixture into a 9- x 5-inch loaf pan coated with baking spray. Bake at 375°F for 40 to 45 minutes or until a toothpick inserted in the center comes out with moist crumbs clinging. Cool in pan on a wire rack 5 minutes. Remove bread from pan; cool completely. Serves 16 (serving size: 1 slice)

CALORIES 209; **FAT** 9g (sat 1g, unsat 7g);
PROTEIN 5g; **CARB** 26g; **FIBER** 3g; **SUGARS** 13g
(added sugars 2g); **SODIUM** 362mg; **CALC** 6% DV;
POTASSIUM 4% DV

Cranberry-Ginger Shrub Cocktail

Gluten Free • Make Ahead
Vegetarian

Hands-on: 10 min. Total: 2 hr. 10 min.

1 cup apple cider vinegar
1/2 cup water
1/2 cup sugar
2 tablespoons grated peeled fresh
  ginger
1 pound fresh or frozen cranberries
  (about 4 cups)
6 (2-inch) strips fresh orange rind
8 cups prosecco or other sparkling
  wine, chilled (about 2 1/2 bottles)

1. Bring first 6 ingredients to a boil
in a large saucepan over high; cook
10 minutes or until cranberries
begin to burst, stirring occasionally.
Remove pan from heat; cool to room
temperature. Place in an airtight
container, and refrigerate 2 hours or
overnight. Strain cranberry mixture
through a fine-mesh sieve over a
bowl, pressing solids with back of a
spoon. Discard solids. Package for
gifts, or continue with recipe.
2. To prepare each cocktail, combine
1/2 cup prosecco and 3 tablespoons
shrub in an ice-filled shaker; stir.
Strain into a martini glass. Serves 16
(serving size: about 1 cup)

CALORIES 122; FAT 0g; PROTEIN 0g; CARB 12g;
FIBER 1g; SUGARS 8g (added sugars 6g);
SODIUM 1mg; CALC 0% DV; POTASSIUM 1% DV

HOW TO PACKAGE

For the Cranberry-Ginger Shrub, use a
small funnel or foil cone to divide the liquid among small clear bottles or jars.
Add a label with the cocktail recipe.

Spiced Rum-Caramel Sauce

Fast • Gluten Free
Make Ahead • Vegetarian

Hands-on: 25 min. Total: 25 min.

1 1/4 cups sugar
1 1/4 cups water
3/4 cup half-and-half
1/4 cup unsalted butter
3 tablespoons dark rum (such as
  Myer's)
2 teaspoons kosher salt
1 1/2 teaspoons vanilla extract
1/2 teaspoon finely ground black
  pepper
1/2 teaspoon ground cloves

1. Combine sugar and 1¼ cups water
in a large saucepan over medium-
high; cook 20 to 25 minutes, without
stirring, or until bubbles form and
mixture turns a light amber (between
honey and maple syrup color).
2. Carefully add half-and-half, stirring constantly with a whisk for 1
minute or until smooth (the mixture will bubble vigorously but will
smooth out).
3. Remove pan from heat. Stir in
butter and remaining ingredients.
Divide caramel among 6 (3-ounce)
jars. To reheat, place caramel in a
microwave-safe bowl; microwave
at HIGH until warm, stirring
every 15 seconds. Serves 24
(serving size: 1½ tablespoons)

CALORIES 73; FAT 3g (sat 2g, unsat 1g); PROTEIN 0g;
CARB 11g; FIBER 0g; SUGARS 11g (added sugars 10g);
SODIUM 164mg; CALC 1% DV; POTASSIUM 0% DV

HOW TO PACKAGE

Place the Spiced Rum-Caramel Sauce
in 3-ounce glass jars, and attach a label
with reheating directions and suggestions for use—such as serving over ice
cream, pound cake, or bread pudding;
or drizzling over a baked apple pie or
winter fruit cobbler as a delicious finishing touch.

Everything Lavash Crackers

Make Ahead • Vegetarian

Hands-on: 30 min. Total: 2 hr.

17 ounces bread flour (about
  4 1/2 cups)
1 1/4 cups lukewarm water (100° to
  110°F)
1 (1/4-ounce) package active dry yeast
1/4 cup olive oil
2 tablespoons honey
1 1/2 teaspoons kosher salt, divided
Cooking spray
2 tablespoons toasted sesame seeds
4 teaspoons poppy seeds
4 teaspoons dried minced onion
4 teaspoons dried minced garlic
1 large egg white, whisked

1. Preheat oven to 325°F.
2. Weigh or lightly spoon flour into
dry measuring cups; level with a
knife. Place 1¼ cups water and yeast
in the bowl of stand mixer fitted
with dough hook; let stand 10 minutes or until foamy. Add flour, oil,
honey, and 1 teaspoon salt to yeast
mixture; beat at medium-low speed
10 minutes or until a supple dough
forms. Place dough in a bowl coated
with cooking spray; cover with
plastic wrap.

3. Let dough rise in a warm place (80°F to 85°F), free from drafts, 10 minutes or until ¼ larger in size. Divide into 3 equal portions. Cover with plastic wrap; let rise 10 more minutes or until ¼ larger in size.
4. Combine remaining ½ teaspoon salt, sesame seeds, poppy seeds, onion, and garlic. Flip a baking sheet over so that the bottom is facing up; coat with cooking spray. Roll 1 dough portion to an 18- x 12-inch rectangle on a lightly floured work surface (keep remaining dough portions covered to prevent drying). Place dough on prepared pan. Brush with egg white; sprinkle with 2 tablespoons sesame seed mixture, pressing to adhere.
5. Bake at 325°F for 25 minutes or until crisp. Cool on pan 15 minutes; place on a wire rack, and cool completely. Repeat with remaining dough, egg white, and seed mixture. Once completely cool, break crackers into medium-sized pieces. Serves 20 (serving size: 4 crackers)

CALORIES 132; **FAT** 4g (sat 1g, unsat 3g); **PROTEIN** 4g; **CARB** 21g; **FIBER** 1g; **SUGARS** 2g (added sugars 2g); **SODIUM** 148mg; **CALC** 1% DV; **POTASSIUM** 1% DV

HOW TO PACKAGE

Place the Everything Lavash Crackers in sturdy paper bakery bags or parchment paper envelopes, being careful not to overfill (which might break them); secure with a pretty holiday sticker. You can also make a themed gift by placing the packaged crackers in a basket with an assortment of cheeses.

A SLIGHTLY THICKER CARAMEL AND THE ADDITION OF WHOLE ALMONDS TURN TRADITIONAL CARAMEL CORN INTO GIFT-WORTHY POPCORN MIX.

Make Ahead • Gluten Free Vegetarian

Miso-Caramel-Tamari Popcorn Mix

Hands-on: 30 min. Total: 1 hr. 15 min.

Cooking spray
1½ cups sugar
⅔ cup water
3 tablespoons white miso
1½ tablespoons tamari
2 tablespoons unsalted butter
1 teaspoon baking soda
½ teaspoon black pepper
10 cups popped unseasoned popcorn
3 cups toasted unsalted almonds
¼ teaspoon kosher salt

1. Preheat oven to 200°F. Line a baking sheet with parchment paper; coat with cooking spray.
2. Heat sugar, ⅔ cup water, miso, and tamari in a large saucepan over medium. Cook 35 minutes or until golden-brown and bubbly and a candy thermometer registers 240°F. Remove from heat; stir in butter, baking soda, and pepper.
3. Combine popcorn and almonds in a large bowl. Working quickly, pour sugar mixture over popcorn mixture, tossing to coat. Spread mixture in an even layer on prepared pan; sprinkle with salt. Bake at 200°F for 40 minutes or until golden and crisp, stirring every 15 minutes to break up clusters. Cool to room temperature, stirring occasionally. Store in an airtight container up to 1 week. Serves 24 (serving size: about ½ cup)

CALORIES 178; **FAT** 10g (sat 1g, unsat 8g); **PROTEIN** 5g; **CARB** 20g; **FIBER** 3g; **SUGARS** 14g (added sugars 13g); **SODIUM** 204mg; **CALC** 5% DV; **POTASSIUM** 4% DV

HOW TO PACKAGE

For the Miso-Caramel-Tamari Popcorn Mix, label paper ice cream bowls and place inside wide cellophane bags; fill each bag and tie (or skip the bowl, and add a tag to the tie).

NUTRITIONAL ANALYSIS

At *Cooking Light,* our team of food editors, experienced cooks, and dietitians builds recipes with whole foods, whole grains, and bigger portions of plants and seafood than meat. We emphasize oil-based fats more than saturated, and we promote a balanced diet low in processed foods and added sugars.

We use ingredients that are high in saturated fat (butter), sodium (soy sauce), or both (bacon) in small amounts as flavor-boosting solutions, rather than making them the focal point or cutting them out entirely. We don't cook with any products containing artificial sweeteners or trans fats (partially hydrogenated oils).

HOW TO PORTION

COOKING LIGHT ENSURES THAT EVERY SERVING IS A SATISFYING, REALISTIC PORTION THAT FULFILLS ITS ROLE AS PART OF A BALANCED PLATE. THIS INCLUDES THE FOLLOWING IN EACH CATEGORY:

SEAFOOD
5 ounces cooked

BEEF AND PORK
3 ounces cooked

CHICKEN
4½ ounces cooked breast or 3 ounces cooked thigh

GRAINS
About ½ cup, preferably whole

FRUITS AND VEGETABLES
At least ½ cup

ALCOHOL
1.5 ounces liquor, 5 ounces wine, or 12 ounces beer

METRIC EQUIVALENTS

The information in the following charts is provided to help cooks outside the United States successfully use the recipes in this book. All equivalents are approximate.

Cooking/Oven Temperatures

	Fahrenheit	Celsius	Gas Mark
Freeze Water	32° F	0° C	
Room Temp.	68° F	20° C	
Boil Water	212° F	100° C	
Bake	325° F	160° C	3
	350° F	180° C	4
	375° F	190° C	5
	400° F	200° C	6
	425° F	220° C	7
	450° F	230° C	8
Broil			Grill

Liquid Ingredients by Volume

¼ tsp	=					1 ml				
½ tsp	=					2 ml				
1 tsp	=					5 ml				
3 tsps	=	1 tbl	=	½ fl oz	=	15 ml				
2 tbls	=	⅛ cup	=	1 fl oz	=	30 ml				
4 tbls	=	¼ cup	=	2 fl oz	=	60 ml				
5⅓ tbls	=	⅓ cup	=	3 fl oz	=	80 ml				
8 tbls	=	½ cup	=	4 fl oz	=	120 ml				
10⅔ tbls	=	⅔ cup	=	5 fl oz	=	160 ml				
12 tbls	=	¾ cup	=	6 fl oz	=	180 ml				
16 tbls	=	1 cup	=	8 fl oz	=	240 ml				
1 pt	=	2 cups	=	16 fl oz	=	480 ml				
1 qt	=	4 cups	=	32 fl oz	=	960 ml				
				33 fl oz	=	1000 ml	=	1 l		

Dry Ingredients by Weight

(To convert ounces to grams, multiply the number of ounces by 30.)

1 oz	=	⅟₁₆ lb	=	30g
4 oz	=	¼ lb	=	120g
8 oz	=	½ lb	=	240g
12 oz	=	¾ lb	=	360g
16 oz	=	1 lb	=	480g

Length

(To convert inches to centimeters, multiply the number of inches by 2.5.)

1 in	=					2.5 cm		
6 in	=	½ ft			=	15 cm		
12 in	=	1 ft			=	30 cm		
36 in	=	3 ft	=	1 yd	=	90 cm		
40 in	=					100 cm	=	1 m

Equivalents for Different Types of Ingredients

Standard Cup	Fine Powder (ex. flour)	Grain (ex. rice)	Granular (ex. sugar)	Liquid Solids (ex. butter)	Liquid (ex. milk)
1	140g	150g	190g	200g	240 ml
¾	105g	113g	143g	150g	180 ml
⅔	93g	100g	125g	133g	160 ml
½	70g	75g	95g	100g	120 ml
⅓	47g	50g	63g	67g	80 ml
¼	35g	38g	48g	50g	60 ml
⅛	18g	19g	24g	25g	30 ml

BREAKING DOWN THE NUMBERS

Cooking Light recipes adhere to rigorous nutrition guidelines that govern calories, saturated fat, sodium, and sugar based on various categories (main dish, side, dessert). These standards enable you to easily incorporate our recipes into a diet that follows the most recent USDA and ADA Dietary Guidelines (see below).

CALORIES PER DAY

1,600 - 2,000

This equates to three meals that range from 350 to 550 calories and two 100- to 150-calorie snacks.

SODIUM PER DAY

2,300MG OR LESS

SATURATED FAT PER DAY

20G OR LESS

MENU INDEX

A topical guide to all the menus that appear in *Cooking Light Annual Recipes 2018.*

DINNER TONIGHT

25-Minute Dinners

BEEF

Steak, Feta, and Olive Quesadillas with Cucumber, Onion, and Tomato Salad (page 204) *serves 4*

FISH & SHELLFISH

Zucchini and Shrimp Cakes with Snap Pea Relish with Black-Eyed Pea Salad (page 120) *serves 4*

Grilled Mahi-Mahi with Lemon-Parsley Potatoes with Grilled Tomato, Onion, and Olive Salad (page 203) *serves 4*

PORK

Fresh Pea, Prosciutto, and Herb Salad with Lentil Tapenade Crostini (page 144) *serves 2*

Ancho Chile Pork Chops with Pickled Pepper Relish with Charred Snap Peas with Creamy Tarragon Dressing (page 170) *serves 2*

POULTRY

Chicken and Waffles with Kicky Syrup with Ginger-Lime Fruit Salad (page 68) *serves 4*

Pan-Grilled Chicken with Peach Salsa with Tomato, Herb, and Baby Lettuce Salad (page 202) *serves 4*

Quick BBQ Chicken Thighs with Mashed Potatoes with Creamy Carrot-and-Broccoli Slaw (page 204) *serves 4*

VEGETARIAN

Szechuan Tofu with Cauliflower with Orange-Scallion Brown Rice (page 118) *serves 4*

Shiitake and Asparagus Sauté with Poached Eggs with Herbed Roasted New Potatoes (page 118) *serves 2*

Skillet Ratatouille with Pesto Toasts (page 202) *serves 4*

30-Minute Dinners

FISH & SHELLFISH

Seared Cod with Bacon, Braised Fennel, and Kale with Maple-Dijon Roasted Carrots and Mushrooms (page 42) *serves 4*

Dijon-Herb Crusted Salmon with Creamy Dill Sauce with Warm Buttered Radish and Edamame Salad (page 86) *serves 2*

PORK

Miso Noodle Soup with Meatballs with Baby Bok Choy and Cucumber Salad (page 41) *serves 2*

POULTRY

Sausage, Spinach, and Apple Breakfast Sandwiches with Parmesan-and-Herb Roasted Potatoes (page 67) *serves 4*

VEGETARIAN

Farro Breakfast Bowl with Blistered Tomatoes with Kale (page 66) *serves 2*

35-Minute Dinners

BEEF

Carne Asada Bowls with Cilantro and Almond Pilaf (page 43) *serves 4*

FISH & SHELLFISH

Charred Shrimp and Okra Bowl with Toasted Jasmine Rice (page 146) *serves 4*

Summer Salmon Niçoise Salad with Parsley-and-Dill Potatoes (page 172) *serves 4*

PORK

Spinach, Cheese, and Bacon Bread Puddings with Bibb, Radicchio, and Asparagus Salad (page 88) *serves 4*

POULTRY

Lemon and Dill Quinoa Chicken Soup with Ricotta and Sweet Pea Toasts (page 42) *serves 4*

Chicken, Mushroom, and Bok Choy Bowls with Scallion-and-Cilantro Barley (page 86) *serves 4*

Grilled Chipotle Chicken and Sweet Potato Toss with Dilly Cucumber Salad with Yogurt (page 147) *serves 4*

VEGETARIAN

Creamy Carrot and Herb Linguine with Wilted Chard with Red Onion and Pine Nuts (page 40) *serves 4*

Saucy Skillet-Poached Eggs with Grilled Garlic Toast (page 68) *serves 4*

Basil-Ricotta Ravioli with Spinach with Blistered Balsamic Cherry Tomatoes (page 170) *serves 4*

40-Minute Dinners

BEEF

Grilled Chile-Lime Flank Steak with Grilled Corn and Bell Pepper Salad (page 145) *serves 4*

Coriander-Crusted Flank Steak with Cuban Black Beans with Elote-Style Zucchini Noodles (page 171) *serves 4*

PORK

Mostly Veggie Pasta with Sausage with Black Pepper–Parmesan Wedge Salad (page 121) *serves 4*

POULTRY

Grilled Lemon Chicken Salad with Orzo and Herb Pilaf (page 85) *serves 4*

Chicken and Poblano Stew with Polenta with Avocado Salad with Honey-Lime Vinaigrette (page 119) *serves 4*

Cobb Pizza with Watermelon-Basil Salad (page 173) *serves 4*

VEGETARIAN

Zucchini and Spinach Chilaquiles with Sofrito Pinto Beans (page 66) *serves 4*

Broccoli, Cheddar, and Brown Rice Cakes with Sweet-and-Spicy Carrots and Peas (page 87) *serves 4*

Ratatouille Stuffed Shells with Green Bean and Radish Sauté (page 144) *serves 4*

NEW EASTER ESSENTIALS

All the Green Things Salad (page 80) *serves 8*

Spinach-Artichoke Strata (page 80) *serves 9*

Honey-Baked Pork Roast (page 81) *serves 16*

Turmeric-Pickled Deviled Eggs (page 81) *serves 12*

RECIPE TITLE INDEX

An alphabetical listing of every recipe title that appeared in the magazine in 2017. See page 402 for the General Recipe Index.

MONTH-BY-MONTH INDEX

A month-by-month listing of every food story with recipe titles that appeared in the magazine in 2017. See page 402 for the General Recipe Index.

October

GENERAL RECIPE INDEX

A listing by major ingredient and food category for every recipe that appeared in the magazine in 2017